HUMANIZED INFORMATION SYSTEMS ANALYSIS AND DESIGN

People Building Systems for People

McGraw-Hill Series in Management Information Systems

Gordon B. Davis, CONSULTING EDITOR

DAVIS AND OLSON: Management Information Systems: Conceptual Foundations, Structure, and Development

DICKSON AND WETHERBE: The Management of Information Systems

DICKSON AND WETHERBE: Management of Information Systems Casebook

EVEREST: Database Management: Objectives, System Functions, and Administration

KOZAR: Humanized Information Systems Analysis And Design: People Building Systems for People

LUCAS: The Analysis, Design, and Implementation of Information Systems

LUCAS: Information Systems Concepts for Management

LUCAS: A Casebook for Management Information Systems

MEADOW AND TEDESCO: Telecommunications for Management

SCOTT: Principles of Management Information Systems

WEBER: EDP Auditing: Conceptual Foundations and Practice

OF RELATED INTEREST

DORDICK: Understanding Modern Telecommunications

JONES: Programming Productivity

NEWMAN: Designing Integrated Systems for the Office Environment

SENN: Analysis and Design of Information Systems

HUMANIZED INFORMATION SYSTEMS ANALYSIS AND DESIGN

People Building Systems for People

Kenneth A. Kozar
University of Colorado/Boulder
College of Business

McGRAW-HILL BOOK COMPANY

New York St. Louis San Francisco Auckland Bogotá Caracas Colorado Springs Hamburg
Lisbon London Madrid Mexico Milan Montreal New Delhi Oklahoma City Panama
Paris San Juan São Paulo Singapore Sydney Tokyo Toronto

Humanized Information Systems Analysis and Design: People Building Systems for People

INTERNATIONAL EDITION

1 2 3 4 5 6 7 8 9 0 KHLUPE 8 9 4 3 2 1 0 9

This book was set in Baskerville by the College Composition Unit in cooperation with Better Graphics, Inc. The editors were Karen M. Jackson and Edwin Hanson; the designer was Joan Greenfield; the production supervisor was Salvador Gonzales.
Drawings were done by Fine Line Illustrations, Inc.

Library of Congress Cataloging-in-Publication Data

Kozar, Kenneth A.
Humanized information systems analysis and design.

(McGraw-Hill series in management information systems)
Includes bibliographies and index.
I. Management information systems. I. Title. II. Series.
T58.6.K675 1988 658.4'038 88-6836
ISBN 0-07-035600-9

When ordering this title use ISBN 0-07-100512-9

Acknowledgments
Page 53: William E. Howden, "Contemporary Software Development Environments," *Communications of the Association for Computing Machinery,* May 1982, pp. 318-329. Copyright 1982, Association for Computing Machinery, Inc. **Page 157:** Karl Schoenberger, "An Obscene Gesture Is Strictly Business on Tokyo Exchange," *Wall Street Journal,* Dec. 2, 1986, p. 1. Reprinted by permission of The Wall Street Journal. © Dow Jones & Company, Inc. (1986). All rights reserved. **Page 172:** From "How Casino Computers Stretch the House Odds," *Business Week,* July 30, 1984, pp. 112-114. Reprinted by special permission, copyright © 1984 by McGraw-Hill, Inc. **Page 248:** Figure from Martin McClure, James McClure, and Carma McClure. "Normalization of Data," *Software Maintenance: The Problem and Its Solutions,* pp. 135-158. © 1983. Reprinted by permission of Prentice-Hall, Inc., Englewood Cliffs, N.J. **Page 275:** By permission of The Associated Press. **Page 284:** Reprinted with permission of United Press International, Copyright 1986. **Page 322:** Le Courier table, fig. 5.7, p. 90 of Marvin Gore and John Stubbe, *Elements of Systems Analysis,* 4th ed., pp. 74-75. Copyright © 1975, 1979, 1983, 1988 William C. Brown Publishers, Dubuque, Iowa. All rights reserved. Reprinted by permission. **Page 326:** From Blake Ives, "Graphical User Interfaces for Business Information Systems," *Management Information Systems Quarterly,* Special Issue, Dec. 1982, pp. 15-42. Copyright 1982 by the Society for Information Management and the Management Information Systems Research Center. Reprinted by special permission. **Page 352:** Wendelin Colby, "Burnt or Burned," *Infosystems,* Feb. 1985, p. 40. Copyright Hitchcock Publishing Company. **Page 355:** From Ann Reilly, "Computer Crackdown," *Fortune,* Sept. 14, 1984, pp. 141-142. © 1984 Time, Inc. All rights reserved. **Page 356:** From The Indianapolis News. **Page 365:** Pat Frey, "A Surge of Opportunities," *Sales Moonbeams,* Nov. 1984, pp. 3-4 Courtesy of The Procter and Gamble Company. **Page 373:** Figure adapted from Ben Schneiderman, *Software Psychology: Human Factors in Computer and Information Systems,* p. 135. Copyright © 1980 by Scott, Foresman & Company. Adapted by permission of Scott, Foresman & Company. **Page 389:** From Jerry Weinberg, *Infosystems,* Aug. 1983, p. 49. Copyright Hitchcock Publishing Company. **Page 408:** From Tom DeMarco, *Structured Analysis and Specification* (Yourdon Press, 1978), pp. 336-339. © 1979. Adapted by permission of Prentice-Hall, Inc., Englewood Cliffs, N.J. **Pages 411-413:** Courtesy Apple Computer, Inc.

Printed in Singapore

ABOUT THE AUTHOR

KENNETH A. KOZAR has worked in the information systems field for more than 24 years. Because of the rapid changes in the field, he believes that rather than 24 years experience, he has 2 years experience at least 12 times.

Dr. Kozar has held many positions in the systems field, including developer, manager, educator, and researcher. After receiving one of the first MIS PhDs from the University of Minnesota, he has been on the faculties of the Universities of Minnesota, Calgary, Saskatchewan, and Indiana. He currently is on the faculty of the University of Colorado in Boulder. His publications have appeared in the *Management Information Systems Quarterly, International Journal of Man-Machine Studies, Journal of Systems Management, Journal of Information Systems Management,* and the *Journal of Product Innovation Management.* He has given numerous presentations to both academic and practitioner audiences.

Dr. Kozar has managed several systems development projects as either a full-time manager, a full-time independent consultant, or through continued consulting/training activities. Special areas of interest include improved methods for systems development, systems developer workbenches, and the behavioral/organizational issues of automated systems.

TO MY TEACHERS AND STUDENTS:
IT IS DIFFICULT TO DISTINGUISH BETWEEN THEM

CONTENTS

PART II THE SYSTEMS ANALYSIS PHASE: PROCESS AND TECHNIQUES

PART III THE SYSTEMS DESIGN PHASE: PROCESS AND TECHNIQUES

PART IV THE SYSTEMS IMPLEMENTATION PHASE: PROCESS AND TECHNIQUES

PART V BEYOND THE PROCESS AND TECHNIQUES

PREFACE

Computer-based systems seem to be everywhere. We take their existence for granted except when they do not perform as expected. And more often than not, people are the key to both successful development and performance of systems.

The objective of this book on systems analysis and design is to introduce students to processes, principles, guidelines, and techniques for developing more effective computer systems. The intended audience is both users and developers of systems; in today's organizations, it often is difficult to distinguish between the two. Users are developing computer-based systems to aid themselves in job performance, and developers are acquiring computer-based systems to provide aid in building systems.

Writing the book was the result of a belief that there was a need to focus on the people aspect of systems development. The material has evolved over a number of years, a career-long endeavor. Enjoyment of teaching, belief that good was being done, and positive feedback from both students and colleagues has led to a completed book, rather than a stack of notes.

INTENT OF THE BOOK

The intent of *Humanized Information Systems Analysis and Design* is to view the building of computer systems from the person's point of view. People need computer systems. These systems are developed by people. People make the difference between successful and unsuccessful systems development. The major thrust of the book is to aid communication between people through increased trust, understanding, and empathy. Methods that serve as semantic bridges between different organizational role players are the foundation of the material.

Within a college curriculum, the book is intended as a follow-up to a computer systems fundamentals or introductory management information systems course. The assumption is made that the reader is familiar with computer basics. Terms like hardware, software, database, files, telecommunications, batch, micros, K, on-line, and compilers should already have meaning to the reader. Familiarity with computer programming might aid in understanding some development concepts. It may hinder other development skills since programming emphasizes problem solving, often at the expense of problem finding.

CONTENT OVERVIEW

The book is divided into five main parts. A top-down presentation of the material is taken. General knowledge is presented first with an unfolding of increasing levels of detail.

OVERVIEW OF CONTENTS OF TEXTBOOK

Ch 1—Overview of Systems Concepts

Ch 2 and 3—Overview of Methods of Systems Development and the Data Generated

Ch 4—Overview of Systems Analysis

Ch 5—Representing Systems Data

Ch 6—Gathering Systems Data

Ch 7—Reviewing Systems Data

Ch 8—Overview of Systems Design

Ch 9—Design for the Machine

Ch 10/11—Design for People

Ch 12—Design for the Auditor

Ch 13—Overview of Systems Implementation

Ch 14—Managing Systems Development

Ch 15—The Future?

Part I Introduction to Systems Development

The first three chapters introduce systems concepts, overview systems development, and introduce the data necessary to document a system. Chapter 1 assures that students have a clear understanding of systems thinking, components of organizational systems, and what systems development entails. Chapter 2 presents the thread that weaves through the text material, a systems development life cycle, augmented by traditional and structured development techniques. Chapter 3 takes the perspective that information systems builders need information systems to do their job properly. These information systems would contain documentation about the system under development. Each of these chapters includes a case study exhibiting the material.

Part II The Systems Analysis Phase: Process and Techniques

This part of the book introduces the processes and techniques used to define and analyze a system. Chapter 4 provides an overview of the processes and subprocesses needed to conduct a systems analysis. Management topics such as selecting appropriate projects and kicking off a project are included. Chapter 5 includes the techniques used to represent systems. Several techniques are described, and data flow diagramming is detailed for skill development. Chapter 6 specifies the various techniques of data gathering. An important technique is requirements dialoging, a means of linking the information system to business strategy. Chapter 7 presents the techniques needed to present and review material gathered in systems projects.

Part III The Systems Design Phase: Process and Techniques

This part of the book introduces the topic of systems design by reviewing the process and techniques to design for the machine, the user, and to satisfy the auditor. Chapter 8 introduces the processes and subprocesses needed to specify a systems design. A method of evaluating alternative design payoffs is presented. Chapter 9 presents the technical and physical aspects of design. Data specifications and program structure charts are introduced and exhibited. Chapter 10 presents material on achieving human performance, including procedure and job design, training design, and manual design. Chapter 11 is devoted to designing usable person-machine dialogs and input/output layouts. The technique of person-machine dialog representation is introduced and exhibited. Chapter 12 is concerned with the control, security, privacy, and recovery aspects of systems design. A unique method for determining the need for system integrity is introduced.

Part IV The Systems Implementation Phase: Process and Techniques

Getting the system built and installed in the organization is the concern of this part of the book. Chapter 13 examines top-down versus bottom-up approaches to systems building, approaches to systems implementation, and conducts a postaudit of the development project. The need and means of systems testing as well as management of change is included in this chapter.

Part V Beyond the Process and Techniques

This section discusses material that does not fit within the development life cycle. Chapter 14 introduces systems project management and the challenges of planning and estimating. Other project management topics include managing tasks and people on a systems project and how automated aids can provide assistance. The chapter also includes an examination of alternatives to the life cycle such as user-developed systems, prototyping, and use of packaged software. Chapter 15 provides a view of systems development in the future from the author's perspective. The challenge to continue your learning and be a changemaker also is presented.

Appendixes

Appendix A presents a case study that can be used to practice systems analysis. Appendix B presents guidelines for conducting a systems project in a real-world setting. This approach has been used successfully by many student teams. Appendix C presents the results of a student team project based on the guidelines in the previous appendix.

FEATURES OF THE TEXT

The book is a blend of education and training material. It attempts to be a usable book for both students and instructors written using system concepts. And it is hoped that it will even allow you to smile and laugh when reading.

Pedagogy

Each chapter begins with a list of behavioral objectives and a short synopsis. Liberal use of photos and boxes relating real life stories are included to reinforce the material. The author calls on his vast experience to include vignettes and real life cases. He has also included actual student solutions and examples. Each chapter includes review and discussion questions. Review questions relate to the written material while discussion questions require synthesis and thinking beyond what was written. Exercises in each chapter aid learning by doing. Each chapter includes relevant references and further readings to expand learning. The instructor's guide is written by the book author.

Emphasis on People

The emphasis is on the person's role in developing systems: interviewing persons, making presentations to persons, person-software interaction, persons reviewing development deliverables, training persons, person-machine dialogs, procedures for persons, etc. But the text does not omit topics such as program or database design.

Appeal to Visual Senses

Believing a picture is worth a thousand words, the book incorporates graphic techniques wherever they are meaningful. Structured techniques such as data flow diagramming, structure charts, and a new technique promoted by the author called person-machine dialog charting are advocated, described, and practiced. The book presents alternatives to the traditional methods of development and examines knowing when, as well as developing know-how.

Tested Material

The material in the text has been tested through use at both Indiana University and the University of Colorado in Boulder. It has been used for one or two semester sequences and with both undergraduate and graduate students. Other professors have been introduced to the material at the Advanced Management Information Systems Faculty Development Institutes sponsored by the American Assembly of Collegiate Schools of Business where the author has held responsibility for the systems analysis and design track. Many helpful and insightful comments were gathered from these audiences. The author assumes responsibility for any and all deficiencies in the material.

ACKNOWLEDGMENTS

The author would like to thank others who have had an influence on this effort.

- Students at Indiana University and the University of Colorado who made many helpful suggestions. Special thanks go to the students whose work is included in the text.
- Donna Kocialski, who as a student at Indiana University took a real interest in the book and edited and made numerous suggestions.
- Participants at the AACSB Advanced Faculty Development Institutes for their willingness to use the material and to offer encouragement and improvements.
- Milt Jenkins, who not only shared his materials and his knowledge, but boosted my confidence by providing challenges I may not have attempted without his encouragement.
- Bob Bostrom, who caused me to see teaching and education in a new light.
- My family and friends for their support and encouragement, especially Nancy and Cindy, who were without many hours of my time during this endeavor.

This book is a continuing effort to aggregrate ideas, concepts, and methods used in developing information systems. The author would like to hear comments from readers and adopters of the book. Thank you in advance for your inputs. Kenneth A. Kozar, University of Colorado/Boulder, College of Business/MSIS, P. O. Box 419, Boulder, Colorado, 80309.

Kenneth A. Kozar

HUMANIZED INFORMATION SYSTEMS ANALYSIS AND DESIGN

People Building Systems for People

PART I

Introduction to Systems Development

Part I provides a foundation for the rest of the material in the book. It attempts to ensure understanding of what a system is, systems that exist in organizations, what a systems developer does, processes and techniques used in developing systems, and data needed to describe a system being built.

CHAPTER 1

A Review of Systems Concepts

THIS CHAPTER REVIEWS the basic systems concepts of goals/purpose, input/process/output, subsystems, suprasystems, control, and boundaries. The organization as a system is introduced to provide the background for developing systems in organizations. The chapter then examines basic components of computer-based systems: people, organizing structures, technology, and data. A typology of different computer-based information systems is introduced. Finally, the topic of what systems development entails is considered. A case study of a successful systems implementation is included.

CHAPTER OBJECTIVES

You should be able to:

- Describe things in systems terms (think systems)
- Specify the subsystems in an organization
- Specify the subsystems in an information management system
- Specify the types of information management systems
- Specify what a systems developer does
- Specify the people roles needed to do systems work

Systems are everywhere. There are ecologic systems, transportation systems, exhaust systems, administrative systems, computer systems, communication systems, and so on. We criticize, praise, build, and "beat" systems. We cannot avoid them.

Before we can analyze, design, and implement a system, we must establish a common definition of what systems are and the basic concepts that apply to all systems. This common base is necessary so we can communicate about systems development.

A ***system*** is a set of interrelated parts that interact with one another, brought together for a purpose. A car can be thought of as a system. It is composed of a set of interrelated parts (engine, tires, body, suspension, etc.) that work together for the purpose of providing transportation.

Every system accepts ***inputs*** and ***processes*** them into ***outputs.*** Our car must be provided inputs (fuel, driving skill, oil, etc.) which it processes into an output—transportation. Our cars are systems that are parts of a larger system, the transportation system. These larger systems are called ***suprasystems.*** Likewise, our cars are made up of smaller systems such as the exhaust system or electrical system. These are called ***subsystems.*** Depending on perspective, a system to one person may be a subsystem to another person. It depends on each person's needs for viewing and understanding the interrelated parts.

We often try to understand a system by understanding its subsystems. A car mechanic analyzing a stalled car with a gas engine will check for an electronic spark (ignition subsystem) and for a gas mixture (fuel subsystem).

Any system or subsystem has a ***boundary.*** A boundary is the border between the system we are considering and the ***environment*** in which the system exists. The environment could be thought of as another system. One system's output is often another system's input. The electrical system in our car meets the fuel system when the fuel mixture meets the spark at the system boundary. These meetings are called ***interfaces.*** (See Figure 1.1 for a pictorial view of a system.)

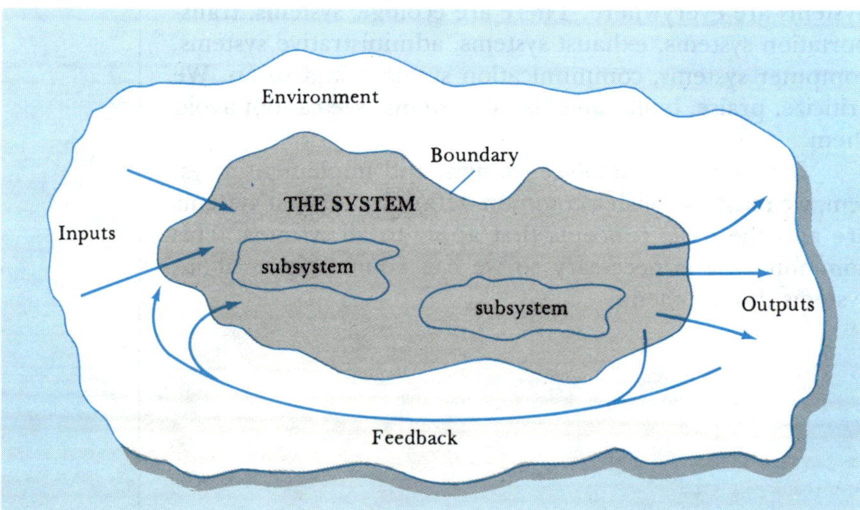

FIGURE 1.1

A pictorial view of a system.

Systems often are conceptual rather than physical things. Sometimes we can't touch them or see them. They are created in our mind so we can think and talk about things they represent. The car, a physical system, is chosen using a ***selection strategy***, a conceptual system. The selection strategy allows a buyer to order and organize needs and wants. ***Systems thinking*** allows us to create a perspective to view, understand, and thrive in the world.

We can, however, touch and see things that represent the system. Since systems are something that we create in our mind, we can draw the conceptual system boundaries wherever we choose to. The boundary may, by our choice, enclose a certain part of an organization, a certain set of tasks or processes, or things physically grouped together (a car). For example, some persons might group all the motion-producing parts of a car together and think of them as the power system. This would be especially true of a person who does not care about each component needed to deliver power to the wheels. A person making a living as an auto body repair person may not be interested in the engine components. But he or she would consider as important the hood system, with its latches and hinges and exterior metal, and would likely view it as a separate subsystem. Engine mechanics may see the entire set of body components as the "body subsystem."

Since systems are created by our perceptions, we must be careful that all persons concerned with the system are thinking and talking about the same things contained within the system boundaries. One person's subsystem may be another person's individual component.

System boundaries are very important in systems development work. We want to make sure that the systems developer and the systems project sponsor are both including the same subsystems in a systems development project. For example, a personnel system could include only the payroll subsystem or it could include a payroll and worker skills inventory.

It is important to have a common understanding of what is within the system boundary in systems project planning and reviewing. Where the system boundary is drawn will affect project size and accordingly, the project budget. If the boundary is not understood, persons reviewing models of the system will constantly bicker over what the system will represent. An example of this would be a group of automotive engineers debating whether tires are part of a new car design if the tire suppliers could be any one of several companies.

The last important concept regarding systems is that the system must adapt to its environment to have a long life. This is the element of ***control***. When the system provides an output, the output must be received by other systems in the environment in which the system exists. If the output is not acceptable, it must be changed. The method for making the change is to change the inputs to and/or the processes within the system.

In essence, the system must receive ***feedback*** and have a control or adapting segment. This control or adaptation is done because the persons responsible for the system's life receive some information indicating that the system is not in control. We keep our car system in control by doing tune-ups if the performance outputs are not satisfactory.

ORGANIZATIONS AS SYSTEMS

Now that we understand some of the basic concepts of systems as they pertain to the familiar object of a car, we will examine another entity that can be viewed as a system, the organization. Since most systems development takes place in organizations, we must understand the organization and its environment.

Organizations exist in an environment which is familiar to most of us. In fact, it is so familiar that we often take the existence of the environment for granted. But since the environment is the source of inputs to and destination of outputs from the systems we will be concerned with, we should be aware of the environment our systems will exist in.

Figure 1.2 shows some of the entities in the environment which affect organizational systems. Regulation, which usually comes from some level of government, is often the reason for an organizational change. This is also the case with competition. When an organization's competition introduces a new service using systems technology, the organization will likely respond with a new system. Banks had to do this when competitors came up with 24-hour teller machines.

The environment is the source of inputs to the organizational system and the receiver of outputs. For example, people are hired from the environment, and data, information, and raw materials are acquired from it. These inputs are used to generate products and services offered to the environment. If the environment does not accept the outputs, the organi-

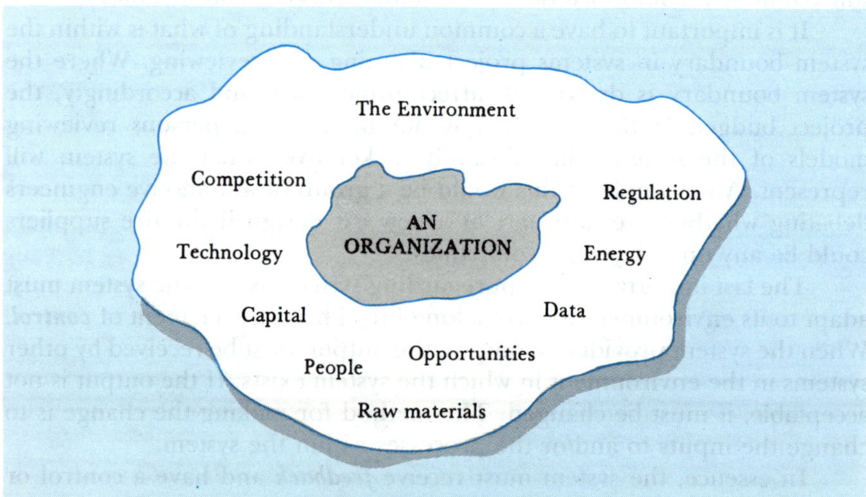

FIGURE 1.2

The environment in which organizations exist is of concern to a systems developer.

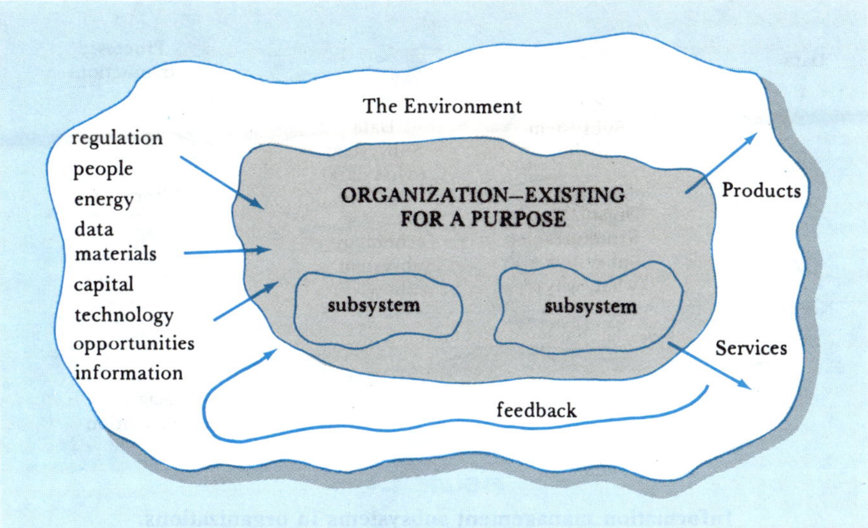

FIGURE 1.3
An organization in the environment.

zational system is changed to make it more responsive to the environment. We alter our organizations in response to the information received. For example, if the information managers receive indicates to them that a product is not selling well, the organization may discontinue or change the product. This feedback is necessary to keep the organization in control. Figure 1.3 shows the organization interacting with the environment.

Organizations, like other systems, are created for a purpose. They utilize the resources in the environment and, as their name implies, organize them to try and achieve the purpose. They add value to the inputs by processing them and introduce the outputs back to the environment by exchanging them for resources. If the organization is compensated for the value it adds, it will obtain more resources and will continue its existence. If not, it must use the information feedback to adapt and change to assure a long life.

By looking at Figure 1.3, we see that to react to the environment, the organization must have information. One of the critical subsystems in an organization is the ***information management system***. In the next section, we will look at the subsystems important to the information management systems.

INFORMATION MANAGEMENT SYSTEMS

As we move from our discussion of systems in general to organizations as systems, and then to information management systems, we are moving closer to the areas or subsystems which we must understand to carry out systems development work. Several subsystems are of critical importance in computer-based information management systems. These are the ***organiz-***

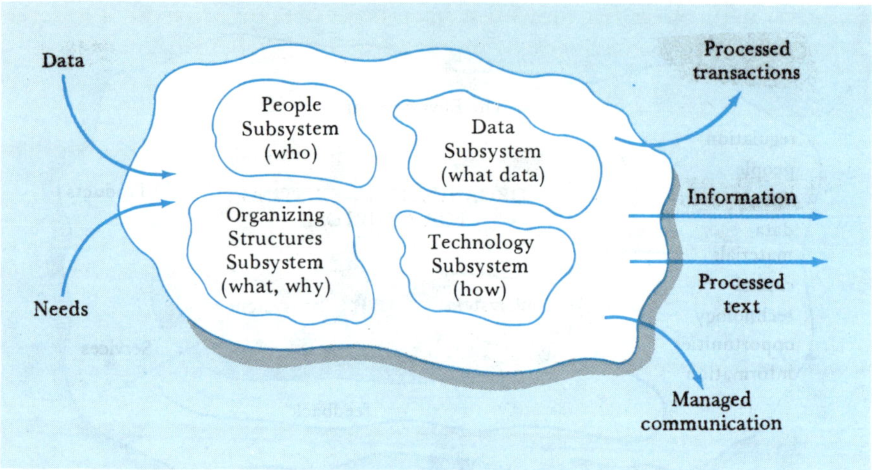

FIGURE 1.4

Information management subsystems in organizations.

ing structures, people, machines/technology, and ***data*** subsystems. As shown in Figure 1.4, the organization's computer-based systems accept raw data and needs as inputs and process them into information, processed transactions, processed text/words, and managed communications.

The organizing structure subsystem includes the organization's plans and activities. This subsystem indicates *what* is done and *why*. The people subsystem indicates *who* develops, operates, and uses the organization's systems. The data subsystem specifies *what data* is stored and processed. The technology subsystem indicates *how* the processing and data storage are done (hardware and software).

It is important to see the relationships between the components of the information subsystems to perform an adequate job of ***systems analysis***. Each systems developer, like a car mechanic, may not understand the intricate workings of each subsystem, but will be aware of the subsystem's existence and the inputs it requires and outputs expected from it. This is how we can study and improve computer-based systems in organizations. Since we will be studying and analyzing systems in organizations, we must have an awareness of each of the information management subsystems. Let us now look at each of these subsystems in more detail.

THE ORGANIZING STRUCTURE SUBSYSTEM

An organization is formed by a person or persons who have an idea they would like to bring to actuality. They have something they want to accomplish and a strategy for accomplishing it. This strategy indicates *what* the organization is to do and *why*. The strategy is brought to life through the process of management. Management activities include planning, organizing, controlling, and leading. To perform these activities, the organization founders determine that they must have some structure to exist. Thus, the strategy leads to a management or organizational structure.

$$\text{Purpose} \rightarrow \text{Strategy} \rightarrow \text{Structure}$$

As seen in Figure 1.5 the structure often takes the shape of a pyramid. Top management is at the top of the pyramid, which is narrower since there are few persons there. The bottom of the structure is where the products get produced and services delivered. Management provides the direction to the producers and assures that resources are obtained from the environment.

As can be seen from the front triangle of the pyramid in Figure 1.5, top management carries out long-range or strategic planning, middle management assures that the plans are carried out by performing management control, and operational management supervises workers to make sure that they have the resources and motivation to do the needed work. The recording of transactions, which forms the base for the structure, is done by financial and accounting functions. Systems developers must work with all levels and functional areas of managers and workers.

There are three basic functional areas in our organizing structure:

1. *Procuring* obtains resources such as people and raw materials from the environment.
2. *Producing* utilizes these resources to produce finished goods and services.
3. *Selling* transfers the products and services to the environment.

People who specify appropriate organizational structures are often titled *organizational designers*. The *systems developer* must have some of the skills of the organizational designer since new or changed systems often affect organizational structure. Job tasks, superior/subordinate relationships, and reward/benefit programs may be influenced by a changed

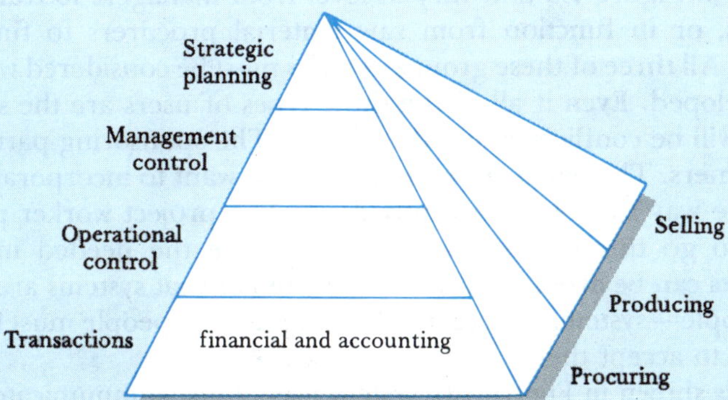

FIGURE 1.5

An organizational structure.

system. In addition, understanding the organizational strategy and goals or *why* an organization exists is a task of the systems developer. The developer must understand and help to document what the mission of the organization is and the functions necessary to accomplish the mission. Systems must aid managers in performing their functions.

THE PEOPLE SUBSYSTEM

The organization contains people who fulfill roles in the organization. Each of these roles requires different information processing to provide people at different levels, with different organization functions, and with different personal needs, the information they need to perform their organizational functions.

From our previous discussion it is clear that computer-based information systems are built to aid people in organizations. There are a number of different "people functions" which must be fulfilled in order for a system to be developed and used. Figure 1.6 shows three of these functions. It should be remembered that these are functions that people perform, and they may actually be performed by one person.

We have already discussed one of these roles, that of the information users who do their jobs better because of better use of technology. These users are distinguished by organizational level, functional area, and individual differences which make their information needs unique. In systems development there are three categories of users:

1. The *project funders,* who provide the resources (people and money) to complete the project.
2. The *project beneficiaries,* who will benefit because the system makes their job easier.
3. The *project workers,* whose job may change as a result of the system but who may not receive any benefits from a new system.

These users may reside anywhere within the organizational structure shown in Figure 1.5 and vary in level from managers to transaction processors, or in function from raw material procurers to finished goods sellers. All three of these groups of users must be considered when a system is developed. Even if all of the three types of users are the same person, there will be conflicts within the person. The sponsoring part will want to cut corners. The beneficiaries part may not want to incorporate the system into the way the job is currently done. The project worker part may not want to go through the trouble to provide the needed inputs. These conflicts can be avoided only if we remember that systems are provided to aid people—systems are created for people. The people must be ready and willing to accept them.

As shown in Figure 1.6, system users must communicate their needs to a person who fulfills the role of information analyst. An *information analyst* examines user requirements and links the user's business needs to a proposed system to make the user's job more effective and efficient. This role also may be known as the *systems analyst,* although in industry a systems

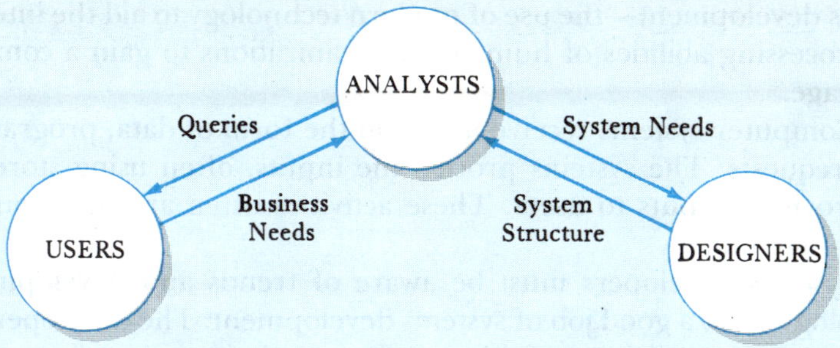

FIGURE 1.6

Roles of user, analyst, and designer are needed to develop a system.

analyst may perform the roles of both the systems designer and information analyst.

Systems design is performed by persons familiar with current technology. They usually are more comfortable and skillful working with machines than they are working with people. The systems designer role also consists of developing or acquiring any needed software, specifying needed data structures, and configuring needed hardware. Thus, the application programmer and database specialist would fit under the roles of systems designer, although a person with an organizational title of programmer may do no real system designing.

The information analyst must communicate with the designers to express the users' problems in systems terms. The information analyst is more of a problem definer, and the system designer is more of a problem solver. The information analyst must have an understanding of the human users. One successful way of understanding users is to view them as human subsystems. Users provide inputs such as data and needs for information to analysts. Analysts must provide systems which produce outputs needed by users and which aid in the implementation of the system once it is designed and constructed. To do this, analysts must interface with the users. This is done through communication—a focus of much of this book.

The above discussion may give the impression of creating stereotypes of persons fulfulling the three major roles in systems development. Our intention is not to "pigeonhole" people. Some users are very technically oriented, while some designers have excellent human interaction skills and are as comfortable working with people as they are with machines. The intention of this discussion is to present the total skill package needed to create information systems.

THE MACHINE/TECHNOLOGY SUBSYSTEM

Another subsystem which exists in our organizational information system is machines/technology. Although information systems can exist without machines, much of our information revolution is a result of advancing technology and the ability to effectively use it. This is one of the objectives of systems development—the use of modern technology to aid the intellectual and processing abilities of humans in organizations to gain a competitive advantage.

Computer systems receive inputs in the form of data, programs, and other requests. The systems process the inputs, often using stored data, and provide outputs to users. These activities often are best done using modern technology.

Systems developers must be aware of trends and developments in technology to do a good job of systems development. The developer should be aware of the availability of processing power in its various forms, such as microcomputer systems or through communications channels.

Hardware is not enough. Tasks will be accomplished only if appropriate software exists. Knowledge of the availability of software packages or where to find out about hardware/software is part of the needed background for a systems developer. Technological knowledge is perishable. Someone up-to-date on the computer technology of 5 years ago would be severely limited in discussions of the state of the art today.

THE DATA SUBSYSTEM

A subsystem that we cannot ignore is the data subsystem. We gather data, input data, validate data, process data, store data, audit data, move data, and disperse data. We must manage data as a resource. Data is the basis for input to machines and to humans to be processed into information.

Data is the link between an organization's subsystems. A critical part of systems development is the study and organization of data. We must:

1. Study data flows needed to run an organization.
2. Determine what data must be stored to keep organization records and have needed history.
3. Know who needs what data to be processed into information, when, from where, etc.

Some still consider the data processing group in an organization as *the* information systems area. As will be explained in the next section discussing different kinds of information management systems, the data processing focus is actually quite narrow. But historically this is where the business computer and technology were located in an organization.

Within an organization, data which concerns many activities and subjects is gathered and stored. Data about activities in functional areas such as procurement (personnel and purchasing departments), production, sales, and financial/accounting are all part of *internally generated* data. *External* data is obtained from information services or by gathering industry statistics. Examples include bibliographic citation services, market research data, or financial data such as that provided by the Dow Jones Service. Much of this frequently used data can be machine stored and manipulated to obtain desired information.

Managers also use informal data to process into information. Informal public data can come from sources such as the newspapers, magazines, radio, and TV. Some persons feel that this data is so important that they require formal means of obtaining it. Data services such as newspaper clipping services have evolved to satisfy this need.

The last data source to be considered is informal private sources. Many decisions are made and actions taken based on what is heard on the grapevine. The grapevine operates both inside an organization and through external sources. People using the grapevine may have to filter and verify any data received. A formal information system may aid this process.

Systems developers, both analysts and designers, should be aware of the existence of these data sources. Executive actions sometimes do not make sense to us because we do not know what data the person is receiving as input. One should not assume that the formal information system is the only source of information. By understanding all sources, opportunities for improving the data gathering and information providing channels through a refined system can be recognized.

TYPES OF INFORMATION MANAGEMENT SYSTEMS

All information management systems developed and maintained in an organization do not have the same characteristics, audience, or purpose. Some systems were developed to process and summarize transactions and some systems exist to support communications between different organization locations. Let us look at a breakdown of the types of most commonly found systems in organizations. This typology of systems is important because different development methods may be appropriate for different types of systems.

Figure 1.7 shows the breakdown of information management systems into three basic categories: ***operational support systems***, ***decision support systems***, and ***communications support systems***. Of course, as with many categorizations, there are systems which do not neatly fall into one category. Let's look at each of these types of systems and break the categories down even further.

OPERATIONAL SUPPORT SYSTEMS

Operational support systems are what most people think of when someone mentions data processing systems. These systems support the operational activities of the organization by processing high volumes of transactions and generating reports about the operational activities of the organization. If we were to look at our organizational structure pyramid in Figure 1.5, the operational support systems would support the base of the pyramid. Some of the typical systems that would fit in this category include payroll processing, accounts receivable, accounts payable, general ledger, and other accounting functions. Depending on the type of business, other systems may be needed to keep the organization running. These would

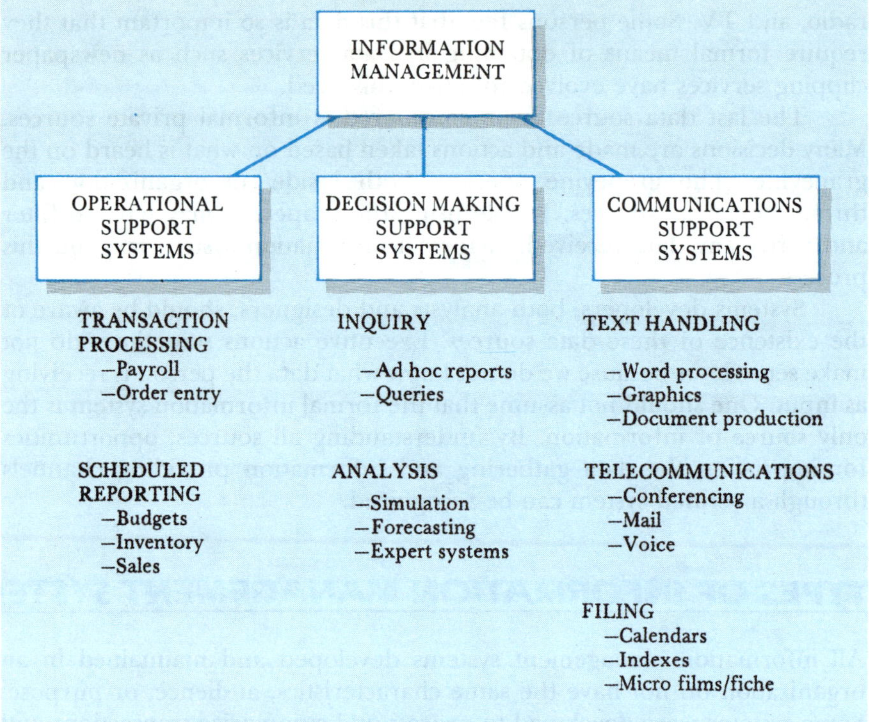

FIGURE 1.7

Types of information management systems.

include systems such as inventory processing, order processing, and sales recording. Specialized industries such as banking would also have some operational support systems that other organizations in manufacturing may not have. These systems have a long life and usually take a long time to build. Many people and organizational units are involved.

Along with the processing and recording of transactions, the transactions support systems would also report on transaction activities. These usually take the form of standardized reports which would be produced as a result of transactions processing. The reports would typically be a by-product of processing and be distributed to those who would be concerned about these activities. Such standardized reports would be produced on a periodic basis that corresponds to the processing period. Examples include budget reports, inventory turnover reports, and sales reports. Transactions could be processed in either a batch or online mode. Although there is a trend to online systems, there are still many systems which process transactions in batch mode.

In a recent survey of over 500 user-managers of systems in 13 organizations, over 63 percent of all systems had the purpose of processing transactions and 16 percent had the purpose of reporting on the transactions (Alloway and Quillard). What was noteworthy in the study was that most of the managers surveyed found that their greatest unsatisfied needs did not fall in these categories. This could indicate a trend toward decision and communication support system development.

Another point that should be noted is that these systems serve the needs of an organizational position more than the personal needs of a manager. If a person is in a certain position, he or she will receive a report, even if it has not been requested. The attitude is taken that if the data is generated, it should be reported to someone. As a result, these systems provide more data than information. In many cases, they do not lead to a surprise or an insight which would trigger a management action. This does not mean that all scheduled reports are not useful. In fact, many requested reports turn out to be scheduled since they prove to be of value to a manager. However, many managers may ask themselves why they are getting certain reports. This often is the result of the bottom-up approach, with the data first being generated and then a purpose or need for the data sought. It is little wonder that many of these reports are never used.

A facsimile machine, allowing an exact copy of a document to be transmitted electronically, may be part of a communication support system. (Courtesy AT&T)

DECISION SUPPORT SYSTEMS

The next category of systems supports the decision making and managerial activities of different levels of managers. This type of system is typically generated from the top-down. This means that a manager in the organizational pyramid has a need which leads to steps to satisfy the need. Since this type of system is a result of a specific manager's request, the information usually is generated to serve a person, not a position. As a result, this type of system may not have as long a life or satisfy as many persons, but it does satisfy the specific need of the requestor. In essence, it is a solution to a problem, while the management reporting systems we discussed above often were solutions looking for problems.

Decision support systems typically are demanded on a short lead time. A manager has a need and wants it satisfied very quickly before the opportunity disappears. As well, the systems often are used once and discarded—they could have a short life. Of course, there are exceptions to this. These types of systems fall into two categories:

1. Inquiries which request some report without data manipulation.
2. Analysis which requires some type of restructuring of the data.

Both of these categories often require data that is external to the organization. For example, a forecast of industry sales would need industry data and a predictive model of the future.

Some examples of decision support systems include simulations, forecasting models, and spreadsheet analysis.

COMMUNICATIONS SUPPORT SYSTEMS

Communications support systems help organization members keep in touch with other persons. These systems support the activities on which managers spend so much of their time, such as talking to others, writing to others, and managing their schedules to be able to meet others. This type of system helps a manager use time more efficiently due to better organization and use of technologic aids.

There are several categories of communications support systems. First, there are the *text handling systems* such as word processing. Another is *telecommunications systems,* which link distant locations by voice or data transmission. Finally, there are *filing systems* such as those which help a manager keep his or her calendar or track essential documents.

IMPORTANCE OF RECOGNIZING THE TYPE OF SYSTEM

When a request is made for a systems project, it will require resources in the form of people and time. The type of system will often determine the amount of time and the type of people that need to be involved with the project. Different types of systems will require a different set of development processes. Even if the same processes are used, the amount of time spent on each will be different. This is an important factor for an analyst/designer.

The analyst/designer must recognize that different types of systems may require different development approaches or techniques. A purchased software package may be appropriate for some developments, a database management system may serve well for other types of systems, and a fourth generation programming language may be appropriate in still other situations. Let us look at the different systems types to understand how they might affect development methods.

Operations support systems often will be tightly coupled together. What is meant by this is that accounts payable will be linked to the general ledger system which will be linked to the payroll system which will be connected to the personnel system, and so on. These projects must be concerned with a systems boundary. It is no wonder that many of these projects never reach any results. The tentacles of one system reach into many other systems.

Operations support systems also involve many organizational members at several organization levels. It is often difficult to manage such a project because of the many user groups that must be satisfied. Systems persons involved in such projects may also have to have better group interpersonal skills and be able to work on a team.

Decision support systems often have only one user. This may make it easier to reach a statement of user needs. However, the decision support system user could be at a higher organizational level, and could have less time to spend with the systems developer. In these cases, quick results by using a fourth generation programming language, or quickly developing a prototype system may be appropriate.

Communications support systems also have their own peculiarities for a systems developer. Often, many geographic locations will have to be considered. Technology will often be very complex and change rapidly. The introduction of such systems also may be met with resistance.

All systems are not alike. This is what makes the work so interesting and challenging and at the same time frustrating. It is helpful for developers to realize that different categories of systems exist and to understand how different development methods may be more appropriate in certain situations.

WHAT IS SYSTEMS ANALYSIS AND DESIGN?

Now that we have defined some of the components of systems in organizations and the different types we will be confronted with, let us proceed to define what we mean by systems analysis and design. There have been some heated discussions by systems professionals about what systems people actually do. There even have been articles written entitled "Is Anyone Here a Systems Analyst?" (Dance) and "There's No Such Thing as a Systems Analyst" (Addleman).

Let us look at the words *analysis* and *design*. *Analysis* means to take something apart to find out more about it. In essence, we are factoring systems into subsystems. In information systems development work, we are studying the inputs to a system, the processing of the inputs, and the outputs the system must provide. We study the *data* movement and storage in the system. We study the machines or *technology* used in the system and the programs that control the machines. We study the *organizing structure,* including the reason for the systems existence and what changes in the environment or in the system itself might cause it to go out of control or not provide the needed outputs. We study the *people* providing inputs, doing processing, and receiving outputs. We look for bottlenecks or delays.

Once we determine what can be done better and what things are not done that should be done, we can take the parts or subsystems and put them together in a better design or structure. "Better" may mean a different organization of the subsystems or may mean using more current technology in some of the subsystems. One or more parts of a subsystem may be replaced by automation. For example, a report may be typewritten rather than handwritten or we may even go a step further and use a small computer and word processor. In our design work, we are always aware of how people, organizing structures, data, and technologies fit together.

To summarize, *analysis* is taking things apart to fully understand them and *design* is establishing a plan to put things back together in a more satisfactory manner (*synthesis*). Once synthesized, the parts can be created, tested, and implemented in the system's environment. One could argue that systems analysis and synthesis may be a more accurate name for the discipline than systems analysis and design.

Development of a new system is very similiar to the creation of a new office building. First, any existing facilities are studied and new requirements are determined by understanding current subsystems and why they do not meet needs. Then, a model or blueprint of a new environment is created by an architect or designer. Finally, the plans are implemented by construction.

Whether we have a simple system for one person or a complex system for an entire organization that exists in many geographic locations, study and understanding is needed of people (*who*), the organizing structure (*what* and *why*), the data that is stored and processed (*what* data), and the technology used (*how*).

SKILLS A SYSTEMS DEVELOPER NEEDS

As we could gather from our discussion of the people involved in systems development, the systems developer needs a variety of behavioral (people) skills and technological (machine) skills. Since there are many courses in technology such as database management, telecommunications, hardware, or programming languages, we will not concentrate on those skills in this book.

Systems developers should be aware of current technology and how specific problems have been solved with the aid of technology. They do not need to be able to manipulate the computer at the machine language level or understand how each technologic device operates, but they should be able to communicate with the persons who have these skills. Systems developers must understand the application of the technology.

Systems developers need problem definition skills. Often, the problem in systems work is defining and communicating the problem. A superb solution to the wrong problem does not serve the problem owner. If the wrong problem is solved, the original problem will still remain.

The systems developer needs communications skills. Once a problem is defined, it must be communicated to others. The problem owner must be assured that the problem is understood. The technical persons who will help solve the problem must understand it to aid in solving it. The skills of interviewing, listening, writing, speaking, presenting, and reviewing must all be practiced to achieve successful systems development.

The systems developer must be a skillful organizer. Large numbers of seemingly unrelated things such as data elements or data flows must be linked together. This skill also includes the ability to relate things so that a model of a system can be put together. This is what is meant by some who say that a good developer can think systematically, linking inputs to processes to stored data to outputs.

The systems developer must have the ability to work with people in organizations. Change must be introduced into organizations to people who often resist the change. Projects must be managed with planning, organizing, controlling, and leadership skills. Systems must be developed with scarce resources for which the developer must compete. The developer must have the skill to work in organizations with many political forces.

If you are thinking that systems developers are a different breed, you are right. It is challenging and exciting work because you get to do a varied number of things with a wide variety of people. It is not a career for those who like to relax and sit on their hands and wait for something to happen.

The following scenario provides an example of a systems development project and the type of persons that were needed to achieve success in the project.

COMPUTER SYSTEM LATEST WEAPON FOR DOCTORS AT WISHARD HOSPITAL

The following article exhibits the characteristics of transaction, decision, and communication support systems and stresses the importance of knowing the users' business to create a successful system.

When patients walk through the doors of Wishard Memorial Hospital's busy general medicine clinic, they're stepping deep into the computer age. Most of them probably don't realize it, for there's little outward sign. The telltale video display terminals are, for the most part, tucked out of sight. But virtually everything that happens to patients in the Regenstrief Health Center, which houses the general medicine clinic and Wishard's other outpatient clinics, is affected in some way by computers.

That's because Regenstrief is the home of a computerized medical records system that's regarded by health-care professionals as one of the two or three most sophisticated in the world. With extensive records on more than 80,000 patients dating back to the mid-1970's, the Regenstrief system is the largest known collection of computerized information on general medical patients, experts say.

But the system does more than simply store information. It can schedule appointments, write prescriptions and alert doctors to unusual laboratory test results. And, it can go a step beyond that. The computer, using hundreds of rules written into its memory, can analyze the medical records of patients coming in for appointments. "Two days before patients' visits," said Dr. Clement J. McDonald, the system's creator, "the computer scans all the records of all the patients who are coming in and applies all the rules to all of those records. The computer's decisions—its suggestions—are printed out and come as a report to the physician."

What that means, simply, is this: The computer takes note of a patient's age, sex, medical history, medications and recent diagnostic test results. Then it compares the answers with guidelines for dozens of diagnostic tests and preventive health measures. If it finds, for example, that a patient hasn't had a vaccination for influenza, fits the profile of people eligible for inoculation and isn't allergic to the vaccine, it will suggest that the doctor administer a shot. Physicians, of course, are not bound to follow the suggestions if they feel they shouldn't or if the patient objects. But doctors say the reminders are helpful. "In a busy practice setting, we all forget lots of things," said Dr. Joseph L. Mamlin, director of medicine at Wishard. "So from a patient care point of view, many preventive health measures are built into the system with consistent reminders."

Those reminders have had a demonstrable impact on the quality of patient care given at Wishard's general medicine clinic, said Dr. William M. Tierney, another physician at Wishard. "We were able to double, in a lot of cases, the physicians' ordering of the preventive care types of things. So, I think, as far as that goes, we've demonstrated time and again in articles in some of the major medical journals that we've been able to affect preventive care. And I think that's important. I think we're finding that things are better for patients and more cost-effective if we can prevent things from happening rather than treating them after they happen," he said.

The computer system has had some other effects, too. For one thing, it has virtually revolutionized the style in which the clinic provides its care. As with most medicine clinics at municipal hospitals, the staff members and residents at Wishard's facility act as the primary, personal physician for most of the patients who walk through the door. "We started out, in the late '60s and early '70s, trying to use the existing medical records system and trying to just sort things out by hand and we really were just a miserable failure," Mamlin said. "I found examples of patients coming to the general medicine clinic who had seen 30 and 40 different doctors over a period of a couple of years."

The system, however, has made it possible to keep track consistently of which doctors are seeing which patients and to make sure those relationships continue, appointment after appointment. "Dr. McDonald's system, as it emerged, created the means to use computer technology to tie every patient very solidly to his primary provider . . . They see the same person every time they come, their appointments are automatically scheduled at the time that physician is going to be there," Mamlin explained. "And so, the patients begin to know the names of their doctors and the doctors begin to know the names of their patients, which is a revolution for a municipal hospital."

The system also makes a patient's medical chart available within seconds whenever a physician needs it, rather than waiting for a file to be pulled from a

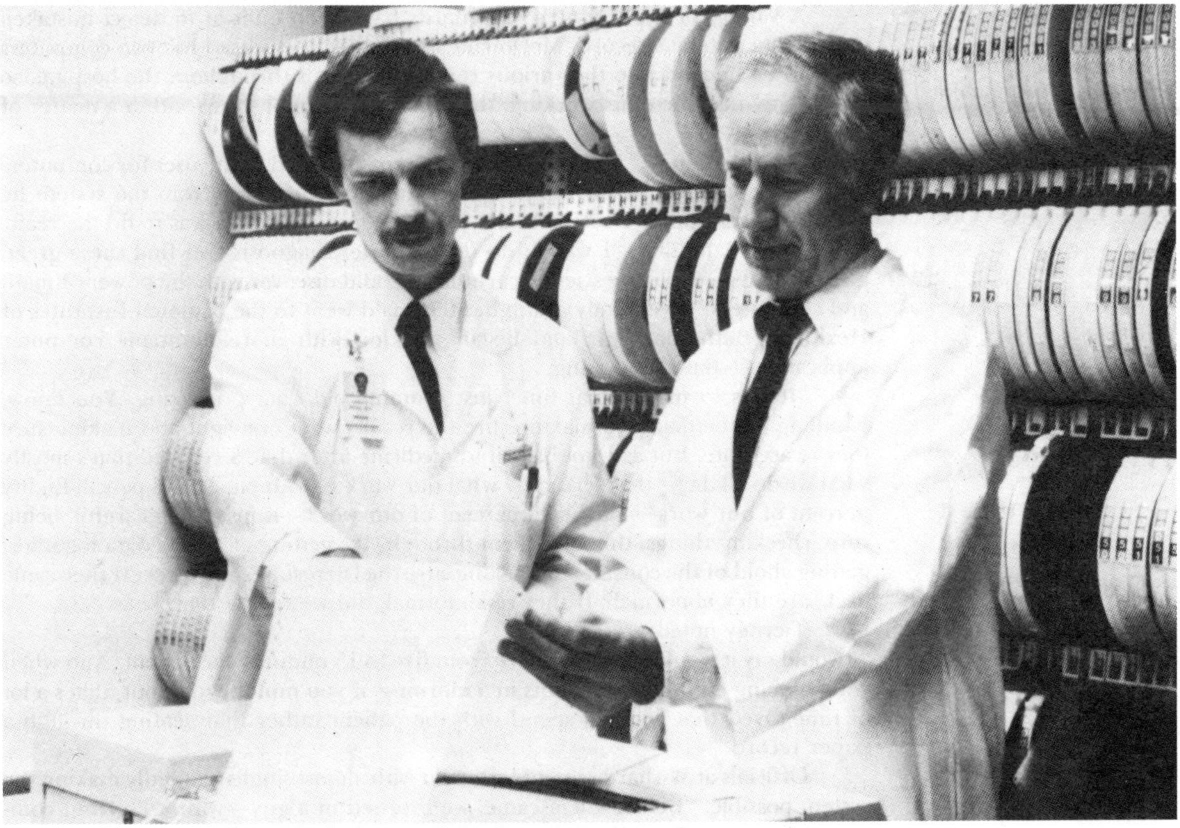

Dr. Clement McDonald, designer of this hospital system for managing patient's records, confers with another staff physician. (Charles Smith, Medical Illustration Dept., Wishard Memorial Hospital)

central records department or chancing that part of a record won't be available. "Using this system, we have 100 percent chart access because it is computer-generated and stationed in the clinic itself. So, that means on every visit and on every phone call, the chart is there. From a patient's standpoint, then, it has added not only the fact that they're seeing the same doctor everytime, but their records are always there. "And a third thing important to patients," Mamlin said, "the system runs the laboratory and it runs the pharmacy. All data that has anything to do with testing of a patient has a final common pathway of being recorded in the computer system. So, all of that data—or any portion of it—can be called up on terminals or printed out on paper for easy reference, with unusual test results marked with asterisks.

Because the system grants easy access to data on more than 80,000 patients, it allows doctors to look at topics that otherwise would be prohibitively difficult to research. "I think a big advantage that a system like this has is in looking for things like drug interactions." Tierney said. "Because we have so many patients registered in the system and so many patients taking both common and uncommon drugs, we have a way of searching for whether or not a certain drug is associated with an abnormal increase in kidney disease or liver disease, for example. Those kinds of studies are, otherwise, very difficult and very time-consuming to do."

A variety of sophisticated safeguards have been built in to detect mistaken entries in a patient's record, McDonald stressed. And Wishard has two computers that can be hooked into the various remote terminals throughout the hospital, so that if one machine quits working, the other can be hooked up within a matter of minutes.

Oddly, when Dr. McDonald first became interested in the uses for computers in medical practice, he envisioned something very different from the system he eventually went on to create. "At the very beginning, my idea was to do the really fancy things," he said. "I wanted to do computer diagnosis and find these great, giant insights—explosive scientific truths we could discover with the power of math and computers." Eventually, though, McDonald went to the National Institutes of Health in Bethesda, Md., and began working with more mundane computer applications—data processing.

"It was to me, at that time, just crummy old data processing. You know, handling all the data and making sure the results went out right and making sure they're accurate. But as I got back into medicine after that, I realized that's mostly what we do all day—that's basically what our work is, with paper and pencil. Eighty percent of our work—maybe 95 percent of our work—is just being careful, being sure, checking things, thinking them through. It's getting all of the data together, getting ahold of the consult and making sure the lab results came back. If they came back, are they abnormal? If they're abnormal, did we realize that?"

Tierney noted:

"I would say it would save anywhere from five to 15 minutes per patient. And when you're seeing eight to 10 patients in a morning, if you multiply that out, that's a lot of time saved that you can spend with the patient rather than leafing through a paper record."

Officials at Wishard credit McDonald with almost single-handedly making the system possible. "Before Clem came, we invested in a guy—with a Ph.D. in computer science—to come in and try to solve some of these problems. It was a disaster because he didn't understand medicine." said Mamlin. "Then we had a couple of doctors say, 'Oh, I can do this.' But they didn't understand computers so we wasted time. But then we got Clem McDonald and we had both in one man—an excellent practicing physician and an excellent computer scientist. "And, of course, we now have a system that everyone nationally recognizes as state-of-the-art."

—From Vic Caleca, in The Indianapolis Star, June 2, 1985, Section A, P. 1.

1. Relate the capabilities of the system mentioned to the three general categories of systems mentioned in Chapter 1. Do you agree that this system is "just data processing"? Is calendar checking, appointment setting, decision rules, checking drug interactions, etc., part of data processing? Does this depend on one's definition of data processing?
2. Who were the people involved in the original systems effort? Do you think there might have been communications difficulties? Relate this to Figure 1.6 in the text. Why did Dr. McDonald have fewer problems? What roles did he fulfill?
3. Do you think the persons who started the systems efforts knew what the final results would be? Do you think Dr. McDonald had a better idea of the people, organizing structures, and data subsystems that would be needed in the system?
4. Do you think there may have been resistance to the original system being developed for physicians by nonphysicians? Why?
5. How have doctors benefited from the system? Patients? Hospital administrators? Anyone else?
6. Find an example of exception reporting, backup/recovery, and controls for correctness in the Case Study.

A CLOSER LOOK AT SYSTEMS DEVELOPMENT

Now that we know what systems are and have a generic definition of systems analysis and design, we must move on and apply these concepts to the specific job of systems development. We have found that certain steps or methods have resulted in more easily accepted and better quality systems. We will discuss these steps in the next chapter. As well, we have found that certain techniques will help in developing systems. We will also overview these in the next chapter. In essence, we will discuss *what* must be done in a systems project and *how* we do these things.

REFERENCES AND FURTHER READINGS

Addleman, E. "There's No Such Thing as a Systems Analyst," *Proceedings of the Fourteenth Annual Computer Personnel Research Conference*. T. Willoughby, ed., New York: Association for Computing Machinery, 1976, pp. 36–43.

Alloway, Robert M., and Judith A. Quillard. "User Managers' Systems Needs," *MIS Quarterly*, vol. 7, no. 2, June 1983, pp. 27–41.

Athey, Thomas H. *Systematic Systems Approach: An Integrated Method for Solving Systems Problems*, Englewood Cliffs, NJ: Prentice-Hall, Inc., 1982.

Boulding, Kenneth E. "General Systems Theory—The Skeleton Of Science," *Management Science*, February 1956, pp. 197–208.

Brody, Howard, and David S. Sobel. "A Systems View of Health and Disease," in *Ways of Health*. David S. Sobel, ed., New York: Harcourt, Brace, Inc., 1979, pp. 87–104.

Dance, D. L. "Is Anyone Here a Systems Analyst?" *Proceedings of the Fourteenth Annual Computer Personnel Research Conference*. T. Willoughby, ed., New York: Association for Computing Machinery, 1976, pp. 29–35.

Pirsig, Robert M. *Zen and the Art of Motorcycle Maintenance*, New York: William Morrow, Inc., 1974.

Vitalari, Nicholas F. "Knowledge as a Basis for Expertise in Systems Analysis: An Empirical Study," *MIS Quarterly*, vol. 9, no. 3, September 1985, pp. 221–241.

Weinberg, Gerald M. *An Introduction to General Systems Thinking*, New York: Wiley-Interscience, 1975.

______, and Daniela Weinberg. *On the Design of Stable Systems*, New York: Wiley-Interscience, 1981.

Weinberg, Victor. *Structured Analysis*, New York: Yourdon Press, 1978.

REVIEW QUESTIONS

1. What is the difference between systems analysis and systems design?
2. What is the difference between data and information?
3. Are all the organizing structures in an organization formal and written? Explain why or why not.
4. Do all systems have a boundary? Explain.

5. What people roles have to be fulfilled on a systems project?
6. What are the four major subsystems in an organization?
7. Why is it important to distinguish between different types of information management systems?

DISCUSSION QUESTIONS

1. *Interfaces* are where one system meets another system. To have a successful interface, knowledge of both systems is important. Explain why this may be true for cars interfacing with road (nonroad?) surfaces. What is the part of the car that touches (interfaces with) the road? Does the road surface influence the selection of the car part?
2. What does someone mean when he or she says, "I'm going to beat the system"? What is necessary knowledge before the system can be "beat"? Be sure to include the components of a system definition in your discussion.
3. Now that you have some knowledge of what systems analysis is, take a side in the argument—"a systems analyst must be very skilled in computer programming."
4. Discuss the difference between data and information. Can information for one person be data for another person?
5. Some persons refer to "communications support systems" as described in this chapter as "office automation" systems. Can an office be automated? Which of the above words do you feel are more descriptive?
6. Why might an undefined system boundary lead to overspending a systems development project budget?

EXERCISES

1. Draw a diagram of an entity as a system. A bicycle, motorcycle, stereo components, etc., may be appropriate. Be sure to label the subsystems, inputs, outputs, purpose, and boundaries.
2. Make an attempt to meet a person in systems development work or who has been involved in a systems development project. Have them describe what they like and dislike about experiences in systems work. Ask them to define "success" in systems work. Be prepared to share this knowledge with other class members.
3. Form two groups of persons with systems developers in one group and systems users in another group. Each group is to come up with two series of statements or words to follow:
   "We see us as . . ."
   "We see them as . . ."
   Compare and contrast the different and same perceptions of how systems developers see users and how users see systems developers. Are there differences in perceptions that could lead to difficulties in communication?

4. Perform a system definition of an organizational work unit. Set the boundaries for the unit (what is inside and outside the system). Define the inputs and outputs. List the key environmental considerations and relationships. Specify the people involved in the work unit and their organizing structures. What data is used by the system? Briefly define the major processes needed to transform the inputs into outputs. What technologic aid is used to perform the processes or manage the data?

CHAPTER 2

Systems Development Methodologies: An Overview

CHAPTER OBJECTIVES

You should be able to:

- Distinguish between a method as a process, and as a technique
- State the processes followed to develop a system
- Explain why systems development is similar to problem solving
- Explain why systems development might be viewed as a system
- Identify structured and traditional development techniques
- Relate development techniques to the development process
- Understand success factors for a systems project

THIS CHAPTER DISCUSSES three main topics: the process of systems development, techniques used to conduct systems development, and how the processes and techniques fit together to accomplish systems building. Structured and traditional development techniques are described and contrasted. The context of systems development as a problem-solving process, managed as a project, is introduced. An example of an actual systems development project using a systems development methodology is included.

Systems are everywhere. But they don't just happen; they must be created. This chapter explores the means for creating organizational information systems. First, an overview will introduce many terms and techniques that may be unfamiliar to you. You will be introduced to methods of systems development which will be detailed later in the book. Hopefully, this chapter will create a "hunger" for more knowledge which you will gain as you continue through the book. In fact, many readers have found that reading this chapter later in their study served as a good review and a reinforcement of material that later became familiar to them.

As discussed in Chapter 1, there are several kinds of organizational information systems. The general development process for each will be very similar. However, the specific subprocesses of development and the techniques used for each of the types of systems may differ. The methods used in different organizations will be different as well. Some of the similarities and differences will be examined in this chapter. Three main topics will be discussed in this chapter: the process of systems development, techniques used in systems development, and how the process and techniques are integrated.

In progressing through the discussion of systems, you will encounter the word ***methodology***. Literally, the word means a study of methods. In the systems development field, the word connotes not a study of methods, but a method, a defined way of doing things. In systems development practice, a method can mean two different things:

1. A *set of processes* required to successfully build a system, *or*
2. A technique or *set of techniques* used in systems development.

To put this chapter in perspective, let's look at these meanings. The first meaning refers to the *processes* needed to develop systems (represented by the largest box shown in Figure 2.1). The collection of these processes is commonly called the *systems development life cycle*. The life cycle indicates all possible activities needed to complete a systems project.

Using the life cycle, a systems project manager plans a project by selecting the needed subset of processes, estimates the time to complete the processes, schedules the start and completion of the processes, assigns people to complete the processes, and controls the project by measuring actual process progress and comparing it to the original plan. These activities are commonly called ***project management*** (see Figure 2.1). Project managers specify when the processes are to be done, in what order, who is to do them, and time estimates. This is called the ***project plan.*** The processes specify *what* is to be done. They indicate there is a need to do something and produce some result. These processes often can be done in many different ways.

The second meaning of methodology refers to the way or *how* a process is to be carried out. These are the specific *techniques* that must be used. A technique specifies one method of accomplishing the process. In the building construction industry, wall construction would be a process. It

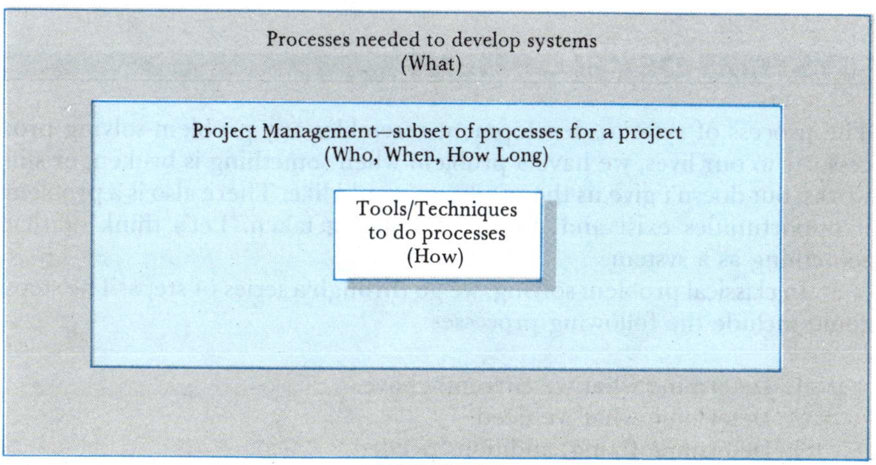

FIGURE 2.1
Systems development components.

tells workers what they must do. Framing in carpentry and bricklaying in masonry would be two techniques used in wall building.

These techniques are sometimes called the tools of systems development. In this book we will discuss many of these tools and techniques including such things as data flow diagramming, product reviews by peers, and screen layout charting. Since a technique specifies how the process is to be done, it specifies a means to achieve the results specified by the process. Different techniques may be used given different conditions. Since the actual doing is in performing the technique, training and skills are associated with tools and techniques, not processes. A full instruction to a systems development person will indicate:

What to do (process)

How to do it (technique to be used)

When it should be started and finished (project management)

An example that may clarify the above discussion is the common process in systems development of writing and documenting procedures. The project plan may require the process (first definition of methodology) of writing a procedure.

The systems developers would need to know what technique was specified in the organization, commonly called the "standard." Techniques could include plain English narrative, look-up tables, decision trees, structured English, or some other procedure-writing technique. The developers must use a technique (second definition of methodology) or techniques that are acceptable in the organization, appropriate in the situation, and in which they have been trained to have adequate skill.

In summary, the word *methodology* can be used to describe the project plans telling what is to be done, and a specific technique which specifies how it is to be done. In the next portion of this chapter, we will discuss the process of systems development from the "what is to be done" perspective.

THE PROCESS OF SYSTEMS DEVELOPMENT

The process of systems development resembles any problem-solving process. As in our lives, we have a problem when something is broken, or still works, but doesn't give us the results we would like. There also is a problem if opportunities exist and no action is being taken. Let's think of that something as a system.

In classical problem solving, we go through a series of steps. The steps could include the following processes:

1. Determine what we currently have.
2. Determine what we need.
3. Determine fixing, additions needed.

4. Determine if changes are worth doing.
5. Plan a new design.
6. Acquire any needed parts.
7. Assemble, test, and use.

The initial step is to understand the current workings and purpose of the existing system. Then we must stipulate the desired results. A determination then must be made if something has to be replaced, rebuilt, or added to produce the desired results. Next, we determine if all or part of the fixing is worth doing. Then, we plan a design to rearrange and/or add the parts to achieve the desired result. We would build or buy the parts needed. Following the design, the parts are reassembled. Notes should be taken throughout the process as to what we will have and how to use it to get the results we desire. Finally, the result is tested and used until a need for change comes again. The previous steps are reiterated if we make discoveries that change the problem or make the solution inappropriate.

This process is commonly called the ***systems development life cycle.*** A system is given life by being conceived, gestated, born, used, maintained, and buried (or reborn).

THE SYSTEMS DEVELOPMENT LIFE CYCLE

The systems development life cycle is an organized process for developing and maintaining systems. It helps establish a systems project plan because it gives an overall " shopping list" of processes and subprocesses needed to develop a system. A project manager can select the pertinent subset of processes to complete the project currently being planned.

There are many variations of the basic development life cycle. An international conference reviewed 13 "information systems design methodologies" (Olle et al.). If there was any conclusion reached by the conference, it was that there is no one formula or recipe for systems development. But there are some essential steps, common to all, to be taken in developing any system. These steps include gathering and analyzing data about the subsystems in an information system. As you remember from Chapter 1, the subsystems of concern are the people subsystem, the data subsystem, the organizing structure subsystem, and the technology subsystem. Once the subsystems and their interrelationships are understood, proposals for an improved design are suggested, a new design is chosen, and a new system is built, tested, and used.

Once you enter an organization and are involved in the systems development process, you should explore the methodology or process followed in the organization. You likely will find that it is different than the one another neighboring organization uses. In fact, in many large organizations (and some not so large), you will find that the actual subprocesses followed and the amount of time spent on them will differ between divisions in the same organizations on very similar projects.

THE LIFE CYCLE AS A SYSTEM

The systems development life cycle might be viewed as a system. It is a set of interrelated parts assembled for a purpose. The parts or processes, which can be viewed as subsystems, receive inputs from each other or the environment. The system receives data from other systems, indicating that the development system has a boundary. The development system, like any other system, has to be changed or maintained to be responsive to the environment. Depending on the type of inputs the system will receive and the needed outputs, a different set of subsystems (subprocesses) must be invoked. Taking this view, it may be more appropriate to call the systems development life cycle a systems development system.

Viewing the life cycle as a system allows analysis of the life cycle from a systems point of view. The life cycle system can be broken into subsystems and the subsystems into sub-subsystems. This systemic view allows the process of systems development to be described in a hierarchical manner.

The most basic building block is the ***process*** which we discussed earlier in the chapter. Processes may be broken into subprocesses. Subprocesses may be further broken into sub-subprocesses. At some point, it does not make sense to decompose a subsystem any further since it is at a basic enough level to be understood and used as part of a plan. Different organizations may use different words for process, subprocess, and sub-subprocess, such as "phase" or "activity" or "task," but the objective is the same. All break down the systems development life cycle into more easily managed parts and pieces.

These hierarchical groupings of processes are used for convenience in both planning and description. Different detail levels allow the process of systems development to be described to different levels of management. For example, strategic level managers may be interested in the progress of a project but only at the process level. A manager who is going to be the recipient of the project in his or her department may be interested to know when a subprocess such as user training will take place.

Another advantage is the clear picture of the inputs to any process and the outputs it should produce. Without the proper inputs, the outputs cannot be produced. This aids in planning and controlling projects. There are a number of commercially sold methodologies that have a different number of processes to develop systems, but all the methodologies serve the same purpose—aiding in the management of systems development.

AN EXAMPLE OF A SYSTEMS DEVELOPMENT SYSTEM

Let us look at a system for developing systems. As can be seen in Figure 2.2, there is a series of seven processes for developing a system. Having seven processes is not mandatory. In fact, other methodologies may have five, eight, 13, or 20 main processes. As mentioned in Chapter 1, a system is detailed with subsystems so we can understand the system better. The system describer must decide how to break the system into subsystems to best serve the purpose at hand.

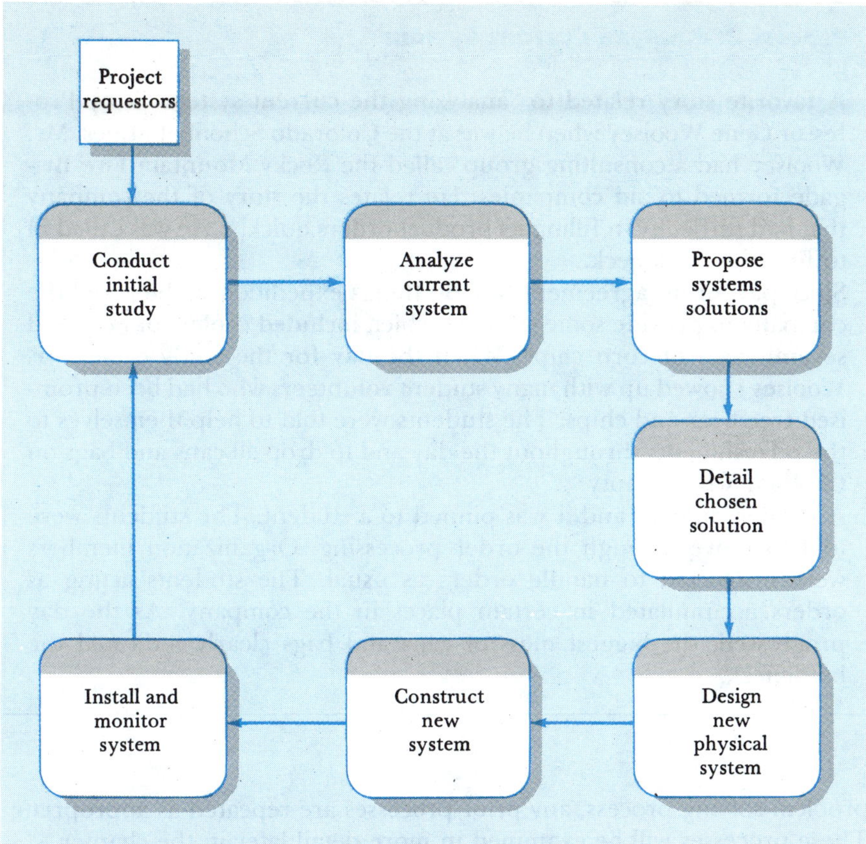

FIGURE 2.2
A systems development process methodology.

Our earlier discussions of the systems development methodology mentioned that it resembled a problem-solving process. Let us look at the seven processes and see how they fit into this definition.

First, we must recognize that we have a problem or opportunity. This is done in Process 1 where we ensure that the project is a viable one, and in Process 2, where the current system and why it is not satisfactory are studied. Next, the size and scope of the problem solution are clearly determined by defining a system boundary, and the mix of technology and people needed to solve the problem is detailed (Process 3). A set of solution alternatives is proposed and one alternative is selected. Then we analyze further within the selected system boundary and constraints (Process 4). In Process 5, the components are put back together in the form of a system design or blueprint. In Process 6, the system components are built and tested. Finally, in Process 7, the problem solution is installed in the organization and reviewed to make sure it really does solve the problem. If not, changes are suggested that would again be evaluated in Process 1 as to whether there was a problem that should be solved. Again, as in our

Process 2: Analyze Current System

A favorite story related to "analyzing the current system" is by Professor Gene Woolsey when he was at the Colorado School of Mines. Mr. Woolsey had a consulting group called the Rocky Mountain Fire Brigade formed to aid companies. He relates the story of the company that had difficulty in filling its product orders quickly. He was called in to find the bottleneck.

Since part of his agreement is to do things expeditiously, he asked the company to provide some supplies which included coolers of beer and several cases of corn chips. When the day for the study came, Mr. Woolsey showed up with many student volunteers who had been promised free beer and chips. The students were told to help themselves to the refreshments throughout the day and to drop all cans and bags on the floor when empty.

An order came in and it was pinned to a student. The students were told to move through the order processing. Organization members were instructed to handle orders as usual. The students acting as orders accumulated in certain places in the company. As the day progressed, the biggest mess of cans and bags clearly indicated the bottleneck.

problem-solving process, any prior processes are repeated as appropriate. These processes will be examined in more detail later in the chapter.

The basic processes can be thought of as *defining, designing, constructing,* and *using.* You can probably relate these processes to the development of a building, an automobile, or any product that can be purchased today. A building is defined in terms of what is needed, designed in terms of developing an architectural plan, constructed in terms of actual building, and then used. If it is not satisfactory, changes are made (remodeling).

A true systems analyst will see systems and the systems building processes in many day-to-day activities. This is an excellent method of becoming an outstanding analyst and will reinforce the advantages of using a systems approach.

ADVANTAGES OF USING A SYSTEMS APPROACH TO SYSTEMS DEVELOPMENT

At one time, systems development was treated as a cottage industry since systems developers conducted their work as craftspeople. Each project was treated as a separate and unique activity. In essence, every system was "cobbled" together rather than using the methods of the industrial revolution, which include interchangeable parts, a standardized process, written procedures, and specialization. With the introduction of some order to the systems development process, it has taken on more of an engineering or scientific approach. We still cannot take an assembly-line approach to systems development, but we can use a more standardized and repeatable set of processes and a better set of tools and techniques.

If we were again to use the car as an analogy to the systems we build, we would find that every car built in a cottage industry would be built from scratch with a newly created plan. We don't want to have the expense of every car being a custom creation. Limited editions are very expensive for a consumer. We want to use some of the advantages of standardization in our systems work. There are a number of advantages to using a planned systems approach to systems development. They include:

Improved Understanding and Tracking of Projects. If we had some standardized and repeatable processes, the project plan would become familiar to both developers and users. It would not be a totally new creation with new names and labels, but would follow a general plan for all projects which would be modified to fit the particular project assigned. Both the development and user groups would be familiar with the general processes and could see where the project was in the development cycle. They would have a visual checklist of what is to be done and what has been completed.

Ease of Collection of Performance Data to Aid in Future Project Planning and Estimating. A standardized and repeatable set of processes in the development cycle would allow for performance data collection. Once there was some performance data, project managers would be assisted in making better estimates of how long processes should take in the future. You might say that they would have a better information system because they had a better database. This is what industries such as printing or auto repair have been doing for many years.

Users Would Have a Better Idea of What Has to be Done to Accomplish a Systems Project. Even a "small change" requested by a user could result in many development processes having to be completed. As well, users would be identified as having an important role in the development process which, if neglected, would result in project delays. History has shown that projects in which users and developers had only a short period of initial contact, and then no contact until a solution was reached, have ended in failure and disappointment. Responsibility for success must be shared by both users and developers. The development system defines the roles that must be fulfilled by each.

Training Needed to Perform a Technique Can Be Included in a Process Specification. If the person assigned to a development process is not trained, the project manager must either assign another person to the project who is trained, or allow time in the project plan for formal or on-the-job training.

To summarize, having a defined systems development methodology aids planning, organizing, staffing, directing, and controlling of systems projects. It leads to organized thinking about a project and minimizes omissions of processes that are necessary for successful systems development. A few persons have believed that an organized process is necessary to avoid a project life cycle that resembles the one below proposed by McLean and Welke, "a life cycle without a plan" (found in Sanders):

1. Good "undefined" idea
2. Wild euphoria
3. Growing concern
4. Disillusionment
5. Unmitigated disaster
6. Search for the guilty
7. Punishment of innocent
8. Promotion of uninvolved

It is important to note that the process of systems development has been changing over the years. Different types of systems will require a different subset of processes to accomplish a project. As well, changes in technology such as the microcomputer revolution, fourth generation programming languages, the office automation movement, and communications service packaging have created additional considerations in the development of systems. Another factor causing great changes is the movement toward establishment of a database environment. All of these factors have created a need to change or add to the processes needed to develop a system.

The discussion in the first part of this chapter has given us an understanding of *what* must be done in the systems development process. To implement these processes, there has been an evolution of new system development tools and techniques. These tools and techniques are all part of the *how* of systems development. This will be the topic of the next part of this chapter.

TECHNIQUES NEEDED FOR SYSTEMS DEVELOPMENT

The techniques of systems are often called ***development tools.*** They are the *how* of systems development. We will introduce these techniques in this section with an overview. In later chapters, we will discuss them in greater detail and practice them, but it is important to understand how all the techniques fit together to know what your systems development tool kit should contain.

The techniques of systems development are often separated into the categories of ***traditional*** and ***structured techniques.*** This categorization may cause some confusion, so we should have an awareness of what is meant when someone in the systems development area mentions traditional or structured. One author (Colter) distinguishes between traditional and structured techniques by stating that traditional techniques concentrate on defining the detail of system input, output, and processing. Structured techniques concern themselves with the general structure of the system and

Processes	*Traditional*	*Structured*
Representing system flows	System flowchart	Data flow diagram
Representing data	Forms, layouts Grid charts	Data dictionary Data structure diagrams Normalization
Communicating	Interviews	Peer/user product reviews
Representing procedures	English narrative Playscript	Decision tree/table Structured English
Representing programs	Program flowchart I/O layouts	Structure charts Warnier/Orr diagrams

FIGURE 2.3

Traditional versus structured techniques.

add detail later. This is a good starting distinction between traditional and structured techniques. Our distinction will evolve as we examine some of the differences more closely. But before we move to our discussion of the traditional techniques, it is important to note that a combination of techniques is needed for a full set of development tools.

Figure 2.3 shows some of the traditional and structured techniques for performing the processes of systems development. The list is not meant to be all-inclusive nor is it intended to show that one set of techniques is better than the other. Some of the techniques also overlap the processes where they have usefulness.

TRADITIONAL DEVELOPMENT TECHNIQUES

Traditional techniques include many of the skills that are often taken for granted when we talk about systems development work. These include skills such as interviewing, making presentations, drawing physical system flowcharts, and laying out input or output documents or screens. Systems developers have been doing these things for many years. They will continue to practice many of these traditional techniques. We will give an overview of each technique and detail some of them in later chapters when we need to practice them to progress on a development project. Try not to feel overwhelmed by this mass of new material.

Traditional techniques include:

1. *System Flowcharts:* A graphic means of representing a system by showing the physical devices and manual activities and the flow of data between them.
2. *Program Flowcharts:* A graphic means of representing the logic of a computer program or human procedure.
3. *Playscript:* A narrative exhibiting human roles and the activities people must perform to execute a procedure.
4. *Input Layout Forms:* A means of exhibiting the format and content of a document or screen that is used to collect input data.

Making presentations is a traditional—and important—skill for systems developers. (c. Joel Gordon 1980)

5. *Output Layout Forms:* A means of exhibiting the format and content of a document or screen that is used to display data or information that is the output of a system to a user.
6. *File Layouts:* A chart of the content, size, and type of data elements stored as part of a system.
7. *Grid Charts:* A chart of the relationship between different system components such as the usage of data elements by different program modules.

By examining the above definitions, it can be determined that traditional techniques concentrate on the inputs, outputs, and technologic processing in a system. They concentrate on *how* things are done and stored. The results of using these techniques are often difficult for nontechnical persons to understand. This technology orientation was one of the reasons that traditional techniques were difficult to use in communicating with system users. This led to a search for better communication means.

STRUCTURED TECHNIQUES

Structured techniques gained popularity in the late 1970s and early 1980s. But many persons are still confused by what is meant by "structured." It is not just an organized way of doing something, but is the *building of something very complex using a few basic structures.* By solidly combining these structures, we can challenge G. Weinberg's assertion that "If builders built buildings the way programmers write programs, the first woodpecker to come along would destroy civilization."

Structured techniques include a set of tools that have evolved in the last 10 or 15 years. These techniques differ from traditional techniques in that they emphasize building structural models of a system that facilitate user–developer and developer–developer communication. The models are often described as serving as a semantic bridge, that is, as something understood by two parties having a different language. They have much more of an engineering orientation in the sense of building models of something that we can evaluate before we actually start physical building. These are called *logical* (versus *physical*) models.

Basic tó the topic of model building and structured systems development is distinguishing between logical and physical models. A logical model exhibits *what* is done by a system. A physical model is one implementation of the logical model. This is very similiar to our definitions of methodology. "Logical" exhibits *what* and "physical" exhibits *how.* If there is more than one way of doing something, it usually indicates that what you have is a logical representation.

Structured techniques are based on the premise that we should have a thorough understanding of the problem before we start to solve it. We gain that understanding by building a model of a system and then sharing it with other developers and users. The model is formally reviewed and changed until it accurately represents an existing system, showing understanding, or a proposed system, giving a blueprint for the future.

As we consider the differences between traditional and structured techniques, it is clear that a *systems flowchart is a physical representation* of a system. It exhibits the physical storage mediums and the physical processing units that are used.

Data flow diagrammming is a technique that we will introduce in the structured tools to present *a logical representation* of a system. The data flow diagram only indicates generically that something is stored, but does not indicate on what medium. It could be on a disk, tape, paper ledger, index card, or in someone's head. All we know is that it is stored. Once we choose the physical implementation of the storage, we then are building a physical model of the system. We know we will have to do this to finally build a system, but if we only see the physical model, it is human nature to see a solution to a problem rather than understanding the problem.

Successful systems developers have found that it is wise to build and evaluate logical models of both data flows and data structures/storage before settling on a physical implementation. However, it is often necessary to understand the system from a physical point before we can represent it logically. The structured tools and techniques give us an easy way to represent a logical model of a system. These techniques include:

1. *Context Diagram:* A graphic representation of system inputs and their sources, and system outputs and their destinations. This diagram will establish and exhibit the system boundary.
2. *Data Flow Diagram:* A jargonless, graphic representation of a logical model of a system. Data flow diagrams (DFDs) describe systems at any level of detail by breaking systems down into subsystems. They describe systems using the four structures of *data flows, data stores, processes,* and *external entities.*
3. *Data Dictionary:* A repository of all data about the system under development. The data dictionary contains detail about data flows, data stores, processes, and the system environment shown on the data flow diagram. The relationships between data elements and the attributes of data elements are shown in the data dictionary. In Chapter 3, we will discuss the data about a system that must be collected and maintained to have adequate system documentation.
4. *Structure Chart:* A graphical representation of the modules, data passing between modules, and the control flows in a computer program. The structure chart is developed by performing a series of manipulations on a data flow diagram. This is the link between structured analysis and structured design.
5. *Process Logic:* A graphic or structured representation of the complex processes needed to perform user procedures. These include the tools of decision tables, decision trees, and structured English.
6. *Data Structuring:* Techniques that tie in with relational database structures and the use of links between the data stores shown on the data flow diagrams. Data structuring also provides a means to exhibit how user requests for information would be satisfied from the databases.
7. *Structured Programs:* The building of programs according to the blueprint shown on the structure charts using only the three basic structures of sequence, repeat,. and if-then-else.
8. *Reviews:* The team process of reviewing products of systems development by users or peers while still preserving the developer's ego. This results in systems products being "owned" by the development team rather than the individual developer. "Bosses" are not allowed to attend peer reviews because they tend to evaluate the person rather than the product.

MISCONCEPTIONS ABOUT STRUCTURED TECHNIQUES

There have been many misconceptions about structured techniques. This section will attempt to clear up some of them by stressing points made earlier:

1. *Structured* does not just mean organized. It means using a few basic structures to build something complex.
2. A model is a *logical model* if it can have more than one physical implementation.
3. A *data flow diagram* is a tool to build a logical model of a system. Data flow diagramming is only one component of structured systems analysis.
4. A *data flow diagram* can show a system at *different levels of detail* through functional decomposition of processes, while a *system flowchart* typically shows a system at *one level of detail.* A set of data flow diagrams is much like a set of maps; a national map shows major routes, a state map shows more secondary routes, and finally a city map shows all streets.
5. A *data flow diagram* typically represents a *logical* model while a *system flowchart* typically represents a *physical* model.
6. *Systems flowcharts* represent physical implementations of current or proposed systems detailing the *hardware/software* representation.
7. A *data dictionary* is more than a data element repository. A comprehensive data dictionary should contain data about a system including who is involved, what the system does, why it exists, when it is needed, and how it does what it must do.

From the above descriptions, it should be clear that structured techniques will not replace traditional techniques. A systems developer who is a real professional will use the strengths of any of the techniques when it is appropriate. He or she must *know when* as well as *know how.*

Now that we have some background on both the process and techniques of systems development, let us move on to see how the two "methodologies" representing processes and techniques can be fitted together.

COMBINING THE DEVELOPMENT PROCESS AND TECHNIQUES

Figure 2.2 is the most generalized view of the processes used in systems development. As discussed earlier, the development process could be considered a system for developing systems. Within the boundary of the system, there are the seven processes mentioned earlier in the chapter. These processes are connected by outputs from one process serving as inputs to another process.

There is a connection shown to the Project Requestors in the environment. These Requestors desire new systems or changes to existing systems. The primary system development output is an application system that would serve the needs of the requestors and other users.

In systems development work, it is essential to have a good understanding of the development process. It is important to have the development process in mind when any systems project is undertaken. This will allow you to know where the project is currently and where it is going.

Likewise, it is essential to know what development techniques are used at different stages of the development process. To understand the relationships of the processes and techniques, we will discuss each of them.

Process 1: Conduct Initial Study

Purpose: Determine project priority by defining problem or opportunity.

Output: A mix of projects with acceptable paybacks that utilize available development resources. Preliminary organizational data, systems documentation, and cost/benefit data.

Subprocesses: Determine who is affected by the system to be studied. Make a rough estimate of the benefits from accomplishing the project. Make a rough estimate of the costs of the project. Draw up a project plan for the later processes.

Techniques and Skills: Interviewing, presenting, peer/user reviewing, data flow diagramming, system flowcharting, requirements defining.

Process 2: Analyze Current System

Purpose: Understand and document the structure and purpose of the current system. Determine requirements of the new system.

Output: A set of user-reviewed and accepted models of the organization, the data movements and storage, the processing needed, and the organization needs that would be served by an improved system. A more refined set of system costs and benefits to determine project continuance.

Subprocesses: Convert any existing physical descriptions of data storage, data flows, and processes to logical descriptions. Gather and analyze data on who is involved with the system, what the system does, why changes are needed, and what data and processes a new system should contain.

Techniques and Skills: Interviewing, presenting, peer/user reviewing, organizational modeling, data flow diagramming, data structuring, requirements defining, procedure writing.

Process 3: Propose Systems Solutions

Purpose: Establish a menu of possible system solutions at different costs to obtain different benefits. Project sponsors must choose the alternative that most closely meets their needs at an acceptable cost.

Output: A defined system boundary for the proposed new system indicating what subsystems will be included. Within the system boundary, the person–machine boundary must be established. This will enable the system designers to propose alternative hardware and software solutions.

Subprocesses: Determine any simplification, compression, modification, and elimination of existing processes and data. Add any new processes and data stores. Generate a set of alternative system boundaries and gain approval on one. Generate a person–machine boundary and get it approved.

Techniques and Skills: Presenting, peer/user reviewing, data flow diagramming, data structuring.

Process 4: Detail Chosen Solution

Purpose: Detail logically the data storage, data flows, and data processing within the chosen system boundary. Decide on system acquisition and make any vendor decisions.

Output: A statement of the selected vendors as well as detailed new system specifications. This may include a statement of the use of specific software packages, programming languages, or system generators.

Subprocesses: Refine and explode subprocesses and data stores and flows for the selected alternative. Include error handling, audit control, and backup and recovery details. Select application software that is to be acquired. Select hardware and systems software and communication network. Select any external data sources. Secure needed contracts.

Techniques and Skills: Data flow diagramming, presenting, peer/user reviewing, vendor selection, contract negotiation, technology configuration generation, audit/control design, backup and recovery design.

Process 5: Design New Physical System

Purpose: Specify, review, and approve the structure of nonacquired software, human procedures, physical facilities, and databases.

Output: A physical representation of the system inputs, outputs, programs, procedures, and storage. Included are program structure charts, human procedures, input and output layouts, file and database structures, and physical site plans.

Subprocesses: Design human subsystem including layout formats, procedures, manuals, and training. Design technology subsystem. Design data structure subsystem. Design physical site specifications. Specify data conversion procedures.

Techniques and Skills: Human–machine dialog design, input and output layout design, structure charting, data structuring, site planning, manual writing, training development, procedure writing.

Process 6: Construct New System

Purpose: Bring working version of the new system to a usable stage.

Output: A working version of the new system that provides users with real benefits.

Subprocesses: Write and test computer programs. Write and test human procedures. Create test data and procedures. Develop human materials and training. Install hardware and acquired software. Conduct training. Conduct integrated current version tests.

Training users is an essential activity in systems development. (c. Joel Gordon 1985)

Techniques and Skills: Computer programming, technical writing, test data creation, training development, software testing, training implementation.

Process 7: Install and Monitor System

Purpose: Ensure that the version of the system operates in the organizational environment. Ensure that future changes are recorded and passed to the project planning function.

Output: An accepted working system version with suggested changes.

Subprocesses: Run system in the organizational environment. Certify usability, operability, standard adherence, controlability, and maintainability. Create operation, maintenance, and training libraries from development documention. Cut over to new system. Monitor installed system. Perform postimplementation review to actually measure expected benefits.

Techniques and Skills: Presentations, peer/user and quality assurance reviews, training implementation.

Reviewing the above processes and techniques, it should be clear that the job of systems development is an exciting one requiring a diversity of interpersonal and technical skills. In the following chapters, we will work toward the goal of detailing the above processes and the techniques required to accomplish them, especially those concerned with human communications. But first, we will try to anchor our findings with a real-world case.

AN EXAMPLE SYSTEMS PROJECT

To more fully understand a systems project, we will review a development case for a hypothetical situation. It will exhibit the growth of an idea into a real working system.

Art Fletcher is a national class steeplechase runner. As with many serious athletes, Art has to walk a fine line between top fitness and injury. The track and field club that provides Art with support decided to help him by using modern technology to develop better training schedules. They commissioned a systems developer, Jim Arnold, to develop a system for Art.

Art's task is to determine the amount and intensity of his training. He has trained so hard at times that he got sick and had to lay off for a period of time. There are some physical measures that would indicate his reaction to the training. In essence, Art would like to correlate his training intensity with his heart rate, resting pulse, blood tests, etc., so he can train and not strain.

We will use the systems development life cycle to trace how this system came to life.

Process 1: Conduct Initial Study

Purpose: Determine project priority by defining problem or opportunity.

Output: Preliminary organizational data, systems documentation, and cost/benefit data.

Jim and Art got together for an initial meeting. Jim determined that Art was serious enough about the project to spend time playing a key role in developing the system. The project was a priority for Art since he was suffering with another injury from overtraining.

Jim gathered some preliminary data from Art and from other persons Art identified. He recorded data about the key persons in the project and their roles in Art's training. He surveyed and recorded data on some of the training and clinical data Art thought was critical. Jim read two articles related to using computers for athletes given to him by the project proponents. He now understood why some people felt this was a real opportunity.

Jim laid out a rough sketch of current data flows from the clinic facilities and other sources. He did a rough cost estimate and listed potential benefits. He then laid out a rough time table to complete the project.

Jim used interviewing skills to gather data from Art, proponents of the project, and a representative from the physicians and trainers who could be data providers. Jim used presentation skills to share initial findings with the funding body and other involved persons. Flow diagrams and layouts of data were used in the presentation. Jim also gave a statement of benefits he felt Art and the sponsoring group would receive if a system was implemented. Based on the information provided, the decision was made to continue the project.

Process 2: Analyze Current System

Purpose: Understand and document the structure and purpose of the current system. Determine requirements for the new system.

Output: A set of user reviewed and accepted models of the organization, the data movements and storage, the processing needed, and the organization needs that would be served by an improved system. A more refined set of system costs and benefits to determine project continuance.

Art's methods of updating pencil and paper logs and of trying to do correlations by hand were recorded on flow diagrams. What Art tried to do with tables, charts, and graphs was recorded. Art's wishes for what "ideal knowledge" would be were uncovered through interviews. New data and processing needs were revealed and recorded.

Organization charts, context diagrams, data flow diagrams and data structure charts that were roughed out in Process 1 were completed, reviewed, and refined. Art gained confidence that Jim understood what information he needed to plan his training. Art's performance objectives were recorded as well as how he intended to change to meet the objectives. For example, these would include diet changes and therapeutic massage. Jim and Art interacted to determine how better information might help Art do the right things. This resulted in a more complete statement of benefits and costs.

Presenting skills were used to share findings. The formal review technique was used to assure complete participation and to save egos. Based on the sharing, the current methods were understood by all, and the potential to improve the situation became clearer. Comments were made by some of the participants indicating that for the first time they understood everyone else's role in Art's training. The reviews led to a consensus opinion to continue the project.

Process 3: Propose System Solutions

Purpose: Establish a menu of possible system solutions at different costs to obtain different benefits. oject sponsors must choose the alternative that most closely meets their needs at an acceptable cost.

Output: A defined system boundary for the proposed new system indicating what subsystems will be included. Within the system boundary, the person–machine boundary must be established. This will enable the system designers to propose alternative hardware and software solutions.

Jim searched for and proposed alternative solutions. He investigated what other athletes had for information management systems. He found varied degrees of sophistication, including telecommunication linkages with a central computer from laboratory sites to track timing devices, and video motion recording devices to study stride efficiency. He also found more mundane applications that linked training, blood and pulse tests, and track performance.

There were various places that a system boundary could be drawn based on what the system was to accomplish. A new logical model was created in the form of a data flow diagram with new processing and data. This gave a better "picture" of options. Alternative boundaries were shown on the diagram. Jim discussed these first with Art and then with the others involved. Of course, each alternative had a different cost associated with it. Each cost alternative was associated with a different set of potential benefits.

Along with the system boundary decision was the agreement on what a human would do and what the machine would do—the person–machine boundary. Options included things such as a microrecorder that would automatically count track laps if Art wore a small sender unit. This could be fed directly into a computer. Or, Art and his friends could count laps and times and record them in a notebook as he usually did.

Reviews of options were held with those involved. The review group made the decision to go ahead with the project according to Jim's revised project plan. The consensus was to start small and simple, with manual recording and input of data. The primary system objective was to provide correlations between training intensity and lab tests. This would help Art realize that he was overtraining before physical symptoms of fatigue set in. The information system was to aid Art to understand himself and his conditioning better.

Process 4: Detail Chosen Solution

Purpose: Detail logically the data storage, data flows, and data processing within the chosen system boundary. Decide on system acquisition and make any vendor decisions.

Output: A statement of the selected vendors as well as detailed new system specifications.

Jim set out to detail the processes, data flows, data stores, and data structures within the designated system boundary. He specified needs for error detection procedures to find bad input data, for control totals and crosschecks, and for backup of any stored data. Art wanted to avoid entering any misleading data or losing any training history or lab test results.

Jim refined the original specifications of data and processing volumes. He simplified the data structures and determined any needed coding of data. He then contacted several software vendors who had packages or services that would aid in data analysis. He provided them with background about the proposed system and they responded with proposals for how they could meet the system objectives.

Jim reviewed these proposals and found that no one had a system that could satisfy the system objectives without a lot of work. He determined that a microcomputer system with an integrated spreadsheet, statistics, and graphics package would satisfy Art's needs. He also found that a local sports foundation had a person knowledgeable about the package who could be contracted to create the actual computer commands.

Jim came up with a cost proposal and a recommended plan for assigning remaining activities. He presented the plan to the funding group and obtained approval to move ahead. He quickly placed an order for the needed microcomputer hardware and started contract negotiations with the person who would do some of the programming.

Process 5: Design New Physical System

Purpose: Specify, review, and approve the structure of nonacquired software, human procedures, physical facilities, and databases.

Output: A physical representation of the system inputs, outputs, programs, procedures, and storage. Included are program structure charts, human procedures, input and output layouts, file and database structures, and physical site plans.

Jim worked very closely with Art to define the exact content of desired reports. They did not spend much time with screen layouts since they felt content was more critical. They also spent some time determining the commands and menus Art would use to enter new data or request outputs. Art was taking an increasing interest in working with the system as he saw results could be near.

Jim shared the results of this effort with Cleo, the person contracted to create the computer commands needed. Cleo was knowledgeable in both the package and statistical analysis. Jim suggested that they meet with Art.

Jim spent some of his time assuring there was a place for the computer system once it arrived. A separate workroom was obtained and a special desk ordered to hold the new microcomputer and printer. He made arrangements for a data entry person to convert Art's logs and lab data into a machine-readable form. He conferred with Cleo to assure formats would be acceptable.

Art, Cleo, and Jim met and shared the output requirements, input procedures, and Art's needed dialog with the new computer. Art got some hands-on usage of the microcomputer Cleo had in her office. Jim was busy developing some written procedures to ensure that Art would not have trouble getting started or get stuck.

All plans for the computer hardware, computer software, needed data, procedures, training for Art, and the new site were in place.

Process 6: Construct New System

Purpose: Bring working version of the new system to a usable stage.
Output: A working version of the new system that provides users with real benefits.

Jim assured the new computer was delivered in working form. Cleo and Jim worked on acceptance and installation of the new software packages. Cleo tested the macro commands that would allow Art to request needed information. Copies of the historic data were used for testing with Art playing an active role in the operation and verification of the data. Art was already interested in making changes to the general query commands and was getting some informal training.

All procedures were tested, including the backup and recovery generation. To protect against losing the database, current backups had to be written weekly or the system could not be run.

Art started to use the system output to plan his weekly training schedule. Some of the frequent blood tests revealed that long, slow training runs were better for his recovery from hard workouts than a complete day of rest. He always felt this, but several coaches said he should take a day off to recover. He also discovered an increased resting pulse would occur if he scheduled for water jump practice that day, something he dreaded. He also found that a fast time for the first two laps of a race was sure to result in a mediocre performance. There were more questions coming up as soon as he had some answers. Art felt he had a real tool.

Process 7: Install and Monitor System

Purpose: Ensure that a version of the system operates in the organizational environment. Ensure that future changes are recorded and passed to the project planning function.
Output: An accepted working system version with suggested changes.

Art was actively using the system. He found he needed more information on his diet and how it affected his perceived energy and motivation to train. Cleo and Jim helped him to make some system modifications to add data that he now felt was important.

Art found that going to a special room to do some of the analysis and data entry was very inconvenient and tiring. His improved performance and the success of the system resulted in the sponsoring organization moving the system to his residence.

Art and Jim met and wrote a short report on their development effort. This review would serve as a guide for development of future systems. Art wanted to continue on the project with Jim since there were new needs and so much potential to be tapped. He started to wonder about biorhythms, sleep patterns, and competition in different time zones. After all, the next Olympics were. . . .

This is a case of a single user and a single developer. The complexity would increase if there were many athletes who had to use the system or if there were several developers who were spending part of their time working on the system.

SUCCESSFUL SYSTEMS DEVELOPMENT

Having a good development process and improved development techniques is not enough to accomplish successful systems development. It is necessary to have a good attitude about systems development. This attitude is formed in part by understanding our objectives when developing systems. We must know what we are trying to achieve.

The following list could serve as the objectives of systems development or what developers are trying to accomplish. A successful information system:

1. Satisfies users of the system
2. Produces useful results and increases human productivity
3. Is understandable to users, maintainers, and operators
4. Satisfies a need that is apparent to those involved with the system
5. Is easy to operate and has a good human interface
6. Uses machines where they should be used and humans where they should be used
7. Is changeable with adequate performance and controls
8. Edits and checks inputs, outputs, and processing at least as well as an excellent employee
9. Doesn't cause chaos in the workplace even though it may cause change
10. Doesn't allow a disaster to take place in terms of failure, security breaks, or recovery
11. Operates in various environments if required
12. Handles exceptions to the normal without chaos
13. Is delivered on schedule
14. Is delivered within budget
15. (Add anything else you feel is important from your own experiences and perspective)

The above list is important because it is what a systems developer needs to accomplish to be successful. Not all of today's existing systems meet these objectives. The systems field is still growing and being refined. Systems developers must accept the challenge of making things better.

SUMMARY

This chapter provided a background understanding of the activities needed to develop systems. The reader must remember we will return to these activities in more detail throughout the rest of this book. Chapter 3 will examine what data the systems development activities need to start—the inputs, what the activities will produce—the outputs, and the data that is stored about the system during its life. This will provide a full picture of a system for building systems.

REFERENCES AND FURTHER READINGS

Berlinger, Scott, and Mike Bealmear. "Systems Methodology Quits Data Processing Doghouse," *MIS Week*, vol. 7, no. 38, section II, September 22, 1986, p. 8.

Colter, Mel. "A Comparative Examination of Systems Analysis Techniques," *MIS Quarterly*, vol. 8, no. 1, March 1984, pp. 51–66.

Davis, William S. *Systems Analysis and Design: A Structured Approach*, Reading, MA: Addison-Wesley Publishing Company, 1983.

DeMarco, Tom. *Structured Analysis and System Specification*, New York: Yourdon Press, 1978.

Dickinson, Brian. *Developing Structured Systems*, New York: Yourdon Press, 1980.

Gane, C., and T. Sarson. *Structured Systems Analysis: Tools and Techniques*, Englewood Cliffs, NJ: Prentice-Hall, Inc., 1979.

Gore, Marvin, and John Stubbe. *Elements of Systems Analysis for Business Data Processing*, Dubuque, IA: Wm. C. Brown Company Publishers, 2d Ed., 1979.

Hartman, W., Matthes, H., and A. Proeme. *Management Information Systems Handbook*, New York: McGraw-Hill Book Company, 1968.

King, David. *Current Practices in Software Development*, New York: Yourdon Press, 1984.

Levine, Arthur. "Selecting a Systems Development Methodology," *Infosystems*, April 1985, p. 72.

Olle, T. W., Sol, H. G., and A. A. Verrijn-Stuart. (eds.) *Information Systems Design Methodologies: A Comparative Review*, North-Holland Publishing Company, 1982.

Orr, Kenneth T. "Systems Methodologies for the 80s," *Infosystems*, June 1981, pp. 78–80.

Sanders, Donald H. *Computers and Management*, New York: McGraw-Hill, Inc., 1974, p. 238.

Semprevivo, Philip C. *Systems Analysis: Definition, Process, and Design*, Chicago: Science Research Associates, Inc., 2d Ed., 1982.

Senn, James A. *Analysis and Design of Information Systems*, New York: McGraw-Hill Book Company, 1984.

Wetherbe, James C. *Systems Analysis and Design: Traditional, Structured, and Advanced Concepts and Techniques*, St. Paul, MN: West Publishing Company, 2d Ed., 1984.

Whitten, Jeffrey L., Bentley, Lonnie D., and Thomas I.M. Ho. *Systems Analysis and Design Methods*, St. Louis, MO: Times Mirror/Mosby College Publishing, 1986.

Yourdon, Edward. *Managing the System Life Cycle*, New York: Yourdon Press, 1982.

———. "The Emergence Of Structured Analysis," *Computer Decisions*, April 1976, pp. 58–59.

REVIEW QUESTIONS

1. What is the difference between a method as a process and a method as a technique?
2. How could a context diagram aid in system boundary defining?
3. Why would a clear definition of system development processes aid in systems project management?
4. Would the existence of a standardized procedure for systems development affect system users? Why?
5. In relation to systems development, what does "structured" mean?
6. Distinguish between a logical and physical model.
7. Is the word "logical" used in a systems context the opposite of the word "illogical"? What is the opposite?
8. Link the scenario of the system development for Art Fletcher to the combined Process/Techniques. Were most of the mentioned Process outputs generated? How can you explain this?
9. Why would the system development effort for Art Fletcher have been more difficult if there were several developers?

DISCUSSION QUESTIONS

1. What characteristics of systems does the the system development system exhibit? Are there any characteristics that are not exhibited?
2. Is it meaningful to receive training in systems development processes? Why or why not? If so, what would be the skills that a trainee would develop as a result of the training?
3. Who are the major players in each process of the systems development life cycle?
4. The definition of systems analysis given so far in this book includes a study of the existing system. Do you think there will always be an existing system? Why or why not? Remember the definition of organizational systems from Chapter 1. Does the existing system have to be internal to the organization? Could it be something like an accounting method accepted by industry?
5. Do you think any one process in the systems development life cycle is ever 100 percent completed? Why or why not? Is is possible to move on to the next processes if total completion is not reached? Why might this be possible?
6. A student suggested that the sport of football was a good example of the differences between processes and techniques. She suggested the "plays" a team executed were similiar to the processes of development. The "plays" were *what* was done. The techniques were blocking, tackling, passing, etc. This is where the players had to have skills since this is the *how* of the game. Do you agree? Why or why not?
7. "Systems development is an iterative, not a serial process." Comment.

EXERCISES

1. Your friend wants to acquire a new stereo component system. He feels the stereo system would enhance his life. He has been dwelling on the technical performance characteristics of many components and has considered both new and used systems. Use the systems development approach to aid him in acquiring a new stereo system. (If you are not into stereo systems, consider a new car or new house or new ? as the system to be acquired.)

2. Share the "life cycle without a plan" from McLean and Welke with an experienced systems developer. Ask them if they have ever had or heard of such an experience. Be prepared to share your findings with other class members.

3. Liken the development of a book to a systems development project.
   a. Could a book be viewed as a system? Why or why not?
   b. What are the processes of book development?
   c. What techniques or skills are needed to develop a book?
   d. Are the processes or the techniques more likely to change?
   e. How would you estimate how long it would take to write a book?
   f. In what ways is systems boundary determination similar to book content determination?
   g. Are user needs determined in the same manner as on a systems project? Who is the user—students or instructors?

CHAPTER 3

CHAPTER OBJECTIVES

You should be able to:

- Give arguments for using a systems development database
- Specify uses of a systems development database
- Specify data about people, organizing structures, data, and technology needed to describe a system
- Specify when data about a system is collected or generated
- Indicate major deliverables in a systems development project

A SYSTEMS DEVELOPMENT DATABASE

THIS CHAPTER INTRODUCES systems development from an information building point of view. The chapter focuses on what data a system developer needs to build and maintain a system. This in essence is a discussion of an information system for systems developers. The building of models using an entity-attribute-relationship approach is introduced. The four models required for any system being developed which detail the *who, what, why,* and *how* of a system are detailed. A real-life case study of the use of a systems development database is included.

The previous chapters have viewed systems development from an action or "doing" perspective. These chapters concentrated on the processes and subprocesses of systems development and the techniques used to perform these subprocesses. In the case of information systems development, each process receives certain data inputs and converts them into data outputs. These inputs and outputs make up much of what is called system ***documentation*** or, in the case of outputs, system ***deliverables***. In this chapter, the data that is collected and generated in a systems development project will be viewed as a database for systems development.

The reader should be clear that the systems development database contains data about the system being developed. It is a systematic and detailed description of the information system. It is not the database that would serve as the focus of processing and storage for the completed system. For example, the development database contains data or documentation about *who* is concerned with the payroll system, *what data* and *processes* are part of the payroll system, *why* the payroll system is needed, and *how* the payroll processes the payroll data. There also will be a database that contains payroll data such as employees' names, pay rates, tax paid, etc. The database about the system has been called *metadata*, which could be taken to mean "data about data." It also has been referred to as a comprehensive data dictionary or data encyclopedia.

This chapter forms the basis for many of the concepts discussed later in the book. At this time, it is important to have a general understanding of what data we will be working with in succcessful systems development. If we do not know what we are trying to collect, analyze, and produce, we will have a much harder time collecting, analyzing, and producing.

The long-term hope is that we can give systems developers an information system which will help them do their jobs. We are working toward an information system for information systems development which, in most cases, is providing shoes for the shoemaker's children. Some persons have believed that, like the shoemaker's children who are the last to receive shoes, the information systems builders are the last to have an information system.

WHY BUILD A SYSTEMS DEVELOPMENT DATABASE?

A recent study examined some contemporary software development environments (Howden). The study also examined some of the tools and techniques used in systems development. One conclusion of the study was that the choice of methods and tools used for systems development was not as important as the resulting database. The database tied all the efforts together.

> The data base provides an integrating and unifying medium for interfacing tools without forcing them into a complex structure of interrelationships. Tools obtain their information from the database and return their results to it without having to interface directly with other tools.
>
> In order to maintain flexibility, it is important to avoid building bridges between pairs of tools rather than bridges into the database (Howden, p. 326).

The database is a repository for documentation. Documentation is often thought of as the curse of systems development. There doesn't seem to be time to do it. But without good documentation, system development and maintenance is very difficult. The systems development database provides aid in the following areas.

LOWERING THE COST OF RESTARTING

When building or repairing something without existing documentation, it often takes a great amount of time to figure out what someone else has done. This is especially true if the creator is not accessible. Many systems developers have found it easier to start over rather than trying to reuse someone else's vaguely recorded ideas, structures, and unexplained detail. This restarting is very costly.

REDUCING THE NEEDED VERBAL COMMUNICATION

Even if the creator of a subsystem is available, it is easier to pick up someone else's work if intermediate results were recorded in an organized and understandable form. This would reduce the syndrome called by Brooks the "mythical man-month." This refers to the slowing down of a project resulting from adding people because of all the communication needed between existing and new project members (Brooks).

GENERATING DOCUMENTATION AS A BY-PRODUCT

With proper planning and definition, documentation can be developed as a by-product of performing a process, not as an afterthought. These by-products can be shared, examined, and critiqued. A database would require standardization and clear definition which would facilitate generating by-products.

AIDING PROJECT MANAGEMENT

Peer developers, project managers, and users will all have an idea of progress because results in the form of data exist in the database, not because someone says they are working on something. Because of this, projects would be easier to manage.

IMPROVING PRODUCTIVITY

Productivity of developers would be improved by using database technology to manage the systems development database. Data entry, updating, maintenance, and access control would all be aided much as in any other database application.

USING AUTOMATION

Generating deliverables would also be aided through automation. The capability of generating graphics such as organization charts or data flow diagrams could exist if hardware and software existed to manipulate and display data. But if data did not exist or was not in a usable form, there would be no potential to do these things. By having easy generation of a project deliverable once data existed, there would be no "crashes" to document after the creative work was done.

There clearly is a trend toward aiding systems development through the use of automated programmer-analyst workbenches. This area is often referred to as ***computer-aided software engineering*** (CASE). Most of these automated aids use a data dictionary as a central repository for data about the system being developed.

PERFORMING REAL ANALYSIS

A last but very important advantage of using a database approach is that *real* analysis can take place. As with any database, the flexibility to examine data in different ways, retrieve selected data, and relate different data to other data is needed. For example, relating people in an organizational position to their job description or to their organizational objectives may reveal inconsistencies. This is *real* analysis that is not usually done because the data does not exist in a form that can be easily manipulated.

USES OF A SYSTEMS DEVELOPMENT DATABASE

Systems development can be aided by maintaining and using an organized database. Systems development processes would be supported if developers knew the data they needed to perform a process existed, and if they had easy access to it in various forms. We will examine some examples of specific uses.

SYSTEMS ANALYSIS

During analysis, we would know who to interview or observe if we had some data about the people involved with a system. We would know how many interviews to conduct and could make a more precise time estimate for carrying out analysis.

COMPUTER PROGRAM DEVELOPMENT

Program testing could be aided by the generation of test data from knowing the range and volume of data elements. Portions of data division *declarations* in COBOL programs could be automatically generated from the database.

SYSTEM TRAINING

We would know who had to be trained if data existed on who performed what procedures. We also could make better time estimates for training if we knew how many people performed a procedure as part of their job and the geographic locations of those persons.

SYSTEM MAINTENANCE

Maintenance would be easier if we knew who performed certain system procedures since we would know who must be notified and trained if we changed the procedure. Changes to a data element would be facilitated if knowledge existed of which programs used the element, what files or schemas contained the element, and who "owned" or could update the element.

SYSTEMS PROJECT MANAGEMENT

Project control would be improved with better data. We would know certain development had been completed if the data existed in the database. Projections of "almost done" would be supported by actual reviewable results.

What could be accomplished if a complete information system existed about a system, one containing data about people, organizing structures, data, and technology? The possibilities are limited only by your imagination. We could search for conflicting business objectives, find what people received what data in what reports or who provided what inputs, or determine the business reasons for completing a process on time. To further understand this concept, it is necessary to specify what information a systems development database would contain.

INFORMATION NEEDED FOR SYSTEMS DEVELOPMENT

If we were to closely examine the systems development process overview in Figure 2.2 in Chapter 2, we would note that something is missing which will appear in most system descriptions we will develop. This is the flow and storage of data we collect during development activities. Figure 2.2 only shows the processes and an external source of data.

Systems developers collect, generate, and store data when building a system. They do this by building ***documentation libraries.*** These libraries typically take the form of paper documents stored in folders and notebooks. It is not critical what storage medium we use, but it is important to know that the data does exist, that we have easy access to the data, and are able to maintain it over the life of the system. But a limiting factor to paper as a medium for storage is that changing data order, relating data elements, or selecting from data becomes very time-consuming and costly.

Since a great deal of data is generated during a systems project, the revision shown as Figure 3.1 may be more accurate. The lines shown with arrowheads coming in and going out of the data store are a flow of data. If we were to organize this data, it should correspond to the subsystems that make up the information system we discussed in Chapter 1: namely people, organizing structures, data, and technology. People correspond to the journalistic guide of *who,* data correspond to *what* people generate and manipulate, organizing structures (needs) correspond to *why,* and technology to *how, when,* and *where* the system does it.

We also know from Chapter 1 that we must relate the subsystems that make up a system. For example, people in organizations have needs, use data to help achieve their needs, and use technology for aid. We must know

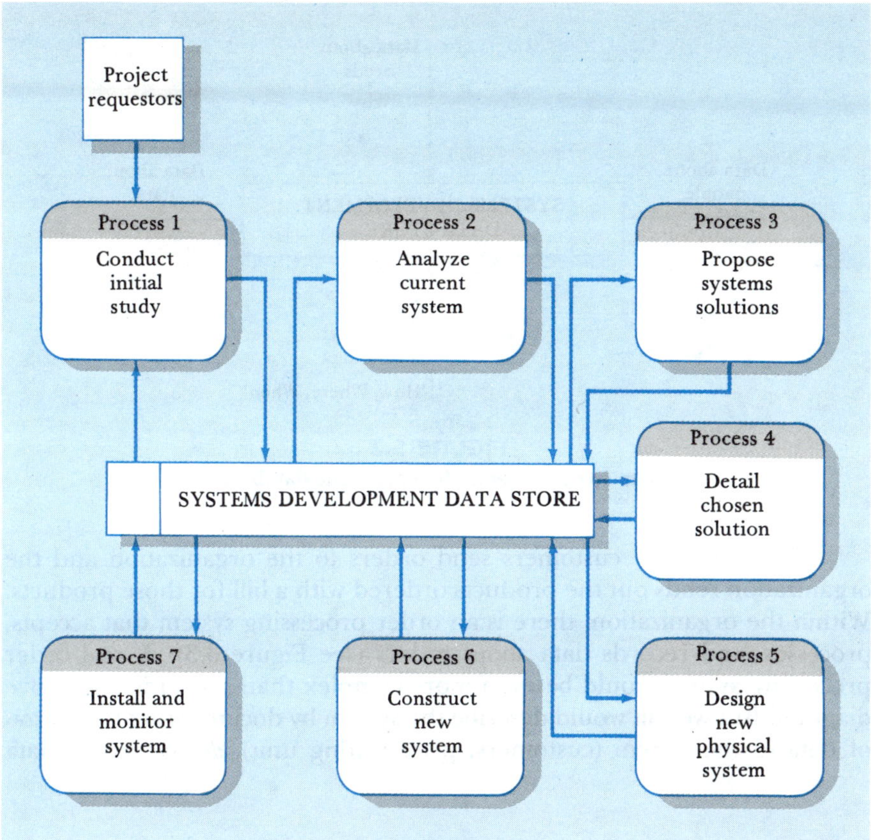

FIGURE 3.1
Systems development processes and data storage.

the *whos, whats, whens, wheres, whys,* and *hows* of any system and how they relate to be able to clearly understand and change the system.

SYSTEM DESCRIPTION USING MODELING

As shown in Figure 3.2, we will collect, store, and analyze data describing the subsystems of people, needs or organizing structures, data, and technology that make up the system we are developing. What we are attempting to do is create a series of models describing each of the different subsystems. We do this by first determining what the important components or *entities* are in each of the subsystems. We then determine what we need to know about these entities, or the *attributes* of the entities. Then we determine how the entities are related, or the *relationships* between the entities. It is also important to know any attributes of the relationships.

Let us see how we can describe a data subsystem using the entity-attribute-relationship method. We will use a customer order processing system as an example.

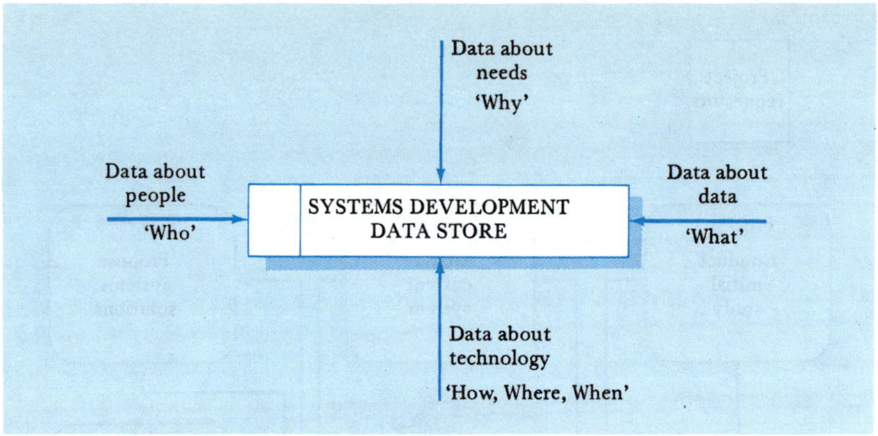

FIGURE 3.2
Data for a systems development database.

First, we know customers send orders to the organization and the organization sends out the products ordered with a bill for those products. Within the organization, there is an order processing system that accepts, processes, and records data about orders (see Figure 3.3). A real order processing system would be even more complex than shown in the above diagram. But we still would describe the system by documenting the *sources* of data to the system (customers, price setting unit), *destinations* of data

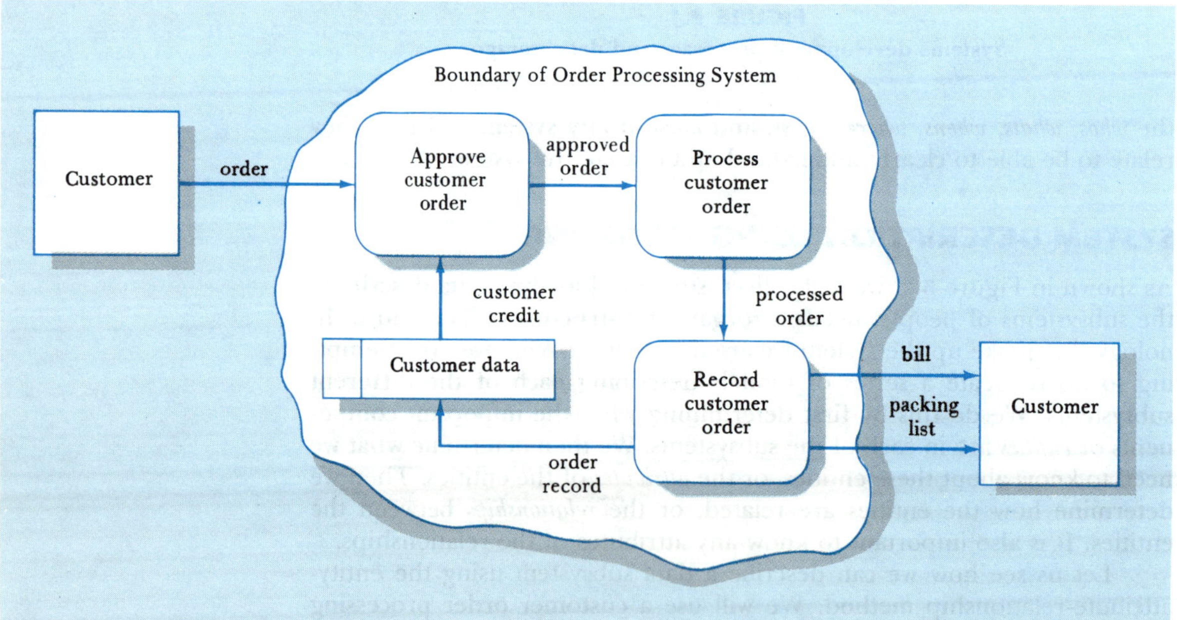

FIGURE 3.3
A simple order processing system.

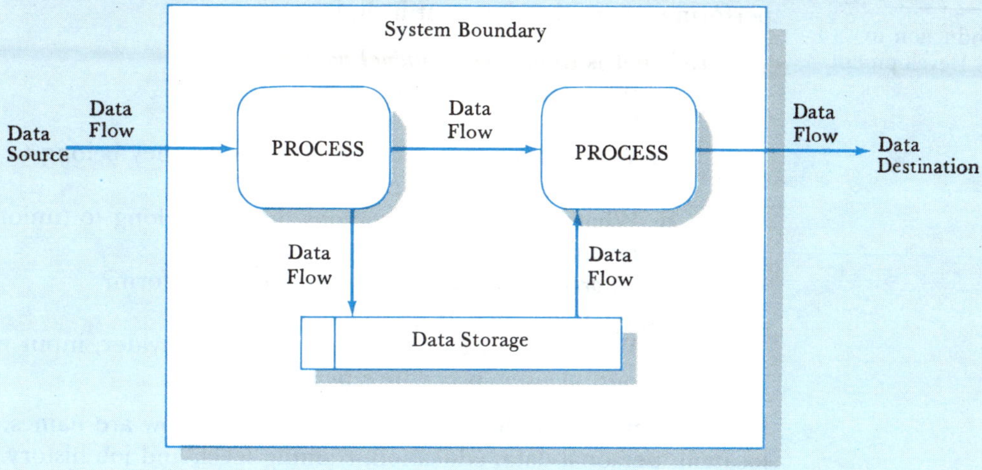

FIGURE 3.4
Entities in a data subsystem model.

produced by the system (customers, order filling department, accounting department), *data flow* within the system (approved orders sent to inventory checks, prices being retrieved from the price data store), *data storage* within the system (customer data storage, product data storage, price data storage), and *processes* within the system (approve orders). The underlined "things" are the *entities* that make up our data model. Figure 3.4 exhibits the general data model in graphical form.

Each of these entities has attributes. The attributes of the data flow entity would include volumes of data moved, when data is moved, frequency of data flow, and what would trigger a flow. A relationship between the "data flow" entity and the "source of data" entity would be that the source sends data to the system via the data flow entity. An attribute of this relationship would be types of data sent such as orders or complaints.

We can create models of people, organizing structures, data, and technology used. Let us look at each of these subsystem models in terms of their entities, attributes, and relationships.

DATA ABOUT PEOPLE

As we mentioned earlier, people are the *who* of the system we want to analyze and describe. These are the users and operators of the system, existing at different levels in an organization. These people hold jobs, have a job history and various skills, perform different tasks, etc. People entities in our database include *organization positions,* or what jobs people hold, and *organization functions,* or what they do in those jobs.

Since we know these people do not exist as islands within organizations, there are characteristics (attributes) of the position holders as well as their relationship to other positions or functions which are important in developing a system. Some questions about people we must answer to perform systems development include:

1. What is their *organizational position?*
   a. Who reports to them?
   b. Who do they report to?
   c. What internal organizational units do they belong to (departments, task forces, committees)?
   d. What external organizations do they belong to (unions, trade groups)?
2. What *organizational functions* must they perform?
   a. What are their responsibilities?
   b. What type of user are they? (funds provider, input provider, output user, procedure performer, etc.)

Other general attributes of people we want to know are names, salaries, location, personal data, education, training level, and job history.

The people subsystem also would include the training programs and skill sets needed for an organizational position holder. This would include

An important part of gathering data is learning who reports to whom and what organizational units the workers belong to.
(Robert Houser/Comstock)

training materials, entry qualification, and tests to indicate mastery. A system can only operate if data gathering people, data input people, data control people, human procedure performing people, technology and computer operations people, and output user people are trained to perform their role in the system's functioning.

In an organization, data about people is found in various places and documents. Organization charts indicate what positions exist and the relationships between the positions. The charts also indicate the names of the position holders. Job descriptions indicate what tasks people, by position, are supposed to perform. As well, union contracts may indicate the activities that people in certain positions can or cannot perform.

All of the above data must be collected and stored so we can fully understand the role of people in the system being developed. The data should be aggregated and organized so questions the developer might have can be answered.

DATA ABOUT ORGANIZING STRUCTURES

Organizing structures are *why* something in the organization must be done. The people, data, and technology subsystems must have a purpose and a means of achieving it. In the long run, organizations have the goal of survival. In most business organizations, this means making a profit. To do this, organizations must have specific objectives and the tactics to reach these objectives.

This model could also be called the ***requirements model.*** The key to this model is to establish relationships between what the organization wants to achieve and what the information system can do to help. The subsystem attempts to link the users' business wisdom with the aid provided by systems performance.

The entities which we must determine and collect data about include quantified *business objectives,* performable *business tactics,* quantified *information system objectives,* and cost-effective *information system tactics.* We also must know what caused a modification to what currently exists which we will refer to as *stimuli.* The relationships between these entities in the requirements model are shown below.

a change of some type
STIMULI
forces changed organization needs
BUSINESS OBJECTIVES
causing changed user behaviors
BUSINESS TACTICS
requiring changed information needs
INFORMATION SYSTEM OBJECTIVES
requiring changed information system activities
INFORMATION SYSTEM TACTICS

Entities in the Organizing Structures/Requirements Subsystem Model

Something in the environment or the organization may force the organization or the system to react and change. These *stimuli* may be actions of the government, a competitor, or a hardware/software vendor. We must know about:

1. The government and its laws and regulations that might dictate some of the specifications of the system being developed.
2. Competitors' actions, especially if the competitors' systems are providing customer services through the use of information systems technology.
3. Standards that the system must abide by. For example, there may be a standard for using a code (such as the universal product code) that could influence the development of the system.

These stimuli cause the organization to try to achieve some cost reduction or revenue increase. These achievements are the *business's objectives*. Quantified objectives that indicate how much, by what time, for what period, and by whom are needed to assure that objectives are measurable. To pursue the objectives, the organization may have to change the way it currently acts. These actions are the *business's tactics*. To provide help in performing the business's tactics and give a competitive advantage, the information system is summoned to assist. To do this, the information system must provide usable results such as reports or screens containing information. These results or achievements are called *information system objectives*. To pursue the objectives, the system may have to change the way it does things. These actions are called *information system tactics*.

In an organization, data about the organizing structures can often be found in mission or strategy statements. Unless an organization makes a conscious effort to record data about goals and objectives, it is necessary to tap the minds of the organization's founders and leaders. This is especially true of new companies going through growing pains. Often, loan applications or documents that appeal for funding can be clues to finding data about the organizing structures.

Data about the organization's needs often can be found if the organization has gone through conscious efforts to arrive at critical success factors or key result areas. These types of statements are often developed and can be used by systems developers. Such statements indicate what the organization members want, and the systems developer then can specify what the system can do to help.

Data about the purpose and tactics of the information system might be contained in systems documentation. Data about current or desired outputs should be found in project requests. How the system is attempting to reach its objectives should be found among the documentation used to maintain the system. The analyst is challenged with the task of recording this data that often is found only in someone's memory—hopefully, a memory that is still accessible to the analyst.

DATA ABOUT DATA

Earlier in the chapter, the data model was discussed in learning about entities, attributes, and relationships (see Figures 3.3 and 3.4). We discovered that the data needed about systems data is basically *what* the organization does—data *processes, what* the organization processes need—*data input flows, what* is produced by the processes—*data output flows,* and *what* the organization must store—*data stores.* We must also know the sources of data from outside the system boundary, and destinations of data to outside the system boundary. These are commonly called ***external entities***. The impetus to start the processing, commonly called a ***trigger***, also is needed.

The data subsystem is represented by logical models containing the inputs, outputs, human processes, automated processes, data storage, and data flows. The primary tools for representing logical models are the context diagram and data flow diagram. The data flow diagram is supported by the logical data dictionary, data structure diagrams, program structure charts, and procedure specifications.

The data dictionary holds all the detail about the data flow diagram. Data store contents, data flow contents, processing logic, and data element detail are all stored in the data dictionary. Attributes of data stores include the data structure, data elements, organization, growth, volumes, key elements, and order.

Attributes of data elements a systems developer needs to collect include alias names, composition, size, type, origin, volume, ownership, permissible values, access, security, and change rights. We will discuss these attributes in more detail in future chapters.

The program structure chart specifies the machine processing modules required by the system. The chart is a graphic representation of the computer program modules and how they are connected by data and control.

Data structure diagrams exhibit links between different levels of stored data. A data store on a data flow diagram is "opened up" to show how the stored data can be broken down and how data elements are linked to other data elements.

The data subsystem also contains data about the human processing needed, referred to as ***procedures***. These will include data entry, data control, data collection, information distribution, data processing, audit/control, recovery, and manual backup procedures. Each of these procedures may be represented by a set of instructions, and will be incorporated in the manuals needed to operate the system in a production environment.

DATA ABOUT TECHNOLOGY

The technology subsystem overlays the other subsystems in the system. It is the actual implementation of the other subsystems. It indicates *how* data is stored and on what devices, *how* computer programs actually process data, *when* or *how often* processing is done, *how* communication devices are linked and *where* they are located, and *how* the systems software is controlled (job control language). The technology subsystem is a physical model of the system, one possible implementation of the logical model of the system.

The physical model is of major concern at two points in the development process. First, the existing system is or should be represented by a physical model. This is the existing system documentation that explains *how* the system currently operates. Since the system actually exists physically, the documentation is a representation of the actual physical implementation. This is appropriate at the beginning of a project since this is when the implemented system must be maintained, and it must be understood to maintain the existing system.

The physical model indicates what processes are automated in the current operation and which are done manually. How program modules are linked and how the programs actually operate are included. Links between hardware, software, and telecommunications are shown. Attributes such as the physical size of data elements and files and the types of storage devices are included.

There is a second time when such a description makes sense. This is when the commitment to a physical representation has been made in the development of a new system. At other times in the development cycle, it is more appropriate to represent the system in a logical fashion to avoid premature physical commitment.

Besides systems flowcharts, program structure can be indicated by program structure charts. These charts indicate the needed modules in a computer program, how the modules are linked by data movement and control, and the hierarchy of the modules. The actual application program and source code are part of the technology subsystem.

Data about the technology subsystem includes the hardware/software (H/S) specification. This document would contain a diagram showing a static view of all the physical components of the H/S configuration. All of the computing devices and interfaces such as channels, controllers, modems, encryption, and switches should be shown. Along with this would go hardware specification attributes stating the speeds and capacities of the devices that are part of the subsystem. Protocols, operating systems, database management systems, utilities, and languages also must be specified.

The environment needed for the hardware/software should also be specified. This would include the needed site preparations. Specifications of space, temperature, humidity, electric power, and ventilation must be developed.

The operations run book is part of the technology subsystem. This material is specific to the technology used in the system implementation. It must be changed if the technology changes. The documentation provides the computer operations unit with the required procedures to install, operate, and control the system.

Test data files are also part of the technology subsystem. If a change is made to a system, it is convenient, efficient, and thorough to have data and a test plan that can be used to test the system to assure that it still operates properly.

OTHER DATA THAT AFFECTS SYSTEM DEVELOPMENT PROJECTS

Project management data does not really describe the system itself, but the progress made in the development of a system. It is part of the data that is kept during the development, but serves little purpose in actual maintenance or operation of the system. Project management data does aid in maintenance planning in that time estimates to do certain development processes can be based on how long it took in the past. As well, knowing who actually did the development may give clues as to the health of the system. The original creator also can provide maintenance assistance.

Project management will be discussed in a later chapter. Now we only need to know that this data is needed to accomplish a systems project.

THE DEVELOPMENT DATABASE AND THE DEVELOPMENT PROCESS

The development database should be a by-product of the systems development process. It is constructed by the systems developers while conducting development activities. Data is collected, analyzed, presented to peers and users, and reviewed for completeness and accuracy throughout the development life cycle. Documentation *should not* be developed as an activity that follows the implementation of the system. Documentation developed as an afterthought often is incomplete, inaccurate, or never accomplished. Adding documentation to the development database as the system is being analyzed, designed, and implemented helps avoid this problem.

In this section of the chapter we will move through the development process and indicate what data is generated at each step. This is an overview of the system *deliverables* that will be expanded when we go through the development cycle in more detail. We can view the building of the systems development database as the generation of a set of libraries about the system that will be used during development, operation, and maintenance.

DATA AND PROCESS 1—CONDUCT INITIAL STUDY

Inputs to Process 1 would include a project request. The request resembles a problem (opportunity) statement stating the current situation and why it is not satisfactory. Data included would identify the organization functions and positions concerned with the system and some reasons why an improved system would be beneficial to the organization. To accomplish the needed subprocesses in Process 1, developers need to obtain data about the system history and maintenance record, expand statements about the potential benefits of a new system, and make some rough estimates of cost to proceed with the project.

Outputs from Process 1 would be preliminary data about people, organizing structures, data, and current technology. Much of this data includes existing documentation on the system, if any exists. One of the most important data entities is the statement of business objectives. Meeting these objectives would mean increased revenues or decreased costs, which would result in benefits to the organization. These benefits must offset estimated project costs for the project to continue.

DATA AND PROCESS 2—ANALYZE CURRENT SYSTEM

Inputs to Process 2 include the data collected in Process 1. This is true for the remaining processes which will access the database to retrieve inputs that had been collected and entered in previous processes.

To perform the needed subprocesses in Process 2, people involved with the system are identified. More data about people is collected and analyzed, and is used to identify persons who must be interviewed to build

Gathering data includes thoroughly analyzing the current system and its shortcomings. (Comstock)

logical data models of the current system. Then, current needs and new requirements are summarized.

Outputs from Process 2 would be the data needed to build current organization charts, data flow diagrams, data structure diagrams, and requirements statements. The ability to relate this data to identify who does what, why, when, and how often is needed. This data is stated in terms of new requirements, analyzing who can't do what, why they should be able to, when, and how often. This will give an estimate of the cost of not having a better information system.

DATA AND PROCESS 3—PROPOSE NEW SOLUTIONS

The data from Process 2 is used to propose new systems solutions. Data flow models are used to show alternative system boundaries. Each different boundary would include a different set of processes and data stores. Within each different boundary would be the processes and data stores which are automated and those performed by humans. This is the start of the design of new system tactics in the organizing structures subsystem. The logical models are converted into more physical models.

Each alternative combination of system tactics would have associated with it the business objectives that could be met by implementing the alternative. Since each system solution also would have a cost associated with it, data is generated to associate a system solution cost with the accompanying business benefit. This cost/benefit data is used by managers to select a set of system tactics.

The final output of Process 3 is data identifying system and automation boundaries and preliminary notes on potential technologic solutions.

DATA AND PROCESS 4—DETAIL CHOSEN SOLUTION

Data on the details of data structures and elements, and automated and human procedures is collected, analyzed, and simplified. The data also is subjected to a technique called *normalization* to ensure simplification. Detailed error handling, audit control, and backup and recovery procedures are specified. This work was not done until this point because effort would have been expended on areas not to be included within the systems boundary. Data generated in Process 4 includes specifications of hardware and systems software, applications software, and human procedures.

DATA AND PROCESS 5—DESIGN NEW SYSTEM

Process 5 generates data that will serve as new system models. The people subsystem is represented by new organization charts, job descriptions, and human/task procedures. New physical implementations are generated. The new data model is represented by data about "physicalized" data flow diagrams, program structure charts, data structure charts and schemas, file layout charts, and input/output layout charts. "Physicalized" is a term that indicates that the logical descriptions are now stated in terms of the one physical implementation which would include sizes, speeds, and vendors. The technology model is represented by system flowcharts, physical site specifications, and hardware and systems software specifications for the chosen vendor.

DATA AND PROCESS 6—CONSTRUCT NEW SYSTEM

Data generated in Process 6 includes user reference manuals, operations personnel procedures, training materials, computer program code with accompanying data dictionary or directory, file layouts and schemas, and data on installed hardware and software.

DATA AND PROCESS 7—INSTALL AND MONITOR SYSTEM

Process 7 extracts data from the existing development database to move the system from a development to a production mode. A production library is established for the operations personnel who must run the system and a maintenance library is established for those who must keep the system running.

IMPLEMENTING THE SYSTEMS DEVELOPMENT INFORMATION SYSTEM

There are various ways of physically implementing the development database. One way is to collect and record data on paper. People have used notebooks with an entity on each page with the descriptions included. Others have used index cards since they could be sorted and handled more easily, and are quite durable. These simple procedures gave way to text processing to keep data more up-to-date and in an easily edited form. People used text editors to manage all the words within the system libraries.

Automated data element directories and dictionaries have been used to support the managing of the data descriptions for a database. The capabilities of data dictionaries vary, but most do not include comprehensive descriptions of all the data needed to develop a system. This type of extended capability has been proposed (Kozar and Smith; Mendes; Stohr).

Finally, there are some automated systems which combine text processing with data manipulation (sorting) and retrieval capabilities. Database technology is used to enter, manipulate, relate, and display data collected about a system. These aids are often called *analyst's workbenches*. Some of these systems can graph the relationships between entities and actually draw diagrams such as Figure 3.3. We will discuss some of these developments in a later chapter.

AN EXAMPLE OF A DEVELOPMENT DATABASE

This section gives as an example a project which used a systems development database approach to develop an information system.* A critical information management project representing $13 million in payments due to clients is described. Up-to-date payment processing was needed to satisfy waiting clients and to provide information valuable in generating increased organization revenues. The project approach included the task of building subsystem models which resulted in an information system to build the needed system.

BACKGROUND

The 3M Company Health Care Products Division is one of 3M's 40 divisions. Each of the divisions is run as a nearly autonomous business. National Accounts, a part of Health Care Products, is responsible for promoting the sale of 3M health care products to hospitals which are members of purchasing groups. These groups give the member hospitals special considerations, including rebates on certain products or for quantity purchases. While this business strategy of using rebates increases sales and gives a competitive advantage, it brings with it special information processing needs.

The growth in Health Care Products sales and rebates has been substantial. The existing rebate processing and sales reporting system quickly grew due to increasing business success, resulting in fragmented processing done in several physical locations. This included both internal processing and use of a service bureau. The existing system needed attention. Documentation was scattered, considered personal, or was nonexistent. There was little overall structure or coherence recorded except in the minds of user groups. This "mental documentation" went home each night. A means was needed so users could record their knowledge about the system.

THE REBATE AND SALES REPORTING SYSTEM—PROBLEM AND OPPORTUNITY

The rebate and sales reporting system is not a typical system found in most organizations. It is meant to support a particular business strategy that is appropriate for some industries and markets. Since this is not a common system, it is necessary to describe its activity.

To help readers understand the system, a context diagram created during system development will be used (see Figure 3.5). This diagram exhibits the links with other systems and sources and destinations of data. The labeled lines with arrows indicate Flows of Data (caps on first letters in

*This example is based on a paper by Kozar and Mahlum.

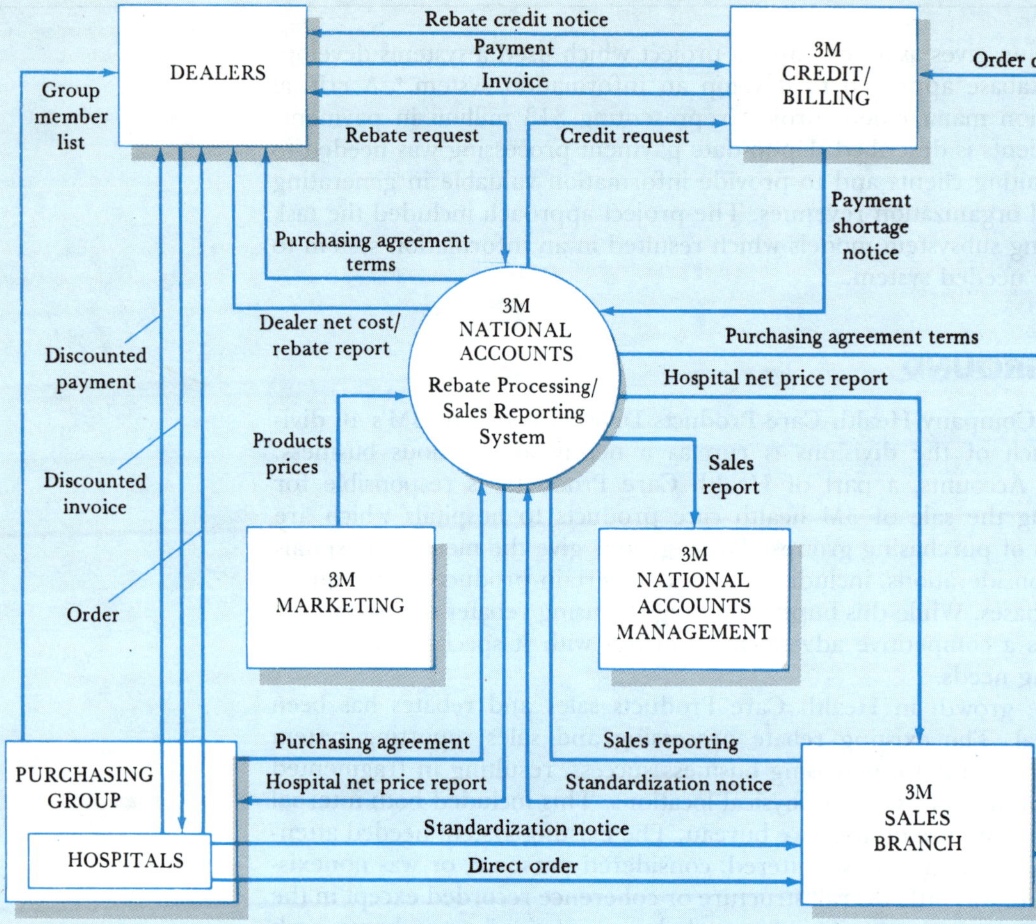

FIGURE 3.5

Context diagram of rebate processing/sales reporting system.

text) between ENTITIES shown as squares on the diagram (caps on all letters in text). The following describes the diagram:

PURCHASING GROUPS of HOSPITALS are formed to allow HOSPITALS to increase purchasing power. 3M's purpose in negotiating Purchasing Agreements with the PURCHASING GROUP is to provide incentives to HOSPITALS to buy 3M Health Care Products. The incentives are in the form of Discounts the HOSPITALS receive from selected DEALERS as a result of being a member of a PURCHASING GROUP. Discounts are received on specific products, for volume sales, for agreeing to commit to a 3M product (standardization), and for just being a member of a PURCHASING GROUP.

3M agrees to protect DEALERS from losing money from 3M's action in negotiating the Purchasing Agreement. This price protection is offered through Rebate Credits made to DEALERS by 3M.

The DEALERS make Rebate Requests to 3M NATIONAL ACCOUNTS. The DEALERS provide proof to 3M NATIONAL ACCOUNTS of discounts given to HOSPITALS with documents indicating sales of 3M products to individual HOSPITALS. This proof is verified by 3M NATIONAL ACCOUNTS, and if approved, a Rebate Credit Request is made to 3M CREDIT/BILLING, which issues Rebate Credit Notices.

In some cases, DEALERS make payments to 3M CREDIT/BILLING, which deducts their expected rebate. In this case, 3M CREDIT/BILLING issues a Payment Shortage Notice. NATIONAL ACCOUNTS must verify these Payment Shortage Notices, and ensure that the Rebate Credit Request from DEALERS subtracts the already taken amount.

HOSPITALS also make Direct Orders to a 3M SALES BRANCH, rather than through a DEALER. 3M NATIONAL ACCOUNTS must be aware of these Direct Orders since they contribute to sales volume which could affect discounts.

3M MARKETING notifies the system if any Price or Product Changes take place.

The system provides information to NATIONAL ACCOUNTS MANAGEMENT, PURCHASING GROUPS, DEALERS, and the 3M SALES BRANCH. An important type of reporting is a Sales Recap which can specify sales dollars of 3M Health Care Products for each HOSPITAL. Another report is the Hospital Net Price Report which indicates whether DEALERS are abiding by the Purchasing Agreements.

Thus, the 3M National Accounts' price protection, rebate, and sales reporting system is critical to maintaining a competitive advantage through purchasing agreements and providing timely information to focus revenue generating efforts by salespersons. Without the information from rebate processing, 3M would not really know which hospitals are buying its products, since most purchases are made through 3M dealers.

The system problem and opportunity was to bring this system up-to-date to handle growing volumes of rebates and to provide the information needed to focus sales efforts.

BUILDING A SYSTEMS DEVELOPMENT DATABASE ABOUT THE REBATE SYSTEM

One of the critical tasks of the development group was to build a systems development database (known to many as "documentation"), providing information to make decisions on system design and implementation.

The database included:

who was involved with the system

what the system did

what data was required

what users could not do that they would have liked to do

why this system was needed in "bottom-line" business terms.

Subsystem modeling techniques were used.

People Subsystem

An organization chart detailing *who* was involved with the system was developed. The chart showed organization units and positions within the system. *Who* also was shown on the organizational and environmental context diagram shown in Figure 3.5. The relationships between the different organizational units were specified and formally reviewed. This information served as a directory of who should be interviewed or trained, or be part of a review team, etc.

Data Subsystem

As well as the context diagram, which showed data movement between organizational and external groups, data flow diagrams and data dictionaries detailing *what data* were developed. These models were presented to and reviewed by several levels of managers in different functional areas. These data flow diagrams served as the index to any existing or developed system documentation. A portion of one of the diagrams is shown in Figure 3.6. Four basic symbol types are represented: a square, representing a source or destination of data to or from the system; a rounded-corner rectangle, representing the processing of data; an elongated rectangle, representing the storage of data; and a line, representing the flow of data, with an arrowhead indicating flow direction.

The data dictionary was more than a data element description and directory. It expanded on the data, processes, persons, positions, and units denoted in the data flow and context diagram. This led to standardization of names and in identifying aliases (same things called by different names).

Organizing Structures Subsystem

Organizing structures were detailed with a set of requirements models. The models specified *why* the system was needed in the organization. The requirements models linked:

Business objectives—desired business accomplishments expressed in terms of reduced costs or increased revenues

Business tactics—business actions done by people to accomplish business objectives

System objectives—system achievements (reports and screens) to support businesspersons in performing business tactics

These requirements would allow systems personnel to specify potential system tactics to allow the system to achieve system objectives. The following is an example of the relationships between the factors:

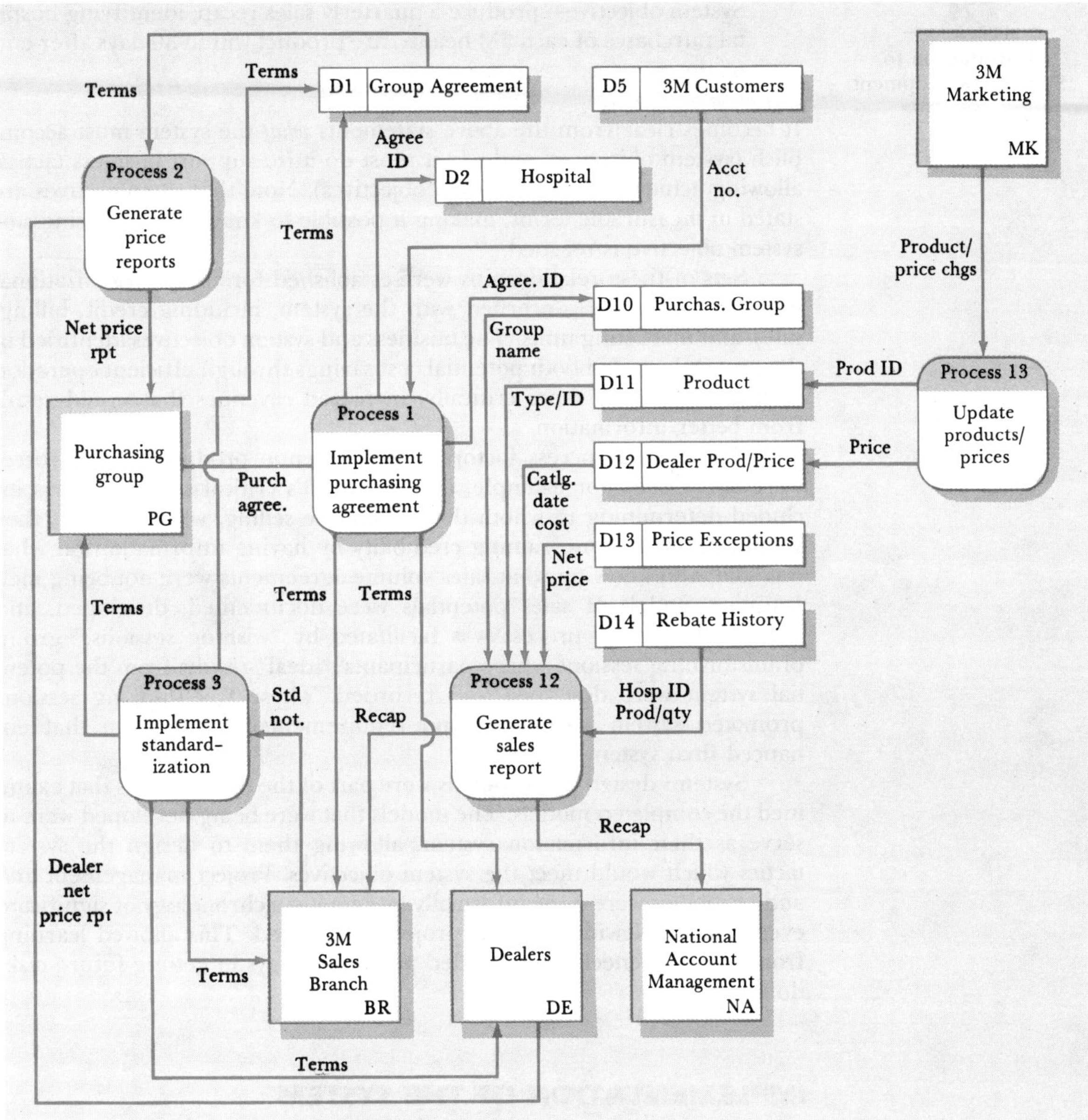

FIGURE 3.6

A data flow diagram segment.

Business objective—increase sales revenue of health care products by 5 percent from purchasing groups not fulfilling current purchasing agreements.

Business tactic—identify hospitals not purchasing specific 3M products as agreed, and contact them regarding these deficiencies.

System objective—produce a quarterly sales recap, identifying hospital purchases of each 3M health care product within 30 days after end of the quarter.

It becomes clear from the above statements *what* the system must accomplish (system objective), and *why* it must do it (to support business tactics, allowing achievement of business objectives). Note that the objectives are stated in measurable terms, making it possible to know when a business or system objective is reached.

Sets of these relationships were established for all the organizational units and positions concerned with the system, including credit, billing, sales, and marketing units. The business and system objectives identified in the project included both potential cost savings through efficient operation of the system and, more critically, increased revenues that would result from better information.

The critical success factors of the revenue producers (sales force) were addressed. For example, the sales staff's critical success factors included determining to whom they should be selling, what products they should be promoting, gaining credibility by having information on what was sold, and knowing what sales volume agreements were not being met. Intuitive models of sales potentials were documented, developed, and implemented. The process was facilitated by "wishing sessions," group brainstorming sessions where participants' "ideal" results from the potential system were described and recorded. These free-thinking sessions promoted system acceptance and requirements identification that enhanced final system quality.

Systems design professionals were part of the review teams that examined the completed models. The models that were being developed were to serve as their information system, allowing them to design the system tactics which would meet the system objectives. Project management and audit activities were done informally by keeping a chronology of significant events and reviewing it as the project progressed. This allowed learning from past bottlenecks and avoided potential delays in getting future tasks done.

IMPLEMENTATION OF THE SYSTEM

Once the three models that described *who, what,* and *why* were built, the fourth model that included *how* the system would be implemented was built. Development of this model, representing technology, was facilitated with the database about the existing system, its deficiencies, and new needs. The systems designers could propose alternative designs using modern technology once they understood the problem and its environment. The new systems design was done with excellent information. The shoemaker's children had shoes!

SUMMARY

This chapter has provided knowledge about the data needed to create the information for accomplishing systems development. With an understanding of the high-level processes of development, the techniques used to perform the processes, and the data input to and output from the processes and stored in the systems libraries, we have a good overview of systems development. In the next chapters, we will explore these processes, techniques, and data in more detail.

REFERENCES AND FURTHER READINGS

Brooks, Frederick P., Jr. *The Mythical Man-Month,* Reading, MA: Addison-Wesley, 1975.

Howden, William E. "Contemporary Software Development Environments," *Communications of the ACM,* vol. 25, no. 5, May 1982, pp. 318–329.

Kozar, Kenneth A., and Harry R. Smith. "METADATA: An Approach for Managing an Organization's Data Environment," *Proceedings: Canadian Information Processing Society Session '78,* Edmonton, Alberta, May 1978.

Kozar, Kenneth A., and John M. Mahlum. "A User Generated Information System: An Innovative Development Approach," *Management Information Systems Quarterly,* vol. 11, no. 2, June 1987, pp. 163–174.

Mendes, Kathleen. "Structured Systems Analysis: A Technique to Define Business Requirements," *Sloan Management Review,* Summer 1980, pp. 51–63.

Stohr, Edward A. "The Systems Development Process: A Data-Theoretic Approach," *Proceedings of the First International Conference on Information Systems,* E. McLean (ed.), December 8–10, 1980, Philadelphia, PA, pp. 144–164.

REVIEW QUESTIONS

1. Why might information systems professionals be considered to be "shoemaker's children"?
2. What is the "mythical man-month" phenomenon?
3. Assuming an automated systems development database existed, how could a project manager determine how much of a systems development process was complete without asking the project team?
4. Explain how automation could help produce system deliverables.
5. What data in a systems development database as proposed in this chapter could help a systems trainer?
6. What are some entities and attributes of the:
   a. People subsystem
   b. Organizing structures subsystem

c. Data subsystem
d. Technology subsystem

7. Sources and destinations of data to or from the system are called *external entities*. What are they external to? (*Hint*—see Figure 3.3 and Figure 3.4.)

8. What is the difference between a program and a procedure?

DISCUSSION QUESTIONS

1. What might be some arguments for not developing a database for systems development? What types of persons might object?

2. Would a database as suggested in the chapter be useful for all systems development projects? For what kinds of projects may a database be less appropriate?

3. How would each of the following use a systems development database?

   a. Information/systems analyst
   b. Systems designer
   c. Application programmer
   d. Systems project manager
   e. Database administrator
   f. User manager

4. Some of the data recorded about a system may need to be protected from unauthorized use, just like any database. What data in each of the four subsystem models might be sensitive? Why?

5. Based on the "new view" of the systems development processes shown in Figure 3.1, why might it appear that more than one process could be conducted at any one time? What would limit starting a process?

EXERCISES

1. Describe a model of a family by listing the entities, attributes of the entities, relationships, and attributes of the relationships. Entities may include parents, siblings, pets, homes, etc. Attributes may include age, height, eye color, etc. Relationships may include born to, brother of, owns, etc. Attributes of the relationships may include when, where, miles apart, etc.

2. Interview a systems project manager. Find out when documentation is generated in his or her organization in terms of the systems development life cycle. Is it a separate activity or is it a by-product of systems development? Has completion been a problem? What improvements has the organization tried to make to improve the situation? Describe the systems development database idea to the person. What is his or her reaction?

3. Seek some documentation or promotional literature about a systems development workbench. Examine the material to determine if a systems development

database concept is used. What is included in the storage about the system under development in the workbench you examined? How does it compare with what is recommended in this chapter?

PART II

The Systems Analysis Phase: Process and Techniques

Part II addresses the challenge of defining information system problems and/or opportunities. It examines in detail the analysis portions of the systems development methodology introduced in Part I. After the techniques for representing the collected systems data are presented, techniques for gathering and reviewing the collected data are examined.

CHAPTER 4

The Processes of Systems Analysis

CHAPTER OBJECTIVES

You should be able to:

- Specify what processes are needed to launch a systems project
- Specify the processes needed to define a systems problem or opportunity
- Describe the different human roles that must be fulfilled to launch a systems project and to more fully understand the problem or opportunity
- Specify the models of existing and proposed systems that must be included in systems analysis
- Defend the need for user commitment on a systems project

A systems project manager was stressing the importance of having user commitment, not just user involvement. When one of the users asked the difference between involvement and commitment, the project manager replied: "Well, I like to think about it in terms of my morning breakfast of bacon and eggs. The chicken was involved, but the pig certainly was committed!"

THIS CHAPTER DISCUSSES the initiation of a systems development project and its continuance by specifying the problem/opportunity and its environment. The chapter breaks down the general analysis processes introduced in Chapter 2 into more detail. The material discusses what is done at each stage and what the desired outputs would be.

This chapter introduces the activities in the initial stage of a systems project and stresses the importance of people who must be committed to the accomplishment of a project. The chapter discusses the varied types of systems projects and how scarce systems development resources are allocated to projects. The chapter builds on conceptual foundations examined in previous chapters by describing the *what* of systems analysis. The *how*, or techniques of systems analysis, will be presented in later chapters in this section.

BEGINNING A SYSTEMS DEVELOPMENT PROJECT

Systems development is done on a project basis. Each project must be assigned resources. Since the resources of time and money are not unlimited, an organization must select a mix of projects that use the available resources to maximize benefits for the organization.

There are many variations of systems projects. Projects may be big or small, have solutions using various mixes of people and technology, and be either new systems or reworkings of existing systems. Rework may be a "fix" of an existing system that is not working, or an enhancement or addition to the current workings. This rework commonly is called *maintenance*. All of these activities consume resources and must be part of the systems plan.

Management should set systems project priorities based on contribution to the organization. Users must sponsor the projects with a sincere commitment, with systems developers acting as experts to help obtain needed results. *Involvement* with a project may only mean a loose association, but *commitment* means that a person will do everything in his or her power to make the project a success.

Some of the discussion in this chapter tends toward the ideal. It proposes what should be, but is not always done in today's organizations. For example, it would be nice to believe that projects are selected in a rational manner, but this may not be totally true. There are political implications, beliefs that first come are first served, and "squeaky wheel" project selection that could result in diminished long-term benefits for the organization. If the chief executive officer of an organization says a particular project will be worked on, it likely will happen. The beginning analyst will discover that a balance of rationality and emotionality is most realistic in selecting and managing projects.

SOURCES OF SYSTEMS DEVELOPMENT PROJECTS

The systems development unit accepts systems project proposals from various sources. Figure 4.1 shows some of these sources. User groups in the organization may generate a need for a new system based on increased awareness about what new information could do for them. Use of an

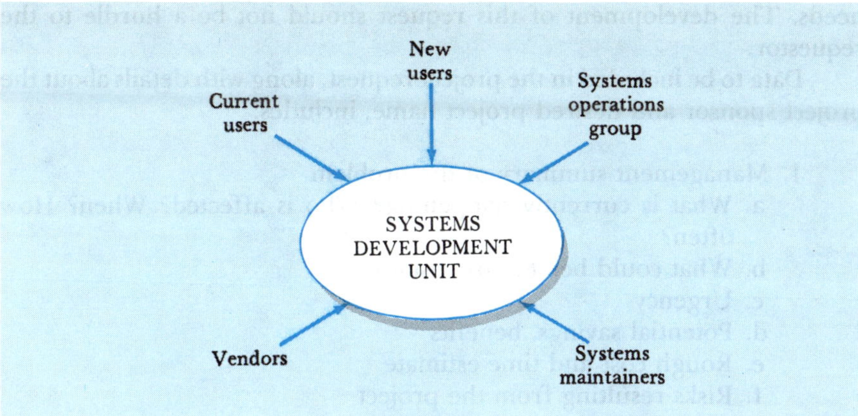

FIGURE 4.1
Project requests could come from varied sources.

information system often generates desires for additional capabilities. This could mean an existing system might have to be enhanced.

Existing systems must be repaired if there is a breakdown and operation is hindered. Repair requests likely would come from users if incorrect output is generated. The requests could come from the computer operations unit if an existing system was inefficient in operation or caused an operations problem.

Systems development persons who must maintain existing systems may make project requests. This is often analogous to the car mechanic suggesting some rebuilding work rather than just doing patching to keep the car running.

Vendors of currently used hardware or software might be sources of a project request by supplying a new version or release of an existing system. The revision of an existing system may cause other changes to programs and procedures that must be made by the systems development unit.

All of the above project requests would consume resources and must be planned and controlled. All project requests cannot be honored. Good management dictates conscious inclusion or exclusion of a project in the workload.

THE PROJECT REQUEST

The project request should be a formal written request to the systems department for services from a project sponsor. The sponsor is a person or organizational unit wanting the project done and willing to commit resources to complete the project. The request may be jointly completed by the requestor and a person from the systems unit, usually a project manager. The project manager should act much like a service advisor at an auto dealership. He or she should help record the system background and the needs. The development of this request should not be a hurdle to the requestor.

Data to be included in the project request, along with details about the project sponsor and desired project name, includes:

1. Management summary of the problem
   a. What is currently happening? Who is affected? When? How often?
   b. What could be? Future visions
   c. Urgency
   d. Potential savings, benefits
   e. Rough cost and time estimate
   f. Risks resulting from the project
2. Current situation in more detail
   a. What is currently happening in terms of inputs, processing, storage, and outputs? Any existing documentation?
   b. Why are current happenings deficient?
   c. Where or who the idea for the project came from? (This will often give some information sources to the future developers.)
   d. Who is affected by the system?
   e. Who could provide more information about current situation?
   f. Project priority compared to other systems projects of requestor?
3. Proposed situation
   a. Desired conditions? Scenario of an excellent workplace environment?
   b. Why things would be better? Potential achievements not now possible?
   c. Problems perceived in achieving new environment?
   d. Time constraints? Money constraints for project?
   e. Specific persons who must be involved? (Both developers and users.)

This preliminary document should not attempt to present all the detail about a project. It should be a rough first draft to give the systems developers some direction in conducting the initial study. The effort that the requestor puts in will indicate a commitment to the project. The project will get a good start by putting ideas in writing and starting the systems documentation.

MANAGING THE PROJECT MIX

Before a systems development project is officially started, a decision must be made to include the project in the planned systems work, often called the organization's *project portfolio* or *project mix*. The project must be important enough to be allocated scarce resources managed by the systems development unit.

Before starting a new project, workers selected to be on a steering committee meet to determine the need for the project and how it will fit in with other company functions. (Comstock)

Project approval and resource assignment are decisions that are made by systems and user management. Often a corporate steering committee is established for this purpose. To assure that projects critical to an organization's existence are being developed and maintained, it is important that the selection group have the information necessary to make wise decisions on which projects are to be pursued, in what order, and with how many resources. Only if all projects are handled in this way can systems department budgets be planned and controlled.

It is important to select a varied mix of projects. This is similar to managing a personal investment portfolio. Some projects should be more risky, with a higher potential payoff, while some are merely work required to keep an essential system in operation. Some projects should result in short-term benefits, while others may prove to be viable in the long run. A proposed project must be compared to all other projects that are competing for resources. Only projects which have an acceptable payback, expressed as rate of return in an investment sense, should have resources assigned to them.

Care must be taken to assure that enhancements or "fixes" to existing systems, commonly called maintenance, are included in the resource allocation assignments. Otherwise, the workload of systems personnel will grow without official recognition. These "little" additions add up and swamp the systems workers. Work will unofficially grow and put a burden on the systems staff.

An organization will have a specified number of projects with persons assigned to the projects. The projects should have development schedules fully utilizing these persons. If new projects are added to the schedule without consciously including them in the systems plan, several things could happen:

1. Previously scheduled projects can be eliminated or delayed.
2. Persons doing systems work can work longer hours.
3. Resources (persons) can be added to the systems work group.

Managers must decide which combination of the above factors they are willing to support, and the risks associated with the factors. And, most importantly, this must be done in a conscious manner.

Good systems personnel are hard to find. They should not be abused with inappropriate workloads. Overworked people could quit, or at a minimum, work at less than optimal efficiency and effectiveness. Adding work without changing plans does not make any sense and should be avoided. Projects can "creep" into the workload and swamp the systems staff.

Sometimes projects may require immediate attention. For example, an essential existing system may fail for some reason. If so, slack resources might be assigned to handle the problem. If the human resources are taken from another development project, then that project's schedules should be adjusted.

The project mix must be reevaluated as development proceeds because increasingly better information is collected about the resources needed to complete the project. For example, in Process 1 when projects are initiated, an accurate estimate of resources to complete the entire project would be impossible. Processes 2 and 3 will generate information that will include how bad a problem really is, how great an opportunity is, and what alternatives exist in terms of scope and automation potentials for changing the current system. This new information could increase or reduce the payback on a project.

The resources to complete the project will depend on factors such as whether software can be purchased or has to be developed, whether the existing system must be replaced or merely enhanced, or whether the project will require new hardware or changed physical facilities. Only after these factors are considered can more accurate estimates for project completion be made. But before a project can be evaluated for inclusion in the project mix, initial data on the system must be gathered. This is the purpose of the initial study.

CONDUCTING AN INITIAL STUDY TO START THE PROJECT

Each of the processes of systems development will be discussed in more detail as we proceed through the book. This may overwhelm the reader if he or she attempts to memorize the detail on the first reading. An attempt first should be made to take a high-level view of what organization members are doing and the results of their activities. Then, the reader should refresh his or her memory by trying to fit all the activities together. Finally, when confronted with a real project, the material can serve as a reference and guide to development activities.

Process 1: Conduct Initial Study

Purpose: Determine project priority by defining problem or opportunity.

Output: A mix of projects with acceptable paybacks that utilize the available development resources. Preliminary organizational data, systems documentation, and cost/benefit data.

Subprocesses: Determine who is affected by the system to be studied. Make a rough estimate of the benefits from accomplishing the project. Make a rough estimate of the costs of the project. Draw up a project plan for the later processes.

Techniques and Skills: Interviewing, presenting, peer and user reviewing, data flow diagramming, system flowcharting, requirements defining.

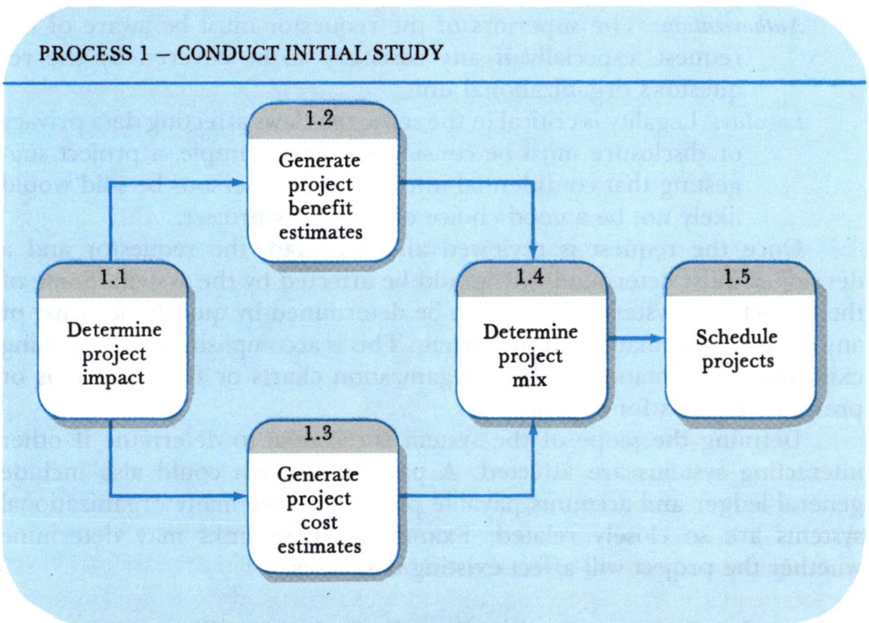

FIGURE 4.2
Subprocesses within Process 1.

Activities within Process 1 of a systems development project are shown in Figure 4.2. They include determining who would be affected by the project (Process 1.1), why the project is needed in terms of avoided future costs and/or increased organization revenues (Process 1.2), some rough cost estimates for the project (Process 1.3), how the project would compare in worth with other proposed projects (Process 1.4), and, finally, development of a revised schedule including all projects (Process 1.5).

Process 1.1-Determine Project Impact. All submitted project requests must be screened for completeness, authorization, and legality. The project requestor provides this information in a written statement which then is reviewed by the systems unit. The systems unit must attempt to work with the requestor to enhance information which would give the project a greater chance for success. The review includes an examination of:

Completeness: The problem to be avoided or the opportunity to be pursued by a new or revised system must be understood by both the requestor and the systems unit. This would include who likely will be affected, a brief description of the problem or opportunity, and why ignoring the problem or opportunity would be detrimental to the organization.

Persons or organizational units affected by the project must be recorded. This would include internal groups such as current input providers, output users, or data processors, and outside groups such as suppliers, customers, or unions. This information is critical, not only to conducting the development work, but also to having the system accepted once it is completed.

Authorization: The superiors of the requestor must be aware of the request, especially if any costs are to be covered by the requestor's organizational unit.

Legality: Legality is critical in the sense that laws affecting data privacy or disclosure must be considered. For example, a project suggesting that confidential information on persons be sold would likely not be a good choice of a systems project.

Once the request is reviewed and accepted, the requestor and a developer must determine who would be affected by the system. Some of the impact of a systems change can be determined by quickly perusing of any existing information on the system. This is accomplished by examining existing documentation such as organization charts or flow diagrams or previous requests for systems work.

Defining the scope of the system is essential to determine if other interacting systems are affected. A payroll problem could also include general ledger and accounts payable problems since many organizational systems are so closely related. Examining these links may determine whether the project will affect existing databases.

Process 1.2-Generate Project Benefit Estimates. The general statement of why the project is deemed important from the project request must be expanded. The degree of urgency and an estimate of when project completion is needed must be included. The reasons the project is needed should be stated in both systems and business or organizational terms.

Systems reasons for resource expenditures may include limitations in speed, response time, storage, vendor support, etc., or because the existing system is becoming too costly to maintain. The processing or information system often will require changes to take advantage of new technology or to respond to changed business practices.

Business reasons for a project may include changing laws or statutes, new markets, competitor actions, new products, new accounting methods, new organizational structure, and new competitor services (for example, banks and automated tellers). As changes take place in the environment in which a system resides, changes in the system may become necessary. A request such as "wanting a terminal on my desk" must be addressed with the question of "why will the organization benefit if this were to happen?"

Process 1.3-Generate Project Cost Estimates. A general statement of proposed project cost is needed so a decision can be made on whether to include the project in the project mix. It should be clear that such a statement will not have much detail at this stage.

Project cost will be influenced by many factors. The number of persons affected will influence development tasks such as the number of interviews or training needed. The number of interacting systems that would be affected by changing the system will influence project size and scope. The state of the system's current documentation will influence the time needed to analyze the current system. The state of the actual system in terms of solidness of structure and amount of patching done will reveal whether parts of the existing system can be reused. Systems including new technology such as pioneering hardware or telecommunications equipment likely will cost more because of the organizational learning that must take place.

Subprocesses to help cost determination should include:

1. Perusing and assessing existing documentation
2. Roughly stating desired system results, noting hardware, software, and vendor constraints
3. Determining existing system condition
4. Determining database or shared file implications;
5. Generating a rough draft of potential alternatives with accompanying costs for hardware, software, and telecommunication combinations
6. Estimating total costs to continue project based on 1 through 5 above.

At this stage, only rough approximations that will be refined by more thorough systems analysis are the best that can be expected. Ranges of costs for systems development, hardware and software strategies, and user time for development and work stoppage should be developed.

All of the above steps are needed to estimate the resources which the proposed project will require. Then it is necessary to review these findings with those who will be involved in the potential development effort. This includes persons who must commit resources to the project, such as database administrators, systems software specialists, and user management, and others whose time, effort, and commitment is necessary.

Users must be reminded that:

1. They share responsibility for project success.
2. It is their system.
3. The project will cost them time and money.
4. They must furnish information and review intermediate results.
5. They will be asked many questions about how they do their jobs.
6. They likely will have to change as a result of the system.

Since these are realities, they must be brought out early and understood before the project is officially sanctioned. Some users might feel this is too high a cost to pay for a system.

At this stage, the systems developer will likely have some suggestions as to what type of development method is appropriate for the project. The classic life cycle approach or alternatives such as a user-generated system, prototyping, or package acquisition may be suggested by the developer. For example, a decision support system project using existing data may be most appropriately approached with a prototyping approach using a fourth generation language. This topic will be discussed in much more detail in Chapter 14.

Process 1.4-Determine Project Mix. Information gathered in the previous subprocesses will be used to make decisions on which projects will be allocated systems development resources. Usually, these decisions will be made by an executive steering committee. This group periodically will review all projects to ensure adequate progress and a good use of organizational resources. The project mix is part of the information systems unit's plan for the future.

As part of this subprocess, progress on existing projects must be collected and summarized. The planned tasks that were scheduled to have been completed are viewed against the actual completion. Any revisions in terms of costs and benefits that would affect economic feasibility must be noted. As well, changes in technical or operational feasibility should be noted for the decision makers. For example, a vendor may have delayed a delivery date on a piece of software, or some potential users of the project results may have stated their reluctance to participate in the project. These factors will affect continuance of any project.

All of this information should be prepared for the decision makers in a format that will allow comparison across projects. Each project must have an evaluation of economic benefit based on the current present value of cost expenditures versus potential benefits. All projects should be summarized in rank order based on economic benefits. Any other notes such as risk estimates, special urgency, or doubts about future use should be added. If new or altered projects change the original ranking, potential reassignment of personnel should be evaluated. Project mix alternatives should be suggested for evaluation by decision makers.

The strategic decision makers also may have private information that could alter the suggested project mixes. For example, a confidential business strategy of product line expansion could nullify a project that assumed a constant product line.

Once the project mix has been selected, the original project requestor must be notified of the decision of the steering group. Options include rejection, pending based on lack of resources, or acceptance for the next steps of systems development. For an expanded discussion of selecting an appropriate project mix, see the articles by McFarlan and Gremillion and Pyburn in the references at the end of the chapter.

At this point, a project leader likely will be selected. Many organizations insist that part of the leadership be assumed by the user body. Again, such a move will assure commitment from the user group.

Process 1.5-Schedule Projects. Once resources are assigned to projects, a schedule and plan are established for each project in the project mix. The human resources available must be balanced across the proposed project mix. Skills must be matched with needed tasks. Plans must include training if skills are needed, but are not available.

Building project teams can be a difficult task. Of course, personal desires and personality conflicts should be considered. Avoidance of changing assignments if there is no current problem on a project team will assure project continuity. For further discussion of these management issues, see Semprevivo and Thomsett in references at the end of this chapter.

Actual project scheduling is beyond the scope of this book. Some organizations will use automated project planning and scheduling systems and some will accomplish this activity manually (Cleland and King; DeMarco).

Once the schedules are completed, it is essential to assure that all involved developers and users understand their roles in the development process. This will help avoid misunderstanding later when questions come up about who is supposed to do what. A "kickoff document" such as the one shown in Figure 4.3 may clear the path and give the project legitimacy. The document should include:

1. An announcement of the existence of the study
2. The purpose of the study
3. The proposed participants
4. The intended objectives
5. A request for persons' involvement

MEMORANDUM

DATE: August 11, 198?
TO: All Accounting Group Managers and Supervisors
FROM: Names and Positions of Persons on Steering Committee
RE: Enhanced Accounts Receivable Systems Study (EARSS)

We have requested that the systems development unit of our Information Systems Department initiate a study of the feasibility of enhancing our present accounts receivable system. As some of you are aware, we are experiencing problems in billing customers promptly. There also are needs for better identifying and collecting delinquent payments. We do anticipate additional growth in this area based on our business success in the past two quarters. We will have to handle additional new accounts and an increase in the daily volume of invoices.

Sandy Alter has been assigned the responsibility of conducting an initial investigation of the current system. Sandy will be working most closely with Art Revers, Manager of the Accounts Receivable Department. As part of the assignment, we have asked Sandy to visit with each of the Accounting Group leaders. We will appreciate your aid to Sandy in helping to understand the current accounting operations and documentation related to accounts receivable.

We expect that you will direct Sandy to other persons in your unit if further information is needed for the study.

Enhancement of the accounts receivable area can aid us in improving our profit picture. Thank you for your efforts in keeping the team effort going.

FIGURE 4.3
A project kick-off memo.

CONTINUING THE PROJECT

Once a project is approved as part of the organization's project mix, a more detailed study of the existing system and its problems and deficiencies is needed. The detailed study may take place immediately or be delayed due to lack of available resources. Some of the same tasks that were done in Process 1 now are done in more detail. A very important need is to understand the existing system from a logical point of view, that is, what the system does, why it must do it, and who is involved. This contrasts with physical understanding, or knowing and documenting how any existing system operates and with what devices. As in the previous process, all of the data that is collected and generated about the system is recorded in the system database.

In gathering data, it is essential for the systems designer to understand what workers currently do and how this may change under the new system. (Lou Jones)

Process 2: Analyze Current System

Purpose: Understand and document the structure and purpose of the current system. Determine requirements of the new system.

Output: A set of user reviewed and accepted models of the organization, the data movements and storage, the processing needed, and the organization needs that would be served by an improved system. A more refined set of system costs and benefits to determine project continuance.

Subprocesses: Convert any existing physical descriptions of data storage, data flows, and processes to logical descriptions. Gather and analyze data on who is involved with the system, what the system does, why changes are needed, and what data and processes a new system should contain.

Techniques and Skills: Interviewing, presenting, peer and user reviewing, organizational modeling, data flow diagramming, data structuring, requirements defining, procedure writing.

Process 2 does not require collecting all the detailed data about the current system. Since there will be many options for drawing system boundaries, it is better to wait until a boundary decision has been made before doing detailed analysis. Thus, more and more detail is collected, but the greatest detail will not be sought until the project scope and degree of automation is defined. The same is true for error and exception handling. What should be understood is what happens most of the time (85 percent is

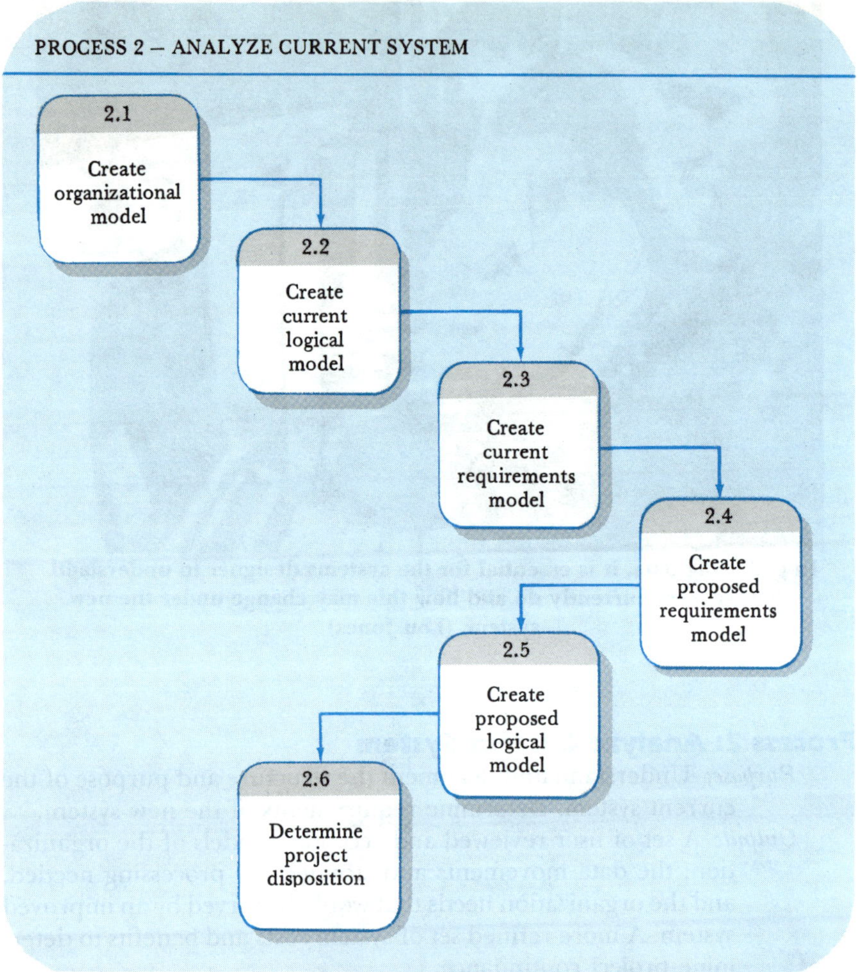

FIGURE 4.4
Subprocesses within Process 2.

a rough guess). We do not want to lose the "forest for the trees" at this early stage of the project.

Figure 4.4 breaks Process 2 into more detail. It should be remembered that this is not the only way to conduct the analysis of a system. There could be variations of the processes shown. This figure only illustrates one acceptable way of studying a system.

Note in Figure 4.4 that first a model is developed of the organizational setting. This will define the organization positions and units concerned with the system and the organizational functions they perform. This will define *who* is involved in terms of people, and begins to define *what* is done. *What* the system does is refined and enhanced when a logical model of the system processes and data is created. The model is called "logical" since it describes "what" is done, not "how," as with a physical model. Techniques for creating logical models include data flow diagrams and data description entries. These techniques will be detailed in Chapter 5.

Once the logical model details *what* is currently done, a current requirements model specifying organizing structures is created to specify *why* current processes are done and *why* data is stored in the existing system. Next, the reasons *why* a changed system is needed are explored. A partial requirements model of the proposed system is developed. This will state:

New business objectives—achievements desired by the business

New business tactics—actions to be performed by organizational members

New system objectives—achievements by the system that will aid in performing business tactics

Further definition of these concepts and how data on them is obtained and detailed will be discussed in Chapter 6.

Once the requirements model defines *why* in business terms the new system is needed and what aid will be provided by the information system, a new logical model can be proposed to support business needs. This new logical model will delete unneeded processes and data, modify existing processes and data, and add new processes and data. During this development stage, the analyst must avoid the temptation to begin proposing system designs or hardware and software. The challenge at this point is to fully understand the problem or opportunity. Otherwise the developer will fall into the trap of "computerizing before systematizing."

Finally, all developed models are reviewed, evaluated, and changed by sharing them with all persons who will be involved with the system.

Process 2.1-Create Organizational Model. This process documents the organizational setting the system is to support. The organizational positions or jobs, organizational units or departments, and functions performed by the positions or units are determined, recorded, and reviewed. The organizational functions are the activities done to produce and deliver goods and services to the marketplace as well as any support needed to perform these functions.

This subprocess provides much of the information to be used to complete a systems project. Information on who to gather data from, who is to review collected data, who to train, who can provide system results, who can provide needed system inputs, etc., is determined at this stage of the project. The collected data will constitute a directory of further sources from which data can be gathered. Understanding what employees currently do and how this may change because of a system alteration also is essential for performing job or organizational design.

It may be necessary to contact the project sponsors before starting this subprocess. This is an assurance that the "kickoff memo" from Process 1

Involved developers and users hold a kick-off meeting to share information and enthusiasm. (Pierre Kopp/West Light)

reached all the appropriate persons. The analyst must assure that permission is granted to interrupt people, who already have assigned duties, to conduct data collection activities.

Data to complete this subprocess will come from many sources. Existing organization charts (see Figure 4.5), job descriptions, policy statements, union agreements, organization job surveys, and newly collected data from interviews or questionnaires all will aid in completing the organizational model. If existing documentation is found, it is necessary to verify that it is correct through a review by the involved personnel. Often, tasks get added to job positions or organization unit responsibilities without being recorded.

The formal organizational structure should be supplemented with any data about the informal structure. Some of this data can be determined by observing things like group social behavior to determine informal leaders. Questions such as "Who would you go to if you had a problem?" may also reveal informal communication structures.

Another valuable source of data about the system and organization that is often overlooked is former position holders. These persons may still be in the company, but be a member of another organizational unit. Permission should be obtained from both the project sponsor and the person's supervisors. If there is a real need for information that does not seem to exist, it may be necessary to pay to interview a former position holder no longer with the company. Of course, care should be taken to avoid any legal ramifications due to conflict of interest.

It is important to determine how changeable the organizational setting is. For example, existing union agreeements, job contracts, or accepted industry standards may add constraints to suggesting new system changes.

It also may be possible to collect some data on how receptive persons and units are to change. This can be done informally by "gut feel" or by hiring experts to study and report on the organizational climate. Although many persons may believe this is a drastic step, many systems have turned out to be failures because of the "people problem" of reluctance to accept a new system.

On many occasions, there will be questions as to whether an organization unit is within the scope of the systems project. It may be necessary to

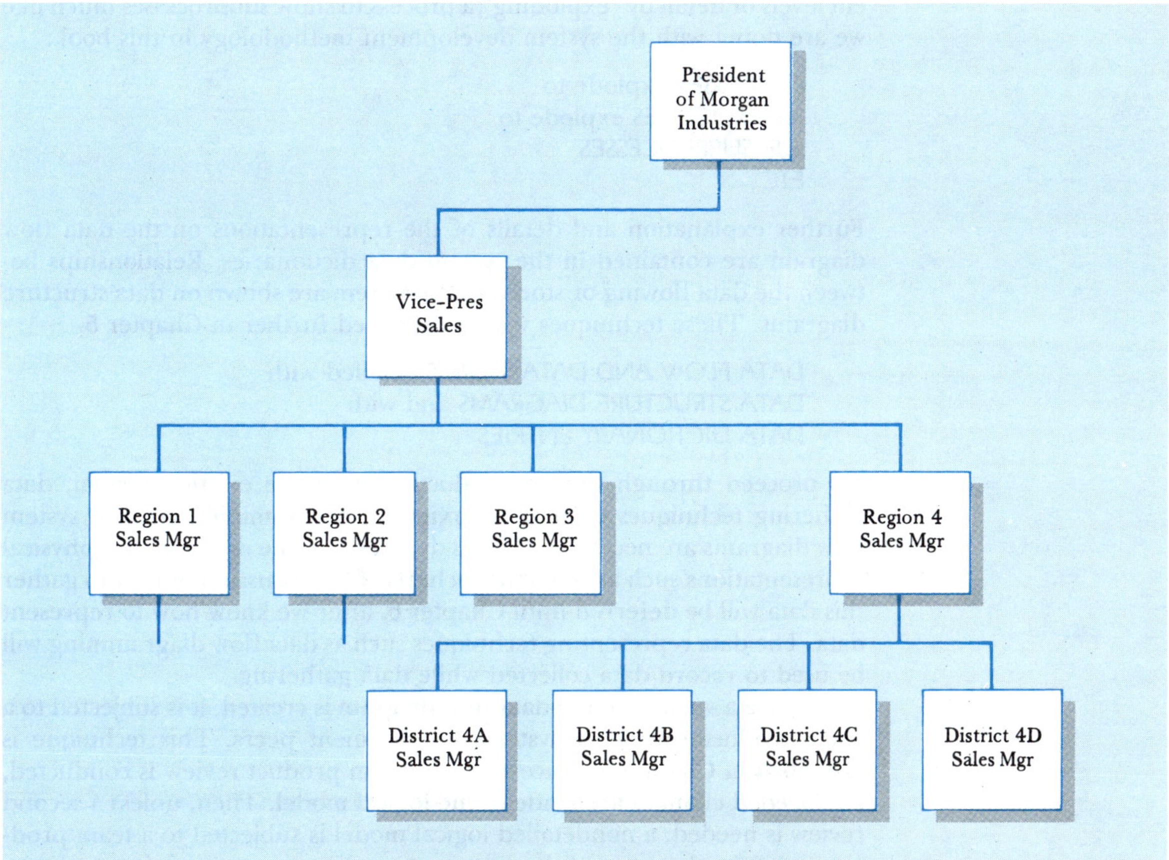

FIGURE 4.5
Morgan Industries organization chart for sales management group.

get higher-level management or the information systems steering committee involved if there is a question about the organizational boundary included in the systems project. For example, if a payroll system project is to involve personnel data, there will be a question whether the personnel unit in the organization should be involved in the study.

The results of the subprocess will be the data needed to generate organization charts, organization unit and position descriptions, and organization functions performed by the persons in organization positions or units.

Process 2.2-Create Current Logical Model. This process produces a representation of the processes and data movement and storage included in the existing system. It does this with a logical representation, including what is done rather than how it is done. It should be remembered that what a system does is much more stable than how it is done due to the rapid changes in technology.

The predominant techniques for creating the logical model are the data flow diagram and the system data dictionary. You will learn about data flow diagrams in the next chapter. You will find they can represent different levels of detail by "exploding" a process to show subprocesses much like we are doing with the system development methodology in this book.

PROCESSES explode to
SUBPROCESSES explode to
SUB-SUBPROCESSES
ETC.

Further explanation and details of the representations on the data flow diagram are contained in the system data dictionaries. Relationships between the data flowing or stored in the system are shown on data structure diagrams. These techniques will be discussed further in Chapter 5.

DATA FLOW AND DATA STORES detailed with
DATA STRUCTURE DIAGRAMS and with
DATA DICTIONARY ENTRIES

To proceed through the act of documenting the existing system, data gathering techniques such as interviewing or examining current system flow diagrams are necessary. This is done even if the diagrams are physical representations such as system flowcharts. The discussion of how to gather this data will be deferred until Chapter 6, after we know how to represent data. The data representing techniques such as data flow diagramming will be used to record data collected while data gathering.

Once a version of the data flow diagram is created, it is subjected to a team product review by systems development peers. This technique is described in Chapter 7. Once the peer team product review is conducted, any needed changes are made to the logical model. Then, unless a second review is needed, a nondetailed logical model is subjected to a team product review by the users of the system. A quality assurance review to assure adherence to organizational standards may also be needed. Once a general, or top level, logical model is created and revised, more detailed "explosions" are created.

Data stores and structures are also defined and documented. Data flowing into a data store is verified against the data needed from the data store. This may require revision of system database entries. Data is refined into its simplest form by attempting to remove complex relationships. The data definitions are reviewed by peers, database administrators, quality assurance groups, and knowledgeable users. This discovery and review process is continued until the system is adequately modeled.

This iterative process may take more "up-front" time than some other traditional development methods. In fact, some experienced persons may get nervous because there is no computer program code being produced. However, the reason for this modeling effort is to understand the system and adequately define the problem so that the right problem is being solved. Remember from Chapter 1 that we must understand a system before we can "beat it," or, in our case, improve it.

Maintenance costs over a system's life have classically been 50 to 80 percent of total system cost (Boehm). Much of this cost can be attributed to solving the wrong problem and to real communication between users and developers only starting once an operating or physical version of the system is delivered. Logical models will allow a mutual understanding of the system and its deficiencies.

Some persons have believed that the amount of communication during a development project that takes place between users and developers

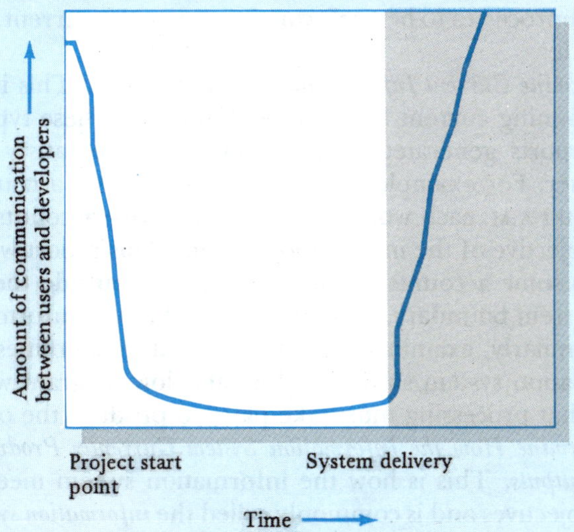

FIGURE 4.6

Probable user/developer communication over the project life without the use of structured techniques and modeling.

during classical systems development (without structured techniques and modeling) may appear as in Figure 4.6. They have felt that developers have had a great deal of interaction at the beginning of a project only to disappear until they had a finished product. Once users saw the finished product, communication immediately increased as they told developers what they really wanted. Building models of the system thus may improve needed communication and make communication more constant over time. This will improve the chances that systems meeting user needs will be built

Process 2.3-Create Current Requirements Model. This process produces a statement of the organizational justification and need for the existing system. The statement links the current organizational needs to the objectives the existing information subsystem satisfies to aid the organization in meeting needs. In essence, Why? things are currently done must be discovered and recorded. This includes why processes are done, why external entities are involved, why data is sent or received, and why data is stored. It also is important to determine why certain persons or positions perform processes and if this is appropriate.

This subprocess uses a technique called *requirements defining*. More detail on this technique, its terminology, and how to create the requirements model is given in Chapter 6. In general, existing outputs from the information system are identified from the logical model. Each output is examined to determine who uses it, and why in business terms. Criteria such as when the output must be produced and what data for what time period are also examined. The purpose of all of this activity is to ensure that what is currently being done by the information system contributes to the mission of the organization.

The subprocesses to be performed to create the current requirements model include:

1. *Determine Current Information System Objectives.* This is done by examining current logical model outputs. These typically are the reports generated or processing done to satisfy some system user. For example, producing a delinquent accounts report by 9:00 A.M. each working day for all active accounts would be an objective of the information system. This report would likely go to some accounts person who may be outside the information system boundary, an entity external to the information system. Similarly, examining inputs from external entities to the information system shown in the data flow diagram will determine what processing must take place to produce the outputs.
2. *Determine How the Information System Currently Produces the System Outputs.* This is how the information system meets the system objectives and is commonly called the *information system strategy or tactics*. This often is found in current system documentation such as system flowcharts. Detail is not important here since the current technology will likely be replaced by some emerging

technology. It only is important to generalize to describe the system in terms of approach such as batch versus online, application files versus subject databases, centralized database versus distributed database, centralized versus decentralized data entry, or micros versus mainframe.

3. *Determine Current Business Tactics.* This is done to determine how the system outputs are used by the receiver of the output. In some cases, when the system outputs are not used, the intended user will not have a business tactic. If so, there is serious question as to whether the organization should continue to expend resources to produce the output.
4. *Determine Current Business Objectives.* This is done to ensure that the preceding activities which consume resources also produce benefits. Business objectives should contribute to the organization's "bottom line" by increasing revenues or by reducing costs.

The above activities should lead to a justification of the current information and business subsystems. Weaknesses in the current subsystems likely were the impetus for the existing project work. Now that the existing system is understood, the next activity is to detail why the current subsystems are not satisfactory.

Process 2.4-Create Proposed Requirements Model. This process justifies new information system needs. The data about what changes are needed and why, collected in Process 1 when the project was initiated, is enhanced. The technique of requirements defining again is used to create the model of new needs. The order of proceeding through the requirements defining model is changed. The model serves as a guide for proceeding from the business reasons for a change to a rough idea of how the system would perform to provide needed outputs. In the case of new or changed needs, we are not searching for information system deficiencies, but are starting with the changed business achievements an organizational member desires.

First, the economic reasons for the proposed information system are determined by recording changed or new business objectives that would result in increased revenues or reduced costs. The change in business objectives could be either a major revision or just a small change in the quantification of an existing objective. Then, the business tactics or means to achieving the business objectives are recorded. Next, the aid the system can provide is documented by recording new information system objectives. Finally, alternatives to achieving the information system objectives, called the *information system tactics,* are recorded.

The new requirements model should state what is needed in a new system. This may include performance of processes by different persons or units, whether the work environment needs to be changed, whether the system boundaries may have to be enlarged or narrowed, whether the system has adequate control or audit trails, and whether the system must produce changed inputs or outputs.

Process 2.5-Create Proposed Logical Model. This process produces a new logical model of the system incorporating any needed changes to satisfy newly identified requirements. The original logical model from earlier processes is modified to accommodate performing new or changed business tactics, achieving different information system objectives, and performing new information system tactics.

Consideration must be given on the current logical model to the following:

1. Simplification—making existing tasks easier to do
2. Compression—merging and combining functions to save resources
3. Modification—changing sequences or locations of activities
4. Elimination—removing functions not really needed

The new logical model usually is shown as data flow and data structure diagrams with accompanying systems development database (data dictionary) entries. The new logical models will incorporate new processes and new data flows and stores. Several levels of detail may be needed to represent the proposed system completely and accurately. Finally, the data structures included in the proposed logical model are constructed and reviewed.

Process 2.6-Determine Project Disposition. Once the existing system has been studied, it is necessary to reexamine the original cost/benefit statements, update them, and determine if the project should continue to receive development resources. This project management activity is needed since new and more accurate estimates of future costs and benefits will be a result of the system study. The revenue figures only should reflect net increases in business revenues as a result of an improved information system. The costs that are reduced include both reduced information operating costs and reduced costs of performing business tactics. All of these figures are converted to present values in a financial sense.

Better estimates should also be possible for the costs of continuing systems development. There will be alternative costs of completing the development depending on what information system tactics are pursued. Likewise, different sets of system tactics will allow achieving different levels of benefits. This will be discussed in more detail in later sections.

The systems developer plays an active role in this process by developing presentations to organization management. The developers either deliver the presentations, or aid the project management, including user project sponsors, in presenting the material to decision making management. This information may cause the management, often the information systems steering committee, to alter the project mix or portfolio. If a project continues to be part of the portfolio, the systems development work proceeds to Process 3. This process will be discussed in a later chapter after we learn more about the techniques of systems analysis needed to accomplish Process 1 and Process 2.

SUMMARY

This chapter traced the processes and subprocesses used to initiate a systems development project and to develop documentation about the system and its deficiencies. This is done through discovery of who is involved with a system, what the system does and with what data, and why the system is needed for organizational survival. The processes of analysis could differ from organization to organization, but the major thrust is to define the system problems and opportunities and to record them accurately. This can be accomplished by the commitment of all involved organizational members to sharing and communicating about the system. The ability to gain mutual understanding of the system by the entire development team is facilitated through the development of system models which are shared and reviewed by all participants.

As was discussed in previous chapters, the processes now must be accomplished through the use of systems analysis techniques. These techniques will be presented in following chapters.

REFERENCES AND FURTHER READINGS

Boehm, Barry W. *Software Engineering Economics,* Englewood Cliffs, NJ: Prentice-Hall, 1981.

Brooks, Frederick P. *The Mythical Man Month—Essays on Software Engineering,* Reading, MA: Addison-Wesley, 1974.

Cleland, David I., and William R. King. *Systems Analysis and Project Management,* New York: McGraw-Hill, Inc., 3d ed., 1983.

DeMarco, Tom. *Controlling Software Projects,* New York: Yourdon Press, 1982.

Gause, Donald C., and Gerald M. Weinberg. *Are Your Lights On? How to Figure Out What the Problem Really Is,* Cambridge, MA: Winthrop Publishers, Inc., 1982.

Gremillion, Lee L., and Philip J. Pyburn. "Justifying Decision Support and Office Automation Systems," *Journal of Management Information Systems,* Summer 1985, vol. 2, no. 1, pp. 5–17.

McFarlan, F. Warren. "Portfolio Approach to Information Systems," *Harvard Business Review,* September–October 1981, pp. 142–150.

Metzger, Philip W. *Managing a Programming Project,* 2d ed., Englewood Cliffs, NJ: Prentice-Hall, 1981.

Semprevivo, Philip C. *Teams in Information Systems Development,* New York: Yourdon Press, 1980.

Thomsett, Rob. *People and Project Management,* New York: Yourdon Press, 1980.

Yourdon, Edward. *Managing the System Life Cycle: A Software Development Methodology Overview,* New York: Yourdon Press, 1982.

REVIEW QUESTIONS

1. Give an example of project mix selection being specified by reality rather than rationality.

2. Who might request initiation of a systems project?
3. What might be different distinguishing characteristics of systems projects in a project portfolio?
4. What should be the contents of a project request?
5. Who should develop a project request?
6. Who should determine what projects are appropriate for a project portfolio?
7. What might happen to the systems development group if they did every "little" job that was requested?
8. Why can't an accurate estimate be made of resources needed to complete a systems project when the project request is made?
9. What are some systems reasons for a project request?
10. What are some business reasons for a project request?
11. What are some factors affecting project cost?
12. What is meant by computerizing before systematizing?
13. What techniques are used to develop a logical model of a system?

DISCUSSION QUESTIONS

1. Why might development of a physical model of an existing system hinder future logical model creation?
2. Discuss the differences between involvement and commitment. Which requires greater risks for the project requestor?
3. A systems development project manager said that his staff would not give any aid to new project requestors. His reasoning was that if the users could not put the project request together, they were not committed to the systems effort. Several users argued that many questions asked on the request form were confusing. Would you agree with the project manager that the requestors just did not want to put in any effort?
4. One MIS manager argued that an "initial study" for a systems project was unnecessary. Another said that the study was needed to allocate resources appropriately. Who is right?
5. A project manager told a user that an initial study for her proposed decision support system project would take 6 person-months. The user asked you if this was appropriate. What would be your reply?
6. Why is it inappropriate to collect all the detail about a system during the initial analysis processes?
7. Why is the order of progressing through a requirements model different for justifying an existing system versus justifying a proposed system?

EXERCISES

1. The use of logical models to represent systems is a relatively recent concept. Talk to some working systems analysts to find out if they make attempts to create logical models. Share your finding with your classmates.
2. This chapter discussed some of the realities that users must face to have a system developed (see section on Process 1.3). Do you feel the points made are reasonable? Discuss the points with both systems users and developers. What is their reaction?
3. Meet with an MIS manager to find out how his or her organization determines the project mix. How does it differ from the approach advocated in this chapter? How is it similar? Why might there be differences?

CHAPTER 5

Representing Systems Data

MORAL: It's not know-how that counts; it's know-when.
—Gerald M. Weinberg, Rethinking Systems Analysis and Design, Boston: Little, Brown and Company, 1982, p. 24.

THIS CHAPTER DISCUSSES techniques used to represent data gathered in systems definition. System flowcharts, presentation graphs, context diagrams, data flow diagrams, Warnier-Orr diagrams, and data models (including organizational, logical, and requirements models) are discussed. The chapter specifically focuses on representing logical organizational models using data flow diagrams. A specific example of building a logical model is included in a step-by-step scenario.

CHAPTER OBJECTIVES

You should be able to:

- Determine when to use a data flow diagram versus a system flowchart
- Create a data flow diagram of a moderately complex system
- Specify what a data flow diagram should include and exclude
- Specify the attributes of data flows, data stores, data structures, and data elements to be included in a data dictionary
- Recognize and read a Warnier-Orr diagram, a system flowchart, and a set of SADT diagrams
- Recognize and read models of data structures and data accesses

Now that we understand some of the processes involved in analyzing a system, we will learn about some of the techniques a systems analyst uses to represent systems. The techniques include both graphic and narrative means to describe what an analyst discovers when exploring existing systems or needs for systems that users propose. The techniques present a standardized method of documenting systems and sharing this documentation with others who need to know about the system. However, a skilled analyst must know when to use the techniques, as well as knowing how.

This chapter will be broken into several complementary sections. First, physical system flow will be introduced with an overview of systems flowcharting and presentation graphs. Logical system flow will be described with an overview of context diagramming, data flow diagramming, Warnier-Orr diagramming, and Systems and Analysis and Design Technique (SADT) diagramming. Then the discussion will move to representing data structures and models with data access diagrams and data dictionaries. Finally, a detailed technique description of data flow diagramming will be presented.

REPRESENTING SYSTEMS

Before a systems developer can study a system in an organization, it is necessary to be familiar with accepted techniques for representing systems. Then the analyst will understand his or her desired result from the analysis. As recalled from Chapter 2, there are both traditional and structured approaches for representing systems. (Figure 5.1) This chapter will present some of the traditional and structured approaches for representing system flows and structured methods for representing data within the system. Representing procedures and programs will be covered in later chapters since those techniques are used more frequently in the design phase of systems development.

Many of the approaches employed to represent system flows and system data are in the form of diagrams and graphics that are a by-product of user–developer communication. Using the "picture is worth a thousand

Processes	*Traditional*	*Structured*
Representing system flows	System flowchart	Data flow diagram
Representing data	Forms, layouts Grid charts	Data dictionary Warnier-Orr diagrams Bachman charts Normalization
Representing procedures	English narrative Playscript	Decision tree/table Structured English
Representing programs	Program flowchart Input/output layouts	Structure charts Warnier-Orr diagrams

FIGURE 5.1

Some traditional versus structured techniques.

words" concept and appealing to the visual nature of many persons has been a trend in representing systems. Relationships between entities are more vivid when shown in graphic form. The symbols used in the diagrams are intended to communicate. Both users and technicians can read graphic diagrams if they are built simply from a few basic structures—thus, the word *structured.* Narrative then is used to support the graphics. This trend has also been enhanced by automated tools to represent diagrams and accompanying documentation on electronic mediums. This makes the diagrams, which are part of documentation, easier to develop and maintain. These automated tools will be discussed more fully in a later chapter.

REPRESENTING THE PHYSICAL SYSTEM

As discussed in Chapter 4, the physical system might be represented if it currently exists. This is done to obtain an understanding of how the system currently operates and what mediums are used. If documentation of the physical system does exist, it likely will be in the form of a system flowchart. The next section will discuss enough system flowcharting for a minimum reading knowledge of the diagrams.

Other physical data about the system may exist. This might include physical data dictionary descriptions such as what medium data is stored on, field lengths, and internal coding. The analyst should collect and index this data, but not dwell on it in great detail.

Processes also may be part of physical documentation. Human procedures would detail what humans are to do to play their role in system operations. The physical description would include when the procedure is to be performed, using what devices, by which persons, and how often.

Programs would detail what the machine would do. Programs likely would be represented by program flowcharts or listings of the actual program code. Often, the only existing documentation is the computer code used to operate the system.

SYSTEM FLOWCHARTS

System flowcharts are a graphical representation of the data movement in a system showing prescribed physical processes and data sources and destinations. They represent a macro view of a system and should not be confused with program flowcharts. Program flowcharts present specific algorithms and processes, especially those to be executed by computers. The program flowchart details the sequential and logic processes shown on the system flowchart.

There has been a great effort made to standardize the symbols used in system flowcharting. In the 1960s, several standards existed. Some of these reflected international differences. Finally, in 1970, the American National Standards Institute (ANSI) was able to obtain agreement on an accepted standard. This struggle reflects the difficulty of getting many groups of vendors, users, and educators to agree to change from their comfortable way of doing things to a standard abided to by all. This has been and likely will continue to be typical for the systems field.

Figure 5.2 contains the symbols used in system flowcharts. These symbols are linked with relationship lines that usually are represented on paper in a top-to-bottom and left-to-right fashion. Note that the symbols represent physical items—tapes, disks, actual programs, specific procedures, etc. For this reason, some persons refer to system flowcharts as "visual jargon" since so many actual devices and technical items, unfamiliar to many nontechnicians, are represented.

Figure 5.3 shows a simple systems flowchart. The system flowchart does not represent generic transformations and processes or data storages. All items are represented physically. The diagrams show control and timing and typically include a great deal of detail.

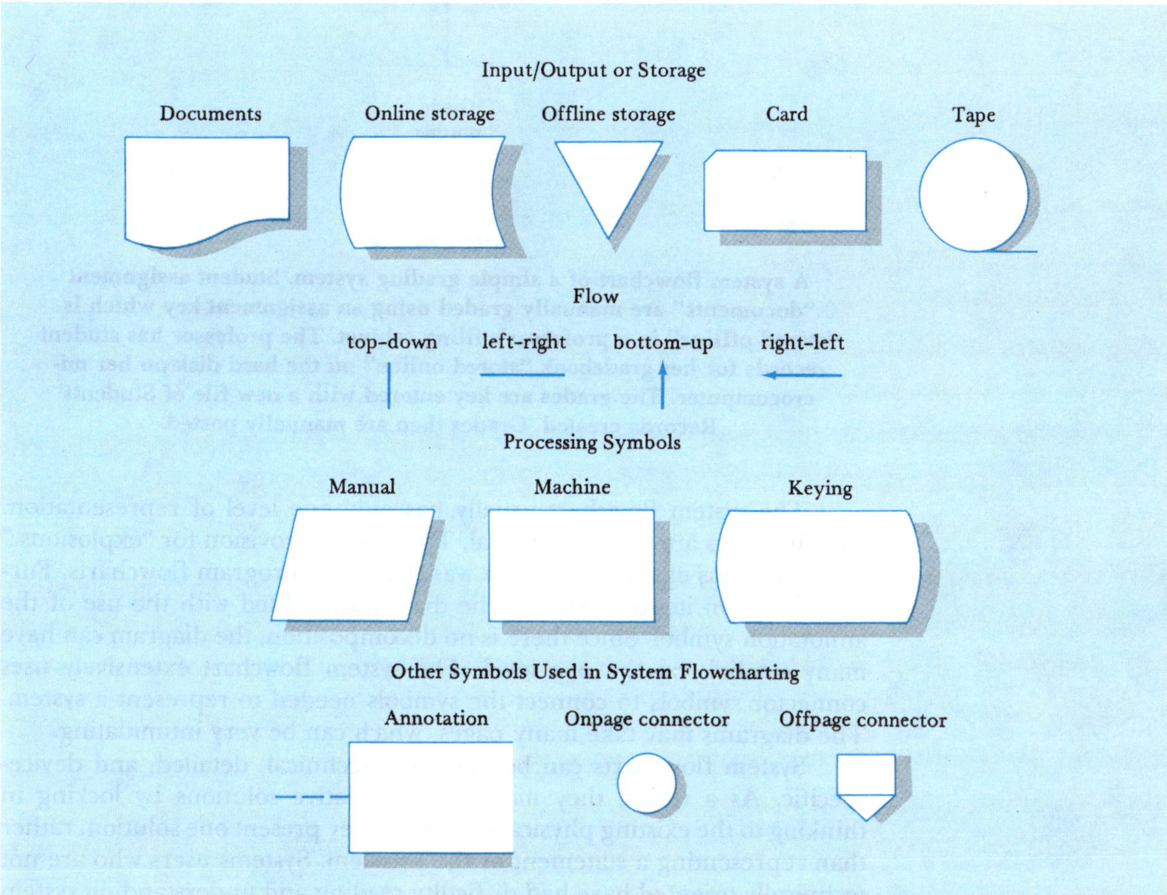

FIGURE 5.2
Symbols used in systems flowcharts.

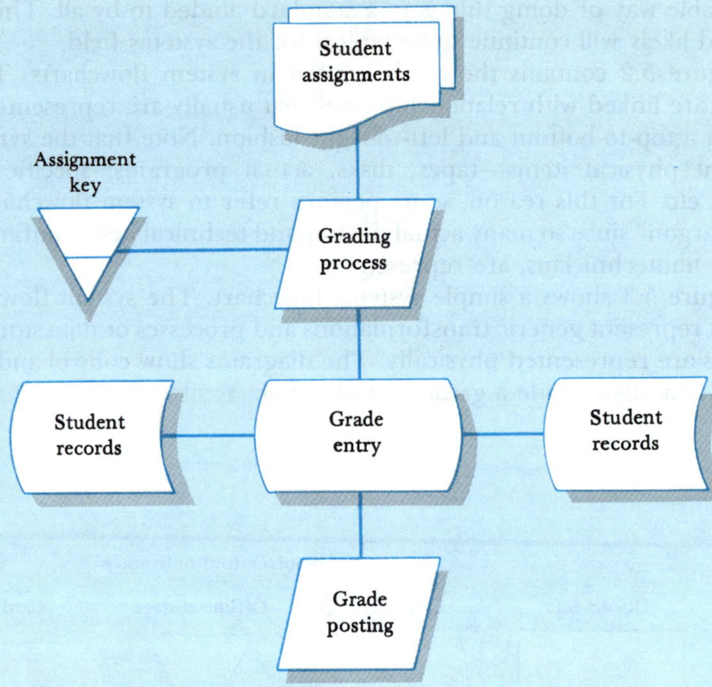

FIGURE 5.3

A system flowchart of a simple grading system. Student assignment "documents" are manually graded using an assignment key which is "stored offline" in a professor's filing cabinet. The professor has student records for her gradebook "stored online" on the hard disk on her microcomputer. The grades are key entered with a new file of Students Records created. Grades then are manually posted.

The system flowchart usually has only one level of representation. The diagrams are not hierarchical. There is no provision for "explosions." Actual process explanation often was done with program flowcharts. Further detail on items shown on the diagram is added with the use of the annotation symbol. Since there is no decomposition, the diagram can have many symbols on the one level. The system flowchart extensively uses connector symbols to connect the symbols needed to represent a system. The diagrams may take many pages, which can be very intimidating.

System flowcharts can become very technical, detailed, and device-specific. As a result, they may restrict creative solutions by locking in thinking to the existing physical solution. They present one solution, rather than representing a statement of the problem. Systems users who are not technically oriented have had difficulty reading and understanding system flowcharts. However, they have been useful for more technically oriented persons to represent and share systems knowledge.

PRESENTATION GRAPHS

Presentation graphs are another means of representing the physical system. The graphs are more human-oriented, using familiar objects. Figure 5.4 shows some commonly used objects in presentation graphs.

The purpose of presentation graphs is to aid communication about physical objects that people are familiar with. The graphs typically are used in a presentation to give visual reinforcement to the spoken word. Figure 5.5 shows an example of a simple presentation graph of a payment processing system.

STRUCTURE CHARTS

Structure charts present computer program modules and the data and controls that connect the modules. Structure charts ideally are developed from data flow diagrams with a prescribed procedure which will be described in a later chapter. A variation of the structure chart is called a ***visual***

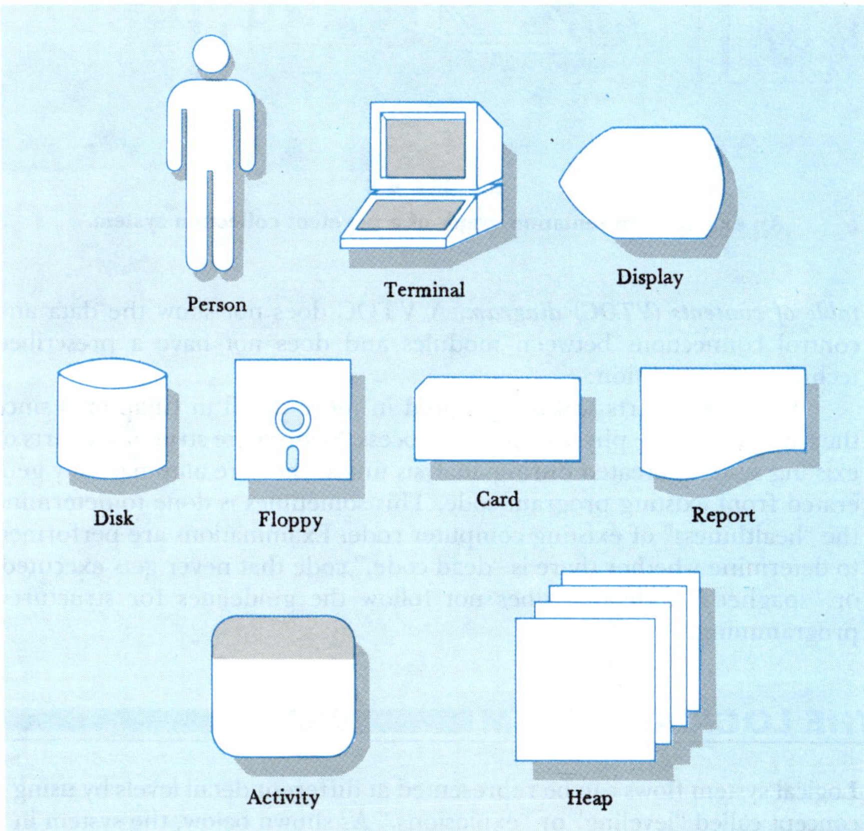

FIGURE 5.4

Objects used in presentation graphs.

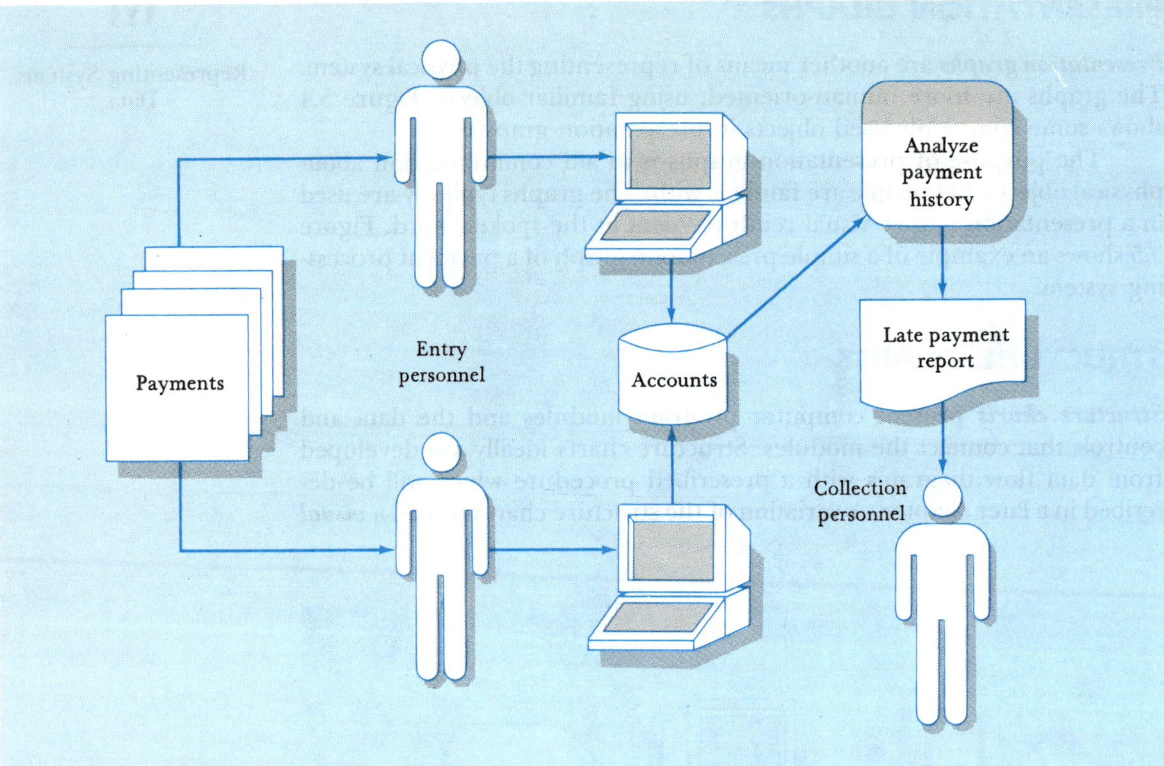

FIGURE 5.5

An example presentation graph of a payment collection system.

table of contents (VTOC) diagram. A VTOC does not show the data and control connections between modules and does not have a prescribed technique for creation.

Structure charts will be explored in more detail in Chapter 9 since they are part of the physical design process. Seldom are structure charts of existing systems created during analysis unless they are automatically generated from existing program code. This sometimes is done to determine the "healthiness" of existing computer code. Examinations are performed to determine whether there is "dead code," code that never gets executed, or "spaghetti" code that does not follow the guidelines for structured programming.

REPRESENTING THE LOGICAL SYSTEM

Logical system flows can be represented at different detail levels by using a concept called "leveling" or "explosions." As shown below, the system in a context diagram can be "exploded" into processes in a more detailed, leveled diagram. Then, this more detailed diagram can be broken into more detail by specifying the contents of the processes. As this detail is

When completed, a flow chart will represent the entire physical system. (Innervisions)

	Context Diagram	
	Contains	
External entities	Flows to System Flows to	External entities
	Leads to	
	Top Level System Data Flow Diagram	
	Contains	
Above external entities	Processes/data flows, stores (within above system)	Above external entities
	Leads to	
	Next Level Process Explosions	
	Contains	
Above/new external entities	Processes internal to above Above/new data stores Above/new data flows	Above/new external entities
	Leads to	
	Next Level Process Explosions	
	Contains	
Above/new external entities	Processes/internal to above Above/new data stores Above/new data flows	Above/new external entities

FIGURE 5.6

The hierarchical breakdown of systems descriptions.

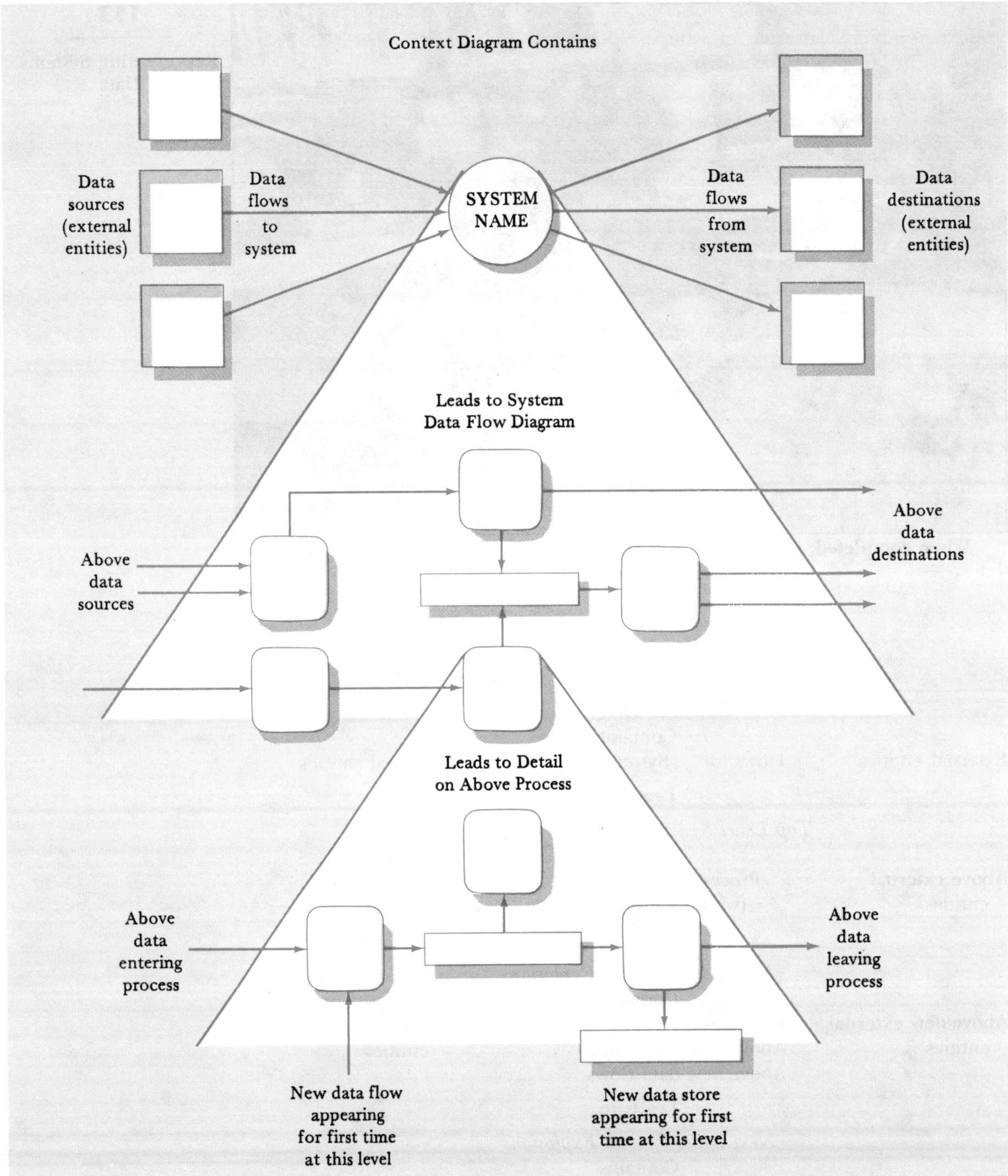

FIGURE 5.7

A graphical view of levels of detail in flow diagrams.

increased, more data stores, sources, and destinations may appear because they are only explanatory at a more detailed level. At a less detailed level, they would only be confusing.

This concept is similiar to an auto parts book where the first diagram may show the whole auto. This would serve as an index to a page where you might find more detail on the fuel system. Within the fuel system, there may be an exploded diagram of a carburetor where each part is shown. Showing every specific bolt or valve on a general overview diagram could result in a very complex and cluttered diagram. Figure 5.6 shows the hierarchical breakdown of system descriptions using the context and data flow diagramming approaches while Figure 5.7 shows a graphical view of the same concepts.

CONTEXT DIAGRAMS

A ***context diagram*** is the highest level graphic representation of a system. It shows data along with the data's sources and destinations to and from the system. These sources and destinations are called *external entities,* since they are external to the represented system boundary. In some cases, the diagram also may show data flow between external entities, especially if a system boundary is unclear to the analyst. Figure 5.8 shows the form and content of a context diagram.

Figure 5.9 shows a context diagram for a system that should be more and more familiar to students of systems analysis and design. The squares are external entities. The letters in the lower right-hand corners of the squares are short identifiers. The diagonal lines in the external entity corners indicate that the external entity is duplicated somewhere on the page.

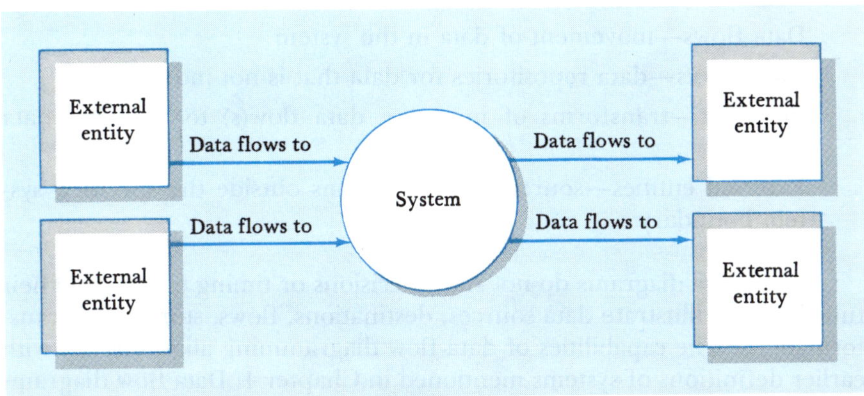

FIGURE 5.8
Contents and form of a context diagram.

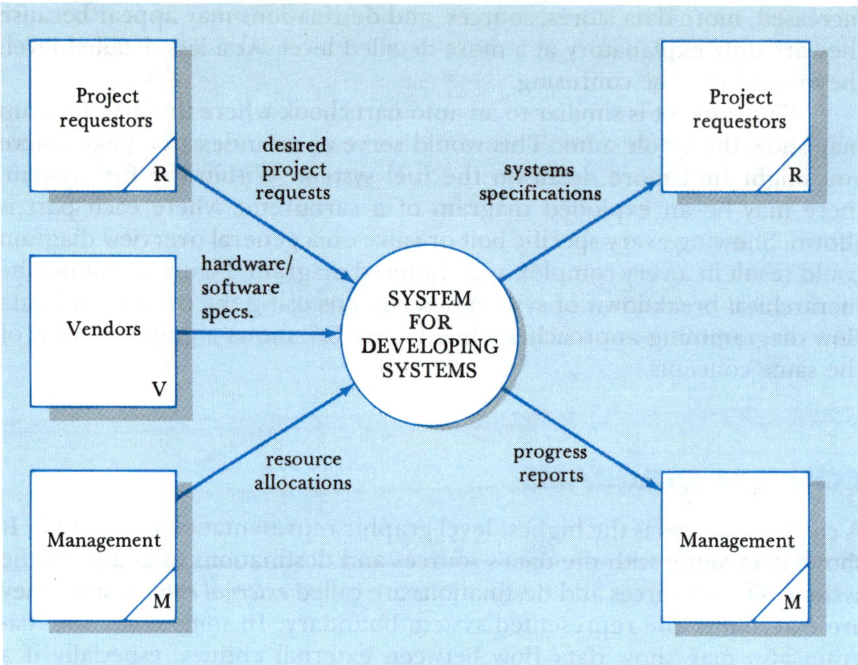

FIGURE 5.9
A context diagram of a system for developing systems.

DATA FLOW DIAGRAMS

Data flow diagrams are a network representation of a system. They are the cornerstone for structured systems analysis and design and the primary development technique used in this book. The diagrams use four symbols to represent any system at any level of detail. The four entities that must be represented are:

Data flows—movement of data in the system

Data stores—data repositories for data that is not moving

Processes—transforms of incoming data flow(s) to outgoing data flow(s)

External entities—sources or destinations outside the specified system boundary

Data flow diagrams do not show decisions or timing of events. Their function is to illustrate data sources, destinations, flows, stores, and transformations. The capabilities of data flow diagramming align directly with earlier definitions of systems mentioned in Chapter 1. Data flow diagrams are an implementation of a method for representing systems concepts, including boundaries, input/outputs, processes and subprocesses.

The data flow diagram is analogous to a road map. It is a network model of all possibilities with different detail shown on different hierarchical levels. The process of representing different detail levels is called *leveling* or *partitioning* by some data flow diagram advocates. Like a road map, there is no start or stop point, no time or timing, or steps to get somewhere. We just know that the data path must exist because at some point it will be needed. A road map shows all existing or planned roads because the roads are needed. If we were to add usage patterns or great detail to the road network on a state road map, it would become unusable to plan routes. When we look at the road map of Illinois, we know we could find more detail of the Chicago vicinity, and then even find more detail of the street network within the Chicago vicinity.

Figure 5.10 is a data flow diagram of the systems development process. Note that the diagram is a detailing of the context diagram shown in Figure 5.9. The data flows to and from the external entities shown on the context diagram all appear on the data flow diagram. Note that only four symbols are used. The diagram differs from the diagrams of the system development system shown in earlier chapters by having all the data flows labeled. The diagram should enhance your knowledge about the systems development activities. The diagram shown in Figure 5.10 is not the only correct diagram of a system for developing systems. As you develop data flow diagrams, you will find that there are many ways of representing the same ideas and concepts. The important thing is that the diagram is useful to the viewer.

Actual procedures, such as those to accomplish a specific task, would be detailed in a procedure specification. Procedures will present not only data manipulation, but also control, such as deciding which path to take in performing a procedure. Data flow diagrams present all possible paths. Control, or how to select a specific path, is not shown on the data flow diagram. We will discuss procedure specifications in a later chapter. These procedures would be analogous to a "Trip-Tik" that the American Automobile Association uses for getting from a specific location to a specific destination. The Trip-Tik would have very detailed maps if detail was needed to avoid getting lost.

Repetition, or how many times a procedure is performed or when it is performed, is not included on the data flow diagram. Remember that the data flow diagram only presents a network of paths. It presents the network at a degree of detail that is understandable and usable for a select set of users. Different views at different levels of the same system are needed for users at different levels of authority and responsibility to understand and review their relevant system portion.

Detail that is not shown on the different levels of the data flow diagram, such as volumes, timing, and frequency, is shown on supplementary diagrams or in the data dictionary. For example, data store contents may be shown in the data dictionary, and usage patterns may be shown on a data access diagram. These concepts and techniques will be explained in more detail later in the chapter.

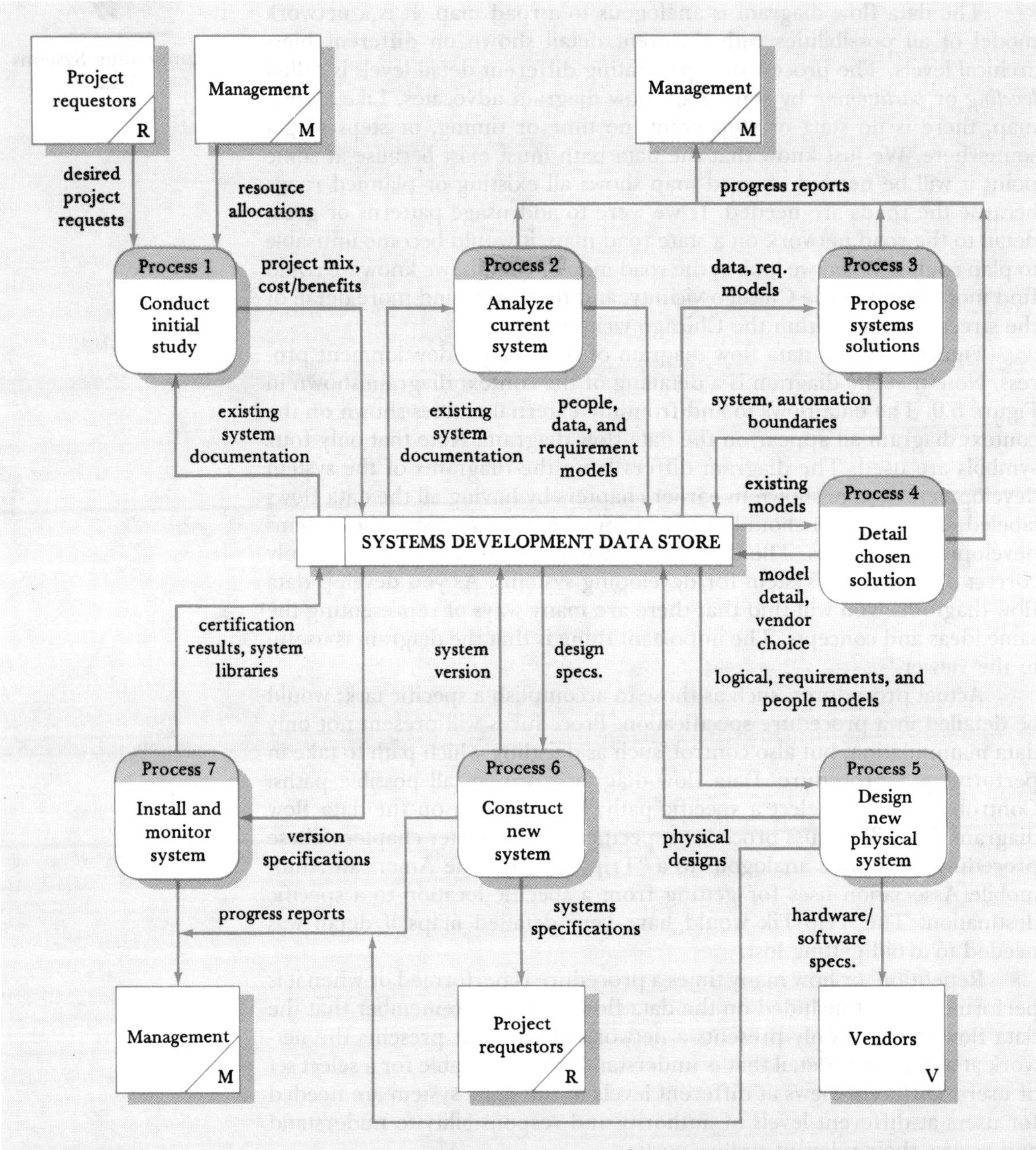

FIGURE 5.10
A data flow diagram of a systems development process.

SADT DIAGRAMS

Systems Analysis and Design Technique (SADT) is a proprietary technique that represents the processing activity of a system in one diagram, and the data aspects of the activity in an similar accompanying diagram. SADT uses hierarchical representation to represent several levels of detail. The SADT activity diagrams (ACTIGRAMS) contain more detail than a data flow diagram. As can be seen in Figure 5.11, constraints, controls, and work mechanisms are shown as well as inputs and activities. No data stores are shown on the diagram. The activity box should contain a phrase starting with a verb. The constraints or controls influence the activity but do not contain data which is transformed by the activity. The work mechanisms are the means for accomplishing the activity. As can be seen, the diagram contains more information than a data flow diagram.

Data diagrams in SADT (DATAGRAMS) as shown in Figure 5.12

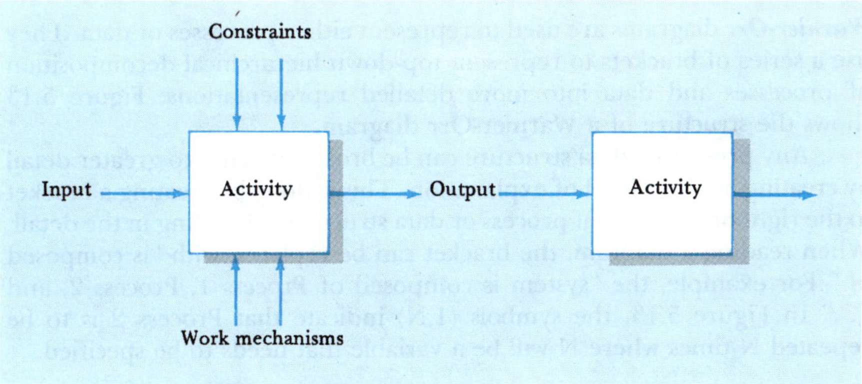

FIGURE 5.11
SADT activity diagram (ACTIGRAM).

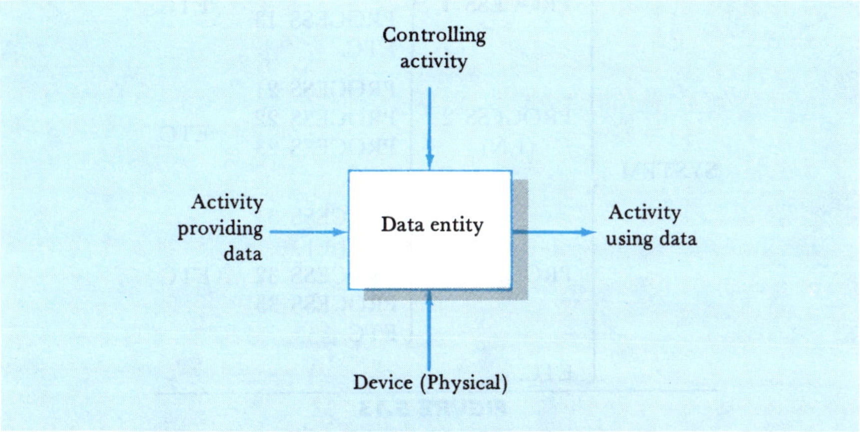

FIGURE 5.12
SADT data diagram (DATAGRAM).

have a similar appearance to the activity diagrams. The arrows, boxes, and leveling all are used but have different roles. The boxes represent entities, containing nouns, and the flows represent activities. Thus, the input activities create parts of the data entity and the output activities use parts of the entity. There is no one-to-one linking between a data and activity diagram for the same system. One type of diagram expands on the other type of diagram, but the diagrams cannot be overlayed. Decomposition of the data diagram is based on the data entity decomposition. Some persons have found this lack of correspondence difficult to comprehend.

Each of the diagrams has a label. "A" labels for activity and "D" labels for data diagrams are done by level. For example, the top level activity diagram would be labeled A0 while diagram A2 is the further explanation of activity 2. Activity 2 then would be more fully explained by diagrams labeled A21, A22, A23, etc.

WARNIER-ORR DIAGRAMS

Warnier-Orr diagrams are used to represent either processes or data. They use a series of brackets to represent top-down hierarchical decomposition of processes and data into more detailed representations. Figure 5.13 shows the structure of a Warnier-Orr diagram.

Any process or data structure can be broken down into greater detail by creating another level of explanation. This is done by creating a bracket to the right of the present process or data structure and filling in the detail. When reading a diagram, the bracket can be replaced with "is composed of." For example, the "system is composed of Process 1, Process 2, and . . ." In Figure 5.13, the symbols (1,N) indicate that Process 2 is to be repeated N times where N will be a variable that needs to be specified.

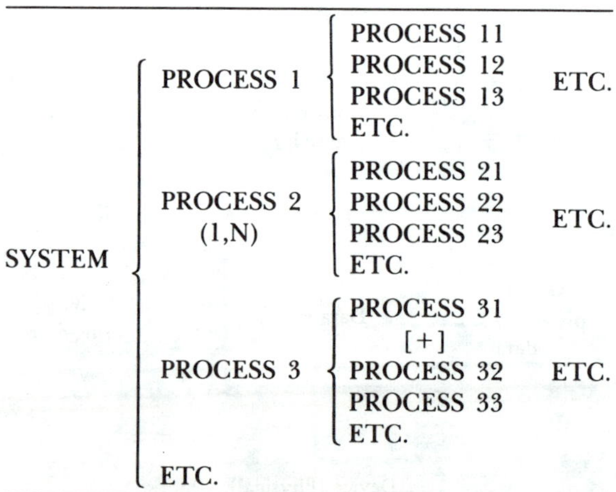

FIGURE 5.13

The structure of a Warnier-Orr diagram.

```
                    ⎧ READ A STUDENT RECORD
                    ⎪ SORT CLASSES IN ALPHA ORDER
                    ⎪ VERIFY REGISTRATION
                    ⎪                       ⎧ SELECT DEVICE
FOR EACH STUDENT    ⎨ PRINT ERROR REPORT    ⎨ FORMAT DATA
                    ⎪   [+]                 ⎩ OUTPUT RESULTS
                    ⎪ PRINT NAME/ID
                    ⎪ PRINT CLASSES WITH GRADE
                    ⎩   (1,N)
```

FIGURE 5.14
An example of a Warnier-Orr diagram.

The symbol + indicates an "or." In the case above, either Process 31 *or* Process 32, 33, etc., are performed. Otherwise, every process is performed in a left-to-right and top-to-bottom fashion. This means every subprocess is performed until the right margin is reached, then processing moves back to the left and down.

As can be seen in Figure 5.14, the diagrams can be quite useful for breaking down the processes or data in a system. However, there is not a direct linking between the process and data diagrams Thus, it is difficult to make links between the processes and the data stores or input/outputs in a system.

The diagrams may be best for modeling physical systems that already exist or for proposing new physical program code. The diagrams are convertible to computer program code with clear rules. They force the developer to think temporally or in a serial fashion with an exhibition of the required processing. However, they do not show the links to data needed to execute the processes. Some persons have viewed the diagrams as program flowcharts that can be decomposed into different levels. This may aid their introduction to those persons who are devout program flowchart users.

COMPARING TECHNIQUES

There are advocates of all of the above techniques of systems representation. There are even differences in the means of using the same technique. For example, on data flow diagrams, DeMarco advocates 7 plus or minus 2 (5 to 9) processes at each level while Gane and Sarson advocate 15 to 40. The DeMarco data flow diagrams use circles for process representation while Gane and Sarson use rounded-corner rectangles ("roundtangles?"). Some of this is taste (or marketing distinction) and some of it is philosophy.

Some of the techniques are easier to learn and use, but may stifle creative thinking. For example, Warnier-Orr diagrams are easy to explain to a nonsystems person, but they may encourage serial or procedurelike thinking. The developer is easily led to writing a procedure rather than representing the system. This may lead to solutions being proposed before the problem or opportunity is understood. SADT and data flow diagrams can represent branching networks more vividly than Warnier-Orr diagrams. SADT can represent a great deal of detail, but the detail can also be confusing.

A person's introduction to the approaches and personal means of problem solving may fit better with one or another of the techniques. Very likely, however, the standard that an organization chooses will dictate which will be used.

The data flow diagram has been widely used for representing systems. Since it is an easy technique to understand by both developers and users, and automated aids exist to support its use, it will be the technique that we will examine in more detail later in the chapter. However, the intent of the data flow diagram is not to furnish *all* the detailed data about a system. The representation of the system shown on the data flow diagram must be supplemented with more detail. The next section will expand on the means for doing this.

DETAILING SYSTEM FLOW MODELS

The representation of the processes, data flows, and data stores in a data flow diagram must be enhanced to provide enough information about a system. There are two principal means for providing more detail. One is to create graphic data models. The other is to provide more detail describing the system with a descriptive data dictionary.

During the analysis stage of the development process, logical representations of data are needed. This means that at this time there is not a need to specify which physical storage devices are needed or desired. Even though these characteristics may be known or may be of concern to a physical designer at a later stage, it is premature to specify solutions (physical storage) when the problem or needs are not clearly understood. The concern first is to specify what must be done, with how much data, and how often, rather than *how* these needs can be satisfied.

The scenario on page 123 exhibits that physical designing can be a time-consuming process with many compromises. These physical design decisions should be delayed until later in the project when needs are more clearly defined.

It would be presumptuous to believe that systems analysts design most large databases. However, the analyst must provide the database designer with data about the data, and desired outputs from stored data, to enable the database designer to accomplish his or her tasks. The user or owner of the data must understand the data representations to participate in reviews to assure correctness and completeness. The analyst also must retain the data in a vivid and accessible form to assure maintainability if designing a small system on a microcomputer where the analyst actually does the database design. This data representation is the focus of the next section.

WHAT IS A DATE?

Physical Versus Logical Representations

A group of users could agree on the content of the data structure named "DATE", but were spending many hours arguing over what a "DATE" was. They all agreed that a "DATE" should include month, day, and year. (There was an argument by one person who thought that the date could be represented by year and the day of the year from 001 to 365. This person was overruled by the rest of the group.) The variations for "DATE" included:

DDMMYY
DDMMYYYY
YYDDMM
MMDDYY
MMDDYYYY

A user manager stepped in when she found out what was happening and specified that the decision on the physical positioning and field lengths would be decided at a later date when everyone had less "fight" in them and needs were better understood.

DATA MODELING

The primary purpose of ***data modeling*** is to provide representations of the system's data objects, their interconnections, and descriptors of the objects and connections. There are several methods for representing the data in a system. Before we examine those methods, we will discuss the language we will use to describe data.

Describing Data

There are many words that can be used to describe data and its components. You may have heard words such as files, records, fields, items, elements, occurrences, instances, or attributes. Many different groups can use different words for the same thing or the same words for different things. For our purposes, we will attempt to take a simplistic approach to describing data.

We must collect data about things in our system. ***Entities*** are the things in a system about which data is collected and stored. Entities could be customers, orders, vendors, machines, or students. The most basic descriptive unit of an entity is a ***data element.*** A data element details some attribute, or is a descriptor, of the entity. Data elements could include age, size, sex, or model. It is not meaningful to break down a data element into smaller constituents.

Data elements that are meaningfully grouped together are called ***data structures.*** For example, it usually is not meaningful to break down a street

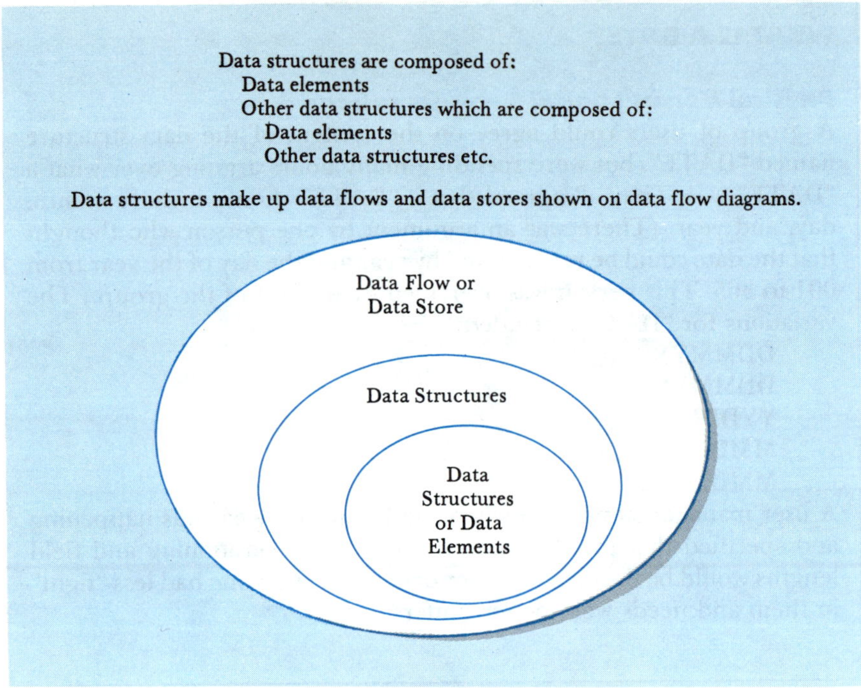

FIGURE 5.15
Representing data in systems.

address into street name and street type (avenue, boulevard, etc.). But it often is meaningful to combine street address, city, state or province, postal code, and country into a data structure called *mailing address.* "Mailing address" may be an attribute of an entity called *customer.* Figure 5.15 exhibits a means of representing data.

Figure 5.16 shows an example of the description of an *entity* named Student. There are many *occurrences* of students, each uniquely identified by a data element or *attribute* of Student called Student ID. Student ID is called a *key identifier* since it uniquely identifies a student. Each student, referred to as an *instance,* takes many classes so the data structure classes is called a *repeating group.* When we try to find out more about classes, we may find that it also is a thing we collect data about. It could be considered

Entity Name = Student

	Attributes (Data Structures and Data Elements)					
	Student ID	*Name*	*Graduating Year*	*Class 1*	*Class 2*	*Class 3*
Occurrences	S1	Joe	86	mis2	fin3	acc2
an instance-	S2	Ted	87	mis1	fin4	acc4
	S3	Joy	86	mis2	acc4	fin3

FIGURE 5.16
Attributes and occurrences of an entity named student.

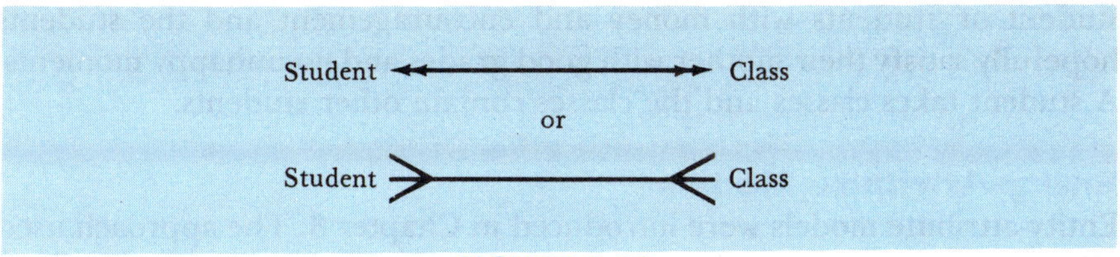

FIGURE 5.17

A many-with-many relationship between students and classes.

another entity. There could be a table of data about classes, including the data elements of class name, section, term, instructor, and grade. We may also find that the entities named "students" and "classes" could be related. There is a graphic notation for representing this relationship (Figure 5.17). The notation is a many-with-many relationship. This means each student is associated with many classes, and that each class is associated with many students.

If one of the school organizations collected data about each student's mother, we would have another entity. When we were talking about the relationship between the entity of "mother" and the entity of "students," we would think of this as a one-with-many relationship. Each student could have one mother, but each mother could have many children who were students (Figure 5.18).

Likewise, when speaking about "husbands" and "wives," we would assume in our culture that this is a one-with-one relationship. Putting together a series of these relationships results in a diagram called a *logical data model diagram*. Others may call the diagram a *conceptual schema*.

A logical data model diagram for some of the above relationships is shown in Figure 5.19. This figure shows that a mother may support a

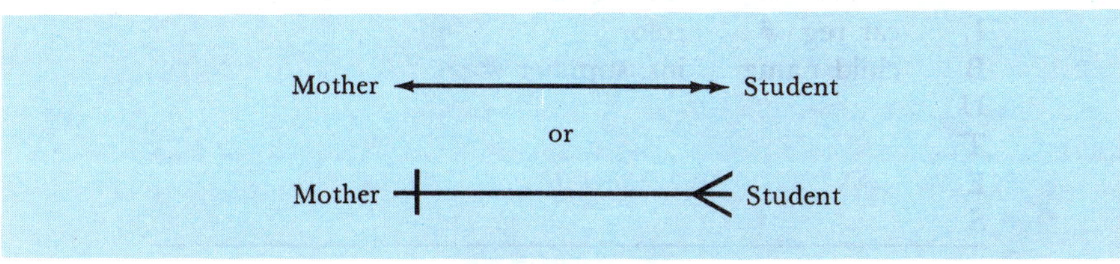

FIGURE 5.18

A one-with-many relationship between mother and students.

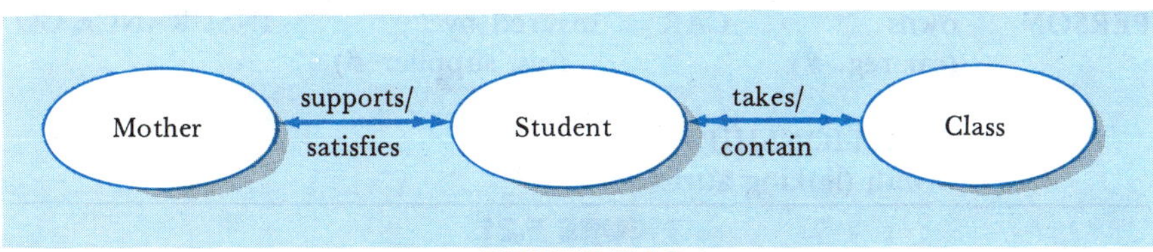

FIGURE 5.19

A logical data model diagram.

student or students with money and encouragement and the students hopefully satisfy their mother with good grades and no unhappy moments. A student takes classes and the classes contain other students.

Entity-Attribute Models

Entity-attribute models were introduced in Chapter 3. The approach used is based on work by Chen (see References). The purpose of entity-attribute modeling is to provide a graphic representation of the primary data entities and their linkages. ***Entities*** represent a class of objects which are meaningfully described by the same attributes. ***Relationships*** are the links between the entities. ***Attributes*** are data elements used to describe entities or relationships. Figure 5.20 shows some entities and their attributes.

One way of viewing relationships between entities is shown in Figure 5.21. This would likely be the "view" of the data from a "person." More than one person could own a single car, one person could own several cars, an insurance company would insure many cars, but each car would likely be insured by only one company. The logical data model diagram representing these entities and relationships would look like Figure 5.22.

The "view" of the user is critical in describing the data. The needs of the user, the desired outputs, will aid in specifying the physical data structure needed to permit the requested accesses. These accesses are represented on data access diagrams.

		ENTITIES	
	Person	*Car*	*Insurance Company*
A	name	make	name
T	address	year	address
T	birthdate	model	ins. supplier #
R	soc. sec. #	car reg. #	cust. car reg. #
I	car reg. #	color	
B	child name	ins. supplier #	
U			
T			
E			
S			

FIGURE 5.20

Entities attributes of persons, cars, and insurance companies.

PERSON owns (car reg. #) CAR insured by (ins. supplier #) INSURANCE CO

RELATIONSHIP
with (linking attribute)

FIGURE 5.21

Relationships between persons, cars, and insurance companies.

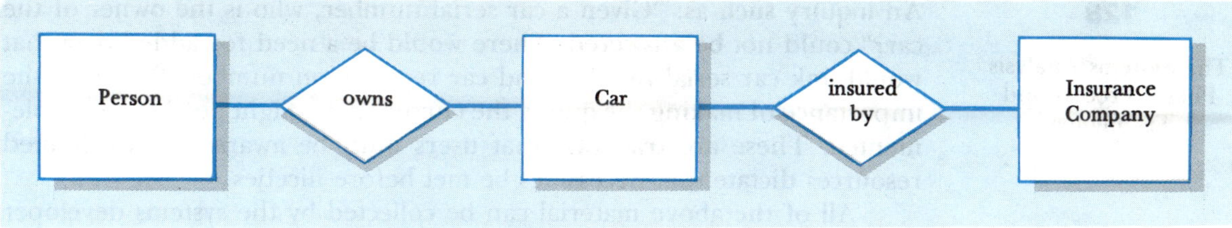

FIGURE 5.22
An entity-relationship model.

Data Access Diagrams

Data access diagrams are also called *data structure diagrams, data immediate access diagrams,* or *user views* (*subschemas* to some persons). The purpose of the diagrams is to present a graphic representation of a specific user's data needs in terms of data structures. The user needs are specified in terms of queries, information to perform business tactics, and the information needed to make decisions. These needs can differ because of organizational level, functional area, position, or personal perspective. The data access diagram is an implementation of the above entity-attribute concepts.

Figure 5.23 shows a data access diagram. The diagram contains the three entities that we mentioned earlier in the chapter. With the three labeled arrows shown, the diagram exhibits the linkages needed to satisfy three user requests:

1. Given a person's car registration number, what is the name of the person's insurance supplier?
2. Given a car registration number, who owns the car?
3. Given a car registration number, who insures the car?

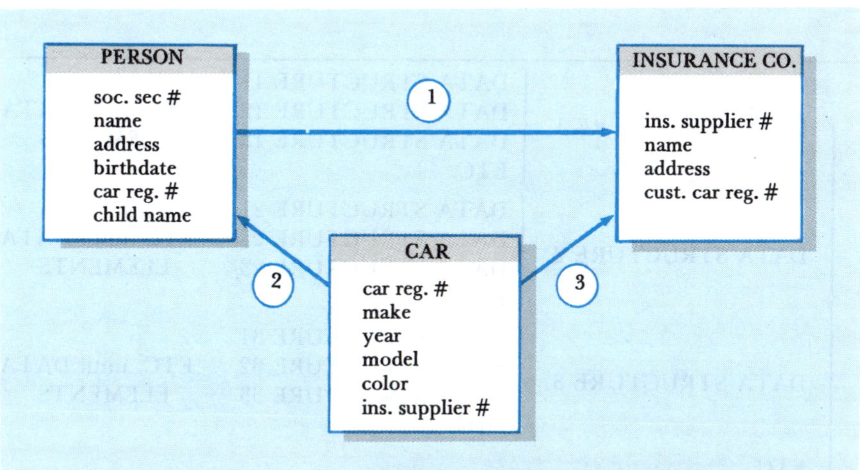

FIGURE 5.23
An example of data access diagram.

An inquiry such as: "Given a car serial number, who is the owner of the car?" could not be answered. There would be a need for added data that would link car serial number and car registration number. Based on the importance of making the query, the current data might need to be supplemented. These are tradeoffs that users must be aware of since limited resources dictate that necessities be met before niceties.

All of the above material can be collected by the systems developer when analyzing systems. The material will document existing systems, specify needs to be satisfied by future systems, and serve as a guide for persons doing logical and physical data base design.

Warnier-Orr Diagrams

Warnier-Orr diagrams also are used to represent data. They use a series of brackets to represent top-down decomposition of data in more detailed representations (Figure 5.24). Any data structure can be broken down into greater detail by creating another level of explanation. This is done by creating a bracket to the right of the present data structure and filling in the detail. Figure 5.25 shows data broken down using the Warnier-Orr approach.

As can be seen, the diagrams can be quite useful for breaking down the data in a system. However, they do not have a good linking between the processes and the data stores or input/outputs in a system.

DATA DICTIONARIES

Besides all the diagrams describing the system data, a place is needed to represent narrative about data in a system. The function of a data dictionary is to supplement the logical model of the system shown in the data flow diagram and data description diagrams. Detail about the system is shown in

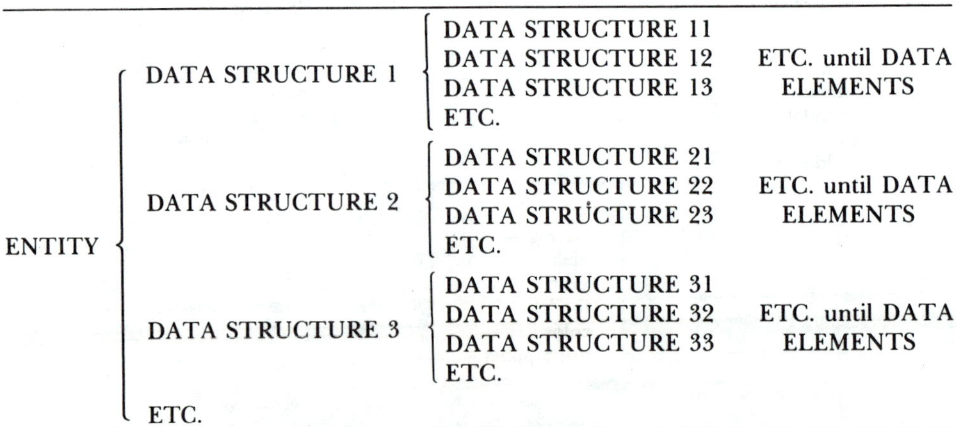

FIGURE 5.24
A Warnier-Orr approach to representing data.

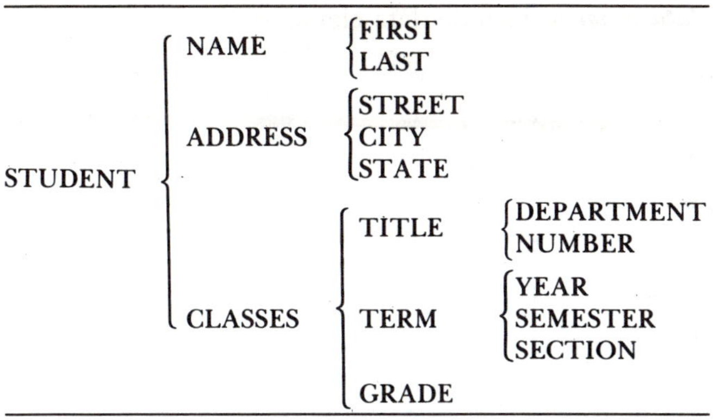

FIGURE 5.25

An example of a Warnier-Orr representation of data.

the data dictionary. This keeps the diagrams simple and easy to read. The diagrams serve as the outline of the system while the data dictionary fleshes out the outline.

Description of Logical Systems Data

The data dictionary is used to provide more information about the models describing the system. For example, data about data flows, data stores, processes, and external entities shown on the data flow diagram would be detailed in the data dictionary. Following is some of the data that would be contained in the data dictionary.

For each ***data flow***, include data flow:

- name
- alternative name/alias
- number
- description
- reason for existence
- sources
- destinations
- volumes
- periodicity (time period covered)
- composition data structures/elements

For each ***data structure,*** include data structure:

- name
- alternative name/alias
- description
- composition data structures/elements

For each ***data element,*** include data element:

name
alternative name/alias
description
purpose
type (A, N, AN, B)
encoding
length
domain of values

For each ***data store,*** include data store:

name
alternative name/alias
number
description
reason for existence
input data structures/elements
output data structures/elements
volume
access frequency
access security
owner

For each ***external entity,*** include external entity:

name
alternative name/alias
description
type—system, person, database/source
total occurrences

Organizational Data

All of the data on the organization chart should be more fully described in the data dictionary. The users of the system, their attributes, their link to business tactics, the data they own or maintain, etc., should be included in the data dictionary.

Requirements Data

As described in Chapter 3 and to be more fully described in Chapter 6, the requirements of each of the users described in the user model must be described. The data will consist of different levels of detail of business objectives, business tactics, information systems objectives, and information system tactics.

Simplifying Data Structures

Data structures included in data stores can become very complex and unwieldy. There are several means of simplifying data structures. First, the analyst should match the needed outputs from a data store with the data store contents. If a data structure or element is not needed, it should not be stored. This "extra" data causes complexity, and if everything is stored "just in case" it is needed, the elegance of the system is lost and results in high operating overhead. Second, data structures can be simplified through normalization. This technique will be explained in a later chapter. Suffice it to say that all attributes should fully describe only the entity they are associated with.

DETAILING THE TECHNIQUE OF DATA FLOW DIAGRAMMING

This section describes in detail the data flow diagramming technique. It is intended to serve as a handbook to guide the reader in developing data flow diagramming skills.

Definition

Data flow diagramming is a means of representing a system at any level of detail with a graphic network of symbols showing data flows, data stores, data processes, and data sources and destinations.

Purpose and Objective

The purpose of data flow diagrams is to provide a semantic bridge between users and systems developers. The diagrams are:

Graphical, eliminating thousands of words

Logical representations, modeling what a system does, rather than physical models showing how it does it

Hierarchical, showing systems at any level of detail

Jargonless, allowing user understanding and reviewing

The goal of data flow diagramming is to have a commonly understood model of a system. The diagrams are the basis of structured systems analysis. Data flow diagrams are supported by other techniques of structured systems analysis such as data structure diagrams, data dictionaries, and procedure-representing techniques such as decision tables, decision trees, and structured English. Data flow diagrams are not an end in themselves, but lead to structure charts, the basis of structured systems design.

Data flow diagrams have the objective of avoiding the cost of:

User or developer misunderstanding of a system, resulting in a need to redo systems or in nonuse of the system.

Having to start documentation from scratch when the physical system changes since the logical system, what gets done, often remains the same when technology changes.

Systems inefficiencies because a system gets "computerized" before it gets "systematized."

Being unable to evaluate system project boundaries or degree of automation, resulting in a project of inappropriate scope.

Description

Data flow diagrams are composed of the four basic symbols shown in Figure 5.26.

1. The *external entity* symbol represents sources of data to the system or destinations of data from the system.
2. The data flow symbol represents movement of data.
3. The data store symbol represents data that is not moving (delayed data at rest).
4. The *process* symbol represents an activity that transforms or manipulates data (combines, reorders, or converts).

Any system can be represented at any level of detail by these four symbols.

External entities:

1. Are named with appropriate name and identified with a capital letter in the southeast corner (Figure 5.27).
2. Can be duplicated one or more times on the diagram to avoid line crossing. As shown in Figure 5.28, this is done with a diagonal stripe across southeast corner with the same identifying letter within the created triangle.
3. Determine the system boundary. They are external to the system being studied, and are often beyond the area of influence of the developer.

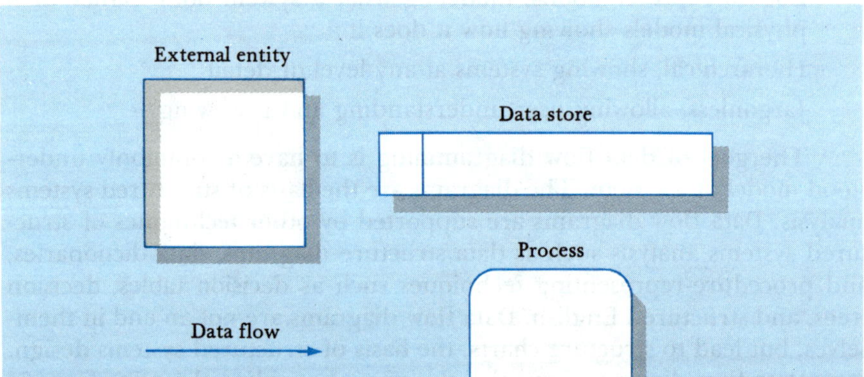

FIGURE 5.26
Symbols used in data flow diagrams.

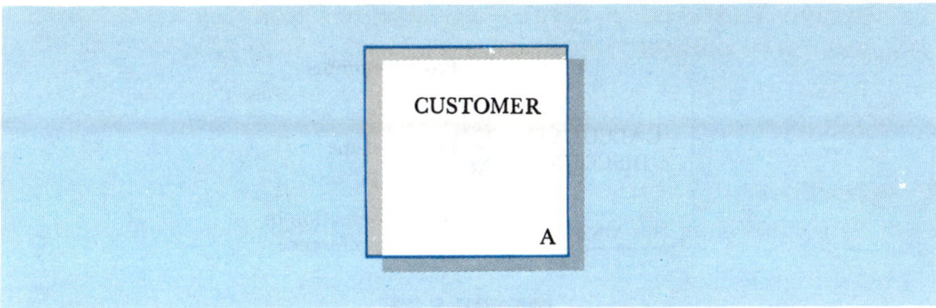

FIGURE 5.27

External entity customer with identifier "A."

4. Can represent another system or subsystem.
5. Go on margins or edges of data flow diagram.

Processes:

1. Show data transformation or change. Data coming into a process must be "worked on" or transformed in some way. Thus, all processes must have inputs and outputs. In some (rare) cases, data inputs or outputs will only be shown at more detailed levels of the diagrams. Each process is always "running" and ready to accept data.
2. Are represented by a rounded corner rectangle (Figure 5.29).
3. Are named with one carefully chosen verb and an object of the verb. There is no subject. Name is not to include the word "process." Each process should represent one function or action. If there is an "and" in the name, you likely have more than one function (and process).
4. Have physical location shown only for existing physical systems or if a physical design is being represented.
5. Are numbered within the diagram as convenient. Levels of detail are shown by decimal notation. For example, a top-level process

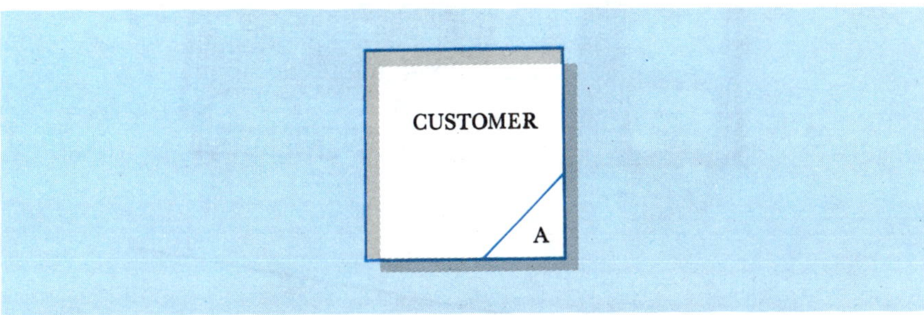

FIGURE 5.28

Diagonal corner slash indicating external entity duplication.

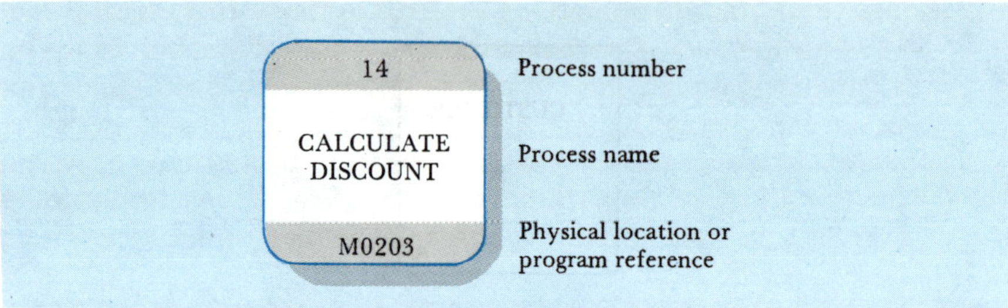

FIGURE 5.29

Process symbol.

would be Process 14; the next level of detail would be Processes 14.1 to 14.4, and the next level Processes 14.3.1 to 14.3.6.

6. Should generally move from top to bottom and left to right.

Data flows:

1. Are represented with a line with an arrowhead on one end. A fork in a data flow means that the same data goes to two separate destinations. The same data coming from several locations can also be joined.
2. Should only represent data, not control.
3. Are *always* named. Name is not to include the word "data."
4. Are referenced by a combination of the identifiers of the constructs that the data flow connects (14-A references a data flow from Process 14 to external entity A).
5. Cannot directly connect two external entities, two data stores, or an external entity to a data store. Data cannot "magically" move. A process is needed to move the data. And, no external entity should have direct access to a data store. A process is needed to monitor

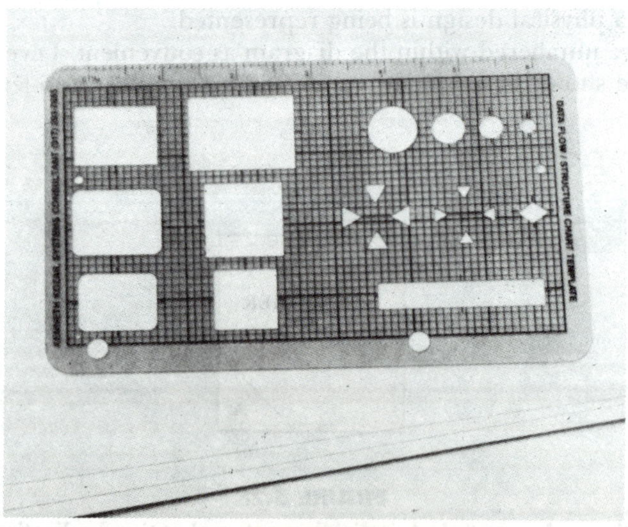

A template like this is used to draw flow diagrams by hand. (Innervisions)

and verify that the something external to the system is authorized to access the data. External entities, especially if systems shown on a context diagram, may transmit data between them. Since this would be outside the system of concern, this is only done if the analyst has some reason to believe the connection should be within the boundary of the system. Then there is a need to include a process between the external entities. The process would be within the system boundary.

6. Crossing should have one flow line with a semicircle at crossing point (Figure 5.30).
7. Leaving the process boundary when doing a process explosion and not appearing on the higher-level diagram, is marked with an X at the exit or entry point from the higher-level process.
8. Can connect to another page by using circles as off-page connectors (Figure 5.31). Within the circles, indicate the identifier of the construct the data flow is going to or coming from. This usually is done when connecting detail levels of data flow diagrams.

Data stores:

1. Are generic for physical files (index cards, desk drawers, magnetic disk, magnetic tape, shirt pocket, human memory, etc.)

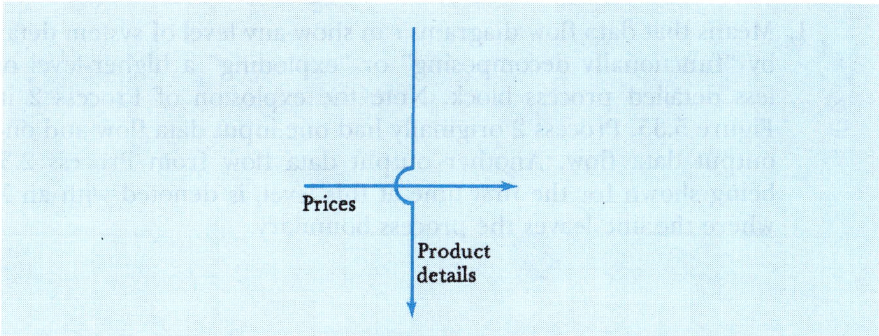

FIGURE 5.30

Crossing data flows.

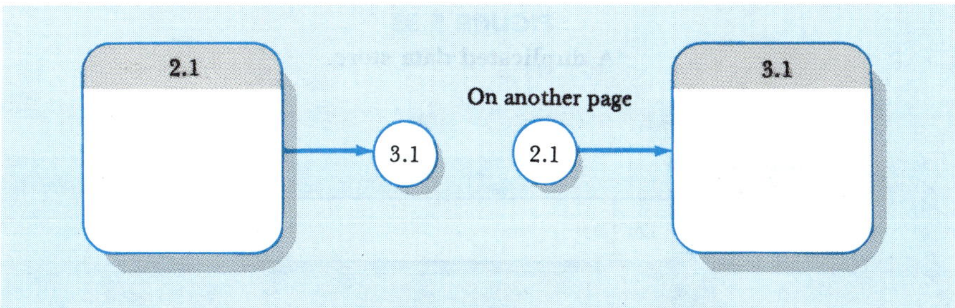

FIGURE 5.31

Use of connector symbols.

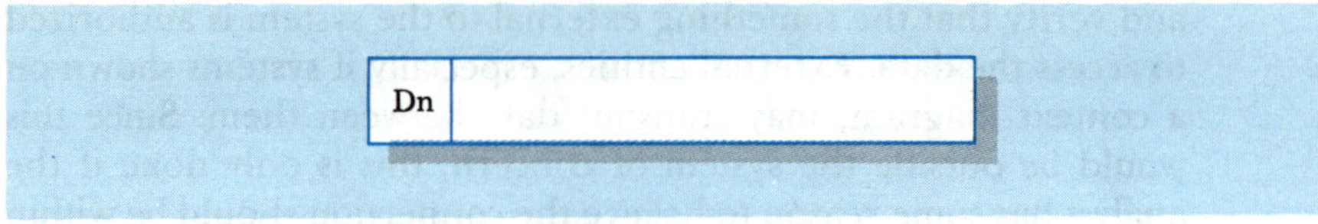

FIGURE 5.32
The data store symbol.

2. Are named with an appropriate name, not to include the word "file," and numbered with a number preceded with a capital letter D (Figure 5.32).
3. Can be duplicated one or more times to avoid line crossing. This is done by adding a stripe on the left boundary (Figure 5.33).
4. Can show two or more systems that share a data store. This is done by adding a solid stripe on the left boundary (Figure 5.34). This can occur in the case of one system updating the data store, while the other system only accesses the data. For example, the data store could be a freight rate book that one system builds and maintains, but is used by the represented system.
5. Are detailed in the data dictionary or with data description diagrams.

Leveling:

1. Means that data flow diagrams can show any level of system detail by "functionally decomposing" or "exploding" a higher-level or less detailed process block. Note the explosion of Process 2 in Figure 5.35. Process 2 originally had one input data flow and one output data flow. Another output data flow from Process 2.3, being shown for the first time at this level, is denoted with an X where the line leaves the process boundary.

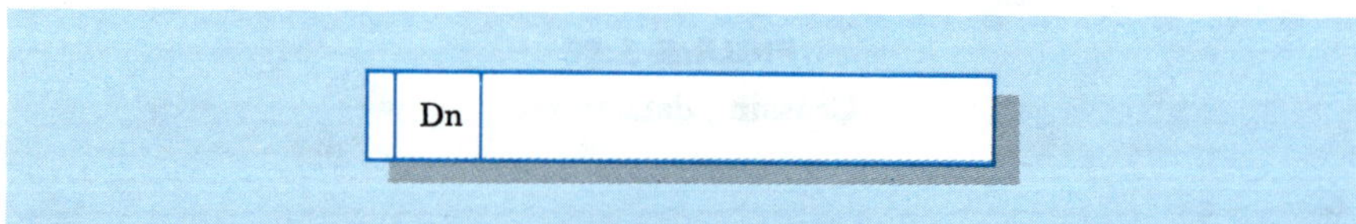

FIGURE 5.33
A duplicated data store.

FIGURE 5.34
A data store shared by more than one system.

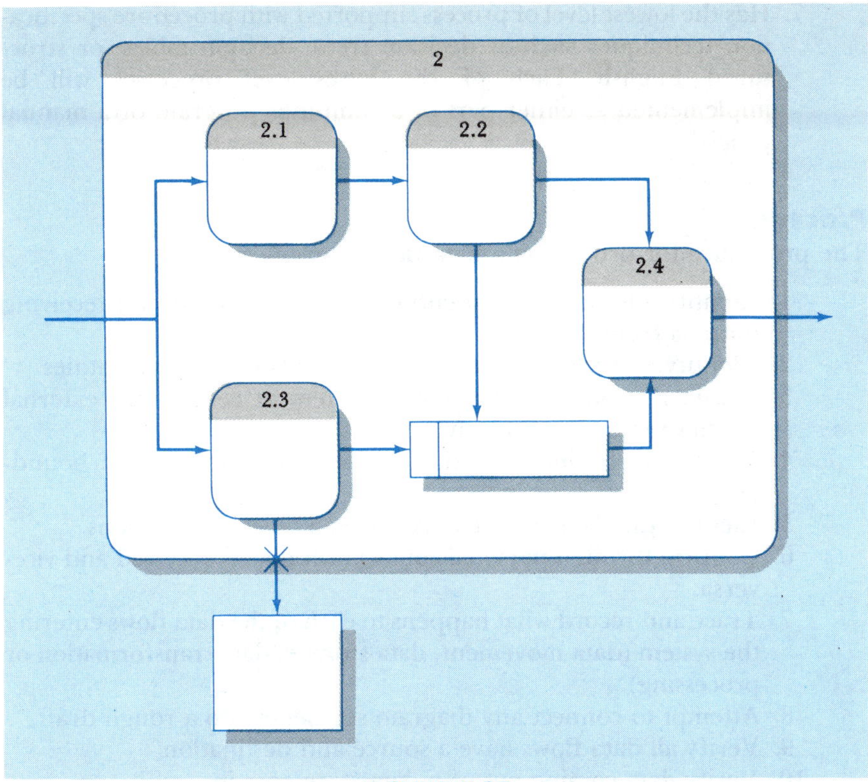

FIGURE 5.35

An exploded process with a data flow to an external entity appearing for the first time at this level.

2. Usually go to three or four levels depending on purpose. The top level is a business view, often called the *system context,* that shows the system at the center with external entities providing data to and receiving data from the system. The next level, the first level where processes are numbered, will contain a breakdown into major subsystems (4 to 20 processes). The third level breaks these processes into subprocesses. One or more breakdowns could be needed.
3. Requires processes to be numbered by level with decimals (2, 2.1 to 2.6, 2.1.1 to 2.1.4, as shown above).
4. Requires judgment on the part of the developer as to what to put on each level. This is an art that depends on the purpose of the diagram and the nature of the viewers. Each level must communicate understanding of the system to the user who will view the diagram.
5. Requires the top levels to show what happens to a good transaction. Error and exception handling go on the lower levels.
6. Requires validation of inputs to and outputs from a process to ensure consistency.

7. Has the lowest level of process supported with procedure specification techniques such as decision trees, decision tables, or structured English. Each of the lowest-level processes will be implemented as either part of a computer program or a manual procedure.

Procedure

The procedure for producing a data flow diagram is:

1. Identify and list external entities providing inputs and receiving outputs from system.
2. Identify and list inputs from and outputs to external entities.
3. Create a context diagram with system at center and external entities sending and receiving data flows.
4. Identify the business functions included within the system boundary.
5. Identify the data connections between business functions.
6. Confirm through personal contact sent data is received and vice-versa.
7. Trace and record what happens to each of the data flows entering the system (data movement, data storage, data transformation or processing).
8. Attempt to connect any diagram segments into a rough draft.
9. Verify all data flows have a source and destination.
10. Verify data coming out of a data store goes in.
11. Redraw to simplify—ponder and question result.
12. Review with "informed."
13. Explode and repeat above steps as needed.

Guidelines/Gumption Traps: (Places where DFDing can go astray)

1. System boundary establishment is an important judgment call. External entities aid in determining where the boundary is established. An interfacing system can be shown as an external entity. It may be necessary to dictate the input of the external entity to assure system control. For example, customers may be required to submit orders or refund requests containing specific information which may require that the system aid in completion of a form. Use of output such as reports by management may require some agreement on tactics to be performed, which may mean the entity becomes part of the system, not external to it. When in doubt, include the external entity as processes within the system and then evaluate with those concerned.
2. Label your processes carefully and vividly. A process that is labeled "Produce Report" and has the output of "Report" tells a reviewer very little. If you have trouble labeling anything on the diagram, it

often is because you do not have adequate understanding. Choose names carefully.

3. Think logically, not physically. Ignore media, color, font, layout, packaging, time, and sequencing. Think "what," not "how." Something logical can be implemented physically in more than one way. Including "when," "where," and "how" means you are getting physical.
4. Think data, not control, flow. Data flows are pathways for data. Think about what data is needed to perform a process or update a data store. A data flow diagram is not a flowchart and should not have loops or transfer of control. Think about the data flows, data processes, and data storage that are needed to move a data structure through a system.
5. Concentrate first on what happens to a "good" transaction. Systems people have a tendency to lose sight of the forest because they are so busy concentrating on the branches of the trees.
6. Reviewers will not be convinced by confusion. A quality data flow diagram will be so simple and straightforward that people will wonder what took you so long.
7. Data store to data store, external entity to external entity, or external entity to data store connections do not make sense. Data flows with an arrowhead on each end cause confusion in labeling. Do not use them.
8. Do not try to put everything you know on the data flow diagram. The diagram should serve as as index and outline, which will be fleshed out in the data dictionary, data structure diagrams, and procedure specification techniques.

USING DATA FLOW DIAGRAMS—AN EXAMPLE PROBLEM

A university professor was asked by a systems analyst friend how she managed data about students enrolled in her classes. She started to talk about the processes she went through. She quickly realized she was confusing her friend. The professor agreed to help her friend who thought he might be interested in developing a system to sell to professors. They agreed to use a procedure found in a systems analysis and design textbook to try and represent the system using a data flow diagram.

Procedure: The procedure for producing a data flow diagram is to:

1. *Identify and list external entities providing inputs and receiving outputs from system.* The professor said that she got data from publishers, students, the registrar, and school administrators. She provided data to the registrar, other colleagues, and to potential employers of the students.

2. *Identify and list inputs from and outputs to external entities.* The publishers provided books and reference materials so she could keep up in the field. The students handed in assignments, answers to exam questions, and asked her questions. The registrar sent her the student class lists and received student grades at the end of a term. The school administrators set guidelines for grade assigments and standards for what had to be included in a class. Potential employers of students asked for reference letters. She shared excellent student work with her colleagues as she was proud of her students.

3. *Create a context diagram with system at center and external entities sending and receiving data flows.* The professor's analyst friend took with this information and developed the diagram shown in Figure 5.36. The professor and the analyst reviewed the diagram and agreed that it was a reasonable first draft. They wanted to get on with the procedure and come back and make any changes later. The analyst had learned that too much time could be spent polishing something that might have to be changed later when more learning about the system took place.

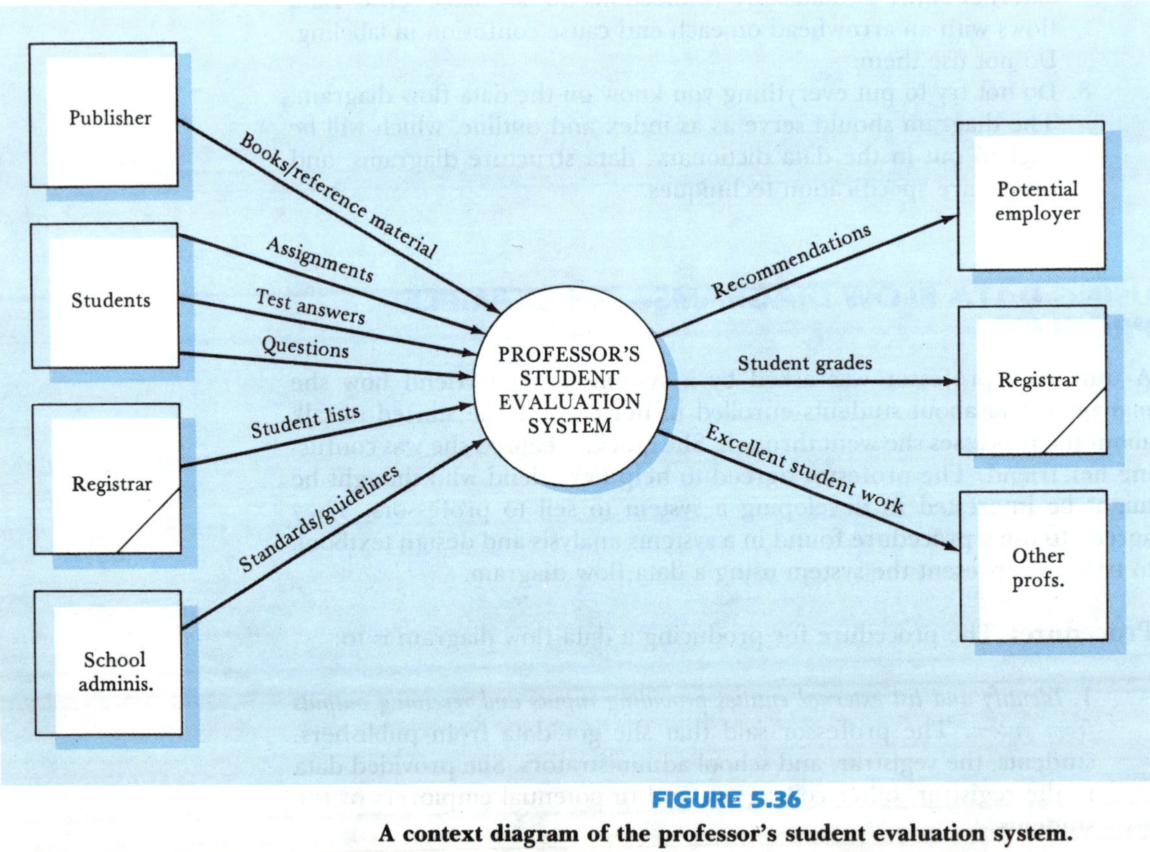

FIGURE 5.36

A context diagram of the professor's student evaluation system.

4. *Identify the business functions included within the system boundary.* The analyst told the professor that business functions were like processes or procedures she went through to get the needed outputs from the inputs. She said she had to develop a syllabus which was the course plan and policies, develop assignments to assure student understanding, teach classes to give students knowledge, grade assignments, counsel students, develop exams, grade exams, create a gradebook, and record all grades to summarize and assign final grades. The analyst started to draw some rounded-corner rectangles with one of these activities in each rectangle (Figure 5.37).
5. *Identify the data connections between business functions.* The analyst found the following data connections:
The syllabus was needed to weight class work to assign grades.
Developed assignments were needed to grade assignments.
Developed exams were needed to grade exams.
All grading was required to assign final grades.

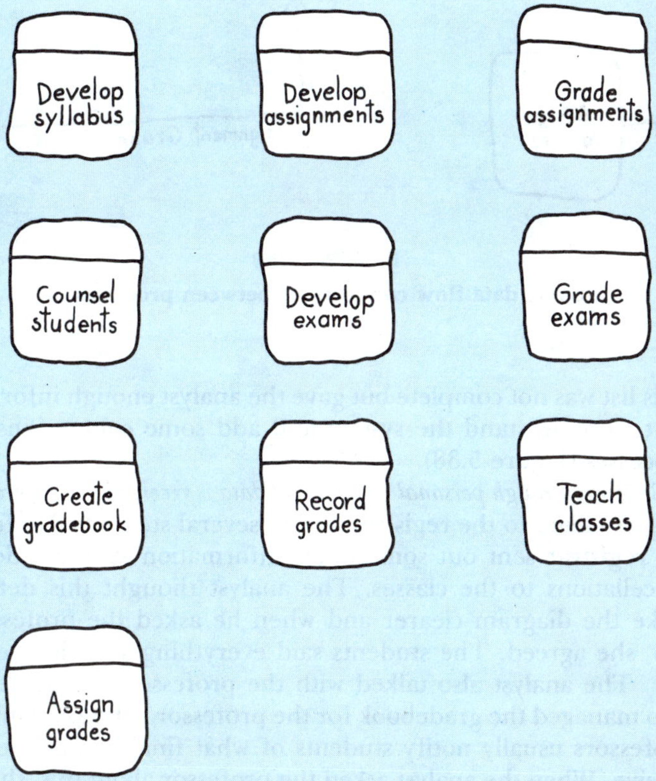

FIGURE 5.37
The business functions or processes in the system.

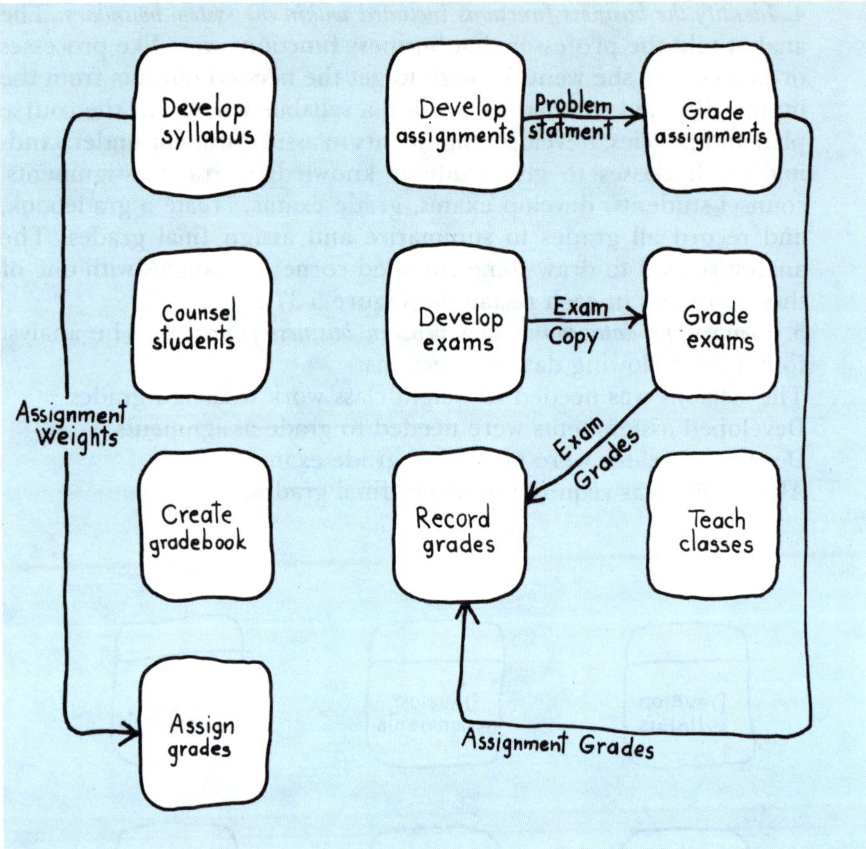

FIGURE 5.38
Some data flow connections between processes.

This list was not complete but gave the analyst enough information to start to understand the system and add some connections between processes (Figure 5.38).

6. *Confirm through personal contact sent data is received and vice-versa.* The analyst talked to the registrar and to several students. He found that the registrar sent out some other information such as additions or cancellations to the classes. The analyst thought this detail might make the diagram clearer and when he asked the professor about this, she agreed. The students said everything sounded reasonable.

The analyst also talked with the professor's graduate assistant who managed the gradebook for the professor. The assistant said that professors usually notify students of what final grades the students receive. When the analyst asked the professor about this, she said she had a policy of not posting final grades since the registrar mailed them out. She did say that the context diagram should indicate that she did distribute assignment and exam grades to students and gave them counseling if necessary. As shown in Figure 5.39, the analyst added the grades data flow to the context diagram.

7. *Trace and record what happens to each of the data flows entering the system (data movement, data storage, data transformation or processing).* The analyst examined the context diagram and tried to determine which processes received data from or provided data to the exhibited external entities. Connections included:

Information found in books was used to develop the syllabus and assignments and to teach class.

Standards and guidelines were used to develop the syllabus.

Graded assignments that were excellent were shared with other professors.

Information from student work was used to compute grades.

Information from registrar was used to determine class list and as basis for recording grades.

Information from school administration was used to establish course requirements and as a guideline to measure level of student achievement

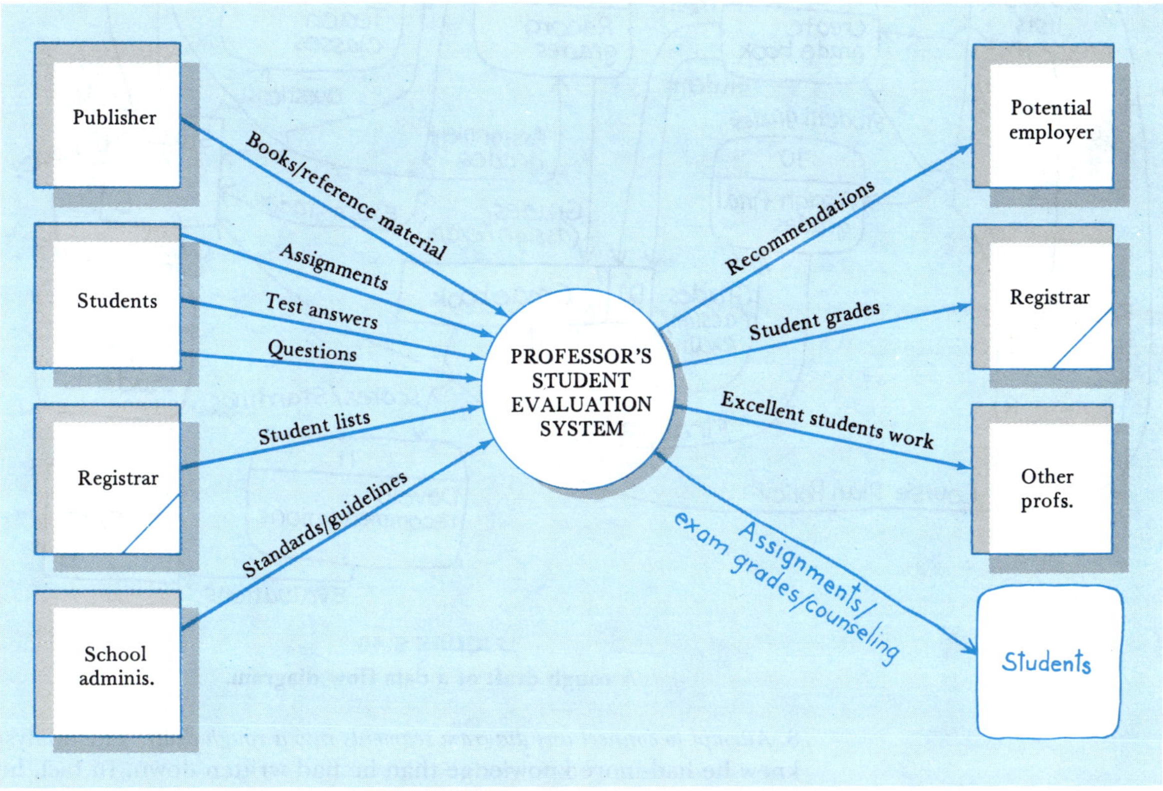

FIGURE 5.39

A revised context diagram.

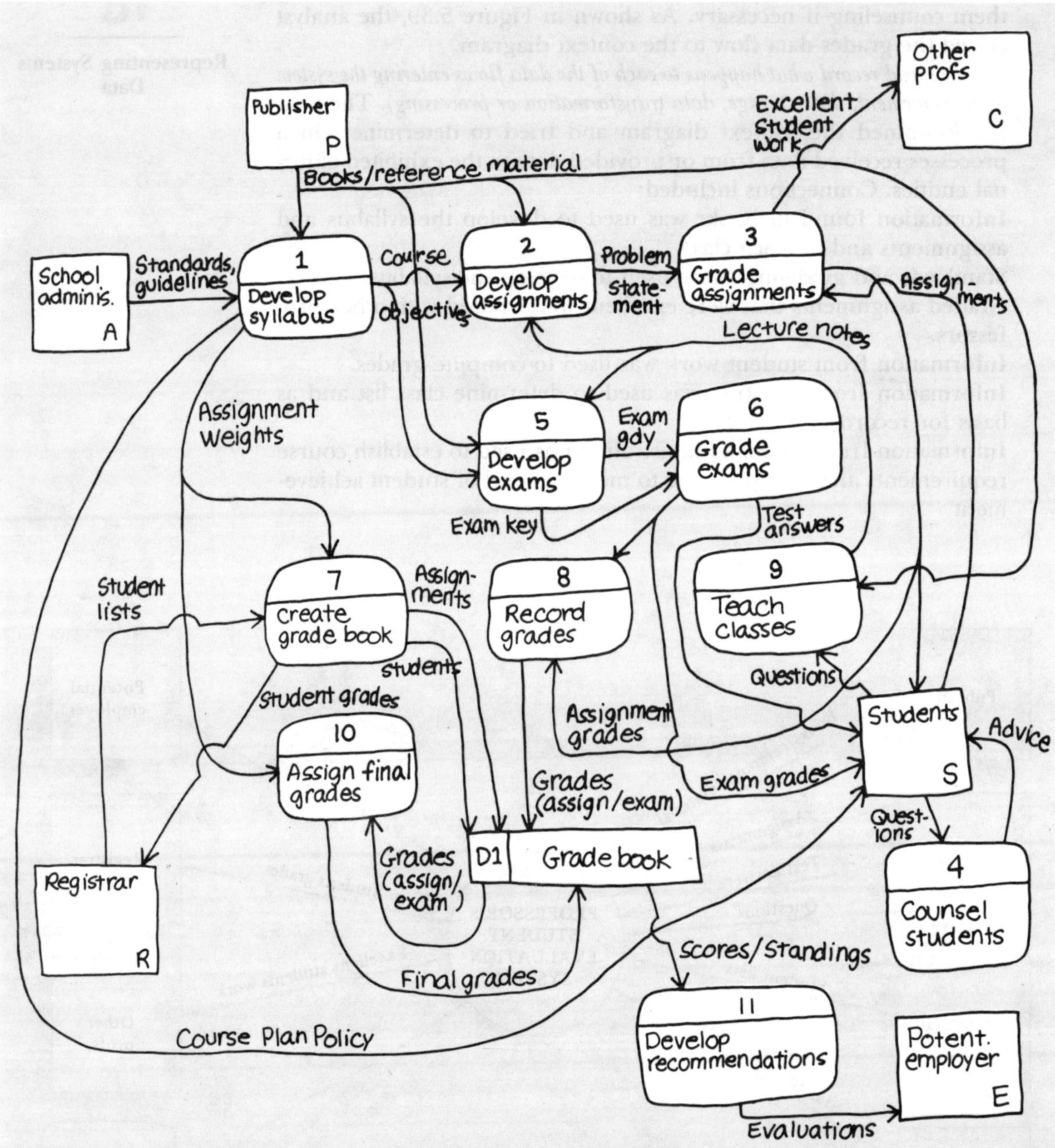

FIGURE 5.40

A rough draft of a data flow diagram.

8. *Attempt to connect any diagram segments into a rough draft.* The analyst knew he had more knowledge than he had written down. In fact, he felt like he was suffering from overload. He used the context diagram and other notes to try to develop a data flow diagram and came up with the rough draft shown in Figure 5.40.

9. *Verify that all data flows have a source and destination.* The analyst verified the diagram and could not detect any deficiencies.

10. *Verify data coming out of a data store goes in.* The only data store on the diagram was the gradebook. The analyst wondered if the textbook and other reference materials should be a data store or a data flow. Then, he wondered if the syllabus was a data store. He was very confused and sought help from an experienced data flow diagrammer. The experienced person told the analyst that there was no "one right solution" and if the data flow diagram helped in sharing a model of the system, then it was ready to share with others. The analyst felt better.

11. *Redraw to simplify—ponder and question result.* The analyst contemplated the results and attempted to simplify some of the crossing lines. (*Note:* This exercise is left to the student! You will learn by doing it.)

12. *Review with "informed."* The professor got a couple of her professorial friends together along with her graduate assistant and reviewed the diagrams. The analyst presented the material to the group in a semiformal fashion. A few needed changes were found, but the professors were very excited about having a documented record of their activities. They intended to use the diagrams the next time some "taxpayer" commented on "just showing up to talk to the kids a few times a week."

13. *Explode and repeat above steps as needed.* The analyst decided that more detail was needed about the professor's procedures and started to gather more detail about each of the processes on the data flow diagram.

SUMMARY

The representation of systems is a key activity of systems developers. There are many techniques for representing systems. Different systems development groups use different techniques or combinations of techniques. There will continue to be an evolving set of techniques for systems developers. This will require continued knowledge and skill development.

REFERENCES AND FURTHER READINGS

Bostrom, Robert P., and Peter Nault. "A Comparison of Structured Design Methodologies for Logical System Design," Indiana University Working Paper, Bloomington, Indiana, 1982.

Chen, Peter P. *Entity-Relationship Approach to Systems Analysis and Design,* Amsterdam: North-Holland Publishing, 1980.

Chapin, Ned. "Flowcharting With ANSI Standard: A Tutorial," *Computing Surveys,* vol. 2, no. 2, June 1970, pp. 119–143.

DeMarco, Tom. *Structured Analysis and System Specification,* New York: Yourdon Press, 1978.

Gane, Chris, and Trish Sarson. *Structured Systems Analysis: Tools and Techniques,* Englewood Cliffs, NJ: Prentice-Hall, Inc., 1979.

Orr, Kenneth T. *Structured Systems Development,* New York: Yourdon Press, 1977.

Ross, Douglas T. "Structured Analysis: A Language for Communicating Ideas," *IEEE Transactions on Software Engineering,* vol. SE-3, no. 1, January 1977, pp. 16–34.

Shevlin, Jeffrey L. "Evaluating Alternate Methods of Systems Analysis," *Data Management,* April 1983, pp. 22–25.

Teague, Lavette C., Jr., and Christopher W. Pidgeon. *Structured Analysis Methods for Computer Information Systems,* Chicago: Science Research Associates, Inc., 1985.

Warnier, Jean-Domininique. *Logical Construction of Systems,* New York: Van Nostrand Reinhold Company, 1981.

Weinberg, Victor. *Structured Analysis,* New York: Yourdon Press, 1978.

REVIEW QUESTIONS

1. Where are representations shown on a data flow diagram "detailed"?
2. What are the differences between data flow diagrams and program flowcharts?
3. Why might system flowcharts be called "visual jargon"?
4. Why are there no "start" and "stop" symbols shown on a data flow diagram?
5. Why might less detailed data flow diagrams have to be changed once more detailed (exploded) views are developed?
6. Why does the system flowcharting approach make representing data flows at different levels a difficult task?
7. Relate the data flow diagram to the following concepts of system description from Chapter 1:
   System boundaries
   Inputs
   Outputs
   Subsystems
   Interfaces
   Environment

DISCUSSION QUESTIONS

1. Why might "flowchart thinking" hinder data flow diagram production?
2. Why do you think it is so hard to obtain agreement from vendors, users, and others on standards for the systems industry? Do you think groups are trying to distinguish themselves for good reasons?

EXERCISES

1. Create a logical model of a system you are familiar with. This could include a system at your place of employment or the university. The registration process may be a good system to model.

2. Represent the system by which you get an education at your school. Create a context diagram to put the system in perspective. Create a top-level data flow diagram from a student's perspective, including the processes of obtaining counseling, registering for classes, attending classes, filing for degree completion, etc. Explode one of the processes such as attending classes to another level of detail—such as buying books, reading books, attending classes, doing assignments, and taking exams.

3. Use the systems development process as an example to exhibit to someone the Warnier-Orr process representation diagram. Use the following abbreviated description for a start. For each project, analysis, design, and implementation take place. *Analysis* consists of building a current physical model, current logical model, and new logical model. *Design* consists of specifying hardware, building software structures, and specifying human procedures. *Implementation* consists of installing the system and doing the conversion.

CHAPTER 6

CHAPTER OBJECTIVES

You should be able to:

- Describe several data gathering techniques
- Specify when each data gathering technique is appropriate
- Discuss difficulties faced in data gathering
- Specify decisions data gatherers must make
- Conduct a data gathering interview
- Develop a data gathering questionnaire
- Determine whom to interview and in what order
- Conduct a requirements defining dialog

Gathering Data about a System

THIS CHAPTER DISCUSSES techniques used to gather data about an existing system. It examines interviewing—including questioning and listening skills, questionnaires, and observing. A technique for accomplishing a requirements statement through the use of a dialog which links a proposed system to the organization's objectives is introduced.

When a systems analyst starts a project, he or she has many unanswered questions. The analyst may wonder:

> What happens to a transaction processed by the system? Are there exceptions?
>
> What reports does the system generate? How often?
>
> How many people work in the area being studied?
>
> What do these people do?
>
> What information for managerial decision making does the system provide? How often?
>
> Why, in business terms, is the system justified?

And the questions go on and on.

In systems analysis, such data must be gathered from many sources. Gathering data requires use of our senses to see, ask, hear, and feel what is happening in a system that concerns us. Entire books have been written about some of the methods to be discussed in this chapter, such as interviewing or developing questionnaires. The intention of this chapter is to present a good base for performing data gathering duties and for continued learning about this critical part of systems work.

AN OVERVIEW OF DATA GATHERING

Before proceeding to data gathering techniques, some background information is needed which is common to all data gathering methods. It should be kept in mind when any data gathering plans are established. Let's start with a definition.

WHAT IS DATA GATHERING?

Data gathering is the process of communicating actions, facts, feelings, interpretations, intentions, and plans regarding a system. It increases knowledge about an existing system and its deficiencies, and can build rapport between development team members. Data gathering is important because it is a means of generating information for decisions on systems design.

Since data gathering involves a great deal of personal contact, it will leave others with an impression of the systems development group. This impression should be positive and professional. Rapport and confidence built during this stage of systems development will pay off later during systems design and implementation.

Data gathering is practiced throughout the systems development activities. It usually is done in the initial stages of a project, but may continue in later stages as well. For example, system testing in the later stages of development requires that data be gathered on the results of the administered tests. Techniques used to gather data about a system include studying existing material, observing the existing system, participating by performing the users' jobs, questioning persons through written queries, and interviewing persons knowledgeable about the system.

Data gathering is practiced throughout the systems development activities. It usually is done in the initial stages of a project, but may continue in later stages as well. For example, system testing in the later stages of development requires that data be gathered on the results of the administered tests. Techniques used to gather data about a system include studying existing material, observing the existing system, participating by performing the users' jobs, questioning persons through written queries, and interviewing persons knowledgeable about the system.

Data gathering requires a careful plan. The analyst should not rush into the collection process. Thinking is needed before doing. Often, when we hurry, we make mistakes and have to do tasks over. In other words, "Slow Down! We're in a Hurry."

CONSIDERATIONS AFFECTING DATA GATHERING

Some considerations affect many of the data gathering techniques. Since these considerations create options for the data gatherer, they should be kept in mind when creating a data gathering plan. These considerations are discussed below.

Depth versus Breadth of Collection

Depth collection probes much detail on one topic (market potential specifics), while *breadth collection* seeks more general data on more topics (general marketing data needs). Breadth first, then depth, is a general guideline to follow.

Open versus Closed Questioning

Open questions are like essay questions where the respondent may interpret and answer in a general way (in their own words), while *closed questions* have a limited set of responses to choose from (choosing from menu). Open questions are helpful in an undefined environment where definite categories do not exist, but data gatherers may have difficulty analyzing the unstructured collected data.

Direct versus Indirect Questioning

Direct questions ask how respondents or interviewes would feel or act, while *indirect questions* would ask how respondents would see someone like themselves feeling or acting. Indirect questions are appropriate for sensitive topics since the person may express more openly his or her true feelings by projecting them to someone else.

Structured versus Nonstructured Collection

A *structured collection* has a prescribed procedure such as an interview that has a specific set of questions to be asked in a defined sequence, while a *nonstructured collection* has a general goal with very few guidelines. Structured data gathering is easier for an unskilled person to administer and analyze but takes longer to develop and may result only in what is asked for. An unstructured approach is more spontaneous, more flexible, more likely to build rapport, and can result in unexpected insights but takes more time to administer and needs a skilled person to administer.

Data gatherers are confronted with many decisions on methods and options to be used. The environment in which data gathering is done and the skill of the data gatherers will suggest what is appropriate. Judgment by the data gatherer is required.

CHALLENGES OF DATA GATHERING

There are some obvious challenges that one can run into when gathering data:

Approaching the Wrong Persons: In general, it is best to start with the project requestor to seek direction. To minimize risk, it is best not to depend on one informant.

Biasing the System or Person by Being There: By observing the system or interviewing a person who is part of the system, you influence the system. For example, making a note can imply to the person that what he or she just said or did is of importance.

People Telling You What They Want You to Hear: This could be based on human bias, recency of a happening, or purposeful omission. Human bias is especially strong. Biases could include seeing someone else as too old, too young, too thin, too heavy, bearded, smoking too much, etc.

Not Sensing All the Stimuli That Are Presented: We do selectively perceive. We could miss things we should have sensed. Data providers may have different interpretations of the same event or situation.

Not Interpreting Correctly the Things You Sense: Did the crossed arms posture indicate closedness or was the person chilled by the air conditioning? Do you understand the jargon? Do they understand yours?

Not Uncovering Feelings or Intentions: People may believe you just want the facts.

Handling some of these challenges can only come from experience. Practice in role playing settings while being evaluated by others can help a person develop data gathering skills.

BEFORE STARTING THE COLLECTION

A prerequisite before any data gathering takes place is to make certain that you are sanctioned by the group where you are collecting data. This means that management has approved your intrusions, the collection participants are aware of your process and intentions, and any other groups such as unions have been approached and given approval. A briefing of all participants may be necessary to avoid misunderstandings. The briefing should let participants know what is expected of them and why they are being asked to participate. Concerns about job elimination should be handled by user management.

Before using any data gathering technique, it is important to carefully think through the implications of its use in the workplace. This includes pretests of interview and questionnaire formats with a pilot group to discover and eliminate any weaknesses.

Agree to anonymity if necessary on the project. Keep your promises. Do not take sides with any group. You need to be accepted to acquire any data of value. Achieve acceptance first, then get the quality data. You must *trust* that the data provider has something to contribute and they must *trust* that you can help them (or at least not cause them distress).

TECHNIQUES OF DATA GATHERING

Techniques for data gathering include:

Reading and studying written material

Observing an activity
Participating (doing someone's tasks)
"Questionnairing" (asking for written response)
Interviewing (asking for verbal response)
Brainstorming ("wish" sessions or group interviews)

It is likely that a combination of techniques will be required to collect data needed about a system. For example, a questionnaire may give a general indication about potential improvements, brainstorming may generate some specific suggestions, and interviews will give an indication of the usefulness of the suggestions for a particular manager. The analyst should attempt to use the strengths of each of the techniques and at the same time try to minimize the disruption of the user or client. (For further discussion on when to use different requirements defining methods, see Davis, and Naumann et al. references.)

READING AND STUDYING WRITTEN MATERIAL

Existing documentation on a system is a great source of information. But the major drawback to using this technique is that current and accurate documentation is often not available or complete. If documentation does exist, it is important to determine if it is up-to-date. Often the material in existence is some representation of the system at a previous stage of development. What was proposed and what finally was developed often are not the same.

Current operating manuals can contain data of value. Other items that may be of help include organization charts, job descriptions, input documents, system outputs, file descriptions, flow diagrams, data element descriptions, maintenance requests, vendor suggestions, auditor recommendations, customer complaints, and other material related to the system.

Reading and studying forms and requests to a system can lead to valuable data. Both blank and completed forms should be analyzed. A cross section of the completed forms or documents rather than one "typical" example should be collected.

Since the collection and analysis of existing documents does not take much of the user's time and can be a good introduction to a system, it is often a good place to begin the data gathering activities.

OBSERVING

Observing is a powerful technique for gathering data. Observing is best suited to human or machine processes that currently exist. Most often, these are the transaction or office processing activities. An example is to watch a process such as the recording of orders or the inputting of data. Observation also can be used to substantiate or clarify data that has been

Existing documentation can aid in understanding a system. (Science; Source/Photo Researchers)

collected in another manner, such as interviewing. Obviously, the activity must currently be done to be observed. In the study of human decision making, such as for a decision support system, the only thing that exists is an intuitive model, something inside someone's mind. Observation of someone "thinking" may lead to few insights.

The analyst should remember that by being there to see an activity, he or she influences the activity. In fact, people may change the way they do something if they know they are being observed. The observed persons should be at ease and *trust* you if you are to collect accurate data.

You should be aware that what you observe may or may not be the normal case. Experienced workers often have "special tricks" to react to different situations. For example, orders from certain companies may be handled with different procedures. Workers may have the "written way," the "boss' way," the "Friday afternoon way," the "catch-up way," and "our usual way."

Permission to observe activities is critical. Not only should supervisors be contacted to gain permission, but the workers or activity performers should be consulted as well.

The time when observation can take place is of great importance. Peak activity periods may lead to different observations than a slow period. As well, representative workers should be observed. You do not want to observe the one local expert or the slowest person who performs the activity.

PARTICIPATING

Participating is really an advanced form of observing. Rather than just watching someone do something, the data gatherer actually performs the activity. This will often lead to greater understanding of the activity and an appreciation of the real situation. Many discoveries have been made by participating. This follows the adage that "I hear and I forget, I see and I remember, I do and I understand." You can't really understand work at a fast food restaurant until you have stood behind the counter during a busy lunch hour.

One form of participating is to attach yourself to a document and trace its path. You may find some obvious bottlenecks in the system. Another means of participating is to try and provide inputs to a system, or try to use the outputs from a system. This may lead to the asking of some perceptive questions and the making of significant discoveries.

If done without threatening workers, participation may lead to rapport with current users. They will believe that you do understand what

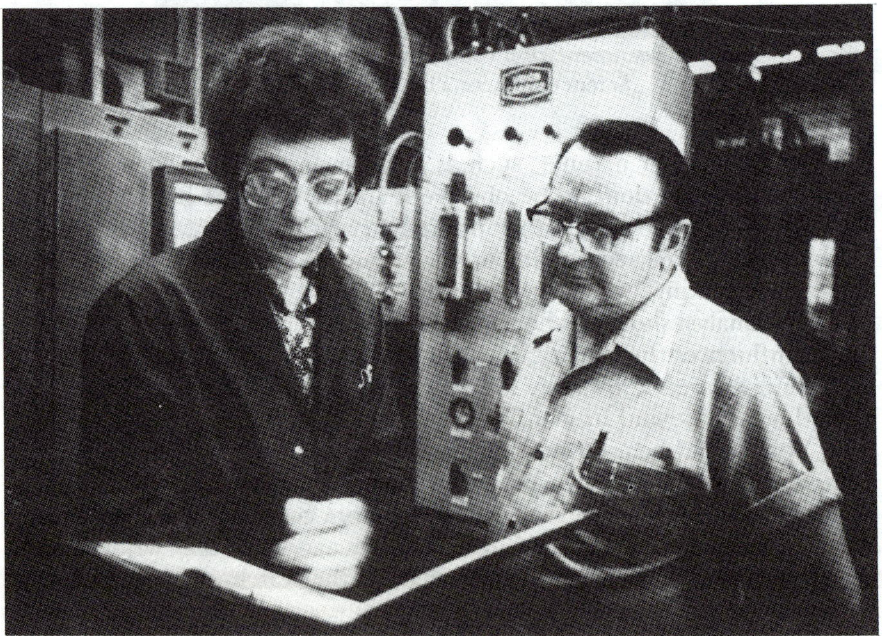

To understand what workers actually do under the current system, a systems analyst may need to try to do their job for an hour or two. (c. Joel Gordon 1983)

their work entails. You may discover that what is written about the work and what is actually done are very different.

"QUESTIONNAIRING": ASKING FOR WRITTEN RESPONSE

Developing, administering, and interpreting questionnaires often is part of the job of the systems developer. Questionnaires have certain advantages over other methods of data gathering, but they also have certain disadvantages. Questionnaires work best when the analyst needs a small amount of data from a large number of people.

It is easy to get wide coverage at a low cost once a reliable questionnaire is built. The elapsed time to administer a questionnaire is usually less than to carry out a large number of interviews. Questionnaire administration can be more uniform than interviews since interview results depend on the skills of the persons conducting them. There is less pressure on respondents since they can fill out the questionnaire within their available time. Questionnaires are more anonymous. The respondent does not have to be identified thus people can be more open in volunteering their interpretations, feelings, and intentions while remaining anonymous.

However, good questionnaires are difficult to build. They must be pretested to ensure that the questions are clear and really collect the data that is desired. There is a longer time before any data is collected. You usually cannot answer questions or modify a questionnaire once the questionnaire has been sent out. You really have only one chance with each respondent. And, once questionnaires are sent to respondents, the data gatherer will live in anticipation, worrying about response rates.

Some decisions the questionnaire developer must face include:

Open versus closed questions—closed questions (such as multiple choice) are best if there are defined choice points and a known range of responses; otherwise you will have many of the "none of the above" or "all of the above" responses.

Indirect versus direct questions—indirect questions (pertaining to another person) are best if the topic is embarrassing or threatening; giving a short case study of another person exhibiting some behavior or feelings and asking about the behavior may uncover the respondent's feelings. For example, in a company where workers were believed to be unhappy, questions asking why "Carol," a worker in the hypothetical company, was unhappy may reveal more data than if the person is asked "Why are you unhappy?"

Ordering of questions—get background facts first to ease into the questionnaires; go from general to more specific; go from less sensitive to more sensitive.

Pretesting with a representative sample *must* be done. A representative sample does not mean using systems development colleagues. It means using persons who are actually in the same situation as, with the same abilities as, and with attititudes similar to your future respondents.

1. Decide on objective. What data do you need?
2. Prepare by reviewing any written documents.
3. Decide who might have needed data and create a distribution list.
4. Decide on the question type (open or closed, direct or indirect).
5. Outline topics to be covered.
6. Write questions to cover topics.
7. Review for completeness, bias, and clarity.
8. Pretest and revise.
9. Administer and await responses.
10. Aggregate, summarize, and analyze.

FIGURE 6.1
A procedure for using questionnaires.

You must be sure questions can be understood without explanation or rewording. You must also determine if the answers you receive indicate correct interpretation, and that the respondent believes the questionnaire makes realistic demands. Several iterations may be needed before this happens.

Based on the above material, Figure 6.1 outlines a general procedure for using questionnaires. Note the planning of *what is needed, what do we know now, who can help,* and *how can the data best be collected* before actually writing the questions. After the questions are written, the important step of *pretesting* cannot be forgotten to ensure that your questions are clear to the reader and that the data you collect is really the data you intended to collect.

The next section on interviewing gives some guidelines on developing questions. Whether the question asked is written or verbal, some of the same concepts apply.

INTERVIEWING: ASKING FOR VERBAL RESPONSE

Interviewing is a technique used to gather data by verbally asking questions and listening to responses. Both the activities of asking and listening are of importance. Asking the right questions, in the right order, of the right people, in the right way is difficult. Just as difficult is hearing the answers and interpreting them correctly. Interviewing is really a difficult skill to master. It requires more skill than just being a "good talker."

Interviewing is a good method of collecting data on feelings and interpretations. It is a flexible method in which the speed, tempo, or order of questioning can be changed, depending on the responses being received. Interviewing should not be approached as an interrogation. It should be a pleasant experience for both the interviewer and interviewed.

Being face-to-face in an interview has many advantages. You can observe interviewee reactions, making it possible for many nonverbal indicators to be collected and analyzed. You can compare the words said to how they are said. Intonation, how someone's voice sounds, and emphasis can give data that a questionnaire does not allow you to collect. Most of us can

THE UNSPOKEN LANGUAGE

The trader on the floor of the Tokyo Stock Exchange isn't holding his nose because he smells something bad. He is dealing in shares of Mitsubishi Gas Chemical Co. The gesture signifies the odor of leaking gas. Traders in Tokyo also rap their heads, lick their wrists, pat their chests and sketch mountains in the air to deal in about 250 other stocks still traded by hand. From behind the glass of the visitor's gallery, the activity down on the floor looks like well-organized chaos. Swarms of young men in identical white shirts and blue blazers flail their arms in a babble of gesticulation—rapid-fire semaphore without flags. And sometimes they get dirty down there, flashing bawdy gestures at one another as they move billions of yen of stock. Japan's spoken language, it should be noted, is remarkable for its lack of obscenities.

From the *Wall Street Journal,* December 1986.

recognize interest or disinterest by a person's tone of voice. You also know who is giving you the data you are collecting, something you can never be sure of when you receive a completed questionnaire. For example, you may have directed a questionnaire to the vice-president of marketing, but may have collected the opinions of the person's administrative assistant or secretary.

Care should be taken not to do counseling during interviewing sessions. Trying to convince an interviewee that change is needed or suggesting solutions to some perceived problem should not be part of a data gathering interview.

Questioning

A good question is understood by the person who hears or sees it, compels the person to answer completely, allows the person to answer without feeling threatened, and imparts knowledge to the questioner. Developing good questions is very difficult. One means of asking good questions is to ask the person being interviewed what questions he or she thinks should be asked to really learn about the system. This method assumes that you will still do "your homework." You should prepare to show that you have learned about the system from available sources.

Questions that can be answered with a "yes" or "no" can result in misleading data. The explanation behind the "yes" or "no" usually reveals more than a single-word response. You must allow for explanations of the "why," so it is best to try to work this into your questions. Weinberg suggests avoiding:

Leading questions: "You're not going to expand this file, are you?"

Loaded question: "Are we required to preserve this clumsy format?"
"Is your boss (co-worker) doing a good job?"

Groucho Marx asked the loaded question: "Are you still beating your wife?" Either a "yes" or a "no" would trap you.

Self-answering questions: "How many entries will there be in this table? I think 50 will be more than enough."

Parting shots: The question asked when everyone is ready to leave that should get more attention. "One more thing, . . ."

Controlling questions: Breaking the interviewee's flow by returning to a preset list of questions. "That may be important, but it is not on my list of questions."

Closed questions, or selecting from a limited set of answers, are best when there is a limited set of responses and clearly defined choices. An inappropriate closed question is usually reacted to by the respondent with a feeling of "none of these, but maybe several of them," or, "I've got to explain my answer."

Getting the right answer is more likely if you wait for an answer. Don't answer your own questions. Wait for a response. Most unskilled interviewers have a great fear of silence. Assume that the silence is the result of careful thought and contemplation.

Listening

There is a high cost of not hearing or incorrectly interpreting what is heard. Not listening has been the cause of wasted actions such as incorrect order filling, retyped letters, labor strikes, and even some tragedies such as airplane or automobile crashes. You might recall someone saying "Guess I didn't hear you right."

Listening is a skill that must be learned just as reading, writing, and speaking. We assume that we know how to listen, but this usually is not true. Studies have shown that our listening skills are poorly developed. There is a difference between hearing something and listening. *Listening* is interpreting correctly. We know what is said, why it is being said, and what it means to the situation at hand. We truly understand what is being communicated. To really listen, we must turn on all our senses. We must:

Focus on what is being said

Hear words, intonations, and emphasis

Note phrases such as "their system" rather than "our system"

Correctly interpret both facts and feelings

Observe and interpret the body language of the interviewee

Be aware of why something is being said

Effective listening means listening hard and watching hard. It means that we must have enough rapport to feel free to ask more questions.

One difficulty we must overcome when conducting interviews is being so consumed with thinking of what to say next that we do not listen to what is being said. Use pauses to gather your thoughts. This may give both you and the interviewee a chance to think.

There are some aids to effective listening and understanding. You can:

Paraphrase what is being said to see if the meaning is correct: "Let me repeat that back to you to see if I understand."

Give feedback by acknowledging that you are hearing: "OK, I've got it."

Give encouragement: "That's interesting. Tell me more."

Use silence: "Let me think about that for a minute."

Use summarizations: "So far, this is what we have . . ."

Ask for clarifications: "I need help understanding that."

The listener has the power to turn the speaker off. Poor listeners:

May fidget to the point of distraction

Exert power by interrupting

Intimidate speakers by intense staring

Give the impression of being insincere

Make the speaker feel he or she has little to contribute

Will communicate biases and immediate judgments

Influence through nonverbal clues such as frowns or raised eyebrows

Listening is an unselfish act. You are giving yourself fully to another and are recognizing the importance of the other person, rather than focusing on yourself.

Interviewing Hints

Plan to Go From General to Specific. Topics should follow this pattern. You should try to gather data from persons with overall general knowledge and then go to persons with more detail (*top-down* approach). Be sure to ask persons being interviewed who else you should talk to.

Know Your Person. You should have some information on the person from organization documents such as organization charts or job or department descriptions. You may be helped by being aware of such things as hobbies or the type of car a person drives. One interviewer of top-level executives suggests calling the person's secretary to not only learn about the interviewee, but to gain favorable reception through recognition of the secretary. An observation of objects in an office (trophies, art objects, pictures, etc.) and a question may break the ice and show interest in the person.

Asking questions about personal items in the office—such as a painting, a tennis trophy, a photo of family members—may aid in gaining acceptance with a user. (c. Joel Gordon 1983)

Plan, Prepare, and Act Like a Professional. Get clearance, make appointments, explain your purpose, and think out your actions. Allow one or two times the scheduled interview length to do your summary and prepare for the next interview. (For a 30-minute interview, allow 30 to 60 minutes for writing a summary and for preparation for next interview.)

Plan Where and When. Alternative locations for interviews include your office, the interviewee's office, or a neutral location such as a conference room. A neutral location can provide isolation from phones or other distractions. However, a person may be more comfortable in his or her own office, and you can learn about people by their office contents. A location where one can shut a door is helpful. Certain times may not be good in some situations—immediately before or after a vacation, Monday mornings, Friday afternoons, or during peak business days or hours. Ask the interviewees for help in setting a time and place and consider their desires.

Be Aware of The Person's Reasons for Participating. You must aid the person in answering the question, "What is in it for me?" Exhibit some care with interviewees who have all the answers, who just want to talk to someone, or who want to downgrade all others.

Connect, Agree on Process, and Then Proceed. "Connecting" means that both you and the interviewee are on the same wave length and are ready to share. Make sure the person is ready to be interviewed. Has something come up that would make your interview an intrusion? If so, it may be better to reschedule. (This is like catching someone with a phone call while he or she is cooking an omelet. Do you think you will have the person's full attention?) The process agreement could include permission to take notes, use a tape recorder (usually not recommended unless you are just collecting facts), or to deviate from the list of questions you may have. Do not smoke unless invited.

Listen and Make Notes. Have your notebook ready before the conversation starts. Take as few notes as you can get by with. Do not try to transcribe the interview into your notebook. You will not be able to listen. Use techniques such as flow diagram segments to record processes or requirements templates (business objectives, business tactics, etc.) to record needs. Share your notes with the interviewee as you are composing them, especially if it is a graphic representation.

Keep It Moving, But Do Not Rush. You should attempt to meet the objective you set for the interview, but be flexible enough to address any of the interviewee's concerns. You should allow your subject enough time to think through your questions and organize his or her answers. You may ask for time to make some notes or to think through your next question. By doing this, you will not have to be thinking of your next question when you should be listening. Silence in a conversation can be of great value.

End Slowly and in a Friendly Fashion. Do not be abrupt in the end. It is appropriate to wind down. Do not open new topics.

Summarize. You need to reach closure. One excellent way to aid both yourself and the interviewee is to do a brief review. Once you leave the interviewee, write your summary and fill in any points not previously

1. Set interview objective. What do you want to accomplish?
2. Prepare by reviewing any written documents.
3. Decide who might have data.
4. Find out about the person to be interviewed including function and position.
5. Decide on the type, length, and form of interview (structured? detailed?).
6. Decide on location.
7. Make an appointment.
8. Appear on time for appointment.
   a. Connect (ask if now still ok, introduce self with business card.
   b. Provide purpose/stage of project.
   c. Agree on process.
   d. Question and listen.
   e. Gather samples.
9. Close and summarize verbally. Express appreciation.
10. Summarize on paper and send copy to interviewee.

FIGURE 6.2
A procedure for conducting interviews.

noted. It is best to seek a quiet place to do this. This summary should be shared with the interviewee.

Based on the above material, Figure 6.2 outlines a general procedure for using interviews as a data gathering technique. Similar to use of questionnaires, the approach includes a number of planning steps that are necessary before the interview is conducted. Remember what some persons refer to as the five P's—*P*rior *P*reparation *P*revents *P*oor *P*erformance.

Not all interviews are done with individuals. Sometimes it may be beneficial to have a group of persons from whom you gather data. The next section discusses such an approach.

BRAINSTORMING: "WISH SESSIONS" OR GROUP INTERVIEWS

Often persons are reluctant to express their views in the one-to-one setting of the typical interview. What is often needed is free and uninhibited thinking. A means of loosening up ideas and using people to motivate each other is the *group interview.* One specific type of group interview is the "wish session." This type of session works particularly well for requirements defining.

In a wish session, participants are instructed to put themselves in a "future frame" and express their wishes. As in most brainstorming sessions, the wishes are not evaluated or debated. Participants must take the attitude of "If my wishes came true, I would achieve these things in the business . . . , I would do the following . . . , and the system would be helping me by providing the following . . . ." This will lead to statements of business objectives, business tactics, and information system objectives.

Much of the stimulus for ideas in such sessions comes from other participants stating their wishes and someone else "bringing the idea" to their world.

SOME DO's AND DON'Ts IN DATA GATHERING

Here are some hints on things to do and not to do to make your data gathering more effective and fun.

Don'ts include:

Don't make promises you can't keep (promises could haunt you later).

Don't waste users' time.

Don't counsel (remember you came to gather data).

Don't argue.

Don't try to show your brilliance.

Don't try to sell a solution you like.

Don't criticize or blame anyone or anything.

Don't make the interview into a social event.

DOs include:

Smile.

Make appointments and be on time.

Inform and agree on a process.

Use the person's name (first name with permission).

Feel confident you can do well.

Dress and act like a professional.

Make other persons feel important.

Be a diplomat.

REQUIREMENTS DEFINING: A SYSTEMS DEVELOPMENT TECHNIQUE

This section will discuss a specific technique used in data gathering. This technique is useful when written or verbal questioning is needed to determine user requirements. Since this portion of systems analysis has caused great difficulty for analysts, we will give it special attention. The data collected will fit in the organizing structures subsystem discussed in earlier chapters.

WHAT IS REQUIREMENTS DEFINING?

Requirements defining is a means of specifying information management system needs through a methodic examination of what users need to achieve (*business objectives*), the means of achievement (*business tactics*), what the information system must achieve to help users (*system objectives*), and the means the information system will use (*system tactics*). It allows linking business and information management.

The purpose of requirements defining is to link the information systems plans to the organization plans. This is done to offset the cost of information system technology and personnel with improved organization performance. The technique promotes:

Interaction between project users and developers

Orientation to an organization's profit motives

Commonly understood motives by those with differing perspectives

Quantified, measurable objectives

The goal of requirements defining is to have a commonly understood set of both business and information system objectives and a means of achieving those objectives. The role of users *and* the technology subsystem will be defined. This will aid in avoiding the cost of:

Developing and operating a system for the systems developers' rather than the users' sake.

Producing information system outputs that are not used.

Providing a system satisfying 99 percent of users' needs for $2,000,000 when 80 percent of these needs could be satisfied for $60,000.

Disagreements on when a systems project is finished.

Developing a system satisfying user wants, rather than user needs.

Blaming an information system for nonperformance, when the information system is actually meeting its objectives.

WHAT DATA DO WE COLLECT?

Requirements defining is a means of determining and linking four entities:

1. *Business Objectives*—what the users want to achieve expressed in increased revenues or reduced expenses or costs.
2. *Business Tactics*—what the users intend to do to achieve business objectives (tactics make up business strategies).
3. *System Objectives*—what the information system must achieve to help the user.
4. *System Tactics*—what the information system must do to achieve the system objectives.

The basic model for requirements defining can be summed up in one very long sentence: A problem or opportunity creates a need to avoid some business costs or increase some revenues (business objectives) which require changed user behavior (business tactics) which is supported by different information system achievements (system objectives) which require changed system behavior (system tactics). A change to any of the entities will start a chain reaction to each of the other entities.

An Example

A new union contract with higher wages causes a need to reduce overtime costs by 10 percent over the next quarter (business objectives). The means to do this is by hiring more temporary people for peak loads (business tactics). The information system must report predicted labor shortages four working days prior to the actual shortage (system objectives). The information system must keep labor availability and predicted labor needs based on existing and predicted product demand (system tactics).

AN OVERVIEW OF THE ENTITIES

Business Objectives

Business objectives represent the desired states system users would like to achieve. Since organizations exist in a changing environment, desired states change. Avoidance of some cost is one state users try to achieve (problem avoiding). Increasing revenues is another state (opportunity pursuing). Achieving these states will affect the bottom line through increased profits. They are critical success factors. Business objectives *must* be stated in terms of *increased revenues* or *reduced costs* to follow this method.

To discover business objectives, developers must examine what instigated a project. This could include factors such as changed laws, competitor action, changed products, changed markets, or acquiring subsidiaries. The reasons should be part of a business plan. Someone wants to make something better. The "someone" and the systems developer must work together to define that "something" and what "better" means.

Besides defining business objectives in terms of avoiding costs and increased revenues in measurable terms, the developer must aid in recording and viewing objectives to determine consistency, conflict, and duplication among user groups. The developer is not to judge who is right, but to point out differences to allow users to take action. (THIS MAY SOUND ACADEMIC, BUT IS ONE OF THE REASONS THAT SYSTEMS FOR MULTIPLE USERS WILL BE A FAILURE FOR SOMEONE.)

Business Tactics

Business tactics can be viewed from two perspectives—as a means of accomplishing business objectives or the means of using an information system result. The two perspectives should be consistent. Business tactics must be specified by users with the aid of developers. The tactics must be performable by the designated organization members. The examination of required business tactics could lead to changed job descriptions, pay, training, physical environments, or union contracts. Remember, business tactics are what an organizational member must carry out as part of his or her job.

System Objectives

System objectives also can be viewed from two perspectives—what users must get from the system or what the system must achieve or avoid. These objectives include both one-time achievements such as conversions or developments, and continuous achievements such as performance or security. Typically, systems objectives will be stated in terms of outputs from the information system such as reports or accessibility to stored data.

For some system objectives, there will be no matching business tactic. A system objective may merely specify the system environment that must be used. In this light, the objective has the appearance of a constraint. For example, accepting a new form of input such as the universal product code would be an achievement, but also would be a constraint on system design.

There are two major groupings of system objectives. One is the typical system improvement because the current system is too slow, too small, too insecure, too inaccurate, or too unreliable. (Problem). The other grouping is to take advantage of some new software, new information source, or new hardware/software. (Opportunity).

Since system objectives are achievements by the system, they often appear to users as improved outputs or improved processing. This would include reports with different content, order, format, time period, circulation, or availability. Inquiries may have different response time, freshness of data, security, or media. Processing could include new models or forms of analysis.

System Tactics

System tactics are the means of achieving system objectives. They are really preliminary design with no vendor, hardware specifics, or physical details. Tactics must be combined to define a system strategy. Tactics and strategies cost money.

Examples of different tactics include batch, manual, or online processing, networks or centralization, database or files, distributed data entry, distributed databases, distributed processing, micros, minis, or various combinations of the above factors. All these potential combinations have different costs. With today's technology, there are many different ways to solve a problem.

PROCEDURE FOR REQUIREMENTS DEFINING

The procedure for using the requirements model consists of the dialog shown in Figure 6.3 which must take place between the developer and the user. The questions in this Figure can be used as a template when talking to a potential user of a system. The questions are also appropriate if the systems analyst decides that a questionnaire is appropriate for data gathering. In any case, the questions are intended to guide the analyst and user through a meaningful dialog linking the business to the information system.

These questions may be hard for the user to answer and may not be an activity he or she expected to engage in with a "computer type of person." This is why it is wise for the analyst to explain the intentions of the dialog and make it clear to the person answering the questions that this linkage is needed to benefit the organization. The questions and desired outcomes must be apparent to both parties to assure mutual direction and understood motives.

If the user and developer roles are assumed by the same person, such as in developing a system for oneself, the dialog can be used for self-inquiry.

Using the Dialog in Justifying An Existing System

To justify an existing system (why we're doing what we're doing):

1. Examine existing system outputs. This will result in a statement of system objectives. Record performance criteria.
2. Determine any existing technology that must be retained. This will give you a set of constraints which are part of the system objectives.
3. Determine what the system does to meet the objectives mentioned in step 1 above (in generic terms). These are the system tactics.
4. For each user, determine what the user/receiver would do once he or she receive a system output. This will give you a business tactic.

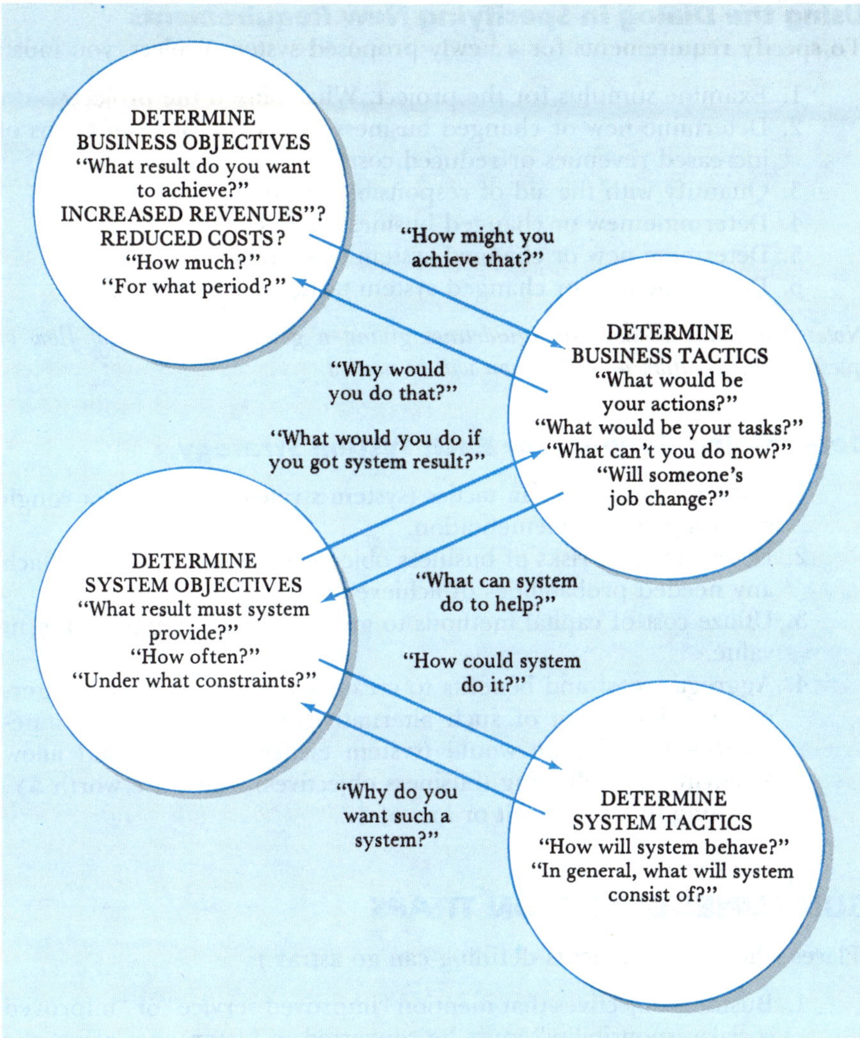

FIGURE 6.3

Questions asked in requirements defining.

You may find that there is no current action. This may suggest that the system output or objective is not needed.

5. Determine why the user performs the business tactic; this will give you the business objectives, and should be stated in terms of avoided costs and/or increased revenues.
6. Aggregate business tactics and examine for consistency.
7. Examine system objective performance criteria for rigidness. For example, if someone says he or she needs a report in one day, find out if more than one day really would be acceptable. Many persons quickly state that they need a reply in "real time" when the next day would really be fine.

Using the Dialog in Specifying New Requirements

To specify requirements for a newly proposed system project, you must:

1. Examine stimulus for the project. What caused the project?
2. Determine new or changed business objectives. State in terms of increased revenues or reduced costs.
3. Quantify with the aid of responsible person.
4. Determine new or changed business tactics.
5. Determine new or changed system objectives.
6. Determine new or changed system tactics.

Note: The above sections are guidelines giving a general direction of flow of questioning. Iteration and repetition will be needed.

Determining Benefits for Each System Strategy

1. For each set of system tactics (system strategy), establish a rough cost range for implementation.
2. Determine any risks of business objective achievement and attach any needed probabilities of achievement.
3. Utilize cost of capital methods to give all dollar figures a present value.
4. Aggregate cost and benefits to create a matrix of potential alternatives. The form of such alternatives would follow the statement—"For $X, we would (system tactics), which would allow achieving the following (business objectives) which are worth $Y, resulting in a net profit or loss of $Z."

GUIDELINES/GUMPTION TRAPS

(Places where requirements defining can go astray.)

1. Business objectives that mention "improved service" or "improved social responsibility" must be converted to factors that affect the bottom line. In fact, these may be business tactics, not business objectives. A good test to apply to these intangibles is to ask the question, "So what? What would be the result in terms of increased revenues or reduced costs?" Many hidden agendas likely will appear.
2. Quantification of objectives is necessary to assure measurement. Words such as "more," "quicker," "fresher," etc., must be replaced with precise statements including when, how many, to whom, by whom, and for what period. If there is room for debate, there will likely be a debate.
3. Requirements defining must involve several levels of users.
   a. Strategic users include those persons providing funding for the project. They are most concerned with long run plans.
   b. Tactical users include those persons who are likely the "tactics determiners" at the operational level. These persons also will

assure that tactics are performed. They are most concerned with short-run plans.

c. Performing users gather and record inputs, perform manual processes, and carry out many of the tactics.

Since each of these user groups is needed for systems project success, they must be included in the requirements determining process.

4. In many cases, successful entrepreneurs operate only by "gut feel" and are not ready to go through the efforts needed to develop a requirements statement. It is difficult to force someone to disclose plans when success has come in the past without a publicized plan. As a systems developer, you must be realistic and often proceed with imperfect information about "why" the system is needed. A rigorous defense for a "quick and dirty" decision support system may be a waste of time. In this case, do the project and let the user react. This is a form of prototyping.
5. The same methods and formats for justifying a new system can be applied to any suggested changes to an existing system. The newly created costs must be offset with new benefits.
6. Goal setting is difficult. Goals must be achievable, but not too easy. Stating and accomplishing short-term goals ("inch-pebbles") will give positive feedback to help accomplish long-term goals ("milestones"). Going public with goals is a risk and is difficult in a nontrusting environment. In a trusting environment, knowing others' goals or motives can explain actions and facilitate helping each other.

SUMMARY

As we end this chapter, the beginning analyst should keep in mind that there is much to learn about the methods of systems analysis. This learning and skill development cannot happen overnight. There is so much to learn and practice that it can be discouraging, but at the same time it is fun. Discouragement should be countered by the challenge to continue learning and make new discoveries. Experience will aid in this growth.

REFERENCES AND FURTHER READINGS

Davis, G. B. "Strategies for Information Requirements Determination," *IBM Systems Journal,* vol. 21, no. 1, 1982, pp. 4–30.

DiGaetani, John L. "The Business of Listening," *Business Horizons,* October 1980, pp. 40–46.

Gildersleeve, Thomas P. "Conducting Better Interviews," *Journal of Systems Management,* February 1976, pp. 24–28.

Grassel, Milt. "The Power of Questions," *Nation's Business,* November 1986, pp. 56+.

Jenkins, A. Milton, and Randall D. Johnson. "What the Information Analyst Should Know About Body Language," *Management Information Systems Quarterly*, September 1977, pp. 33–47.

Kahn, Robert L., and Charles F. Cannell. *Dynamics of Interviewing*, New York: John Wiley & Sons, 1957.

Kulp, William C. "Involvement of People: The Ideals Way," *Journal of Systems Management*, June 1970, pp. 22–25.

Miller, Sherod, Daniel Wackman, Elam Nunnally, and Carol Saline. *Straight Talk: A New Way to Get Closer to Others By Saying What You Really Mean*, New York: Signet New American Library, 1982.

Naumann, J. David, Gordon B. Davis, and James D. McKeen. "Determining Information Requirements: A Contingency Method for Selection of a Requirements Assurance Strategy," *The Journal of Systems and Software*, vol. 1, 1980, pp. 273–281.

Orr, Kenneth T. *Structured Systems Development*, New York: Yourdon Press, 1977.

Weinberg, Gerald M., and Daniela Weinberg. "The Fuzzy Early Stages," *Journal of Information Systems Management*, Winter 1984, pp. 71–75.

Review Questions

1. What is another objective of data gathering besides the gathering of data?
2. What will the data gathered during systems analysis be used for?
3. Give an example of:
   a. A closed question; an open question.
   b. A direct question; an indirect question.
4. What are some of the challenges data gatherers must face?
5. What role does trust play in data gathering?
6. What are some sources of written data to read and study?
7. What are some cautions about data gathered from observation?
8. Give some hints on how to start an interview.
9. Give an example of a:
   a. A loaded question
   b. A leading question
   c. A self-answering question
   d. A parting shot
   e. A controlling question
10. What is a general guideline for the amount of time to allow between interviews to do your interview summary and prepare for the next interview?
11. What is the difference between hearing and listening?
12. What are some hints for getting full understanding while conducting an interview?
13. How many notes should be taken during an interview?
14. In requirements defining, how is the business linked to the information system? What are the "interfacing" entities?

15. What is the difference between an objective and a tactic as used in requirements defining?

DISCUSSION QUESTIONS

1. What might be some of your personal biases that could influence your data gathering activities? Do you feel that it is necessary to be conscious of these biases in your data gathering activities?
2. What might influence where an interview should be held?
3. What might you do in the following situations?
   a. Interviewee constantly looks at watch or clock.
   b. Interviewee constantly gripes and groans about the company.
   c. Interviewee is unhappy and wants you to help with a rebellion.
   d. Interviewee refuses to talk.
4. Who would you use for a pretest of a questionnaire? Would your systems development peers be able to determine whether the questionnaire is written in appropriate language?
5. Should you use a tape recorder during an interview? Why might an experienced interviewer argue that tape recorder usage and note taking would be of less concern if persons allowed enough time between interviews?
6. Why might a group interview or wish session produce more results than a one-on-one interview?
7. Examine the requirements defining dialog in Figure 6.3. Is there any set way one would have to proceed through the questions?

EXERCISES

1. A construction company was having trouble keeping track of which workers were assigned to which projects for billing purposes. One of the owners of the company felt this information could be obtained via the payroll system being run by a local service bureau. Since a relative of the owner just recently got into the systems consulting business, the owner felt the relative could help analyze the problem. The two met and Artie, the new consultant, was hired and told to figure out a solution to the problem.

   Artie immediately headed out to the service bureau, and on arriving, asked to see the "person in charge." He was told that the person was not in, so he replied that he would check again later. Since he was in the area, he thought he would interrogate a few people to find out about the system. He saw a door marked "Systems and Programming," and walked in. He turned on his hidden tape recorder and asked a couple of programmers about the system. Artie sat down and coaxed some valuable opinions about the system and made some suggestions on how they could improve the system from what he could remember from the programming class he took. The programmers became uncooperative, so he decided to leave.

With his new knowledge about the system, Artie headed back to the construction company. He proceeded to the bookkeeping area and began to ask about the payroll system. Again, people were not cooperative, so he had to remind them that he was sent there by the company owner. One person immediately became helpful and told Artie how he could help get rid of some of the other employees. Artie supported this since those persons were so uncooperative.

Since Artie had now collected all kinds of data, he thought he would quit for the day. 'This systems consulting sure is fun,' he thought, 'and not as hard as people make it out to be.'

a. How do you think Artie will do in his career as an analyst? Why?
b. What advice would you offer him?
c. Point out some attitudes that Artie may have to change.
d. Are there any dos and don'ts that Artie should heed?
e. If you were asked to continue the project, how would you proceed?

2. Determine a bias you may have (smoking, exercise, politics, 55-mph speed limit, etc.). Prepare a counterargument to your bias to share with another person. Sit down with another person and present your argument. Did you learn anything about yourself? Is your bias stronger or weaker?

3. The following is a case study of a business that identified its business objectives, business tactics, system objectives, and system tactics. Read through the case study and create the answers to as many of the questions in Figure 6.3 as you can.

HOW CASINO COMPUTERS STRETCH THE HOUSE ODDS

When singer Lionel Richie performed in June at the Golden Nugget casino in Atlantic City, 2,500 people in the audience were attending "on the house." A computer had generated their names from a list of the casino's high rollers.

During last January's Super Bowl weekend, Caesars Palace flew 170 of its best customers to Las Vegas, where on Saturday night they heard a "chalk talk" by New Orleans Saints head coach Oail A. "Bum" Philips and watched the Super Bowl the next day on wide-screen television, eating complimentary hot dogs and waving pennants in the casino's plush surroundings. These big spenders, too, had all been picked with the help of a computer.

As casinos in New Jersey and Nevada have watched their once-typical 15% profit margins halved in the past five years, they have had to scramble for an edge. And casino managers are finding that they can get that edge by keeping better track of information on the customers, the odds, the statistics, and the dollars that make up their $5 billion industry. That way, they can better spot and woo the big spenders, as well as control costs. "A professional information systems approach is finally coming into the gaming industry," reports John M. Boushy, director of systems development for Harrah's five casino properties.

The gaming business has not always been as competitive as it is today. "In the 1960s and 1970s, all the casinos had to do was put gaming equipment in a reasonably accessible building," says Stuart E. Curtis, financial analyst for the Nevada Gaming Control Board. But in the late 1970s, recession ushered in tough times for the 165 casinos in the two states with legal gambling. And since then, more than a dozen smaller casinos have surrendered their licenses, while many more have changed hands.

To avoid a similar fate, many casinos in the past five years have begun to add their actual gaming functions to existing accounting, hotel, and restaurant management systems. Once, credit for a high roller rested virtually on the nod of a pit boss with a good memory. The casino's credit accounts—typically listing between 50,000 and 100,000 players—were kept on cards and filed by hand by cashiers, wasting two valuable casino commodities, space and time.

Now the accounts are stored in computer memory and include much more data. Many casinos record such variables as a player's preferred games, the time spent at each, betting patterns—and even favorite drinks, restaurants, hotel rooms, and entertainers.

All that information gives casino managers their most potent marketing tool. On-line credit limits are computed with "ruin factor"—the probability, based on the way the customer typically plays, that he will lose a certain amount of money. Depending on a player's probable loss, a "complimentary" limit is established. Casinos often spend an astounding 20% of revenues on complimentaries—free services ranging from providing rolls of nickels for players on a church group excursion to travel via Lear Jet for high rollers from anywhere in the world to the casino.

THE RIGHT PEOPLE

If a casino does not lavish its money on the right people, though, it will show quickly on the bottom line. Explains one data processing manager: "We used to determine complimentaries by credit limits. If somebody had a $50,000 limit, we might be giving him free travel to the hotel, free lodging, and free meals. The trouble was, if he was only cashing a $5,000 marker, we'd be losing money."

Thus, putting together better data on gambling customers becomes crucial to a casino. When Caesars Palace developed a new player-rating system, for example, it dropped its complimentary budget by more than 20%. At the two Golden Nugget casinos in Las Vegas and Atlantic City, management has used its player-rating system to target a more upscale clientele. The company raised its complimentary allocations by $12.8 million to $45.5 million in 1983 and watched income increase by $31.1 million to $108.6 million, up 40% from the year before. "When comps go up, it's not all bad," says Clyde T. Turner, chief financial officer for Golden Nugget. "But if you don't understand which of your customers are your best, you're misallocating your resources."

Bally's Park Place Inc.'s Atlantic City casino management believes that it has worked out a system that enables it to lavish complimentaries only on crap shooters from whom it is likely to win the most money. The pit bosses observe the duration and betting patterns of the players at their table and then compare those patterns with pre-established guidelines. A player betting an average of $25 for 15 minutes will be given free parking; a player betting an average of $1,000 a hand need play for only 2 ½ hours before the pit boss will graciously offer him free lodging in the casino's executive suite, a limousine, and meals in the casino's best restaurants.

'WIN IT BACK'

By maintaining specific player information in their computer, the casinos can target almost miniscule market segments for their promotion. For instance, they can pinpoint all players between 40 and 50 years old who spent more than $10,000 the last time Frank Sinatra performed in the casino. The next time "Ol Blue Eyes" is in town, the casino may fly in 100 of his high-rolling fans as well. The Golden Nugget sends out birthday and anniversary greetings to its high rollers and invites them to celebrate in the club.

To track who is spending what, pit bosses fill out a card for every player betting amounts of any significance. That way, the casino knows what individual tables and players are doing. In the larger casinos, a pit clerk enters the information into a video display terminal in the gaming pit, where credit information can be updated on an hourly—rather than daily—basis. Most casinos store their credit data files on minicomputers in the back office. "On-line credit allows us to put money in a man's hand and get him back in action; you've got to have money in his hand before you can win it back," says Philip D. Griffith, president of both Harolds Club in Reno and the Sands Hotel & Casino in Las Vegas.

Computer surveillance can pay off in security situations as well. Harolds Club has a program that models blackjack card-counting systems used by professional gamblers. If a player seems to be winning too consistently, his betting patterns are entered and analyzed.

The 10 Atlantic City casinos, all built within the past six years, are "significantly ahead of the casino industry as a whole" in terms of sophisticated information management, says Harrah's Boushy. "Given the level of regulation [by the New Jersey Division of Gaming Enforcement], it would be impossible to do business here without an [information] system." explains C. Patrick McKoy, vice-president and treasurer of Bally's Park Place.

In Nevada, where gaming dates back to the 1930s and the commission has fewer regulations, managers are nonetheless anxious to gain the business benefits from better information management that is being developed in Atlantic City. In most large casinos, three-person crews may spend four hours a day reading individual machine meters, disrupting play, and creating a massive data-entry job to get those numbers into a data base. But at Bally's in Atlantic City, where each slot machine's performance is monitored by computer, personnel costs have been reduced and programs that monitor slot machine performance can determine which slots do best in which areas. They can also produce deviation reports on machines that are paying off outside of normal probability curves. Mechanical failures, an honest run of luck, or even tampering can cause these deviations.

WITCH DOCTORS

One reason for such relative backwardness is that gambling is a superstitious and tradition-laden business. Pit bosses, for example, used to sell their services to casinos based on the number of high rollers they could attract. With the freedom to determine complimentaries for individual players, the pit bosses became favorite hosts whom gamblers would follow from club to club. Now, with customers on computers, "it destroyed the goodwill of pit bosses," notes Donald E. McGhie, a partner in Kafoury, Armstrong & Co., a Reno accounting firm. "When we first started doing computer consulting a few years ago, these guys were thought of as witch doctors who had an understanding of the magic [of gambling] that nobody else had. They'd practically stand there and shake gourds at you."

Casinos are still at the early stages of automation, McGhie says. "Only in the past three or four years has the industry begun to analyze itself. Before, everybody was running on intuition," he adds. Of course, notes Thomas P. Flynn of the New Jersey Casino Control Commission, "If a game is honest, a house doesn't need to do anything to make money. Inevitably, the odds are in the house's favor." But as the casino business becomes more competitive, more effective management of the elements that are outside of Lady Luck's domain will increasingly be the difference between boom and bust.

—From Business Week, July 30, 1984, pp. 112-114.

CHAPTER 7

Reviewing the Data: Assuring Mutual Understanding

CHAPTER OBJECTIVES

You should be able to:

- Give arguments for using team processes to assure quality
- Indicate studies that support the use of reviews in systems development
- Specify objectives that reviews can aid in achieving
- Specify the types of reviews used in systems work
- Specify proper review behavior for participants

"If you can't convince them, confuse them."
"If they can't understand it, they can't critique it."
"If the basic structure is weak, give it a lot of polish. The glare will baffle them."
"Since 90 percent of the processing is done by 10 percent of the system, delay that or we will look too far ahead."

—*Words of Devious Danny, The Noncaring Analyst*

THIS CHAPTER EMPHASIZES achieving quality in systems building through effective team communication. The chapter discusses giving effective presentations on collected systems material to assure mutual understanding by team members. The processes and techniques used to conduct reviews of systems deliverables by peers and users is presented. The chapter emphasizes giving constructive criticism to assure high-quality systems development products without destroyed egos.

Systems development work is not conducted in isolation. Besides a data collection activity such as interviewing, which usually is a one-to-one activity, there is a need for team processes to review, enhance, and approve collected and generated data about the system being developed. There are numerous opportunities for systems analysts to share the results of their efforts with other interested persons.

Systems are completed by creating a series of intermediate products, often called *deliverables,* that together lead to the ultimate product, a completed system satisfying the organization members' needs. The deliverables exhibit the progress being made on the project. Usually, the deliverables consist of portions of the different system models that were first introduced in Chapter 3. These models should be understood by different groups within the organization and are shared through semiformal team gatherings called *reviews.*

The objective of sharing systems development data is to improve the quality of the systems development deliverables and, in turn, the resulting system. An objective is *zero defects*—a deliverable that has nothing wrong with it and meets users' needs. Even if a zero defects state is not achieved, minimizing defects at a reasonable cost will improve systems development results.

This chapter discusses methods of reviewing collected data. It describes how the reviewing process fits into the project life cycle. Who should be involved in reviews and what roles they must fulfill is discussed. What can and should be reviewed and the general concepts governing reviewing are introduced. Finally, the techniques to be followed in making presentations to groups attending reviews and the specifics of conducting team product reviews are covered.

WHAT IS REVIEWING

Quality comes from people who care about their work and who believe that any product or service can be improved. This improvement can result from giving and accepting *constructive* criticism. However, behaving properly when giving and receiving constructive criticism is a skill that must be groomed. One of the principal means of doing this is by conducting team product reviews, a focus of this chapter.

Another common name for reviews is "walkthroughs." Historically, this was the early name for team processes of reviewing, but many of the walkthroughs were conducted without proper attitudes and training. They turned into opportunities to "get the presenter or producer" and then that person or persons waited to "get those that got them." This resulted in some persons calling the technique "walk*overs*" (see Lippard). To counteract this unfortunate period of history and to ensure a more conscious attitude of quality through team efforts, the techniques here will be referred to as *team product reviews.*

A team product review is the semiformal process of subjecting project deliverables to an examination by a small group of competent persons to detect errors early and at a low cost. Let us examine some of the words in the definition. *Semiformal* means that there are certain rules and protocols for behavior. It is not a free-for-all. There is a procedure that must be followed. But the formality is dismissed if it hinders reaching the review objective. In essence, there are rules to give structure but freedom to make judgments to get the job done. *Project deliverables* are the results that are achieved in doing systems work. These include data flow diagrams, structure charts, data structure diagrams, organization charts, and procedures. A *small group* usually means three to six people who are competent in that they will understand the deliverable and can contribute by giving both positive and negative feedback. An attitude of seeking team success by giving constructive criticism is needed.

Reviews are done early in the development of a deliverable to make sure an inappropriate structure is not refined and polished at great expense to the project. The required review attitude is: "I got this thing started, but before we get too far let's get together and see if I'm going in the right direction." The destruction of the developer's ego is likely if a product is polished, since a great investment of time and energy has been made. This ego destruction can be costly to an organization since it could result in reduced human productivity. Teamwork and an attitude of "we all work for the same company" are essential to a successful review process.

WHY DO REVIEWS

In performing systems work, we humans do many things quite well. But it also is human to make errors. Pencils come with erasers because we may not do everything right the first time. The only time we do not make errors is if we do not do anything, hardly an acceptable approach for a systems developer. It often is difficult to see our own errors. Others may see things we have done incorrectly more quickly than we can ourselves. Many a programmer can testify that the one "bug" he or she was blind to glared out at someone else.

We make many kinds of errors. They include errors of:

Commission, or doing something wrong

Omission, or leaving something out

Standards violation, or not doing something in the acceptable or required way

Boundary misinterpretation, or having too much or too little in the system

Mislabeling, or calling something by an inappropriate name

If these errors are allowed in our models and representations of systems, they may end up in our physical systems. Studies have shown that errors not found in the analysis stages of a systems project can cost ten times more to correct in the maintenance stage (Boehm). Thus, it is critical to find errors early.

Although there are many means of finding errors in systems deliverables, formal reviews are one of the more effective means (Connell and Brice). Studies have shown that of total errors detected during systems development, peer reviews uncovered 83 percent while machine testing uncovered only 17 percent (Fagan).

Our goal in systems work is to keep the good, and find and correct or discard the bad. If others help us locate our errors, it must be done in a friendly and nonantagonistic way. Giving and receiving criticism can be very ego-destroying to sensitive and insecure human beings.

Reviews have many advantages. Properly conducted reviews can:

Create wider awareness of a system as it is being developed, since data about the system is not kept private but is shared with others

Provide a formal means for getting feedback which many developers never receive and thus remain in doubt about the soundness of their work

Build a team spirit through the act of helping one another

Use the knowledge and varied observation powers of several persons

Formally transfer ownership of a deliverable from a person to the project team making the development effort less personal and more of a group effort

The goal of a review is a deliverable with no serious deficiencies, understood and accepted by relevant organization members, and preserved egos for all review participants. Reviews have the objective of avoiding the cost of:

Individual polishing of a deliverable that will have to be "recarved"

Users feeling left out of the development process by only getting final results

"Personal," rather than team, ownership of a deliverable, resulting in privately held documentation which is not accessible if the documentation holder does not volunteer

Professor J. David Naumann of the University of Minnesota relates an instance of developing an instructional videotape to demonstrate appropriate review behavior to students. He got together with four colleagues who were team-teaching a class on software engineering to do a "mock" review. The product to be reviewed was five pages of data flow diagrams that each of the professors had independently reviewed and approved. They had used the diagrams as classroom exhibits for 2 years. In conducting the "mock" review, the professors found 12 errors on the diagrams, about half of them being serious enough to cause the "correctly specified" system to be inoperable! All of the professors were surprised and had new insights into the benefits of team reviews.

Destroyed egos when an improperly conducted review turns into a "walkover," resulting in decreased productivity, increased absenteeism, and employee turnover

Not finding errors until late in the development cycle, when they are costly to correct

Errors remaining in implemented systems

Reviews can be destructive as well as constructive. Incorrect use of reviews by teams in systems development has led to some very destructive behavior, much like the abuse of individuals in mismanaged group encounter sessions. In one organization, the improper use of the technique contributed to 100 percent turnover of systems employees during a 2-year period (Lippard).

Wider understanding of a system under development is an important objective of reviews. Organization members who send data to, or receive data from, other persons in the organization get to meet these persons and understand their roles and needs. Frequently, the result will be a statement such as, "*Now* I know what you do with that, and why it has to be in the form requested." This clarification of interfaces and relationships can help organization members perform as a team rather than as units of competing individuals.

WHEN TO REVIEW

Reviews should be done when the developer feels a draft of a needed deliverable is achieved. Before polishing the deliverable, the team product review should be employed. An appropriately sized result can be reviewed in 30 to 60 minutes. Time should be taken to ensure that the deliverable is on track before too much time and energy is spent in refinement. Of course, judgment is needed so time is not wasted by either too much refinement or reviewing too soon. The systems development project leader should aid analysts in determining when to review.

A series of reviews may be needed for any of the products of systems development. The team product review by peers allows the developer of the product a chance to share it with fellow workers to inform, practice before meeting users, and find errors and omissions. The review process shown in Figure 7.1 assures a quality, accepted, and team-owned product.

Once the product is created and the producer feels comfortable with it, a team product review by peers is conducted. This acquaints colleagues with the product and gives them the opportunity to offer suggestions. The producer then does any revisions and, if needed, subjects the product to another review. If approved by peers, the product is accepted as a developer team product. The product is next reviewed by members of the user community until it satisfies them. Then the product will be owned by all members of the project team.

A team product review should not be conducted if a group situation does not provide advantages. There are some activities that are best han-

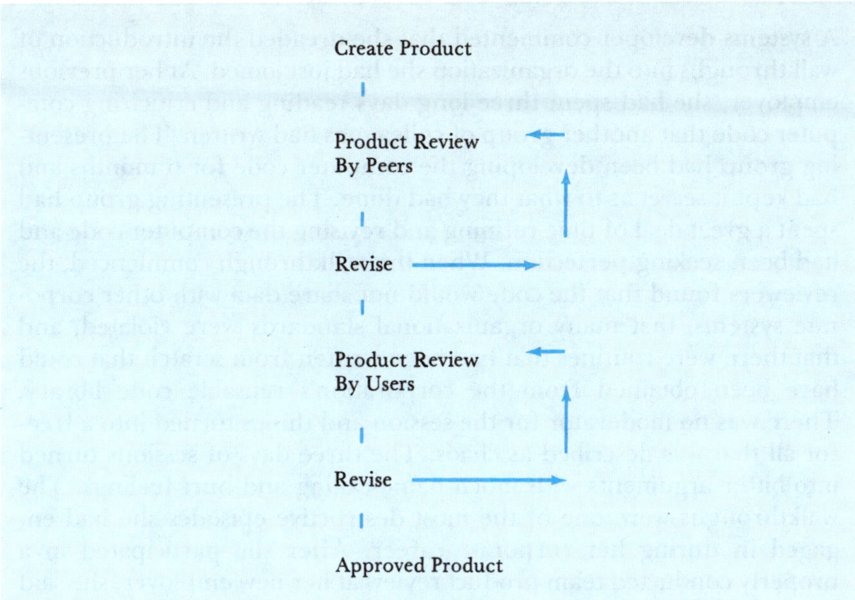

FIGURE 7.1

A review cycle to assure a quality deliverable.

dled on a one-to-one basis. For example, a supervisor of a group may review a proposed procedure as an individual rather than as part of the group. This may be done to assure that the group is not stifled by peer or supervisory pressure when conducting a review. The presence of a supervisor may inhibit honest feelings of individuals who would speak up in front of their peers, but not in front of supervisors. If it is necessary to have a supervisor review the product, have it done on a one-to-one basis.

WHAT CAN AND SHOULD BE REVIEWED

Reviews are made of the deliverables or products of systems development. These products are generally intermediate results that need to be verified by others to assure correctness and completeness. It is best to review in a top-down process where the total structure is reviewed first, then the structure with more detail, and then on to greater levels of detail.

Small pieces that can be covered in 30 to 60 minutes are appropriate for a review. A mistake some reviewers have made is to spend a great deal of time producing a deliverable and then to ask the review team to spend a half-day or more to do a review. This creates information overload and impedes project progress. There also may be a great investment made in the product, so developers are less willing to change it.

The most likely products to be reviewed are portions of the models of the system that are being assembled—people, data, organizing structures, and technology, as discussed in Chapter 3. These would include organiza-

> A systems developer commented that she dreaded the introduction of walkthroughs into the organization she had just joined. At her previous employer, she had spent three long days reading and criticizing computer code that another group of colleagues had written. The presenting group had been developing the computer code for 6 months and had kept it secret as to what they had done. The presenting group had spent a great deal of time refining and revising the computer code and had been seeking perfection. When the walkthrough commenced, the reviewers found that the code would not share data with other corporate systems, that many organizational standards were violated, and that there were routines that had been written from scratch that could have been obtained from the corporation's reusable code library. There was no moderator for the session and things turned into a free-for-all that was described as chaos. The three days of sessions turned into bitter arguments with much name-calling and hurt feelings. The walkthroughs were one of the most destructive episodes she had engaged in during her corporate career. After she participated in a properly conducted team product review at her new employer, she said the processes and attitudes did not resemble her previous experiences.

tion charts, data flow diagrams, data dictionary entries, data structures, requirements statements, input layouts, output layouts, output distribution lists, user manuals, person and machine dialogs, and procedures.

Different criteria may be needed for reviews done at various stages of a project. Likewise, the type of project and the scope of the system will affect who is to attend the review. Some examples of objectives of a review and participants who can help meet these objectives are shown in Figure 7.2.

Review Participant	*Focus*
Peers	Improve product Share results Avoid premature user review
Users	Assure accuracy, appropriate requirements, ease of use
Quality/standards	Organizational guideline adherence
Operations	Avoid hardware/software degradation
Database group	Assure data integrity
Auditors	Appropriate controls
Communications group	Data transfer between locations

FIGURE 7.2

The focus of different review participants.

Management reviews have a different process and objective. They are held to determine project continuance and to assure that proper resources are adequate. The management review is held at the end of a phase of development. There is less focus on quality and more focus on actual versus planned progress and adherence to budgets.

PERSONNEL ROLES IN REVIEWING

A general guide for review attendance is to include persons who can contribute to a more meaningful end product in a nondisruptive manner. This could include creative persons with good ideas, persons who may see something from a different perspective, those who must approve the results, or those who have to implement the results of an effort. Roles in a review include the producer, presenter, moderator, recorder, and reviewer.

The *producer* of the product being reviewed may not always be the *presenter*. It may be advantageous to have someone else present the product, allowing the producer to avoid the tension of doing the presentation. The producer may take more notes and think while the review is taking place. In some cases, presenting one's own product could lead to extreme cases of defensiveness since the presenter may perceive product criticism as personal criticism. The producer could also fulfill the role of recorder to maintain an active role in the review.

The most critical role in review conduct is that of *moderator*. The moderator can make the difference between whether the review turns into a glowing success or a total disaster. The moderator can change the tone of a review from a "walkover" to a spirit of sharing. The choice of moderators is critical, especially when introducing reviews to an organization. Some special training may be needed, often done by conducting "mock" reviews under supervision.

There are a number of characteristics that are important when choosing a moderator. The moderator must have the respect of all the persons in the review. The moderator will influence and exert power over participants. He or she should not be afraid of bringing everyones' attention to improper review behavior. Control must be exercised by adhering to the standard set for reviews. The moderator must be an "alive" person who has spirit and enthusiasm. He or she should be firm, but fair, to everyone in the review.

The moderator should try to assure that everyones' opinions are being recognized. Favorite or powerful persons must not be given partial treatment. Reading body language to detect clues such as eyebrow-lifting may reveal that someone has something to say. A good moderator would detect this behavior and encourage the person to speak up.

The *recorder* must be very attentive during the review and hear and interpret what is going on. The recorder must be able to think on his or her feet. He or she must be able to summarize points with help from the group, and also be able to print clearly. After the review is completed, the recorder

PRODUCT REVIEW FORM

PRODUCT PRODUCER: __________
PRODUCT NAME: __________ Product-ID __________
PROJECT NAME: __________ Project No. __________
DEVELOPMENT PROCESS NAME: __________ Process-ID __________

TYPE OF REVIEW	PRODUCT DISPOSITION	SCHEDULE
___ Peers	___ OK	Date __________
___ Users	___ OK with Revisions	Place __________
___	___ 2nd Review	Start Time __________
	___ Rethink	Stop Time __________

PARTICIPANTS

Presenter __________	Reviewer __________
Moderator __________	Reviewer __________
Recorder __________	Reviewer __________
Reviewer __________	Reviewer __________

ACTION POINTS

FIGURE 7.3

A product review form.

is responsible for completing the product review form as shown in Figure 7.3.

Further definition of the role of each of these participants is included in the procedure for reviewing later in the chapter. Persons participating in a review should examine the procedures. This will allow each of them to think through what they will be required to do in the review.

SYSTEMS MANAGEMENT'S ROLE IN REVIEWING

Systems management has an important role in reviews, but it does not include actual participation in the review. Unless the manager will be the actual user of the system, he or she will likely have little to contribute and can actually stifle desired review behavior. However, management can aid the review process. It can:

1. Encourage including time in schedules for reviews
2. Budget for materials and supplies to conduct reviews
3. Examine review summary reports to determine participation and product disposition
4. Respond to any volunteered feedback on review behavior
5. Reward good reviewers
6. Attempt to correct behavior of poor reviewers
7. Allow and encourage the use of valued persons in reviews

Good review behavior includes appropriate preparation and abiding by the guidelines set for reviews. Good reviewers are perceptive to strengths and weaknesses of the product and sensitive to the producer. They are good team members. Managers will likely find out who is good or poor by others' requests for more or less participation by certain individuals.

Although it is beyond the scope of this book, it is important to remember that team behavior and project leadership are critical to having group processes work well. Many managers will find that the team will use social sanctions to get team members to contribute. The manager must be perceptive to the needs of the team and provide aid by using authority not possessed by the team members.

ASSURING PROPER REVIEW BEHAVIOR

The most critical factor in assuring successful reviews is for all participants to understand and be aware of the objective of the review. Participants must know whether they are reviewing for adherence to standards, efficiency, adequate documentation, technical advancement, or operating ease. The moderator can aid the review process by redirecting the discussion if the review strays off the subject.

Attitudes are an important part of the review process. Two general sets of attitudes are those of the producer of the deliverable and that of the reviewers. We will examine each of these to assure proper understanding of the behavior needed for successful reviews.

REQUIRED PRODUCERS' ATTITUDES

Deliverable producers, the persons who created the product to be reviewed, must believe that others are participating in the review because they want to help both the persons and the team. Included as required producer attitudes are:

"I make mistakes, doesn't everybody?"

"Others will help me find my mistakes."

"Others will not attack me."

"I will present the material clearly if I do the presentation."

"I will respect others' questions."

"What I do is project property."

"A deliverable is not complete until reviewed."

The producer must try to feel part of the helping and caring team. Trust that others feel the same way must exist. Too many persons in the systems area will not share their work because others have caustically humiliated them.

REQUIRED PARTICIPANTS' ATTITUDES

Participants—including moderator, recorder, and reviewers—also must enter the review process with a proper attitude for reviews to be successful. Included in these attitudes are beliefs that:

"I must preserve the developer's ego by being a charitable critic."

"I will seek and mention positive aspects of the deliverable."

"I will spend time critically appraising the product."

"I will not use the review to exhibit my brilliance."

"I will notify a producer prior to the review if there is a serious flaw."

"I will not debate style."

The most frequent type of improper review behavior is to debate style. This is frequently expressed as, "I wouldn't have done it that way," when the real question is "Does it work or not?"

Reviewers must remember that *facts* needed to build a system should be correct, but *judgments* must be reasonable. For example, a volume figure on the number of accounts or clients to be handled by the system should be accurate, but whether a report title is printed in bold or plain font is a style judgment and opinion with no "right" answer.

EGO SAVING

Reviews can turn into very destructive episodes. People who do not concern themselves with other person's egos and their need to belong can say things, even though subtle, that can be very damaging. Some guidelines can be of aid.

Itemized Response

Studies have been done of groups that were able to accomplish a task and those that were not able (Chopra). One critical factor found was that successful groups gave value to other persons' work. The study found that, in unsuccessful groups, much energy was expended in establishing and instituting a defense of work already done. Chopra suggested a technique called *itemized response* to aid groups in being successful. *Itemized response* is composed of several main ideas:

Any item mentioned must be specific. Statements like "that's a good (or bad) idea" must be restated specifically by explaining why.

> **IS OUR SOCIETY A NEGATIVE WORLD?**
>
> **Worst News About News**
>
> "Bad news is reported on TV 20 times more than good news," according to the Media Analysis Project of George Washington University. After evaluating 85,000 words in hundreds of broadcasts over 100 days, the project found only 47 positive statements.
>
> From *Parade—The Sunday Newspaper Magazine*, January 5, 1986.

> A critiquer first must concentrate on what is useful in a product or idea. He or she must itemize the merits.
>
> Next, the critiquer can list negative elements.

This technique ensures that reviewers keep two columns, both good and bad, and that the producer finds out about both of them.

"You" versus "I" Statements

Care in using language also is needed in reviews. Statements made by reviewers that begin with "You . . . " usually accuse someone of doing something unacceptable. "You" statements are blaming statements. They put people on the defensive. "I don't understand . . . " statements are usually perceived by the listener as asking for help. The person receiving the statement likely has an explanation that the asker would like to hear. Having knowledge that others seek is an ego booster. Someone is admitting that you have knowledge he or she would like. This gives confidence and strengthens the entire team.

Care should be taken not to disguise "you" statements in "I" statements. For example, saying "I don't know why you . . ." is blaming, not asking for an explanation.

One means of embedding an "understanding" question and combining it with itemized response is to:

1. Repeat your understanding back to the presenter (paraphrase).
2. Listen for clarification.
3. Ask for further clarification if needed.
4. Mention specific items you feel are strengths of the product or idea.
5. Mention specific items you feel could lead to future problems with the product or idea.

Error Correcting

Correcting errors is not an objective of reviewing. The reviewers must have confidence that the producer of the deliverable can make the needed corrections. Besides the producer's ego boost from others having confidence in his or her ability, it takes a great deal of time to get agreement on

A supervisor of systems development in a paper products firm felt he could find out more about development projects by attending team product reviews by peers. He went to his first review and felt a great degree of discomfort. A data flow diagram was being presented. Every time there was an issue or question, everyone looked at him for his opinion. He vowed he wasn't going to intervene, but one of the more open workers later commented to him that he had nonverbally communicated his approval or disapproval. He has never attended one of the reviews again. If he is curious, he schedules a one-on-one meeting with the project leader.

how to correct errors. This often turns out to be a long discussion on style where there are no really happy participants.

Management Participation

Managers may be tempted to attend team product reviews by peers to "see how things are going." This is detrimental to the review process. Peers are gathered to help each other and improve the team product. It is hard for managers to avoid doing a performance appraisal during a review. Personal experience has shown that active and helpful review atmospheres are changed into performances for the boss. Sometimes managers insist on attending reviews by peers. What will often happen is that peers will hold preliminary reviews and then have another review with the manager attending. This turns out to be a time waster and contributes little to the quality of the product.

The systems development team usually has no say as to who will attend team product reviews by users. The user manager of the project should try to use good judgment as to who can make a contribution. Reviews are not management decision points, but are the putting together of many minds to share and improve the product.

REVIEW TECHNIQUES

Now that the reader has a good background about the team processes of doing reviews, including what reviews are, why they should be done, when they should be done, what products should be reviewed, who does reviews, and appropriate behavior, we will proceed to the actual techniques or *how* to do reviews. There are three major systems development techniques associated with assuring deliverable quality. The first is the technique of ***presenting a deliverable*** to a group. The second is the technique of ***conducting team product reviews by peers.*** The third technique, ***team product reviews by users,*** is similar to reviewing by peers. Remember that these technique sections are presented in an outline and point form to serve as future reference sections when you actually have the opportunity to practice the technique.

The skill of presenting is best developed by observing those good at it, and by practice and then more practice. It is important to be conscious of what makes a good presentation and what makes a mediocre one and how to plan a presentation. This will be covered in the next section.

Team product reviews then will be discussed. In keeping with a general guideline for writing procedures, team product reviews by users will repeat some of the material from team product reviews by peers. The reason is that the entire procedure should be included in one place to eliminate the "go to another location" problem that causes us to have our fingers stuck marking locations in a manual. By having a complete procedure in one location, copies of the technique procedure and guidelines can be distributed to all participants.

THE TECHNIQUE OF PRESENTING

Definition: Presenting is a means of verbally and visually communicating ideas, intentions, and proposed actions to a group of persons.

Purpose and Objective: The purpose of presentations is to provide information, gather information, or convert others to your way of thinking.

Team product reviews by peers can improve the quality of computer program solutions. (Comstock)

Procedure: The procedure for presenting includes:

1. Gather background about:
   a. Audience, including aptitudes, attitudes, biases, and interests.
   b. Constraints, including time, facilities, and conventions.
   c. Material that will be presented.
   d. Objectives, or what presentation should achieve (intentions).
2. Develop outline of material (content and order).
3. Determine strategy for presentation:
   a. Slick versus draft?
   b. Attack existing system?
   c. Handout what, when?
   d. Timing?
4. Determine medium (overheads, 35-mm slides, flip chart, computer projection, nothing).
5. Develop material and test (notes, visuals, handouts).
6. Arrange facilities (Seating number and arrangement, size, noise, sightlines).
7. Deliver and review.

Guidelines/Gumption Traps (Places where Presenting Can Go Astray)

1. PREPARE! Mark Twain said "It takes 3 weeks to prepare a good ad-lib." *Think* the presentation. Try to imagine as if it is actually taking place and the audience is loving it. It has been said that speaking in front of a group is one of the biggest fears people face. Preparation and rehearsal will "make the butterflies fly in formation."
2. Be tasteful and avoid being negative toward any group or faction. If you do not know everything about your audience, you may have offended some or all of them.
3. Do not read your presentation. Your audience can do this themselves. It is not a speech.
4. Involve your audience. Use props to appeal to senses other than hearing. Seeing, hearing, touching, and feeling are all important.
5. Watch your audience to get nonverbal feedback. If you detect negative feedback, it may be necessary to do some exploration using questions, or have a short exercise, or take a break. Make eye contact with every member of a small group.
6. Watch your time. Be sure to *finish before your audience finishes.*
7. Repeat questions that are asked. This will assure getting the question right, will share it with others who may not have heard it, and give you time to think over your answer. If

others in your audience look like they would like to answer, you may want to let them respond.

8. You must develop your own presentation style. You can learn from others, but you must be yourself. Be confident, friendly, human, enthusiastic, smiling, and rested. Do not apologize unless there is a reason to do so ("I know others can do a better job than me."). *Do not degrade yourself.*
9. Listener distractions can include nervous pacing, shifting, nonwords ("um, ah"), monotone, no eye contact, and physical appearance that detracts from your presentation. Dress to feel comfortable with your audience. Face your audience at all times.
10. Use transparency backing sheets or mounting frames for your notes. Notes are legitimate prompts. Do not be afraid to use them.
11. Visuals will aid your presentation but make sure only key words are included, that words are bold enough to be read, and that the medium will work with your audience in the room to be used. Choices include transparencies, flip charts, display boards, video tape, slides, or display screen projection.
12. Room setup is critical. You should be the focus. A screen should go in a corner without distracting outside light on it. Arrange seats to have the audience where you want them—with a good view, not too close, not too far, and no neck craning.

Now that the reader has some idea of how to present a deliverable to an audience, we will discuss the process of actually conducting a team product review when peers are the reviewers.

THE TECHNIQUE OF TEAM PRODUCT REVIEWING BY PEERS

Technique Name: Team product reviewing (peers); also known as structured walkthroughs, peer reviewing

Definition: Team product reviewing by peers is a formal means of giving and receiving constructive criticism of system project deliverables, by a small group of competent peers, to detect errors early and economically.

Purpose and Objective: The *purpose* of team product reviewing is to detect (not correct) errors of omission, of commission, or of deviation from standards and to validate judgments made by the deliverable producer. The objectives of a review are a deliverable with no serious deficiencies ready for review by users, one that is understood and accepted by peer developers, and preserved egos for all review participants.

Procedure: The procedure for conducting a team product review is:

1. Initiate review:
   a. Deliverable producer notifies project leader that product is ready for review.
   Producers should be informed that this should be done early, soon after something has "taken shape" and before refinement is done.
   b. Project leader confirms deliverable is reviewable and gets agreement on objective of review.
   The project leader must ensure the deliverable is not embarrassing.
   c. Project leader schedules review, determines time duration, assigns reviewers, moderator, and recorder, and does notification.
   d. Deliverable producer distributes deliverable materials to participants.
   Time can be saved if review materials are distributed several hours before the review. Reviewers must pledge to reserve time to study materials before the review. This prevents material loss, promotes a fresh product, and prevents prereviews.
   e. Participants study material prior to start of review.
2. Conduct review:
   a. Moderator assures room is ready and that supplies, including flip chart, pens, review forms, and time piece, are in place.
   A flip chart or large sheet of paper taped in view of everyone is required. Black or white boards cannot be carried off just the way the team saw them, preserving visual images.
   b. Moderator calls review to order, assures understanding of the review objective, and allocates budgeted time.
   c. *All* review participants acknowledge proper review behavior and pledge to behave accordingly.
   It may be valuable to review appropriate review behavior by either reading aloud or having a printed sheet of proper behavior for silent review.
   d. Presenter gives a general introduction to the deliverable (for first review) or gives past action points (for second and subsequent reviews).
   e. Presenter presents deliverable.
   It is usually best if the presenter is not interrupted and is allowed to complete the entire presentation.
   f. Recorder records action points on flip chart.
   g. Moderator calls for vote on disagreements (majority rules).
   Team product reviews are kept on the subject by the moderator. If disagreements occur and the discussion rambles, the moderator must ask the questions: "What is the issue?", "What are the

pros?", "What are the cons?", and "What could be the consequences of a positive or negative vote?" All reviewers' opinions must be recognized and respected. Then a vote can be called. After this procedure, the issue is not to be brought up again.

h. Recorder reviews action points by reading out loud to the entire group.
i. Reviewers vote on deliverable disposition.
   Several categories including "OK as is," "OK with action point revisions," or "OK only after another review" are usually adequate.
j. Project members assume deliverable ownership if deliverable is accepted.
   This step is valuable for building team efforts and products.

3. Complete review:
   a. Recorder transcribes action points to a review form.
   b. Recorder distributes review form to participants and project leader.
   c. Project leader updates project management.
   d. Deliverable producer incorporates action point items into deliverable.

Guidelines/Gumption Traps (Places where Team Product Reviewing Can Go Astray)

1. Team product reviews can result in walkovers if improper review behavior is exhibited. The most common failing is a reviewer "blaming" a presenter or producer. Blaming statements usually begin with "You" or "I think." Uncertainty statements, beginning with "I don't understand," are required to preserve a presenter's ego and avoid defensive behavior. An ego preserver is to have each reviewer make a positive comment on the product. The belief must exist that the product has some merit.
2. Team product reviews are not used for performance evaluation. *No* managers are allowed.
3. A flip chart or large sheet of paper taped in view of everyone is required. Black or white boards cannot be carried off just the way the team saw them, preserving visual images.
4. Time must be carefully managed. This is the responsibility of the moderator. The moderator must keep the review moving and on the subject. The team must:
   a. Save error correction until after review.
   b. *Focus* on one point at a time.
   c. Cover all major points; then, if there is time, move to the minor points.

   Time can be saved if review materials are distributed several hours before the review. Reviewers must pledge to reserve time to study materials before the review. This prevents material loss, promotes a fresh product, and prevents pre-reviews where reviewers informally influence each other.

5. Team product reviews are kept on the subject by the moderator. If disagreements occur and the discussion rambles, the moderator must ask "What is the issue?", "What are the pros?", "What are the cons?", and "What could be the consequences of a positive or negative vote?" All reviewers' opinions must be recognized and respected. Then a vote can be called. After this procedure, the issue is not to be brought up again.
6. Team product reviews with peers can be successful only if a trusting team spirit exists, and a producer or presenter believes:
   a. I make mistakes, doesn't everybody?
   b. I will be helped by the reviewers in finding my mistakes.
   c. I will not be attacked by the reviewers.
   d. I am not being reviewed, the product is.
   e. The product is not my personal property, but belongs to the project.
   f. Reviews are necessary before the product is completed.
   And then acts according to the beliefs.
7. Team product reviews with peers can be successful only if a trusting team spirit exists where a reviewer believes:
   a. I must work to preserve, not destroy, the producer or presenter's ego.
   b. I must not use the review to demonstrate my brilliance.
   c. I must not debate style, or the way I would have done something.

   And then acts according to the beliefs.

THE TECHNIQUE OF TEAM PRODUCT REVIEWING BY USERS

Much of the material in the next section may seem repetitious. It is included in the standard format for techniques to assure that a procedure for team product reviewing by users exists in one place. In your reading, it may be wise to peruse the material and look for differences, rather than to dwell on material that already may be familiar to you.

Technique Name: Team product reviewing (user); also known as structured walkthroughs, user reviewing.

Definition: Team product reviewing by users is a formal means of giving and receiving constructive criticism of system project deliverables, by a small group of relevant users, to detect errors early and economically.

Purpose and Objective: The purpose of team product reviewing is to detect (not correct) errors of omission, of commission, or of deviation from standards and to validate judgments made by the deliverable producer.

Procedure: The procedure for conducting a team product review by users is:

1. Initiate review:
   a. Deliverable producer notifies project leader from systems development that deliverable is ready for review.
   b. Project leader confirms deliverable is reviewable.
   c. Systems development project leader works with user project leader or user representative and schedules review, determines time duration, and assigns reviewers, moderator, and recorder.
   Notice that the user and development project managers must work together to assure review success.
   d. Deliverable producer distributes deliverable materials to user representative.
   e. User representative distributes notifications and materials to participants.
   f. Participants study material prior to review.
2. Conduct review:
   a. Moderator assures room is ready and that supplies, including flip chart, pens, review forms, and time piece are in place.
   b. Moderator calls review to order and allocates budgeted time.
   c. *All* review participants acknowledge proper review behavior and pledge to behave accordingly.
   d. Presenter gives a general introduction to the deliverable (for first review) or gives past action points (for second and subsequent reviews).
   e. Presenter presents deliverable.
   f. Recorder records action points on flip chart.
   g. Moderator calls for vote on disagreements (majority rules, developers present have no votes).
   h. Recorder reviews action points.
   i. Reviewers have secret vote on deliverable disposition (see product review form). A consensus is required for deliverable to be "OK" or "OK with revision."
   Note that a secret vote is taken on disposition of the product. This is done to prevent any user managers who may attend the review from influencing their subordinates when an open "show of hands" vote is taken. Remember that systems developers cannot prevent user managers from attending if they are part of the user community concerned with the product. Also note that a consensus vote is needed to get a favorable disposition. This is done because ALL users must be pleased with the product. The product must be

Users have an opportunity to contribute to system quality through team product reviews. (Courtesy Motorola Information Systems)

redone with inputs from all users, especially those who felt the product was not acceptable.

   j. Project members assume deliverable ownership if deliverable is accepted.

3. Complete review:
   a. Recorder transcribes action points to review form.
   b. Recorder distributes review form to participants and project leaders.
   c. Project leaders update project management.
   d. Deliverable producer incorporates action point items into deliverable.

Guidelines/Gumption Traps (Places where Team Product Reviewing by Users Can Go Astray)

1. Team product reviews can result in walkovers if improper review behavior is exhibited. The most common failing is a reviewer "blaming" a presenter or producer. Blaming statements usually begin with "You" or "I think." Uncertainty statements, beginning with "I don't understand," are required to preserve a presenter's ego and avoid defensive behavior. An ego preserver is to have each reviewer make a positive comment on the product. The belief must exist that the product has some merit.
2. Time must be carefully managed. This is the responsibility of the moderator. The moderator must keep the review moving and on subject. The team must:
   a. Save error correction until after review.
   b. *Focus* on one point at a time.
   c. Cover all major points, then if there is time, move to the minor points.

Time can be saved if review materials are distributed several hours before the review. Reviewers must pledge to reserve time to study materials before the review. This prevents material loss, promotes a fresh product, and prevents pre-reviews.

3. Team product reviews are kept on the subject by the moderator. If disagreements occur and the discussion rambles, the moderator must ask "What is the issue?", "What are the pros?", "What are the cons?", and "What could be the consequences of a positive or negative vote?" All reviewers opinions must be recognized and respected. Then a vote can be called. After this procedure, the issue is not to be brought up again.
4. A flip chart or large sheet of paper taped in view of everyone is required. Black or white boards cannot be carried off just the way the team saw them, preserving visual images.
5. Team Product Reviews with users can be successful only if a trusting team spirit exists where a producer or presenter believes:
   a. I make mistakes, doesn't everybody?
   b. I will be helped by the reviewers in finding my mistakes.
   c. I will not be attacked by the reviewers.
   d. I am not being reviewed, the product is.
   e. The product is not my personal property, but belongs to the project.
   f. Reviews are necessary before the product is completed.

   And then acts according to these beliefs.
6. Team product reviews with users can be successful only if a trusting team spirit exists where a reviewer believes:
   a. I must work to preserve, not destroy, the producer or presenter's ego.
   b. I must not use the review to demonstrate my brilliance.
   c. I must not debate style, or the way I would have done something.

   AND then acts according to these beliefs.

Note that the above guidelines are very similar to those for team product reviews by peers. They were included to make the point that for training and execution purposes, the entire explanation of the technique should be in one place.

SUMMARY

Reviewing and team processes for improving systems quality is critical to systems development work. But skill in the techniques required to use the processes can only be developed by practice and concentration on the actions used in team meetings. It is helpful to videotape or have observers who understand the processes critique early sessions. Only by concentrating on exhibiting proper behavior and by having the proper attitudes mentioned in the chapter can the techniques provide maximum benefits.

REFERENCES AND FURTHER READINGS

Boehm, Barry W. *Software Engineering Economics,* Englewood Cliffs, NJ: Prentice-Hall, Inc., 1982.

Chopra, Amarjit. "Motivation in Task-Oriented Groups," *Journal of Nursing Administration,* January–February 1973, vol. 3, no. 1, pp. 55–60.

Connell, John, and Linda Brice. "Practical Quality Assurance," *Datamation,* March 1, 1985, pp. 106+.

Fagan, M. "Design and Code Inspections to Reduce Errors in Program Development," in E. Yourdon (ed.), *Writings of the Revolution: Selected Reading on Software Engineering,* New York: Yourdon Press, 1982.

Freedman, Daniel D., and Gerald M. Weinberg. *Handbook of Walkthroughs, Inspections, and Technical Reviews,* Boston: Little, Brown and Company, Inc., 1982.

Humes, James C., and Alan Paller. *How to Give the Best Presentation of Your Life,* Integrated Software Systems Corporation, Publication AR 831, 1983.

Keller, Arnold E. "Quality Assurance in DP," *Infosystems,* vol. 32, no. 3, March 1985, p. 28.

LeRoux, Paul. "Mastering the Art of the Winning Presentation," *Working Woman,* February 1985, pp. 84–86.

Lippard, Mark S. "Structured Methods: The Impossible Dream?" *Computerworld,* Dec. 1, 1980, InDepth section, pp. 1–15.

Podolsky, Joseph L. "The Quest for Quality," *Datamation,* March 1, 1985, pp. 119+.

Semprevivo, Philip C. *Teams in Information Systems Development,* New York: Yourdon Press, 1980.

Weinberg, Gerald. *The Psychology of Computer Programmer Programming,* New York: Van Nostrand Reinhold Company, 1971.

Yourdon, Edward. *Structured Walkthroughs,* Englewood Cliffs, NJ: Prentice-Hall, Inc., 1979.

REVIEW QUESTIONS

1. Distinguish between a team product review and a management review. What is the difference in objectives?
2. What kinds of errors might show up in system deliverables?
3. Why might the review process be called "semi-formal?"
4. What should a systems developer do if he or she is not sure a deliverable is ready for review?
5. What can systems management do to aid the review process?
6. Why was the name "team product reviews" chosen rather than "walkthroughs" or "peer" or "user reviews"?
7. What are required review participants' attitudes? Required reviewer attitudes?
8. What is "itemized response?"

9. Why might the producer of a deliverable not be an appropriate presenter for a review?
10. What is the difference in procedure between a team product review by users and by peers?
11. Why is error correction not part of the review activity?

DISCUSSION QUESTIONS

1. Some persons have said that persons who are really critical of others in a review with few positive comments about the product are usually very insecure persons. Do you feel there is credibility in this belief? Why or why not?
2. The chapter mentions that reviewing small chunks in a top-down fashion is better than reviewing all the detail at once. How could this be done if the project was to write a textbook on systems development?
3. Why is listening to a presentation different than reading a book? What advantages does a presenter have over an author?
4. You have been told that you have been chosen to be a moderator for a team product review by peers. What are you going to do to prepare?
5. Why is it important for deliverables to belong to the development team rather than to an individual?
6. Why is it that persons who work for the same company have to be reminded of that fact?

EXERCISES

1. Use a product from one of the other exercises you have done in this book as a deliverable to be reviewed. Prepare a short presentation and schedule a review of the deliverable. A data flow diagram, procedure, structured interview format, or questionnaire would be ideal as the deliverable. Use the procedure for a peer review and your classmates as participants.
2. Write a very specific procedure to get a "robotlike human" from the room you are in to the final state of having a drink of water. State your assumptions. You may do this in groups of up to three persons. You have only 15 minutes to develop your procedure. Use the review process to improve your procedure. Test the procedure. Did the review help? In what ways?
3. Positive feedback is unnatural for many people to deliver. In the next 2 days, sincerely compliment two of your friends, family, or acquaintances. Record the events. Describe what you said and what the other person's reaction was. Were you surprised? Do you think this would be a valuable thing to do?

PART III

The Systems Design Phase: Process and Techniques

This section addresses the challenge of solving information system problems and examines information system opportunities made possible through new systems design. The design portions of the systems development methodology introduced in the first section of the book will be detailed. Hardware design, data, and programs needed for a system are discussed. Then, design for people is examined. Finally, topics concerned with designing to maintain system integrity are introduced.

CHAPTER 8

CHAPTER OBJECTIVES

You should be able to:

- Understand the challenges of completing a systems design
- Specify what processes are needed to specify a systems design
- Specify what deliverables result from systems design activities
- Specify who should perform the processes of systems design
- Specify the order of the processes of systems design

The Processes of Systems Design

THIS CHAPTER INTRODUCES the topic of systems design and why design is a challenge. The general design processes introduced in Chapter 2 are broken down into more detail. Included is a discussion of what is done at each stage and what the desired outputs would be. Choosing automation alternatives and presentation of alternatives to management through use of an alternative payoff matrix ($ benefit from business objectives met vs $ cost from system strategies purchased) is examined.

An earlier chapter mentioned that systems design may be more appropriately described as *systems synthesis*. The architecture of the new system is specified by establishing a plan for combining subsystem components that will represent the entire system. This means that a description is needed of procedures, programs, data, hardware, person/machine interfaces, and controls which can be combined to represent a revised, coherent system to meet new and future needs.

This chapter will describe the processes that are performed to accomplish systems design. This is the *what* of systems design. The following chapters will describe the design of program and data structures (Chapter 9), some of the techniques used to specify people roles and interfaces (Chapters 10 and 11), and controls to assure appropriate system integrity (Chapter 12).

Once an analysis is completed and the decision is made to continue a project, the systems developer must propose new systems solutions. These solutions may have been in the back of the developer's mind when analysis was being done, they may result from the study of other organizations' solutions, or they may be the result of vendor proposals. The design process is a creative one that is hard to describe and prescribe. In fact, the greatest challenge of design is to "make something out of nothing." The developer should take the attitude of an artist with a blank canvas, knowing there are constraints but not ruling out new possibilities and opportunities. This differs from analysis, where the developer is "taking things apart," since design is a prescriptive rather than just a descriptive activity. The developer must propose a meaningful combination of people and technology to meet the needs of the organization.

Before getting into the design processes, a definition is appropriate. *Design* is an activity to produce a plan which, when implemented, should achieve specified goals without creating unacceptable side and aftereffects. The goals should have been determined by analysis. Implementation will take place once the design is reviewed and accepted. Some considerations must be apparent before we start discussing design.

DESIGN OCCURS WITHIN A BOUNDARY WHICH DETERMINES SCOPE

One of the most difficult activities in designing a system is agreeing on the system boundary. There are tradeoffs in choosing a small or large boundary. A smaller boundary could mean that a working version of the system is completed earlier. Fewer resources are needed to achieve results, which usually will be more limited. There will be fewer people involved with the development effort. This may increase the chances for success. But a small boundary may disappoint those who will not receive the results they expected from a new system.

A larger boundary could mean that more people are receiving outputs from the system, thus receiving results which would enable them to do their jobs more expeditiously. But a larger boundary also means that more persons must agree on system specifications. This could delay development efforts and increase resources needed to complete the system.

The systems developer must try to balance the rational and economic reasons for the system's scope with the emotional and political reasons. Above all, the organization must benefit. One way to accomplish this is to have a task force representing different factions which will help the systems development team decide on an appropriate boundary, rather than leaving it to chance or political clout.

Attempts to satisfy a greater number of system users has led to a ***versioned approach*** to systems development, where the decision is made to develop the system in versions of increased scope and automation. Documented plans of the system versions will allow users to understand when they would receive their desired deliverables. If there is a structurally sound design, this type of modular development is possible.

DESIGN IS LIMITED BY CONSTRAINTS

The systems developer must be aware of the resource and governing constraints on design. ***Resource constraints*** would include factors such as organizational buy or make policies with regard to software, budget constraints, and available development personnel. ***Governing constraints*** include factors such as compatibility with currently used hardware and software, acceptable hardware and software vendors, union restrictions, personnel policies, and laws which must be considered.

DESIGN IS ITERATIVE

A designer must understand that the first draft of the design may have to be revised many times. Like the architect with the plans for a new building, reviews with involved parties will result in suggested changes, additions, and deletions. Following procedures for team product reviews can aid in iteration until an acceptable design is achieved.

The initially proposed design must be viewed as a draft that should be easy to modify on paper, or, in the case of a prototyped system, within the physically represented system. Once the system is built, it is not as easy to change. The attitude of the designer is most important. The designer must not let his or her ego become involved in the design, but must believe that reviewing early and often will result in the most acceptable design.

DESIGN USUALLY CANNOT BE PLANNED PRECISELY

Because design is iterative and creative, it cannot be planned precisely. It is difficult to predict how long creativity will take and hard to put a time estimate on "coming up with a good idea." This is comparable to an artist saying that "it is done when it is done." However, some estimate or constraint must be put on the process, or it could take forever.

A first draft of a design may be approved, or it may be sent "back to the drawing board." The design is finished when it is approved by the reviewing parties.

DESIGN CAN BE VIEWED HIERARCHICALLY

Design must be accomplished at different levels of detail. It may be ideal to complete a design from the top-down with approval of each level of detail. But there will be constraints such as prespecified, detailed procedures that will force the designer to move from the bottom-up or the middle-out. Once the design is finished, it may be presented and documented as a hierarchical set of subsystems like any good systems model.

DESIGN CAN BE EITHER LOGICAL OR PHYSICAL OR BOTH

An idealistic view of design is to move from a logical model to a physical model. For example, data storage specification ideally would move from a specification of what entities are stored, to what attributes are associated with the entities, to final decisions on physical storage medium and field length of elements. Realistically, there will be predetermined physical specifications since often there are no choices on things such as physical devices to be used or attribute field length. The designer must accept these limitations as givens and consider them as constraints.

A meaningful progression is to stay as "logical" as possible until it is necessary to be "physical." But sooner or later it will be necessary to be vendor- and device-specific in terms of hardware. The designer must balance "analysis/paralysis" with making too early a commitment to hardware and software that will constrain the needed solution. The governing factor is to understand the problem and its environment well enough to propose solutions.

DESIGN INCLUDES BOTH PEOPLE AND TECHNOLOGY

Although a primary consideration is to propose hardware, systems software, communications technology, and application software as part of the design, the designer must not forget that people are part of the system. Job design, human procedures, and person–machine dialogs must be designed into the proposed system, not added as an afterthought. The new system will be sociotechnical, not just a mass of technology.

Designers must not lose sight of operational feasibility—whether the new system will be accepted. Humans must be able to perform new business tactics that will lead to business achievements of increased revenues and/or reduced costs.

GETTING THE DESIGN STARTED

Once the data is collected on the current system, its limitations, and some alternative logical models, we must define the project size and scope by examining different system boundaries and getting agreement from management and users. Since many alternative solutions are possible, how well each meets the organization needs must be examined. This is like picking from a menu of different types and sizes of meals for different prices.

Once the system boundary is selected, the degree of automation is decided. The mix of people and technology necessary to implement a new system of a certain scope often is called "physicalizing."

There are two major factors to consider in specifying design alternatives:

1. Specifying the System Boundary. This is a determination of which subsystems the system will include. Often, this discussion will include what business functions will be included in the new system. For example, is this a payroll system; a payroll and personnel system; a payroll, personnel, and training system; a payroll and general ledger system; or a payroll, personnel, and general ledger system? From our definitions of systems in Chapter 1, we know that many subsystems are interconnected. When investigating one system, we often find that persons in interfacing systems also feel a change could be of benefit. To adequately plan a new system and specify a budget, we must know what the system includes.

2. Specifying the Physical Implementation of the System. This decision will specify the technology that will be used in the design of the system. At one time, the physical system was not difficult to specify. There were not many alternatives. Now there are a multitude of vendors, computer sizes, terminals, data storage types, networks, workstations, etc. The decision is no longer as simple as it once was.

Alternatives must be established for distribution of processing power and data. Distributed processing versus centralized processing must be evaluated on the merits for the system under study. This is done by determining which business tactics can be performed and business objectives can be achieved by an alternative physical implementation.

The need for information in different locations is a primary consideration in making distribution decisions. What new revenues can be generated or what costs can be avoided with improved information will influence the decision.

The physical implementation decision also must establish a person–machine boundary, also called an ***automation boundary***. This will include what people will do and what machines will do. It will also show where humans interact with machines, thus identifying locations where person–machine dialogs must be developed.

Establishing the boundary is done by examining the processes on the logical model and data flow diagram, and determining which ones require the strengths of humans and which ones require the strength of machines. This critical decision has led to new views of many processes such as manufacturing. The introduction of robotics has changed the nature of many systems.

Often, human tasks are found on the more detailed levels of data flow diagrams. Handling exceptions or errors, answering questions from people in atypical processing situations, and dealing with irate people are handled best by humans. Machines handle best repetitious activities or processes that require much memory.

The decision on physicalizing is based on the feasibility of each system alternative. Economic, technical, and operational feasibility must be examined for each alternative. The requirements model built in Process 2 provides information on both costs and benefits for each alternative. The value added/cost displaced must be weighed against system cost. The system investment must have an adequate return on resources expended, just like any organizational investment.

If the project continues to be part of the project mix, and an alternative has been selected, the project again is planned and scheduled.

We will now look at Process 3 in more detail.

Process 3: Propose Systems Solutions

Purpose: Establish a menu of possible system solutions at different costs to obtain different benefits. Project sponsors must choose the alternative that most closely meets their needs at an acceptable cost.

Output: A defined system boundary for the proposed new system indicating what subsystems will be included. Within the system boundary, the person–machine boundary must be established. This will enable the system designers to propose alternative hardware and software solutions.

Subprocesses: Determine any simplification, compression, modification, and elimination of existing processes and data. Add any new processes and data stores. Generate a set of alternative system boundaries and gain approval on one. Generate and get approved a person–machine boundary.

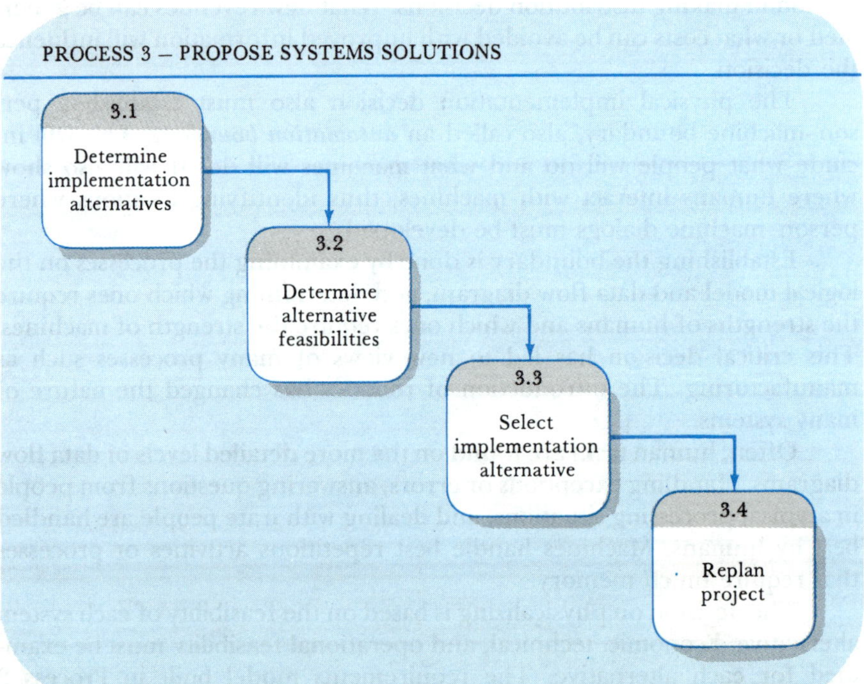

FIGURE 8.1
Subprocesses within Process 3.

Techniques and Skills: Presenting, peer/user reviewing, data flow diagramming, data structuring.

Activities within Process 3 of a systems development project include determining the implementation alternatives (Process 3.1), determining the feasibility of each proposed alternative (Process 3.2), selecting an alternative that best meets organizational needs (Process 3.3), and replanning the project with more certainty (Process 3.4). (See Figure 8.1.)

The reader must remember that not all processes are carried out for each project. For example, there may be so many organizational constraints that only one design is possible. Each of these processes may take a different amount of time and require different skill sets. These factors are part of the reason that systems development work is so challenging.

PROCESS 3.1 - DETERMINE IMPLEMENTATION ALTERNATIVES

As mentioned earlier, implementation alternatives include two considerations, system boundary and the degree and type of automation. Since the alternative mix has two dimensions, it makes sense to represent the alternatives as a two-dimensional table with one dimension being subsystem boundaries and the other being the degree of automation (see Figure 8.2). The intersecting points would have a value for benefits and costs for each alternative combination. This table is the end result of each of the design proposals and should be kept in mind while generating alternatives.

An example of what an actual implementation alternatives matrix might look like is shown in Figure 8.3. Note that the payroll and benefits reporting system with decentralized entry and centralized processing may provide the most value. A manual system that would attempt to manage a personnel database may actually cost more than the benefits it would

The more detailed levels of data flow diagrams often include the tasks that are done by humans, such as interacting on a personal level with customers. (Innervisions)

			Automation Alternatives		
			Automation Alternative 1	*Alternative 2*	*Alternative 3 etc*
Subsystem Boundary Alternatives	Subsystem Alternative	1	$$$	$$$	
		2	$$$		
		3			
		etc			

FIGURE 8.2

The implementation alternatives matrix.

provide. Some combinations that include decentralized processing may be very costly due to distributed computing power and communications networks and may not be as cost-effective since they would not provide substantial offsetting benefits. Computing the above costs and including them in a tabular form would assist the project team in making an implementation decision.

The system boundary consideration requires examining the logical model of the proposed system to determine which processes, data stores, and data flows might fit together to comprise a reasonable alternative. Only a small part of the system proposed in Process 2 may actually be pursued. The "biggest" may not be the "best" when benefits are measured against costs. The most costly alternative may provide only marginal benefits.

The logical model, represented by the highest-level data flow diagram, is reviewed by the analyst and the project sponsor to determine reasonable alternatives to a full-blown system. The funding authority may make a decision to provide resources for some subset of the larger system proposal. Two methods can be used for defining subsets:

	Automation Alternatives			
	Manual	*Centralized Entry/ Processing*	*Decentralized Entry/Central Processing*	*Decentralized Entry/ Processing*
Boundary Alternatives				
Payroll check writing	$13K	$26K	$29K	$16K
Check writing and payroll history	$7K	$29K	$37K	$11K
Payroll and benefits reporting system	$5K	$36K	$42K	$29K
Payroll and personnel database system	–$23K	$32K	$34K	$32K

FIGURE 8.3

Alternatives for the proposed payroll/personnel system. (Amounts shown indicate present value dollars of system alternative benefits minus costs in thousands of dollars.)

1. Defining sets of processes which, when considered together, will make up a sensible whole.
2. Defining sets of deliverables or outputs, also considered as systems objectives, which would be achieved by the alternative.

This set of alternative boundaries is needed if a decision is made to contact outside vendors. The proposals which vendors make must include a clear statement of the system boundary their proposals are supporting. This is the only sensible way to have common comparisons.

The degree and type of automation consideration requires examining currently available automation alternatives. These considerations include sequential versus random file structures, batch versus online entry from the data source, batch versus online processing, file versus database organization, processing capacity distribution, data storage distribution, and various communication strategies.

This book is not meant to be an exposition on the latest technology or processing methods. It is assumed that the reader has a working knowledge of technology alternatives and will call on vendors as well as organization technology experts to define these strategies. Many of the actual choices between technical alternatives will be dictated by existing information systems plans, actual capabilities existing in the organization, or policies, either written or unwritten. In a few cases, a new system proposal could cause this plan to change.

The focus for creating alternatives is the requirements model. The goal is to propose reasonable sets of systems tactics (how the system will behave) to meet different business objectives (what the organization desires to achieve in terms of increased revenues or reduced costs).

There are many sources of information on technical solutions. Besides going to vendors with information system objectives and allowing them to propose means (systems tactics) to meet the objectives, there are information services that specialize in comparing and contrasting technologic capacities and prices. These include Datapro, Auerbach, or publications such as the ICP Quarterly.

The organization also may have constraints that are part of the system objectives. For example, there may be favored vendor lists or policies that prohibit the use of service bureaus. The organization also may have guidelines on making or buying software.

The desired or needed capacities of processing volumes, speeds, or response times may be met with existing hardware, software, and telecommunications facilities. Even if this is true, it is necessary to determine how much a new system will tax existing capacities or alter current processing priorities.

PROCESS 3.2 - DETERMINE ALTERNATIVE FEASIBILITIES

Each of the alternatives must be evaluated for feasibility. This includes:

Technical feasibility: "Can we do it with today's technology?"

Economic feasibility: "What is the alternative's payback?"

Operational feasibility: "Will the alternative be used if implemented in our organization?"

One of the things that must be done is to eliminate unreasonable alternative combinations. For example, if there were three possible system boundaries and five possible technologic implementations, fifteen total possibilities would exist. Some may not make sense and should be eliminated. For example, a sophisticated technical solution with a wide system boundary might not use human strengths, and thus would not be a wise alternative.

Feasibility assessments must include a statement of risk for any alternative. There will be technical risks, such as in using pioneering technologies; economic risks, such as potential high gains but with high chance of failure; and operational risks, where an excellent system is not used. These risks are part of the feasibility assessment. Notes should be made if the designer believes an alternative includes a high risk.

Technical Feasibility

As we learned in Chapter 1, there are different ways of arriving at the same systems output. This factor must be considered in examining technical feasibility. Some systems solutions are more technically feasible than others, yet provide the same output. For example, logically, data must be input to a system. Physically, this can be done in several ways. Keys can be struck, menus can be invoked, or voice can be detected. But, depending on voice to enter masses of data may not be a technically feasible alternative. The technology may not exist that ensures the volume and accuracy that is needed. However, if a few commands are needed to choose previously generated screens of data, the technology may exist.

The task of the analyst is to view needed capabilities in light of currently available technology. Care should be taken not to trust everything vendors or trade publications promise. "Vaporware" is a term that resulted from unfulfilled promises for hardware and software which existed only in spoken or written words.

The availability of needed expertise must be considered in the technical feasibility analysis. Proposing a new system using satellite communications technology if no one is available organizationally or on a consulting basis to recommend or support such a decision may influence technical feasibility.

Economic Feasibility

As with any investment, the investment in a new or changed system must provide a reasonable return. An expenditure for system development, new hardware and software, and new positions must be offset with increased revenues or avoided costs from meeting business objectives.

New costs which must be considered include:

1. Costs of implementing the proposed system tactics (hardware, software, communications, site changes, rentals, supplies)
2. Costs of continuing the systems development (designing, constructing, implementing)
3. Costs of performing new organization tactics (job redesign, new hires, union contracts, relocation costs)
4. Costs of preparing persons and machines to perform new tactics (training, parallel operation, conversion, data preparation)
5. Costs of maintaining the proposed system alternative over its life (fixes, enhancements, supplies).

New benefits would include:

1. Increased marginal revenues from reducing existing:
   a. Organizational operating costs
   b. System operating costs
2. Increased marginal revenues from new opportunities (revenues minus the cost of generating the revenues)

These costs and benefits must be examined on a period by period basis over the projected life of the system. Accounting and financial persons should aid in both defining an appropriate period (monthly, quarterly, yearly) and in determining the "present value" of economic considerations. Since we are dealing with estimates, best versus worst case scenarios with sensitivity analysis should be applied.

Operational Feasibility

Operational feasibility determination ensures that proposed alternatives will be accepted without destructive resistance. When considering operational feasibility, it is reasonable to use the technique of behavioral auditing. This approach is described in Chapter 10.

Many systems have failed because they did not fit within existing job descriptions or duties or within the organizational structure. The need to redefine jobs or organizational relationships must be specified. Personnel department members should be included in this activity. Considerations of factors like government regulations or union rules may make proposed system alternatives unreasonable.

Upsetting social or work group patterns, destroying individual self-worth or ability to grow, or reducing economic security could all turn into real problems. Further consideration of these factors will be done in Chapter 10. There will be resistance to change, and the systems developer must make sure that the change is managed.

Consideration must be taken of clerical level persons whose job may change, middle management persons who could get different system outputs or have to change their management methods, and top management who will need to direct the organization in an environment they may find uncomfortable due to a perceived loss of control.

PROCESS 3.3 - SELECT IMPLEMENTATION ALTERNATIVE

The purpose of this subprocess is to assemble and present information on the system alternatives to the funding body. Exhibits of the logical configurations and technological considerations are created. Financial implications of the alternatives are presented in tabular and graphical formats. Contents of the presentation include why the alternative should be considered, why the alternative is feasible, what would be done by the alternative, how it would be done, and the impact and risk for the organization.

Such a presentation will allow users and funding authorities to integrate their plans with the systems work. The systems project could be considered an intrusion unless conscious integration into the workplace is planned. The actual implementation decision *must* be made by management and users, not the systems department. The system is being built for the users.

If the user groups cannot agree on the size or scope of the project, the role of the systems developer is not to take sides or to settle arguments, but to provide information that will aid in reaching a consensus. If needed, the developer might recommend to his or her superiors that there is a conflict that will require intervention by a higher authority. Conflicting units may have to be reminded that they all work for the same organization.

The alternatives matrix mentioned earlier in the chapter is used here as a conscious attempt to provide a stimulus for data collection, a framework for data aggregation and presentation, and an aid in using data in a decision provoking format. The matrix helps increase comfórt after a decision is made. By consulting the information used, the justification for the decision can be supported.

A project may be discontinued at this stage of development. It is more appropriate to cut off future funding if the return on investment does not look favorable. The benefit gained from the initial systems development work is the documentation of the system. This will aid in maintenance of the system and any other future development considerations.

The alternative selection will lend more certainty to the rest of the systems development project. System size and scope, technology to be used, and make/buy contract decisions will give a clearer picture of the end result.

PROCESS 3.4 - REPLAN PROJECT

Once an alternative has been selected, remaining tasks can be selected and estimated and the human resources needed to complete the project can be assigned. Keeping continuity by assigning persons familiar with the project is usually a good idea. Attempts also should be made to schedule any specialists that will be needed in the next development processes.

Information that will be aggregrated at this stage will include:

Hardware and software needs

Training or hiring needs (required people skills)

Test needs

Installation needs

Conversion needs (new files and formats)

Development needs (needed development activities)

The specifications will indicate the needed outcomes so that design work can continue in the next development processes.

DETAILING THE SELECTED ALTERNATIVE

Since the system boundary or degree of automation has not been decided until this point, it has not been necessary to describe the current or proposed system in great detail. The detail is added at this point, and is done in a logical manner to establish long-lasting documentation, since the logical system likely will not change very much.

Since this process is adding to the documentation on the existing logical models and at the same time proposing physical solutions, there is a gray area here whether the process is really detailed analysis or generalized design. This only exhibits the point that there are more gray areas in the systems field than there are blacks and whites.

In this process, the areas that are not included in the selected system boundary are removed from the work plans. This would include reduction of the logical, requirements, and organizational documentation that will not be part of the newly revised system. Of course, this documentation is not destroyed. It is moved from active, day-to-day working and revision status to information-providing status to aid in maintaining the unchanged system components.

Next, two concurrent subprocesses take place. The logical data flow model is detailed down to the lowest level of "explosion." Data stores and data flows are also detailed. The data structures and data elements are described. If needed, application software is selected. Necessary hardware and systems software is selected. Final contracts are drawn up and secured at this time for any acquisitions of hardware and software.

Process 4: Detail Chosen Solution

Purpose: Detail logically the data storage, data flows, and data processing within the chosen system boundary. Decide on system acquisition and make any vendor decisions.

Output: A statement of selected vendors as well as detailed new system specifications. This may include a statement of the use of

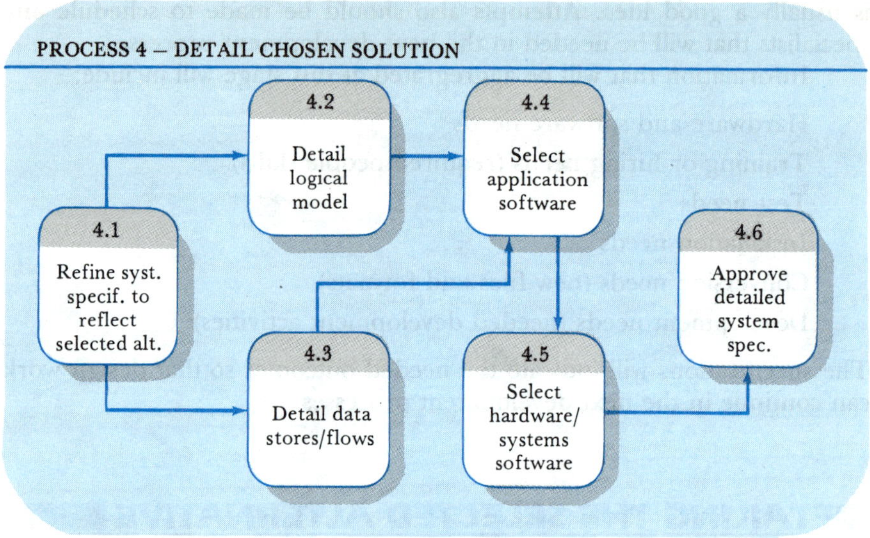

FIGURE 8.4

Subprocesses within Process 4.

specific software packages, programming languages, or system generators.

Subprocesses: Refine and explode subprocesses and data stores and flows for the selected alternative. Include error handling, audit control, and backup and recovery details. Select application software to be acquired. Select hardware and systems software and communication network. Select any external data sources. Secure needed contracts.

Techniques and Skills: Data flow diagramming, presenting, peer and user reviewing, vendor selection, contract negotiation, technology configuration generation, audit and control design, backup and recovery design.

Activities within Process 4 of a systems development project shown in Figure 8.4 include refining the system specification to include only data on the selected alternative (Process 4.1), detailing the logical model (Process 4.2), detailing the included data stores and flows (Process 4.3), selecting any application software that has to be purchased (Process 4.4), selecting any hardware or systems software (Process 4.5), and approving the revised system specification (Process 4.6). It should be noticed that not all of these processes may need to be done for a project. For example, there may be no application software to be purchased, or existing hardware or systems software may be sufficient to meet systems needs.

PROCESS 4.1 - REFINE SYSTEM SPECIFICATION TO REFLECT SELECTED ALTERNATIVE

Usually, the system specification is developed at a general level of detail with a wide system boundary. The system models represent all possibilities for the new system. Now that the boundary is selected, it is necessary to refine the logical, requirements, and business models to represent only the selected alternative.

The logical model is refined by creating an appropriate subset of external entities, data flows, data stores, and processes that reflect the selected alternative. Revised data flow diagrams and data dictionary entries are created. All the logical model entities that are not within the boundary are referenced and saved for use in maintenance of the system that will not be changed, but may still be operational within the company.

The requirements models are changed to include only relevant system objectives and tactics, and affected business objectives and tactics. A good starting point may be the system objectives, or what the system will produce, then moving to the business tactics and objectives. When examining the business tactics, it may be wise to note who performs the tactics so changes can be made to the people subsystem.

In reviewing the above three models, it is appropriate to note whether any physical resources may need to be acquired. This could include hardware, systems software, communication services or devices, application software, and supplies. Since these aspects have been consciously ignored until this point, a more conscious effort now can be made to start thinking of the system in terms of a final configuration.

In conducting this subprocess, there may be some cases where the boundary may not have been drawn wide enough. In this case, the models may have to be expanded. This is an example of some of the iteration that is needed since this actually means going back to perform some of the activities in Process 2 to gather and record appropriate information.

PROCESS 4.2 - DETAIL LOGICAL MODEL

One of the required processes in any systems development project is to detail the logical model that was refined in Process 4.1. The steps followed include explosion of normal processes, explosion of error and exception processes, detailing of support processes such as audit, control, and security and backup and recovery, creation of process logic descriptions, and approval of the logical model details.

We begin the process by exploding the normal processes. The focus is to concentrate on mainline processing. The details are needed to handle good transactions or data that must be transformed or stored. This really is the detailing of the business and system tactics from the requirements model which are supported by the processes in the logical model. As we had discussed in earlier chapters, there are relationships between the entities in the models used to describe a system.

Next, we add and detail the error handling and exception processes. These are the activities needed if everything does not go perfectly—exceptions to the mainline processing. Error handling is especially important in designing an interactive online system. Persons dealing with a system in an interactive mode must be treated as if the system could handle any of their activities. The technique of dialog designing, which will be described in Chapter 11, will be especially useful to help in create these interfaces.

Processes for handling audit, control, and security must also be detailed. These are the additional overhead that must be added to a system to maintain integrity of data and processsing. These will be discussed in more detail in Chapter 12.

Needs for backup and recovery processing must also be specified at this time. This is to ensure that in the event of a system failure, the system will be able to reconstruct the needed databases and files.

In the "explosion" of logical processes, a point is reached where it is not meaningful to break the process down any further. This is often referred to as a "primitive" representation. At this stage, the logic to complete the process may still be complex. In that case, process logic descriptions may have to be developed. These descriptions may be done using techniques such as decision tables, decision trees, structured or "tight" English, and grids or tables which will be discussed in Chapter 10.

All of the detailing of the processes must be reviewed using the techniques of peer and user team product reviews. It is critical to have users of the processes review the processes, not only to improve the quality of the activities but also to improve the chances of acceptance and resulting operational feasibility.

PROCESS 4.3 - DETAIL DATA STORES AND FLOWS

The purpose of this subprocess is to create a complete logical description of all data stores and flows to help the database designer make decisions on the actual design of data storage. This will include complete descriptions of the data structures and data elements for each of the data stores and flows. Attention also must be given to the requirements for:

Accesses to data and their frequency

Privacy and security

Frequency of backup of each data structure

Editing to assure accuracy

Coding

Volatility or frequency of change

Time that old editions must be kept

Design decisions will become more physical as needs are matched against actual storage devices. Factors such as data element lengths, mediums for storage of backups, and encrypting of data will be determined with the aid of a database designer.

The needed output data flows from a data store are matched against the data store contents to specify the data flow inputs. The developer must keep the systems objectives in mind, since they are the results or outputs which the processing must provide. The data must exist to provide the outputs. Data access diagrams are also used to specify data store entities and relationships. The data needed to satisfy user requirements for data accesses is matched against the data available as part of stored or derived data.

The data store contents are then simplified through a technique called *normalization,* which will be discussed further in Chapter 9. Normalization will present the data in simplified tabular form so that both the database designer and the users of the data can meaningfully communicate about the data. An argument can be made to keep the data in second normal form to eliminate confusion about derived data elements. At the final design stage, the derived data elements may either be calculated or stored depending on the tradeoffs between extra storage and time to calculate the element.

The results of Process 4.3 should provide enough information to commence database or file design.

PROCESS 4.4 - SELECT APPLICATION SOFTWARE

Process 4.4 is one of the subprocesses that is not always done. It only needs to be done if the decision is made to investigate the purchase of application software. If this is the case, much time could be spent on this subprocess.

The subprocess converts a general statement of needed application software to a detailed specification, gathers data on viable options, and selects a vendor that best meets the set criteria. Since there may be a combination of make/buy to obtain needed application software, careful coordination of needs and compatibility is needed. It may be necessary for consultants, information services, and legal staff to be involved in specifying and contracting for new software.

Existing documentation, usually part of the system objectives stated in the requirements model, must be viewed and understood to obtain information on functions needed, performance needs, output requirements, constraints, standards, costs, vendor support, and modifiability rights. These criteria should be stated as "must haves," "like to haves,", and "nice to haves" so vendors can understand priorities. All criteria that are measurable or "benchmarkable," such as response time, capacities, and hardware performance characteristics should be recorded. These criteria must be reviewed by "experts" such as database adminstrators, quality and standards groups, technical support staff, audit staff, and others.

A request for proposal (RFP) may be needed to state in standard form needs to vendors. Vendors could include hardware vendors, software houses, network services, and user groups.

Documentation exists on software available for purchase. It can be found in trade magazines, in promotional material, from current users, from consultants, and from rating services such as Data Pro, Auerbach, or International Computer Programs (ICP). Care should be taken to interpret facts as facts, and opinions as opinions.

The RFP should request a standard set of criteria and format for submission. If not, it will be impossible to compare proposals. Unacceptable bids should be sent back if content and/or format are not presented as requested. Resubmission is allowable if schedules can be met. All of these practices should be clearly and frankly communicated to bidding vendors. An RFP should contain at minimum:

1. A cover letter explaining why the RFP is being sent and an identifying résumé for your organization.
2. A procedure specification with a schedule of dates and time for response, an explanation of how vendor questions will be handled, a common format for response, and a proposed installation schedule.
3. A statement of contractual terms and conditions, including payment and penalty clauses.
4. A statement of existing facilities and specific site requirements.
5. A statement of evaluation criteria to be used and the evaluation method.
6. Any supporting detail such as logical models, data dictionary entries, etc.

Vendors, who have a great deal to gain by selling software, may become a nuisance. There may be a need to have potential vendors contact you only at times you specify. Otherwise, vendors can be bothersome. Vendor conferences where vendors have a set time to make a presentation, phone calls only on specified days between specified hours, and site visits to other software users may reduce the intrusions.

All of the data on the proposed software must be aggregated, reviewed, and evaluated. Evaluation criteria include:

1. Does the package do what we need? Are the processes as indicated on the data flow diagrams supported by the package? Is there adequate control and editing?
2. How installable is the package? Does it fit our hardware with regard to storage and peripheral devices? Does it fit our systems software?
3. How good is predicted performance? Can we meet our systems objectives with regard to throughput, response time, down-time, etc.?
4. How usable is the package? Are the input and output formats acceptable to users? Are written procedures understandable and performable? Can the system be audited?
5. How changeable is the package? Is the software structure acceptable?
6. How do you and your company feel about the vendor? Reputation, time in existence, aid promised, training promised, quality feeling generated, representatives and service personnel image?

Some of the data received may need to be reworked to be meaningfully compared. If multiple vendors are needed to satisfy requirements, a compatibility review must be conducted.

There are many methods for evaluation of proposals. Some type of weighted-point technique with minimum thresholds of performance or features may be appropriate. The weighted-point technique takes the criteria from the RFP and gives each feature a numeric weight to indicate importance. Each competitor then is scored on the criteria and a summary score is calculated.

The successful vendor must be contacted to negotiate any scheduling needs and other unsettled terms and conditions. The legal staff may need to be involved in establishing such a contract. Needless to say, unsuccessful vendors also must be contacted to assure that the systems department is not bothered any further and to retain cordial relations for future contact.

PROCESS 4.5 - SELECT HARDWARE AND SYSTEMS SOFTWARE

This step involves collection and evaluation of hardware and systems software alternatives in order to choose an appropriate alternative. Even if no acquisition of new hardware and systems software is needed, an estimate of the added burden on existing facilities must be done. This will prevent each new system from reducing total capacities which could degrade total system throughput. The process involves specifying criteria and needs, determining alternatives, collecting data on alternatives, and making a choice.

The process begins with an examination of the stated system objectives and tactics in the requirements model. The system objectives should include constraints such as allowable vendors or systems compatible with the existing environment. The objectives also will give performance criteria such as response times or capacity requirements such as volumes of data and projected growths. The system tactics may give some clues to the type of processing environment that will be required.

Some of the same activities that governed Process 4.4 to select application software will be needed in this process. We must specify mandatory thresholds of performance and storage as "must haves," moving on to optional "like to haves." Measurable criteria such as response times, processing speeds for masses of transactions, and storage must be quantified. All of these specifications may be put together in a document which may serve as a request for proposal (RFP). These specifications must then be reviewed by appropriate groups such as computer operations, technical support groups, and others with special technical skills.

Documents such as Auerbach reports, ICP reports, and other sources of vendor information are used to create potential vendor lists. Vendors are asked to submit proposals. In some companies, only one vendor is dealt with, so it is a matter of asking that vendor for a bid. If there is a competition among vendors, data is collected and evaluated, further questions are clarified as in Process 4.4, vendor claims are substantiated by benchmarks or site visits, and a choice is made.

PROCESS 4.6 - APPROVE DETAILED SYSTEM SPECIFICATION

This subprocess includes the review activity needed to communicate and approve the work accomplished in Process 4. The specifications must be reviewed by groups such as technical services to ensure that any plans will fit into hardware and systems software plans, and quality assurance groups must see that organizational standards are followed. Users must be certain needs will be met, and management must ensure that the proposed alternative will align with organizational strategy. Special groups such as human resources will have to see that there will be no violations of personnel practices and labor agreements.

The subprocess begins by aggregating all specifications for the system. Reviews are planned for each of the relevant subgroups mentioned above. Finally, any contracts are secured with agreement on delivery schedules, return privileges, penalty clauses for late delivery, and any other legal considerations. Once all these activities take place, a more elaborate plan is established for the remaining development processes and subjected to review by the development resources allocation groups.

CREATING THE PHYSICAL DESIGN BLUEPRINT

Now that all the data is collected for the selected alternative in terms of system scope and degree of automation, the actual physical design begins. This will be the blueprint for the final system. The previous processes have all provided the information necessary to do an adequate job of design.

The systems designer is responsible for physical design, including inspecting the building for adequate support facilities such as wiring and ventilation. (Innervisions)

Now is the time to design the physical structure of the programs, human procedures, person and machine interfaces, input/output layouts, and files and databases. File and/or database conversion programs must also be designed. This work is likened to that of an architect who makes certain the builders have a good blueprint to work from when "construction" starts in Process 6.

Process 5: Design New Physical System

Purpose: Specify, review, and approve the structure of nonacquired software, human procedures, physical facilities, and data bases.

Output: A physical representation of the system inputs, outputs, programs, procedures, and storage. Included are program structure charts, human procedures, input/output layouts, file and database structures, and physical site plans.

Subprocesses: Design human subsystem, including layout formats, procedures, manuals, and training. Design technology subsystem. Design data structure subsystem. Design physical site specifications. Specify data conversion procedures.

Techniques and Skills: Human and machine dialog design, input/output layout design, structure charting, data structuring, site planning, manual writing, training development, procedure writing.

Activities within Process 5 of a systems development project shown in Figure 8.5 include designing the human subsystem (Process 5.1), designing the basic automated subsystem (Process 5.2), designing the file and database structures (Process 5.3), designing new physical site facilities (Process 5.4), designing the input/output subsystems (Process 5.5), designing the file and data subsystems (Process 5.6), designing the data conversion specifications (Process 5.7), and assembling and reviewing the aggregated system design (Process 5.8).

PROCESS 5.1 - DESIGN HUMAN SUBSYSTEM

Up to this point, the system models represented the human subsystem in a logical fashion. For example, correct content was more important than format in specifying reports and screens. Now, with a complete understanding of what must be produced and when, attention must be paid to specific "hows."

System objectives are reviewed to obtain report and screen contents. The data dictionary will be useful in doing this. Then with the aid of the users of outputs, layouts are established. It may even be possible to have users do the layout design. Consideration must be made of regulations which may dictate layouts. For example, tax forms filed with the government may have to follow prespecified formats and layouts. The topic of layout design will be addressed in Chapter 11.

Procedures must be written to perform human processes. Procedures will be needed for input providers, output users, actual process performers, and operations personnel who run automated devices. The procedures

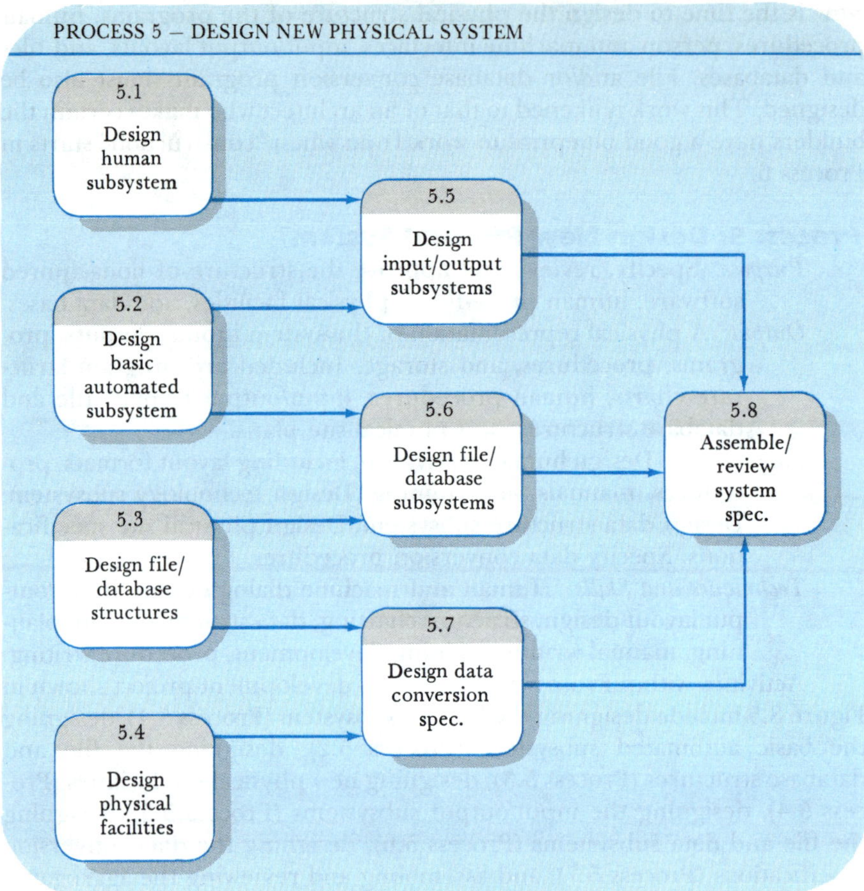

FIGURE 8.5

Subprocesses within Process 5.

will be developed using some of the procedure specification techniques to be addressed in Chapter 10. If vendor-provided packages are used, they already may include the needed procedures or be the basis for modification. Some of the procedures involve interaction with an automated device. Design of these person/machine dialogs will be discussed in Chapter 11.

All of the procedures will probably fit in either training or reference manuals, which will be designed at this time. They will include what the content and order will be and is similiar to a book proposal where an outline of the content is presented, even though the specific paragraphs still have to be written. A training plan to allow needed performance objectives to be met is also specified at this time. The establishment of such a plan is discussed in Chapter 10.

Once the human subsystem is designed and assembled, it must be reviewed by performers, human resources persons, and trainers to assure performability. Quality assurance personnel may also review the subsystem to ensure adherance to organization standards.

PROCESS 5.2 - DESIGN BASIC AUTOMATED SUBSYSTEM

The purpose of this process is to transform detailed data flow diagrams into a basic structure chart which includes data transformation processes. This means that processes to accept input, generate output, and access the files and database are delayed until file and database structures are established.

The subprocess begins by isolating the processes on the data flow diagrams that actually transform the data, rather than obtain, access, or display it. Next, a modular design is created using the technique for developing a structure chart. Structure charting will be discussed in more detail in Chapter 9. The structure chart is reviewed by a group of peers for appropriate coupling between modules and cohesion within modules. Quality assurance reviews take place to ensure adherence to standards, and audit specialists review to ensure that adequate controls are included. Supporting documentation is included in the systems development database.

PROCESS 5.3 - DESIGN FILE AND DATABASE STRUCTURES

The purpose of this process is to design the files and databases required within the system. This process likely will be performed by a person specializing in file and database design. A specific outline of physical storage and layout is needed along with a specification of backup and recovery activities to assure data integrity. The designer must consider factors such as size, growth, and security to determine the static aspects of the stored data. Then the dynamic aspects such as processing activity, access activity, and ordering must be considered to assure that data movement is possible with alternative designs. Finally, reviews are done to assure that requirements can be met.

Since database design is a discipline in itself, it will not be discussed in much detail in this book. See some of the references at the end of this chapter for sources of more information. This exemplifies the many skills a systems developer personally must have or have available from experts.

PROCESS 5.4 - DESIGN PHYSICAL FACILITIES

The purpose of this process is to establish a plan to provide needed physical facilities within the office or physical site. This could be as simple as buying some new desks and chairs for a microcomputer or may be as complex as erecting a new building. It is essential that the physical environment be ready for new hardware and people.

This process should commence as soon as a commitment is made to the completion of the system and an alternative for automation is chosen. There have been some lengthy system delays waiting for the physical space and furniture needed for a system to become operational. Again, this can

> A large utility suffered some embarrassment when they realized that their new "showplace" computer facilities had some limitations. The new freight elevators would not accommodate the company's mainframe computer. The solution of removing outside windows and using a crane to get the computer to the appropriate floor attracted some significant press coverage. A few observers said they had a vision about the boat builder who built a "dream boat" in a basement workshop and then could not remove it.

be a complex activity where experts exist to aid in site planning. Experts have saved organizations from potential tragedies such as when a large computer system was initially planned to be installed on a floor beneath the company cafeteria where a spilled soup cauldron could have caused a system shutdown.

An installation plan is essential to coordinate the completion of the physical environment. The plan should include:

Site specifications, including air conditioning, offices, electric power for normal and emergency usage, storage space for supplies, and security, including new locks, and insurance

Modifications to existing hardware and systems software

Location sequences if multiple sites are included

Installation sequences so a raised floor is ready before hardware arrives

Training sequences to assure new hardware and software can be operated and maintained

These plans must be coordinated with testing plans so that hardware and systems software are available when application software is to be tested.

The objective of this process is to have a clear plan ready to accept any new acquisitions, have space available for them, be able to operate them, and be able to keep them maintained.

PROCESS 5.5 - DESIGN INPUT/OUTPUT SUBSYSTEMS

The purpose of this process is to specify the input/output computer program modules needed to accept data for, and display data from, the system. The reason for delaying this process is to have both the input/output layouts from Process 5.1 and the basic structure chart from Process 5.2. Completing this as a separate activity will assure a significant amount of independence between the input/output modules and the processing modules.

Both data flow diagrams that show input and output data flow and dialog flow diagrams will aid in adding modules to the basic structure chart. The focus of the designer is to ensure that the data is available in a correct and edited form for processing, and that processed data can be output to satisfy the system objectives, which now will include the layouts specified in Process 5.1. Again team product reviews by peers, quality assurance, personnel workers, and auditors are performed to maintain system stability and integrity.

PROCESS 5.6 - DESIGN FILE AND DATABASE SUBSYSTEMS

The purpose of this process is to add any modules to the basic structure chart for file or database accesses that are needed to satisfy user queries. This is where systems development goes beyond transaction processing and reporting systems to satisfy management support needs.

Data structure and data immediate access diagrams are useful at this stage as checklists of needed retrievals. System objectives should give the designer any criteria for needed reporting. As well, the objectives will hold information on items such as passwords for security, authorized access lists, message identification needs, and controls needed in the system.

Specification of needed programs to test database security should also be done at this time. An independent group may be designated to perform this task if sensitive data is concerned. This group may play the role of "system busters" to ensure that real intruders cannot illegally access the system. Much of this work will be done by persons who specialize in database design and administration. Reviews by experts could also be done; these might be expensive in the short run, but could help avoid tragic situations at a later point.

PROCESS 5.7 - DESIGN DATA CONVERSION SPECIFICATION

The purpose of this process is to specify the procedures and programs needed to convert existing files and databases into a form usable with the new system. There must be a specification of a means to collect and establish databases which currently do not exist but will be needed for the new system. For example, outside data services may provide industry data which will need to be "massaged" to be usable in the new system.

Care must be taken at this stage to verify that data which the documentation says exists actually does exist. Some spot checks of actual data files might be done to assure that inputs to conversion software are clean and usable.

The developer must develop the processes which accept data and convert it to new forms and mediums of storage. This could include code conversions, field expansions, internal representation changes, and ordering changes such as changing dates to new formats. Programs also may be needed to calculate or derive new data elements from varied sources of input data.

Once conversion specifications are completed, a conversion plan must be started. A clear specification of how much historic data is needed and the timing of when outside data will be extracted and inserted must be done. A great challenge will be to do this type of conversion and maintain work in process. For example, it is no easy task to do inventory file conversions while files are actively used to keep the business running.

PROCESS 5.8 - ASSEMBLE AND REVIEW SYSTEM DESIGN

The purpose of this process is to assemble all the design components, check them for completeness, and subject them to rigorous reviews to assure all the pieces fit together before actual system building commences in Process 6. A plan for implementation of the system is completed and reviewed at this time.

A great danger at this stage of the systems development project is an attitude of "we'll figure it out later" toward questions of design specifics. A good feeling about adequate performance, changeability, and control should be felt at this time. If there are questions about the blueprints for the system, get them answered before construction begins. Any bridge or building engineer would certainly do this.

SUMMARY

This chapter has led us from taking the results of analysis to carrying them through to a specified system. There is much art as well as some science in coming up with a solid design. But now the project requestors should have a good idea of what they will receive from the system and what roles people in the organization must fulfill for success.

Excitement could be rampant at this stage of the project. Most of the system is specified. The situation is similar to placing an order for a new automobile after contemplating all the options, models, and colors. Once we know what we are getting, we impatiently wait for the final result. Now it is a matter of building the system—not an easy undertaking, but the "light at the end of the tunnel" should be apparent.

REFERENCES AND FURTHER READINGS

Adams, David R., Powers, Michael J., and V. Arthur Owles. *Computer Information Systems Development: Design and Implementation,* Cincinnati: South-Western Publishing Co., 1985.

Adams, James L. *Conceptual Blockbusting: A Guide to Better Ideas,* Reading, MA: Addison-Wesley Publishing Company, Inc., 3d ed., 1986.

Dickinson, Brian. *Developing Structured Systems: A Methodology Using Structured Techniques,* New York: Yourdon Press, 1981.

Everest, Gordon C. *Database Management: Objectives, System Functions, and Administration*, New York: McGraw-Hill Book Company, 1986.

Harris, James H. "Decision Making in the System Development Process," unpublished paper, Graduate School of Business Administration, University of Minnesota, June 1982, 34 pp.

Keane, John F., Keane, Marilyn, and Mark Teagan. *Productivity Management in the Development of Computer Applications,* Englewood Cliffs, NJ: Prentice-Hall Inc., 1984.

King, David. *Current Practices in Software Development,* New York: Yourdon Press, 1984.

Kroenke, David M. *Database Processing: Fundamentals, Design, and Implementation,* Chicago: Science Research Associates, Inc., 2d ed., 1983.

McFadden, Fred R., and Jeffrey A. Hoffer. *Data Base Management,* Menlo Park, CA: The Benjamin/Cummings Publishing Company, Inc., 1985.

Yourdon, Edward. *Managing the System Life Cycle: A Software Development Methodology Overview,* New York: Yourdon Press, 1982.

REVIEW QUESTIONS

1. Why is it difficult to precisely plan the design processes?
2. What is the difference between logical and physical design?
3. Why is it necessary to decide on the system boundary before proposing the degree of automation?
4. What is the difference between an automation and a system boundary?
5. What kinds of tasks should be assigned to humans when establishing an automation boundary? To machines?
6. Describe the three kinds of feasibility.
7. Why is risk important in proposing system requirements?
8. Where would a developer find information on technical solutions to a systems problem?
9. Why is it necessary to continually replan the project?
10. Why was the system detail not collected until Process 4?
11. What experts may have to be consulted when application software is acquired?
12. What is an RFP? Is one always developed? Why or why not?
13. Why is the physical design compared to a blueprint for a building, rather than the actual building?
14. What will happen to human procedures? Where will they be used?
15. What would be the role of a "system buster"?
16. Why would a systems project leader be worried if one of the developers commented that we will "play it by ear and figure out any design specifics later"?

DISCUSSION QUESTIONS

1. An experienced systems designer said: "It is more important to be able to present a design in an understandable manner and accept constructive criticism than it is to come up with a 'perfect' first design." Comment.
2. Based on what you understand about team product reviews from Chapter 7, why is it important to present designs early even though they may not be polished?
3. "A system that is not used provides no benefits." Discuss this statement in terms of the types of feasibility.
4. An ideal may be to design levels of a system from the top-down in a hierarchical fashion. Why might this not happen in the real world?
5. A person discussing systems design said his company bought software packages so it was not necessary to be concerned with systems design. How would you react to this? Would you agree that design is not needed in this case?

EXERCISES

1. A friend of yours is overwhelmed with data when trying to make a decision on a new microcomputer system. The system could be either a basic system with no software for $1689, the same basic system with a manual modem for $1785, or the basic system with an auto-answer/dial modem for $1825. With any of these systems, desired word processing software would cost $149, a desired spreadsheet would cost $99, a communication program would cost $79, and a database system would cost $219. Your friend definitely wants word processing, but only wants the communication program if a modem is bought. If she buys the spreadsheet program, she will also buy the database system. Present an alternatives matrix for the different alternatives such as the one shown in Process 3.1 of this chapter. Even though this matrix presents costs, your friend must be confronted with associating benefits of each configuration to make a meaningful decision.
2. Contact a systems development group for information on how it determines system and automation boundaries. Is the actual decision made by the project sponsors and users or the systems development group? Try to find out why it is done this way. Share your findings with the rest of the class.

CHAPTER 9

Designing for the Machine

CHAPTER OBJECTIVES

You should be able to:

- Understand the components of a physical system plan
- Understand the availability of physical devices and sources of information about them
- Understand the criteria for data file design
- Simplify data structures through inspection and normalization
- Understand the objectives of computer program design
- Convert a simple data flow diagram into a structure chart
- Recognize and avoid the pitfalls of poor computer program maintainability
- Review a computer program design and determine if it is good or bad

THIS CHAPTER INTRODUCES the physical and technical aspects of systems development. Hardware, telecommunication, and data specification is examined. File and database issues are introduced, including logical simplification using data store inspection and normalization. Program design using structure charts is introduced. Examples of data normalization and developing structure charts are included.

Up to now, most of the systems activities in this book have considered the *who, what,* and *why* of a system under development. Now the emphasis will turn to *how* the system might actually be implemented. With small systems or single-user decision support systems, reaching this stage of the project may come very quickly. There is not as much concern with *who* if there is only one user; *what* if the one person has a specific, even though unclear, need; and *why* if the person has an intuitive belief that the project has value and there is funding to support the project.

How is partially specified by system tactics in the requirements model. From the model we know that the information *system tactics must allow achieving system objectives,* which help users perform business tactics, which allow achievement of business objectives. Achieved business objectives allow the organization to achieve its goals, resulting in increased profits. The analyst must not lose sight of the overall objective—proposing system tactics that allow the achieving of system objectives.

Designing physical system tactics has become very complicated due to the development of a growing number of technology alternatives at reduced prices. As well, more new technologies at reduced prices are being introduced at a rapid rate. In many organizations in the past, it was a matter of verifying that the IBM salesperson had prescribed the hardware and software that you needed.

Today, the decision is a more complex and visible action. There are more vendors, sizes, devices, and systems software, that can meet requirements, plus organizational standards and recommended vendor lists. Adding to the complexity are decisions such as purchase versus lease versus rent, or the tax implications of physical equipment acquisition. These complexities make actual selection of a significant system a complex decision rarely made by a beginning analyst.

Rather than discussing how specific technologies are engineered, this chapter will explore general concepts and principles. The belief is that you don't have to know how it works to purchase and use it. This certainly is true in our increasingly technological world. There is a greater need for systems developers to understand the advantages of alternative technologies as well as the criteria for selecting a specific technology to satisfy system objectives. We assume that the systems developer will not be an expert in all the technical aspects of systems development. Moreover, the student of information systems will receive more detail on the topics in this chapter in courses in database, telecommunications, hardware and software, and programming methods.

ESTABLISHING A PHYSICAL SYSTEM PLAN

Before delving into the specific topics of hardware, software, and telecommunications, it is necessary to understand that the physical system architecture should be planned, much like any other activity that is to be successful. This section explains the components of a physical system plan and the criteria by which such a plan would be judged.

COMPONENTS OF A PHYSICAL SYSTEM PLAN

The physical systems plan must include a description of the physical devices and architecture that must be installed in the organization. Physical aspects include the following areas, which will be presented in more detail in this chapter:

Hardware and systems software (devices and operating systems)

Telecommunications (voice, data, text, and graphics transmissions)

Data structures and storage (architecture and devices)

Computer programs (program architecture)

The plan must indicate what physical components will go in which locations, a sequence for installations in different locations, an installation sequence within each location, and the criteria or tests that the system must perform to be acceptable.

The usual sequence of developing a plan is as follows:

System strategy specification	→	Hardware/storage telecommunication configuration design	→	Files database design	→	Program design

The system strategy specification is the general guide for establishing the physical system. It will indicate the type of devices, their locations, whether application software is to be built or bought, and the general storage approach. It will not specify vendors or specific model numbers unless there will be no choice. Much of this specification is a result of the activities that took place in Process 3 of the development cycle.

Of course, there will be iteration and repetition in the above steps. Most systems projects require a basic database or file design prior to specification of hardware storage devices. Other projects may have hardware or telecommunication specifications limited to what is currently available within an organization. This may mean that the first step is to gain an understanding of the current configuration and then establish the system strategy. In any case, all of the above steps will have to be considered to specify a physical design, but the order may vary depending on existing availability and the specific project.

An information analyst may not be specialized enough to develop detailed specifications for all of these components. But he or she must be knowledgeable enough to communicate requirements either to a vendor, possibly in the form of a request for proposal, a telecommunications expert, a database design expert, or a consultant.

One of the strategic decisions that must be made before proceeding is the degree of centralization versus distribution or decentralization of:

Data—storage at one site versus many sites?

Processing—a mainframe site versus mini- or microcomputers?

Development and control of input and output—who does this where?

Advantages of distribution are:

Potentially better response and service of needs since decentralized sites are closer to those with the needs

Local concern and caring since local sites may be more personal and accessible

Potentially more reliability with more nodes

Disadvantages of decentralization include:

Less economy of scale with scattered sites and devices

Loss of control and security due to need for networks and having more physical sites that need to be secured

Less centralized expertise where persons learn from others by association

These advantages and disadvantages must be balanced to achieve the most critical user needs at the lowest cost. Again, the developer must not lose sight of the system objectives.

Thus, a large portion of a physical plan will be what devices are located where and how they are connected, what data is located where and how it is organized and stored, and how the software is designed to obtain system results.

CRITERIA FOR A PHYSICAL SYSTEM PLAN

A physical systems plan must consider the appropriateness of devices for hardware processing, data storage, and telecommunications. In any specification of a system strategy for the *devices* in a systems plan, the developer must be concerned with:

Compatibility—ability to "talk" to one another

Capacity—being large enough to meet current and future system objectives

Transparency—no user concern for what is behind their interface

Performance—having adequate throughput and response time

Serviceability—ability to be repaired

Serviceability is one of the factors that must be considered in planning physical systems. (Courtesy Grumman Systems Support)

Availability—current and future purchase and delivery

Expandability—growth potential

Security—protection from unwanted sources

Reliability—operability when needed

At one time, emphasis was placed on physical performance. Now, with processing and storage capability coming down in price and more organizational dependence on system results, there is an increased emphasis on having a system available when needed that can be networked with other devices or data. This means a greater emphasis on telecommunications of data, text, voice, and graphics.

Computer *software criteria* also have changed. The concern once was with efficiency and optimizing performance. Although this is still a consideration, the cost of maintaining software has been found to be so great that changeable software has emerged as a major consideration. Many developers believe that the primary goal of software development is maintainability with adequate performance and control. If a program is maintainable, it can easily be "tuned" for performance and controls can be added.

In studying what makes a complex object maintainable, whether it is a car or a software program, persons have found the following:

A good architecture or framework is needed (a good structure)

A good set of documentation should describe the object (good manuals)

The object must be divisible into small pieces (modularity)

The pieces must perform only one function (known output)

The pieces must be small (understand the purpose and operation)

The pieces must not be too tightly connected (a car all welded together)

An understanding of the internal workings of each component is not needed to understand the entire object (the black box)

Most of the car maintenance that a backyard mechanic can handle will fit the above requirements. A good design and a repair manual are desired. Small, simple parts whose internal workings need not be understood in detail are what auto parts stores specialize in for home mechanics. Parts that perform only one function make finding a problem easier. Parts that are less modular, such as engine blocks with "hidden" components, make a repair job more difficult.

The developer should consult the above lists when considering any physical device or in purchasing or constructing software. Many of the above concepts will be applied to systems development and will appear as words like *coupling, cohesion,* and the *blackbox concept.*

Now that an understanding has been established for the components as well as the criteria necessary for a physical systems plan, each of the major components will be explored.

HARDWARE

A systems developer must determine input devices, output devices, processors, storage, and telecommunications to adequately specify the systems plan. The devices often are graphically displayed by using a system flowchart. The devices must be combined as part of system tactics to allow satisfaction of system objectives. Acquisition of hardware could mean purchasing an entire system or upgrading existing equipment. This could mean adding or upgrading input devices, processors, storage, or output devices. Each of these areas will be considered.

Input Devices. There is a great variety of input devices. The developer must consider who will be operating the device and how much input must actually be done. Experienced full-time input operators may work with devices such as key-to-tape, key-to-disk, or terminal devices. Terminal devices could include "dumb" terminals, intelligent terminals, or microcomputers. Terminals could have keyboards and other devices such as a mouse or light pen with a pointing stylus. The standard Touchtone telephone should not be ignored as an input device. Special-purpose input devices could include optical readers for either bar codes or text, magnetic ink readers, point-of-sale terminals, or devices such as automated teller machines or badge readers. In some applications, voice input could be a possibility. Finally, the developer should not ignore the use of card input, especially in the case of a turnaround document with preprinted or prepunched data. The input devices should fit the organization, the application, and the individual users.

Processors. The developer must determine processing needs for the project at hand and then see what processing is available within the organization. He or she must also determine where processing power is needed and if portability using microcomputers is a consideration. It is difficult to categorize processing power, but in general there are microcomputers, minicomputers, and mainframe computers. However, with the distribution of processing power in a network, a series of minicomputers may actually have more processing power than a single mainframe computer. Wit each of the processors, there also will be options in memory size and processing capabilities. There are special-purpose devices that can offer nonstop processing for those who cannot be without processing, even for a few moments. Since systems software such as an operating system or database management system are tied closely to processors, it often is necessary to consider the processor and systems software as one package. It is most critical to state the problem and then allow vendors to supply their processing solutions. Asking a vendor what they have available without the vendor understanding what you must achieve (your system objectives) is not making the vendors do their homework.

Storage. In general, there are several categories of storage. There is fixed and removable storage, and sequential and direct access storage. The main storage mediums are magnetic tape and magnetic disk. Magnetic tape is used for storage in either a sequential processing environment or for off-site backup generation. Tape media come in various capacities and read/write speeds. Magnetic disks are used to support direct access storage environments. Magnetic disk drives also have various capacities and read/write speeds.

Output Devices. Output devices generally are broken into screen and hard-copy devices. Screens vary in size, resolution, and color versus monochromatic. Hard copy can be printed or put on media other than paper, such as microfilm or microfiche. Printers can be impact, such as dot matrix or daisy wheel; or nonimpact, such as laser, ink jet, or thermal devices. Less expensive impact printers are character printers while high-speed impact printers typically print a line at a time. Other hard copy can come from devices such as plotters. Finally, other forms of output such as voice or tones should not be ignored. Amount of output, quality, and use are important criteria to consider in selecting output devices. For example, if output must be carried to many locations, screen or microfilm output probably would not be satisfactory.

The developer must come up with a viable combination of hardware that fits with the need of the application. For example, input may be done on a microcomputer with intelligence to edit and verify data. Data may be batched together and sent via a modem and phone line to a minicomputer that aggregates data from various locations. Then data may be sent to a mainframe for processing of all transactions. Or a terminal may be connected directly to a minicomputer where all storage for a certain location is kept. Data may be processed online to assure instantaneous updates. Again, the processing and storage that is needed depends on the objectives of the system and organization.

For each device included in the system, the capacity, speed, vendor, and model, must be specified. All of the devices must be aggregated into a physical site plan, as described in Chapter 8. This includes everything from floor plans, power, cabling, and furniture to lighting and supplies.

Explaining how each of the hardware devices operates is beyond the scope of this book. As well, model numbers, speeds, and storage capacities would likely be out of date by the time you read the information. The important thing to know at this stage is where you can find more information on hardware.

There are several sources to seek information on current technology. They include:

Internal Experts—employees who try to keep up with what is available. There is a danger in relying too heavily on such information, since a person's familiarity with existing equipment may bias any opinions. Bias also may be introduced by advertising, small sample sizes for data collected (a few horror or praise stories), or salespersons who can be more convincing than their products.

Literature—trade journals and newpapers are a source of information. These sources may include reviews of hardware and telecommunications equipment. Also included are beta test site reports where early testing users report their results. Some of the reports are accurate and some may have to be read with a critical eye. Newpapers include *ComputerWorld* and *MIS Week;* popular trade journals are *Datamation, Infosystems, Computer Decisions,* and many microcomputer publications. Research subscription services include Auerbach reports, DataPro, and ICP Quarterly.

Vendors—actual sellers of the sought items. Vendors may serve as sources of information. However, it will be clear that the answers obtained will only be as good as the questions that are asked. Questions should focus on facts, not opinions. Besides primary vendors, devices also are available from original equipment manufacturers, (OEMs), which are organizations that sell devices compatible with other vendors' processors. These organizations may furnish good comparative data to evaluate input/output and storage devices.

Consultants—persons who specialize in different areas of hardware, software, and telecommunications. Consultants should maintain their openmindedness by not serving as a representative for any vendor. If their living is earned by commissions from sellers, they may make recommendations based on the highest commission, not the best solution. Consultants can lend expert advice, but they can be costly. It should be remembered that most consultants will not be around the organization after the decisions are made, but the organization will have to live with their decisions for a long time.

Existing Customers—organizations which have already made and are living with a decision similar to the one you are facing. Vendors may be sources of such information. Beware of too glowing a report, however; the existing customer may be getting a premium if you sign a contract. Again, it is dangerous to generalize from someone else's experiences, as your organization and its members may be totally different. On site visits may be the best way to gather the information you need and determine if the other organization is similar enough for you to make well-founded generalizations.

User groups—existing customers of a certain product who may band together to get the benefits of sharing with one another. An example of this type of group at the microcomputer level may be a local user group of a specific brand and model of computer. These groups also exist for mini- and mainframe computers.

One of the challenges to a person in the systems field is to stay better informed about the marketplace and continue to use the above sources during all of his or her career. Only constant reading and inquiry will keep you up to date in the field.

Besides merely specifying devices, components located at different locations must be connected. This brings us to the topic of telecommunications.

TELECOMMUNICATIONS

Telecommunications has developed into a critical component of physical design. Distributed databases and processing power must be linked. Beyond simple movement of data has come the need to move text (written words), voice (both live and stored), and images and pictures (both still and moving) to support communications between persons within and outside an organization.

General options could include:

Terminals or microcomputers linked to a computer

Devices such as copiers or facsimile machines linked to one another or to a computer

Computers to computers all in one location (local area network)

Computers to computers through outside lines

The combination of all these possible options and the means of *networking* them is overwhelming. There are innumerable vendors and technologies, especially since the 1984 breakup of American Telephone and Telegraph (AT&T) and the deregulation of the telecommunications industry.

The complexity of telecommunications can grow very quickly, especially when there are many devices that can be linked and many vendors providing both devices and linking services. There are choices between devices, speeds, and types of connections. For example, communication lines use one or more of the following methods:

Physical connection (often called *conductive media*)

Twisted pairs of copper wires

Shielded wires

Coaxial cables

Fiber optics

Nonphysical connections (often called *radiated media*)

Microwave stations

Satellite

Radio

Cellular nets

This exhibits why complete courses are needed to understand the linking of sites and the connection of devices within sites (local area networks).

However, there are important management considerations when deciding on telecommunications. These include the ability to service all loads at reasonable cost and a system reliable enough that the business will not be "down" if the system is down. This includes a need for compatibility between equipment, upgradability, maintenance, and backup.

Much of the telecommunication dilemma can be simplified by hardware planners taking a corporate-wide view, and looking beyond the needs of one systems project. For example, one of the considerations when investigating new systems needing communications is the possibility of integration of voice and data networks. Leasing high-speed lines that would carry both voice and data often is justified because the combined need requires volumes that allow less expensive rates.

Overall, the role of the analyst is to aid in development and review of a configuration chart showing all devices and connections, including modems, controllers, concentrators, and switches, to assure that user needs for the system at hand will be met.

One of the things that must be organized and moved between locations as part of the physical system plan is data. The storage of data will be considered next.

DATA

Data is the lifeblood of most processing systems. The developer must work with the logical representation of the data to create a physical specification. This means viewing logical definitions of data stores and flows in the data dictionary, the data structure diagrams, and data access diagrams to convert them to a physical specification.

The developer must realize that each data store on the data flow diagram may represent either an entire physical file or database or just one physical portion. Physical packaging of the data may differ from the logical representation. There may be many physical stores making up one logical data store, or vice-versa. Physical design of data used in a system involves the following considerations.

Classification and Coding of Data

Codes are prevalent parts of our life. We deal with zip codes, area codes, and product codes. Codes are groups of digits, characters, or symbols that identify and describe an attribute of a data element. Some codes like a telephone area code are readable by both machines and humans, while a code like the universal product code may be best read and interpreted by a scanner such as the ones you see at grocery stores.

The analyst may be called on to establish a coding system for some data. Usually, this code is the result of some classification or categorization of data according to some common attributes. For example, all persons from 20 to 29 years of age may be coded as a "2," or all females may be coded as an "f." This type of classification may make it easier to manipulate and retrieve data, but if the original data is not kept, there is no way of reconstructing it. For example, if all data was coded in age categories and original age was not kept, it would be impossible to know how many people had a specific age.

There are some guidelines in establishing a code. The code should be:

Consistent (the same data occurrence should always get the same code)

Comprehensive (all data should fit in a category)

Unambiguous (an element should fit in only one category and have only one code)

Expandable (future data should be accommodated in the coding scheme)

Understandable (humans and/or machines should be able to read and interpret the code depending on need)

Standardized (new coding schemes should not be created where one already exists, as in the case of library call numbers)

Descriptive (contain some information about the data element)

Some examples of codes include:

A ***sequential code***—a social security number which is assigned to uniquely identify a person but contains little other information

A ***block code***—a number which uniquely identifies a college course, for example and if 500 or greater identifies a graduate course (this code may be "blocked" further with a prefix like "IS" indicating an information systems class)

A ***numeric group code***—a zip code which identifies the state, state postal region, and local postal zone groups (for example, 80301, with an 8 for state, 03 for state postal region, and 01 for local postal unit); this code will be expanded to 9 digits to link to a city block

An ***alphabetic code***—the two-digit state code (CO, MN, etc.)

An ***alphanumeric code***—the Canadian postal system code which can identify an address down to the postal carrier route (T3A 1C3)

Note that the use of alphanumeric codes allows more items per position (0–9 versus 0–9 and A–Z). Alphabetic codes also seem to be easier to remember, especially if they represent an abbreviation for a physical object, such as the airport codes for Denver being DEN, rather than 634. But the tradeoff is that alphanumeric codes may take more storage space than numeric codes.

There also is a tradeoff in using codes for representing data categories. Coded data takes less storage space and may be easier to process, but it may be more difficult for the user to understand. People constantly complain about being represented by a number, which usually is a code. As storage and processing capability become less costly, there is a trend toward greater "humanization" of the data representation and less use of codes just to save storage.

The result of classification and coding is a complete entry in the data dictionary for each data element specifying its name, type, format, length, and a key for any coding used.

Understanding the Aggregated Data

Now that all the data is coded and classified, the analyst must gain an understanding of the data in terms of the processing needed. The data must be physically stored so that it can be obtained in a correct, accurate, and usable form whenever it is needed. As well, it must be stored cost-effectively. The purpose of this effort is to simplify the data, eliminate unjustified redundancy, and ensure that all needed data elements are present. Two methods for simplifying data include *inspection* and *normalization*.

Inspection. The analyst must check to see that all data that flows out of a data store flows into the data store. This can be done by visual *inspection*. The end result should be a specification of all the data structures and elements that are needed in the logical data stores.

Data going into a data store = Data going out of a store?

The analyst should be alert for inconsistencies and inefficiencies in the data. Turk (see References) believes these could include:

Homonyms—the same name for different data elements

Synonyms—different names for the same data element

Derived data elements—data elements that can be created from other data elements (these elements should be noted so that a decision can be made to either store or derive them when physical design is done)

Mutually exclusive data elements—data elements that cannot occur simultaneously (for example, separate payroll data elements indicating salaried or hourly employees with a "yes" or "no" could be combined into one element with a code for type since an employee cannot be both salaried and hourly at the same time.

The analyst should eliminate synonyms, homonyms, and mutually exclusive data elements and merely denote derived data elements. The decision of whether a data element should be derived or stored should be a decision made when actual physical design is done. This is a tradeoff between storage savings versus processing time.

Next, we must determine some of the characteristics of the data. The characteristics for each data structure record or data elements include:

Amount and size—how many of each data structure and lengths of data elements

Growth—the number of records to be added to a file over time

Volatility—number of records added to or deleted from a file of data

Variability—number of adds, deletes, and changes to a record within a file

Activity—percentage of total number of records referenced when processing is done ("hit rate")

The analyst also must determine what constraints exist in dealing with data structures. For example, some processing or updating can be done on an overnight basis as in the case of customer orders, while other situations such as bank withdrawals should result in immediate updating of the customer records.

The analyst should aggregate all the data from all data stores in an attempt to see the data as a comprehensive whole. The next step is to simplify the data through a process called ***normalization.***

Normalization. Normalization is an attempt to present a clear view of the data to the designer of file and database structures. The results of normalization are:

Data structures without repeating groups (repeating groups result in variable-length records, which some persons believe give a third dimension to the data, rather than simple two-dimensional tables)

Data structures with data elements dependent on the entire primary key, and only the key (a primary key is one or more data elements that uniquely identify a data structure occurrence)

Simpler views for data designers of complex relationships and dependencies between data elements

Reduction of fact (as opposed to data) redundancies

Data elements describing data entities to which they are most closely related

Normalization accomplishes the above by manipulating data structures about the system under development. There are different levels of normalization, called *first normal form, second normal form, third normal form,* etc. Usually the objective of the system developer is to express data in third normal form.

First Normal Form: Remove Repeating Groups. For example, in dealing with customer orders, each order could have a different number of products on the order.

ORDER1 contains an order for:
product1 and
product2 and
product3

ORDER2 contains an order for:
product1 and
product2 and

product3 and
product4 and
product5

ORDER3 contains an order for:
product1 and
product2
ETC.

These sets of data structures that are variable in number are called *repeating groups*. If these were all contained in one data structure, variable length records would be created.

Let us look at an actual case of the data we would have to store if we had an order processing system. This would be typical data placed on a mail-order form in a catalog. The entity ORDER would be described as follows:

Entity ORDER consists of the following data structures/elements:
ORDER-NUMBER (a primary key)
ORDER-DATE
CUSTOMER-NUMBER
CUSTOMER-NAME
CUSTOMER-ADDRESS
PRODUCT-NO (for each product ordered)
PRODUCT-NAME (for each product ordered)
COLOR (for each product ordered)
PRICE-PRODUCT (for each product ordered)
QUANTITY-ORDERED (for each product ordered)
TOTALCOST-PRODUCT (a derived data element for each product ordered)
TOTAL-MERCHANDISE-COST (a derived data element)
TAX-ORDER (derived)
DELIVERY-COST-ORDER (derived)
TOTAL-ORDER-COST (derived)

Note that we would have data about "orders" and data about "products" that must be stored in the data structures. In this case, the product data is a repeating group. To bring the data structure to first normal form, we would break the structure into two entities, one for ORDER and one for PRODUCTS-ORDERED. The resulting data structures would look like the following:

Entity ORDER consisting of:
ORDER-NUMBER (a primary key)
ORDER-DATE
CUSTOMER-NUMBER
CUSTOMER-NAME
CUSTOMER-ADDRESS
TOTAL-MERCHANDISE-COST (derived)
TAX-ORDER (derived)

DELIVERY-COST-ORDER (derived)
TOTAL-ORDER-COST (derived)

Entity PRODUCTS-ORDERED consisting of:
PRODUCT-NO (a key data element identifying the product ordered)
PRODUCT-NAME
COLOR
PRICE-PRODUCT
QUANTITY-ORDERED
TOTALCOST-PRODUCT (derived)

Since we broke PRODUCTS-ORDERED from a specific order, we must link it back to that specific order. To do this the data element ORDER-NUMBER is added to the data structure. ORDER-NUMBER is needed to uniquely identify the "line items" for ordered products from the original order. The key of PRODUCT-NO would not be unique since there are likely many other orders that contain orders for that product. The data structure for PRODUCTS-ORDERED now looks like:

Entity PRODUCTS-ORDERED consisting of:
ORDER-NUMBER (key data element)
PRODUCT-NO (key data element)
PRODUCT-NAME
COLOR
PRICE-PRODUCT
QUANTITY-ORDERED
TOTALCOST-PRODUCT (derived)

We no longer have repeating groups and have a relationship between the two data structures. Now we will attempt to simplify further by going to second normal form.

Second Normal Form: Remove NonKey Data Elements Not Fully Dependent on All Data Elements in the Key. This means that we must first look at the primary key to see if it contains more than one data element, called a *concatenated key*. If a data element in a data structure does not need all the primary key data elements to identify it, then we must separate those elements not fully dependent on the whole primary key and create new data structures.

Again, back to our example. We do not have to deal with entity ORDER since it does not have a concatenated key. But, we must deal with the the entity PRODUCTS-ORDERED since it does have a primary key consisting of two data elements, ORDER-NUMBER and PRODUCT-NO. Let us look at each of the data elements that are not part of the key and determine if they are fully dependent on the whole key.

Entity PRODUCTS-ORDERED consisting of:
ORDER-NUMBER (key data element)
PRODUCT-NO (key data element)
PRODUCT-NAME (dependent only on PRODUCT-NO)

COLOR (dependent only on PRODUCT-NO)
PRICE-PRODUCT (dependent only on PRODUCT-NO)
QUANTITY-ORDERED (dependent on both ORDER-NUMBER and PRODUCT-NO)
TOTALCOST-PRODUCT (derived—dependent on both ORDER-NUMBER and PRODUCT-NO)

We must take the data elements that are dependent on only one of the primary keys and create a new entity. This new entity is linked back to the PRODUCTS-ORDERED entity since the primary key of PRODUCT-NO is common to both data structures. We end up with the following:

Entity PRODUCTS-ORDERED consisting of:
ORDER-NUMBER (key data element)
PRODUCT-NO (key data element)
QUANTITY-ORDERED
TOTALCOST-PRODUCT (derived)

Entity PRODUCT consisting of
PRODUCT-NO (key data element)
PRODUCT-NAME
PRICE-PRODUCT
COLOR

Of course, we still retain the entity called ORDER from our first normal form definition. Now we move on to third normal form.

Third Normal Form: Remove Data Elements Uniquely Identified by Another Non-Key Data Element. Now we must examine the data elements to see if they are dependent on both the primary key and on one another. When examining the data structure for ORDER, we find that

Entity ORDER consisting of:
ORDER-NUMBER (a primary key)
ORDER-DATE (dependent on primary key)
CUSTOMER-NUMBER (dependent on primary key)
CUSTOMER-NAME (dependent on CUSTOMER-NUMBER)
CUSTOMER-ADDRESS (dependent on CUSTOMER-NUMBER)
TOTAL-MERCHANDISE-COST (derived—dependent on primary key)
TAX-ORDER (derived—dependent on primary key)
DELIVERY-COST-ORDER (derived—dependent on primary key)
TOTAL-ORDER-COST (derived—dependent on primary key)

CUSTOMER-NAME and CUSTOMER-ADDRESS are primarily dependent on CUSTOMER-NUMBER, and *transitively* dependent on ORDER-NUMBER. This is reasonable since CUSTOMER-NUMBER would uniquely define CUSTOMER-NAME and CUSTOMER-ADDRESS. Thus, we create a new entity to move these two data elements to a separate data structure. This leaves us with the following entities and data structures:

Entity CUSTOMER consisting of:
CUSTOMER-NUMBER (a primary key)
CUSTOMER-NAME
CUSTOMER-ADDRESS

Entity ORDER consisting of:
ORDER-NUMBER (a primary key)
ORDER-DATE
CUSTOMER-NUMBER
TOTAL-MERCHANDISE-COST (derived)
TAX-ORDER (derived)
DELIVERY-COST-ORDER (derived)
TOTAL-ORDER-COST (derived)

Entity PRODUCTS-ORDERED consisting of
ORDER-NUMBER (key data element)
PRODUCT-NO (key data element)
QUANTITY-ORDERED
TOTALCOST-PRODUCT (derived)

Entity PRODUCT consisting of
PRODUCT-NO (key data element)
PRODUCT-NAME
PRICE-PRODUCT
COLOR

Martin and McClure (see References) use a diagram that exhibits the steps of normalization. This diagram is shown in Figure 9.1.

Data in third normal form should be clear to designers who must use the data. The reason that the systems analyst might do the normalization is that a good understanding of the data is needed. Since the analyst has been working with the data, he or she may have a better understanding of it than a database designer. Thus, even if the analyst does not do the file or database design, he or she is putting the data in the best form for the designer. The analyst should be aware that this may not be the clearest presentation to a data user. For example, users may see the mail-order form as the clearest view for their purposes.

Not all data is physically stored as specified in third normal form. It may be more efficient to physically store the data differently. But it is still desirable to simplify the data through normalization.

File and Database Designation

Physical file and database designation depends on usages of the data including activity, volatility, needed accesses, response time, and growth. The designer must make certain that all demands for use of the data can be met efficiently and at an acceptable cost. Up to this point, we have completed activities that should give the designer the background to proceed with the design work.

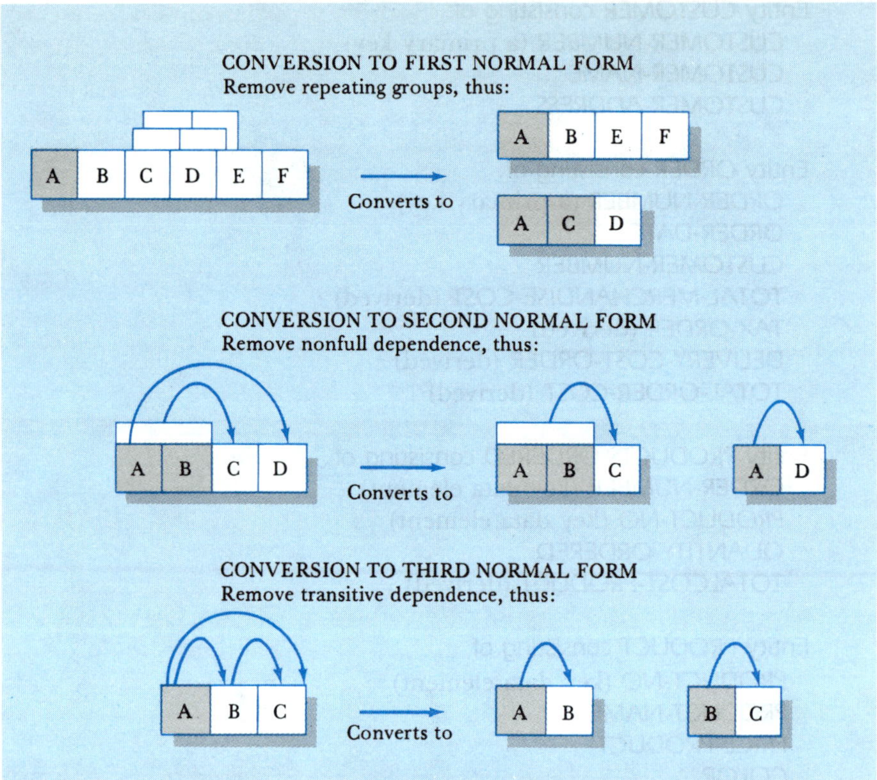

FIGURE 9.1

A graphic view of the normalization process. (Lettered boxes indicate data elements. Shaded data elements are primary keys. Arrowed lines indicate dependence. Taken from Martin and McClure, p. 153.)

The designer must know the data intimately before embarking on the actual physical design. This was the reason for completing the prior activities. The designer also must realize that file and database design is an *iterative* process. You may not get it right the first time.

The analyst must decide on the location, content, and organization of master files, transaction files, and scratch files (files created for a specific process to either hold some data temporarily or to generate a specific output). Or, if a database approach is appropriate, the database structure and storage must be specified. Much of this material is beyond the scope of this book, but there are some basics that the designer must understand.

Sequences of the data and access methods are choices the designer must make. Alternatives to data storage include consideration of sequences and access methods. Sequences include:

Sequential—the data is kept physically in a specified sequence usually ordered by record key as on a magnetic tape. The logical order is identical to the physical order.

Direct/Random—the data is added without regard to physical sequence and has a physical location calculated by mathematical means, usually a repeatable manipulation of the record key.

List—the physical storage location of data is determined from physical pointers derived from the logical organization. Data structure occurrences with like characteristics point to each other. These pointers result in linked lists of related data occurrences.

Access methods include:

Sequential File Processing—this method is useful for batch processing where there is a high activity level. This results in storage efficiency since there is no overhead for indexes or pointers. Finding a single record means searching the entire file, but the updating process is efficient if there is a high "hit rate." The process is easy to program. It also is easy to assure data integrity by keeping archival versions of master files and transaction files since a new file is written as a result of a processing run.

Direct/Random—this method allows easy access of any single record. This is needed for handling random updates and inquiries in a quick response time. A manipulation of the record key gives the physical location where the record is stored. This results in storage overhead. If the manipulation results in more than one record with the same specified physical location, we must create overflow areas. If there is a high volatility, this storage organization can create many overflows in storage and be very inefficient.

Indexed Sequential—this method contains tables of keys called indexes that give the approximate location of a record. These *indexes* allow access of a sequentially stored file. The index links a logical record key to a physical location. This is similar to the phone book which contains the range of names on each page. If we put these ranges in an index, we would first search the index to get the correct page, then would search the page sequentially. This method is favored if there is a need to do both sequenced and unsequenced operations. The method is relatively easy to program and files are easily reorganized.

The designer must examine the above to determine which would best fit the needs of the application at hand. Some of these decisions are obvious and may have been made earlier in the development process, such as in Process 3 when preliminary system tactics were stated. Likewise, the physical devices that can be used to implement the methods may have already been determined when a hardware specification was developed.

The designer must perform some size calculations for storage to assure that current and future storage needs will be satisfactory. To do this, the designer must understand the storage structure and organization on any devices being considered. As a simple example, floppy disk storage may have a sector or block length limitation. If 256 characters were allowed per sector and each data structure required 119 characters, then one could have 256/119 = 2.15 or 2 complete records per sector. If there were a possibility of 450 of the 119 character records, then 450/2 or 225 sectors would be needed. A disk with 400K storage character storage would have about 1600 sectors so there would be adequate storage on one floppy disk.

The above example is provided to show that the designer must understand the structures of devices such as magnetic tape or mass storage. This can only be done by examining the technical details on the devices. In some cases, vendors who propose equipment for use in the application can be a great aid in doing such calculations. In any case, the designer must not ignore the overhead for pointers and links between data occurrences if a complex storage structure is used.

The designer also could be saddled with making a decision on whether to build software to access and maintain data or to obtain a packaged solution in the form of a file or database management system. File or database management systems are costly, but can result in development cost savings. The file or database management system serves as a source of functions that otherwise would have to be developed by the application developer. Data integrity is maintained by having the database management system maintain data relationships and physical file details aiding actual access to the data. However, all of this comes at a cost due to the package expense and the high amount of overhead to maintain data relationships.

Another important consideration in file and database design is access control, backup, and recovery. These topics will be covered in Chapter 12, which will discuss at length maintenance of data integrity.

The total objective of file and database design is to provide needed capacity, response time, expansion needs, and retention capability at the most reasonable cost. The developer must attempt to balance a number of tradeoffs, including:

Equipment costs versus operating costs (will new storage equipment costs be offset by lower costs of processing runs?)

Operating costs versus maintenance costs (will run cost savings offset file maintenance costs?)

Operating performance versus maintenance costs (will lower run costs result in higher costs of file maintenance?)

Program complexity versus data structure complexity (is the programming maintenance cost offsetting any storage cost efficiencies?)

Balancing these tradeoffs is a never-ending challenge for a designer, but the design decisions are very important. The designer must never forget that changing the processing of the data is much easier than changing the structure, organization, and storage of the files or databases.

Although the systems developer often will be provided assistance by others in hardware, systems software, communications, and database design, the task of software or computer program design often will be totally in the domain of the developer. We will discuss this topic in the next section.

COMPUTER PROGRAM DESIGN

A good computer program is one that minimizes the cost of its existence over its life. These costs include creation, operation, and maintenance. Studies by Boehm (see References) have shown that over a program's life, the highest cost is for maintenance, which includes changes and testing.

Maintainability of a program is facilitated by having a program broken into modules that have good readability, small size, independence, and a "black box factor," which means the ability to understand the module by understanding its inputs and outputs. Structured system design attempts to minimize maintenance costs by trying to achieve the above factors.

Software design is not just programming. It involves establishing the architecture for the software. Some persons consider this to be more and more of a scientific endeavor. It is not just "art." Thus, the name *software engineering* has evolved.

The systems designer is responsible for showing the data base administrator that the system delivers adequate capacity, response time, expansion and retention capability with reasonable cost. (Dick Luria/Science; Source/Photo Researchers)

Although it is suggested that an architecture exist for software, this step often is ignored in actual systems development. In some cases there is little need for rigorous software planning. This especially is true when decision support systems are being built using prototyping, when small systems are involved, or packaged software is being purchased. Some persons also believe they can use detailed data flow diagrams for developing modular designs and do not go through the extra effort to develop structure charts to express the program architecture.

Structured Design Requires Structured Analysis

If the suggested processes and techniques of structured systems analysis have been followed, data flow diagrams representing the proposed system will exist at the design stage of the development project. The lowest level (most detailed) data flow diagram is used in program design. Each of the processes on the lowest-level data flow diagram should represent independent functions. The data flow diagram will serve as the basic input to the program design process.

Detailed DFD → Structured design process → Structure chart

The primary output of the structured design process is the structure chart. The structure chart is a hierarchic, graphic representation of the modules in a program and the connections between modules. These modules represent the functionally independent modules in the detailed data flow diagram. But, as you will discover, structured design:

Is an approach that follows from structured analysis

Has definite means of evaluation

Follows the guidelines for maintainability mentioned earlier in the chapter

Is more than modular design

Structured design is called "structured" because any very complex program can be designed using only a few basic structures which are shown on the structure chart.

Structure Charts

Structure charts are an improvement over hierarchy charts, often called VTOCs or visual table of contents, which display hierarchies of modules, but no data or control connections between the modules. As shown in Figure 9.2, a structure chart resembles a hierarchical organization chart with the workers at the bottom and management toward the top. Much of the actual processing takes place toward the bottom of the chart while control over the processing starts at the top of the chart.

The modules on a structure chart are shown with rectangles. Each module represents a set of contiguous computer program statements. The statements are packaged as a meaningful unit which is given a name. On

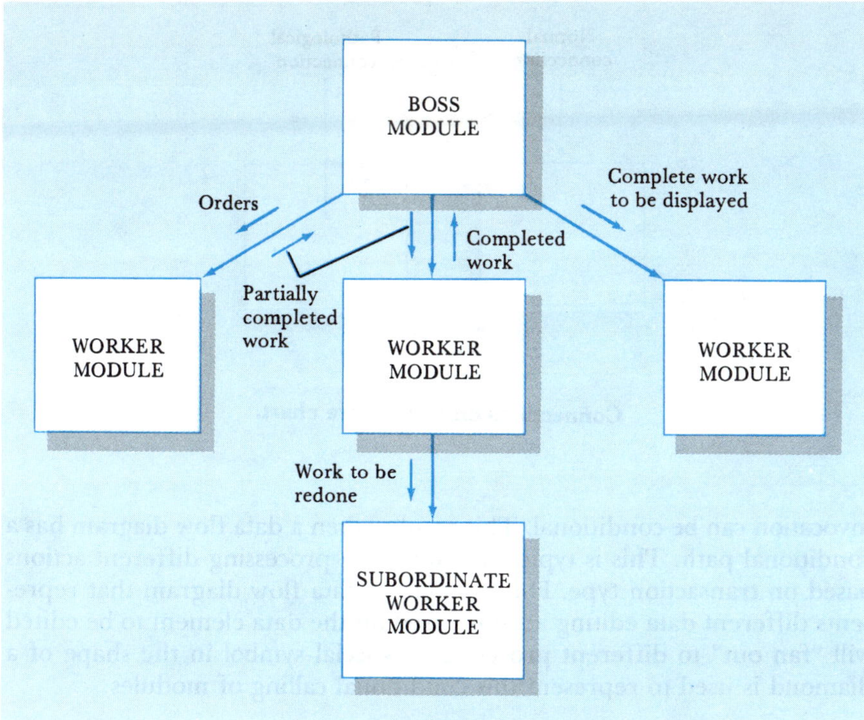

FIGURE 9.2
A structure chart resembles an organization chart.

the above diagram, the arrowed lines linking one module to another module are not flows, but are *invocations,* which means a module "calls on" another module.

Much like a building architect, a system architect will not be concerned with detailed construction, but with the overall general structure. In systems terms, this means each module is treated as a black box at this point. This means that the inputs and outputs are known, but the actual processing is an unknown at this point. The important thing is that the modules are small enough to remember at one time and ideally perform only one function.

Connections

The structure chart shows connections between modules. A ***connection*** is any reference from inside one module to something outside the module. A ***normal connection*** is a reference to another module by name such as in a CALL or a PERFORM. A ***pathological control connection*** is a reference to any secondary entry point within another module. A GO TO statement is such a connection (see Figure 9.3).

As mentioned above, normal connections typically are called invocations. One module "invokes" another module. As shown in Figure 9.4, this

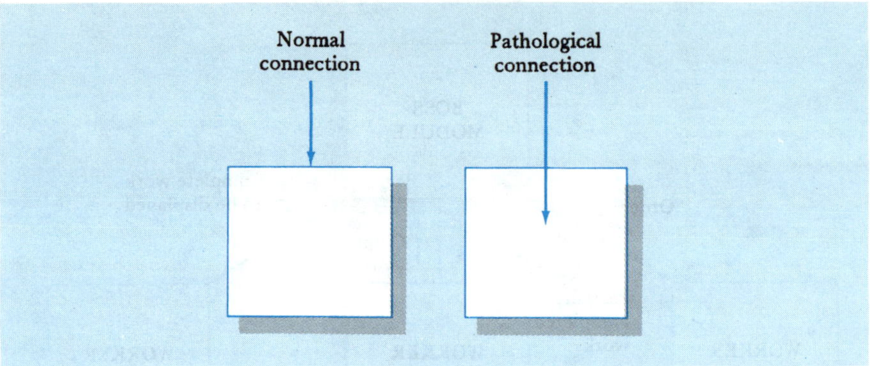

FIGURE 9.3

Connections on a structure chart.

invocation can be conditional. This results when a data flow diagram has a conditional path. This is typical when we are processing different actions based on transaction type. For example, a data flow diagram that represents different data editing actions based on the data element to be edited will "fan out" to different processes. A special symbol in the shape of a diamond is used to represent this conditional calling of modules.

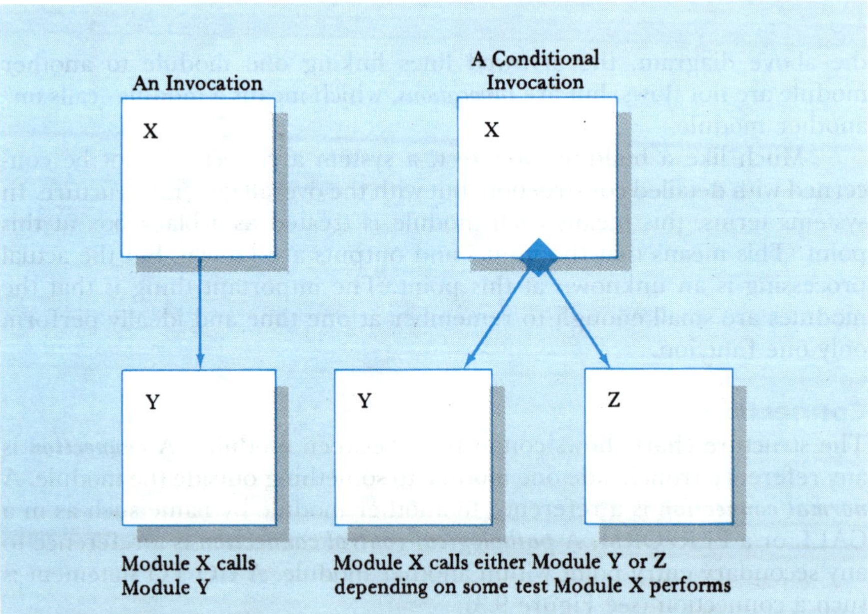

FIGURE 9.4

Two means of a module invoking another module.

MEDICAL TALK IN SYSTEMS DESIGN

Much of the original work done on finding designs for maintainable programs was done by Larry Constantine. Larry was a medical student hired by IBM to find characteristics of maintainable programs. As a result, much of the original writing by Constantine is laced with medical terms such as afferent, efferent, pathological, and morphology.

Couples

Coupling is a measure of strength of interconnection between modules. ***Loose coupling*** is preferred to ***tight coupling*** because a change in one module does not affect another module or modules. Independence of modules is an objective of structured systems design. All connections should be apparent and kept as simple and standard as possible.

A ***couple*** is a data element shared between modules. A ***data couple*** is used by the receiving module for calculation or indexing. A ***control couple,*** often called a flag, is used by the receiving module as input for making a decision. A general rule is that most decisions should be made by manager modules, not worker modules.

A data couple can flow either up or down in a hierarchy without causing complications, but a control couple should only flow back up to a "boss" module. If a control couple or "flag" is passed down to a worker module, the first thing that the worker module will have to do is make a decision, something we would like to reserve for boss modules. If the worker module did receive a control couple, the first thing it would have to do is test the "flag" and then transfer control. This means the module would likely have to contain more than one function, ruining its single purpose. In programming talk, the first thing the module would have to do is perform a test and then execute the undesirable GO TO statement. These types of "weaving paths" result in the commonly termed *spaghetti code.*

THE DREADED "HYDRA EFFECT"

Greg Grosch of Improved Systems Technologies often spoke of the dreaded "hydra effect" operating in tightly coupled program modules (named for the Greek mythological monster that grew two heads whenever one was cut off). Greg believed that tightly coupled programs acted the same way. The person "fixing" one error found two more errors appear. When one of those errors was "fixed," two more errors appeared. This continued ad infinitum.

The ideal coupling situation occurs when a module is changed and there is minimal need to change another module. One ideally would like to change any module without knowing anything about the contents of any other module. Normal connections, rather than pathological connections, usually result in less coupling.

Cohesion

Cohesion is a measure of strength of the internal purpose of a module. Cohesion is contained *within* a module, while coupling is *between* modules. There are a number of types of cohesion, some better than others.

The worst to best types of cohesion are:

Coincidental Cohesion—statements put together for no good reasons (which are usually random happenings). Splitting a 2000 statement program into 40 modules of 50 contiguous statements each, because a programming standard of "no modules over 50 statements" was instituted, results in coincidentally cohesive modules.

Logical Cohesion—putting statements that perform similar functions together in a module. For example, all error routines may be put together and would share some code. But if changes are needed and if some of the functions have to be moved, maintenance time and cost can be very high.

Temporal Cohesion—putting together program statements that are related in time. This includes initialization and termination modules, often indicated by words such as "first," "next," and "finally" in describing functions performed. If these modules have to be changed, care has to be taken to avoid "ripple" effects where modifying one function affects another function. If such a module produces an error, it is usually difficult to find the source.

Procedural Cohesion—putting together program statements that may not perform a single function, but would fit in a sequence as control passes from one segment to another. This is similar to what is found on a program flowchart. For example, a procedurally cohesive module might open existing files, reset switches, and prepare newly needed files. These various activities might deal with different data and be parts of several functions. This could make activities difficult to find and change.

Communicational Cohesion—putting program statements together that reference the same data. For example, a set of statements performing several functions on the same file would have communicational cohesion. Again, if one of the functions had to be chosen from among the many in a module, there would be a need to set switches and transfer control to execute the appropriate statements.

Functional Cohesion—a set of statements that together perform one function. Examples are: read a transaction, edit a transaction, print a transaction, or computation of a single data element.

A module may combine the forms of cohesion. Ideally, a module would have only functional cohesion. But, the less severe types of cohesion seem to creep into developed software.

Stevens, Myers, and Constantine (see References) suggest a method of examining module cohesion. First, they suggest you write a statement accurately describing what the module does. Then they suggest you analyze the statement. If, for example, the statement:

Is a compound sentence, there likely is *procedural* cohesion.

Contains "timing" words (first, next, then, etc.), there likely is *temporal* cohesion.

Contains more than one object after the verb, there likely is *logical* cohesion.

Contains words such as "initialize," "clean-up," or "terminate," there likely is *temporal* cohesion.

Contains none of the above, there likely is *functional* cohesion.

It might be added that if you cannot come up with one statement describing what the module does, you may have *coincidental* cohesion.

Care should be taken not to add what are called side effects, the adding of a "by the way, the module also does this other thing, too." The critical and most important factor is to make certain that the person who must maintain the program can find things that must be changed by looking at either the module name or the structure chart.

Notations of Structured Design

Figure 9.5 exhibits some of the basics of structured system design and structure charts.

Manager module M calls worker modules W1, W2, and W3 one or more times each. These are normal connections. In calling W1, M passes the data couple D1 and receives the couple D2. The open-ended tail on the arrow indicates that this is a data couple. M calls and sends couple D2 to W2. W2 sends back control couple C1, indicated by the filled-in tail on the arrow. All of these connections are normal and acceptable.

Worker module W2 contains a pathological control connection to W3. This is likely a GO TO from inside W2 to somewhere inside W3. This will create spaghetti code, where a program maintainer likely will end up wondering "Where did we come from to get here?" W1, W2, and W3 are workers who should only communicate through their manager, M.

However, not all communication between manager modules is acceptable. For example, W3 is pathologically connected by data couple D3. This is similar to a worker leaving a message for a manager by leaving it in a stack on his or her desk rather than passing it through proper channnels. In structured design notation, D3 would overwrite M's private data element also named D3. Again, this is how mysterious errors creep into computer code.

Another poor design is the passing of control couple C2 to W3 by M. This forces W3 to make a decision based on C2. The first thing W3 would have to do is a test and then likely would perform a transfer of control. A

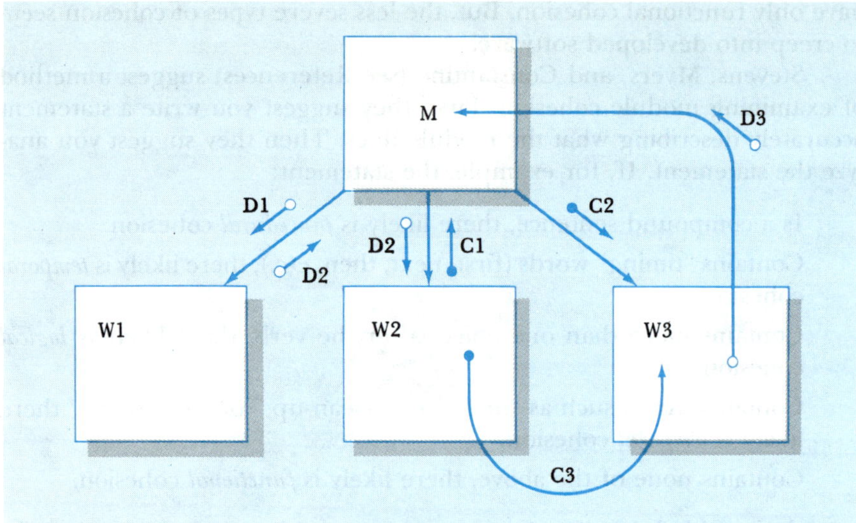

FIGURE 9.5

The components of a structure chart.

good general rule is that control couples should only pass up to higher-level modules.

Figure 9.6 exhibits a structure chart for some basic payroll functions. If we continued to add detail to the diagram, each of the three worker modules would have subordinate modules providing assistance. For example, the "Get Valid Time Data" module might have subordinates that "Get Time Data" and "Validate Time Data." The "Compute Pay" module might have subordinates to "Calculate Gross Pay," "Calculate Deductions," and

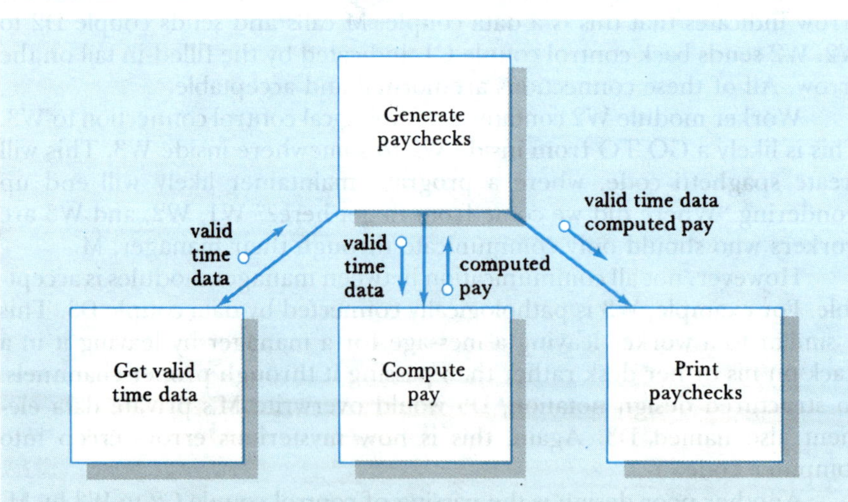

FIGURE 9.6

A structure chart for basic payroll processing.

"Calculate Net Pay." The "Print Paychecks" module might have subordinates to "Format the Paycheck" and to "Output Checks." Each of these functions would be based on the processes that are part of the data flow diagram for the system.

The next section will describe a procedure for creating a structure chart from a data flow diagram.

The Steps of Structured Systems Design

1. Obtain a copy of the most detailed DFD of the system that requires software to be developed, (Figure 9.7).
2. Determine major input and output streams on the data flow diagram. This is done for the input stream by examining inputs at the source of data to the system and examining each process to determine if it is an input activity or actual processing of the data. Then the output stream is examined by starting at the destination and working backward, examining each process to determine if it is preparing for output or doing actual processing (Figure 9.8).

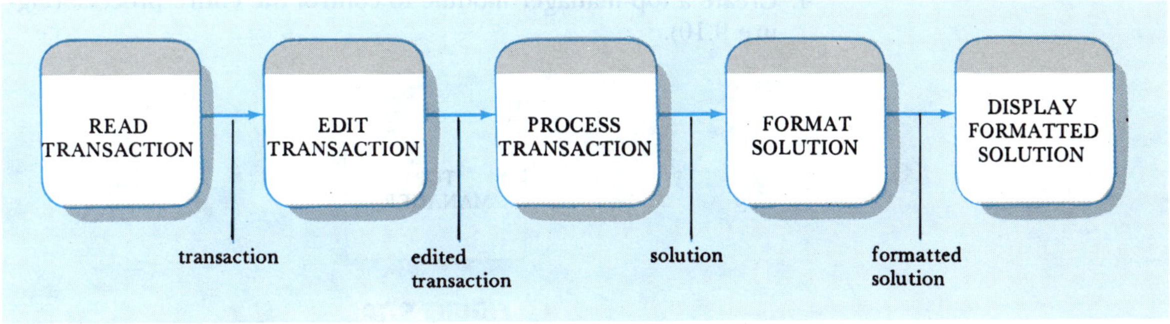

FIGURE 9.7
Copy of detailed data flow diagram.

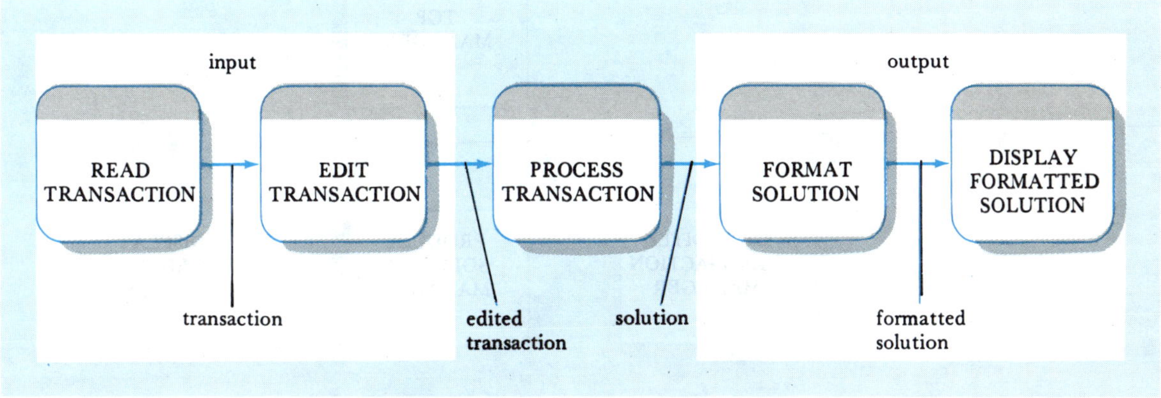

FIGURE 9.8
Denoted input and output streams.

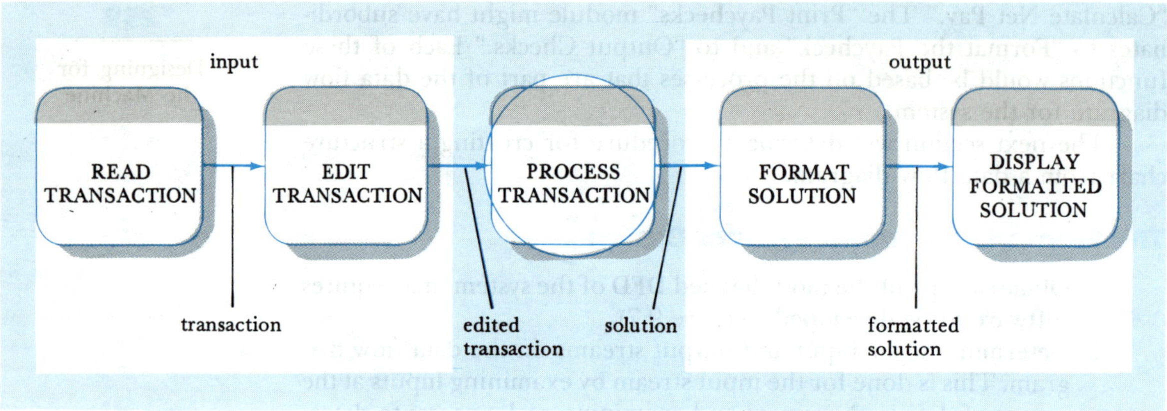

FIGURE 9.9

Denoted transform process.

3. Denote the middle-most processes that actually transform inputs into outputs and mark this on the data flow diagram (a circle may be appropriate) (Figure 9.9).
4. Create a top-manager module to control the entire process. (Figure 9.10).

FIGURE 9.10

A top manager module.

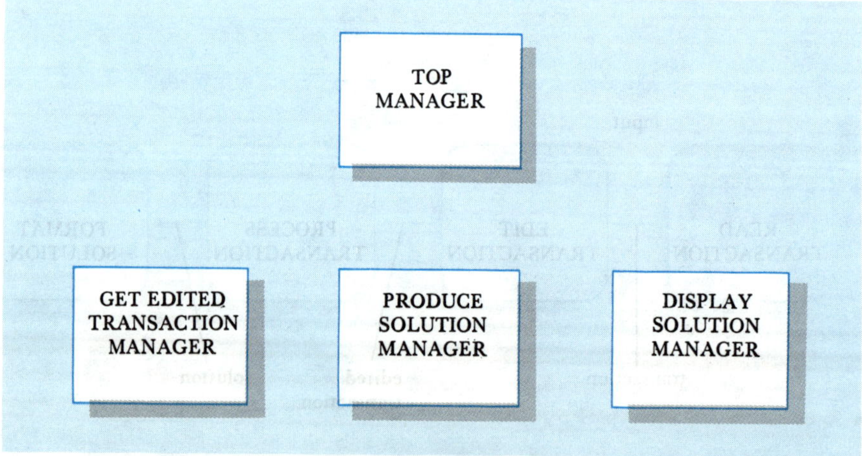

FIGURE 9.11

Adding managers.

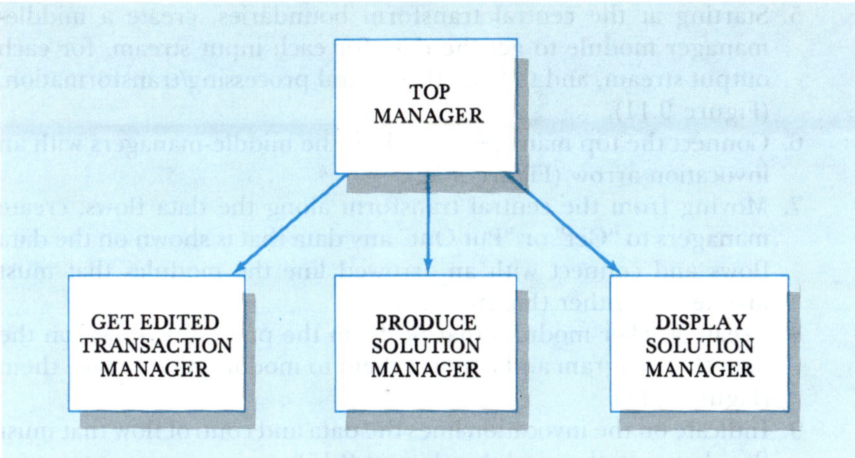

FIGURE 9.12

Adding invocations.

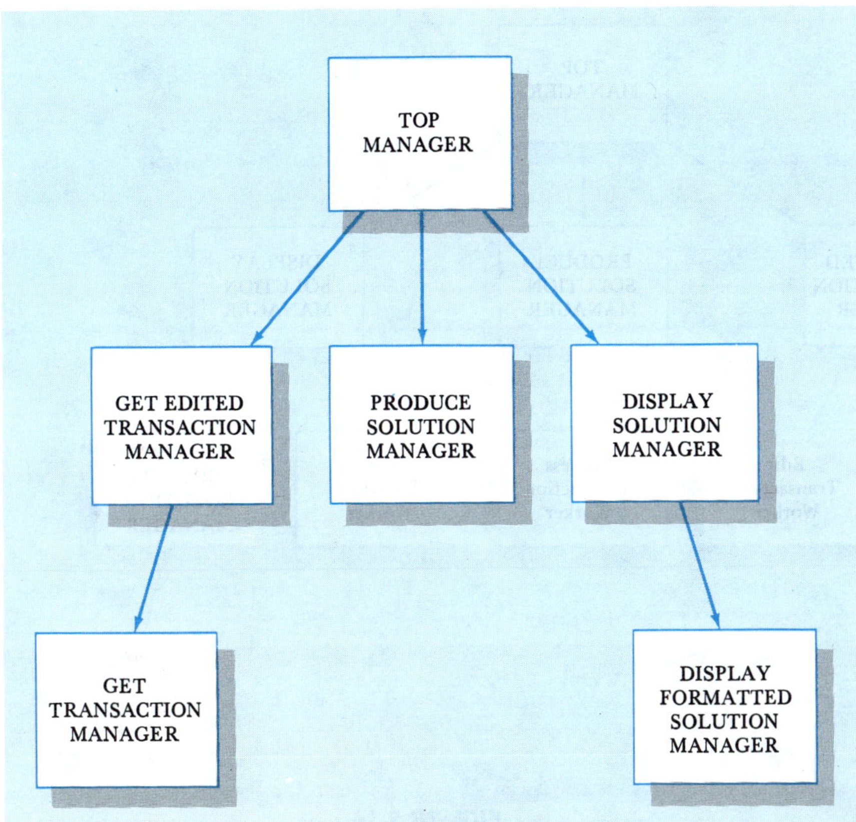

FIGURE 9.13

Adding additional functions.

5. Starting at the central transform boundaries, create a middle-manager module to get the data for each input stream, for each output stream, and to head the central processing/transformation, (Figure 9.11).
6. Connect the top manager to each of the middle-managers with an invocation arrow (Figure 9.12).
7. Moving from the central transform along the data flows, create managers to "Get" or "Put Out" any data that is shown on the data flows and connect with an arrowed line the modules that must invoke each other (Figure 9.13).
8. Create worker modules that perform the processes shown on the data flow diagram and connect them to modules that invoke them (Figure 9.14).
9. Indicate on the invocation lines the data and control flow that must flow between the modules (Figure 9.15).

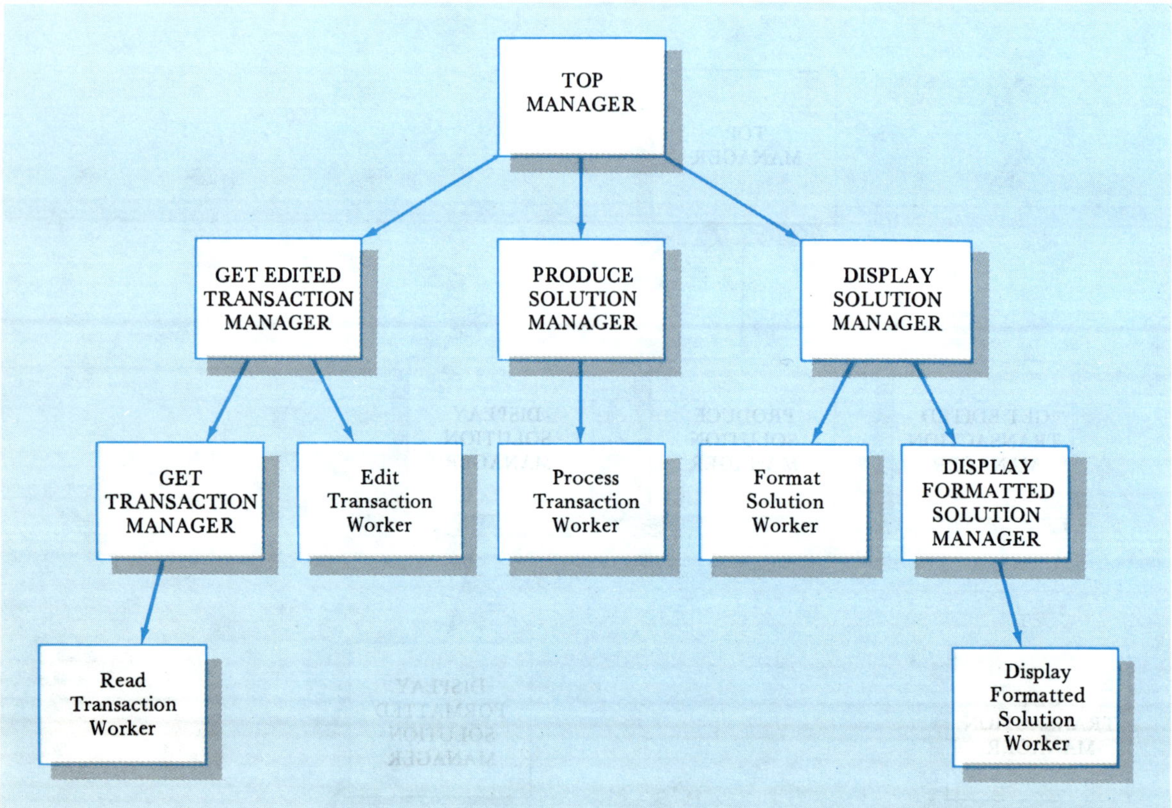

FIGURE 9.14
Creating worker modules.

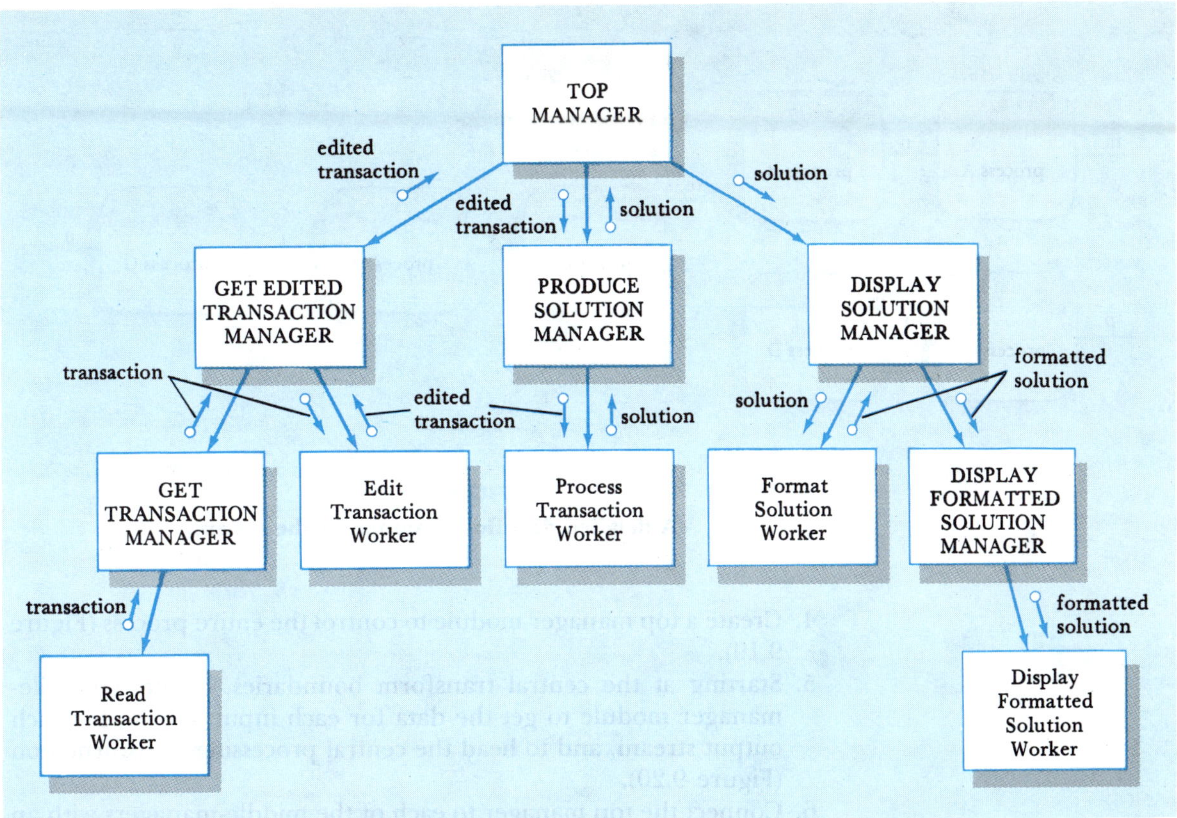

FIGURE 9.15

Indicating data and control flows.

Another Example of the Use of the Procedure

To anchor the above method, we will exhibit how the procedure is used to create a slightly more complex structure chart.

1. Obtain a copy of the most detailed DFD of the system that requires software to be developed (Figure 9.16).
2. Determine major input and output streams on the data flow diagram. This is done for the input stream by examining inputs at the source of data to the system and examining each process to determine if it is an input activity or actual processing of the data. Then the output stream is examined by starting at the destination and working backward, examining each process to determine if it is preparing for output or doing actual processing (Figure 9.17).
3. Denote the middle-most processes that actually transform inputs into outputs and mark this on the data flow diagram (a circle may be appropriate) (Figure 9.18).

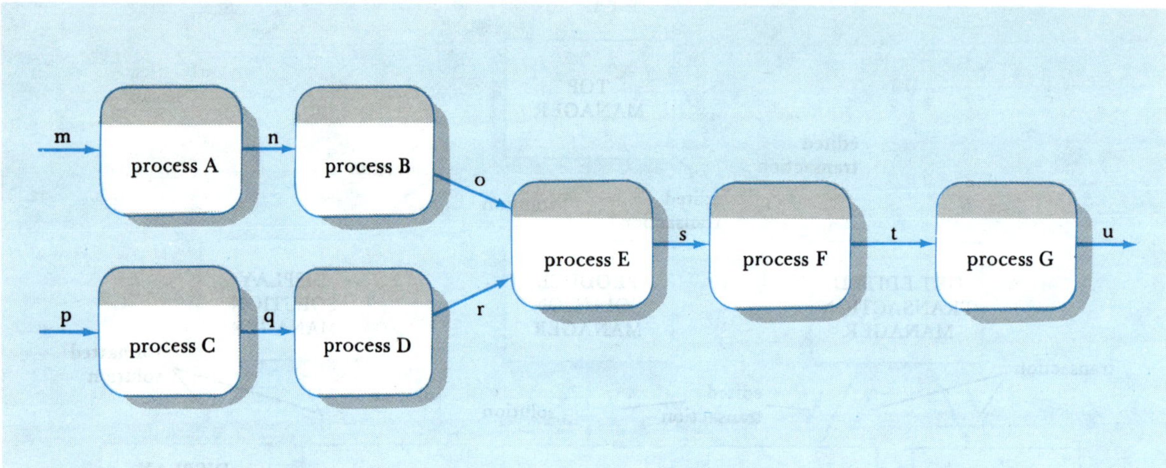

FIGURE 9.16
A detailed data flow diagram for the system.

4. Create a top manager module to control the entire process (Figure 9.19).
5. Starting at the central transform boundaries, create a middle-manager module to get the data for each input stream, for each output stream, and to head the central processing/transformation (Figure 9.20).
6. Connect the top manager to each of the middle-managers with an invocation arrow (Figure 9.21).

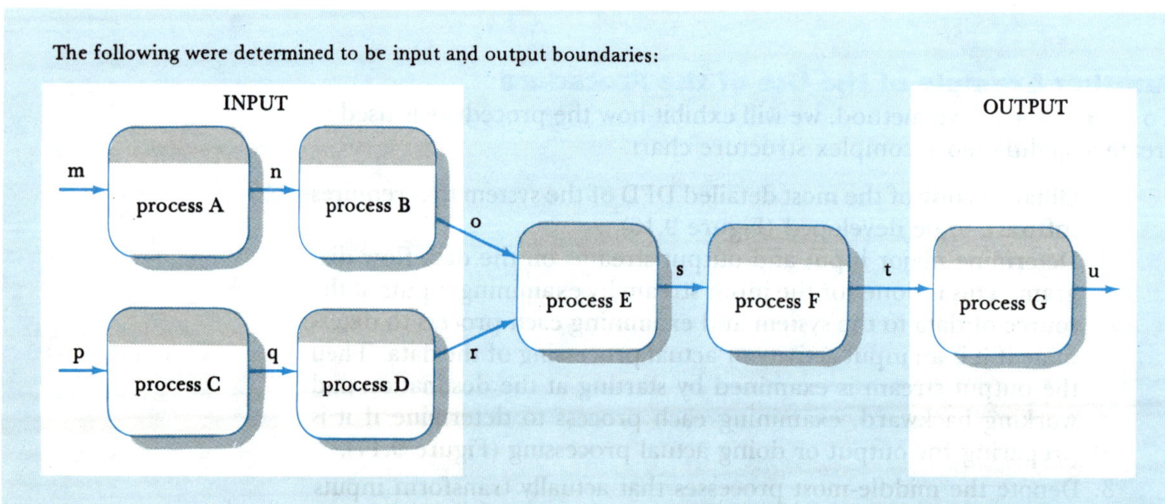

FIGURE 9.17
The data flow diagram with denoted input and output boundaries.

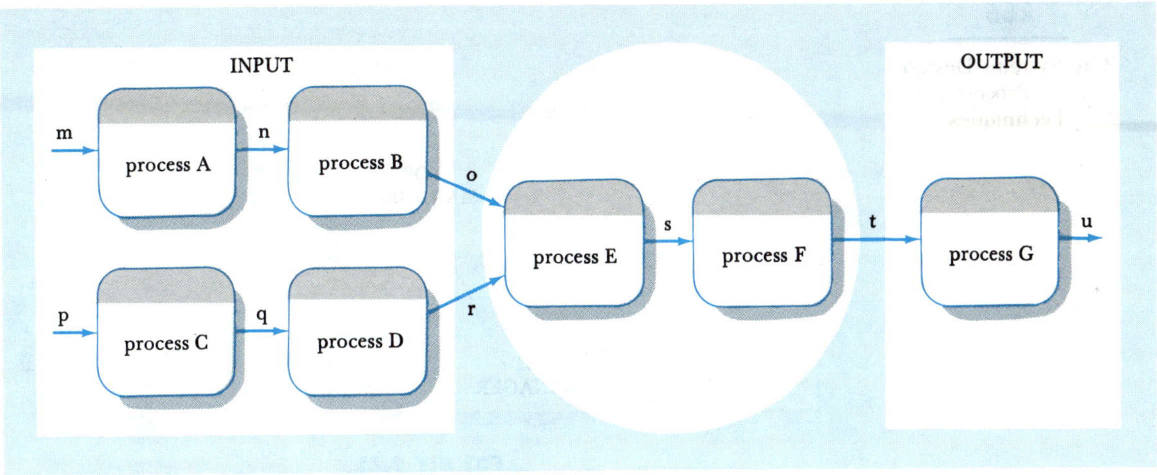

FIGURE 9.18
Denoting the transform processes.

FIGURE 9.19
Creation of the top manager.

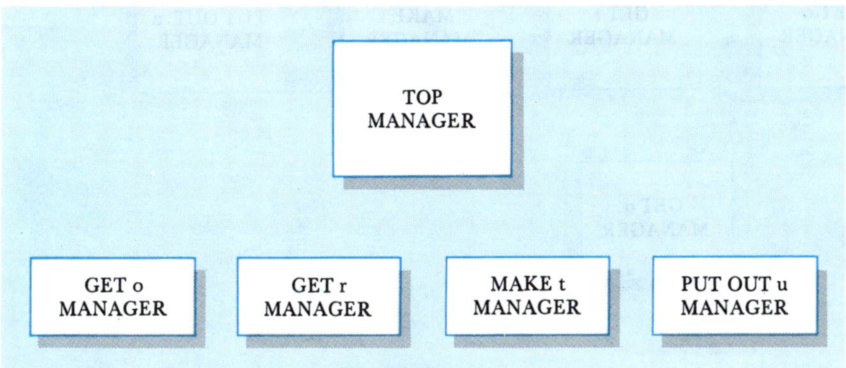

FIGURE 9.20
Creating middle managers for each input, output, and processing stream.

7. Moving from the central transform along the data flows, create managers to "Get" or "Put Out" any data shown on the data flows and connect with an arrowed line the modules that must invoke each other (Figure 9.22).

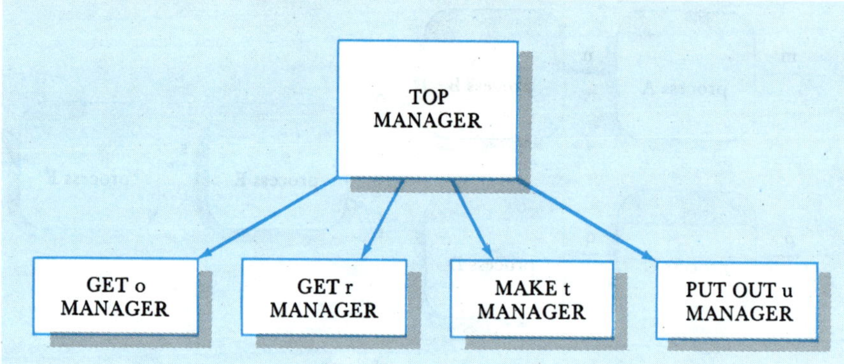

FIGURE 9.21
Giving the top manager "invocation privileges."

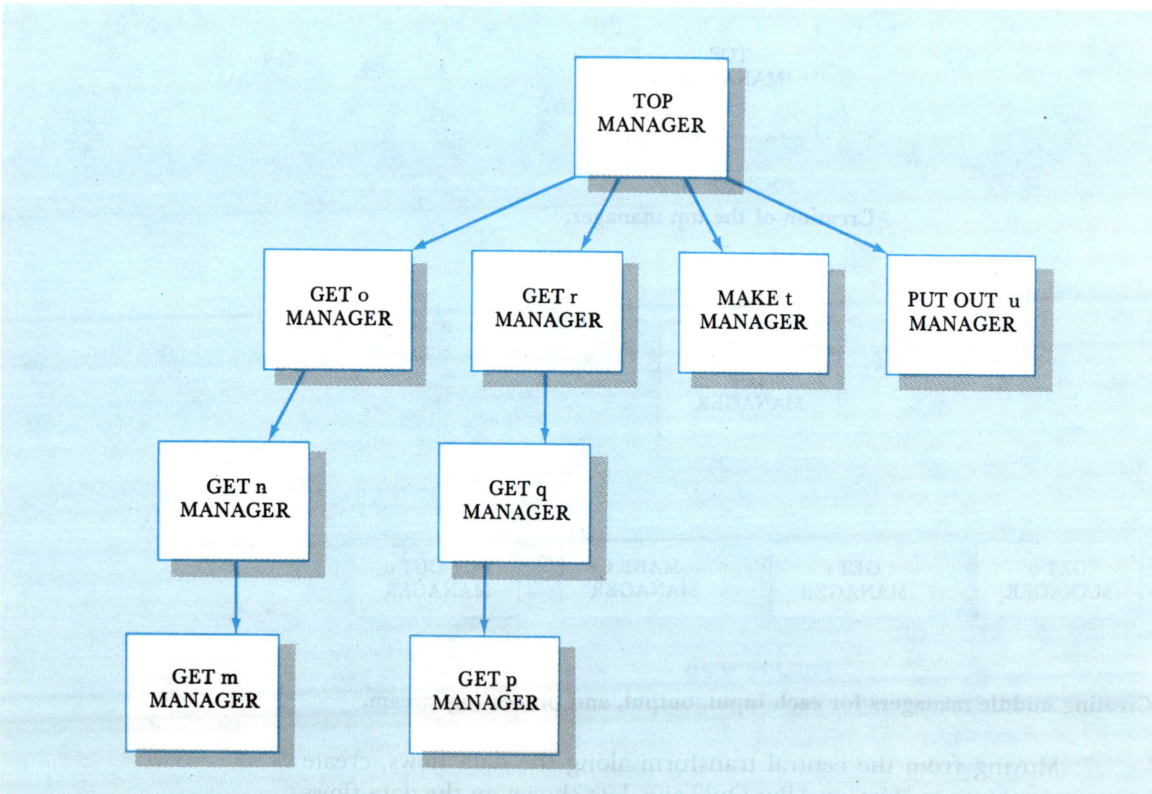

FIGURE 9.22
Creating "Get" and "Put" managers.

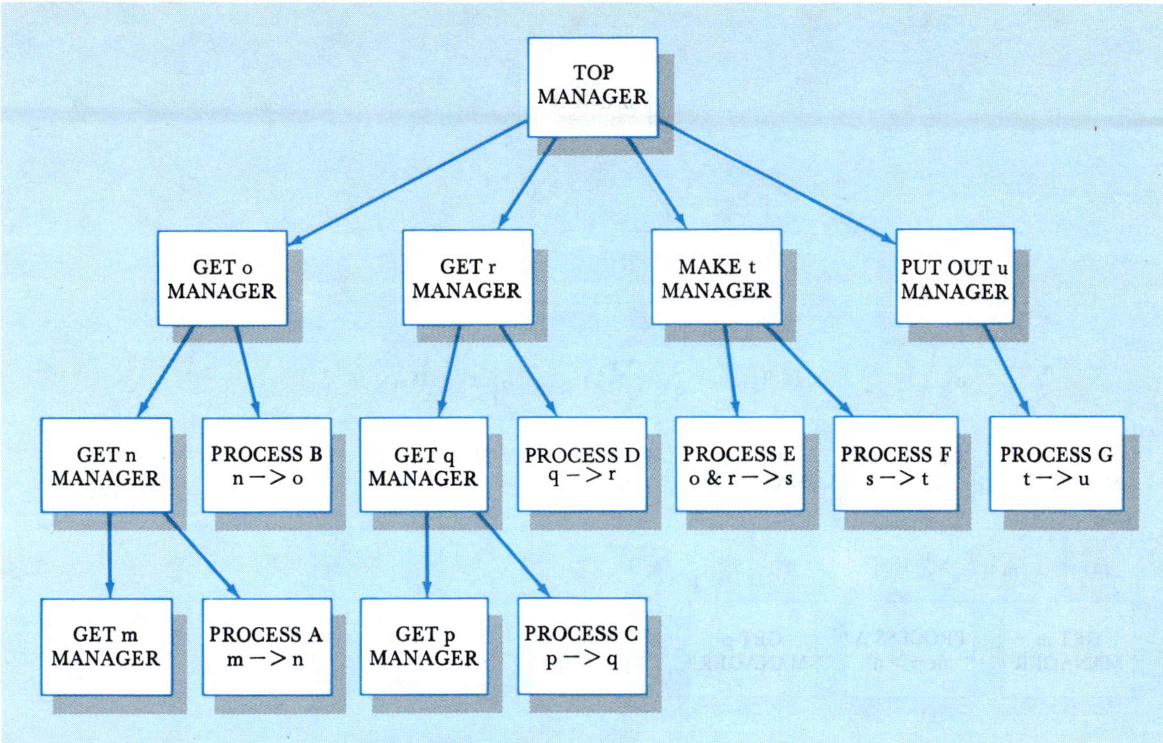

FIGURE 9.23

Adding worker modules.

8. Create worker modules that perform the processes shown on the data flow diagram and connect them to modules that invoke them (Figure 9.23).
9. Indicate on the invocation lines the data and control flow that must flow between the modules (Figure 9.24).

Transform- versus Transaction-Centered Design

Not all data flow diagrams contain a sequential set of processes. Often there is a need to execute different modules depending on some condition. For example, there may be a need to decide among several types of transactions. Such a data flow diagram might look like Figure 9.25.

Process A would obtain a transaction. Process B would determine the transaction type and dispatch it to either Process C, D, or E, depending on the transaction type. The processing would take place and Process F would display the result. This would be represented on a structure chart as shown in Figure 9.26.

In more complex structure charts of larger systems, both transform- and transaction-centered portions likely would appear.

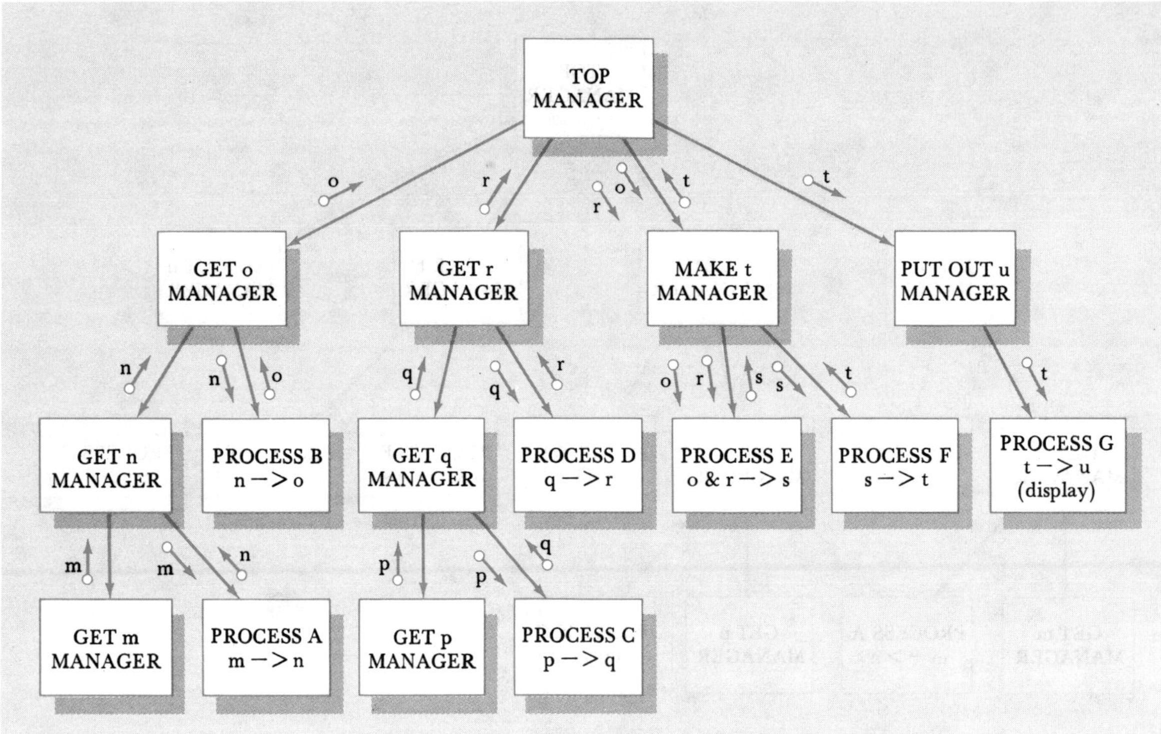

FIGURE 9.24

Adding data and control flows.

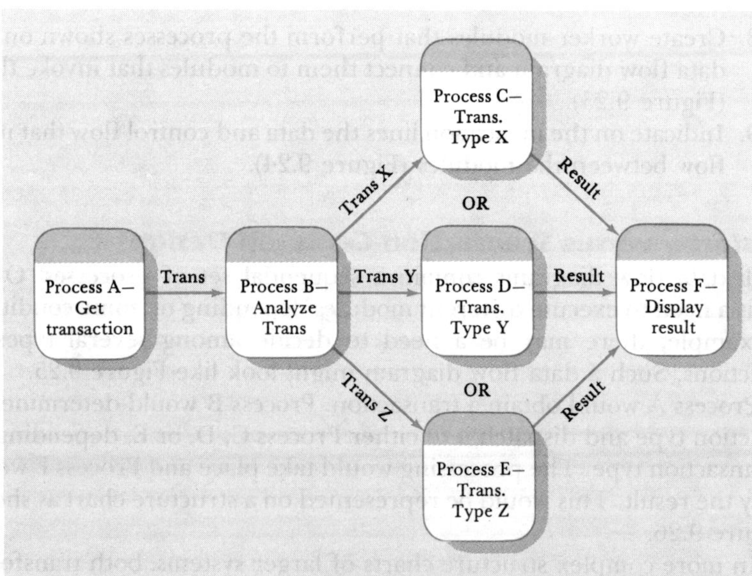

FIGURE 9.25

A transaction-centered data flow diagram.

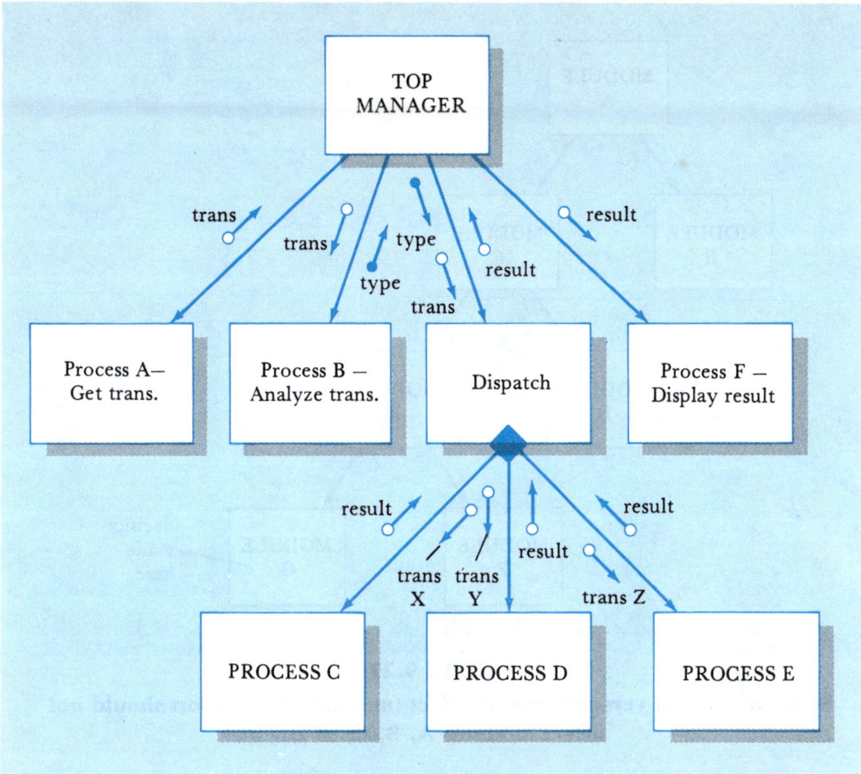

FIGURE 9.26
A structure chart based on transaction-centered processing.

Other Structured Design Terminology

There are some other terms that the student may run across when reading further. They are introduced here to for some basic background and understanding.

Morphology. *Morphology* is a medical term derived from the Greek language that means the general form and structure of an organism. In systems terms, it means the general shape of the system. Constantine found that afferent-oriented morphologies which are heavy on the input stream are hard to maintain. He also found that efferent-oriented morphologies which are heavy on the output stream are difficult to maintain. (In medical terms, *afferent* means "to the brain" while *efferent* means "from the brain.")

Scope of Effect versus Scope of Control. The ***scope of control*** of a module is the module itself and all of its subordinates. The ***scope of effect*** of a decision (by a module) is the aggregation of the modules containing any processing that is conditional upon that decision. Scope of effect of a decision by a module should not exceed its manager's scope of control. This could occur when one module does something that has an effect on

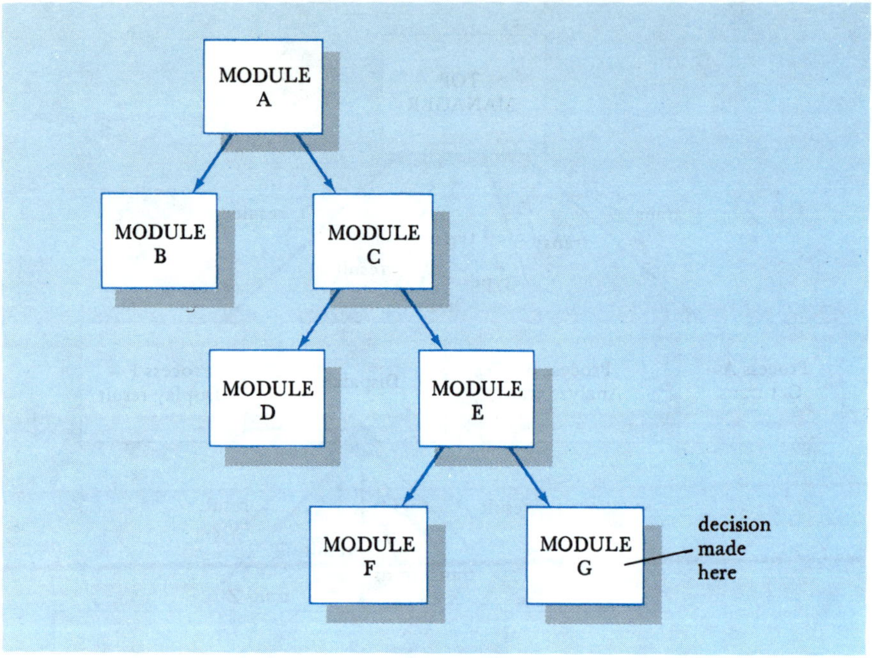

FIGURE 9.27

Scope of control versus scope of effect (module G's decision should not affect modules A, B, C, or D).

another module and the second affected module is not under control of the same manager module. This is equivalent to a low-level worker making a decision that has an effect on another worker who works for another manager. Another way of stating the principle is that if a module A is affected by a decision, then the module A should be subordinate to the decision making module's boss. In Figure 9.27, if the decision made by module G affects module A, B, C, or D, it is beyond the appropriate scope of control.

Span of Control. The *span of control* is the number of modules that can be invoked by a managerial module. This span should not be too great. This can occur when a boss or manager module has too many worker or other boss modules under its control. The boss module can become very complex. Some systems designers believe the seven plus or minus two rule should apply to the number of modules beneath a manager module.

Packaging and Lexical Inclusion. Even though modules are logically represented as separate and distinct units, the actual physical implementation may include them as separate. To maximize performance, it may be necessary to physically aggregate different modules. For example, it may be more efficient to include two logical modules into one physical module if this makes it possible to include them both in active computer memory at

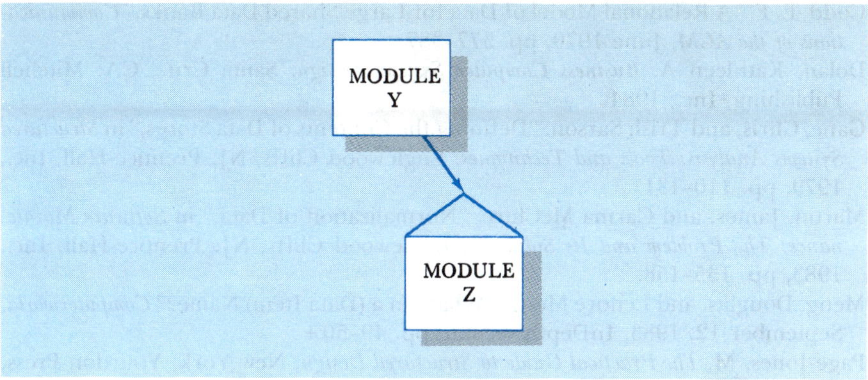

FIGURE 9.28
Module Z is lexically included in module Y.

one time. Some persons advocate using a special symbol to exhibit this phenomenon which is called lexical inclusion. For example, Figure 9.28 shows module Z is logically separate, but physically included in module Y.

This concludes the material on program design. It is hoped that the student will look at programs and programming in a different light, and realize that there is a difference between good and bad programs. Most of us likely have created some of each. The hope for the future is that we, as beginning programmers, now know the difference between good and bad.

SUMMARY

This chapter was not intended to make you an expert at specifying a physical design for a new system. This expertise can only come with much knowledge and experience. But the reader should understand the components of a physical plan and the important role others will play in establishing such a plan. Students should also realize that other courses in their curriculum will aid them in building expertise, and that learning in this area will continue as long as a person is in systems development work. Technical knowledge is perishable and must be constantly updated. Other topics, such as the design of software, are based on some conceptual foundations that the student should absorb and attempt to apply to any software development activities.

References and Further Readings

Boehm, B. W. "Software Engineering," *IEEE Transactions on Computers,* vol. C-25, no. 12, December 1976, pp. 1226–1241.

"Bringing Voice into the Long-Distance Data Network," *Infosystems,* November 1984, pp. 46–48.

Codd, E. F. "A Relational Model of Data for Large Shared Data Banks," *Communications of the ACM,* June 1970, pp. 377–387.

Dolan, Kathleen A. *Business Computer Systems Design,* Santa Cruz, CA: Mitchell Publishing, Inc., 1984.

Gane, Chris, and Trish Sarson. "Defining the Contents of Data Stores," in *Structured Systems Analysis: Tools and Techniques,* Englewood Cliffs, NJ: Prentice-Hall, Inc., 1979, pp. 110–131.

Martin, James, and Carma McClure. "Normalization of Data," in *Software Maintenance: The Problem and Its Solutions,* Englewood Cliffs, NJ: Prentice-Hall, Inc., 1983, pp. 135–158.

Meng, Douglas, and Lenore Meng. "What's in a (Data Item) Name?" *Computerworld,* September 12, 1983, InDepth section, pp. 49–50+.

Page-Jones, M. *The Practical Guide to Structured Design,* New York: Yourdon Press, 1980.

Pressman, Roger S. *Software Engineering: A Practitioner's Approach,* New York: McGraw-Hill Book Company, 1982.

Stevens, W., Myers, G., and L. Constantine. "Structured Design," *IBM Systems Journal,* vol. 13, no. 2, 1974, pp., 115–139.

Turk, Thomas A. "Using Data Normalization Techniques for Effective Data Base Design," *Journal of Information Systems Management,* Winter 1985, pp. 36–49.

Yourdon, E., and L. Constantine. *Structured Design: Fundamentals of a Discipline of Computer Program and Systems Design,* Englewood Cliffs, NJ: Prentice-Hall, Inc., 1979.

Review Questions

1. What are the four components of a physical system plan?
2. Why is physical system planning more difficult than it was 10 to 15 years ago?
3. What are some of the criteria for *devices* in a physical systems plan?
4. What is meant by the word *transparency?*
5. What are the major criteria for software design? Which of the criteria has been shown by research to be very costly?
6. What is meant by the words *black box?* Why is it important in systems development?
7. Why might it be detrimental for an organization to depend on an outside consultant to make a hardware decision?
8. What kinds of things might be moved via telecommunications in an organization?
9. Why might people resent being represented by a code?
10. Why might coding be less critical than it was 10 years ago?
11. What is the difference between a VTOC and a structure chart?
12. In general terms, what kind of coupling is desired in a software design?
13. What is the difference between a data and a control couple?

14. Why is it not advised to have a control couple flow from a boss module to a worker module?

15. Give an example of coincidental cohesion.

16. Why might a program flowchart lead to procedural cohesion?

17. What are *side effects?* How might they be detected if someone wrote a sentence describing a module?

18. What is "morphology?

Discussion Questions

1. A programmer said software design and programming are synonymous. What would be your reaction?

2. What other classes that you will take or have taken build on or support the material in this chapter? What topics covered in these classes will aid you to be a better systems developer?

3. Why would building a car radio and a clock into one device violate some of the rules for good maintenance? Why might this still be done today?

4. Give an example of some commonly used device that uses the black box concept to improve maintainability. How would modularity affect a purchasing decision for something like an automobile or a home appliance?

5. Does it really matter if coupling and cohesion guidelines are violated if the system works?

6. Do you think it would be possible to develop a structure chart without a data flow diagram?

7. Explain how coupling and cohesion are related.

8. Does coincidental cohesion really exhibit cohesion?

Exercises

1. Convert the data flow diagram segment shown below to a structure chart.

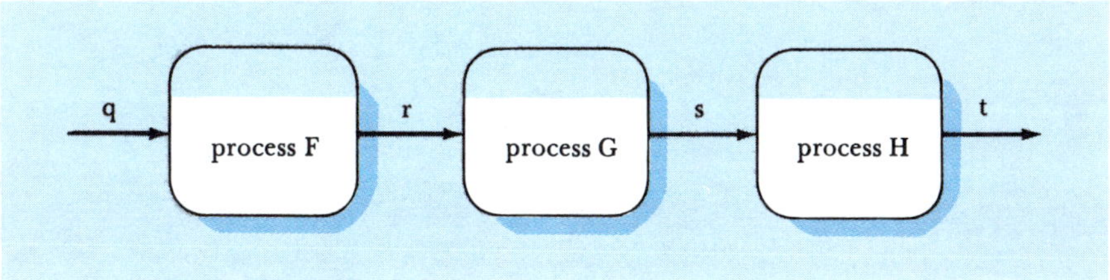

2. Convert the following data structure to third normal form. Make any reasonable assumptions you need to make, but be sure to state them.

Entity called STUDENT which contains:

Student-ID (primary key)
Student-Name
Student-Address
Student-Major
Student-Year
  Class-ID
  Class-Name
  Class-Instructor-Name
  Class-Credit
  Class-Grade
Student-Gradepoint (derived)

3. Investigate your university's or organization's hardware and telecommunications facilities. See if you can obtain performance specifications for the devices in the configuration.

CHAPTER 10

CHAPTER OBJECTIVES

You should be able to:

- Defend the need for careful development of the people subsystem
- Specify the systems activities to develop the people subsystem
- Understand how to use a data flow diagram to determine people–machine boundaries
- Specify when to use which procedure specification technique
- Compose a decision table, decision tree, Playscript, and "tight" English procedure
- Organize, write, and review a user reference manual
- Specify, organize, and review a user training plan

Woodridge, Ill.—A clash between a left-handed clerk and a grocery chain's work rules has resulted in a jury's judgment . . . in favor of the clerk. "It didn't make sense," said Crystal Sagen of the requirement by the Jewel Food Stores that she check out groceries with her right hand. "It was discrimination against left-handers." Miss Sagen . . . said that until the store . . . switched to computerized checkout scanners in 1981, she was one of the fastest clerks, working with her left hand. After the scanners were installed Miss Sagen said she was told that all checkers had to check right-handed . . . . After a year and a half at the store she quit. She sued Jewel and last month a Du Page County Circuit Court jury, all right-handers, awarded her $136,700. —From an Associated Press Dispatch (in Fortune, March 18, 1985, p. 165)

THIS CHAPTER INCLUDES an introduction to the human aspects of systems design. Included are the topics of determining person–machine boundaries, procedure and job design, training design, and manual design. The techniques of decision trees, decision tables, structured and tight English, and Playscript are examined.

As stressed in Chapter 1, people make up a critical subsystem in organizations. Very few systems have no people in them. People must perform procedures, provide and use data, and work with technology to amplify people strengths and support human weaknesses. To have excellent systems, the people subsystem must be designed as carefully as any other part of the system.

In today's systems, people may be hindered if they don't use technology; but without people, much technology is useless. Systems developers must assure that people are doing the tasks for which they are best suited. And the tasks must be done in an accepted, efficient, and meaningful way.

Excellent organizations lead from their strengths. We must use "people strengths" in designing systems. These strengths include being adaptive and creative, being intuitive and having feelings, handling unstructured situations, using judgment, and dealing with other humans in a sensitive manner.

Along with the strengths of people come very different needs. People need to be motivated and recognized for their contributions. They tire easily, get bored, are slower calculators and processors than machines, have smaller short-term memories, and are often imprecise. We must design systems to use people strengths and support human weaknesses.

The overall objective of this chapter is to help the future systems analyst and designer give users of systems a comfortable, efficient, and meaningful role in a newly designed system. This includes appropriately designed procedures aided by tested manuals and training programs. Chapter 11 will expand the human role by introducing the design of person-machine interfaces and input/output layouts.

DESIGNING FOR PEOPLE PERFORMANCE

In studying the history of systems, we see that three types of *feasibility* have been discussed (McKinsey study):

1. *Technical*—whether something is possible with current technology
2. *Economic*—whether something makes sense from a cost/benefit view
3. *Operational*—whether something will be accepted and used

Historically, we have been very conscious of technical feasibility and have tried to economically justify systems. However, some of our technical successes were never used. A system that is not used—not operationally feasible—provides no benefits. This destroys the proposed economic feasibility.

This gaining of acceptance should not start when the system is ready to be implemented, but at the time user contact first is made, while the system is being developed. This means constant feedback and intermediate product reviews throughout the development of the system. There is no magic to developing accepted systems. However, there are some common themes running through all successful people subsystem development work. They include:

1. *Empathy for the User*—the developer must constantly think about how the user perceives the system. Perceptions count! The user must never be put in the position of thinking about the developer, "You really do not understand me or my job or needs."
2. *Action-Orientation*—the developer must tell the user what steps are needed to accomplish tasks that must be performed. If actions are required, the developer must specify those actions. The developer should not inform the user about topics and then expect the user to ferret out what he or she must do.
3. *Testing of All Developments and Documentation*—the developer must dispel a user's fear of new activities by making sure the performer will not get into trouble and will not experience unnecessary anxiety. The developer must make sure the new procedures, manuals, and training get the job done by actual performance evaluation, not armchair speculation.

These three guidelines take advantage of the strengths and weaknesses of people. We must treat people as humans, not as machines.

DETERMINING THE PERSON-MACHINE BOUNDARY

The first thing we must do when developing the people subsystem is to identify it. A useful aid for determining the person-machine boundary is the data flow diagram. Each process and data store can be examined to determine whether it makes sense to automate the processing or storage or have a person carry out the needed activity or maintain the storage.

The analyst should look at the strengths of people and machines mentioned earlier in the chapter and make recommendations based on the best use of available or obtainable resources. The analyst probably will not make the final decision on the degree of automation since that is a matter of information management plans, but, he or she might draw up a set of alternatives to aid in this decision.

The simplest and most vivid way to identify person activities is to draw identifying lines on the data flow diagram (See Figure 10.1). By this stage of the project, the diagram should be familiar to concerned users and developers. Once the boundaries are agreed on, the analyst will have the task of determining what people must do to contribute to the operation of the system.

MEANS OF OBTAINING PEOPLE PERFORMANCE

People involved with systems must do things—perform tasks or tactics—to accomplish some objective. How well people carry out these tactics is termed *performance.* The systems developer plays an important role in getting things done by people who are part of the system, and can assure that they have meaningful and understandable tasks to perform.

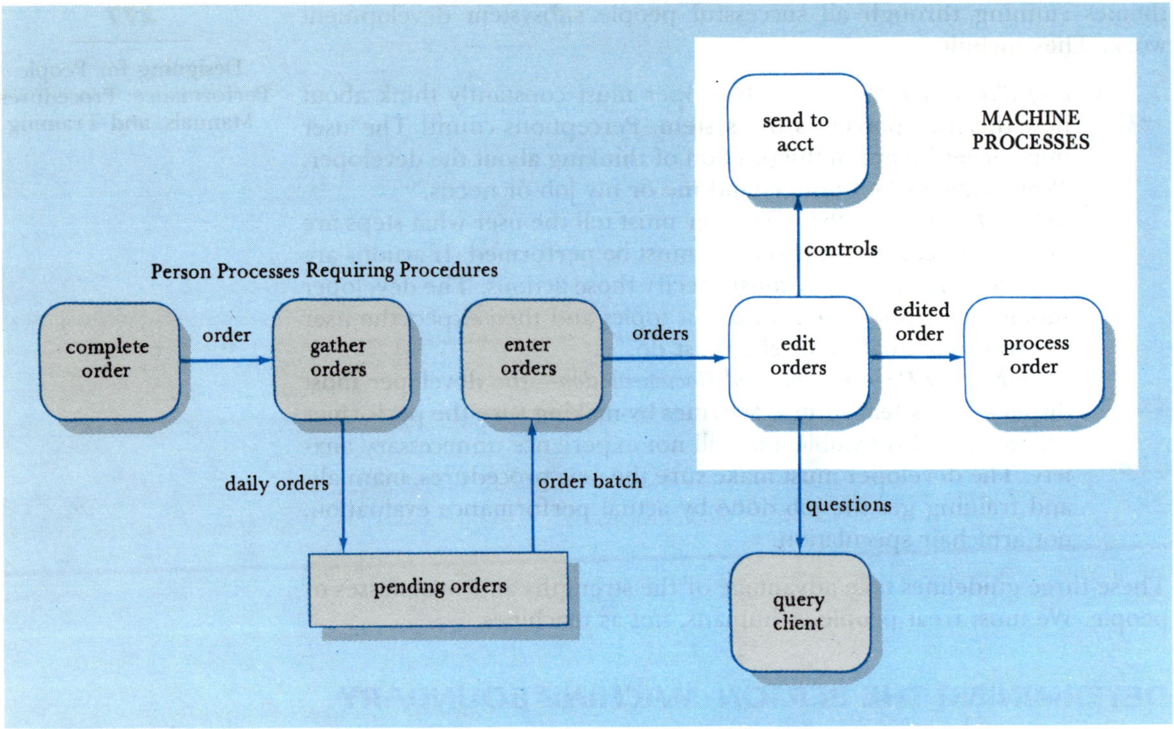

FIGURE 10.1

Person–machine boundary for an order processing system.

From our earlier discussions on defining the requirements of systems, we should be aware that we must define people performance in measurable terms. The developer's objective is to narrow the gap between employees' present and desired performance. There are three overruling factors that influence people performance:

1. *Knowing* what to do, how to do it, and when to do it
2. *Motivation* to want to do it
3. *Environmental conditions* to perform in

Each of these three states must be present to have people perform.

There are a number of ways of achieving improved people performance:

1. Improved people *selection* by a change in selection method or criteria
2. *Training* on what to do, how to do it, and when
3. *Performance aids* such as checklists, procedures, or manuals
4. Redesigned *jobs* or task sequences
5. Redesigned *tools,* equipment, or forms
6. Changed *supervision*

7. Changed *reward structure*
8. Changed work *environment* (heat, light, social interaction, etc.)

We must first realize that formal training is only one method of increasing performance. The analyst must take a *holistic* view of the person in the work environment and examine all of the above factors. Then, the analyst must determine what factors are under his or her control. For example, the reward structure might be fixed by a labor contract, or there may not be the opportunity to change people currently on the job, or hire new employees.

In examining people performance, it often is wise to plan for formal training only as a last resort. Other methods to achieve performance should be considered before formal training. Alternatives to formal training such as guided reading or computer-based tutorials often are less costly and more effective than gathering everyone into a training room. Formal training just before implementation is often a last attempt to fix a poorly designed system.

A more reasonable approach is involving users or representatives of users as the system is being developed, doing informal introductions and tests as part of development activities, using performance aids such as checklists or task lists, and including self-explanatory dialogs within automated parts of the system. The most effective means of learning is by doing, and this should take place as the system is being developed.

Job Design

Systems work can involve changing peoples' jobs. If business tactics performed by humans change, the tasks to be performed change and result in changed job descriptions. Designing peoples' jobs is an entire field of study. A useful model of viewing a person's job is presented by Hackman and Oldham (see References). The model states that *desirable personal and work outcomes* include:

High internal work motivation
High-quality work performance
Low absenteeism and turnover

These are outcomes managers desire.

To achieve these outcomes, a person must be able to achieve some *critical psychological states,* including:

Experienced work meaningfulness
Experienced outcome responsibility
Knowledge of activity results

These states mean that people must believe that what they are doing is important and that somebody cares, that he or she can affect results by what is done on the job ("I did it!"), and that they will get feedback on the results of actions. This leads to a statement of core job dimensions that can result in the above psychological states. *Key job core dimensions* include:

Skill variety (different tasks allowing challenge and interest)

Task identity (understandable tasks that are performable)

Task significance (useful tasks that require human attention)

Autonomy (freedom on what, when, and how tasks are done)

Feedback from job (mutual respect and support)

These factors may be under control of the analyst during system design or alteration.

It may be helpful to see if any of these core job dimensions can be changed. This could lead to more positive psychological states which in turn could lead to better personal and work outcomes. People do differ. They may or may not have a great need for job growth, challenge, social interaction, or job security. Groups of workers must be viewed both as individuals and as work units.

It is beyond the scope of this book to delve into this topic too deeply. Often experts in the organization are called in to aid in such a situation. It is also a good area in which the student should take elective courses in organizational change and job design.

Operationalizing Empathy—The Behavioral Audit

The ***behavioral audit*** is a means of operationalizing empathy. ***Empathy*** is the intellectual or imaginative identification with another person or persons. In the case of systems development, the person the analyst must empathize with is the proposed system user. The user may not think and act like you do. Fun for you could be hair-raising for another person.

The intent of the audit is to give systems developers a review list they can use during the processes of designing for people. It is a means of checking out business tactics, job specifications, and procedures for operational feasibility. The analyst must try to predict whether the proposed activities will be performed or resisted. To conduct a behavioral audit, the analyst should assume the role of a user and ask:

Will I have to work harder? Do I want to?

Will I have fewer workers reporting to me? Is this good or bad for me?

Will I have less authority? Will this upset me?

Will I have less responsibility? Do I want less?

Will I have to supervise more closely? Do I want to?

Will I have less freedom? Will that upset me?

Will I still be able to talk to the "gang"? Will I miss them?

Will I have to attend "school"? Is that fear-producing?

Will the fun go out of the job? Will I want to go to work?

Will new, younger persons threaten my status?

Will my earning go down? Will that upset me?

Will I get less overtime? Do I depend on it now?

Will my promotions be threatened?

What is going to happen next?

Remember that you are dealing with perceptions, which may or may not be reality, but are what the persons affected will have to deal with. It is best to incorporate as many factors as possible in the design that will lessen Fear, Uncertainty, and Doubt in users' minds. FUD has caused many systems to go unused.

Performance Aids

A ***performance aid*** provides a person with help when he or she is confronted with a task. Procedures, recipes, manuals, and checklists are all performance aids. Situations where performance aids are useful include:

When memory is overloaded (a simple scratch pad next to the phone)

When the task is done infrequently ("save the instructions for the artificial Christmas tree" or trying to do year-end reporting)

When tasks are complex (assembling Christmas toys or setting freight rates)

When a calculation may be repeated often (sales tax table next to cash register)

When workers begin using a new system, they will need memory aids. These should be prepared by the systems designer. (c. Joel Gordon 1986)

Note that many of these situations are often best performed using the strengths of machines. But we do not have machines for all tasks. They may not exist or may be too costly. Thus, we must support the actions and intellect of human performers.

In assembling performance aids, it is critical to organize them by task, not topic. For example, a page of instructions on how to bake a cake should have all the instructions in sequential order. The baker should not have to go to another page that discusses the topic of choosing pan size, then to another page that discusses the topic of mixing, and then to another page that discusses oven preheating, etc. Performance aids such as procedures, reference manuals, and checklists are meant to be used, not to be read for learning about a topic. Thus, organize them by task. This practice will eliminate the four fingers stuck in a manual, marking our places in different topics to try and get a task done.

A unique form of performance aid is an annotated form. This simply means that instructions to fill in a blank are next to the blank. It is frustrating to have a form with the blanks on one side of a page and instructions on the other side. To get the job done, the form completer has to flip from one side to the other.

In developing performance aids, we should note that people who can perform a task well may resist having others learn their "tricks", and what they do, which may be the use of performance aids. People may pride themselves on having their job and how they do it remain a mystery to others. They may not want others to be able to achieve the performance they are achieving. The analyst should be aware of this and attempt to enlarge the job of these threatened persons to give them added security. This topic will be discussed further in Chapter 13 under the section Managing Change. Now, however we will move on to writing and recording procedures.

PROCEDURES

Good written procedures should be performance aids. ***Procedures*** are written instructions for the accomplishment of tasks by humans. They usually are written for repeatable tasks. Procedures promote routine by doing things the same way. A goal is to have uniform actions done in the most economical way. A *manual* is a collection of procedures organized with indexes so we can find the needed procedure.

We have heard persons refer to "SOPs." These are Standard Operating Procedures. SOPs are the way tasks typically are done. Depending on the organizational culture, there may be very specific structured procedures or there may be hardly any written procedures at all. For example, McDonald's hamburger chain has a 19-step written procedure for making their french fries.* There are likely other food establishments that do not have that degree of standardization.

Written procedures record standard operating procedures and help achieve standard results, make sure the right instructions are followed,

Written procedures record standard operating procedures and help achieve standard results, make sure the right instructions are followed, help when training new people or when experienced people have to do a task infrequently, and allow for review because a written procedure can be reviewed better than one in someone's mind.

An example of procedure changing for better performance is the task of finding a fuel line leak in an auto. If the procedure required the mechanic to check under the hood, then near the gas tank, then under the hood again, then under the car, and again under the hood with no good reason for the sequence, the procedure should be examined and changed. The sequence could probably be changed to follow a path of proximity. We have all encountered procedures and after having performed them, ask ourselves, "Isn't there a better way?"

There are some distinctions that must be made between words we use when talking about procedures. These distinctions include:

Procedure versus policy (a policy is a general guideline which sets the scene for writing the procedure)

Procedure versus process (a process can be performed by a machine or by a person—such as on data flow diagrams—while a procedure is performed by a person)

Procedure versus program (a program is a process performed by a machine)

Procedure versus business logic (a procedure contains all the sequential steps while business logic only includes branching and decision making)

Procedure versus minispec (a *minispec* is a term used to represent a process in some systems development training circles)

PROCEDURE DESIGN CONSIDERATIONS

There are several things that should be considered when designing procedures. We must take into account the need for empathy, action orientation, and testing, which were mentioned earlier as guidelines for design. The considerations include:

Individual Differences—One example is the procedure designed by a 6-ft 6-inch-tall analyst for picking materials off a shelf. This task was performed by a group of persons, none of which was taller than 5 ft 5 inches. They couldn't reach. We should also be aware that manual procedures are often performed by left-handers. We must assure this is considered.

Complex Logic—the use of logic techniques discussed in this chapter are often superior to narratives.

Needed Materials or Data—you can't do the job if you don't have the tools or the input.

Suitability in the Work Environment—don't give someone in an unclean environment a form to fill out that you want kept clean. The study of the engineering of equipment and work environments is called **ergonomics.** This includes consideration of proper desks, chairs, computer terminals, lighting, sound, and decor for best performance.

WHY NOT USE ENGLISH NARRATIVE?

Many people do not have the ability as writers to use the English language precisely enough to give specific instructions. Nor is the language as we usually speak and write it condensed enough for computer expression. We may take many words to say something. The words are often confusing, so we use more words to try and clarify them. Then we need more words to clarify the added words. The result is chaos. For example, consider this sentence from a systems requirement statement:

> On the report entitled 'Customer Purchases by Month' on which the title is centered eight lines from the top of the page, with 3 blank lines before the body of the report, columns one through seven contain the customer number, and columns nine through fourteen contain . . . with summary totals for the last three fields . . . .

This is attempting to create a visual image in someone's mind. Most people are not very good at using language to do this. An analyst will in most cases better serve the person trying to visualize a layout by developing a mock-up of the report or screen.

We may fall into more traps when writing instructions:

Undefined adjectives (what is a "favored" supplier or a "regular" customer?)

Missed conditions ("less than 20 years of age, or 21 years or older"—what about the 20-year-olds?)

WORDS, WORDS, WORDS

NASA walked away with this year's Doublespeak Award, conferred annually by a national panel of English teachers, for its muddled account of the Challenger spacecraft disaster. The winning comment was: "The normal process during the countdown is that we tag up the operational loops and face to face with the firing room to ascertain the facts that project elements are monitoring the data and that are understanding the situation as we proceed are still in the go direction."

U.S. Defense Department jargon put the Pentagon in the running by calling temporary coffins "aluminum transfer cases," a hammer a "manually powered fastener-driving impact device," a flashlight an "emergency exit light," a steel nut a "hexiform rotatable surface compression unit," and a tent, part of the "Marine Corps Expeditionary Soft Shelter System," a "frame-supported tension structure."

From United Press International, November 25, 1986

Sentences that can be interpreted in different ways ("morc than 2 hours away and having a car or not having an airline discount are to contact company headquarters"—do you make contact if you are more than 2 hours away *and* have a car? Or do you make contact if you are more than 2 hours away *and* don't have a discount or just what do you do?)

We need ways of representing business procedures that are more precise. Some of the tools and techniques that analysts use will be described in the next sections.

Playscript

Playscript is a method advocated by Leslie H. Matthies (Matthies, Schultis). It is similar to the script of a movie or play. To visualize what a Playscript looks like, think back to your early school days when participating in school plays. Playscript denotes the performer and what the performer must do. For example, the first performer's name is included along with his or her actions, then the second performer's name is included along with his or her actions, and so on. This notation is usually preceded by a statement of policy that governs the procedure.

The general form of a Playscript procedure is:

"A Policy Statement Governing the Following Procedure"

Who (Actor1)	1. Step to Be Done by Actor1 (Script)
	2. Next Step to Be Done by Actor1
	3. Next Step . . .
Who (Actor2)	1. Step to Be Done by Actor2

ETC.

Playscript is useful when there is a sequence of actions that are performed by several persons with different job titles. Playscript breaks down when there is a break in the sequence which requires branching.

Some guidelines for developing Playscript include:

Use of simple, not compound, sentences

Action verbs beginning each sentence

One action per sentence

Leaving white space on paper, not crowding

Using simple Arabic numbering, no Roman numerals

See Figure 10.2 for a specific example of Playscript.

Decision Tables

Decision tables can represent complex logic in a tabular form. These tables can document and display appropriate actions if certain conditions exist, but they do not show sequence of actions. An advantage of decision tables is exhaustiveness. This means it is possible to show all possible combinations of conditions and then determine what the appropriate actions are.

Merchandise Returns Policy and Procedure

Date Issued: October 3, 1983 Date Effective: October 6, 1983

Store Policy Regarding Merchandise Returns
Any returned, undamaged merchandise that we sell can receive a full cash refund. Any questions on the policy or procedure must be referred to the department manager.

Procedure

Department sales clerk	1. Examine merchandise to verify no damage.
	2. Obtain master merchandise list.
	3. Locate merchandise item on list.
	4. Record item number and price on refund request.
	5. Calculate sales tax.
	6. Record sales tax on refund request.
	7. Calculate total of refund.
	8. Ask returner to complete refund request.
Returner	1. Fill in name and address on refund request.
	2. Sign refund request.
	3. Turn request over to department sales clerk.
Department sales clerk	1. Verify existence of name, address, and signature of returner.
	2. Refund full amount in cash.
	3. Give pink copy to returner.
	4. File white copy in inventory drawer.
ETC.	

FIGURE 10.2
An example of a Playscript procedure.

Decision tables are often viewed as complex by nonanalytic people. However, they can serve as excellent guides and communication aids for programmers and analysts when complex logic must be represented. There are even decision table processors that can convert decision tables to computer programming code. The analyst may be asked to create a decision table. There are a number of steps that should be followed to create a decision table.

1. Determine possible conditions and list in upper left quadrant of table.
2. a. Determine all possible condition entries and include in upper right quadrant of table. These sets of conditions usually are

called *decision rules*. If a limited-entry table is used (either Yes or No for any condition, which is the simplest form of decision tables), then the number of decision rules must be 2# of conditions. For example, if there were three possible conditions than the number of decision rules would be 2^3 or 8 decision rules.

b. List alternate possibilities for last condition starting with rule one and moving out to last rule (Y N Y N Y N Y N, etc.).

c. For each repeating group of possibilities, cover with alternating possibilities (Y Y N N Y Y N N, etc.).

d. Repeat for each condition (if three conditions, then Y Y Y Y N N N N, etc.).

3. Determine possible actions and list in lower left quadrant of table.
4. Determine specific actions for each decision rule and include in the lower right of the quadrant.
5. Simplify by combining redundant decision rules. Do this by finding pairs of rules for which:
   a. The action in the lower right quadrant is the same.
   b. Only one condition in the upper right quadrant differ.
   Continue this until no "indifference" exists. This really says that if condition 1 and condition 2 are the same, condition 3 makes no difference in what action we take. We still take the same action. Indifference is indicated by combining the decision rules with a "–" (dash) in the one condition box where there was a difference.
6. Reorder decision rules to best suit users of table.

The above steps will be illustrated with a simple example. Do not be concerned with understanding the techniques that are mentioned. Focus on the above procedure and the conditions and actions that are described in the following statement:

> A company has a decision process to cover most cases for determining whether to use a decision table, decision tree, "tight" English, or a combination of these techniques. If the user of the procedure is a clerk, either a decision tree or "tight" English should be used. If the procedure is for a clerk and includes sequential steps as well as logic, "tight" English should be used. If the procedure is for a clerk and also will be converted into computer code, "tight" English should be used with decision tables representing complex logic. If not for a clerk, use decision tables and "tight English." If the above rules don't cover the situation, see your supervisor.

1. Determine possible conditions and list in upper left quadrant of table. Conditions include:
   User is Clerk
   Sequential Steps Included
   Computer Code Needed
   Or ELSE
2. a. Determine all possible condition entries and include in upper right quadrant of table. These sets of conditions usually are

called decision rules. If a limited-entry table is used (either Yes or No for any condition), then the number of decision rules must be 2# of conditions. For example, if there were three possible conditions then the number of decision rules would be 2^3 or 8 decision rules. Since there are three conditions, there are 8 possible decision rules. The ELSE rule will be handled separately.

b. List alternate possibilities for last condition starting with rule one and moving out to last rule (Y N Y N Y N Y N, etc.).

	Rules							
	1	*2*	*3*	*4*	*5*	*6*	*7*	*8*
User is Clerk								
Sequential Steps Included								
Computer Code Needed	Y	N	Y	N	Y	N	Y	N

c. For each repeating group of possibilities, cover with alternating possibilities (Y Y N N Y Y N N, etc.).

	Rules							
	1	*2*	*3*	*4*	*5*	*6*	*7*	*8*
User is Clerk								
Sequential Steps Included	Y	Y	N	N	Y	Y	N	N
Computer Code Needed	Y	N	Y	N	Y	N	Y	N

d. Repeat this for each condition (if three conditions, then Y Y Y Y N N N N, etc.).

	Rules							
	1	*2*	*3*	*4*	*5*	*6*	*7*	*8*
User is Clerk	Y	Y	Y	Y	N	N	N	N
Sequential Steps Included	Y	Y	N	N	Y	Y	N	N
Computer Code Needed	Y	N	Y	N	Y	N	Y	N

3. Determine possible actions and list in lower left quadrant of table.

	Rules							
	1	*2*	*3*	*4*	*5*	*6*	*7*	*8*
User is Clerk	Y	Y	Y	Y	N	N	N	N
Sequential Steps Included	Y	Y	N	N	Y	Y	N	N
Computer Code Needed	Y	N	Y	N	Y	N	Y	N
Use Decision Tree								
Use Decision Table								
Use "Tight" English								

4. Determine specific actions for each decision rule and include in the lower right of the quadrant.

	Rules 1	2	3	4	5	6	7	8
User is Clerk	Y	Y	Y	Y	N	N	N	N
Sequential Steps Included	Y	Y	N	N	Y	Y	N	N
Computer Code Needed	Y	N	Y	N	Y	N	Y	N
Use Decision Tree				X				
Use Decision Table	X		X		X	X	X	X
Use "Tight" English	X	X	X		X	X	X	X

5. Simplify by combining redundant decision rules. Do this by finding pairs of rules for which:
   a. The action in lower right quadrant is the same.
   b. Only one condition in the upper right quadrant differ.
   This really says that if condition 1 and condition 2 are the same, condition 3 makes no difference in what action we take. We still take the same action. Indifference is indicated by combining the decision rules with a "–" (dash) in the one condition box where there was a difference.

	Rules 1	2	3	4	5	6	7	8
User is Clerk	Y	Y	Y	Y	N	N	N	N
Sequential Steps Included	Y	Y	N	N	Y	Y	N	N
Computer Code Needed	Y	N	Y	N	Y	N	Y	N
Use Decision Tree				X				
Use Decision Table	X		X		X	X	X	X
Use "Tight" English	X	X	X		X	X	X	X

First, rules 1 and 3 can be combined. Then, rules 5 and 6 can be combined. Finally, rules 7 and 8 can be combined. This leaves us with:

	Rules 1/3	2	4	5/6	7/8
User is Clerk	Y	Y	Y	N	N
Sequential Steps Included	–	Y	N	Y	N
Computer Code Needed	Y	N	N	–	–
Use Decision Tree			X		
Use Decision Table	X			X	X
Use "Tight" English	X	X		X	X

Continue this until no "indifference" exists.

	Rules				
	1/3	*2*	*4*	*5/6*	*7/8*
User is Clerk	Y	Y	Y	N	N
Sequential Steps Included	-	Y	N	Y	N
Computer Code Needed	Y	N	N	-	-
Use Decision Tree			X		
Use Decision Table	X			X	X
Use "Tight" English	X	X		X	X

Rules 5/6 and 7/8 can be combined leaving:

	Rules			
	1/3	*2*	*4*	*5/6 7/8*
User is Clerk	Y	Y	Y	N
Sequential Steps Included	-	Y	N	-
Computer Code Needed	Y	N	N	-
Use Decision Tree			X	
Use Decision Table	X			X
Use "Tight" English	X	X		X

The table cannot be further simplified.

6. Reorder decision rules to best suit users of table. Rule 4 is put first. Then, rules 2, 1/3, and 5/6/7/8 follow. An ELSE condition is added.

	Rules				
	1	*2*	*3*	*4*	*5*
User is Clerk	Y	Y	Y	N	
Sequential Steps Included	N	Y	-	-	
Computer Code Needed	N	N	Y	-	
ELSE					Y
Use Decision Tree	X				
Use Decision Table			X	X	
Use "Tight" English		X	X	X	
See Supervisor					X

If the decision table is used as a supplement to a procedure, the "ELSE" should be used if there is a chance that there may be conditions for which no prespecified action can be determined. Note that in the above treatment, the procedure user is directed to his or her supervisor for help.

Extended entry tables are those with more than just a "YES" or "NO" for a condition. For example, a decision table representing shipping rates could have the country broken into four shipping zones. The same rules for creation exist except the number of decision rules would be increased. The tables can quickly become unwieldy and difficult to understand.

Decision Trees

Decision trees are a graphic representation of complex logic. Nodes are used to represent decision points and lines branch out to represent either further conditions or, finally, the actions to be taken based on the conditions expressed in the tree branches. (See Figure 10.3.)

If the procedure is written in English narrative, try to take each sentence and mark or highlight each condition and action. Build a "subtree" for each sentence in an attempt to parcel the logic. Look for the most frequent decisions that users must make first and try to move them toward the beginning of the tree. Move out on the tree following the sequence of decisions that users would use. Examine this sequence to see if changes might be facilitated. However, do not make changes until you ask why the procedure is not done in the manner in which you feel is more expeditious. You may find some "hidden agendas."

Structured and "Tight" English

Writing structured English can be a challenge for those persons skilled in writing complete and flowing sentences. Adverbs, punctuation, and compound sentences must be avoided in structured English. The writer should be as terse as possible. Only nouns, verbs, numbers and numeric qualifiers, and procedure specification words (IF, EQUALS, LESS THAN, etc.) should be used.

The structured statements should be combined using only:

Simple sequences

Repeated sequences with repetition qualifier at top of sequence (REPEAT . . . UNTIL . . .)

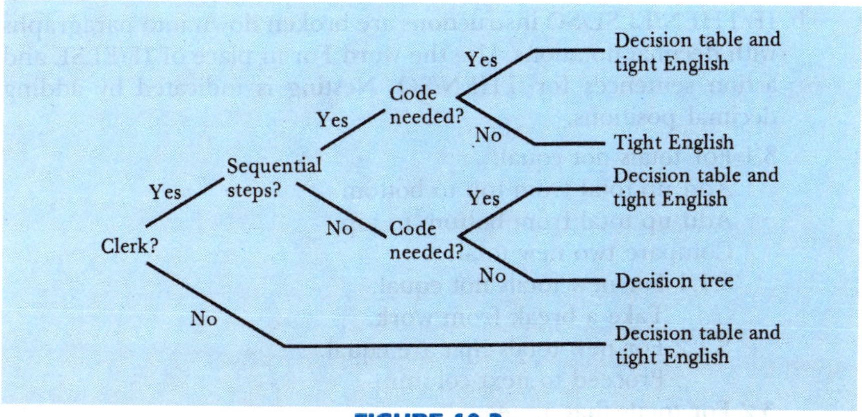

FIGURE 10.3

Decision tree for determining procedure specification technique.

Conditional sequences with condition stated at top of sequence

IF condition
THEN action
ELSE (not condition)
SO another action

"Actions" can be sets of other structured statements. Indentation should be used to distinguish groups of statements.

```
IF condition1
THEN IF condition2
        THEN actionX
        ELSE (not condition2)
        SO another actionY
ELSE (not condition1)
SO another actionZ
```

Care should be taken when "nesting" these conditions since confusion can quickly be created. A general guideline is to not use more than three levels of nesting. The action to be done most often should be found first by the performer. Groups of statements that fit together can be "chunked" as paragraphs. These modules should be associated with performing one function creating functional cohesion. This will facilitate changes and updating.

Structured English becomes very stilted and machinelike. An alternative is a technique called *tight English,* which has been advocated by Gane and Sarson (see References). They suggest making the following changes to structured English:

a. Sequential instructions are steps written as action imperatives. A manual worksheet procedure for a gradebook may include:
   For each column in worksheet:
   - Step 1: Add up total from top to bottom.
   - Step 2: Add up total from bottom to top.
   - Step 3: Compare two totals.

b. IF/THEN/ELSE/SO instructions are broken down into paragraphs with decimal notations. Use the word For in place of IF/ELSE and action sentences for THEN/SO. Nesting is indicated by adding decimal positions.

3.1 For totals not equal:
    Add up total from top to bottom.
    Add up total from bottom to top.
    Compare two new totals.
    3.1.1 For new totals not equal:
          Take a break from work.
    3.1.2 For new totals that are equal.
          Proceed to next column.
3.2 For totals that are equal.
    Proceed to next column.

c. If there are situations that never occur in combination, create a table with the series of situations and the resulting action. This is called *case structure*, since there could be several cases, none occurring at the same time.

Step 4: Determine grades:

Column Total	*Grade*
90–100	A
80–89	B
70–79	C
60–69	D.
59 or lower	F

Step 5 : Enter grade on gradesheet

Note that the end result is very similar to a succinctly written set of instructions to be used by a person, not a machine.

SELECTING A PROCEDURE WRITING TECHNIQUE

The analyst will often have a choice of technique. Communication should be of prime importance. If communicating with a user, a look-up table, decision tree, or "tight" English are good choices. If communicating with a computer programmer, a decision table or structured English may be more concise and compact, and will allow the programmer to establish the sequence that meets performance needs.

If there are multiple performers with no branching, Playscript is an excellent tool. A single performer dealing with complex branching may be happiest with a decision tree. "Tight" English is good if there are both sequences and a few conditional branches. A decision tree or table can be embedded in "tight English."

Often, a combination of techniques is used in development. A decision table can be used to ensure exhaustiveness. Then, if there is a small number of actions, the table can be used to create a decision tree that can be used with a less skilled audience. The choice is up to the analyst. Good judgment and empathy for the audience are needed.

REFERENCE MANUALS

Many of the procedures which systems analysts develop will end up in manuals. Manuals are used for both training and tutorials and for reference. The following discussion will focus on manuals that will be used for reference once training has taken place.

FUNCTIONS OF A REFERENCE MANUAL

A *reference manual* is a performance aid to allow a person to better perform a task. The manual can help a new person once a general understanding of a process is achieved through training. It also can aid an experienced person who only has to perform a task occasionally. The manual can serve as an aid to someone who is currently "stuck" on a problem and needs some ideas as to how to proceed.

A reference manual should not be treated or written as a textbook. A textbook typically discusses "worldly" subjects and once read and understood may leave the reader thinking, "I believe I understand, but I don't feel I can do anything new." This is the topic orientation that we talked about earlier in the chapter. A manual must aid someone in performing, not just in understanding.

The reader may ask whether the book you are reading is a textbook or a manual. The answer is "both." The general material and discussion are written in a textbook fashion. The procedures and helpful hints or reminders are included as references for future endeavors when you have to actually perform the general activities described in the book. The hope is that you will keep the book for future reference when you must actually use your newfound knowledge.

WRITING A MANUAL

To write a manual, the writer should have answers to the following questions:

Why am I writing this?

Who is going to be using it?

What tasks will users want to accomplish by reading this?

What don't readers care about that I might be tempted to include?

What is the *minimum introduction* readers need?

What tasks are done by the user most frequently?

This will give the writer the basic material to put in a manual. The writer should collect any policies and procedures that have been written which are appropriate for the manual. The writer should then make note of any missing procedures so that they can be developed.

ORGANIZING THE MANUAL

The previous sections give an idea of what must go into the manual. However, the organization of the manual is as important as the content. If someone cannot find something, they cannot use it. *The most important objective in manual organization is to put things in the manual so the user can get them out.*

The manual should be organized in a task-oriented manner. "To do xxx task, you should do the following steps:" is a set of words to be found in the manual. More frequently performed tasks should be listed first. If there is a great number of tasks to be performed, it may be beneficial to group them into categories. It is essential to have both an index of tasks in alphabetical order and and a table of contents which lists tasks in order of presentation.

A good exercise to help evaluate a reference manual is to examine the introductory section of your phone book. Does it have a task orientation? Is there a table of contents? Is there an index? What is the order of presentation of the tasks? Is the most frequently used task presented first? How might this "reference manual" be improved?

In developing a manual, be sure to check for any in-house rules, guidelines, outlines, or standards. They may dictate order, content, heading format and size, and spellings.

HINTS FOR MANUAL DEVELOPMENT

1. Use functionally cohesive modules to facilitate changes and updates. Functionally cohesive modules are "chunks" of writing that address one and only one task. There is one task or function to be accomplished, not several of them. This will facilitate changes since you can "unplug" one module and replace it.
2. Keep sections, paragraphs, sentences, and words simple. Remember the letters KISS—*K*eep *I*t *S*uper *S*imple. (but not so simple it would offend someone).
3. Include adequate referencing, indexes, and, if needed, a glossary.
4. Write for content, not bulk. Be concise, but also repeat materials to eliminate the "four-fingered bookmark problem" where the reader must "see this section" or "go to page xx." Remember the repetition in an earlier chapter when procedures were presented for team product reviews by both peers and users.
5. Utilize process logic tools such as decision trees, decision tables, or "tight English" if appropriate. Include illustrations, pictures, checklists, or tables if they help clarify.
6. Avoid jargon, abbreviations, theory, technical discussions, complexity, and items of poor taste such as puns or dialect.
7. Test the manual with practical exercises with representative users. Your own peers may not be representative of future users. Very few computer programs work on the first draft. Very few computer programs are completely debugged. About the same number of user manuals work on the first draft and are completely debugged. So, test any manual you write.
8. Before developing the manual, be aware of organization rules, guidelines, outlines, formats, and other standards that exist for reference manuals. The standards may include help in deciding on spellings, content, order, and other decisions with which the developer may be confronted.

ONCE WRITTEN AND TESTED

A manual is of no use if it is not accessible at the time it is needed. You should ensure that the manual is available to the task performers when the system is implemented. The user management should be made aware that

A Take-home Exam Question—"Analyze a manual you use frequently"—and A Student's Response.

Through rather unusual circumstances, I recently acquired a pool table. With the table came a small rule book, and since I knew virtually nothing about pool, I turned to the book for help. I had to discard the book and buy another one. The material on manual writing aided me in analyzing why this happened.

Book #1 was written in narrative format with very few captions or subtitles. Book #2 is broken into modules, and each different game is described in the same format. This makes #2 more convenient when disagreement over rules erupts around the table. The narrative in #1 is not exhaustive and always seems to leave something out, like what to do about jumped balls (not infrequent in my game), or how to place the balls in the rack.

Book #2 utilizes underlining, italics, and various font techniques. This makes finding things much easier as they stand out.

Book #1 seems to be written for the novice, beginning with the proper stance and ending with lists of champions and tournament records. Book #2, however, seems to have conflicting goals. It begins with information about the Billiard Congress of America (the publisher), moves to BCA equipment specifications, then beginner's instructions, followed by the different games, and ending with BCA champions and records. As a beginner with a new table, I really didn't need or want all that extraneous information—I just wanted to learn how to play. From the publisher's point of view, I think the primary purpose of the book may have been promotion of the BCA rather than instruction in billiards.

Both books featured diagrams that are simple and explanatory. However, Book #1 always seems to place the diagrams a page or two beyond the refer-

FIGURE 10.4

A critique of two manuals.

new persons performing the tasks included in the manual will need access to the manual.

Manuals must be updated when changes in procedures are made. Some organizations store their manuals in text processors to allow easy changing. A distribution list can also be maintained on electronic media to ensure that updates to manuals are made.

Some manual writers and testers will identify themselves in the manual. Usually this is the case if the writers and testers are proud of their work and feel partial ownership of and responsibility for the system. This is an organizational decision that can keep reference manuals current and where developers can learn from those who actually use their work. See Figure 10.4 for an analysis of two manuals.

TRAINING

Training users or others to have a role in creating an operational system is not just "laying on a course". Some people envision training as assembling a group of people in a room and going through a stack of slides and ence. Pictures of people to indicate stance and hand position are photos in #2, as opposed to sketches in #1, which seems less human and more difficult to emulate.

Book #1 makes a point of using numbers when listing tasks to be performed in sequence and alpha characters for unsequenced lists of related items. Book #2 makes no such distinction; all lists were numbered. This was confusing since I had to determine if the list was a procedure or not.

Book #1 contains a section on how to replace the cloth on your table. The job is broken up into manageable parts in task order with good diagrams. All that is missing (and I think is really important) is a list of needed materials at the beginning. But, I wondered if I needed to know this before I started to play?

Both books contain complete glossaries, although #1 buries it in the back of the book among facts and figures and #2 buries it in introductory material in the front of the book. Neither book features an index, but both books have included a good table of contents which makes things easy to find.

In summary, I think a good billiards rule book would contain the following characteristics of a manual:

1. Modular, subtitled narrative using techniques that enable quick reference.
2. Diagrams of tables and balls, but photos of people.
3. A complete glossary in the very back, perhaps with a border around the pages.
4. Clear differentiation between a list of sequenced tasks and a list of related items.
5. A detailed table of contents.

Students response by Winnie Walsh, Indiana University.

FIGURE 10.4 (*Continued*)

transparencies. This type of "formal training" is just one way of improving performance. In fact, if improperly done, it may offend people and actually decrease performance.

A clear distinction should be made between training and education. *Education* emphasizes topics while *training* emphasizes acquiring skills to perform tasks, education emphasizes theory while training emphasizes practice. This is why many college graduates may feel that they know a lot of things, but are not sure if they can do anything. Both education and training have a role in our personal development. A good example of the distinction between education and training is the different reactions of parents when their 14-year-old comes home and announces, "We are getting sex education at school" versus the statement "We are getting sex training at school."

MEANS OF TRAINING

There are many ways to impart knowledge and develop skills. They include the following:

One method of training on a new system is role-playing, wherein one developer takes the role of a customer or other outside party. (Brent Bear/ West Light)

Personal guidance by a manager or specialist
Films or videotapes
Computer-assisted tutorials
Online computer-generated help
Meeting or conference attendance
Guided reading
Special project work
Presentation or "paper" preparation
Teaching others
Visits to other organizations
Attachments to interfacing departments
Discussion groups
Experiential exercises such as role playing

In fact, the approach of trainers is to avoid doing formal classroom training unless there is no other solution. A critical factor to keep in mind is that training should take place throughout the development of a system. If formal training is saved until the implementation stages of a project, it often turns into a session explaining why the system is needed, answering objections to the system, and explaining the changes it will bring, and will turn into a large selling effort. A better way is to keep users and others involved through review sessions, having short, practical exercises as the system is being prepared and tested.

REASONS FOR TRAINING

Some type of formal training is needed when activities are not obvious and it would be difficult for a trainee to get started or if he or she would require help. Some systems that are easy to use and can be approached from a "discovery" viewpoint may not require training. For example, for our homes we purchase complex devices such as video recorders and yet we "discover" the features of the device. The trainer has to decide what is best in an existing situation.

In some cases, sharing with others in a formal training environment is beneficial. People can learn from others' questions and discoveries. People are often motivated when they see that others can do something, gaining confidence that they can do it too. This often is done in the classroom with young persons, but it also works for adults. Another reason for formalizing training is that people will not take the time to train themselves. Their time must be structured by someone else. It often is necessary to set aside a block of time away from the normal work environment for busy people.

The current workplace or job may not allow for on-the-job training. The risk of making a mistake while doing actual work may be too high. The technical environment may not exist or be appropriate. Interruptions may be too frequent. It sometimes is necessary to bring persons into a new or different environment to teach them new or different things. A formal training setting also may be needed if practice sessions or demonstrations are needed. A separate room may be needed that is not possible in the workplace.

A training plan must be established and used to guide the training effort. Training is not usually successful if it is done as an afterthought.

MANAGING TRAINING

A book by Christopher Gane (see References) specifies a number of activities that should help in planning, organizing, and controlling the training process. Training, like other activities that are to be managed, must start with establishing a plan. Gane suggests the following activities:

Define:
- The target population
- Tasks the target population must do
- Desired peformance on the tasks

Design training process including:
- Clear presentation of facts
- Graded acts of mastery (exercises)
- Performance aids

Implement, test, and iterate:
  Conduct training
  Measure actual performance
  Modify training process

When viewed from the problem-solving perspective discussed in Chapter 1, the process is very similar to the systems development life cycle. In fact, it may be seen as the development of a training system.

TRAINING GUIDELINES

1. Center training around tangible things. Use actual forms, documents, terminals, and manuals.
2. Trainees must respond actively and receive timely feedback.
3. Training objectives must be expressed in performance terms. The question to be answered is, "What is the trainee able to do?" Objectives should state the conditions in which the performance is to take place, the criteria for measurement, and the desired level of performance.
4. Training should attempt to respond to the individual trainee. Every person who attends training sessions should be able to perform at some level of competence. Persons with more difficulties in achieving acceptable performance should be helped.
5. Training should allow for questions, be evaluated for effectiveness, and adapted as needed. If trainees are not able to perform, it may not be the trainees who have failed.
6. Topics that are often overlooked in systems usage training include the meaning and use of system outputs, and the performance of failure and recovery techniques. Occasional "fire drills" may be needed to assure that people are still able to perform seldom used processes.

ISSUES IN TRAINING

Trainee motivation is often a problem. Trainees must see the need for the training, and management must see that people are rewarded for excellence. Severe anxiety should be avoided. However, some anxiety can be a motivator. A general rule of thumb may be to allow trainees the freedom to make any mistake once (or even twice?). This may remove some of the barriers to participation.

Another means of motivation is to see that trainees understand the human interfaces with the subsystem with which they work. Trainees will realize that there are humans who depend on them to provide good outputs, and that the persons providing them with inputs really do care about the final product. By meeting persons in an interfacing subsystem, trainees will better understand the whole task and see the reason for receiving inputs in a certain form, or ensuring that outputs meet some standard.

Training is often difficult to schedule. People still have their jobs to do and the world does not stop to allow training to take place. An experienced trainer expects that some training sessions will be interrupted or need to be rescheduled. A difficult decision is whether to train people early and risk their forgetting or the system changing, or to train people close to actual use and not allowing time for practice or absorbing the material ("the jell factor"). The trainer must try to balance tradeoffs much like in other systems work.

Even experienced systems developers may call on an internal organizational trainer or an external consultant for assistance. The systems person cannot hope to be an expert on everything, but should have the wisdom to call on experts if needed.

SUMMARY

Having people perform tactics is critical to system success. Understanding why people may or may not want to fulfill their role in a system is something a systems analyst must constantly be thinking of during systems development. Appropriately designed procedures that fit into meaningful jobs, with available and well-designed manuals, will allow trained persons to achieve objectives that user and system teams specify. Since this area has been the cause of much wasted systems development effort, a fledgling analyst can aid an organization by keeping his or her eyes open to developing and enhancing the people subsystem.

References and Further Readings

Carnegie, Dale. *How to Win Friends and Influence People,* New York: Simon and Schuster, 1936.

Gane, C. *Managing the Training Function,* London: George Allen and Unwin Ltd., 1972.

———and T. Sarson. *Structured Systems Analysis: Tools and Techniques,* Englewood Cliffs, NJ: Prentice-Hall &·Co., 1979.

Hackman, J.R., and G. Oldham. "Development of the Job Diagnostic Survey," *Journal of Applied Psychology,* vol. 60, 1975, pp. 159–170.

Haga, Clifford I. "Procedure Manuals," in *Ideas for Management,* Cleveland, OH: Systems and Procedures Association, 1968, pp. 127–154.

Matthies, Leslie H. *The Management System: Systems Are For People,* New York: John Wiley & Sons, 1976.

Rubinstein, Richard, and Harry M. Hersh. *The Human Factor: Designing Computer Systems for People,* Burlington, MA: Digital Press, 1984.

Schneiderman, Ben. *Software Psychology: Human Factors in Computer and Information Systems,* Cambridge, MA: Winthrop Publishers, 1980.

Schultis, Robert L. "'Playscript'—A New Tool Accountants Need," *NAA Bulletin,* vol. 45, no. 12, August 1964, pp. 3–10.

Review Questions

1. Name and describe the three types of feasibility mentioned in this chapter. Why is economic feasibility dependent on operational feasibility?
2. Distinguish between task and topic organization. Which is preferred for reference manuals? Why?
3. What are means of obtaining people performance besides formal training?
4. What is the "four-fingered problem"? How can it be eliminated?
5. When should a training plan for users be started?
6. Distinguish between education and training.
7. What are the three themes running through all successful people subsystems development?
8. What is an advantage of decision tables over other decision representation techniques?
9. What three things are needed before people performance can be obtained?
10. What is an "annotated form"?
11. What are "SOPs"? Are they the same for all organizations?
12. Distinguish between a policy and a procedure. A procedure and a program.
13. What is ergonomics?
14. What are weaknesses of using English narrative for procedure representation?
15. When is it most appropriate to use Playscript? When does Playscript break down?
16. What is meant by the ELSE condition when developing a decision table?
17. What is case structure? When is it used in "tight English"?
18. What are the three structures used to create structured English?
19. What is the primary consideration when selecting a logic or procedure representation technique?
20. Is there a difference between training and reference manuals? Explain.
21. What are questions a reference manual writer should be able to answer?
22. What must a systems developer do once a manual is completed?
23. What are some alternatives to formal classroom training?
24. In what way must training objectives be stated?
25. What are some topics often overlooked in systems usage training?

Discussion Questions

1. What should a systems analyst do if, when developing people procedures within the user organization, he or she finds:

a. A policy with which he or she disagrees (the analyst thinks the department store's merchandise return policy is unfair)
b. Something illegal (the analyst finds that the procedure includes contacting "competition" to fix prices)
c. Something that does not seem reasonable (the analyst feels time is wasted by having a manager do errands that a messenger could do)

2. What does your university provide—education or training? What do you think it should provide? Why?

3. Guidelines were given for developing manuals in this chapter. Why might they not apply to this textbook?

Exercises

1. Please read all of this assignment before starting. There are two parts to the assignment. You may work in teams of up to three if you choose.
   a. You are to develop a *procedure specification* to help the volunteer personnel answering phone calls from persons who want to know if they are eligible for the UnBoston Marathon, and to aid in accepting or rejecting applications. Use a technique you feel is appropriate. The narrative below has resulted in rejecting several applications that should have been accepted and accepting several applications that should have been rejected.
   b. As you are doing part 1a, you should record your decision process (criteria and actions) in choosing the technique to perform the above specification. Represent this *process* in a manner that would aid another analyst in the future *to choose an appropriate technique.* Be sure to consider all procedure specification techniques mentioned in class.

THE UNBOSTON MARATHON

The UnBoston Marathon will be held on the same day as the Boston Marathon for people who have completed a marathon before, but have not qualified for the Boston Marathon. This means that they have not run a marathon faster than 2 hours and 50 minutes. But, if they are women, they must not have run faster than 3 hours and 20 minutes. However, men 40 years or older when they ran their fastest marathon must not have run faster than 3 hours and 10 minutes. If there is still a question not covered by the above explanation, they should call the phone number NON-BOST (666-2678).

In a future assignment, you will design a new entry form for the race. Keep this in mind as you are working on this assignment.

2. Critique your local phone book as a reference manual. Does it meet the criteria for a good reference manual? Does it use a task orientation? Are things easy to find? How can it be improved?

3. Take a cooking recipe that you use and rewrite it using one of the procedure specification techniques used in this chapter. Why did you choose the technique?

4. The university has a complex decision process for determining tuition. It is based on a basic cost of $46.50 for a credit hour. However, nonresidents pay a premium of $77.00 per credit hour. But, if the nonresident holds an assistantship, they are charged the resident rate. Employees of the university and their families receive a discount of 50 percent. If the person is registered in another university in the conference, they are charged the same rate as his or her home university. Write a procedure to help temporary personnel hired to help with the registration process.

CHAPTER 11

Designing for the User: Dialogs and Displays

CHAPTER OBJECTIVES

You should be able to:

- Defend the need for careful development of person–machine interaction
- Understand different user groups and their interaction needs
- Use the dialog flow diagramming technique to represent a person–machine dialog
- Contrast the hardware available for human–machine interfacing
- Understand the principles of good layout design
- Develop and critique an input form or screen
- Develop and critique an output layout or screen

Electronic Card Catalog Just Doesn't Compute

The computer terminals at the Indianapolis-Marion County Public Library are neither as fast nor as easy to use as the old, familiar card catalog they replaced.

You may not have much trouble looking up an author's book or a book title—if you know it exactly and can spell. If you, like most people, use the catalog to look up a subject, however, chances are good that you won't be able to find what you want. That's true for people who know computers, as well as for novices.

There are problems with "on-line public access catalogs" all over the country. Some industry experts say that every computerized catalog system in use today has one or more serious flaws:

Software is so crude that it doesn't allow for cross references.

Much of it was designed with little research into why and how patrons actually use the catalog.

Subject headings used in the catalog were devised by the Library of Congress years ago. Although the national standard, they are not, as one librarian put it, "user friendly."

The supplier of the $1.2 million Indianapolis system says its systems have been installed in more than 230 libraries of varying sizes around the world. The public library director said, "There is not an on-line catalog on the market that's any better."

—From an article by Carol Elrod, Indianapolis Star staff writer, September 22, 1985.

THIS CHAPTER DEALS with the issues of the human–machine interface, including dialog design, output design, and input design. The technique of person–machine flow diagramming is introduced, and an example of the use of this techinque is included.

The objective of systems development is to have human-machine *symbiosis*—two dissimilar systems dependent on each other, existing in a common space, to achieve a mutually advantageous goal. Each subsystem needs the other to achieve the best results. The above library system was hardly symbiotic. The persons and the machine were antagonistic rather than supportive.

As mentioned in the previous chapter, people have the abilities to be adaptive, creative, and intuitive; they have feelings, handle unstructured situations, use judgment, and deal with other humans in a sensitive manner. These abilities must be supported with machine strengths. These strengths include the machines' abilities to read and write certain documents quickly, store vast amounts of data, do calculations at a rapid rate, follow and execute instructions tirelessly and without question, and be very accurate. But to have success and use these strengths, these unlike entities must support each other.

Much of this support is possible when these two unlike entities can *communicate*. Lately, much attention has been given to these communications, often called *interfaces* or *interactions,* to encourage wider use of machines and automation. Since systems development is a relatively new discipline, we have borrowed from other disciplines to understand communications. This includes the fields of video game design, graphic arts, filmmaking, psychology, sales, and even magic. Heckel describes how all these fields have contributed to understanding human perception and interaction (see References).

The overall objective of this chapter is to allow the future systems analyst/designer to give system users comfortable, nonstressful, and productive interfaces with machines. This includes the design of dialogs, displays, forms, and reports.

WHAT IS MEANT BY PEOPLE-MACHINE SYMBIOSIS?

People interact with machines in different ways. People must:

Provide data on forms for conversion to machine-readable mediums.

Provide data directly to machines for processing through online interaction.

Generate queries where the machine will respond to a specific question.

Carry on dialogs with machines to do analysis.

Receive processed data in the form of documents such as paychecks and bills or informative reports.

If any of these interactions is poorly designed, people will become frustrated with a machine. This frustration is the result of human characteristics, including getting bored with tedious tasks, becoming physically and mentally tired, and seeking better ways of doing things. The person-machine interface designer should attempt to come up with solutions that allow the person and the machine to team up without causing errors, boredom, frustration, and even hate. Above all, a properly designed system will allow the user to focus on his or her task, not on using a machine.

USER FRIENDLY?

A commonly used phrase is "user friendly." Many persons who use the phrase do not take the time to define it. One quip suggested that vendors often make things user friendly "by changing the advertising copy, but not the product." Claiming something is user friendly does not make it so. Brainstorming sessions have led to some characteristics of "friends" which apply to systems. A good friend:

Lets me be me.

Trusts me and allows me to trust him or her.

Is predictable when I need stability.

Shows me respect.

Adapts to me if I need to change.

Pushes me if I need a push.

Helps me define my goals.

Helps me reach my goals.

Helps me stay out of trouble.

Provides aid if I do get into trouble.

Lets me make mistakes and learn from them.

Is natural and not phony.

Doesn't bore me.

Does not greet or treat me like a stranger unless I am one.

Learns from interactions with me.

Adapts to my style of doing things.

Many of these guides for "friendliness" apply to person–machine interactions and dialogs. For example, a good dialog can be both novice and expert friendly by not treating an expert like a first-timer. Ways of doing this could include:

Allowing experienced users who remember commands to bypass menus of options.

Allowing suppression of potential error warnings, but allowing the last command to be undone.

Using defaults by remembering what the user did in a previous situation and asking if they want to do it again.

These are all things a good human friend would do if harmoniously working together with us. It is important to realize that "when people use language to interact with a machine, they behave as if the rules for person-to-person communication apply" (see Rubinstein and Hersh, p. 62). For example, friendly persons are perceived as cooperative and not confrontative, not aloof, interrupting only with care, saying enough but not too much, and not creating new rules (like making me use commas where I normally leave a space). This is the key for building friendly interfaces.

ALLOWING FOR TOLERANCE

When dealing with humans, machines must be perceived to be tolerant. The strategy of humanized dialog design consists of analyzing the users' environment to establish natural communication patterns, determining and establishing natural sequences and codes, and then allowing for normal variations (including shortcuts). Consideration must be given to:

1. *Sequence tolerance*—allowing natural sequences (not last name first!).
2. *Content Tolerance*
   a. Allowing synonyms (T, TRUE, True, t).
   b. Accommodating learning humans with flexible command identification ("not knowing" frustration changing to "overexplanation" frustration as learning takes place).
   c. Allowing for spelling errors (TREU, TREW).
   d. Not forcing the filling of fields such as middle initial (KENNETH NMI KOZAR).
3. *Procedure Tolerance*
   a. Allowing experienced users to use a different order for multiple commands. ([Withdraw, $50, checking account, end] OR [$50, checking account, withdraw, end]).
   b. Not self-destructing or damaging data due to operator error if the machine can automatically build backups, allow recoveries, or permit "undoing" the last command. There should be no opportunity for "self-destructs," and audit trails should be kept for recovery.
   c. Composing alternative "noncomprehension" messages to allow multiple explanations if an operator does not understand an error or "help" message. ("Let me explain it another way.")
4. *Pacing*
   a. Duplicating natural conversation paces by not being too slow, which provokes impatience, or being too fast which pushes the

> It's much cheaper to have 200,000,000 people write their last names first than to program a computer to read them the other way around . . . why can't people just learn to do things the way that's easiest for us to program? Then we could devote ourselves to using the great flexibility of the computer.
>
> from *Humanized Input* by Tom Gilb and Gerald Weinberg.

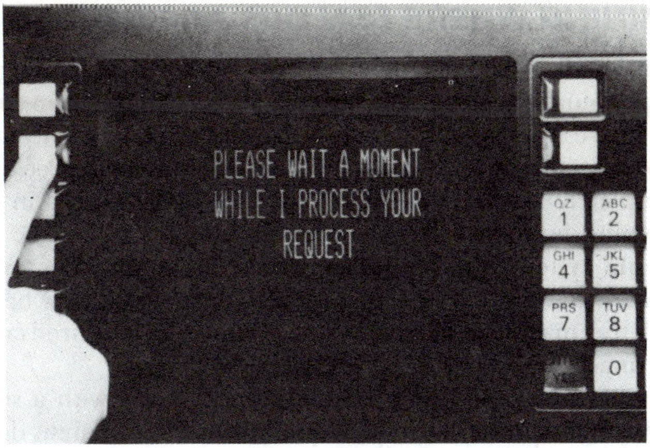

When response time for a particular operation is longer than for others, an interim message will prevent the user from becoming impatient or confused. (Innervisions)

person and provokes anxiety. The range of response times is more critical than the average. Examining distributions of response times to determine acceptability must be done.

b. Providing interim responses just like a human would do ("Hang on, I'm thinking").
c. Keeping track of mistakes and "suggesting" that the operator take a rest break if too many errors occur.

The designer must use judgment in specifying interactions. He or she should avoid dialogs that are so condescending that they are degrading, or so machinelike that they make people feel "robotic."

DEVELOPING PERSON–MACHINE DIALOGS

The general process for developing a person—machine dialog is similar to other problem-solving approaches discussed earlier in Chapter 2. The process includes:

Determining where dialogs are needed

Analyzing dialog requirements

Specifying dialog design

Specifying input/output layouts

Remember that development is not a linear process. Reviews and tests will reveal weaknesses that will cause more analysis and redesign. A prototyping philosophy often is required. These reviews and tests should take place throughout the development process. Constant interaction with the user will assure that the interfaces will fit the needs of user groups and be used once developed. Participation promotes both system quality and acceptance.

DETERMINING WHERE DIALOGS ARE NEEDED

As was mentioned in Chapter 10, a useful aid for determining the person–machine boundary is the data flow diagram. This diagram can be used to identify where humans must provide inputs or receive outputs.

The person–machine boundary will depend on the degree of automation. A completely manual system would have no machines in it and no person–machine boundary. If we were developing an automated bank teller machine system, the boundary would be at the point where the customer entered transactions. This is where data would flow between the person and the machine. Person actions would be required along with responding machine actions.

The interaction could be a simple human query with a simple machine search and response, a complex query with some analysis done by the machine before response, or a series of simple or complex requests and responses. This last case is a true dialog. True dialogs can be broken down into fixed path interactions such as an automated airline ticket dispenser or can be multiple path, such as with data entry where additions, changes, or deletions would create different paths.

ANALYZING DIALOG REQUIREMENTS

Analyzing dialog requirements includes data gathering activities. The developer must gather background about:

Objectives, or what the dialog should achieve

Constraints, including time, facilities, and conventions

Users, including aptitudes, attitudes, biases, and interests

On completing this analysis the developer should have a clear idea of *who* the users are, *what* they do, *how* they do it, *when* they do it, *where* they do it, and *why*.

Knowing Dialog Objectives

The goal of any dialog, whether between persons or machines, is useful communication. A good person–machine dialog will not anger, upset, bore, or confuse the person. There must be some benefit achieved by conducting the dialog. The persons and machines must remain friends.

The developer must first study the system objectives and business tactics to determine what output users must receive and what they intend to do with the output. If the developer can empathize with the user and his or her job, the dialog can be put in a correct perspective.

The developer must not only understand what the user does when things go right, but also when they go wrong. This will aid in designing strategies for backups, recoveries, and audit trails. Unreasonable stress should be avoided. This could be caused by the user feeling that:

Control has been lost.

Unexpected events have confused me.

Novelty or levity is used when seriousness is needed, or vice versa.

Responses are inappropriate, such as using codes when an explanation should have been used.

Hope is lost that recovery is possible.

The developer also must determine if hard copy, soft copy, or both are required for users to accomplish their tasks. These characteristics may be user-specified.

Knowing Constraints

The developer must have a clear understanding of his or her design environment. The physical setting may dictate design decisions. For example, some applications such as field sales entry may require a specific piece of hardware. This could dictate whether features such as full screen entry is possible or if a series of short queries would be needed.

Corporate constraints and standards such as being required to use specific hardware or vendor lines, or whether devices like mouses or touch sensitive screens are possible, must be determined. Often these specifications are denoted in a properly developed systems objectives statement.

Knowing Your Users

A critical consideration in developing a dialog is to know your user. Users can be rugged or temperamental, trained or naive, computer-literate or illiterate, computer lovers or haters, active leaders or reactive followers, typists or "hunt and peck" key-searchers, frequent or infrequent operators, etc.

Think about the differences in needs and capabilities between an automated bank teller user, an airline reservationist, a life insurance salesperson, and a data entry key operator. To illustrate the diversity of users and how this can affect design, consider the following nonexhaustive classes of users:

1. *"Naive" users* using a bank cash card for the first time. These users would not likely have had nor will get formal training, not remember the previous interaction, have varied levels of "ruggedness," would likely be operating in a harassed environment (people in line behind them), and have a low tolerance for frustration. A great fear of this group of naive users would be to "blow up the system" and have their card "swallowed" by the machine.

   A "friendly" dialog would be computer-initiated and computer-commanded, have clear requests and have limited responses or choices, give "help" at any time, and would avoid too fast a response so the user is not "driven." Other people in a bank automatic teller lineup would understand the machine's slowness better than a slow customer. Function keys and menus controlled by the machine are typical means of working with naive operators.

   Understanding a naive user's concern and empathizing with them should give you some direction when doing a design for such a person.

2. *Managerial users* needing computer-stored information would be characterized as wanting little training (maybe some tutoring), being people- rather than machine-oriented, being impatient, being nonrugged, having a lot of "ego," having only short time segments available, and desiring casual usage.

A "friendly" dialog would allow a simple method of getting started, easy restart if the wrong path was taken, little chance of needing help from others, no record that the manager asked for help, little chance of embarassment or frustration, confidence of usefulness and data validity, and the ability to change as new possibilities are seen.

Design considerations include using macro instructions or function keys where a simple action generates a predetermined complex request. Graphics may aid in presenting trends or patterns. Hard copy may be needed to allow results to be studied or

AN EXAMPLE OF A DIALOG FOR A DEDICATED OPERATOR

A customer walks into the Fliver Airlines office in Spokane, Washington, and wishes to book a trip for two from Spokane to Denver, Colorado, on July 17. The Fliver reservations clerk keys in the following request:

A 17JUL GEGDEN

The code A is mnemonic for AVAILABLE, and GEG and DEN are standard airline industry codes for Spokane and Denver. The system responds:

```
A 17JUL GEGDEN
1 FR392   Y11      GEGDEN  07.32  10.23  B 2
2 FR454   F5Y12    GEGDEN  09.45  14.18  L 3
3 FR491   F3Y33    GEGDEN  14.34  16.55  D 2
4 UA243   F11Y06   GEGDEN  08.15  10.29  B 1
```

The list includes the airline abbreviation and flight number, first class (F) seats, economy (Y) seats, cities, departure time, arrival time, meals served, and number of stops. The client desired a morning flight in the economy section. The reservationist keys in the following:

N2Y1

This indicates that two seats are needed in the economy section on flight 1 from the above table. The system responds with the following confirmation:

1 FR392 17JUL GEGDEN Y2 07.32 10.23
PASS. INFO?

This confirms the flight, date, cities, type and number of seats, and references the time for confirmation purposes. The reservation clerk continues with the passenger information needed for flight booking purposes.

presented in another location. Some persons may argue for a human intermediary, rather than direct machine interface. The feasibility of using voice input or output should be a consideration.

3. *Familiar or dedicated users,* such as key entry operators or airline reservationists, are characterized as having device and procedure training, experience, ruggedness, need for frequent and/or continuous dialog use, and potential to operate in an unfavorable physical environment. Some persons have argued that the job of keying data is an "unhuman" one and that key operators are treated like "robots with boyfriends" (Gilb and Weinberg). The analyst must attempt to make this job more appealing and less like sweatshop work.

   A "friendly" dialog would emphasize efficiency, allow learning, the use of shortcuts, and support "mindless" operation. Jargon and codes often are used if they are part of the working language of the user. Designs would be facilitated through development of a humanized, ergonomically designed workstation utilizing current technology.

It is critical to understand your user group. There are many combinations of environmental and human factors, even within a perceived homogeneous group of users in a common setting. The designed interface should be accommodating to operators rather than depending on operators to adapt. Knowing your user group will also aid testing since it will be easier to determine representative users.

SPECIFYING DIALOG DESIGN

The developer must keep the information gathered during the above analysis in mind when creating the dialog design. An objective is to have a vision of the future outcome. In fact, some designers feel that the developer should start the design by attempting to write the users' guide (Rubinstein and Hersh). They believe this method will aid in conceiving and reviewing a design specification.

When designing a dialog, special consideration must be given to getting started (hand shaking), getting stuck ("help me"), and checkpoints (not forcing restarting from scratch). These are the areas where dialogs are likely to break down and cause hostility.

There are two major types of interfaces that will be needed. Each requires a different type of attitude and approach. They include:

1. The machine acts as a boss for a naive operator. The machine is in control and the person must respond to the commands of the machine. There is very little choice left for the person to do a specific task. A bank machine dialog is an example of this type of interface.
2. The machine acts as a powerful coworker for experienced operators. There is tolerance for multiple paths and the operator is in

control within certain rules or constraints. The airline reservation system is an example of a powerful coworker.

The general set of tasks to be conducted in designing include the following:

Specify a starting point and operator choices.

Draft usual sequences of operator actions.

Specify any alternate or error action paths and branches.

Develop alias list for each operator response.

Develop a screen display log.

Detail data movement between person and machine.

Specify hardware and software environment.

Specify screen layouts.

These tasks can be done in various orders depending upon whether an existing hardware and software environment must be used, whether users may be available to do screen layout designs, and whether users want certain branches of a dialog to receive priority treatment.

Dialog Diagramming

One of the goals of dialog design is to develop a model of interaction between machines and humans. The model then can be evaluated in a safe, nonautomated environment. The model can also serve as an index to the screens that must be developed to have a working dialog.

Dialog diagramming* is a technique that is useful in representing person–machine dialogs. It is one of the techniques that a systems developer should have in his or her skill set.

Definition. ***Dialog diagramming*** is a means of graphically representing person–machine interactions. The technique resembles a decision tree showing branching due to human response alternatives.

Purpose and Objective. The purpose of dialog diagramming is to provide a semantic bridge between users and systems developers. The technique is:

Graphical, allowing alternatives in the flow of a dialog to be shown

Comprehensive and exhaustive, showing all needed person and machine responses

Reviewable without programming, allowing users and developers to evaluate dialogs on paper.

Dialog diagramming has the objective of avoiding the cost of:

Unused terminal devices and systems because of proposed users' fears, which may cause avoidance and resistance

*This technique was developed by the author in collaboration with Chris Gane.

Delays because of waiting for dialogs to be machine ready before being tested

Delays while waiting for hardware to start user training

Inefficiency because of unnatural user sequences of interaction

Description. Dialog diagramming consist of using three symbols:

The ***person action symbol*** is a "standing-up" rounded corner rectangle (see Figure 11.1). The word "Enter" or "E" along with a number is used for an identifier. There is no required numbering sequence, but some organizations have found that using grid paper and a grid number, like on a road map, makes it easy to find a symbol.

The symbol can be extended vertically if there are numerous possible person entries. Quote marks should be used if the words are literally what is to be entered. Note in the above illustration that the person is expected to enter one of three responses. If anything else (AE) is entered, a machine response also must be available.

An alias list of acceptable responses ("ADD" or "ADd" or "Add" or "AD" or "Ad" or "A" or "a" should be kept).

The ***machine action symbol*** is a "lying-down" rounded corner rectangle (see Figure 11.2). The word "Display" or "D" along with a number is used to identify screen displays. The word "Print" or "P" along with a number is used to identify hard copy machine actions.

It is likely that the "Display" screen would request the person to take an action. The person would take an action, which would lead to another machine action.

Quotes are used for literal displays. Lengthy displays would not be displayed verbatim. The numeric identifier should serve as a key to a separately kept screen display log.

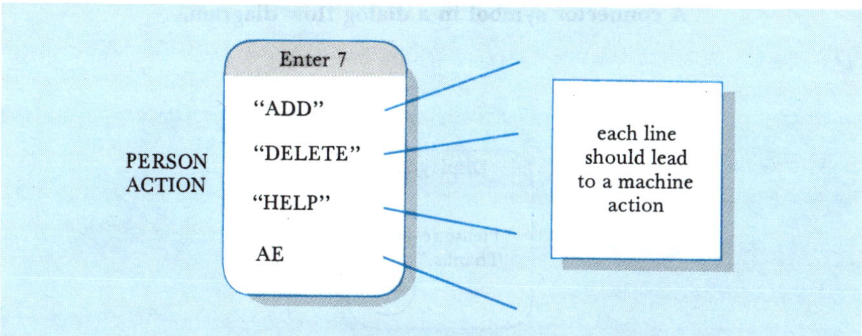

FIGURE 11.1
A person action symbol in a dialog flow diagram.

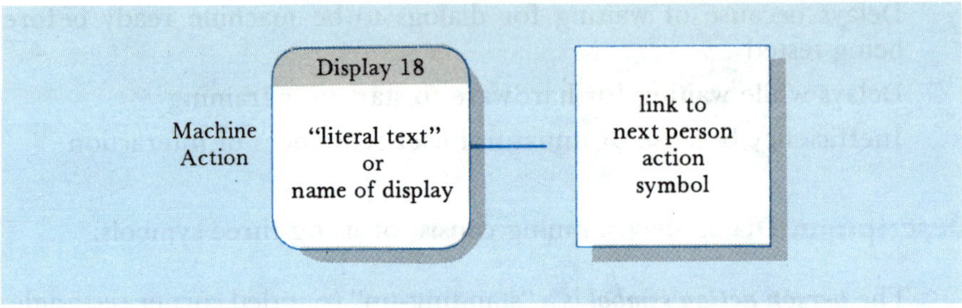

FIGURE 11.2
A machine action symbol in a dialog flow diagram.

The ***on- or off-page connector symbol*** is a circle with an identifier within the circle boundaries. Figure 11.3 represents a return to "Display 18."

To represent similar, but not identical displays, the notation shown in Figure 11.4 is used:

"Display 22" is a machine action that requests reentry from the operator, as well as displaying and returning control to "Display 18."

It is essential that, for every person action, expected or nonexpected, a machine response be available. The machine must be programmed to react to any person action. This includes a reaction to acceptable aliases, a reaction to a plea for "HELP," and a reaction to "anything else." The response should be quick enough to seem natural, but not so quick the person seems "driven." Predictable delays should be announced.

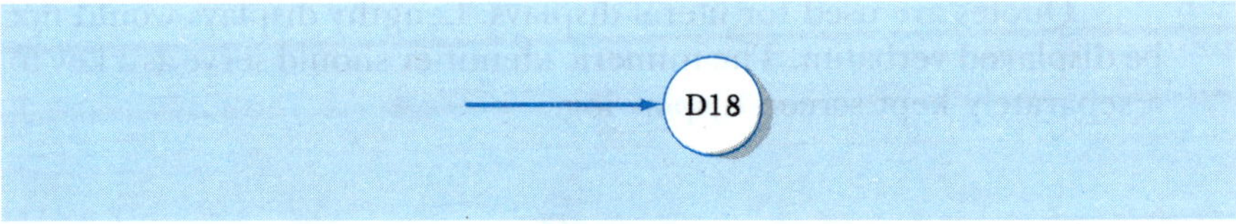

FIGURE 11.3
A connector symbol in a dialog flow diagram.

FIGURE 11.4
Notation for similar, but not identical, displays.

Once the structure of the dialog has been generated and reviewed by users, the designer should concentrate on completing the screen logs and accompanying layouts. This will be supplemented by lists of aliases. These are the alternative acceptable human responses for a specific response situation.

An Example of the Dialog Designing Technique

This problem and solution was created by J. Lunsford, Indiana University MBA student.

Challenge: Design a user friendly dialog between customers and a bank machine.

Environment: The user has access to a keypad with the numerals 0–9, a decimal point, an ENTER key, and an ERASE key. The machine has a visual display device, an alert tone (a pleasant "ding"), and a timer to measure human response time.

Design Tools: Dialog flow diagram, screen log, and display messages.

Dialog Flow Diagram: Figure 11.5 shows a portion of a dialog flow diagram created for this example.

Screen Log and Display Messages:

D1 Welcome to the Friendly Bank Machine.
Please insert your bankcard as pictured
near the slot on your right.

D2 Oops! You inserted your card incorrectly.
Please re-enter as pictured on the diagram.

D3 Hello [customer name]. Please enter your
personal code number, then press the ENTER key.
If at any time you wish to correct a mistake before
you press the ENTER key: you can press the ERASE
key and re-enter.

D4 Oops! You entered the wrong number.
Please re-enter your personal code number,
then press the ENTER key.

D5 Sorry, your card is being retained for your protection.
If the bank is not open, please call your local bank
branch at [customer service phone number].

D6 Tone sounds. Please enter your personal code number,
then press the ENTER key. If you no longer wish to use the
Friendly Bank Machine, enter a "1," then press the ENTER key.

D7 Thank you, [customer name]. Please return to Friendly Bank again.
Don't forget to take your card.

D8 Please enter the number of your desired transaction,
then press the ENTER key. (Remember you can use the ERASE
key when you need to correct errors.)

MAIN MENU

enter:	*if you want to:*
1	**stop** using the Friendly Bank Machine

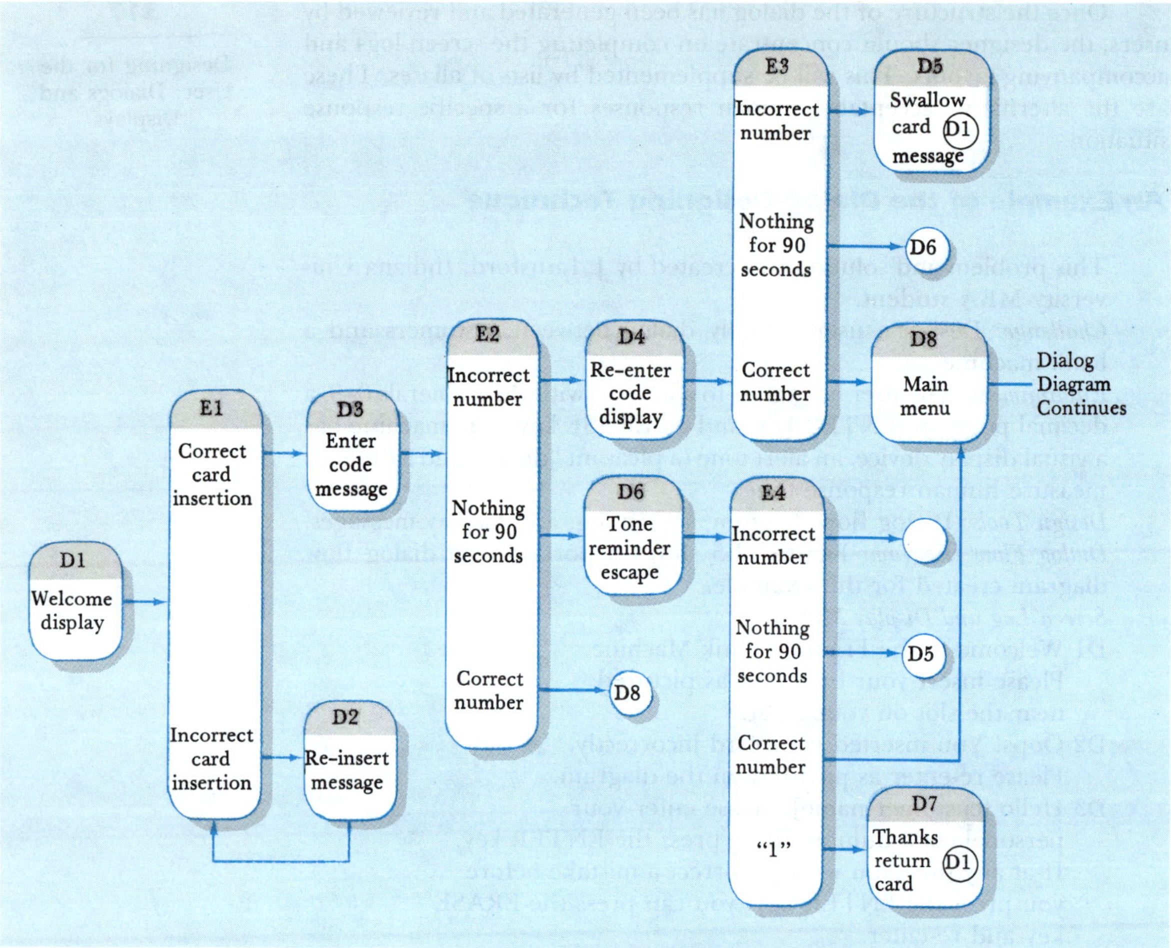

FIGURE 11.5
A portion of a dialog design diagram.

2 make a cash **withdrawal**
3 make a **deposit**
4 **transfer** funds from one account to another
5 see your account **balances**

The developer also must record data that must move across the person–machine boundary. The data flow diagram and data dictionary are used to determine the content of data flows from and to persons and machines. These flows will make up the human responses if they flow to the machine. If they flow from the machine to the person, they indicate data store contents that must be accessed and sent to the operator.

Commands versus Menus

A choice that dialog designers must make is whether to use commands that specify actions, or to use menus from which the user chooses an action.

Menus are appropriate for occasional users who may not remember commands. Experienced operators often like to string several commands together.

Menus allow users to conduct the dialog with little training. Typing can be kept at a minimum. Pointing devices such as a mouse can be used to select from menus. "Pop-up" or "pull-down" menus can be used for a hierarchy of actions. The Apple Macintosh is a good example of these types of menus.

Menus also can be built into hardware devices. Touch screens can display menus. Function keys can be used to specify actions. Automated teller bank machines often use this means to give users a choice. Relevant keys can be lighted to focus on desired user actions. In any case, menus should be kept short, with similar categories of commands kept together.

Prompts versus Screen Filling

Some of the same arguments that apply to menus and commands apply to prompts and screen filling. Experienced operators may prefer to do screen filling where a tab or return key moves one from field to field. Inexperienced operators may prefer to be asked a series of questions, called *prompts,* with the operator response generating the next prompt.

Hardware Choice

Part of the task of the designer is to specify the hardware devices to be used in the application. Often this is predetermined by availability in the organization, or done with the aid of vendors or experts. The number of devices is overwhelming and some persons dedicate their careers to understanding hardware and its capabilities. New equipment is released daily.

Input devices could include phone-linked bar recorders, joysticks, mice, voice readers, image readers, Touch-Tone phones, touch screens, or view control systems where head movement controls the cursor on the screen. Data is usually entered through keying of some type, although

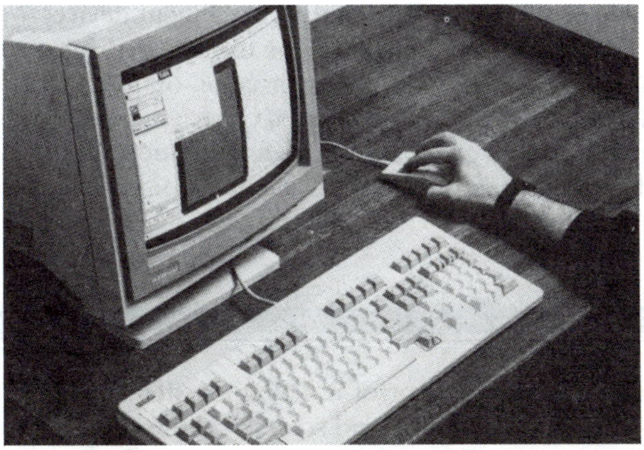

Some systems have more than one input device: a mouse, joystick, or touch screen; as well as a conventional keyboard. (Innervisions)

DESIGNING FOR THE USER—AN EXAMPLE

Let us consider a simple example. We have been given the task of designing a phone that will automatically dial one of 20 stored phone numbers when a button is pushed. But production costs and size dictate that we can only have 10 of the 20 numbers available for display at one time and 10 choice buttons. The user will select one of the 10 displayed by pushing a button next to the name. Our problem is how we are to distinguish the group of 10 that we want to select a person or number from. Various switches have been suggested. Ponder the problem for awhile.

Let us look at some solutions. We could have put the names next to each other in two columns and had a left or right switch. This would take a lot of space on the phone surface. We could have the names in one column of 20 with no spaces in between with a top or bottom switch. This would likely lead to a lot of wrong names since it would have all the names in view at once. It seems that our problem is to have a switch to select from either of two groups of 10 names.

What did one phone maker do about this problem? It had 10 selection buttons next to 10 names that the dialer could see. By pushing a tab, the other 10 names would appear and the first 10 would be covered. But, more importantly, the tab that made the first 10 names disappear also was the switch to activate the second 10 names. So simple that you wonder why you did not think of it, right? The first solutions were workable, but the final solution was humanized.

optical character readers are becoming more accurate and economical. Command selection can be done with a pointing device to allow selection from a menu.

Options for straight data entry applications include key to disk with uploading to another larger computer, local (hard-wired) keyed dumb or intelligent devices, distant keyed dumb or intelligent devices, or local keyed microcomputers that are either online or use batched inputs.

Output could include screens with color or monochrome displays, plotters, video, audio, or other variations. Choice depends on need. Monochrome displays usually give better screen resolution. Color gives another dimension for presentation. Audio is useful if persons have their hands occupied.

LAYOUT DESIGN

Once the structure and content of a dialog are determined, the layout of the input forms, output reports, and screens can be specified. The layout is usually easier to change than a dialog process or the data content of a form, report, or screen. With technology and computing power becoming available at more reasonable costs, designing for machine efficiency has become less critical. What the machine would like versus what the human would like is a contrast that must be considered.

Concerning input layout design:

Machine "Likes"	*Human Response*
Specific locations for each character	"Boxes' are a pain."
Neat capital lettering	"Capitals! That's grade school stuff."
Specific repeatable codes	"It's hard to remember meaningless codes, our shorthand makes sense."
No mix of alpha and numeric	"Alphanumeric gives most flexibility."
No stains on paper	"Our work area is messy."
In order of machine needs	"Our sequence makes sense."
Maximum use of space	"What a crowded mess!"

Concerning output layout design:

Machine "Likes"	*Human Response*
Pack each line	"Wide margins allow notes."
Pack each page	"Hard to read and make notes."
Limited character set for speed	"I need a legend to figure this out."
Use codes	"Like reading with a dictionary in one hand."
Abbreviate	"What does this mean?"
No headings or footers	"What report is this! For what time period?"
Use wide size paper	"Special binders!" "Hard to photocopy."
Legend on one page only	"Suppose I can cut and paste."

Systems development has at one time focused on machine efficiency, especially when machine processing cycles were very expensive. But balance is needed where human needs are considered. This is true for both input and output design.

INPUT FORM DESIGN

We have all experienced poor forms for data collection. They have frustrated us because we did not know what to do, there was not room on the form to do it, our environment did not permit an easy response, or we did not understand what the requestor wanted from us. Forms are part of a system and should be designed as part of it. Forms are usually data collection devices and can exist on hard copy or display screens.

Obvious items should not be ignored. Things such as identification of the purpose of the form, needed instructions, retention instructions, creation/revision dates, phone numbers for help, signatures, what to do with completed form, separate requests for postal codes, etc., should not be forgotten. User reviews and testing with representative users will often find some of these errors.

Designers should be conscious of corporate logos or colors. If appropriate, include these as part of the design to improve corporate image and professionalism.

Multiple copies of a form may be needed. Since there is considerable expense involved with multiple copies, make sure the copies are necessities, not niceties. Each copy should be appropriately labeled. Different colors of paper can be used on different pages to distinguish purpose or destination. Choice of paper is also important. Too flimsy a paper may be destroyed by too much handling. Too stiff a form may be difficult to feed through some printers or other machines such as copiers.

Often, forms must be numbered for control purposes and to determine volumes of usage. If the number is important for manual searching or sorting purposes, make sure the number is visible in one of the corners. This will allow persons to fan through a stack of forms to locate needed items.

Forms should be a standard size to cut printing costs and to allow the use of standard envelopes. Envelopes with windows are often useful for forms to be mailed.

Legibility is an important concern. Leave enough space for people to fill in the form without horizontal or vertical squeezing. If multiple copies are needed, make sure a firm writing surface will be part of the environment. A helpful table of color combination legibility, the result of research by LeCourier, is shown below.

Ranking of Legibility	*Color of Printing*	*Color of Background*
1 (Best)	Black	Yellow
2	Green	White
3	Red	White
4	Blue	White
5	White	Blue
6	Black	White
7	Yellow	Black
8	White	Red
9	White	Green
10	White	Black
11	Red	Yellow
12	Green	Red
13 (Worst)	Red	Green

Note that the commonly used black on white ranks number six in legibility. Maybe this textbook should be printed on yellow paper? Also note that amber or yellow computer screens with black print may be most legible.

A Special Form—The Turnaround Document

Often, a document that you would like returned to your information systems operation is sent to people, who are expected to return the document along with some further information or payment. This identifying document is called a ***turnaround document***. For example, a utility or credit card bill is sent to you with a perforated section to be returned with your payment. The form then is used as an identifier for further transaction processing.

Some of these turnaround documents are machine-readable and others have important identifiers to allow computerized records to be identified. This option should not be overlooked if there is a high cost of determining which master record corresponds to a received transaction.

Some Hints in Input Design

Where possible, the designer should:

Preprint items.

Use multiple choice rather than fill-in blanks.

Use character specification lines or boxes.

Use this

Phone number _ _ _ / _ _ _ - _ _ _ _

rather than

Phone number ______/______-______

Sequence from top to bottom,

Left to right.

Sequence to follow work flow.

Group related items.

Annotate with instructions.

Phone Number _ _ _ / _ _ _ - _ _ _ _

Use color to distinguish multiple copies.

Leave margins around entire form of at least 1 inch.

A wise move is to get advice from internal or consulting forms experts. Attempting to get your forms business, forms companies will often aid in or even develop forms to secure your printing order. Experience with forms development can be invaluable in getting things right.

Software can aid forms design. "Screen painters," which allow interactive and online screen design, can aid the forms development process.

OUTPUT LAYOUT GUIDELINES

The objective of output layout design is to meet the earlier specified system objectives which are part of the requirements statement. The system output should make users' business tactics easier to perform. It is important to review this part of the requirements statement before starting to design the output layouts. Only then can design needs be put in perspective.

The report developer should understand the users' potential actions. The "so what" test in the form of "So what will you do if things appear on the report?" is helpful in doing layouts. Exception conditions that require action should be understood by the developer so they can be highlighted on the layout. Both negative exceptions that require changes and positive exceptions that may require "strokes" for the persons responsible should be pointed out.

Some general guidelines for output design include:

Clear formats

Use columns with adequate spacing.

Numeric data should be right-justified.

Alpha data should be left-justified.

Use short line length.

Newspapers use only 30 to 40 characters per line.

Use highlighting such as dashes and asterisks to direct the reader's attention.

Use care in labeling, including units of measurement.

Include accurate report titles with time periods and date of report.

Make displays similar in format so things will appear in the same places.

Present displays in order of usage to perform business tactics.

Include standard or planned results, actual results, differences, and "flagging" of exceptional differences.

Avoid codes that readers may not understand (a large percentage of the population does not understand what "<" or ">" means).

SCREEN LAYOUT DESIGN

Many systems today will be online with use of video display terminals or personal computers. This requires design of layouts of forms, data, and information for display screens. There are some special considerations to be made when using these mediums. Features such as reverse video (white-on-black display of an item on a page of black-on-white), underscoring, **bold print**, blinking words, color, and different fonts can be used. Besides using the features of new input devices, having an interactive screen-driven environment requires new attitudes and methods to use the environment in a humanized way. These new mediums should not be treated in the same way as mediums of the past.

Breaking the 80-Column Input Mentality

Many persons still believe that input design means breaking data items into blocks of 80 characters as once was done on the 80-column punched card. Today's designer must look beyond this mind set and use modern and humanized techniques.

Gilb and Weinberg in *Humanized Input* discuss a modern humanized input environment as one that takes advantage of defaults, positioning of messages, repeated messages, checkwords, and adaptive checking. We naturally do this in dealing with other humans.

defaults: "Most of them are . . . so we won't have to tell you that." Defaults are based on the premise that if you don't do something, you can't do it wrong. If we know that most of the time hourly employees work 40 hours per week, then we should assume 40 hours unless we are told something different. This will reduce the actual amount of entry work and also reduce errors

Another example is the repeating of record items. If a student took five classes in a school term, there is no need to repeat the entry of the student's name five times. When entering a grade report, the student's identification number could be entered. The system could echo back the student's name, current courses one at a time, and asking for corresponding grade.

positioning of messages: "Why do I have to enter $00.71?" Fixed length fields in specific positions were once required in a punched card environment. Today, blanks or delimiters such as special characters or hitting the return key can be used to specify new fields. Humanization does not include writing unnatural things like "007" when "7" carries the same meaning.

repeated messages: "Sure I write the amount twice on a personal check." Double entries are familiar to all accountants. This same type of control can be applied to critical entry data. Eighty-column verification is a thing of the past.

There are several methods of implementing repeated messages. Critical fields such as account number may have to be entered both at the beginning of a record as well as at the end to assure correctness. A number may be entered both from left to right and then from right to left if it is a critical item (1967 and 7691).

checkwords: "922-3454, that is the J. Johnson if the address is 43rd street." Messages can be "echoed" back to entry persons in different forms (birthdate echoed as age) or on different mediums (account number echoed back in voice output).

adaptive checking: "You sure? That is 20 percent more than anyone has ever ordered." Exceptions to normal patterns can be pointed out to the entry person. This means that experience patterns must be kept and used to find the exceptions.

The 80-column mentality must be not be used with modern technologic environments. Merely filling in forms on a screen when approaches such as defaults and prepopulated entry can be used is not taking advantage of modern technology.

Graphics and Output Design

Tabular data and information can often be enhanced through the use of graphical output. Line, bar, and pie graphs or charts and maps can engender visual images that allow new "looks" at data. And standardized graphics software puts computer generated graphics within budgets of most organizations.

Pie charts are best for showing parts of a whole. Line graphs show changes in a variable over time and the relationship between two variables. Bar charts can be used to show changes over time, parts of a whole, relationships between two variables, and comparisons between several items. Maps are best at showing differences in an item at different geographic locations. Maps also accommodate other charts within map boundaries. For example, bar charts can be located in each geographic area of significance comparing several data items.

Since the choices are so numerous and the outcomes so unpredictable, it is wise to seek assistance from graphic designers to ensure pleasing and effective outputs. Those who work with computers seem to have a tendency to use all available output space. This may result in crowded displays and inappropriate scales. Poor choice of color combinations and other aesthetics such as choice of font sizes or fill patterns often can be enhanced by aid from graphics design experts.

Care should be taken to ensure appropriate titles, labels, and scales. Keys should be carefully designed. All items on the graphs should be carefully located to avoid confusion, misunderstanding, or misinformation. If the graphics package has defaults for establishing these chararacteristics, the defaults should be examined to make sure the results are acceptable.

Ives (see References) presents guidelines for graphic design. He bases the guidelines on empirical research. For someone interested in this area, the original article should be studied. Below is a summary of some of the points made in the article.

Displaying Titles, Labels, and Text

Graphs contain a great deal of narrative data. Placement, content, size, and font type can greatly affect readability of the narrative and, if improperly done, can distract from the main message of the presentation. Ives suggests the following guides:

Content

1. Display no more data than the user needs.
2. Labels should be consistent from display to display.
3. Labels should be readily distinguishable from each other.
4. Labels should be made up from common terms that are familiar to the target user population or from standard lists of terms developed for the particular user population.

5. Avoid humor in accompanying text.
6. Use whole words rather than abbreviations where space permits.
7. If abbreviations must be used, do not include abbreviation punctuation.
8. Avoid contractions such as "won't" in labels and text.
9. Each display should contain enough title material to be comprehensible.
10. If the same chart form is being used multiple times (for example, to compare trends) then use the same set of scales for each instance of the chart.
11. Include zero on scales in which values are being compared; if only a small nonzero part of the scale is used, the chart may be misleading.
12. Values on grid scales should be selected so that interpolation is easy to do.
13. Avoid using two different scales on the same axis.
14. If two scales are used on the same axis, clearly mark (perhaps with an arrow) which scale goes with which curve.

Fonts

1. Generally, a single type face should be employed for a presentation, although different forms of that type face (e.g., bold, medium, or light; condensed, regular, or expanded) may be employed to distinguish among various levels of labels.
2. Such changes should be limited to two or three levels.
3. Proportional variations in type font sizes should be simple and obvious. Primary versus secondary labels, for example, might differ by ratios of 2:1 or 3:1.
4. Use the same family of type styles across multiple charts being used in the same presentation.
5. Simple sans-serif type fonts are preferable (for example, this is sans serif).
6. Avoid italicized, stenciled, or Old English script type fonts.

Position and Size

1. Line curves should be directly labeled if there is room rather than relying on a key.
2. Make scales on line chart axis large enough to easily be read.
3. If room permits, labels should be placed within the colored or shaded areas they represent rather than in a separate key.
4. Use size or color coding to help differentiate between levels of label importance.
5. Use capital letters for labels and short instructions because they can be read at a greater distance than capital and lowercase letters.
6. All labels should read from left to right. Avoid labels that read from top to bottom, that are on their sides, or that go around corners.

Displaying Text

1. Multiple lines of text should be displayed in lines of approximately 40 to 60 characters.
2. Unless the display device is capable of proportional spacing, justified right margins should not be used as they impede reading speed.
3. Normally long lines of text should be displayed with normal use of upper and lower case. This will improve readability as short words of mixed case can be recognized rapidly by their shape.
4. Avoid breaking words by hyphenation between lines.

Using Color

Good taste in the use of color is a challenging task. The designer must make a choice of certain hues, intensities, and combinations. Ives offers some directions based on empirical research.

Color Usage

1. For tasks involving item identification, color is a better coding strategy than anything except alphanumeric codes.
2. If a screen full of alphanumeric characters is broken into groups, blocks, or columns, then each can be made more discrete by separately coloring them.
3. Use color to differentiate two or more lines plotted on the same graph.
4. Color can be used as a prompt to indicate which information should be entered next.
5. Color is a good coding strategy for tasks involving screen searching and counting.

Color Choice

1. Data to be highlighted should be colored with bright colors, while "normal" data should be colored in less noticeable colors. For some IBM devices, colors from most bright to least bright are white, turquoise, yellow, pink, green, blue, red.
2. Use similar colors for similar situations (e.g., red for severe problems, pink for cautionary situations).
3. Color frequently used fields differently from the rest of the data.
4. If important categories must be clearly differentiated, then assign strongly contrasting colors to them first, and then assign colors to the remaining code categories.
5. Avoid red-green, blue-yellow, green-blue, and red-blue color pairs.
6. The color green is often appropriate for representing normal data.
7. Use the color red for error messages, identifying problems, and indicating significant conditions.

8. Apply LeCourier's background and foreground contrasts to color presentations.

Color Cautions

1. Irrelevant colors interfere with an individual's ability to perform a task involving item identification.
2. Use no more than four colors for novice users. Seven colors may be used effectively with experienced long-term users.
3. Red and green are not readily visible in the periphery of the eye. Material to be identified in this area should be coded as white.

Using Icons or Symbols

Icons are pictorial representations of things. They increasingly are being used in designing human-machine interfaces. Icons have long been familiar to persons as labels on charts, signs, and maps. Some guidelines in using icons include:

1. An excellent coding scheme can be developed using up to 20 unique shapes.
2. A particular shape can be varied to indicate some change in an attribute in the object being represented (for example, the wake of a ship can be used to represent both direction of travel and relative speed).
3. The meaning assigned to symbols should remain consistent across displays presented together.
4. Special symbols such as asterisks or arrows can serve to draw attention to exceptional conditions.
5. Limit displays to two or three different sizes of symbols to represent intensity.
6. If multiple sizes are employed for the same symbol, the next larger symbol should be at least 1.5 times as big as the previous smaller one.

Displaying Lines, Grids, and Axes

Choice of lines, grids, and axes can affect readability and clarity of a graphical representation. Guidelines include:

1. A coding scheme involving line widths should employ no more than three different line widths.
2. A coding scheme should consist of no more than four line types (i.e., solid versus varieties of dashed).
3. In plotting data curves, use dotted or dashed lines only for representing projections or extensions.

The above lists may serve as a good review and refresher before engaging in the design of input or output layouts. The lists also are useful when reviewing others' layout work.

The dialog and layouts should be tested as they are being developed. If the system is being developed in a top-down fashion, each increasingly complex version of the dialog and layouts should be tested. This can be considered part of training and implementation. Criteria to be used in tests can be derived from the objectives and tactics included in the requirements definition. The developer must be sure the needed tactics can be performed, and the results stated in the system objectives can be provided.

The dialog flow diagram can be used for early review and testing. This will allow familiarization with the dialog and layouts without the confrontation of having hardware in place. One person can be the "user" and others can "play" the machine. Flash cards can be used to represent screens or responses can be read out loud. Mocked-up screens also could be used. This may lead to unpredicted user actions or discovery of very stilted messages.

Testing also must take place once users become very familiar with the final version of the system. Performance may climb steadily as persons learn and become comfortable with the system. However, once mastery is reached, boredom and frustration could occur and performance may drop. The developer should be aware of this phenomenon, especially if there are changes that can be made that could maintain performance.

A HARDWARE PROBLEM? AN ELEGANT SOLUTION MAY NOT BE COSTLY

Pat was upset. Testing had shown that a new production modeling system was "blowing up." Users were sending off incomplete data which caused historical archives to be built that would be very difficult to recover from except with a complete restart. The reason—the SEND key was immediately adjacent to the RETURN key and the users were hitting the wrong key.

Pat's supervisors didn't know what to do about this hardware problem. Pat investigated keyboard redesigns, history saving to undo the SEND command (which would force buying more computer memory), special switches, and multiple requests once a SEND was made. The solutions were either very expensive or would interrupt users' flow.

After observing users and pondering the problem for a few days, Pat excitedly thought of a solution. Twist-off bottle caps were painted and placed over the SEND key. This would require that users make a conscious action to remove the key and send a complete data set. Users were informed that the system required the "interaction inhibitor" to be in place to be operational. There were no more problems.

Error rates should be recorded during testing. This will not only indicate work throughput, but also the total time operators would take to find errors and correct them. Errors often come at a cost which may be high enough to consider revision of the system.

Testing can be done through observation, recording a log or "trail" of peoples' activities, administering questionnaires to determine confidence and comfort, or even by recording people on videotape. Observation of things like skin flush or head shaking may lead to weak areas in the interface. If the interface is critical, physical measures such as pulse rate can be made. Notes should be made of where in the interface users asked for help. This may indicate a weakness in the dialog, especially if several users have the same problems.

Error logs are great aids for finding spelling or transposition types of errors. Errors often occur in endings of words. Tests for roots of words, and then asking the person if the suspected word is correct is a good practice. Common transpositions can be tested for and corrected on approval from the user (achieve versus acheive). Other confusing phrases or letters should be tested such as "0" or "O," "1" or "I," and "S" or "5" if they are important in avoiding errors.

In interface testing, it is important to:

1. Use representative users. This could include numerous persons to get a cross section of future users.
2. Use all of the types of hardware that will be part of the system.
3. Attempt system saturation to determine degradation.
4. Keep an error log to find frequent breakdown points.
5. Test failure and recovery procedures.
6. Test security with "safe-cracking" attempts.

Developers must keep in mind that a system is not finished until it meets the criteria set earlier in the project. Testing is a critical part of the development process and must be planned, organized, and controlled.

SUMMARY

There are more bad examples of person-machine interactions than there are good examples. Being conscious that the user is a person is a first step in the development of good dialogs and layouts. Empathy for the user, adequate testing, and use of the principles in this chapter should aid developers in being part of a new breed of symbiotic designers.

REFERENCES AND FURTHER READINGS

Foley, James D., and Victor L. Wallace. "The Art of Natural Graphic Man-Machine Conversation," *Proceedings of the IEEE,* vol. 62, no. 4, April 1974, pp. 462–471.

Gilb, Tom, and Gerald M. Weinberg. *Humanized Input: Techniques for Reliable Keyed Input,* Cambridge, MA: Winthrop Publishers, Inc., 1977.

Goleman, Daniel, "The Human-Computer Connection," *Psychology Today,* March 1984, pp. 20–24.

Heckel, Paul. *The Elements of Friendly Software Design,* New York: Warner Books, Inc., 1984.

Ives, Blake. "Graphical User Interfaces for Business Information Systems," *MIS Quarterly,* special issue, December 1982, pp. 15–42.

Martin, James. *Design of Man–Machine Dialogues,* Englewood Cliffs, NJ: Prentice-Hall, 1973.

Meads, Jon A. "Friendly or Frivolous?" *Datamation,* April 1, 1985, pp. 96+.

Mozeico, Howard. "A Human/Computer Interface to Accommodate User Learning Stages," *Communications of the ACM,* vol. 25, no. 2, February 1982, pp. 100–104.

Nesdore, Paul F. "Friendly to All or None," *Computerworld,* In Depth section, Oct. 31, 1983, vol. 17, no. 44, pp. 2–5.

Quirk, William G. "Designing for Novice & Expert," *Computerworld,* In Depth section, Oct. 31, 1983, vol. 17, no. 44, pp. 2+.

Rubinstein, Richard, and Harry M. Hersh. *The Human Factor: Designing Computer Systems for People,* Burlington, MA: Digital Press, 1984.

Schneiderman, Ben. "Designing Interactive Systems," in *Software Psychology: Human Factors in Computer and Information Systems,* Cambridge, MA: Winthrop Publishers, 1980, pp. 247–266.

Thadhani, A. J. "Interactive User Productivity," *IBM Systems Journal,* vol. 20, no. 4, 1981, pp. 407–423.

REVIEW QUESTIONS

1. What is symbiosis? Why is it a meaningful goal for technology-based systems?
2. What is meant by user friendly?
3. What are some suggestions for making a dialog both beginner- and expert-friendly?
4. What is meant by content tolerance? Give some examples.
5. Why should dialog testing not just take place at implementation time?
6. Why has input layout design changed in the past years?
7. How might fields like magic and filmmaking apply to human–machine interface design? What other disciplines might contribute to a systems developer's knowledge?
8. According to Rubinstein and Hersh, what rules apply to interactions people have with machines?
9. Can response time be too short? Explain.
10. What might cause the user of a dialog to experience stress?
11. What are some characteristics of a "friendly" dialog for managerial users?
12. What are the three symbols used in dialog designing?
13. What is an alias list?
14. Why is an "anything else" response needed in dialog design?
15. What are some advantages of command-driven dialogs?

16. What are some obvious items that should not be ignored when designing forms?
17. Why would a number on a form be put in one of the corners?
18. Give an example of the use of defaults.
19. What is adaptive checking?
20. Why are system objectives related to output layout design?
21. What are some options to tabular presentation of output?
22. What are icons? Where have you seen them used?
23. What can error logs be used for?
24. What are some specific subsystems that may not be used very often that must be tested?

DISCUSSION QUESTIONS

1. Review the characteristics of friends mentioned in this chapter. Rank the factors that are important to you.
2. Why might the design of the user interface affect the length of the user training manual?
3. One person–machine interface that has received much discussion is the typewriter keyboard. There has been much discussion about redesigning the QWERTY keyboard to something like the Dvorak-Dealey keyboard, which places vowels on the left, and frequently used consonants on the right. (For example, see the article "The Typist's Touch," by Donald R. Gentner and Donald A. Norman, in *Psychology Today,* March 1984, pp. 66–72.) Do you think this would be a good idea if you were in charge of a keying operation?
4. Discuss how friends greet each other. What might you do differently in greeting a friend you haven't seen in a long time? Can you tell what mood a friend might be in from the greeting you receive? Try greeting a close friend like you would a stranger. What was the reaction you received? What did you learn from the discussion of greeting human friends that applies to human–machine dialogs? What does not apply? Why?
5. What can be done to bridge the gap between "machine likes" and human responses mentioned in this chapter?
6. "A goal of interface design is to allow the user to focus on his/her task, not on using the machine." Explain why this is important. Compare this to using other tools.

EXERCISES

1. Design an appropriate entry form for the UnBoston Marathon mentioned in the previous chapter. Be prepared to have a team product review by peers of your effort.

2. The following is a "pay by phone" dialog instruction. Critique both the instructions provided and the suggested dialog.

Try Bank by Phone for Yourself.

For your practice call, use this special demonstration information:

Call 432-7685.

Bank By Phone Practice Account Number: 987 654 321

Practice Payment Authorization Code: 123

You wish to pay XYZ utility—The Merchant Identification Number is: 16

And you wish to pay them: $38.75 today.

Here's all you do.

1. The voice will greet you and ask you for your *Bank By Phone* account number. Push 987654321 #. The # Button (known as the SEND Button) tells *Bank By Phone* that you have finished your response and are ready to move on to the next instruction.
2. The voice will ask for your Payment Authorization Code. Push 123 #.
3. The voice will ask for the Merchant Identification Number of the merchant you're paying. Push 16 #.
4. The voice will ask for the amount you want to pay. Use $38.75 as an example. Push 3875 #.
5. The voice will ask you to push the Action Button or enter a future payment date. Push * #. The * Button (known as the Action Button) followed directly by the # Button (SEND Button). This indicates that you want your payment or transfer to be processed today.
6. The voice will then repeat the entire transaction back to you for verification.
7. Push * 2 # to complete the call. Do not hang up until you hear the words "Thank you for calling Bank By Phone." This signals that your transactions have been recorded or processed.

   Suggest another technique for repesenting the above procedure and why you might use it.

3. Create a dialog flow diagram for an existing person–machine dialog. Try to find a dialog that includes branching.

4. Find a frequently used form in your school. Review the form in light of the suggestions given in this chapter.

5. Compare and contrast a menu-driven computer such as the Apple Macintosh and another command driven computer. What are the advantages and disadvantages of each?

6. Peruse three computer magazines for advertising for new person–machine interface devices. Visit a computer store and investigate new hardware that can be used to interface with a computer. Report your findings.

CHAPTER 12

Designing for System Integrity

Al Capone, the famous Chicago gangster of the 1930s, allegedly had a bookkeeper who stated he could steal more money with a pencil than a mob of gangsters could steal with machine guns.

THIS CHAPTER CONSIDERS the control, security, privacy, and recovery aspects of systems design. Discussions of who must be involved in systems integrity and a method for determining the need for system integrity are included. A total systems view of vulnerability is presented to assure understanding of the need to protect the system.

CHAPTER OBJECTIVES

You should be able to:

- Understand the criticalness of system integrity
- Understand the components of system integrity
- Specify when integrity is developed and by whom
- Decompose a system to specify the subsystems where integrity is needed
- Specify means used to assure security and recovery
- Understand why the systems developer is concerned with data privacy
- Indicate deliverables that are part of an integrity plan

If Al Capone's bookkeeper could steal with a pencil on a manually oriented system, just think what could be done with modern systems which include huge numbers of transactions, online interaction, and mass storage of data.

Systems developers are not only concerned with crime. There are many systems integrity problems which are not a result of crime. Data or procedures could be lost through carelessness, improper procedures, computer hardware malfunctions, software errors, or natural disasters. Disgruntled employees could be as threatening through sabotage as those attempting to steal. Technology allows activities to happen quickly and with large amounts of data. And since organizations are becoming more and more dependent on their automated systems, it is essential to be sure organizations can depend on the systems.

This chapter is not intended to make one an expert on protecting data and processing capabilities. This would require an entire course or set of courses, and much experience. But it is necessary to be aware of and consider factors which could reduce system vulnerability to abuse or misuse when putting a system design together. These factors must be designed into the system, not added on. Integrity retrofit has been found to be costly and ineffective compared to integrity built into the system. Often, a manager will become concerned that the organization's systems are vulnerable (usually because of some publicized tragedy) and will embark on a "systems control campaign." This is both costly and a major intrusion to the systems development units. Integrity must be a systems design objective supported by management.

BUILDING INTEGRITY INTO SYSTEMS

There are many commonly used words and concepts that describe the integrity or soundness of a system. Each of them must be understood so we can put together a trustworthy system.

Integrity = Control + Security + Privacy + Recovery

CONTROL

There are two ingredients of control: controlling for the *existence* of data and controlling for a certain degree of *correctness*. Existence is usually checked by counting things or by inspecting to see if something really does exist. Correctness is usually checked by having a standard that can be used for comparison. Data can be incorrect because of honest errors or because it was intentionally altered by someone trying to commit a crime.

A teacher exercises control over existence of data when inspecting exams handed in to see that each one has a name on it. If exams are all collected at one time, the teacher also may count the number of exams handed in and compare the total with the number of students present in the room. Control over correctness is exhibited if the teacher added up all the scores for exams recorded in a gradebook, added all the total scores directly from the exams, and compared the two totals.

SECURITY

A system must not be vulnerable to failure because of natural or unnatural acts. This means protection against acts or events such as fire, water damage, or human destruction. Of course, we have different levels of concern in securing a system. A military defense system would have a greater degree of security than a magazine subscription mailing list system.

Teachers exhibit security when they lock up their office, store gradebooks in a locked, fireproof file cabinet, and have passwords on computer files where grades are stored.

PRIVACY

Privacy is protection of access to data that should not be in the public domain. An individual's right to privacy must not be violated. This means that personal data must have limited access and publicly available data should require individual identification. Authorization procedures must exist before someone can view the data.

Security is linked to privacy. If data is not secure and was easily accessed, an individual's right to privacy would be violated. Individuals must be able to see data about themselves and be assured that others cannot see it if it is private.

Teachers respect privacy when they post grades by student number rather than name, and do not post the grades alphabetically to assure that people at the beginning or end of the alphabet cannot be identified.

RECOVERY

If there is an intrusion in the system or if a failure takes place, there must be a means of bringing the system back to a state of stability. One of the primary means of recovery is to use an earlier, totally intact version of a system. Thus, writing backup versions of the system is an essential part of the recovery process.

A teacher exhibiting recovery procedures would periodically photocopy the gradebook, or write a backup copy of automated files on disk and store it in a different location than the working copy.

COMMON EXAMPLES OF INTEGRITY

There are many examples showing how we maintain integrity in our everyday life. We may *control* car engine operation by observing gauges or warning lights and take action if a certain standard is not observed, we *secure* the car by locking the doors and having an ignition key that is needed for operation, we protect *privacy* of owners by not posting names and phone numbers on license plates, and we ensure backup and *recovery* by carrying a spare tire.

Note that these integrity-establishing components are *not* needed for the car to run in normal circumstances. Our cars could still run without door or ignition locks, but would not be very secure. We can drive the car

LEARNING A LESSON THE HARD WAY

An information systems professor assigns and collects a homework assignment dealing with establishing system integrity. The professor returns to the next class and announces that he lost all the assignments. (He really didn't.) He then announces that he will accept either a backup copy of the original assignment (since he actually has the assignments, he can control for originals) or a newly done assignment *and* an essay on backup and recovery. He feels the students who made a copy of the original assignment understand backup and recovery and don't need to write the essay

without a spare tire. Integrity aids are not absolutely needed, but they do ensure peace of mind.

Consider the integrity of your banking activities. You would worry if you had a missing check in your checkbook. You would worry if the bank supplied an account total that did not reconcile with your calculations. You would worry if you lost your checkbook and would take action to bring things back to normal. You would worry if someone stole your wallet with both your bank card and the "secret code" that allows access to bank machines.

System integrity must not be taken lightly. Some might see integrity assurance as a costly burden until an event takes place that makes them thankful these added precautions exist.

WHO HAS A ROLE IN ASSURING SYSTEM INTEGRITY?

The *systems developer* is just one of many persons in an organization who can help protect the information assets and assure system integrity. The developer may also coordinate the activities of others who may be involved.

The *owners* of the data and system have primary responsibility for identifying needed integrity—things they would worry about or that could harm the organization. Owners would work with others to express and review these needs.

Guardians of data, including internal auditors and quality assurance personnel, must review any proposed designs to issue an opinion on the soundness of the system. Guardians may focus on topics such as security or how to build accounting controls into a system.

Custodians of the data, the persons who process and actually keep the data, usually the operations units, must ensure the system is safe and secure.

Organization *management* takes final responsibility and must answer for any tragedies which occur because of an unsound system. Thus, management must ensure that time and resources are available while a system is being developed and not insist on meeting a deadline if it means an unsound system will result.

System integrity calls for a team effort with many specialties. The systems developer must make the system owners aware of the liabilities created by acquiring and installing a system. But, just as in any complex discipline, the systems developer may call on physical security, control, auditing, and legal specialists to assist in the process. This is done by having these persons consult with the designers, or even better, participating in team product reviews specially scheduled to assure system integrity.

There are two major activities in designing integrity:

1. Deciding what to protect—specifying an accurate statement of need.
2. Deciding what can be done to protect it—design the protection.

Owners of data in the system can play an important role in deciding what to protect. Protection often is designed based on what the developer thinks is important. This importance usually is based on the developer's intuition and interpretations of system owners' attitudes. Seldom has there been corporatewide involvement in protection. In most cases systems developers based their security decisions on "gut feel" of what was important.

Today, with critical and sensitive information being stored in many locations, being downloaded to microcomputer systems, or being sent on communication channels, this approach is not reasonable. "Personal" information on personal computers may be more sensitive than general corporatewide data stored in databases. The developer must try to identify any vulnerabilities and ensure protection of data and processing.

The developer can take a systematic approach, based on information, to attach values to the data and information stored within the organization. This will also indicate the need to protect the processes used to generate the organization's data and information. The developers must collect data from individuals and units in the organization to make certain that sensitive information is protected, and that resources are not spent protecting information that does not have a high value. The next section will discuss a method for determining the need for system integrity.

DETERMINING THE NEED FOR SYSTEM INTEGRITY

A method for determining the need for system integrity is to create an ***information asset risk matrix.**** For each *information asset* (subfile, record, data item, etc.), involved organization members are asked to attach a rating value of the need to protect the information against disclosure, modifica-

*This section is based on ideas from a talk, "Information Security's Missing Links," given by Warren Schmitt, Allstate Insurance Co., November 15, 1984, Indiana University Graduate School of Business, Management Information Systems Affiliates Program.

tion, or destruction. When evaluating protection information assets, it is important to consider value to different audiences. Different levels of management, different organization functions, or different staff persons will value information differently. The "custodian" of the information, typically the systems department, may also put a value on the information based on what it may cost to reconstruct it if unauthorized alteration occurs.

DETERMINING DISCLOSURE COSTS

An organization can suffer great costs if data is disclosed to inappropriate groups or individuals. Inappropriate disclosure can affect:

Individuals—releasing private data about an individual which could result in lawsuits

Internal operation—releasing sensitive data about the organization's operations

Competitive advantage—releasing proprietary data the organization needs to maintain a competitive advantage, such as a customer purchases list

Each of the organizational units that uses the information asset must numerically rate the disclosure costs for each asset. One organization uses a 10-point scale which corresponds with the following categories:

Disclosure Requirement	*Numeric Rating*
Registered confidential	10–9–8
Confidential	7–6–5
Internal use only	4–3–2
Unclassified	1

For example, an information asset called the "corporate plan report" might be rated a "9" by one manager and a "2" by another. The reason for this might be the belief by the manager who gave the lower rating that the plan is so out-of-date that its disclosure would not be critical. The important thing is that the *owners* of the data made this decision, not the systems developer. If there are differences between the owners, it is their responsibility to come to a consensus on what degree of protection is needed. It is the owners' needs that must be specified and satisfied.

DETERMINING MODIFICATION COSTS

An organization can suffer great costs if data is modified. Inappropriate actions or decisions could take place. Inappropriate modification can result in:

Losing records—trying to locate master records when identifier fields may have been changed

Lower accuracy of data—assuming data is correct and making a decision or taking action that would have been different if the data was accurate

Each of the organizational units that uses the information asset must numerically rate the modification impact costs. One organization uses a 10-point scale which corresponds with the following categories:

Modification Impact	*Numeric Rating*
Critical impact	10–9–8
Major impact	7–6–5
Minor impact	4–3–2
Acceptable	1

DETERMINING DESTRUCTION COSTS

An organization can suffer great costs if data is inappropriately destroyed. Destruction cost is determined by:

Cost of replacement—data may have to be regathered, regenerated, or may even be irreplaceable.

Time needed to restore the data—if an organization cannot operate without the destroyed data, a high cost is incurred of stopping operations until replacement occurs.

Need for originals—some documents are expensive or even impossible to replace.

Each of the organizational units that uses the information asset must numerically rate the destruction costs. One organization uses a 10 point scale which corresponds with the following categories:

Destruction Impact	*Numeric Rating*
Critical impact	10–9–8
Major impact	7–6–5
Minor impact	4–3–2
Acceptable	1

AGGREGATING THE INFORMATION ASSET DATA

Once all this data is collected for each information asset for each person or unit that is concerned with the asset, it is *aggregated* to develop an overall rating for the asset. This information is used to guide systems developers in designing a protection plan.

	Importance to the Organization Caused by Unauthorized:			
	Disclosure	*Modification*	*Destruction*	
Info Asset	*Aggregated Score*	*Aggregated Score*	*Aggregated Score*	*Total*
Customer #	3	6	7	16
Customer name	5	3	5	13
Customer address	1	3	4	8
Product one purchases	7	7	8	22
Product two purchases for each info asset	7	7	8	22

Once the value of the information exists, the systems developer can establish means of protecting the asset. This information can be used by security experts to ensure that the cost of protection does not exceed the value. The decisions systems people must face include what data, what potential hazards exist, and how much protection is needed. The gathered information can aid in making these decisions

SOME CONSIDERATIONS IN BUILDING INTEGRITY

Before getting into the means of protecting systems, it is important to understand some overruling considerations. These include the need to evaluate the tradeoffs when designing system integrity, realizing that batch processing systems have different needs for integrity than online systems, and realizing that microcomputers bring a whole new set of integrity needs.

TRADEOFFS

As in many design activities, there is a need to evaluate tradeoffs. Two important tradeoffs are discussed below.

Cost of Protecting versus Cost of Loss

System integrity comes at a cost. It is not free. Usually, integrity is established by adding redundancy. This means that operations are performed more than once, data is stored more than once, or multiple copies of equipment exist to ensure availability of working versions. Improved integrity can reduce system efficiency by introducing system access barriers, increasing complexity of operation, and forcing extra computational activities. The disclosure, modification, and destruction costs must be measured against the costs of protection.

For example, frequency of backups of data is based on reconstruction costs of the data. A designer has to compare regeneration costs with backup creation costs. If an organization had to pay overtime wages to recreate data or if it was impossible to "catch up" on processing such as order processing, the value of writing frequent backups may be very great. The developer constantly must be doing this type of cost analysis.

Ease of Use versus Integrity

System designs that incorporate greater integrity can make system usage more difficult. In fact, the easier one makes access to a computer, the less secure it will be. When we had to use many codes and program in assembly language, there was only a small portion of the population that could access and manipulate the data. Now, with easy-to-use terminals, microcomputers, and greater computer literacy, systems are becoming less secure. User-friendly design can make a system more vulnerable.

Safety and risk reduction can degrade performance. The auto makers who had to deal with new safety regulations and pollution control devices can testify to this. However, overall quality of life has been improved with reduced risk to life and improved air to breathe. This same attitude must be taken with systems.

BATCH VERSUS ONLINE SYSTEMS

This activity of control has been made more complex as we have moved to more complex systems holding more complex data. Networks, data communications, and database management have made control more difficult. The one factor that has made systems very difficult to control is online updating, which means that records are rewritten in place rather than having generations of master files and files of updating transactions.

MICROCOMPUTER COMPLICATIONS

The proliferation of microcomputers has brought additional integrity challenges. Many persons managing the micros do not have the "battle scars" that many seasoned systems personnel possess and thus may not take the necessary precautions.

Microcomputers often are very accessible. They occupy places similar to telephones and don't have the security of formal computer centers. Vulnerability of corporate data is increased by this accessibility. Anyone with a little knowledge can access and operate the hardware and destroy or change data. Some organizations have found that integrity can only be achieved by housing micros in separate rooms, providing locks for the on/off switches, providing lockable drawers for keyboards, securing removable storage, and insisting on establishment of backup and recovery policies.

A SYSTEMS VIEW OF VULNERABILITY

One of the easiest ways of viewing system integrity is to examine a figure of the suprasystems the system is a part of and the subsystems within the

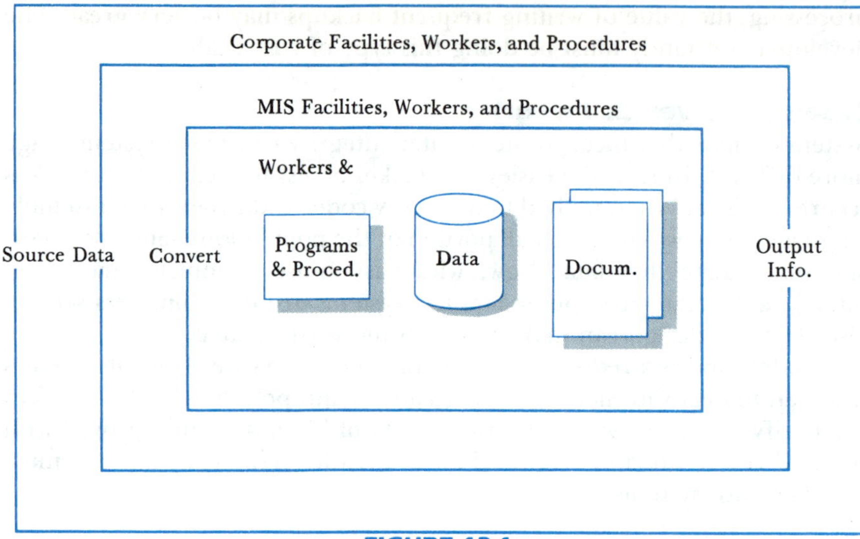

FIGURE 12.1

Points of vulnerability in an organizational system.

system to be designed. Figure 12.1 exhibits a system and its environment. Every word or boundary on the figure shows a point of vulnerability. Each of the boundaries can be treated as an entry to the system, which could make it more vulnerable. Care should be taken in data gathering, data preparation, input to the system, editing of input, processing of the data, and distribution of output.

The system designer or security administrator must be concerned with access to buildings, devices, people, procedures, codes, data views (input, output, and storage), and communication lines. Then, if access is gained, the designer must be concerned with the ability to use and potentially manipulate everything from data to people.

As a system becomes more technically complex, it becomes more difficult to maintain integrity. There could be more entry points to the data and the processing.

PROTECTING THE SYSTEM

This section will discuss areas where a system could lose its integrity by being vulnerable and how the designer can design protection into the system.

PHYSICAL ACCESS PROTECTION

Physical access protection consists of managing attempts to actually touch the hardware and software. Means of providing protection include:

Use of employee badges, coded combination locks, or identification cards for secured areas

Limiting physical access by making access procedures unavailable to unauthorized persons

Security guards or lock devices to keep unauthorized people off the premises

Care as to who will be given tours of the computer room or other facilities

Once the physical barrier is broken, then the next round of protection is preventing access to subsystems.

SUBSYSTEM ACCESS PROTECTION

This consists of managing unauthorized attempts to use certain hardware or software or access certain data. Means of protection include:

Passwords and appropriate attempts to avoid abuse by persons owning passwords:

Passwords can be used to restrict certain operations or access to specific data sets.

Passwords should be changed every 30 to 60 days; organizations may force password changes by denying system access unless there is a record of a recent password change.

Keys to unlock a physical device and operationalize it.

Cards for terminal devices which are similar to credit cards with magnetic strips unreadable to humans.

If data is very sensitive, use of fingerprint, signatures, handprint, voiceprint, eyeball vein patterns recognition (the author heard an unknown quip commenting on combining lip prints and bank teller machines which said: "You can really kiss your money goodbye!").

A NEAR TRAGEDY—"But it *is* just a report!"

An organization learned that security of their payroll data could not be taken lightly. After doing program testing with a copy of a real payroll file, a programmer discarded an intact hard-copy report of the data from a test run. The report was found by a custodian who thought it possibly should be saved and put it on the desk of one of the other employees. The data in the report spread throughout the company and nearly created a shutdown of the company because of the perceived inequities when people knew other peoples' salaries.

—From a student who requested confidentiality.

Dialback devices to protect against those persons trying to gain access from an unauthorized location; the system only will call back to prespecified locations that are linked to passwords.

Precautions to protect data and programs that are used for test purposes.

More sophisticated approaches to detecting unauthorized computer use and abuse will likely be developed. Simulating human detective approaches, means of identifying patterns of computer usage and then detecting deviations from these patterns will often disclose unauthorized use.

The ability to distinguish between change due simply to changed working patterns from that of someone trying to "beat" the system must also be established. A standard pattern could be established for each person who normally accesses the system, including when, or for how long, for how big a change. Then deviations from this standard could be flagged and investigated. For example, someone who has never used his or her authorized computer terminal at 7:00 P.M. may just be doing catch-up work; or, may be either performing devious activities or is being impersonated.

PROCESSING PROTECTION

Processing protection consists of managing the processing of data to assure existence, accuracy, and security. Every good and legal transaction must be processed, but only processed once. Safeguards must be in place to assure this during data input, actual processing, and after output has been generated.

Assuring Input Has Integrity

Inputs are critical in ensuring integrity since assurance is done at a person–machine boundary where the last human contact is made before the machine takes over. Human judgment is still available to avoid any disasters and to ask questions if something does not seem correct. Input controls include:

Editing for reasonableness (checking to see if input data could normally be expected)

Control totals (adding up numeric fields and comparing with an independently calculated standard)

Hash totals (totaling a numeric field that normally would not be totaled, such as a total of employee numbers, and comparing with a known standard)

Record counts (counting the number of records and comparing with an expected number)

Missing data (making sure all needed fields exist)

Proper character types (for example, ensuring only numbers are entered in numeric fields)

Limit or range checks (ensuring data falls in acceptable limits)

Proper sequences (order of transactions is critical, especially in sequential batch processing)

Check digits (suffix number digits calculated by mathematical formula and added to an identification number which is then recalculated each time the number is used),

Tape or disk label checks (verifying internally stored labels to assure proper identification)

Code verification tables (for example, having a table of allowable two-digit state code abbreviations for comparison purposes)

Valid field combinations (for example, comparing postal code with allowable city or state identifiers)

Visual inspection (looking at the data to see if it appears correct)

Feedback in another form (for example, if age were critical, as in an insurance policy, birth date would be entered and age would be fed back)

Pattern detection (detecting and recording patterns and then "flagging" deviations to patterns. For example, an ordering unit check of this type by a human would likely mention that "You never ordered a dozen garden tractors before, are you sure you didn't want to order just one? Or was it garden trellises that you wanted a dozen of?" Our systems could possess a bit of "intelligence")

Source documents control (for example, using sequence numbers on source documents, much like we number our personal checks, to see if there is a check we cannot account for)

Assuring Processing Results in Integrity

Once data is entered into the system, integrity must be assured in the actual processing. Processing controls could include:

Limit checks (ensuring that calculated amounts are within predetermined limits)

Check digit verification (recalculating check digits when a critical variable is encountered)

Crossfooting checks (ensuring that column and row subtotals add up to identical amounts)

Eligible code or data combination checks (checking for illegal codes or for combinations of data that cannot exist)

Redundancy checks (age and birth date)

Record counts (assuring that all records in a batch are still there)

Hash/batch totals (verifying totals from input are still the same)

File label checks (checking disk or tape labels and matching against file libraries)

Write prevention (use of write-prevention tabs or rings on tapes or disks that prevent undesired writing)

Artificial batch creation (once data is correctly entered, online data could be gathered in batches for further processing)

Status logs (maintaining a record of which data has been processed by which programs to focus restart)

Periodic file dumps (files can be written, preferably to remote storage locations, to maintain current backups)

Assuring Output Integrity

One area of the system that often is ignored is assuring output integrity. Output integrity controls include:

Visually checking reasonableness of results.

Verifying that any requests for distribution of reports are authorized.

Ensuring that overruns or extra reports are properly destroyed. This includes maintenance of shredders and making sure that carbon from multiple-part forms is destroyed as part of standard operating procedure.

Establishing inquiry controls only allowing certain data access or processing capabilities based on accessor rights. Database management systems may help by allowing access to data at file, record, or even data item levels.

TELECOMMUNICATIONS PROTECTION

Telecommunications control includes managing attempts to get at software and data from remote locations. It can include the approaches discussed below.

System security should provide for controlled access to confidential data. (Innervisions)

Message Identification

Unauthorized access from remote locations must be flagged and recorded. This could include "real-time checking"—allowing identification of who instigated any changes to databases, and if unauthorized, to flag this in real time. This would be similar to a building with a burglar alarm. Some alarms will be audible so the violator will stop the action very quickly, and some may be silent so the intruder can be apprehended. It may be necessary to maintain "electronic watchmen" to patrol the systems to detect any invaders.

Message Transmission

Encryption devices may be needed to code messages that enter communication networks. *Encryption* means scrambling signals to be sent on a communication line, sending the scrambled signal, and then unscrambling once the appropriate destination is reached. Communication lines and switching centers should not be vulnerable to access by unauthorized persons. Messages may be numbered to assure against gaps in sequences. Persons sending the message can manually keep a record the computer will check. If the two sequence numbers do not match, there can be a review.

AIDS TO DESIGNING INTEGRITY

Some of the techniques that have been discussed in previous chapters can aid in designing integrity.

USE OF FLOW DIAGRAMS

Flow diagrams are an excellent means of identifying and documenting needed and installed controls. The data flow diagram and the systems flowchart can aid in identifying where controls are needed, and may serve as a bridge between systems analysts, users, and control specialists such as security experts or auditors as they discuss integrity controls.

Control designers often include controls on the system flowchart. This will often result in a complex, cluttered, and overwhelming document. A different method of using system flowcharts for control documentation is advocated by Jenkins and Carlis (see References). They advocate the use of dual charts—one illustrating data flow, the other controls. This results in two charts that are similar in graphic appearance, but contain different information.

This concept originally was suggested by Benjamin (see References). The method includes constructing a system flowchart and making an exact replica of the flow symbols without any labeling. Then the blank template is used to add the controls to the represented system. By using the exact positioning of symbols, the reader of the control chart can correspond the system flow and the system controls.

This same kind of approach can be used with structured techniques. Brill (see References) details the use of controls in both the logical model to specify system needs and in the physical model to specify how controls will actually be implemented. A great contribution of structured techniques is to give developers, users, and specialists such as auditors and security specialists a common model for communication and discussion. It is difficult to add controls to a system if the system is not understood.

The dialog flow diagramming technique allows the attachment of access controls by denoting which users can use which paths on the dialog flow diagram. Password control also can be indicated on the diagram and in the screen logs.

USE OF THE DATA DICTIONARY

The data dictionary can be used to document editing allowances on data elements. It can also aid in determining if sensitive data may need to be encrypted. This is done by examining the information gathered during the requirements stages of the project when the information asset protection matrix, mentioned earlier in the chapter, is developed.

The data dictionary also will hold documentation of allowable accesses and procedures to be followed in handling and processing the data. Good updated documentation will enhance system integrity by preventing people from doing the wrong things or doing things wrong. Good documentation such as written procedures can prevent errors in input, processing, or output.

PEOPLE AND INTEGRITY

Besides building in the controls for a system, they must be implemented, managed, enforced, and monitored. We cannot afford to have locks on the car doors and leave the windows open and the keys in the ignition. It is essential to manage the people that have access to the company's facilities, procedures, and data.

It is critical that all the security and control measures that are designed are actually used. Password control that is breached by having the passwords posted in the computer terminal area is of no value. A question you might ask yourself is: "Would I want a cash card at a bank where I could talk someone into giving me my 'secret access code' over the phone?" We must build usable controls into systems we design to make sure that a tragedy cannot take place. And then we must be assured that people understand the controls and why they are in place.

People are the key to control implementation and the resulting integrity. People can break a good system or make a weak one work. They must understand that security and control measures are not senseless paranoia. These measures are the means of preventing a tragedy. Honest mistakes could destroy a company.

Some activities can be taken to ensure that people working with systems will not be the weak link in system integrity.

NEED FOR SEPARATION OF DUTIES

Having system integrity includes examining the duties of persons executing system activities. Duties must be segregated to make sure that there are "checks and balances." Duties such as input preparation, computer operations, systems development and maintenance, and output distribution should be separated and not performed by the same persons. For example, a plan may include the policy of only allowing data librarians to retrieve and mount removable memory devices such as tapes or disks for a job. Operators then would run the jobs. Then the data distributor would have the responsibility for distribution of system output. Programmers would have no access to the data that is used.

Those receiving cash or deposits must not have other duties with sufficient scope to conceal fraud. It is wise to trust people, but at the same time it is not wise to tempt them.

NEED FOR SAFE PERSONNEL POLICIES

Most persons cannot recognize someone who would commit an act of crime or sabotage. Thus, precautions must be taken. Trust must be established, not just granted. Standard credit checks should be run on all potential employees, including part-time or temporary help. If a person has a position or duty change, existing clearances should be examined and revoked if needed. Likewise, precautions should be taken if existing employees are given job transfers which could allow new accesses.

All employees should be required to take earned vacations. It is healthy for the organization to not become dependent on any one employee. And, there have been cases of persons who would not take a vacation because someone might discover the patches they put on a system to commit fraud.

Persons who are to be dismissed from employment and who have had access to sensitive programs or data should be paid severance costs and restricted from the premises. All passwords or other access means to the systems should be invalidated immediately. There are cases of employees who, when given 2 weeks' notice, became disgruntled and sabotaged facilities.

PUBLICITY

Another caution that should be taken is to avoid publicity of an organization's systems. The best way to interest someone in breaking into a system is to tell the world that it is impenetrable. In other words, "Don't issue the challenge!" or someone will accept it. In some cases, it may be wise to prevent knowledge of what kinds of technology exist and where they reside.

At the same time, system integrity should be stressed to all employees who work with the system. This includes data entry, computer operations, output distribution, maintenance, and management personnel. They should be aware of the dire straits the organization could be in if people became careless.

DISASTER RECOVERY

No one in systems work wants to think about a disaster, but plans must exist in case one occurs. The organization's life may depend on having a disaster plan. The computer hardware and software and the data it stores and manipulates is a necessary part of an organization. The organization may not stay in business if it does not have the systems support. Bills will not be sent, workers not paid, and orders cannot be taken. The computer and its support is not a nicety, but a necessity.

BURNT OR BURNED

As the wheels continue to spin on the issue of disaster recovery, John Nugent, senior consultant at Norwest Bank of Minneapolis, finds it especially difficult to deal with executives who don't want to invest in something they think is unlikely to happen. His reasons are well-founded: Norwest Bank burnt to the ground on Thanksgiving day, 1982. If it weren't for a disaster recovery plan then in place, 32 percent of the bank's assets would have been lost and indeed the new facility, as it stands today, may not have become a reality.

To show the impact this disaster had, Nugent has been giving speeches and delivering a slide presentation to top business executives across the country. One of his recent stops was at the Data Processing Management Association conference in Anaheim, CA. His message: "It could happen to you."

The disaster plan at Norwest, which had been implemented only six months prior to the fire, was originally drafted on the supposition that one or two departments might be affected; a disaster of this magnitude was never imagined. That it also might happen on a holiday when employees were out of town or with families also was not expected.

Although perhaps not quite prepared for the worst, within one day, Norwest officials allocated more than 300,000 square feet of space, emptied warehouses and installed a central information phone number, placed ads in the newspapers informing customers that their money was safe, and reordered checks, forms and supplies. Employees were moved to eight other downtown locations.

The disaster area itself was monitored by setting up a color-coded card scheme to restrict the number of people entering the site. Radio communications also were put in place. The idea was first to protect the people, then the data/information and finally the equipment and software.

Looking back at it now, it was quite a feat, Nugent recalled, considering that the on-line operations, personnel and profit sharing, international banking and office support, and financial areas all were shut down. Similar to a fire or smoke in the home, Nugent listed the stages of a disaster: detection, reaction, assessment, authorization, mobilization, restoration, and reconstruction.

One of the key considerations, Nugent noted, was deciding who would be in charge. "If we hadn't had a plan," he said, "we wouldn't have brought some people into the planning process as quickly as we did." He advised that companies address the potential losses that can be sustained; how long they can operate; the recovery cycle; who's legally responsible; financial penalties; and the benefits derived from a contingency plan. He said the assessment phase typically takes the longest: between 3 and 18 months, depending on the size of the company.

By publishing a definition paper and distributing it to key members of the organization early on in the planning cycle, priorities are already set in place, Nugent suggested. In that way, approvals are also solicited from the departments that will be responsible for carrying out certain facets of the plan. Alternative backup sites, whether they are service bureaus, regional processing centers or in-house facilities, also need to be determined.

Nugent pointed out that increased awareness among employees can be facilitated through training and testing of methodologies. He referred to a study performed in Texas which shows that, of the companies which experienced disasters, 43 percent never reopened and 29 percent closed within two years. Ninety-five percent of those that had recovery plans failed to test them beforehand.

Some of the other areas to look into, according to Nugent, are insurance (whether or not personal possessions are covered by the homeowner or the company); and obtaining blueprints so that those unfamiliar with the facility will know which doors have explosives behind them and which can be opened safely. The human response element also cannot be underestimated, he said, adding that stress usually sets in between 90 and 120 days after the disaster has taken place.

In the way of technology, Nugent thinks this disaster, even now, underscored some of the areas that need improvement. He was amazed to see how dependent banking is on paper. The bank then spent an estimated $55,000 to pay a salvage vendor to clean all paper documents. The number of minis and micros throughout the bank "also opened our eyes to getting our arms around the mini/micro explosion going on today," he said. The gives and takes are part of the game, Nugent commented. "But the real issue is survival."

—Written by Wendelin Colby, *Infosystems*, February, 1985, p. 40.

Although disaster planning may be beyond the scope of any single systems development project, it must be considered as a governing force that will determine the integrity of the system. Every systems project must make a contribution to the total plan by assuring that it can be restored in the face of a disaster.

CONSEQUENCES OF NO PLAN

Disaster may come in the form of flood, fire, earthquake, explosion, windstorm, security invasions, power outages, or even an out-of-control automobile. A labor strike may even prevent people from getting to or operating a system. Plans must be established before these events happen, even though people don't like to think about creating a plan because of the realization that such events could really happen. It is as difficult as a human thinking about making plans for burial.

The worst consequence of no plan is that recovery will take place under the most tense conditions. This often leads to the "tense/dense" syndrome. When the pressure gets too great, many haphazard decisions get made, people pay premium prices because there is no time to shop, and there is not time for review by the needed parties. There is a high need for action, and this often turns out to be a case of "any action is better than no action."

WHO IS RESPONSIBLE?

The systems developer has an obligation to protect the corporate assets of data and the means of manipulating it. But the ultimate responsibility is a corporate responsibility and must be established high in the organization. Resources must be available not only to establish a plan, but to implement it. This is as essential as buying insurance policies to protect the corporation's future.

WHAT SHOULD A PLAN INCLUDE?

A disaster plan will include provisions for redundancy and procedures for using the redundancy. Redundancy will include things such as off-premises backups of data, programs, and documentation as well as backup processing sites.

A backup processing plan may involve having another similar installation agree to a reciprocal exchange program, or it may include duplication of existing sites in a remote location. "Hot sites," or locations for which organizations pay a fee for access, include a building with different computers and communications facilities available. Services such as warehouse storage, supplies, office space, fleets of trucks, and conference center facilities to help an organization get back on its feet are available on a contingency fee basis.

Systems persons should be aware that recovery plans are not just a technical problem. A comprehensive plan includes the management activities needed to do the needed processing. If the processing must be done at another site, the procedure for transferring must be included. Likewise, the plan to move back to the original processing site must be established. In essence, the plan is a series of steps, including the persons to accomplish the steps, to get the system running.

Disaster can be lessened through proper site planning. Alternatives to water sprinkler systems such as carbon dioxide or Halon systems may save hardware and software from heat or high humidity damage. The damage from water is often greater than if the fire were allowed to burn out.

There are many interesting stories about disaster recoveries. The article by Thiel (see References) has four case studies of different company's plans for disaster recovery.

CRIME

Our attitude of trust that we have been building as analysts must be dismissed when we consider building in controls. We must believe that not everyone is honest and may not want to accomplish good things for the organization that we are dealing with. There are individuals and groups that will attempt to abuse our system. Someone could tamper with the system by:

1. Stealing or changing the input data.
2. Stealing or withholding the system output.
3. Changing, destroying, or stealing data files.
4. Stealing data from communication lines.
5. Changing the software to alter processing.
6. Stealing, destroying, or changing hardware.
7. Stealing, destroying, or changing procedures or documentation to alter processing.

And people sometimes just make honest mistakes and omissions. *You* as a systems developer must take precautions to prevent these things. If you do not, you are as guilty as the thieves.

> "Bonnie and Clyde were in the wrong business," says Stephen Leibholz, president of Analytics Inc., a Pennsylvania computer security firm. The average bank robber nets $20,000; if caught, he has a 90% chance of being prosecuted, and if convicted is apt to get five years. The thief who pulls off an electronic funds transfer nets an average of $500,000, has a 15% chance of prosecution, and if convicted faces only about five months behind bars.
>
> —From "Computer Crackdown," by Ann Reilly, *Fortune*, September 1984, pp. 141–142.

HACKERS ENTER DATABASE

San Diego—A ring of juvenile computer hackers broke into a database containing financial records of Chase Manhattan Bank, the FBI says.

No arrests had been made Wednesday, but FBI spokesman Gary Laturno said more than 40 agents armed with 23 search warrants, confiscated computers, keyboards, modems and software from the youths' homes Tuesday night.

He said the investigation, which began in July, is continuing. An affidavit filed in U. S. District Court in San Diego says the minors used their home computers to gain entry to records in the computer of the Interactive Data Corporation in Waltham, Mass.

The financial data base is a subsidiary of Chase Manhattan and contains the bank's financial records. It is used by 25,000 subscribers, who pay a fee for the service.

"Some records were modified and-or destroyed," the affidavit said.

From *The Indianapolis News,* Thursday, October 17, 1985, p. 2.

PRIVACY

Since privacy acts were passed in many countries, systems developers have had a special concern with privacy. *Privacy* is an individual's right: A person must be able to protect him- or herself by ensuring the correctness and uses of personal data. A developer is responsible for protecting the personal privacy of stored data about a person. In essence, privacy is a legal problem. A person whose privacy is invaded through negligence could seek damages from a systems developer.

The systems developer must make sure that data collected on individuals for one purpose is not available for other purposes. For example, credit data collected to protect persons granting credit should not be available to salespersons so they can make sales calls. Or worse yet, hospital medical records should not be used to sell medical supplies.

There is an unverified story about an encyclopedia salesperson who obtained access to a report containing school grade records. The report included parent names to enable mailing of report cards. The devious salesperson used information on the report to link low grades and parent names to try to sell his wares to parents of poor performers. He used the line that responsible parents would not let "little Johnny get another 'D'" because he had inadequate educational resources at home.

There should be a defined method for people to verify data you have stored about them. People should be assured that the data you have collected about them will not be used in any other way than was originally intended. The person should have a defined means to correct any data you have stored that is clearly incorrect or misleading.

AUDITING CONTROLS

Auditing controls is a means of safeguarding an organization's processing. A system must be "auditable" to satisfy internal needs as well as external auditors and to satisfy tax regulations. *Audit trails,* also called *processing reference trails,* trace the results of processing back to the operation and original data that caused the results; or forward from a transaction to the end result. Audit trails allow us to answer the questions "What numbers from which transactions make up this total?" and "What totals will this number in this transaction end up being a part of?"

In batch systems, this is relatively easy to do since past generations of transaction files can be saved along with master files that were updated. But with the advent of online processing and in-place rewriting of records that were not part of a "batch" run, the task becomes much more difficult. In these cases, batch logs become things of the past. Thus, auditors must change their methods.

As systems become more complex, it is harder to include adequate controls. Davis (see References) includes a categorization of systems in terms of auditability. He classifies files and processing methods to include complexity levels. *Batch* is the simplest form and is the easiest to control. Audit trails are easily established. *Real-time, online* processing is the most complex. One of the reasons for this is that there are no copies of old files or databases as a result of normal processing. Records are updated in place, rather than entire files being rewritten. There really are not "generations of files," as each change to the file or database creates a new "generation."

There is a need to create "views" of data at points in time and to keep records of the transactions used to change the "views." This can be done in several ways:

> Detailed logs are kept on every transaction including the actual transaction and who entered it, when, and from where to allow reconstruction of the master file at any time. Periodic master file backup files are saved along with clock times. As can be expected, this process is very complex and requires precise timing, especially with high transaction systems such as airline reservation systems.
>
> Hard copy is maintained of all entered transactions for a specified block of time. This creates "time batches."
>
> Batches of transactions per entry terminal are used. These "artificial batches" can be created and used to trace transactions from a specific location.

A "work file" is used during the day to keep a current working master copy for reference and retrieval. Then, at night, the transactions are batched and processed again. This time the transactions will produce a new permanent master file. This file is used for processing the next day and a backup is used for control and rebuilding purposes.

This work requires the special skills of auditors who are skilled in the area of working with automated systems.

SUMMARY

Assuring system integrity is similar to insuring a system. As with any insurance, one is hedging bets by paying now to avoid risks of having to pay later. You cannot buy insurance after a tragedy takes place. Anticipation must be part of the planning process of establishing system soundness. The risks of loss from unsound systems are too great to be ignored. It is easier to make building in of integrity part of the development process than it is to try to "tack on" some controls later. It is necessary be aware of building integrity into systems throughout the development cycle, and have appropriate persons and units involved in the process.

REFERENCES AND FURTHER READINGS

The Auditors Study and Evaluation of Internal Controls in EDP Systems, New York: American Institute of Certified Public Accountants, 1977.

Benjamin, Robert I. *Control of the Information System Development Cycle,* New York: Wiley-Interscience, John Wiley & Sons, 1971, pp. 52–53.

Brill, Alan E. *Building Controls into Structured Systems,* New York: Yourdon Press, 1983.

Campbell, Robert P. "Locking Up the Mainframe," *Computerworld,* In Depth section, vol. 17, no. 41, October 10, 1983, pp. 1–14.

Davis, Gordon B. "An Audit-Oriented Classification of Data Processing Methods," from *Auditing and EDP,* New York: American Institute of Certified Public Accountants, rev. ed., 1976.

Davis, Keagle W., and William Perry. *Auditing Computer Applications—A Systematic Approach,* New York: John Wiley & Sons, 1982.

Guynes, Steve, and Jerry M. DeHay. "Software Security: Legal Aspects and Traditional Considerations," *Journal of Systems Management,* April 1981, pp. 34–38.

Jenkins, A. Milton, and John V. Carlis. "Control Flowcharting for Data Driven Systems," Working Paper, Indiana University Graduate School of Business and Syracuse University School of Management, June 1976.

Mair, William G., Donald R. Wood, and Keagle W. Davis. *Computer Control and Audit,* Wellesley, MA: QED Information Sciences, Inc., 1978.

Martin, James. *Security, Accuracy, and Privacy in Computer Systems,* Englewood Cliffs, NJ: Prentice-Hall, 1974.

Parker, Donn. *Crime By Computer,* New York: Scribner's. 1976.

Reilly, Ann. "Computer Crackdown," *Fortune,* September 17, 1984, pp. 141-142.

Thiel, Carol Tomme. "Disaster Recovery," *Infosystems*, November 1984, pp. 26–32.
Weber, Ron. *EDP Auditing: Conceptual Foundations and Practice*, New York: McGraw-Hill, 1982.
Zimmerman, Joel S. "Is Your Computer Insecure?" *Datamation*, May 15, 1985, pp. 119+.

REVIEW QUESTIONS

1. What is the difference between control, security, privacy, and recovery?
2. What are the two things we control for in a system?
3. Who is ultimately responsible for the integrity of a system? What are some of the other roles that must be fulfilled to have system integrity?
4. Why are the "owners" of data important to establishing system integrity?
5. What are the three types of costs that must be ranked for any information asset?
6. Why might a "user-friendly" system have less integrity?
7. What factor makes control of online systems difficult?
8. What might be done to secure microcomputers?
9. What are some methods of protecting against undesired physical access?
10. How can hardware be protected against unauthorized operation?
11. Why might changed working patterns be an alert to covert operations?
12. If changed working patterns are detected, should immediate action be taken to prosecute the "offender"? Why or why not?
13. What is a hash total?
14. What is a check digit? Why might it add to a processing load?
15. What is meant by write prevention?
16. Why is it essential to manage the disposing of unused reports?
17. What is encryption?
18. How can data flow diagrams be used to aid in building controls and integrity into a system?
19. What duties might be separated in a systems unit to ensure "checks and balances"?
20. Why is it a wise policy to insist on people taking earned vacations?
21. Why is it advisable to avoid public announcement that a system is impenetrable?
22. What should a disaster recovery plan include?
23. What is the difference between security and privacy?
24. Explain the "work file" approach to maintaining an audit trail.

DISCUSSION QUESTIONS

1. You hear a friend complaining about his bank because it compared his signature with his signature card on file, and then asked him to provide more information and to sign his name twice. He feels he is being discriminated against just because he reported some checks missing out of his checkbook. Comment. What types of integrity assurance is the bank using?
2. Why might "dormant" bank accounts be especially susceptible to crime activities? What element of control is lost if customers do not take an active interest in their accounts?
3. A manager says: "We would like to download the following data to microcomputers for further analysis." How might an information asset importance matrix help in determining whether this should be done?
4. Compare and contrast the integrity problems of a decentralized versus a centralized computer facility.

EXERCISES

1. Talk to an EDP auditor. What do they find is the most difficult part of their job? When are they involved in systems development projects? When do they think they should be involved? Share your findings with the class.
2. A salesperson has a name and address book that includes all past customers and potential clients. There are about 150 active names in the book, which includes both friends and customers. She only has one copy of the book. About seven new names are added to the book every month and there are also about six changes every month. The book is turning into a real mess. The salesperson did misplace the book recently when visiting a relative and really panicked. Suggest some means for assuring the integrity of the data in the book. You must come up with a logical design before suggesting any new physical solutions. The person needs portability, simplicity, and ease of use.
3. File-It, Inc. is a supplier of office filing equipment in the Midwest and has salespersons based in 17 regional offices. These salespersons take orders which are sent to the regional office on order forms, or which are called into the regional offices and recorded on the forms by the salesperson's secretary.

   In its regional offices, File-It has 17 terminals connected to its main computer in Minneapolis. The main office stores the customer records. The terminals are used to key in orders and send them into the main office. This initiates the order filling and billing processes. Most customers are regular purchasers who have accounts with File-It.

   File-It management has had some great concerns because of the large number of incorrect orders being sent to customers. Since returns result in great freight charges, a need to correct billings, a need to manipulate inventory, and recalculation of salesperson commissions, the cost of incorrect orders is very great. The order recording system was installed under great duress since there was a computer conversion going on at the same time. The system has little editing or controls.

You have been asked to make some suggestions as to how to control errors such as sending orders to wrong customers, having orders recorded for nonexisting products, having to guess at quantities since the orders were illegible, etc. What is your response?

4. Farsight Bank's president just came storming into the vice-president of Information Systems office. You were having a meeting with the VP of MIS and are sitting in his office while he had stepped out to greet a group of visitors to the bank. The president was concerned about the security and privacy of the bank's data files. She had heard of an insurance company that was bordering on disintegration because a disgruntled employee had destroyed the tape libraries by having a person on a computer room tour drop a smoke bomb with a timer on it in the tape room. She had mentioned this to her acquaintances and each had tried to top each other with horror stories about computer disasters. She heard she could even go to jail for negligence in handling the money of the bank. As the manager of systems development, you know the bank has an excellent security and disaster recovery plan. What are you going to tell the President who clearly is upset and worried about data integrity?

5. Ask your local university computer center if you could get a tour of the computer facilities or if such tours are open to university staff. Find out what you will be able to see and do. Are you surprised? Were you investigated before being allowed to attend a tour? Was there any sensitive data that you could have put your hands on?

PART IV

The Systems Implementation Phase: Process and Techniques

This section completes the systems development life cycle by discussing the processes and techniques needed to successfully construct a system and install it in an organization.

CHAPTER 13

CHAPTER OBJECTIVES

You should be able to:

- Contrast bottom-up and versioned system construction
- Outline the components of project test plans
- Specify the components of implementation plans
- Describe different installation approaches
- Specify advantages and disadvantages of different installation approaches
- Understand the importance of postaudit reviews
- Consider the implementation process as changemaking

Implementation: Constructing and Installing the New System

In 1829, New York Governor Martin Van Buren wrote to President Andrew Jackson: "The canal system of this country is being threatened by the spread of a new form of transportation known as the "railroads." If canal boats are supplanted by railroads, serious unemployment will result. Canal boats are absolutely essential to the defense of the United States . . . Railroad carriages are pulled at the enormous speed of 15 miles per hour . . . The Almighty certainly never intended that people should travel at such breakneck speeds."

. . . the issue of computers replacing people? "Intelligent use of the new technology can contribute greatly to the growth of the business," says Jim Nethercott. "And it's only through growth of the Company that there is real opportunity and job security for our employees." New ideas and ways of doing things are sometimes difficult to accept. But once we get used to doing things the new way, it's hard to think of going back to the old method. (Jim Nethercott is senior vice president of Procter & Gamble and in 1984 was responsible for the Company's computer functions through the Management Systems Division.)

Both of the above quotes are from an article by Pat Frey entitled "A Surge of Opportunities," Sales Moonbeams, November 1984, The Procter & Gamble Company, pp. 3–4.

THIS CHAPTER DETAILS the construction and installation processes of the systems development life cycle introduced in Chapter 2. We discuss bottom-up and top-down system construction, approaches to system implementation, considerations that must be made when using the different approaches, and conducting a postaudit review to learn from the systems project. Other topics examined include systems testing and management of change.

Once a system has been designed and its architecture exists, it must be constructed and installed in an organization. Common names for these activities include *implementation, installation, conversion,* or *integrated system testing*. Our definition will include construction and installation as part of the implementation processes. In the systems development life cycle used in this book, Process 6 activities construct the system, and Process 7 activities actually install the system in the organization.

$$\text{Implementation} = \underset{\text{(Process 6)}}{\text{Construction}} + \underset{\text{(Process 7)}}{\text{Installation}}$$

Implementation of a new system in the organization is the true test of usefulness. The pressures at this time are great. Results will become public. If there is resistance to the system, antagonists will surface. There will be some persons who hope the system implementation will be a struggle and then will say, "I told you so." But if the system development was conducted under conditions of trust and communication, the implementation team will be a supportive group that will receive rewards from achieving greater organizational efficiency and effectiveness. It will be a time for great joy and celebration. Users can be as excited as a child with a new toy.

There are several topics relevant to systems implementation which will be discussed in this chapter along with a description of the activities that take place in development processes 6 and 7. We will examine a number of approaches that might be used in system implementation. They include *parallel, phased, pilot,* or *cutover* approaches.

A new system will bring organizational change. People in organizational units must perform different business tactics. As with anything new, people may resist change and attempt to maintain the status quo. This could lead to a failure to achieve proposed benefits. Thus, the topic of managing system change is included in this chapter.

Once a system has been installed and routinized into an organization, we must examine the installed system to determine if it meets user requirements and if the system builders can learn from an examination of the methods used to develop the system. This process is referred to as the *postaudit* phase of systems development. Why a postaudit is important, who should conduct it, and what should be done are all discussed.

CONSTRUCTING THE SYSTEM

There are two basic methods of constructing the system. One is *bottom-up* and the other is *top-down*. This section will describe each of the methods, but since the *versioned* or top-down approach is advocated in this book, it will be discussed in more detail.

BOTTOM-UP CONSTRUCTION

In some of the traditional approaches to systems development, system construction is accomplished by building and testing all program and procedure subsystems independently. Subsystems then are integrated and tested in combination. This is the ***bottom-up approach***, where the *basic components are built first and then assembled.*

The difficulty with this approach has been that the subsystems did not always fit together as planned. The "puzzle pieces" did not fit very well. There were interface problems. This led to rework of the subsystems at the interface boundaries, which resulted in rippling effects within the subsystems. Many systems ended up being "90 percent done" and remaining that way for a long time.

TOP-DOWN OR VERSIONED APPROACH

The above problems led to a different approach to systems construction. The basic *structure* of the system is built first, providing developers with an opportunity to establish and test interfaces between subsystems. Then, detail is added to the structure by completing the subsystems, resulting in more complete versions of the system.

The ***versioned approach*** dictates that once the structure exists, *the first subsystems built and tested are those that provide the most value to the user.* The premise is that 10 percent of the system likely will do 90 percent of the processing. The idea is to get that 10 percent created, tested, and in use as quickly as possible. Later, other parts of the system essential to safe and secure operation are developed and implemented.

The users and operations persons will be incrementally experiencing more complete versions of the system and receiving benefits from use. This is more of an assimilation process as the system is being built.

In the versioned approach, a skeleton or framework which consists of high-level control and interface modules is created and tested first. Then, versions including the modules which handle normal and error-free transactions or queries are implemented. A simple and most frequent input must be accepted and processed, and a simple and usual output created. This is the processing that is done most of the time for transactions or queries.

The skeleton then is fleshed out as more of the modules and routines are put in place until the system is complete. Versions dealing with error finding, error recovery, and exception handling are implemented. Different types of data, both correct and incorrect, are input to the system. The system may ultimately include online editing and automatic backup routines. This is not to degrade the importance of these routines, but it is similar to believing that if the wheels of the auto cannot be made to roll forward and the auto steered, the windshield wipers or spare tire are of little use.

The structure chart is used as a blueprint for managing versions. Each version can be vividly portrayed by noting which modules will be coded, tested, and interfaced. Figure 13.1 denotes the modules that will be completed on the first version by shading them. This will be enough to test a major and good input, process it, and provide some kind of output. Note the top-down approach.

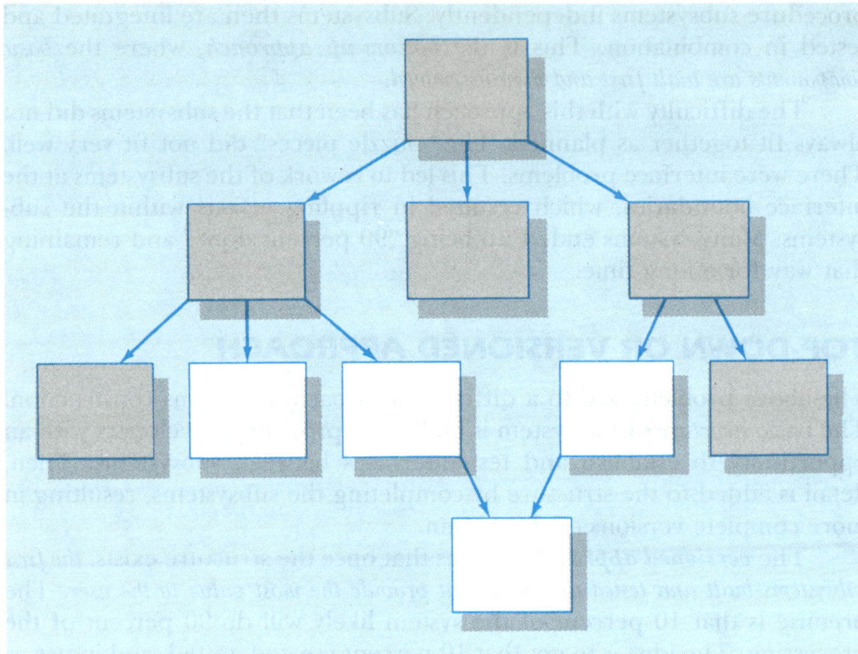

FIGURE 13.1

A structure chart with shaded modules to be implemented on the first version.

Modules which are not completed in initial versions often are called ***stubs***. The unshaded modules in Figure 13.1 are likely stubs. Stubs could do a variety of things. They might return control immediately, display a message that the stub was accessed, return a predetermined test value, or include a performance delay to simulate real processing timing.

Both programs and accompanying human procedures can be created in a versioned fashion. For example, the outline of a user manual could be considered the structure or outline. The fleshing in is done as procedures which correspond to program modules are written and tested. Unwritten manual sections are considered to be stubs. The manual will be more and more complete in incrementally finished versions.

Each version should be delivered in "living memory." This means that the users do not forget what the next version will allow them to do. The time period may be as short as a few days to no more than several weeks. This will keep the project visible in the user environment and demonstrate real and tangible progress. This contrasts with some of the early systems projects where developers would conduct "systems analysis" and then disappear for 1, 2, or 3 years (and sometimes forever) before any results were seen.

There are advantages to using the versioned approach. Incremental learning will get users participating immediately in the use of the system. This will help uncover any weaknesses in the system early and will gain acceptance through communication. User confidence should grow as results are exhibited by demonstrations of actual progress. Other advantages of this approach are the smoothing-out of machine test time since there are incremental demands, rather than one big push. There also are a number of significant milestones which both improve management control and allow changes in the requirements of significant subsystems.

A disadvantage of this approach is that users have to be briefed clearly that the system is not really complete until *all* subsystems are completed and controls are in place. Users might see initial versions as complete since good transactions could be processed. These versions may have many stubs and no controls or backups essential to safe system operation, however.

Another disadvantage is that the hardware and systems software and communications devices have to be in place for early versions. This would require either added rental or capital invested in equipment which was not providing immediate value.

SYSTEM TESTING

Testing is a critical part of system construction. Developers must be assured that the system works as desired. Testing cannot be haphazard; it must be managed. This means that a plan must be established, the effort must be organized, staff must be available to perform the tests, and control must be done to assure the testing plan is accomplished. Two basic types of testing include:

1. Unit testing—independently testing modules and subsystems
2. Integrated testing—combined subsystem tests

There can be various combinations and sequences of unit and integration tests. When using the versioned construction approach, there may be interface testing that first tests links between modules. Then subsystem units are created and unit tested. Unit-tested portions of the system then are combined to create an integrated system. Tests should push the system to its limits. The attitude taken in testing is that there is no way to prove the system is correct, only that it is incorrect.

Myers (see References) suggests the following tests to uncover weaknesses in the system:

Stress tests—presenting the system with large quantities of data over a specified time period

Volume tests—presenting the system with a peak load of data

Usability tests—presenting the user with the system to detect unfriendliness

Security tests—attempting to prove the system does not have integrity

Performance tests—attempting to degrade response and processing times to an unacceptable level

Documentation tests—attempting to demonstrate the documentation is inadequate or inaccurate

Procedure tests—attempting to show the procedures do not allow the user to achieve required performance

Test cases should include:

1. Valid values and valid combinations
2. Invalid values
3. Invalid combinations (for example, closing unopened files)

Testing is becoming an area of specialization in the systems field. A specialist may be needed to aid in establishing a comprehensive plan or to review proposed plans to point out weaknesses. Testing is an important part of constructing the system, which is done in Process 6. This now will be discussed in more detail.

PROCESS 6: CONSTRUCT NEW SYSTEM

The purpose of Process 6 is to construct the designed system by a series of increasingly more complete system versions. One criteria is to get primary system functions working as quickly as possible. This will allow testing of major system functions and obtaining early user reactions.

The first system versions typically will accept a simple and correct input (the normal case), process it using major hardware, software, and human interfaces, and create a simple output. Each successive version is more complete, with more function added until the entire system is complete. This is indicated in Figure 13.2 by the dotted line that loops back to the first subprocess. Some completed versions may be put into production if they can provide benefits at little or no risk.

Process 6: Construct New System

Purpose: Bring a working version of the new system to a usable stage.

Output: A working version of the new system that provides users with real benefits.

Subprocesses: Write and test computer programs. Write and test human procedures. Create test data and procedures. Develop human materials and training. Install hardware and acquired software. Conduct training. Conduct integrated current version tests.

Techniques and Skills: Computer programming, technical writing, test data creation, training development, software testing, training implementation.

Activities within Process 6 include developing a version implementation plan (Process 6.1), developing software for the most current version of the system (Process 6.2), creating test data and software to run the tests (Process 6.3), installing the hardware and acquired software (Process 6.4), developing human materials and training (Process 6.5), performing tests

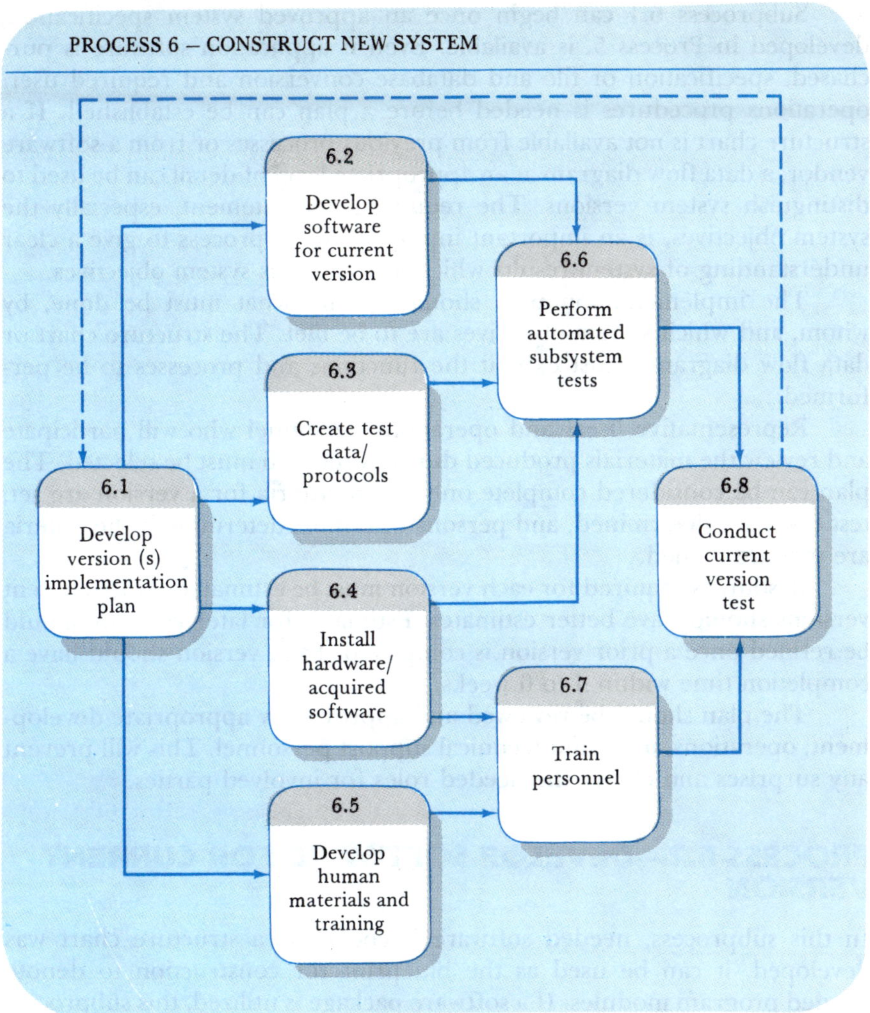

FIGURE 13.2

Subprocesses within Process 6.

on automated subsystems (Process 6.6), training personnel (Process 6.7), and conducting a test of the current system (Process 6.8).

PROCESS 6.1—DEVELOP VERSION(S) IMPLEMENTATION PLAN

The purpose of Subprocess 6.1 is to specify the system functions to be constructed and tested in each version of the system. The plan for this portion of system implementation will include coordinating the availability of hardware, software, and user/operations procedures for each system version. Specifications of program modules, data files, test data, manuals, and training are needed for each version.

Subprocess 6.1 can begin once an approved system specification, developed in Process 5, is available. Even if application software is purchased, specification of file and database conversion and required user/operations procedures is needed before a plan can be established. If a structure chart is not available from previous processes or from a software vendor, a data flow diagram at an appropriate level of detail can be used to distinguish system versions. The requirements statement, especially the system objectives, is an important input to this subprocess to give a clear understanding of system results which are stated as system objectives.

The implementation plan should specify what must be done, by whom, and which system objectives are to be met. The structure chart or data flow diagrams must exhibit the functions and processes to be performed.

Representative users and operations personnel who will participate and review the materials produced during Process 6 must be selected. The plan can be considered complete only when criteria for a version are set, test cases are determined, and persons who must determine if the criteria are met are named.

Resources required for each version must be estimated. More current versions should have better estimates. Estimates for later versions should be refined once a prior version is completed. Each version should have a completion time within 4 to 6 weeks.

The plan should be reviewed and approved by appropriate development, operations, user, and technical support personnel. This will prevent any surprises and clarify the needed roles for involved parties.

PROCESS 6.2—DEVELOP SOFTWARE FOR CURRENT VERSION

In this subprocess, needed software is coded. If a structure chart was developed, it can be used as the blueprint for construction to denote needed program modules. If a software package is utilized, this subprocess will consist of ensuring that the needed modules are installed, debugged, and unit-tested to meet general requirements. Factors such as aligning input and output layouts with module inputs must be considered.

Program development is beyond the scope of this book, but utilization of appropriate approaches such as structured programming, naming standards for program sections and variables, data dictionary construction, process logic denoting techniques (decision tables, decision trees, etc.), and team product reviews will aid in the development of efficient and maintainable software.

Both team product reviews by peers and quality assurance reviews can improve the quality of the developed software. It may only be necessary to sample the actual program code. Reviewing every line of code is costly and usually provides little marginal benefit. A questionnaire similar to the one shown in Figure 13.3 may be used to supplement the review and assure confidence in the code.

Evaluation Form Module Number ________ Program ________

Circle your response. Make any comments after the question or on a separate sheet.

	No ? Yes
1. Are the variable names reasonable?	1 2 3 4 5 6 7
2. Were sufficient and useful comments provided?	1 2 3 4 5 6 7
3. Were spaces and blank lines used to achieve a pleasing format?	1 2 3 4 5 6 7
4. Was the logic of the program comprehensible?	1 2 3 4 5 6 7
5. Was the modular design of the program comprehensible?	1 2 3 4 5 6 7
6. Was the algorithm a good choice?	1 2 3 4 5 6 7
7. Is the program easy to comprehend?	1 2 3 4 5 6 7
8. Would it be easy for you to modify this program?	1 2 3 4 5 6 7
9. Is this program machine-independent?	1 2 3 4 5 6 7
10. Is this program compile-independent?	1 2 3 4 5 6 7
11. Would you have been proud to have written this program?	1 2 3 4 5 6 7
12. Are the data structures used in a reasonable way?	1 2 3 4 5 6 7
13. Would you find it easy to improve the program?	1 2 3 4 5 6 7

Adapted from Ben Shneiderman. *Software Psychology: Human Factors in Computer and Information Systems*, Cambridge, MA: Winthrop Publishers, Inc., 1980, p. 135.

FIGURE 13.3

Some questions to be asked about computer programs.

PROCESS 6.3—CREATE TEST DATA AND PROCEDURES

This subprocess creates test data and accompanying procedures. The procedures are not meant to be part of the final production system. Their purpose is to create a scenario in which the test can take place. For example, a dialog may have to be simulated by creating sets of human responses that can be repeatedly used in different combinations to test human–machine interactions, or variations of orders could be created to simulate arrival at an order processing system.

The subprocess initiates the creation of a test plan library which is part of the final system documentation. Included in such a test plan library would be:

Purpose of test

Environment needed for test

Method for conducting test

Location and volume of test data

Personnel instructions for conducting test

Criteria for evaluating output and performance

Approval procedures

The subprocess can begin once criteria are set for each system version. For example, if backup procedures are to be tested, appropriate test data, scenarios, and correct results are needed to conduct the test. If editing is to be tested, test cases and correct results must be established. Test objectives could include processing normal transactions and queries, exception data and commands, sequence variations, performance and load tests, or other variations. It should be clear what will be required to pass the test. Questions such as how many, how fast, and from what locations must be specified before the test is created.

Test data should attempt to isolate any failures. For example, the people procedures, program modules, communication protocols, computer hardware, or a combination of these must be identified as to what is causing the failure.

The logical model in the data dictionary should be a good source of data variations that are required to conduct the tests. Data about volumes, field sizes, and limits should all exist in the data dictionary. The system objectives should also indicate the requirements the system must meet.

The result of this subprocess will be databases appropriate to test the version at hand along with any procedures needed to implement the test. At no time should a test be conducted using production files or databases.

PROCESS 6.4—INSTALL HARDWARE AND ACQUIRED SOFTWARE

This subprocess results in installed and tested hardware and software. Any contracts for delivery and performance should be examined to understand terms and conditions. The activity may require considerable vendor interaction to assure that deadlines and other terms are met. Records should be kept of the interactions in case any late delivery penalties or negotiations are needed.

Installation sequences must be established to assure that rooms, power, and floors are ready for arriving equipment. Cables and phone connections should be installed. The developer should make certain that all supplies needed for performance tests, such as paper, removable disks, or ribbons are available.

Performance may be tested using ***benchmark tests***, where prespecified performance is compared with actual performance. Benchmark testing attempts to create an environment as similar to the final production environment as possible.

The result of this subprocess will be installed hardware and systems software ready to accept software and data needed to meet version requirements.

PROCESS 6.5—DEVELOP HUMAN MATERIALS AND TRAINING

This subprocess entails development of user and operations personnel materials. These materials then are used to develop any needed training programs for the current version of the system. The materials become increasingly complete with each version of the system.

A training library is created that might contain the following materials:

Training manuals

Presentation materials (notes, transparencies, slides, handouts)

Forms and other samples

Reference manuals

Video/audio tapes and materials

Training computer software

Online help software

Trainer guides

The audience for these materials may include operations employees who actually operate the system, data providers who must fill out forms or fill screens, data users such as managers, who will be receiving new infor-

The systems designer may be responsible for setting up a training facility. Depending on the client's resources and needs, it may not be as elaborate as this one. (Chuck O'Rear/West Light)

mation or information in a new form or on a new medium, or even customers, such as the case of a new online teller system.

Depending on the system version, operations manuals will include procedures explaining how to install, operate, control, restart, recover from failure, and seek help when needed. Data collection, entry, and output distribution must be clearly presented. Likewise, users must be aware of how source data generation, data preparation, forms use, dialogs, output use, system access, and change procedures take place.

An operations library is started at this point to aid computer operators. Typical contents of the operations library would include:

Job run sequence

Job control commands

Job restart instructions

Hardware and software resources

Run commands

Normal action sequences

Application recovery procedures

Contact persons

The developed manuals are to aid users and operators in getting a job done. Thus, they should be task-oriented. General topics that users need as background material, but which are not needed to do the job, should be presented in training materials and sessions.

All materials should be tested with representative users, not just systems development colleagues. The goal of the training package is to provide adequate knowledge and skills so the human portion of the system can operate.

The training package should include a clear definition of what the trainee must be able to accomplish as a result of the training, materials for a clear presentation, a proper choice of presentation media, appropriate peformance aids such as checklists or built-in help functions, and practical exercises to practice, test, and exhibit skills.

This subprocess may entail development of special software for training. For example, online training or tutorials may be needed as well as an environment to accomplish any practical exercises.

PROCESS 6.6—PERFORM AUTOMATED SUBSYSTEM TESTS

The objective of this subprocess is to test the automated portions of the current version. The current version must perform system tests sheltered from users, operations, and entry personnel. Developers must be assured they can get correct system results when they perform the human roles. If developers cannot make the system perform for them, it is not recommended that testing is done with others.

Subprocess 6.6 can begin once programs for the current version are coded (from 6.2 and 6.4), test data and protocols are ready (from 6.3), and acquired hardware and software is installed and tested (from 6.4).

The primary tasks in the subprocess are to run the developed programs on representative hardware, measure and monitor results, compare results with specified test criteria, and make any needed revisions. The result is a version of the hardware and software environment ready for testing with trained users and operations personnel.

PROCESS 6.7—TRAIN PERSONNEL

In Subprocess 6.7, training materials developed in Subprocess 6.5 and installed hardware and software are used to conduct the actual training.

Timing of the training is critical. If presented too far in advance, trainees could forget the material or lose their skills. If presented too close to actual performance, the material may not have had time to jell and be integrated into existing activities.

For a geographically dispersed system, coordination of training at different sites may be needed. There may be a need to survey work schedules to minimize current work in progress. Materials may have to be developed and distributed in advance. In any case, the superiors of the persons to be trained must be aware of any training plans which could cause absence from the job.

Since many system failures can be attributed to weaknesses in the human subsystems, it is critical to assure that trainees can exhibit appropriate performance. This is also a good time to make sure trainees do not exhibit any dysfunctional behavior and system resistance.

The result of this subprocess is a set of users, operators, and entry personnel ready to test the current version of the system. A review may be needed to make sure that people are ready to perform once the version is put in place.

PROCESS 6.8—CONDUCT CURRENT VERSION TEST

The hardware, software, and human elements, are brought together in this subprocess. Actual user and operations personnel must perform using the developed human and technologic procedures. Care must be taken to make tests representative of the real environment. People must be representative, not the exceptional user or operator. Hardware must be what will actually be used, not a close facsimile.

Error logs should be kept to note weaknesses in either the automated or human procedures. For example, note should be taken of where HELP was invoked to detect if a weakness exists in a dialog. Observation of the system in operation can reveal tension or frustration.

The result of this subprocess is an evaluated system version with notes on strengths and weaknesses. Versions which could provide organization benefits with no detrimental effects or risks are transmitted to Process 7 for

CLOSE, BUT NO CIGAR

A data entry test was conducted on a terminal which approximated what actually was to be delivered. After a successful test, 48 of the originally specified terminals were delivered. The delivered terminals were different in that they had dished keys. This resulted in perspiration gathering in the keys, which quickly got sticky and destroyed keying performance. The key entry persons were very frustrated as their error rates increased and speed declined. The search for alternatives commenced. The alternatives were all very costly. Involved persons said the terminals would never have been ordered if they knew the consequences.

—Anonymous Personal Story

installation. Results of the implementation and test are transmitted back to Subprocess 6.1, where the knowledge is used to develop the plan for the next system version. This iteration continues until all system functions are constructed and tested and all system requirements are met.

The final test of any system comes when it is actually installed into a production environment. This is the time when the organization expects the system to provide correct outputs in a timely manner. The organization becomes dependent on the system.

APPROACHES TO SYSTEM INSTALLATION

There are a number of different approaches to systems installation. They include *parallel, phased, pilot,* and *cutover* approaches. However, these approaches are not mutually exclusive. They may be combined to build the entire system. For example, a pilot installation in one location may be operated in parallel with the existing system. As with most systems work, there are tradeoffs in choosing an approach or combination of approaches. The systems developer has to consider carefully the existing environment to choose the means that will be satisfactory.

PARALLEL APPROACH

The ***parallel approach*** to installation is a safe way to check out the new system. System activities are duplicated as the old system and the new system are both operated simultaneously (see Figure 13.4). The results of the new system are compared with the old system results. The new system is "backed up" with the old system for a period of time.

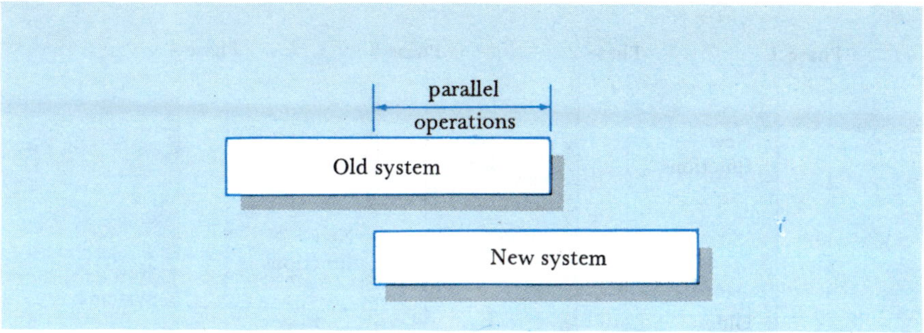

FIGURE 13.4
The parallel installation approach.

Parallel implementation may not always be possible. There may not *be* an old system, or output results may be different for the two systems, or may appear for the first time with the new system. Online systems may produce totally incompatible results if the old system operates in a batch mode. If there is a physical change of hardware, there may not be room to house both sets of equipment. As well, the cost of running duplicate facilities may be prohibitive.

Parallel implementation requires verifying old system results against new system results. Reconciliation of differences must include a determination of whether the old or new system is correct. Taking for granted that old results are correct may be a false assumption.

In summary, parallel implementation is very expensive, but is a safe approach. It requires two work forces and the effort to complete manual procedures twice. As well, it requires the hardware and software and supplies to be expended beyond normal processing.

PHASED APPROACH

The ***phased approach*** brings different functional parts of a system to life, one after another. The idea is to add system features in a function-by-function fashion. The system is "phased in" (see Figure 13.5). Once one part is successfully implemented, another part is activated. This approach often fits quite well with the versioned construction approach.

The phased approach requires factoring the system by function. The approach breaks down if there are complex interfaces between the activated subsystems, preventing a working system after each phase. A problem with this approach is that it is not always easy to factor the system into meaningful subsystems. It may promote "hangers on" to move very slowly with the new system as they are forced to give up progressively larger portions of the old system.

The approach is relatively safe and is not as expensive as the parallel approach since the systems are not duplicated.

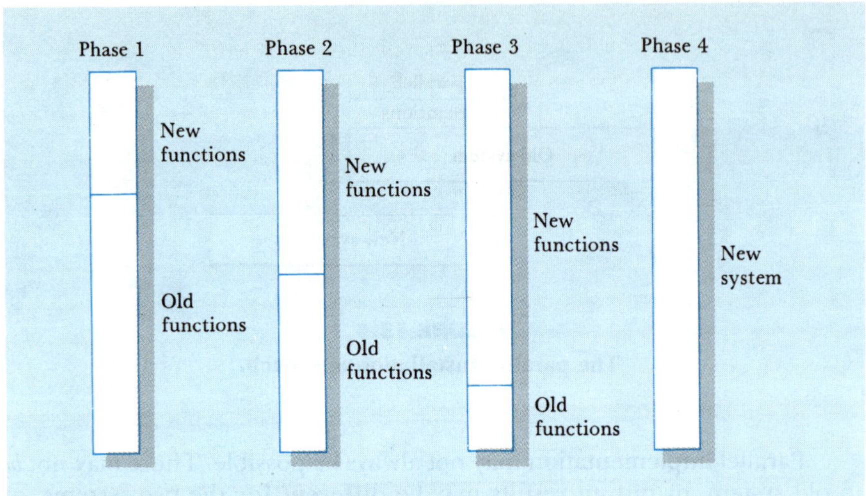

FIGURE 13.5

The phased installation approach.

PILOT APPROACH

The ***pilot approach*** requires the installation of the new system in sites that are representative of the complete system (see Figure 13.6). This could mean selecting certain geographic locations or departments to serve as test or pilot sites. The system is factored by organization unit boundary.

The meaningful selection of pilot sites is essential for this approach to work. There may be no representative sites. Or, there may be many representative sites and it would be politically unwise to favor or disfavor any one site by making a choice. It also may be impossible to decouple one site if it is to be part of a dependent network.

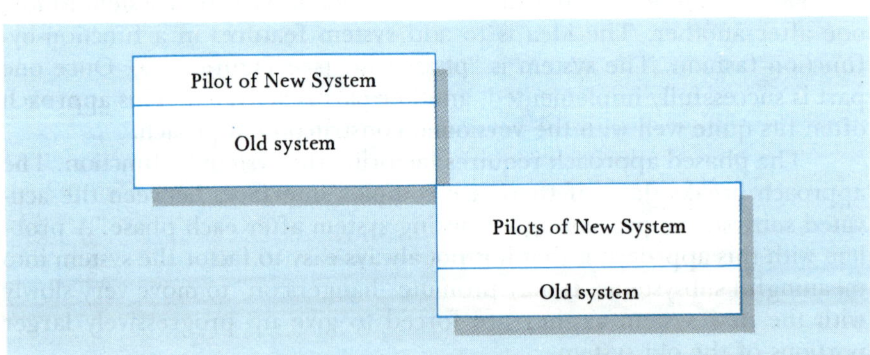

FIGURE 13.6

The pilot installation approach.

The pilot should be run for at least one complete processing cycle. If there are many sites, it may be necessary to have groupings of pilot sites. All sites with common characteristics then may be implemented at once.

CUTOVER APPROACH

The ***cutover approach*** to implementation planning also has been referred to as the "cold turkey" or "burned bridge" approach (see Figure 13.7). This is not to say the approach is not of value. If there is no currently operating system, and other approaches are not possible, there may be no choice but to "flip the switch" and get on with business.

The cutover approach does have advantages. There can be no turning back if there is nothing to turn back to, so resistance is minimized. There can be no hidden noncommitment. If the results are not satisfactory, the system can be revised and activated again.

This approach may be quite stressful for a period of time. But as long as use of system results is not critical for continued existence of the company, the approach can be used with confidence.

CONSIDERATIONS IN PLANNING AN APPROACH

In choosing an approach to the implementation process, there are several criteria to consider. They include stress, cost, duration, and human resources. These factors must be evaluated in terms of the implementation situation. There is no "right or wrong" way to implement all systems, since it is contingent on the specific situation.

Approaches sometimes can be ruled out after examining the situation. There may not be an old system, physical space, or budget to run two systems in parallel. There may not be reasonable phases or versions. There may not be a representative pilot.

As mentioned earlier, a combination of approaches may be most appropriate. For example, a pilot site may be chosen to install the system in a parallel or phased fashion. This may aid in minimizing both stress and cost.

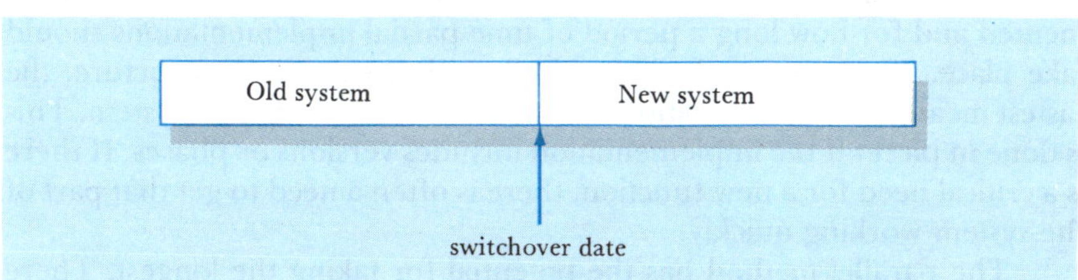

FIGURE 13.7

The cutover installation approach.

The next sections consider the factors of stress, cost, duration, and human resources in regard to planning an installation approach.

STRESS CONSIDERATIONS

The cutover approach to installation is usually the most stressful. There is no turning back to use the old system, or operating the system in a different pilot location if there were serious implementation problems. There only will be an intense effort to get the new system working.

The phased approach also can lead to considerable stress. Worry is generated if portions of the system do not work. Then, people will wonder what else is going to be a problem and what effects the nonworking portion will have on other parts of the system.

The pilot approach generates stress because "all eyes are on the pilot." A good showing is needed to have a smooth transition to other sites. The first pilot site will encounter many of the problems, yet may only have a small workforce to handle them.

The parallel approach creates less stress as there is something to fall back on. The old system can be used.

COST CONSIDERATIONS

The parallel approach is often the most costly. It will require two staffs of people and two sets of hardware and software. Since efforts are duplicated, there is a need to run the systems with less-experienced persons. This may reduce efficiency.

A real cost is to have two different physical sites running in parallel. There simply may not be enough physical room on one site to house two sets of personnel and hardware. This often forces acquiring space at another location, often at a high cost.

The other approaches are somewhat comparable in cost. The phased approach may require having hardware in place earlier. This will require incurring a cost before real benefits accrue.

DURATION CONSIDERATIONS

Duration decisions involve both how fast the new system must be implemented and for how long a period of time partial implementations should take place. If the system has been built with a good solid structure, the fastest means of implementation may be to cut over to the new system. This is done in pieces if the implementation includes versions or phases. If there is a critical need for a new function, there is often a need to get that part of the system working quickly.

The parallel method has the potential for taking the longest. There will be more people "hanging on" to the old system. They may be putting less energy on the new system since they are expending energy holding on to the old.

The suggested period of time to run systems parallel is at least one complete cycle of regular periodic processing. Many systems are run a minimum of two cycles. This will depend on the severity of any errors. Testing is also done on the longer-cycle processing such as quarterly or year-end reporting. If possible, it is wise to try to schedule parallel operation to include these activities.

HUMAN RESOURCE MANAGEMENT CONSIDERATIONS

Behavioral implications must be considered when choosing an installation strategy. For example, if there is a need for the new system and much resistance to change exists, it may be necessary to cut the old system off as of a specific time to force use of the new system. To alleviate resistance, an argument can be made for having the existing persons trained and move them to the new system so they cannot "look back." Being able to depend on the old system may not create the needed sense of urgency to make the new system work.

A real dilemma in parallel implementation is whether to assign acquired temporary personnel to aid in the conversion to run the old system, which they know little about, or to assign them to the new system, precluding "regular" workers from the new experiences. The regular employees probably know the old system best and can handle its quirks. But they will be the persons who will have to make the new system work. An approach to this dilemma is to have teams headed by regular people, and mix the regular and temporaries. The important thing to remember is that this should be a conscious decision with an examination of the implications of each alternative.

In summary, *parallel* implementation is feasible if there is an old system with similar functions for comparison, if you can provide inputs to both systems, and if you can afford the cost of running two systems. *Pilots* are reasonable if pilot locations can be isolated, and sites are representative of the entire system. *Phased* tests are possible if system functions can be isolated and results can be adequately confirmed according to system test criteria. The *cutover* approach is often the cheapest, most intense, and can accelerate conversion since there is no old system to hang on to.

COMPONENTS OF INSTALLATION PLANNING

Finally, we have come to the point where we must make the system part of the operation organization. The components to be considered in establishing an installation plan are similar to the subsystem components of an information system which have been discussed throughout the book. This includes the need to have people, procedures, applications software, data, and hardware and systems software ready to meet the real work world of the organization.

For a small system, such as a decision support system for one user or for a microcomputer spreadsheet package, planning may be fairly simple and straightforward. There is little risk, and coordination should be easy since few resources are needed. There usually is no existing system to worry about. But if the new system is essential to the existence of the organization and replaces an existing system, there will be a need to coordinate activities very carefully. For example, installing a new payroll system for an international organization with remote hardware and communication capabilities is a major undertaking.

Each of the subsystem components will be considered separately. This should create an awareness of the factors which need be be considered.

PEOPLE

The first consideration is the need for human resources. Staff must be available to implement the system. This often requires hiring temporary staff. For example, the parallel approach requires operating both the old and the new system, which requires substantial staff increases. People also are needed to do the actual conversion. This may require people with technical knowledge about both the existing and new systems.

Old files must be converted to new formats and devices. People familar with the data are needed to handle errors and exceptions when the actual conversion is done. There will be cases where people will have to understand the purpose of the system to detect missing data or data which has no matching master records.

Installation of physical equipment should take place only after the systems designer has made sure that support systems such as wiring and ventilation are in place. (Innervisions and courtesy The Computer Studio)

PROCEDURES

The developer must make certain that the procedures are performable in the work environment, all the materials or data are available to perform the procedure, and that individual human differences are considered. It is not unusual to have a procedure, tested in isolation, ending up being unperformable because the designer did not consider human differences such as left-handed or short-statured people.

PROGRAMS

The actual computer programs must be added to the system library for large systems. In small systems, it is necessary to have loaded and tested the program to make sure software is operable on the hardware and systems software available. In more case than one, an application package was found to be inoperable because of insufficient memory or because of an incompatible release or version of the operating system.

DATA

All of the files needed for the system must be converted and backed up before the system can be used. This may require that new data be coded or converted to different formats. New mediums for storage may be required.

HARDWARE AND SYSTEMS SOFTWARE

The hardware and systems software must be installed in each site. This means that the rewiring, air conditioning, and communications needed to make the system operable must be ready.

These final steps of a system project take place in Process 7, which will be discussed next.

PROCESS 7: INSTALL AND MONITOR SYSTEM

Process 7 moves a system from development into operation. "Ownership" of the system is officially transferred from the development group to operations and maintenance groups. Since there may be several usable versions of a system developed in Process 6, Process 7 may be repeated several times for a systems project. This process involves performance testing in a real environment. "Real" means that all other systems in the organization are present and operating.

Process 7: Install and Monitor System

Purpose: Ensure that the version of the system operates in the organizational environment. Ensure that future changes are recorded and passed to the project planning function.

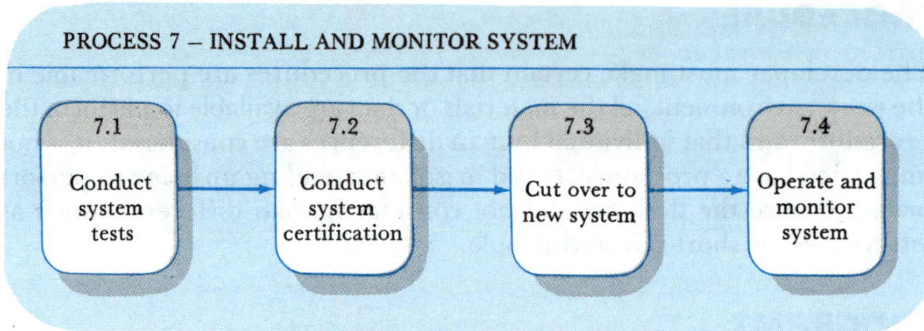

FIGURE 13.8

Subprocesses within process 7.

Output: An accepted working system version with suggested changes.
Subprocesses: Run system in the organizational environment. Certify usability, operability, standard adherence, controlability, and maintainability. Create operation, maintenance, and training libraries from development documention. Cut over to new system. Monitor installed system. Do postimplementation review to actually measure expected benefits.
Techniques and Skills: Presentations, peer, user, and quality assurance reviews, training implementation.

Activities within Process 7 of a systems development project include conducting system tests with other systems present (Process 7.1), conducting system certification (Process 7.2), cutting over to the new system (Process 7.3), and operating and monitoring the system (Process 7.4) (see Figure 13.8 for a graphic view of Process 7).

PROCESS 7.1—CONDUCT SYSTEM TESTS

The purpose of Subprocess 7.1 is to assure that the system operates within the organizational environment. Special care must be taken to make certain that production files and databases are not harmed by this testing. Criteria for these tests should come from the system objectives stated in the requirements models. These objectives can be extended to include factors such as avoiding degradation of other systems.

It may be necessary to run parallel, pilot, or phased operations at this point. Extra resources may be needed such as temporary employees, assistance from a service bureau, or arrangements for overtime by current employees. This is required to avoid having people do two jobs while attempting to climb the learning curve with the new system.

The database administrator should help make certain that data is in place for the tests, and monitor the databases to detect any destructive activities. Training personnel should be aware of any human resources that are not ready to perform in a live environment.

Plans must be made for the actual introduction of the system and informing of affected parties. If new inputs are required or if new outputs are to be delivered, the persons who will need to accept a change must be part of the group informed. This will reduce resistance and also minimize queries once the change is made. Examples include customers having to follow new order procedures or employees receiving a bank deposit pay notice rather than a payroll check.

PROCESS 7.2—CONDUCT SYSTEM CERTIFICATION

The purpose of Subprocess 7.2 is to be sure that users believe the system is usable, operations believes the system is operable, quality assurance believes all standards are followed, auditors believe the system has integrity, and maintenance believes the system is maintainable. This is similar to a formal contracting process, much like making a purchase and getting a certification that certain activities have been done and certain standards have been met.

This is not an opportunity to "nitpick" minor details, like coding within a module. Participants must make sure that there are no components of the system that would seriously compromise its operation. The system must be examined to assure "healthiness." A healthy system would have:

Adequate control over hardware and software, especially remote locations

Adequate implementation and testing of backup and recovery procedures

Compliance with government regulations

"Auditability" by outside auditors

Control of access to any sensitive part of the system or its outputs

Certifiers play an important role. They are committing their organizational unit to expend resources in the future to keep the system operating. If they have actively participated in the development of the system, there should be no surprises at this stage of the project. There are specific areas that the certification meeting must focus on, including:

Users verifying that procedures are performable, training is adequate and comprehensive, customer and consumer groups will not be offended, and there is a high probability of acceptance and usage.

Operations verifying that run manuals are acceptable, backup and recovery procedures are in place and performable, and that all persons are trained to perform required roles.

Quality assurance and standards verifying that standards for documentation, naming, coding, and dictionary entries are followed.

Maintenance verifying that the system design is actually implemented and that documentation to aid maintenance exists and is accessible.

Audit/Control verifying that controls are in place and system integrity exists.

This also is a good time to evaluate the system development methods used and to make any suggestions as to how the methods could be improved. Project activity estimating data can be evaluated and updated. Project managers must remember that the processes and techniques used to build a system are also a system in themselves which must be improved over time to respond to new knowledge and a changing environment.

PROCESS 7.3—CUT OVER TO NEW SYSTEM

The purpose of Subprocess 7.3 is to make final preparation for operation of the new system in a production mode. The result of the subprocess is a production-ready system. A series of finalizing activities takes place at this time. All final file or database conversions are completed. Any needed training refreshers are conducted. Temporary employees are phased out.

Documentation is generated at this time. It must be stressed that *documention is not developed at this stage*. It is "culled" from existing materials. The documentation includes materials for the operations and maintenance units to allow continued "health" of the system. If there is geographic dispersion, all sites must have materials such as data preparation documents, forms, operating procedures, report distribution lists, and report use instructions.

Formal announcement of a new system should be done at this time. For example, persons receiving a different payroll check or customers receiving a new bill format should be informed as to what is or will be happening.

PROCESS 7.4—OPERATE AND MONITOR SYSTEM

The purpose of Subprocess 7.4 is to run the system and conduct periodic audits to ensure that the system is providing maximum benefit to the organization. The system will require both planned and unplanned maintenance. This process may include activities such as periodic training when new employees become involved or refresher training on infrequently performed procedures such as system recovery.

There will be requests for change to the existing system. These requests will be the result of a changing environment, changes in the organization, and the discovery of errors as things are done in different ways and in different sequences. All of these requests for changes must be managed. They cannot be ignored.

Besides preventive maintenance, there will be unpredicted maintenance. We all have to maintain the objects we acquire. Cars may need to be repaired on the day they are driven out of the dealership. The need for maintenance continues throughout the life of the system. Many young persons spend their life savings on an auto only to find they do not have the funds to keep the vehicle on the road. Having to do maintenance should not come as a surprise.

There are various kinds of maintenance:

Fixes—something is broken or does not work (headlight is out or output report needs alignment of titles and columns). If something is broken, it must be fixed if it is to continue doing business. These changes are considered necessities. A fix typically does not require system analysis or design. The problem is well-defined and the basic system structure is not changed. Estimating is quite easy in most cases. Usually fixes are done immediately upon finding a need.

Enhancements—making an improvement to a system that is still operating (adding a new cassette tape player to a car or adding a new report to a system). Enhancements could be delayed without serious consequences. They could be considered niceties. To prevent these types of development changes from consuming all the system development resources, any change must be added to the project mix and available resources assigned to it. If no resources are available (a usual occurence), then resources must be taken from other projects.

A fix may be combined with an enhancement. A new set of tires and wheels could also eliminate the need to fix a flat tire. Care should be taken not to fix things which will be replaced by an enhancement unless there is an intermediate result needed before the enhancement can be done.

The important thing to remember is that maintenance should be managed. A plan should be established, resources should be properly allocated, and efforts should be examined and controlled. Patches should not be put on patches if the organization could suffer as a result.

Scheduled and unscheduled "fire drills" are good tests of the ability of the system to perform. These drills are a form of preventive maintenance where infrequently used, but important, procedures such as backup and

JUST A QUICK FIX

I keep a confidential list of the world's most expensive programming errors. All of the top ten on the current list are maintenance errors. The top three cost their organizations $1,600,000,000, $900,000,000, and $245,000,000—and each one involved the change of a single digit in a previously correct program.

In all three cases, the change was "so trivial" it was instituted casually. A supervisor told a low-level maintenance programmer to change that digit without any written instruction, no test plan or nobody to read over the change. Indeed, no controls whatsoever existed between that one programmer and the day-to-day operations of the organization.

—From a column by Jerry Weinberg in *Infosystems,* August 1983, p. 49.

recovery are practiced. For example, a bank may assure that tellers can perform manual backup activities in case there was a computer shutdown.

Incident reports detailing any problems that occur must be recorded and should be categorized and filed. Care should be taken with making "quick fixes." If the incidents follow a pattern, it may be necessary to request a new systems project to determine if system rebuilding or overhaul is needed.

Once the system is broken in and reaches stability, a postaudit review should be conducted. Postaudit reviews are discussed in the next section.

POSTAUDIT REVIEWS

Once the system has been implemented, there will be a period of time when the system will be on very shaky legs. This is the stage of the project life where the users and operators of the system are at the "conscious competence" learning stage. They must think about what they will do before they do it.

Once the system settles down and unconscious competency is reached, the system is assimilated into the life styles of the persons who are using and operating it. At this time, it valuable to review the new system and the method used to develop it.

WHY DO A POSTAUDIT?

The main reason for doing a postaudit is to learn from past experiences, and hopefully to improve future systems development performance. This learning includes an examination of how well the development system functioned, how the plan for development aided or hindered the development, how well the development techniques worked in the situations where they were used, how team performance could have been improved, and

WHAT LEARNING STAGE ARE YOU AT

A widepread belief is that learning takes place in stages. Stages include:

1. Unconscious incompetence—don't know you don't know
2. Conscious incompetence—know you don't know
3. Conscious competence—know but must think while performing
4. Unconscious competence—know and fluidly perform without thinking

Think about these stages for different activities such as bicycle riding or typing. Note that most experts would fall in stage 4, making expert system development difficult.

how individuals could have been better utilized. Changes to the development methods and means of project management may be a result of the postimplementation audit.

Another reason for doing the postaudit is to determine if the system needs to be changed in any way. The actual meeting of user requirements is examined to determine if revisions to the system should be proposed.

WHO SHOULD DO POSTAUDITS?

There is much controversy over who should do the postaudit of a systems development project. Much of the controversy can be addressed by stating the objective of the review. If the objective is to find fault and punish, the review would be done by someone other than the original development team. But if the objective is to learn from the experiences of doing the project, it is of value to have the same project team do the review.

Since close involvement with a project can narrow peoples' vision, this group can often be aided by other people who can lend an objective view of the system development project. These persons are often part of a quality assurance or quality review group.

By stating the objective of the review and rewarding people for finding the good as well as the bad, the postaudit can add value to the systems development effort in the organization.

WHEN SHOULD POSTAUDITS BE DONE?

Evaluation of the developed system should not be done until the system settles down into somewhat of a routine and employees have learned how to perform the procedures. If the system is not allowed to stabilize, we will be measuring a system that is not representative of the end product.

Another factor to consider is the statement of the business and system objectives. It makes little sense to try to predict if the objectives are met if the required time to meet the objectives has not passed. Only then can system performance objectives such as response time or number of transactions handled be measured with some certainty that these results will not change.

WHAT SHOULD BE DONE?

There are numerous factors that should be examined during the postaudit of a system. They fall in two main categories:

1. Evaluation of the system development methods
   a. Processes including a review of the development approach used?
   b. Techniques including if technique was effective and whether persons had adequate training to achieve needed performance?
   c. Project management including time and cost?

2. Evaluation of the developed system
   a. Overall performance including:
      System tactics cost and reasonableness?
      System objectives including performance such as response time, report delivery, system availability, and query availability?
      Business tactics performance improvement?
      Business objectives met including increased business revenues and reduced business costs?
   b. Usability—outputs being used including:
      Reports being read and used to perform business tactics?
      Queries being made when they should be made?
      Turnover in user groups because system created chaos?
      Bootleg systems appearing?
      Requests for changes? (if none, no one may be interested in system?)
   c. Maintainability—are changes possible including:
      Response to incident reports?
      Reaction of maintenance group?
      Documentation being kept up-to-date?
   d. Dependability—system available when needed including:
      Delays in processing?
      Deadlines being met?
      Number of incident reports?

The team should be sure they have answers to the above questions from an adequate sample of persons who can provide accurate responses.

MANAGING CHANGE

The topic of implementation and installation of systems would not be complete without a discussion of change management. If we lived in a totally rational world, change management would not be a problem. But we are working with people possessing emotionality as well as rationality. Status, power, ego, self-fulfillment, and security must be considered.

Social forces as well as forces in the individual must be evaluated. A system may influence the ability of persons to interact and could destroy social groups. A cohesive work unit must be approached as a unit, not as a set of individuals. Group dynamics can be a powerful force in accepting or resisting change.

If the systems developer waits until the system is in the testing stages to think about acceptance and change, it is already too late. The change process will be facilitated if persons who must change are involved throughout the development of the system. If the developer waits until it is time to implement to think about change, the effort will become a "selling job." Those required to change must have had some influence on the changes they will endure.

A new system represents change, which is stressful for many people at all levels in the company. Frustrated workers may revert to manual methods of getting work done, such as a calculator. (Comstock)

A UNIQUE VIEW OF CHANGE

Tannenbaum (see References) refers to change as a "little death"—the giving up of something you currently know about to accept something you know little about. He believes that to have "rebirth," you must have an appreciation of what the future has in store for you.

Dying may include the following stages:

1. Denial that it is happening ("No, not me")
2. Anger, resentment, and envy ("Why me?")
3. Bargaining ("I need some time.")
4. Grief with things already lost. ("I should have . . . ")
5. Grief with future losses. ("I wish I could . . . ")
6. Acceptance and peace with the loss.

The persons who must accept a system change are going through the same process. They are losing a part of themselves. This may be self-identity or power, but the task of those advocating the change is to identify and help the person address the loss. Tannenbaum believes that we must work with the letting go as much as the accepting of the new. Changers must aid changees going through mourning by allowing a view of comfortable future before rebirth and new living can start to take place. The resistance may not be to accepting the new as much as it is to giving up the old.

For a person to accept change, there must be a realistic challenge and some excitement and anticipation in dealing with the unknown. There must be a recognition of new identity and power. The changer must believe there is a fuller life ahead, and the ending should be seen as a new beginning.

THE ANALYST AS A CHANGE AGENT

The system implementor is a change agent. Bronsema and Keen (see References) believe that education must *precede* the implementation process, rather than employees being trained *after* the implementation process. They advocate the following principles:

1. Use data from the participants' world. This will allow association with something familiar.
2. Senior management must demonstrate its commitment by public investment of time, prestige and attention.
3. Provide a forum for expressing concern and answering questions.
4. Provide an opportunity for action, not just words.
5. Move the sequence of events from concrete to abstract to reflective to active.
6. Limit participants to a small, heterogeneous group whose members can share with one another. A homogeneous group may only see things one way and form a resistance coalition.
7. Use a leader with a consulting action-orientation who exhibits teaching and trust-building skills.
8. Conduct followup activities to learn from the past.

CHANGE INFLUENCES POWER BASES

One reason people may have difficulty accepting new or changed systems is that the system may change power bases. Perceived losers of power may resist the introduction of the system.

French and Raven (see References) believe that power can be obtained in one or more of the following ways:

1. *Reward Power*—power granted because of the ability to grant positive benefits. A person could lose the ability to grant existing rewards.
2. *Coercive Power*—power granted because of the ability to punish. A person could lose the ability to punish.
3. *Expert Power*—power granted because of the ability to perform or to provide knowledge or information. "Old experts" are likely to resist if they will not become "new experts."
4. *Referent Power*—power granted because the person is admired for his or her accomplishments or contacts. "Old" accomplishments could become passé.

5. *Legitimate Power*—power granted because the person holds a job or position that gives them authority (for example, the President of the country). The system could change a person's perceived legitimacy.

The systems developer must examine these power bases and try to detect if any of the bases will be upset. Likewise, systems developers must realize the power that they themselves have to influence the changes needed to implement the system.

Martin (see References) states that the analyst must be aware of forces in the individual person (psychological), forces in groups of individuals (sociological), and forces in power redistribution (political) that affect system introduction. Every employee realizes that political forces are very powerful and influence getting things done in organizations. It must be remembered that it takes less power to prevent a change than it takes to institute a change.

GUIDELINES FOR MANAGING CHANGE

When planning change-making activities to put a new system in place, the interconnections with other systems must be considered. A system will influence not only people and groups within the organization, but also those entities which provide input to or receive output from the system.

For example, the data flow diagram at high levels should be examined to see if the external entities will be affected by the introduction of the change. Even if the entities are outside the system boundary, they will be interacting with the persons inside the system who are giving something up and possibly mourning. The pain of the changees can be lessened if others they are dealing with accept their changed behavior and give them support.

In summary, things to remember about change include:

1. A need for the change must be understood by those to be changed.
2. User-directed change and active (not sham or token) participation is more likely to be accepted. An example of sham participation is to ask people to attend a meeting to gather their opinions and then not really listen to any suggestions made because your mind was already made up.
3. Task accomplishment must be balanced with the perceived quality of work life.
4. Change more likely will be accepted if persons understand added value is sought rather than just cost displacement. This means concentrating on increasing revenues through effectiveness—doing the right things, rather than concentrating on efficiency, or doing the same things better or with fewer people. Cost reduction smacks of people reduction, rather than corporate growth. (This relates to the quote by Jim Nethercott at the beginning of the chapter.)

5. Change may be more likely accepted if persons affected can visualize and understand what things will be like if the change was actually in place. People fear the unknown.
6. Change must be managed. Do not expect people to be grateful to you for making things more complex for them. Change will cause an expenditure of energy, both mental and physical.
7. Social groups are as important a consideration as the individual in proposing change. Conformity to group norms or accepted group behavior must be considered. Individuals will not risk being ostracized by the group to perform tasks the group would frown on. For example, being close to the boss may be an unacceptable form of behavior. You would not expect persons to readily accept a task which would require this behavior because the group would discourage members from behaving this way.

The systems developer must have empathy with the people being changed. Identifying with how a person will feel and then acting in a fashion that will minimize the negative effects is necessary. Long-term benefits must be clear to the changee before short-term suffering will be accepted. Every college student should identify with this phenomenon.

SUMMARY

It often is too late to worry about implementation if it is not considered until the system is ready to install. Rapport is built all through the development of the system. The most critical task is to make sure the implementation plan is thorough. Both the technical and behavioral components of the system must be carefully considered. Individual and social needs must be understood and dealt with. If the project was a success, this is a time for sadness on the part of some of the team members. It is comparable to the sports team finishing a winning year and then parting at the end of the season.

REFERENCES AND FURTHER READINGS

Bronsema, Gloria S., and Peter G. W. Keen. "Education Intervention and Implementation in MIS," *Sloan Management Review,* Summer 1983, pp. 35–43.

DeMarco, Tom. *Structured Analysis and System Specification,* Yourdon Press: New York, 1978, pp. 325–331.

Dickson, Gary W., John K. Simmons, and John C. Anderson. "Behavioral Reactions to the Introduction of a Management Information System: Some Empirical Observations," MISRC Working Paper 69-3, University of Minnesota.

———, and ———. "The Behavioral Side of MIS," *Business Horizons,* August 1970, pp. 59–71.

Feeney, William, and Frea Sladek. "The Systems Analyst as a Change Agent," *Datamation,* November 1977, pp. 85–88.

French, J. R. P., Jr., and B. Raven. "The Bases of Social Power," in Dorwin Cartwright, ed., *Studies in Social Power,* Ann Arbor, MI: University of Michigan Press, 1959, pp. 150–167. Found in Wickesberg, Albert K. *Management Organization,* New York: Appleton-Century-Crofts, 1966, pp. 32–33.

Glaser, George. "Commitment . . . the Unreachable Star," *Datamation,* June 1, 1971, pp. 38–41.

Hetzel, William. *The Complete Guide to Software Testing,* Wellesley, MA: QED Information Sciences, Inc., 1984.

Lamb, Clement A. "DP and the User: A Matter of Planning," *Datamation,* November 1, 1978, pp. 169+.

Martin, E. W. "The Politics of System Development," Discussion Paper #264, Indiana University, Bloomington, Indiana, April 15, 1984.

Myers, Glenford J. *The Art of Software Testing,* New York: John Wiley & Sons, 1979.

Srinivasan, C. A., and Paul E. Dascher. "Information Systems Design: User Psychology Considerations," *MSU Business Topics,* Winter 1977, pp. 51–57.

Tannenbaum, Robert. "Some Matters of Life and Death," Working Paper #76–2, Human Systems Development Study Center, University of California, Los Angeles, April 1976.

Weinberg, Victor. *Structured Analysis,* New York: Yourdon Press, 1980, pp. 208–231.

REVIEW QUESTIONS

1. What are the two main activities included in system implementation?
2. Distinguish between bottom-up and versioned construction approaches.
3. Why might the bottom-up construction approach lead to a system that was 90 percent done and remained that way for a long time?
4. What does the "10-90 premise" mean in regard to system construction?
5. What are stubs? What might be acceptable actions for a stub?
6. State some advantages and disadvantages of the versioned construction approach.
7. What are the tests that Myers suggests to find weaknesses in the system?
8. Is there always a progression from Process 6 to Process 7? Why or why not?
9. What might be some factors to be considered in reviewing developed software?
10. What is meant by a test scenario? Why is it necessary to have both test data and a test scenario?
11. What might be a good source of data about the needs for test data?
12. What are some of the things that users must be trained to do before a system is ready for installation?
13. Why is timing of training essential? What are problems of training too early? Too late?
14. Briefly describe each of the approaches to system implementation.
15. Give an example of combining the approaches to system implementation.

16. Why might the parallel approach to implementation not be appropriate if a quick transition to the new system is needed?

17. Why might parallel implementation not be possible?

18. How is one implementation phase different from a past phase?

19. Why might selection of a pilot implementation site be a political decision?

20. What are some advantages of the cutover implementation approach?

21. What are the components of an implementation plan?

22. Why might Process 7 be repeated several times for a systems development project?

23. What factors would you consider in deciding who to assign to teams when temporary persons are hired to aid with a parallel installation?

24. Where should the criteria for system tests done in Process 7.1 come from?

25. Who are the different groups involved in system certification? What should each group certify?

26. Is it accurate to state that documentation is not created in Process 7? Why or why not? Explain.

27. What are the two major types of maintenance? Which one might require a complete systems development effort?

28. What is meant by a system "fire drill"? What purpose does it serve?

29. Why might a person be alerted if a programmer said that a fix was "no problem, that it only required changing a line or two of computer code."

30. What is the main purpose of a postaudit of a systems project?

31. What are the primary activities in a postaudit with regard to evaluation of the newly developed system?

32. Why should change be considered well before the implementation process?

33. What are ways a person's power base may change by introduction of a new system?

34. Why is it important to consider looking outside the system boundary when considering system change?

DISCUSSION QUESTIONS

1. An analyst stated that the versioned construction approach involved repetition of both integrated and unit testing. Do you agree or disagree? Why?

2. An analyst was trying to argue that Process 6 was not needed. He believed that since a software package was being purchased, there was no need for system construction. What is your response to this person?

3. Why is the attitude taken in testing that you can only prove the system incorrect, rather than believing you can prove it correct?

4. A systems development manager said that she believed that development teams should learn from past experiences. What would you say to convince her that a good means of doing this is the use of postaudits? How would you counter the argument that "there is not enough time to do postaudits"?

5. Do you agree or disagree that the change process involved with a new system is similar to the dying process? Why or why not?

6. A new systems analyst has proposed a system which will improve corporate efficiency, but will require all assembly line workers to take breaks at three different times. What do you think might be the reaction of the line workers?

7. Why might a systems project be compared to a phoenix? (From a dictionary: Phoenix—*In Egyptian mythology, a bird of great beauty, said to live for 500 or 600 years and then consume itself by fire, rising from its ashes in youthful freshness to live through another cycle.*)

8. How could empathy serve as an aid to successful system implementation?

EXERCISES

1. Establish a plan for writing a book using both a bottom-up and a versioned approach.

2. Create a table with your own personal rating from 1 to 5 for each of the four installation approaches for the factors of stress, cost, duration, and human resources needed.

3. The following is a brief description of an organization implementing a new system. After reading and analyzing the situation, you must evaluate the plans of the information systems group. Predict what will happen when the system as currently specified is implemented. Why do you believe this?

    Reelfast Incorporated builds fishing reels for several different brand names in five plants throughout the United States. Each plant is quite similar. Reelfast has about 495 employees in total. Each of the plants uses the workstation principle. The workers move from workstation to workstation depending on production schedules and the materials available to build the products. Each plant works two shifts daily. Each shift has a shift manager over about six supervisors. The supervisor is responsible for a workstation and leads teams of about 5 to 10 workers at each workstation.

    Workers do not require high skill to do their jobs. There is much turnover in the plants. The workers don't feel there is much of a future at the plants and know that most of the supervisors will not come from the ranks of the workers. But the company pays decent wages and has good benefits due to strong union involvement. The union–management and worker–management relations are not good.

    Since the company must bid for new contracts, it is essential to know how much labor goes into each batch of fishing reels. This makes it necessary to monitor workstation productivity to know how many workers actually were working on what product and for how long. The current means of doing this is to have supervisors record worker hours at each workstation for each day. The reports have not been very accurate and the supervisors are spending much of their day keeping track of people. Workers seem to spend more time between workstations than at them. The company plant layouts dictate the keeping of the workstation concept.

The information systems staff convinced management that an automated information system linking workstation check-ins to the currently automated payroll was the way to go. A badge recorder is to be put at each workstation and workers would be required to check in and check out as they were reassigned to different workstations. Recording of actual productivity would be done by supervisors so that correlations between how many and which workers were associated with what production batches could be recorded. Quality could be linked to employees and supervisors.

The hardware and software has already been acquired and tests out well. The informations systems staff has had no problems operating the recorders and building the links between hardware components. The information systems staff plans to introduce the workers to the use of the badge recorders once the rest of the recorders arrive. Supervisors would be told how to submit the productivity data. The information systems staff believe they could generate all the possible reports that management could ever want since they have a new report generation language.

The information systems group will use a pilot location in Freeport, Wisconsin, as the first implementation site. They plan to run the new and old systems in parallel since they feel it would be good to compare the results.

PART V

Beyond the Process and Techniques

This section goes beyond performing typical life cycle processes and techniques. Managing systems development introduces the reader to the challenge of "putting a project together." Alternatives to the classical life cycle are introduced. Finally, the future of systems development and the systems developer is discussed with some hints on survival in the long run.

CHAPTER 14

CHAPTER OBJECTIVES

You should be able to:

- Explain the components of project management
- Give arguments for careful project management
- Understand the advantages of using an automated project management package
- Indicate when alternatives to the traditional life cycle development method should be considered
- Specify the developer's role in assuring user-developed software
- Specify factors that must be considered in acquiring packaged software
- Specify how and when to use prototyping as a development method

Managing Systems Development Projects

15% of all systems development projects deliver nothing of value and cost overruns of 100–200% are not uncommon.
—DeMarco, Tom. Controlling Software Projects, New York: Yourdon Press, 1982, p. 3.

THIS CHAPTER DISCUSSES the topics of project management including planning and estimating. Management of the tasks and people included in a project is explored. Automated project management aids are introduced. Alternatives to the traditional life cycle such as user-developed systems, information centers, prototyping, and packaged system acquisition are discussed.

Most users would find it appalling if their own organizational units had a success record like the one DeMarco describes. A housing contractor would not stay in business for very long if a proposed $80,000 house had a final cost of $160,000 to $240,000 or if one of seven houses started could never be lived in.

Only astute systems development management can prevent the situation described above by DeMarco. Systems development does not just happen by having proposed projects and people with the title of systems developer. There is a need for thoughtful managers to have a satisfactory systems development effort within an organization. Management of systems development includes (1) management of project activities, and (2) management of alternative methods of systems development. This chapter will discuss these topics.

PROJECT MANAGEMENT

Although the words "project management" may sound ominous, most of us have performed project management without realizing it. Completing a school project requires management. Repairing a car, bicycle, or an appliance requires project management.

Project managers must ask themselves and other project team members the following questions:

"What activities have to be completed to get the whole thing done?"

"How long will each of these activities take?"

"Do certain activities have to be done before others?"

"Who do I need to help me and when?"

"When do I have to be done with certain activities?"

"If any activity gets delayed, will it delay the whole project?"

These are questions any project planner would ask when confronted by any complex project.

A *project* is a set of activities or tasks that must be completed to obtain some final result. The final result sought in a systems project is a working system. Project management is the human activity needed to allow orderly completion of required activities or tasks in a minimum of time with a minimum of resources. The activities that must be completed are the systems development processes and subprocesses discussed in earlier chapters in this book.

Projects involve the management of:

Activities or tasks (a "to do" list)

People with skills to perform the tasks (systems developers)

Timing, including start times and projected completion times (a schedule)

Intermediate results from completing a task (reviewable deliverables)

Review points to assure quality is maintained in the results (milestone management)

Management includes the classical activities of planning, organizing, staffing, directing, and controlling of a project. Systems development projects are done with scarce resources. There is not unlimited time or people or dollars. The project resources must be managed.

Projects such as a space launch, building a new office building, or creating an airline reservation system are very complex. They must be carefully planned and organized to assure appropriate breakdown of activities. They must be staffed with appropriate people, and directed to make sure people know what to do and want to do it; and they must be controlled, to assure the project is going according to plan. Project plans are essential to project management. The plans lay the groundwork for the entire project.

PROJECT PLANNING

Planning is an attempt to predict and attain a desired state of reality. A project manager's job is to establish a plan, to implement the plan, to measure reality as it happens, compare reality with the plan, and to revise the prediction of future reality and the means of attainment. Planning must be treated as *successive approximation,* not as precise contracting.

Without a plan, management control cannot take place since there is no shared expectation or plan to control against. Many people will argue that "if you can't plan it, you can't do it." This fits in with the belief that if you do not know what you are going to do, it is very difficult to do it or know when you are done.

Good project managers have found that:

Plans must be approved by those involved, including those who must produce the results and those who will finally approve the results.

Plans are not carved in stone, they can and should be revised.

Replanning takes time and should be included in the project's future time estimates.

Plans have more detail about tasks to be done in the nearer future.

People will move to and from the project team both by plan and because of crisis.

Iteration will be necessary (things you think are done may have to be done again).

Any project must be planned, scheduled with people and resources, and monitored. But project management is not a static and linear activity. The monitoring will reveal deviations from the plan and additional planning, scheduling, and monitoring will be required.

The project leader should attempt to set milestones for the project.

Milestones are quantified and measurable states of completion, in essence a verifiable deliverable. A milestone is either reached or it is not reached—it is a binary situation. There is no such thing as 90 percent done when using milestones. The manager must be sure that if the project scope changes, budgets also are changed. The project manager must guard against creeping commitment.

A worker would know when he or she had reached a milestone, such as when a certain database was established and tested, or when a certain number of users were trained to access a database. Milestones should be assigned to a person who is responsible for achievement of the milestone. Then, there will be no "buck passing" where one person points a finger at another and says that others were responsible.

Milestones work best when the assigned person specifies the milestone and is not told when the deliverable must be achieved. The person must use a management-by-objectives approach and specify the result and when it will be achieved. The project manager must ensure that this is satisfactory and work it into the comprehensive project plan.

Staffing is part of the project plan. Staffing may be a recurring task of the project manager as people are removed from the project for special duties or if different skills are needed to continue the project. The project manager must be responsible for assuring that all persons assigned to projects have necessary skills or are slated for training to obtain the skills.

A systems project plan must be revised as a project progresses since new information will be discovered. The systems development database discussed in Chapter 3 will continue to grow. This data will provide new information which results in new knowledge which will provoke a change or addition to original plans. For example, analysis of the business organization may reveal that 23 persons will have to be interviewed. This will allow the manager to more accurately estimate the time required for interviews. Thus, as a project becomes more defined, the plan should be better defined and estimates should become more accurate.

Project planning consists of representing tasks or activities in some sequence and optimally allocating resources to the activities. The tasks for establishing a systems project plan come from the systems development methodology.

Using a Systems Development Methodology in Project Planning

To plan a systems project, the planner must break the project down into individual activities. The systems development life cycle provides aid in creating such a breakdown. The life cycle includes a comprehensive list of activities needed to complete any systems project. The project planner must choose a subset of activities needed to complete the project at hand. Then the planner would attach a time estimate, often called *duration*, to each of the activities. The next step is to assign resources to accomplish the activities.

An organization often will have a standard methodology—such as the one presented in this book by processes 1 through 7 and their detailing in

Chapters 4, 8, and 13—installed and accepted in the organization. It is the organization's way of doing systems projects. The methodology does not just happen; it must be consciously implemented in the organization. There is a need for acceptance of standards, policies, and for management commitment. Specific forms must be developed, approved, and adopted. People must be trained in how to use the methodology. Like any system, the system development system must be adapted to fit the organizational culture and setting before there can be any hope of adoption and use.

If a project does not go as intended, management should not blame the methodology any more than a craftsperson should blame the tools for an unsatisfactory product. Much as a craftsperson has to maintain and replace tools, systems management must assure that the methodology is "working" and is accomplishing its purpose. If not, then maintenance is needed, as with any other aid people use. Craftspeople must take time to keep their tools sharp.

The methodology is intended to aid, not replace, management. A methodology is not a recipe to be followed that assures success. It requires knowledgeable and aware managers who know the benefits and limitations of its use. The methodology provides a guide and basis for communication between the systems staff and between users and the systems unit.

The systems development methodology is not rigid. Management must select the needed activities from the entire set of those available. Not all projects need to have all activities performed. A program fix requiring a report title change would involve fewer activities than a new inventory system. But the decision not to do an activity should be a conscious one. Deviations from the standard plan must be conscious, not because of neglect. We must learn from history or we will allow history to repeat itself, including the disasters.

Once the list of activities is created, an estimate of time and resources needed to complete the activity must be made. Making accurate estimates is one of the greatest challenges a project manager will face.

Estimating

Estimating establishes the time duration needed to complete a task. Estimates are easier to make if some history exists of how long a similar task has taken in the past. The difficulty is that not all tasks are exactly the same as past tasks, nor are they performed in an identical setting with identical people.

One of the objectives of project planning is to ensure that there will be no surprises for the users. A good estimator would attempt to consistently predict when a product will be delivered and do this far in advance of the delivery date. The objective is to be more accurate earlier.

The project manager must estimate or obtain an estimate of the number of worker hours or person hours a systems development task will take. These person-hours, which estimate how many hours of employees' time are needed to complete a task, are then aggregated into "man-months" (Brooks). But developers must remember that authorities such as Brooks (see References) have declared the "man-month" to be a myth. The reason for this is that people and months are not interchangeable. A month of work by one person is not equivalent to a month of work by some other person. Brooks believes that factors such as individual skills or the number of persons on the team must be considered.

Certain activities will take a certain amount of time no matter how many people are involved. Brooks sums up this argument by saying "the bearing of a child takes nine months, no matter how many women are assigned to the task."

Brooks also says there are other fallacies concerning the man-month. For example, when a project gets behind schedule, managers often will add more people to the project. But Brooks believes this will actually slow a project down. This is due to the geometric increase in the number of communication channels and interactions needed between people assigned to the project. Brooks believes this is true because the added people first have to be introduced to the project and then will add to the number of communication channels that must be maintained. This will take time that the original persons on the project would have spent completing productive tasks. Thus, caution should be used when creating estimates of man-months.

In making estimates, the planner must consider many factors. Factors include:

Management commitment and interest in the result (great interest could create great team spirit)

Size of the activity (for example, number of interviews to be done)

Environment of the activity (must it be done in various locations requiring travel? Is there existing documentation?)

Whether the task has been done before in the organization (is there anyone to provide help based on past experience?)

How many persons are working on or influence the result (is more communication needed?)

Previous experience of task completers (did they learn by doing it before?)

Skill level of task completers (are they good at it?)

Amount of interest and motivation of task completers (are they excited or reluctant?)

Whether the team previously has worked together

A good estimator must consciously or subconciously consider these factors.

DeMarco (see References) makes some observations and suggestions about how to achieve reality in estimating. He reminds project managers of the following:

1. *Estimating is not regurgitating.* "I need your estimate for how long it will take you working full-time without help to finish this project between now and this time next year."
   (Someone already seems to know the answer.)

2. *Estimating is not negotiating or subject to bargaining.*
   "This is required in a year."
   "I estimated it would take me 14 months."
   "Let's split the difference and you can do in 13 months."
   (Seems that someone has made a new estimate of 13 months?)
3. *A slip in one phase implies a proportionate slip in all subsequent phases.* If you think you can make up time, does it mean your original estimate was incorrect? Or are you adding resources?
4. *Since an estimate is a probabilistic assessment, a useful estimate is a projection that is as likely to be too pessimistic as it is to be too optimistic.* A reasonable estimate would mean that a project is as likely to finish 50 percent early as it is to finish 50 percent late. A pessimist would always estimate high (longer than it would actually take). An optimist would always would estimate low. A *realist* would be low in some cases and high in others.
5. *When someone is responsible for a project, his estimating ability is destroyed.* It seems that close involvement biases the person in the direction of either hopeful optimism or destructive pessimism. Therefore, estimate by committee with committee members being everyone who understands the activity. Throw out the estimate of the person directly responsible, and average the others.

There are other factors an estimator must be aware of. Some seem obvious, but often the obvious is ignored. The first fact an estimator must realize is that it is impossible to estimate if you don't know what you have to do. Thus, the estimator must consult the project plan to see what activities must be performed.

In creating the estimate, it may be a bad idea to be too optimistic or too pessimistic. Too high an estimate to complete a project could result in not getting project approval. Too low an estimate may result in cost overruns and loss of respect (or even loss of job) for the estimator. Optimists who believe that all will go well may end up being victims of "Murphy's law"—if something can go wrong, it will. Pessimists who believe everything will go wrong may cause things to go wrong. Optimism and pessimism are best replaced by realism.

One cannot estimate too far into the future. The estimate should be thought of as an output from the estimation process. The estimation process requires certain inputs. Without these inputs, the estimator is using the W.G. technique (Wild Guess). The inputs may not exist early in a project.

The estimator must consider all time consumers when making an estimate. Often ignored is the time it takes for meetings, transportation, vacations, training, or even time for reestimates. Each component or subtask should be estimated separately.

Some tasks are very difficult to estimate. For example, how long will it take a painter to create a great painting? Or, how long will it take an author to write a book chapter? Unless there is some base of past data on these activities, the only thing an estimator can do is to try to come up with the most realistic minimum and maximum times. But, in cases of great uncertainty such as writing one's first book chapter, the range may be from two months to "never"if that task has not been done before.

Every project differs, so that accurate estimates for developing a system are very difficult. If a measure such as lines of computer program code is used, there is little equivalency between 100 lines of code on a 200,000-line project versus 100 lines on a 1200 line project.

Using a measure such as lines of code may be a poor indicator of productivity. "Lines of what?" is a question some persons will ask. Is it assembly language lines, COBOL lines, or fourth generation language lines, where a complete system may be written with a few hundred lines of code? Productivity is a complex measure that some persons have tried to measure with a "rubber yardstick."

Productivity is a function of time, complexity, technology, skills, and objectives. This has led to a unit of measure called ***function points.*** Jones (see References) describes function points as aspects of information systems that are visible and important to users such as inputs, outputs, inquiries, data files, and interfaces. The function points are counted and weighted by empirically derived weighting factors to obtain an adjusted function point total for the system. The function point total then is used to predict source code size based on the programming language used.

There are various aids to help project managers manage software projects. There is computer software to assist in estimating function point totals as well as in converting to projected lines of source code. There also are aids for keeping track of project tasks, the people assigned to tasks, and deviations from the project plan.

PROJECT MANAGEMENT AIDS

Planning and tracking a project with many dependent tasks and a varied group of people working on the tasks is a difficult endeavor. With the potential for hundreds of tasks and many different specialists working on the tasks, a dynamic means of making changes and then evaluating these changes is needed. A project management system provides aid in planning, scheduling, staffing, budgeting, and monitoring a systems development project.

A standard means of representing projects is to create a network diagram that represents the relationships between tasks. Two widely used network planning techniques used for project planning are the critical path method (CPM), and the program evaluation and review technique (PERT). The critical path method shows start and end times and the path of activities which, if delayed, will delay the entire project. These critical activities are on the critical path. Other activities have "slack" in that they would not delay the entire project if not completed on time.

A ***project management system*** is a software package that can help in defining, assigning, tracking, and revising task networks. These software packages are available for both mainframe and microcomputers. Usually a microcomputer-based system does not allow assigning people across several projects, but does allow managing a single project.

To use a project management package, the project manager first indicates all tasks that must be accomplished. Then the manager assigns people to the tasks and makes an estimate of how long tasks should take. A small example of a task planning network is shown in Figure 14.1. The diagram represents the tasks in Process 6 for our systems development methodology.

Figure 14.1 is read from left to right. The task numbers do not indicate the order in which the tasks take place. The lines and squares indicate which activities have to be completed before another activity can start. This is referred to as ***logical precedence.*** For example, Task 6.1 must be completed before any other tasks can take place. Some activities can take place simultaneously. These are called *concurrent activities.* Tasks 6.2 through 6.5 can take place concurrently.

Each of the boxes showing a task also displays other information. In the upper left-hand corner of the box is the *earliest start time* for the task. In

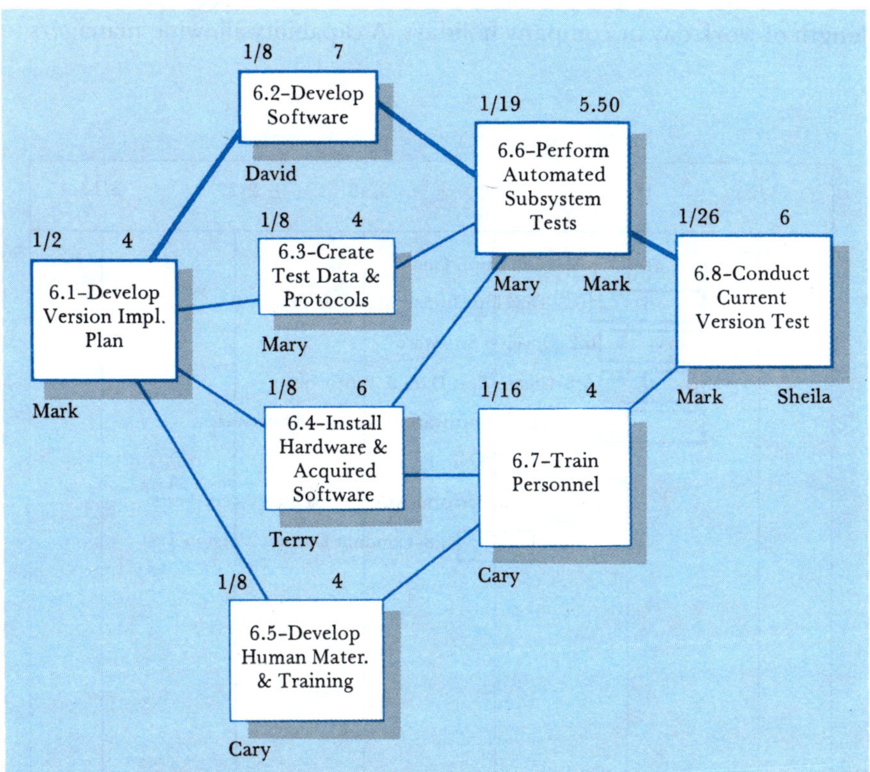

FIGURE 14.1

A project planning network diagram for Process 6 (this figure was created on an Apple Macintosh™ using MacProject).

the upper right-hand corner is the *duration* or number of days required to perform the task. In the lower corners are the *person(s) assigned* to the task. The darkened path through the network is the *critical path.* If any of the tasks along the critical path is delayed, the entire project will be delayed. Tasks not on the critical path have slack time, which means they could be delayed an amount equivalent to the slack time before the entire project is delayed.

Figure 14.2 is another way of viewing project activities. The diagram is commonly called a ***task timeline*** or ***Gantt chart.*** The task timeline allows viewing project tasks over time. Slack time is shown in the shaded portions of the task box. Boxes which have no shading are on the critical path.

Figure 14.3 shows what each of the people assigned to the project will be doing over time. This will allow a manager to reallocate resources as he or she sees fit.

All of the charts and tables can be easily changed using the software. A change in one part of the data will show up in all the other tables and charts. For example, if the manager decided that one of the tasks would take more time, making this change would show up as changes in completion of any tasks which are dependent on the changed task.

The software packages also allow the manager to set variables such as length of work day or company holidays. A capability allowing managers to

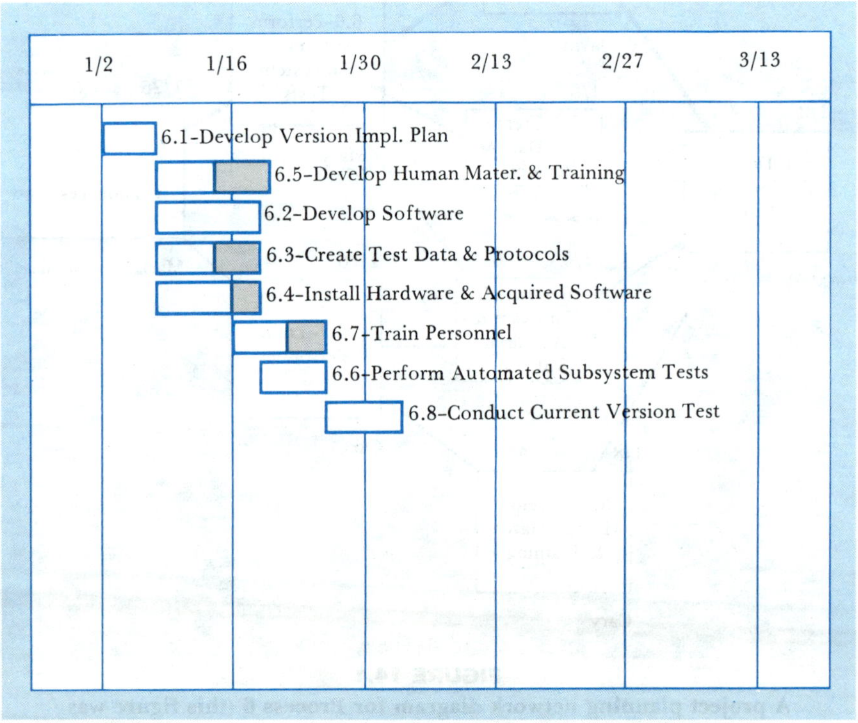

FIGURE 14.2
A task timeline for Process 6 (created using MacProject).

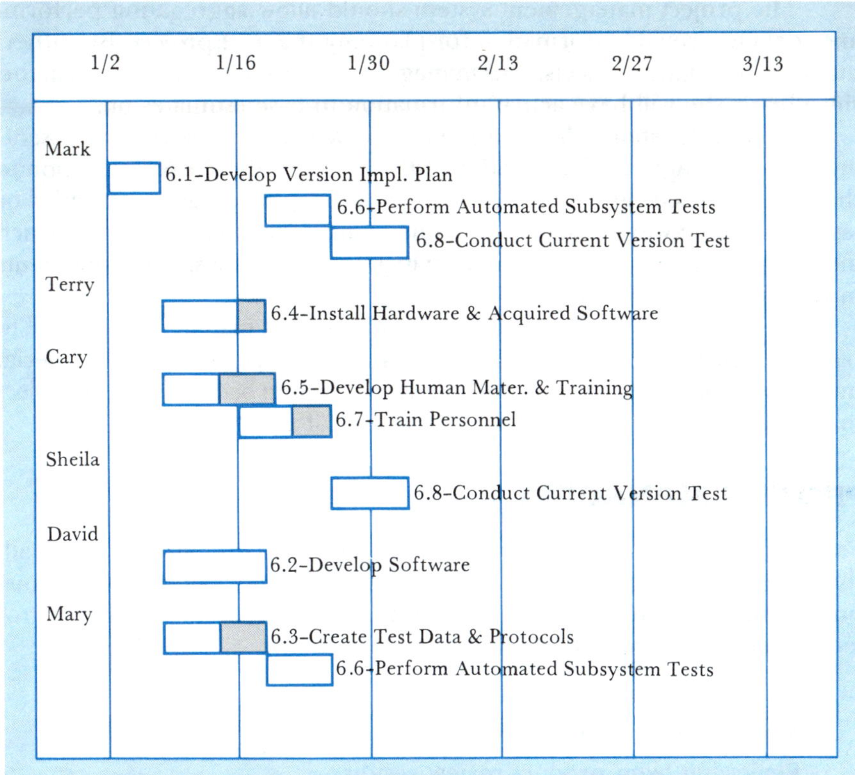

FIGURE 14.3
A resource allocation timeline (created using MacProject).

change the length of the work week (e.g., working overtime on weekends) also is needed. This flexibility is required to integrate realism into the schedule and final completion dates. In most instances, it is wishful thinking to believe that time can be made up by working harder. If the original schedule was a good estimate when established, it only can be revised to incorporate any gained knowledge by doing some of the tasks. One means of speeding up a project is to have people work more hours in a fixed time period, such as by working overtime.

The project management system should facilitate data collection on actual workers progress to allow the manager to compare against the plan for control purposes. Once actual work is done and progress reporting takes place, the project management system allows the plans to be revised and rescheduled.

As these changes are made, all affected tasks and resources also are changed. A good project management system allows project managers to ask "what if . . . " questions in establishing and revising the project plans. It allows alternative schedules or personnel assignments to be evaluated. This is where the power of the computer and the project managment software come into play.

The project management system should allow aggregating performance data to provide information for planning the next project. By gathering data on many projects, the manager can become a better estimator, since he or she will have actual information to base estimates on.

The reader should be aware that there are other means of representing network diagrams. The reader of the diagram should pay attention to the notation used. For example, some approaches represent activities or tasks with a line with an arrow. The lines connect to a box or a circle which indicates a point in time when an activity starts or finishes. These moments in time are called *events*.

As can be gathered from the tasks that project managers are asked to perform, there are some real challenges for project managers. A special mix of skills, knowledge, and attitudes is required to become a good project manager. The next section will discuss some of these characteristics.

PROJECT MANAGERS

Project managers must be more than good technicians. In fact, above all, they must be *managers* trained in management skills. The manager must understand planning, organizing, staffing, directing, and controlling. Project managers are responsible for:

Establishing project plans

Monitoring project progress

Reviewing team product review results

Managing requests for changes in the project

The project manager must keep project funders informed of progress. (c. Joel Gordon 1984)

- Assuring that personnel are recording time spent and progress made on the project
- Determining why variances from the plan have taken place (inaccurate estimates, lack of cooperation, "bottleneck-creating" users, not working on an assigned project, etc.)
- Holding project status meetings as part of the process review and planning sessions

Systems development persons may object to having their progress monitored. This is especially true if there is no progress. Projects get behind schedule one day at a time. But with a good plan that is obvious to those who must execute the plan, the project manager can work with the plan executors to accomplish the needed results.

Bander and Giber (see References) have studied what makes a good project manager. They found that excellent project managers:

- Build a shared sense of purpose among the project team. All project team members know the objective of the team.
- Build client and user ownership of the project. The system being developed belongs to the user and the user realizes this fact.
- Involve others in goal setting. It is not the project manager's goals that are being pursued. The excellent project manager does not commit the team to the impossible task.
- Monitor, diagnose, and reestimate. The project is "live" and needs attention and revision.
- Constantly thinks of "what if . . . " situations and plans for contingencies. The manager is concerned with deviations from the plan and consciously thinks of alternate possibilities.
- Perceive themselves as managers and in charge. The manager is not just another worker, but also leads the team when leadership is needed and pitches in when help is needed. He or she understands that responsibility ultimately falls on the manager. Authority can be delegated, but responsibility cannot.
- Exhibit self-confidence and believe in themselves. They know they can do the job.
- Are flexible in approaches and willing to adapt. There is more than one right way. However, at the same time, the manager is consistent and predictable in guidelines, deadlines, and policy.
- Are results-oriented and do not lose sight of objectives. They realize that there is a job to do.
- Are interpersonally astute negotiators and team builders. They realize that people make the difference.

The manager must assign and use the skills of persons available to work on the project. Motivation of workers must be of prime importance.

The project manager must:

Make decisions about items such as personnel assignments

Resolve conflicts between project workers and systems and user personnel

Encourage loyalty and trust by praising in public and criticizing in private

Have technical respect even though the manager may not be technically superior to his or her subordinates

Understand higher management and steering committee perspectives

Project management is not just filling out forms and reprimanding persons who have not met schedules. It requires close scrutiny of not only what is or is not happening, but why, and what one can do about it.

A SUMMARY OF PROJECT MANAGEMENT

Keane, Keane, and Teagan (see References) provide some good principles for systems project management. The principles include:

1. *Define the job in detail:* Know exactly what you will have to do. Determine the project scope and what activities must be done. Specify the deliverables to be produced at each stage of the project. Understand the project characteristics and environment. Establish verification and validation procedures.
2. *Get the right people involved:* Know who can do it. Get the users and management team active in the project. Get the best systems people available on the team. Have involved persons set their own goals.
3. *Estimate time and costs:* Know how long it will take. Develop estimates before starting the task. Estimate each component separately. Avoid premature cost precision. Avoid planning back from a deadline if your resources are fixed. Avoid incomplete estimates.
4. *Use the 80-hour rule:* Manage "manageable" chunks. Break the project into tasks that take 80 or less hours. Each task should have a tangible product or result.
5. *Establish a change procedure:* "A change will mean . . . " Establish and get agreement on a procedure for instituting project changes before starting project. Changes in plans mean changes in budget. The project leader must manage design changes and time and cost changes.
6. *Establish acceptance criteria:* "We know we are done because . . . " Determine in advance what an acceptable system will include. This is where the system objectives from the requirements model will provide guidelines. Systems acceptance is gradual throughout the project, not all at once.

The systems development unit should be sure it doesn't deliver a system before it should be delivered. This is like serving an uncooked meal because someone demanded it meet a deadline.

Not all projects use the classical life cycle development as described earlier in this book. For example, not all projects will use conventional programming and languages such as COBOL, nor will all projects involve a systems professional to conduct the work, nor will all projects do a classical detailed requirements analysis. The next section describes some of the alternatives to the classical means of development.

ALTERNATIVES TO TRADITIONAL DEVELOPMENT METHODS

Before we discuss the topic of alternatives to classical life cycle development, it is necessary to understand one of the primary technologies that has made the alternatives feasible. This phenomenon is the growth and availability of fourth generation languages.

FOURTH GENERATION LANGUAGES: TOOLS FACILITATING ALTERNATIVES TO THE CLASSICAL LIFE CYCLE

Programming languages have evolved through several generations. Popular opinion considers the first generation as machine language (1s and 0s that the machine understands), second generation as assembly language (symbolic representations of machine language), and third generation as high-level procedural languages such as COBOL or FORTRAN. Fourth generation languages (4GLs) are computer programming languages that are nonprocedural, or problem-oriented.

4GLs aid the user in getting at data and manipulating it. The computer must understand the user while earlier generation languages forced the user to understand the computer. The user specifies what is to be done, not how to do it. In essence, the programmer does not write a list of steps to do something, but states what it is that he or she desires. Some popular fourth generation languages include RAMIS, NOMAD, FOCUS, IDEAL, and MANTIS. These languages allow complete development of a program, not just providing some functions such as LOTUS 1-2-3 providing spreadsheet functions, or IFPS providing financial modeling functions.

A true fourth generation language includes:

A good user interface allowing use by both systems professionals and nonprofessionals

A host language interface allowing utilization of routines written in a third generation language such as COBOL

Query facilities in an English-like format

A comprehensive data dictionary allowing description of all data elements and structures in all relevant databases

Accesses and queries of data in other databases without conversion of the established database

Screen design facilities

Facilities to manipulate data such as a report generator and a graphics generator

The 4GL has features of a database management system with the ability to establish links between data elements in different databases. The 4GL user builds a schema of data elements from many different physical files to create a selected subset to manipulate. This allows great flexibility, but there is a high data storage overhead to store all the pointers and links between data.

Since fourth generation languages allow creation of programs with few lines of code, it is necessary to assure that the programs are sound and accurately process the data. As with any powerful tool, the user must exhibit care since larger mistakes can be made more quickly.

Fourth generation languages have allowed some alterations to the classical life cycle methods. But one should not forget that systems development in any form requires a problem solving approach as was discussed in Chapter 2. Programming is only one small part of the development process. Fourth generation languages should not be seen as a substitute for programming without understanding the problem.

One critical aspect of systems development that has been stressed in this book is not only "knowing how," but also "knowing when." The next section will discuss "when" different systems development methods might be used.

CHOOSING A DEVELOPMENT METHOD

Sophistication of development tools and organization members has made possible alternatives to the traditional life cycle method of building systems. Three primary alternatives include:

Packaged software: buying software that will be adapted for use in the organization

User-developed systems: having users develop their own applications without assistance from systems professionals

Prototyped systems: having the user and systems developer build systems using fourth generation languages that will be evaluated and revised in quick iterative cycles

Each of these methods has its place in an organization in the creation of the desired system.

There are a few other options in creating a working system. For an organization that has no current systems function, such as a small start-up company, it may be wise to consider either a turnkey system or a service bureau. A ***turnkey system*** consists of all the hardware, software, and procedures for an operational system. The purchaser only has to "turn the key." Of course, there is little flexibility with how things are done with a turnkey system. A ***service bureau*** will handle an organization's applications for a processing fee. For example, a company can have its payroll done by a service bureau for a fee based on the number of employees. Many organizations begin their processing functions using turnkey systems or service bureaus and take over functions themselves as they become cost-justified and internal expertise is developed.

Gremillion and Pyburn (see References) discuss factors that must be considered when examining alternatives to the traditional methods. The factors include:

Commonality—whether the problem and system requirements are common to a large number of organizations. There are some problems or functions that are common to most organizations. For example, every company has to pay its employees (payroll), pay its bills (accounts payable), and collect bills from other organizations that owe it money (accounts receivable). Great commonality will lead an organization to consider packaged software packages.

Structure—whether it is easy to understand and define the problem and requirements. If there is a low amount of structure, building a prototype of a system may be an aid in requirements definition.

Impact—whether the problem affects the whole company or has strategic implications for the company. Problems with little impact affect only a few people and would not affect the company if the system failed. If there is little impact, the application may be developed by users with little intervention from the systems development units. If there is great impact, the systems development unit should be involved and use either traditional life cycle, packages, or prototyping methods.

Figure 14.4 exhibits the three factors affecting choice of a systems development method.

Another consideration in deciding on an approach is advocated by Linder (see References). Linder contrasts the needs of two contrasting types of organizations, one youthful and growth-oriented, and another mature and control-oriented. She feels that a growth-oriented company that does not have established procedures and policies may be better off adapting to the procedures of a service bureau or packaged software for standard applications. The older, more traditional organization may be more suited to an approach like the one suggested by Gremillion and Pyburn.

Many organizations may decide to use a software package if they currently do not have a programming staff. Even if a staff exists, there may not be needed expertise to develop certain kinds of applications. In that case, it may be wise to investigate software purchase. This topic will be explored later in the chapter.

The greatest choice in systems development is whether to use a traditional technique such as the development life cycle with packaged or

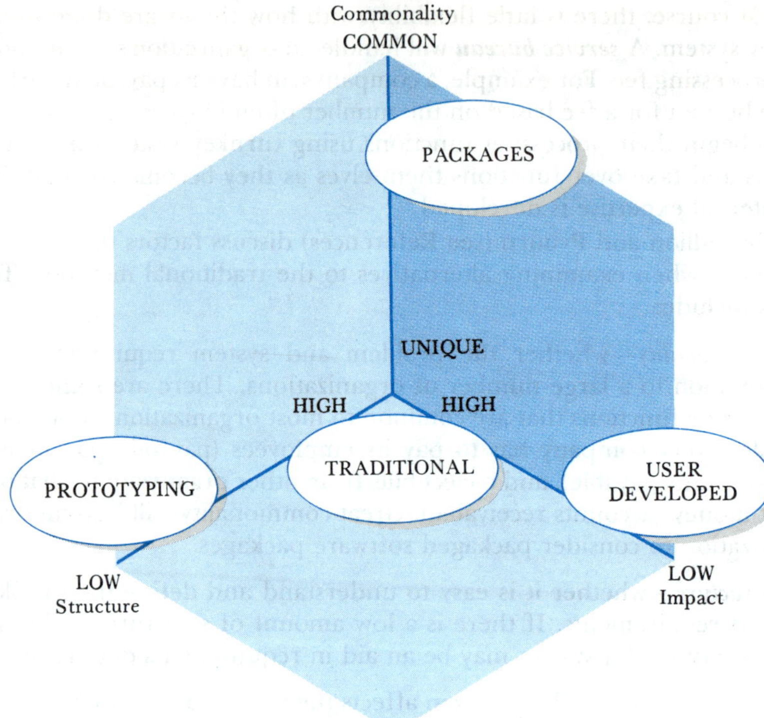

FIGURE 14.4

Project characteristics and suggested development methods.

custom-built software, or whether to use a more radical approach such as prototyping or user-developed systems.

The traditional approaches are best if:

There are multiple users.

The project is large and complex.

The problem cannot easily be partitioned or decomposed into smaller segments.

There is a fixed set of definable development activities.

Users want an early cost estimate and a contractual agreement.

The traditional approaches are bad if:

Users are unsure of requirements.

The project is simple with one time usage.

The traditional approaches allow discussion and consensus among multiple users for large projects which are hard to manage. But the overhead of using the traditional approaches is high since there is a systematic sequence of steps to be followed to assure a system with integrity is built. If this integrity is not essential, it may be more beneficial to use an approach such as prototyping.

An approach such as prototyping or user-developed systems is best if:

It is hard to define requirements for the system.

System efficiency and performance is not important.

There is a great deal of user–machine interaction and dialog.

Prototyping or user developed systems are not good if:

The hardware, software, and data environment to use the approach does not exist.

The key user is not committed to the project (of course, this can be a detriment to any development effort).

Systems have high impact and would receive widespread use in the organization.

The following table summarizes some guidelines for choosing between the two general categories of development. Using the alternative development methods will be discussed in the next sections.

FACTORS DETERMINING DEVELOPMENT METHODS

Tend to Life Cycle or Packages if:	*Tend to Prototyping or User-Developed if:*
Many users	One user
Batch-oriented	Interactive
Many other systems interfaces	Few system interfaces
Large size project	Small size project
Little output with much processing (scientific application)	Much output
Third generation development environment	Fourth generation environment

PACKAGED SOFTWARE

Buying a software package from a commercial vendor may be a viable alternative in systems development. Widespread availability of software packages has been a reason for the growth of microcomputers, but it also applies to large computer environments. The seller of the software assumes the high development costs with the intention of selling a large number of the packages at a fraction of the actual development cost.

Cost is a primary consideration in buying a package. It is often cheaper to buy a package than to develop custom software. Having multiple users of a single package not only reduces development costs, but saves on maintenance costs as well. Vendors can spread maintenance costs over many users.

Purchasers of packages should be aware that there are great costs beyond the purchase price of the software. Some purchasers have found that a rule of thumb may be to spend two or three times the package cost for installation and implementation. These costs result from software modification, human procedure modification, training, and management of organizational change.

Organizations purchasing a package must realize that a requirements definition must be done before vendors are approached. This means development of a logical model to clearly understand what processes, data storage and data movements are needed. A requirements model must be developed to understand both systems objectives like hardware/systems software constraints and desired outputs. Unless needs are carefully spelled out, it is like shopping for a car without knowing what roads you will be driving, under what conditions, how often, and what your personal desires are (low cost or luxury?).

The logical and requirements models must have as much detail as those for software developed in-house, especially for mature organizations where current methods are well established. In the long run, a mature organization may find it easier to adapt the package to fit the organization than to adapt the organization to fit the package. Organization change comes at a high cost, especially if there is resistance.

The major challenge in packaged software acquisition is to match actual needs with a package that will satisfy these needs at the lowest total cost. There must be a detailed specification of what the software package must be able to do. For example, will the package allow online updating while a batch run such as check writing is taking place? If these discoveries are made after acquisition and installation, major modifications may have to be made or the package may even have to be abandoned.

Criteria for Packaged Software Selection

Criteria for packaged software should include:

A fit with the current installation environment including hardware, operating system, storage, interface requirements, and database links.

Performance of package including speed and amount of storage needed.

A solid architecture which may include an evaluation of things like modularity, cohesiveness of modules, and coupling between modules if changes must be made to the source code.

Documentation content to allow both using and changing the software.

Documentation organization to assure that material is not only in the documentation, but can be found when needed. Some vendor documentation is not even indexed.

A solid vendor reputation, including length of time in business, support staff, support hours, support staff location, and responsiveness.

Vendor ability to make needed modifications or to allow purchaser enhancement.

Installation aid and training provided by vendor.

Guarantees offered by vendors, especially if the package is changed by the purchaser.

Update policy and charges.

Often, vendors will not allow the purchaser to obtain source code that can be modified. The vendor will only provide object code to operate on specified hardware and systems software. The purchaser should be aware that any changes to the package must be done by the vendor at an added charge. Some organizations have contracted to have original source code held in escrow, such as in a safe deposit box, to be opened if the vendor goes out of business.

Some vendors will furnish source code, but will not allow changes to be made to the programs or modules. Making changes can result in legal action or can void any contracted vendor support. Some organizations have gotten around this problem by insertions or additions of program code that will add functionality.

Another approach is parameterization. This means that package users can select features by setting parameters. For example, a two-digit state code can be the parameter to select which state payrolls are needed or depreciation type is set by parameters such as an SL code for straight line, or DDB for double declining balance. In these cases, it is critical to understand what the vendor is both offering and supporting.

When evaluating a package, user involvement is critical. Users should review inputs and forms to be sure they will fit in the application. Report and screen users should carefully study outputs from different packages to be clear what they will be getting with any potential purchase.

Purchasers should be aware that vendors often advertise software that is not fully developed. This software that exists only in promotional materials or in verbal presentations is called *vaporware*.Some vaporware has never reached a developed state. Likewise, purchasers should use caution when vendors talk about future software or software versions that are currently being tested. *Alpha tests* are done within the vendor's organization. *Beta tests* are done in organizations other than the vendor's, on a limited distribution test basis. Some have called this software *betaware*. Betaware has not always made it to market. Thus, purchaser's must make sure they are not buying some salesperson's promise.

Modifying the Life Cycle to Accommodate Package Acquisition

Software acquisition should follow the classical problem-solving life cycle as mentioned in earlier chapters of the book. The major modification to the life cycle is that the actual program coding is not done from scratch. However, a major portion of the life cycle remains the same. This means following the processes discussed earlier.

Process 1—Conduct Initial Study. The initial study results will determine whether the project is feasible. The study may reveal that the application is one with high structure and great commonality, which would suggest an examination of software packages in later phases of the project.

Process 2—Analyze Current System. This process will determine:

- Who the audience will be and if they are in one location or distributed
- What must be done (desired functionality)
- What data must be used
- Why the system is needed in business terms
- What constraints must be met such as the hardware and systems software environment
- What system tactics allow reaching system objectives

In general, requirements developed at this stage will be used to determine if proposed solutions may be appropriate. The solutions could include purchased software.

Process 3—Propose Systems Solutions. At this stage, some preliminary solutions are proposed to meet different sets of objectives. If the solutions include acquiring packaged software, the developers must generate a list of packages that might provide solutions. A preliminary screening of packaged software is done based on literature, vendor reputation, and features.

Process 4—Detail Chosen Solution. This process is where the primary tasks of acquiring the packaged software take place. Process 4.4, discussed in Chapter 8, is dedicated to selecting application software.

The development team must compare needed functions to package features. Vendors may be contacted for more information. This can be done informally, or more formally with a request for proposal. Care should be taken in dealing with vendors. The purchaser should be demanding enough to get the data needed to make a comparison, but not so demanding that the best vendors are driven off. One must remember that it is costly for a vendor to respond to a request from a potential purchaser.

Once all data is collected, the development team must select a vendor. This is often done using a weighted point technique. An example of such an approach would consist of the following steps:

- Segmenting selection criteria into measurable subcriteria
- Weighting each subcriterion from 1 to 5 in terms of importance
- Rating each subcriterion from 1 to 5 for each package
- Multiplying the weight times the rating for each subcriterion to get a score
- Considering minimum threshold scores for any subcriterion
- Tallying total points for each package and determining significant competitors

Dividing package cost by total points for the package to get a value index

Analyzing and making a decision based on above collected data

Finally, any contractual agreements are made with the chosen vendor.

Process 5—Design New Physical System. The environment needed to support the package is designed at this time. This includes design of the human subsystem, including procedures, training, and input/output layouts. The design of the hardware and systems software environment is established as well as design of the needed data structures and conversion routines. A design is established for any software package modifications.

Process 6—Construct New System. Once the hardware environment is established, delivery and installation of the software package is next. The package may have to be modified, either before or following installation. Test data and procedures are established. Human materials are written and training plans are implemented. Testing is done with both the software and the human subsystem.

Process 7—Install and Monitor System. The system is now put into the organizational environment and monitored. The package is certified and approved by relevant organizational units such as operations, quality assurance, auditing, and maintenance units. It is necessary to be in touch with vendors to obtain updates and revisions to the package.

Information on packaged software was discussed in earlier chapters. This information can be obtained from vendors, current users, competing vendors, user groups—especially a product change request subgroup, or trade associations such as bankers' associations for software used in that environment. When making a substantial acquisition, it may be of great value not only to telephone other sites, but also to make site visits. People may be more candid in person and you can actually see the package in action.

From review of the above approach, it can be seen that packaged software acquisition takes a great deal of the systems professional's time. If that time is not available, users may resort to other means, such as developing the system themselves.

USER-DEVELOPED SYSTEMS

Users who have been anxious to have a system developed quickly have often turned to themselves as developers. Users have created systems on personal computers, have made retrievals from a database, or acquired and installed packaged software. Users can program in a procedure-oriented language such as BASIC, FORTRAN, or PASCAL; can use aids such as a spreadsheet or a modeling package; use a fourth generation or query language in conjunction with a database management package; or use a report writer.

Some advantages of user developed systems include:

Systems development starts when the users want it to. There is no wait for systems developers' time to free up.

Reduced development time since there are few communication difficulties. There is more action and less talk since the user understands the problem or opportunity.

Satisfaction with the results is greater since users produce the systems themselves. There is great likelihood that the system will meet the users' needs.

No overhead for training or implementation since the users accept the system they develop and are intimately familiar with the system.

Immediate attention to any maintenance or enhancement needs.

Users clearly understand their needs, can satisfy them, and can take great pride in their own accomplishments.

Along with the advantages of this approach are some disadvantages, including:

Inefficient use of human resources since users likely were not hired for their systems development skills

Inefficient use of computing resources and a real challenge to provide capacity for all users

Questionable controls and security measures

Little documentation which makes transferability unlikely to other persons who may benefit

Users have often produced systems without help from systems professionals, which has been a mixed blessing for information systems managers who do not have to commit the resources to build the system but who later are asked to maintain or enhance a system that may have little documentation or that followed few standards. The systems could suffer from the use of solid systems integrity and maintenance. The user must assure that the system is using correct inputs, does processing correctly, and that outputs are correct and reliable.

The key to making the most of the advantages of user-developed systems, and avoiding the disadvantages, is to carefully manage the process. Factors that must be managed when end users engage in systems building include:

Documentation—if the organization is dependent on the system in any way, the system must go beyond being a personal system. Documentation must be provided for others to continue using the system.

Validation—both input and output must be certified as correct. Verification of processing routines must be done to make sure the results are not being improperly altered.

Back-up—data that the company relies on must be backed up by the person altering the data. A specified backup cycle must be established and enforced.

Recovery—if the system malfunctions, there must be a means for reestablishing the data and restoring the system to the previous condition.

Resource Usage—the system must be protected from unwise use of corporate computing and storage resources.

Inconsistency of Data—the system must have a means of verifying that redundant data is consistent.

The systems development unit can have a role in aiding users. There should be a spirit of helping, not controlling. One approach is through the use of an organizational unit created to aid users who want to develop their own systems. These units are called *information centers.*

The information center is a physical location managed by the information systems unit that assists users in "growing their own" systems or getting the information they need. The information center personnel are MIS department members who help users access or obtain data and use "friendly" software to satisfy their own needs. Access may come through terminals to a mainframe or through microcomputers where software such as spreadsheets can be used to manipulate the data. Information center personnel may help users acquire microcomputers to use within the user departments or even at home.

Maintaining data integrity can be managed through the information center. Information center personnel can assist users in acquiring "downloaded" data from corporate databases and ascertaining that this data is correct and fresh. The personnel also can manage any "uploads" that users want to do to corporate databases.

The systems development unit must attempt to establish harmony with users involved in development, and manage, not control them. Experienced information systems managers know that users will find ways around rules they feel are burdensome.

Another alternative systems development method, *prototyping*, requires close relationships between users and developers. Prototyping is an alternative to user-developed systems that calls on the strengths of both users and developers.

PROTOTYPING*

Prototyping is a method for developing systems that requires a new philosophy or set of beliefs about systems development. Systems are built rapidly and are enhanced and changed as they are used until the system satisfies users. The method resembles engineering approaches to systems design, where a physical model of a system is built to allow user reaction. The user

*Much of this section is based on the work of Jenkins (see References).

exercises versions of the system to understand and refine his or her needs. Prototyping calls for a less rigorous requirements definition. Since users may not be able to define requirements, the assumption is made that by giving them some physical results to react to, they will be able "zero in" on what they would find useful.

The thoroughness of the life cycle approach is traded for quick developer action and increased user reaction. The analysis, design, and implementation is rapidly done, with the goal of delivering a working physical model of the system for users to try and then suggest changes. Iteration of this rapid development is planned, since the intention is to refine user needs with many versions of a working system, each coming closer to what the user really wants.

Prototyping fits well with the life style of a critic. In fact, Jenkins states that prototyping is "based on one simple proposition: users can point to features they don't like about an existing system (or indicate when a feature is missing) more easily than they can describe what they think they would like in an imaginary system" (Jenkins, p. 2).

Prototyping allows reality testing. In essence, prototyping is based on the premise that people have trouble putting themselves into a "future state" and trying to imagine what the future would be like.

Many persons attempting to find an ideal microcomputer package for an application such as word processing may be unconsciously prototyping. They buy a reasonable, but low-priced, package with the intention of examining what the features are and whether they are important to them. By using such a package, the persons will more clearly understand their needs and be able to specify a package that suits them best.

A corporate information center provides help in accessing data and in finding or adapting software to meet users' needs. (Innervisions and courtesy The Computer Studio)

One should be sure what is meant when hearing the word "prototyping" since it can mean different things to different people. There are different degrees or levels of prototyping. One degree is that the *output only* is created in a mock-up screen or report. For example, screens are shown to users who can react to them, but the screens were not created with actual data from a database. This approach also is called *heuristic development.*

Another level of prototyping is using a fourth generation language to actually create a working system using representative and "live" data. This type of prototyping leverages modern software tools and decreasing costs of hardware.

Roles in Prototyping

Prototyping is most ideal with one user and one developer. This eliminates the multiple communication channels which hinder full communication. Jenkins makes the point that the constant user interaction places the user in the role of designer and the developer in the role of builder. The user/designer sets the tempo of the development process. The user drives the process of prototyping with his or her reaction to the prototype version. The user cannot just sit back and observe. An active role is critical or the process will stop. The user is rewarded for finding deficiencies in the system. After all, they are criticizing of their own design, not the developer/builder's.

In prototyping, the user:

Must be the key user and not a substitute such as the key user's subordinates.

Is competent in his or her functional area.

Must approach the MIS organization with the desire to develop a prototype.

Sets the tempo and pace of development.

Has a greater role in project success than in a life cycle approach.

Is rewarded for criticism and suggestions for improvement.

Must operate ("drive") the prototype rather than observing someone else operate it.

The user must not only request the system, but must be willing to commit time and energy to work with the builder.

The builder has new roles. Speed is essential once a new "design" is specified. More iterations lead to a closer approximation to what is desired. The builder must be willing to "throw one away", which could also mean that more than one will be thrown away due to the iteration process.
The builder of the prototype:

Has access to a modern program development environment and database management tools and experience in using them.

Uses "brute force computing" with fourth generation languages, rather than finesse, if needed to deliver the prototype quickly.

Consciously leaves out security, documentation, backup, etc., to quickly deliver early versions of the prototype. (Of course, these considerations are not forgotten, only delayed.)

Must explain the prototyping process to the user before any prototypes are built. This briefing must be clear about the iterative nature of prototyping and that the prototype is not done until integrity and documentation features are completed.

Must ensure project scope does not change a great deal without a budget revision.

The developer must have special skills including fourth generation language skills and database usage skills. The developer must be aware of the data resources of the organization.

There may be more than one potential user if the system has a wide boundary. In this case it may be wise to attempt to decompose the system and develop a prototype for each subsystem. Another possibility is to sequentially take one user at a time and build a prototype. This approach must be compared with working with several users at one time. The tradeoffs may not be clear, but generally, the one-user/one-builder approach is desirable to reduce communication and negotiation.

If one builder does not have the expertise to build the prototype, another builder may have to be involved. The decision must be made whether all the builders will interact with the user or if the additional builders merely act as consultants to the primary builder.

Prototyping should not be used if the builder does not understand prototyping tools or technology, if data resources and software resources are not well managed, or if the user is not willing to spend time on the project.

The Prototyping Process

Prototyping cannot be done in a haphazard fashion. There must be a certain routinization of the basic problem-solving process that was mentioned in Chapter 2. In fact, some persons believe that prototyping needs rigor and have felt there was a prototyping "life cycle." This has been referred to as *protocycling*.

According to Jenkins, prototyping has four main steps:

1. *Identify the user's basic information requirements.* This step is intended to capture the essential needs of the user. The process should not take more than a few hours. One or two meetings are held to introduce the prototyping process, capture desired features of the prototype, identify data elements needed, determine data availability, and estimate costs which are based on system scope and degree of uncertainty of the requirements. The builder must be careful to avoid computer jargon and keep initial requirements as simple as possible.

2. *Develop a working prototype system.* The builder will use a modern hardware and software environment to create a working system very quickly. The database must be designed, models must be built, the database must be loaded, menus and dialogs created, and programs written. The ideal is to develop the initial prototype in a matter of hours, not days. Some "semi-instant" results should be readied for the user. The goal of this step is to create the essential processes and outputs quickly without focusing on a finished system that operates with efficiency.
3. *Use the prototype and refine user requirements.* This step includes delivery, training, operation, and use of the developed prototype, and obtaining the user's reaction. The user works with the system for as long as he or she desires and records likes, dislikes, and desired additions. The user is in control of this step and must contact the builder if changes are desired. This could take place at the delivery or could come after a period of use. The builder should be elated if the user does ask for changes, since this indicates a continued interest. The user decides if another iteration of the prototype is needed or if the prototying will end at this step.
4. *Revise and enhance the prototype system.* The builder changes the prototype to better suit the user's requirements. This could mean changes to the programs, database, or dialogs. The changes should be made rapidly, and hopefully will not take more than a few days. The builder should not fix anything the user does not request, should use modules and reusable code as much as possible, and not change the scope of the system without an appropriate change in budget.

Steps 3 and 4 are repeated as often as necessary to satisfy the user. Jenkins says five iterations is not unusual before a satisfactory result is achieved.

When a prototype is delivered there is installation, training, and use of the prototype. This interaction aids in refining the system. Change is planned for, not avoided. Use determines both desired and undesired characteristics, which leads to refinement.

The Prototyping Environment

Prototyping is only appropriate in certain situations. The prototyping project is typically a small project where data already exists and is managed so it is retrievable, the system will be used infrequently and irregularly, and the user is unsure of what he or she really needs. Jenkins mentions that a small project would have 30 or less output screens, with four or five being desirable, and not more than 50 data elements. The user typically wants the system delivered in a short period of time. Decision support systems fit many of these requirements.

Prototyping is similar to version implementation mentioned in Chapter 13. Both work toward delivering a series of more complete and more correct products. Both require active user participation. However, there are some differences. Prototyping employs modern technologic aids to develop the product. Systems prototyping is best suited for infrequently and irregularly used systems for one user. The product from prototyping is delivered in hours, not weeks.

Prototyping depends on a number of factors:

The data needed to run the prototype must exist.

The data must be available in an organized database format.

The software environment to create prototypes quickly must exist.

The software environment is critical in prototyping. The environment would include:

An active data dictionary and directory that describe entities such as data elements and structures. The data dictionary is a catalog of what data exists and where.

A database management system should exist with capability for data modeling, updating, and security handling. The database management system should be integrated with the data dictionary.

A nonprocedural fourth generation language to allow quick generation of programs.

A query language with English-like commands for retrievals, accesses, queries, and manipulations such as statistical summarizing. The query language should have many defaults for simple operation and should have some capability for parameter-driven operation. The language should be integrated with the data dictionary and database management system.

Report generators and screen generators and painters to lay out reports on a screen.

Statistical capabilities beyond simple operations within the query language.

Graphics capabilities to display outputs in many forms.

Simulation capabilities to allow generation of simulation models.

Editing routines to allow quick checking of inputs of data.

As can be seen, this is a sophisticated environment that does not exist in all organizations.

Why Does Prototyping Work?

Prototyping works for a number of reasons. One reason is that harmony is created between users and developers. Each has an opportunity to use his or her strengths. There is no power struggle and both parties can win. No one person holds the key to success, everyone holds a part of it.

Creative solutions are encouraged by prototyping. The team does not make a huge time investment to "try something." Real working models encourage reaction and comment, with all the senses brought into play.

A short development period keeps up interest. There is a great deal of intensity for a short period of time. There is a single, short-term goal, with a focus on results. It is like sprinting—you cover a lot of ground, but only for a period of time.

What Happens to the Developed Prototype?

There are several disposition possibilities with a completed prototype. These possibilities include:

Throw it away after using it for a specific task. Once the prototype serves its purpose, it is disposed of.

Use it "as is" in the future. This should only be done after examining the impact of the use of the prototype. For example, if the prototype influences a large part of the organization, it may be necessary to document the system, write cautions on its use, and establish any necessary controls. Or it may be necessary to build a production system.

Use it to define requirements and then build a production system. The production system is built to gain greater efficiency. The prototype may replace the requirements definition phase of development since systems objectives and tactics should be clear from the developed prototype. Since the user has an active role in the development, the business tactics and objectives should be obvious to the user.

Use it as a basis for further prototypes. The prototype may be usable, but also may serve as a model for further prototyping work which may expand the system capabilities or the number and types of users. The basic prototype can serve as a demonstration device to garner further resources.

The disposition of the prototype depends on several factors, including:

Amount of change in the work environment. If there is a great deal of change, it is best to discard the prototype after it serves its usefulness and create new prototypes as needs arise.

Amount of user turnover. If the original user changes jobs and no longer requires the system, it may be best to discard the prototype.

Life expectancy of the system. If the system will be used repetitively over time, it may be wise to keep the prototype and modify it or to turn it into a production system.

Frequency of use. If the prototype receives frequent use, it may be wise to rewrite it to operate more efficiently.

Integration with other systems. If the prototype must be integrated with other systems, it may be best to redevelop the system as a production system with needed controls and documentation.

Cautions with Prototyping

Prototyping should only be used under the right conditions. As mentioned earlier, the type of project makes a big difference in choosing when to prototype. But there are other considerations as well.

Users must understand the prototyping philosophy and method. If users are familiar with the classical life cycle approach, they will not understand their role in the prototype development process. They must realize that they are in the driver's seat. They must know what outputs they will be receiving and what they should be doing with them. Users must understand that just because the system provides output, it does not mean that it is completed. Documentation and integrity measures may need to be taken.

Developers also must be trained in prototyping methods and in use of technologic tools such as fourth generation languages, screen painters, and database management. Developers also must be familiar with the organization's data resources and other external sources of data.

Overall, prototyping can be a powerful addition to the systems development environment, but it must only be used when appropriate and then managed carefully.

SUMMARY

For successful systems development, a project *must* be managed. Development tasks must be done in a planned and controlled environment. This environment is created by having real leaders of systems development teams. Without leadership, a team will flounder and lose sight of its goals. Although students of systems development will not likely move into a management position in an initial job, they should keep in mind that they can have influence by aiding their systems development group in managing projects they work on.

Good management begins by not being rigid in the way systems are developed. Alternatives to the classical life cycle can be suggested and evaluated to ensure they are used in the appropriate situations and in an appropriate way.

Above all, all of us who are students of systems development must learn from the mistakes of others and from those we make ourselves. This is the real key to building systems development experience.

REFERENCES AND FURTHER READINGS

Bander, Diana O., and David J. Giber. "In Search of the Excellent Project Manager," *Data Training,* January 1985, pp. 14–15+.

Benbasat, Izak, and Iris Vessey. "Programmer and Analyst Time/Cost Estimation," *MIS Quarterly,* June 1980, pp. 31–43.

Brooks, F. P., Jr. *The Mythical Man-Month: Essays on Software Engineering,* Reading, MA: Addison-Wesley, 1975.

Cleland, David I., and William R. King. *Systems Analysis and Project Management,* 3d ed. New York: McGraw-Hill Book Company, 1983.

Davis, Gordon B. "Caution: User Developed Systems May Be Hazardous to Your Organization," *Proceedings of the 17th Annual Hawaii Conference on Systems Science,* January 1982.

DeMarco, Tom. *Structured Analysis and System Specification,* New York: Yourdon Press, 1978, pp. 336–339.

Gremillion, Lee L., and Philip Pyburn. "Breaking the Systems Development Bottleneck," *Harvard Business Review,* March–April 1983, pp. 130–137.

Jenkins, A. Milton. "Prototyping: A Methodology for the Design and Development of Application Systems," *SIM Spectrum,* vol. 2, no. 2, April 1985, pp. 1–8.

Jones, Capers. "Function-Point Metrics: Key to Improved Productivity," *Information Week,* February 23, 1987, pp. 26–27.

Keane, John F., Marilyn Keane, and Mark Teagan. *Productivity Management in the Development of Computer Applications,* Englewood Cliffs, NJ: Prentice-Hall, Inc., 1984.

Kidder, Tracy. *The Soul of a New Machine,* Boston: Little, Brown and Company, 1981.

Klinger, Daniel E. "Rapid Prototyping Revisited," *Datamation,* October 15, 1986, pp. 131–132.

Lee, Alan F. "Why Prototyping Works," *Infosystems,* vol. 32, no. 3, March 1985, pp. 88-89.

Linder, Jane C. "Avoiding Information Systems Failures," *Infosystems,* October 1984, pp. 98–100.

Metzger, Philip W. *Managing a Programming Project,* Englewood Cliffs, NJ: Prentice-Hall, Inc., 1981.

Snyders, Jan. "In Search of a 4th Generation Language," *Infosystems,* October 1984, pp. 28–32.

———. "The Architectural Plan," *Infosystems,* November 1984, pp. 66–70.

"The Information Center," INFORUM Column, *Infosystems,* November 1984, pp. 36–38.

Sweet, Frank. "Milestone Management," *Datamation,* October 15, 1986, pp. 107–108+.

Systems, E. Z., as told to Ken Orr. *The One Minute Methodology.* Topeka, KS: Ken Orr and Associates, Inc., 1984.

REVIEW QUESTIONS

1. What things must project managers manage?
2. Why are plans so important to project management?
3. Who should establish project plans? Why?
4. Who should approve project plans?
5. What are milestones? Why are milestones never 90 percent done?

6. Why must project plans constantly be revised?
7. What role does a systems development methodology play in establishing project plans?
8. Not all tasks in a systems development methodology are performed for each project. Why?
9. Why are estimates made in systems development projects inaccurate?
10. Why might "man-months" be mythical?
11. Why might a project manager use caution when attempting to speedup a project by adding people?
12. What factors should be considered when making estimates?
13. What are "function points"?
14. What is a critical path in terms of a project network?
15. What advantages would an automated project management software package provide?
16. What is the "80-hour rule"?
17. What is a turnkey system? When should it be considered?
18. What are three factors that Gremillion and Pyburn propose as influencing choice of a development method?
19. Why is it important to know if a vendor furnishes source code when purchasing a software package?
20. What is "vaporware"? "Betaware"?
21. What are some disadvantages of users developing systems?
22. What factors must be managed when users do the systems building?
23. What is an information center?
24. What is the difference between heuristic development and prototyping?
25. When should prototyping be considered for a development project?
26. Why is the user considered the designer when doing prototyping?
27. What are the requirements for the user when prototyping is used?
28. What hardware and software capabilities are needed to do prototyping?
29. What can be done with a completed prototype?

DISCUSSION QUESTIONS

1. Ted is a systems project manager. He says that workers who are assigned to his projects never like the plans and estimates he establishes. He asks you what he might do differently to get people to accept the plans. What will you tell him?
2. DeMarco states that when someone is responsible for a project, they lose the ability to make good estimates. Do you believe this is true? Why?

3. Does a project manager have to be an excellent technician? Why or why not?
4. Some persons feel acquiring software packages is a systems development methodology? What do you think.
5. Why might prototyping be liked by a person who does not like to do systems analysis? Are there any cautions that should be taken if this is the case?
6. The Widgets Company just acquired a copy of a personal computer-based "fourth generation language." Next week the systems group plans to send out an announcement to all potential users that the group is ready to prototype some systems. What do you think will happen?
7. Jack Murray, a forceful vice-president of finance at the Artful Crafts Company, desires a new financial planning model. The company has the environment and personnel for prototyping. They have had several successful prototyping projects. Jack says he does not have time to be involved with the project, yet he is the primary user. How would you handle this situation?
8. A consulting company president said she recently turned down a potential contract with a client. The client had wanted a fixed-price contract for a project. This meant that the consulting company would have to accurately project their costs. The president said the potential client heard prototyping was a good means of developing systems and wanted to be sure the company would use prototyping on the project. What was the inconsistency in the potential client's desires that led the consulting company to turn down the contract?

EXERCISES

1. DeMarco in Chapter 14's beginning quote makes some claims about poor performance in systems development projects. Find his book and explore some reasons DeMarco believes cause this poor performance.
2. Find a real project manager and ask him or her how project management is done in his or her organization. Be sure to ask how tasks are determined for each project, how estimates are determined, and who does project planning and estimates.
3. Investigate a project management software package. Does it operate similarly to the one described in this chapter? What criteria might be used to judge such a package?
4. Review the literature for a language that claims to be a fourth generation language. Does it have the capabilities of fourth generation languages discussed in this chapter?

CHAPTER 15

Future Directions in Systems Development

"I do find the future of interest. After all, I must live in it."
Source Unknown

CHAPTER OBJECTIVES

You should be able to:

- Identify the environment and challenges you will face as a systems analyst
- Predict some directions for systems development in the future
- Find sources of future learning about systems development
- Specify characteristics of a well-prepared systems developer

THIS CHAPTER MAKES predictions about the future of systems development, including changes to the systems development environment, activities, and applications. The future roles of people involved in systems development are discussed. Tools to aid systems developers are introduced, including computer-assisted software engineering (CASE) tools and systems generators/regenerators. The need to continue to learn about systems development is discussed. Finally, the challenge of change by systems developers is presented.

Writing about the future is a real challenge. After all, the present has come so quickly. The advances in technology and development of new methods and approaches to systems development have come at a rapid rate. These indeed are exciting and challenging times.

This chapter will discuss the future and make some forecasts with regard to changes in:

Environments in which systems will be developed—the setting of systems development

Activities of systems development—how the work will be done

Applications—what will be worked on

Developers—who will perform systems development

Tools—assistance that will be provided for developers

Your own future will depend on your ability to continue to learn about systems development. This chapter offers some sources so you can continue your learning. Characteristics of a good systems developer are presented. Finally, the chapter will present some views of change in systems development and how you can help shape the systems development future.

SYSTEMS DEVELOPMENT IN THE FUTURE

Writing, rather than talking, about the future leaves one with a record to compare with actuality when the future becomes the present. Forecasts should not only stimulate readers to think about the future, but to shape it. We must remember that we not only will live in the future, but can influence it.

THE SYSTEMS DEVELOPMENT ENVIRONMENT

The environment of systems development will be rapidly changing. There will be a "new world" in which to conduct systems development. A major factor is that the cost of personnel will grow while the cost of hardware and technology will continue to decrease tremendously. Computer power has become more widely available and will become even more ubiquitous. This will give rise to many more applications of technology that once would not have been cost-effective. Along with these changes will come challenges.

Changing Objectives

At one time, systems developers were predominately programmers, and systems with superb performance were their primary objectives. In fact, with machines that were slow and had limited memory by today's standards, it was necessary to seek out every bit of performance and attain efficient storage from the scarce and costly hardware. Performance objectives will still be important, but will be only one of the many objectives that must be considered in the future. This leads us to some realizations.

First, the future will bring an increased emphasis on getting a real payoff from developed systems. A superbly running system that minimizes run times and storage but is not used has a value of zero to the users and to the organization. Such a system is a great solution to a "nonproblem." Developers must avoid this situation by making sure they are solving the right problem. Effectiveness or doing the right things will be as important as efficiency or doing things right. Thus, the future will bring increased emphasis on defining and meeting business objectives as well as assuring that the system meets its performance objectives.

Second, changeability of systems will receive increased emphasis in the future. This will be due to the increasing volatility of the business environment. Systems of the future may sacrifice performance for the ability to respond to change. Of course, there still will be applications where system performance is critical, such as in online real-time airline reservation systems or other systems where response time is critical. The developer of the future will have maintenance in mind when building a system.

The development environment will require systems that will meet the users' needs, are easy to maintain, and have adequate internal control and performance. Performance alone will be not enough to have a successful system.

Greater Dispersion of Computing Power and Data

Departmental computing, where each functional area can afford computer power once only available to the entire organization, will change systems development. Each department or functional area may have a systems development unit specializing in specific areas of development. This dispersion of computing and development power will mean an even greater challenge to manage the lifeblood of an organization—the data. Better documentation of data existence and usage will be needed as data becomes more dispersed.

More Persons Who Perceive They Understand Systems

Systems developers and projects they work on will be more closely scrutinized. Many more persons will be knowledgeable about technology and its use. Some persons will in fact have real knowledge, while others will know only enough "to be dangerous." Systems developers will have to answer to an increasing number of persons who will feel they understand the work of systems development better than the professional developers.

New Government Rulings

The government also will have an effect on the systems area. A factor that cannot be ignored is the recent tax reform law that will change the incentives for investment in technologic solutions. Equipment acquisition will have to be approached more carefully since tax writeoffs for technology investments will not be as prevalent in the future.

New laws about privacy will appear in the future. Data is being stored in more and more places, becoming more accessible, and is easier to manipulate, which will cause concern about data usage. The developer must respect any privacy concerns when creating systems.

Liability of developers will be a concern in the future. If a system provides misinformation that an organization bases its future on, the developer may have a lawsuit on his or her hands. Systems must do what they are supposed to do and developers will be asked for product guarantees which will protect users of a system.

The systems developer of the future must have widespread knowledge or consult with experts to keep informed about government actions that affect systems development activities.

"Disappearing" Vendors of Technology

Within the technology environment, vendor existence is very volatile. Mergers and acquisitions will continue to change who will remain in the hardware and software industry. More vendors may disappear, leaving organizations with purchased products which no longer will be supported. If the trend of takeovers in the 1980s continues, long-term vendor support will be difficult to find. This will make system maintenance more difficult when there is dependence on any outside vendors.

Systems developers who must evaluate and purchase services and products must be aware of the potential changes in the technology industry as a whole. Industrial forces having tremendous effect on acquisition of technologic services can best be evidenced by the changes in the communications industry since the AT&T divestiture. There once was one predominate vendor in the communications industry. Now, there are numerous competing factions, making acquisition of communication services a complex task.

Now that we have some idea of the systems development environment in the future, we must try to understand how development work will change in the future.

SYSTEMS DEVELOPMENT ACTIVITIES—HOW WILL WORK BE DONE?

Currently, systems development is more of an art or craft than a science (see Grant). Artists and craftspeople have certain characteristics. Think of painters or potters. The following may describe their work:

> They treat each work as a unique application. They do not want to mass produce results.
>
> There are no measurable standards of quality. Much beauty is in "the eye of the beholder."
>
> Artists or craftspersons are possessive and proud, as is indicated by signatures on their works. There are no serial numbers as on mass-produced products.
>
> Artists self-manage themselves and act very independently, rather

than having formal management which would establish a plan and control via the plan.

The work "is done when it is done." There are few schedules or timetables.

The artist must be inspired to get results. He or she cannot "force" a work of art.

There is no formal training that will assure good artists—style only evolves over time.

An artist or craftsperson often learns by serving as an apprentice.

Artists know and build the entire product.

Systems developers in the past have had many of the characteristics of artists or craftspersons. They are very independent and do not follow a defined method, but "go with the flow." They treat every application as unique. Many developers have learned by watching others and still "cobble" a product together.

In the future, systems development will become more of a science with uniform quality and features. It will use specialization, where different persons perform parts of the whole task, and parts which are interchangeable and reusable. For example, there will be "sort" or "merge" functions that will have wider use. No one person will build the entire system, and few contributors will understand the total end product. Developers will only make a contribution to the final product in their area of specialization.

Many of these beliefs fit with the increasing emphasis on an engineering approach to systems building. But we must remember that engineering in the classical sense applies to physical objects such as roads, machines, electronics, or chemical compounds. Once a human with feelings, tastes, and perceptions enters the picture, development becomes more complex and resembles more of a consumer marketing function. But in any case, the future will bring more structure and standards to systems development activities.

With regard to developing systems, the future will include wider use of:

Standardized methodologies for processes and techniques. There will be less "winging it."

Standardized deliverables.

More rigorous development methods, including software and information engineering approaches.

Alternatives to classical life cycle methods such as prototyping and user-developed systems.

Structured approaches, especially for systems analysis where logical models will be developed.

Human-oriented approaches to development.

Approaches to increase interaction with users.

Systems development will be seen as less of a technical endeavor and as more of an organizational improvement campaign to aid in reaching business objectives.

Many of the changes in development methods will focus on the area of systems analysis, which in the past has been an area that was very difficult to describe and specify. One quip was that a definition of systems analysis was talking to people while "resting up to do the computer programming." With the widespread availability and definition of techniques for data, process, amd requirements modeling, this certainly will not be true in the future. There will be defined deliverables that will fit certain classes of projects.

Systems analysis is the stage where users' problems are defined and organizational opportunities are understood. Analysis must serve as the basis for the remaining portions of the development work. If analysis is not done properly, the rest of the project will suffer and analysis will have to be redone.

Along with changes in how projects are carried out, there will be changes in the kinds of projects that will receiving attention in the future.

SYSTEMS DEVELOPMENT APPLICATIONS—WHAT WILL BE WORKED ON?

Currently, much of the systems development budget is spent on maintenance of existing transaction processing systems. Many of these systems will become more stable and structured in the future, allowing changes to the systems to be made more easily. Packaged software also will become available and will be used for more and more applications.

There will be less focus on the transaction or data processing portions of systems development. Good transaction processing systems will be assumed in the future. This will allow more time to be spent on decision support systems, expert systems, and communication support systems.

Systems projects in the future will become more exciting and have a greater impact on the strategic mission of the organization. The systems development area will have greater involvement higher in the corporate structure and will assume more higher-level challenges. With greater understanding of systems by users, there will be a greater likelihood, and necessity, for information systems to influence the competitive strategy of the firm.

A select group of systems developers will evolve who will receive great respect from the rest of the organization. These developers will understand the business of which they are a part and recognize where information technology can be used to gain competitive advantage. Knowledge of the business beyond accounting applications will be essential for the excellent analyst of the future.

Not all future projects will result in tangible, long lasting products. There will be more projects of a research and development nature. Experimentation will be more prevalent, which will produce more risk. But along with the risk will come some greater rewards for both the developers and the organization.

The types of applications we will work on in the future will influence the types of persons who will develop systems.

SYSTEMS DEVELOPERS IN THE FUTURE—WHO WILL DO THE WORK?

Harmony has been a missing ingredient between the persons involved in systems development. Developers often have viewed systems users as persons who did not know what they wanted, who did not want to spend time and effort to help the systems effort, and who were reluctant to learn about technology. Some developers have stated that they could "really build some great systems if the users did not get in the way." Conversely, users have viewed developers as "techies" with no knowledge of what it takes to make a profit in a business. The future will bring a greater degree of team building where these factions work together.

The roles played by persons involved in systems development will change. There will be less distinction between users and developers. Users will become more knowledgeable about systems and system capabilities. They will know more about the capabilities of technology. Developers, including analysts and designers, will know more about the business. The roles of those involved in systems development as described in Chapter 1 will continue to overlap.

There will be some specific changes in the jobs of developers. These changes will include a trend toward greater job specialization within the systems professional function and an increased role of users in performing systems development.

Increased Job Specialization

As the systems development field matures, there will be an increased specialization of jobs. There will be more lower-level support functions such as data librarians and graphic diagram maintainers. Data librarians will keep the systems development database current. Graphic diagram maintainers will keep documentation such as data flow diagrams, entity-relationship diagrams, and structure charts up-to-date under the direction of a senior analyst.

Experts will evolve in various functions including hardware selection, database administration, screen design, person–machine dialog design, procedure writing, security specification, and test specification. There will be people specializing in behavioral and organizational activities such as job and organization design for changed systems. This specialization will be accompanied by the increased involvement of systems users. Systems activities will be of increasing interest to users since they will be using the systems as support tools.

Increased User Role in Development

The users' role in systems development has changed over the years. The user has gone from observer of development and recipient of outputs, to reviewer of documents at significant milestones, to active project members working with systems developers, to project leaders who actually have responsibility for project success. Users will have a greater role in actual development activities. Activities they will be involved in will include:

- Model building including construction of data flow diagrams and requirements specifications
- Layout design, including forms, report, and screen designs
- Training of other users
- Manual writing for other users of the system
- Testing, establishing test data and reviewing test results
- Implementation, including preparing for installation of the system
- Managing projects, including setting of milestones and making reports to project funders

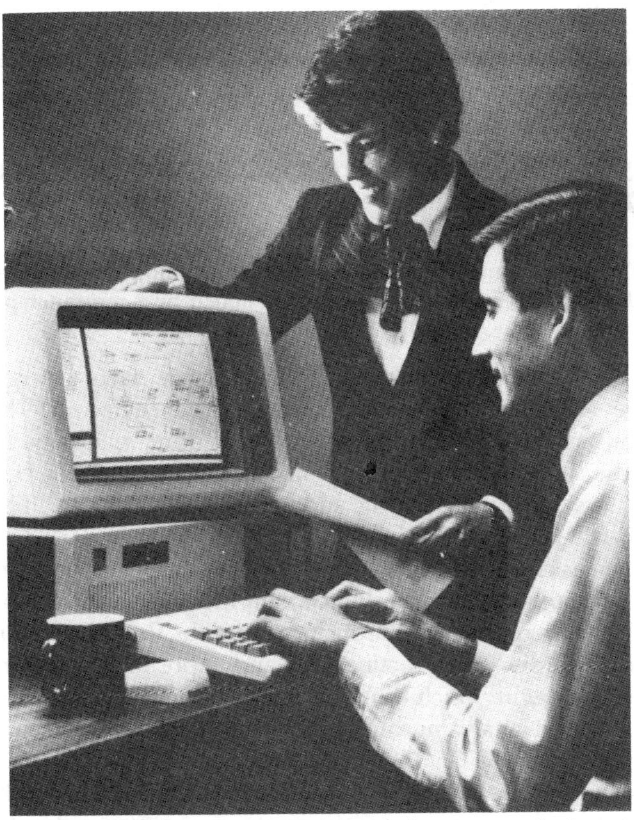

Users may now play a more active role in systems design, even constructing their own data flow diagrams. (Courtesy Index Technology Inc.)

A real exhibition of user commitment is to have users serve as project leaders responsible for obtaining needed participation and commitment to assure project success. This means *all* levels of users—project sponsors, output recipients, procedure performers, and systems input providers—must be committed to the systems development project.

As increased emphasis is put on decision and communication support systems, more systems will be developed using a prototyping approach. This will require a very active role by users, since the user is really in control of the speed of the development process.

Besides users assisting with systems development, there will be increased responsibility for the entire development by users. Many of the decision support systems have short "need" times and serve only one user. Users will not wait for the systems development unit to develop systems for them. They will take off on their own. The trends in easy-to-use software and computing power availability through microcomputer systems or networks will facilitate this movement. Systems developers still will have a role in this process. It will not be one of control, but they will serve in an advisory and review capacity to assure that the developed systems have required integrity.

Whether used by a professional systems developer or a user, the facilities of the future will become sophisticated. The next section will forecast what this environment will be like.

SYSTEMS DEVELOPMENT AIDS—NEW TOOLS FOR DEVELOPERS

> Jake the programmer commenting to Tom the noncomputer user: "Tom, someday soon everyone's job will be threatened by a computer program."
> Tom replies: "Jake, does that mean your job too?"

Although systems developers have explored many parts of organizations with an eye for automation, they have ignored their own "house and family." Many systems developers' activities are done manually. It clearly is a case of the shoemaker's children not having any shoes because the shoemaker was too busy making shoes for everyone else. This will be changing in the future.

Tedious tasks presently performed by systems developers will provide many of the opportunities for enhancement through automation. Some of the tasks that will receive attention include data flow diagramming and maintenance; building data dictionaries and repositories; generating test data; project managing, including task estimation and recording; designing databases; and analyzing and improving the soundness of program code.

Automating these tasks will be done to improve people productivity in systems development. Currently, the tools of a systems developer only include paper, pencils, and drawing templates. There will be an increasing number of technologic aids for systems developers. These aids will help productivity, but people also must help themselves by using them.

Heretofore systems analyst's main tools have been paper and pencil, but computerized workbenches are now becoming common. (Courtesy Index Technology Inc.)

Two of the major aids for systems developers are *regenerators* and *developer workstations.*

Regenerators

A major consideration for any automated system is the degree of maintainability. System maintenance cost is estimated as ranging from 50 to 80 percent of the total system cost over the system's life. It is estimated that $20 billion per year is spent on maintenance costs (see Carlyle in References). In fact, the present author believes that one of our largest national debts is the estimated 77 billion lines of poorly written COBOL code. Estimates to manually rewrite this computer code range from $10 to $30 per line. To redo all this code to create more maintainable systems is a huge endeavor, but would be very costly. Thus, organizations will spend large sums of money on other means of structuring computer code to make a system more maintainable.

There is some hope of reducing this problem through the use of automation. A class of automated development aids called *regenerators* has evolved. ***Regenerators*** are software packages that attempt either to create a new system from given specifications or structure and reconstruct existing systems to a "healthier" state. There are different subclasses of generators and regenerators. They include:

Code and Program Analysis Packages—these are automated software products that examine existing applications programs and attempt to draw a structure chart of the program. This examination will give an analyst an idea of the health of the program and how maintainable it may be. This is especially useful in examining and evaluating software packages for acquisition, or in making estimates of resources required to make a program change. The developer then would attempt to structure the code manually.

Code and Program Restructuring Packages—these packages not only examine program code for the degree of structure, but also attempt to recreate the code in a more structured form. "Dead" or unused code is removed and attempts are made to "modularize" the remaining code.

Code Generators—these packages will create program code from a set of data structures and systems specifications. The specifications often are written in a generalized language called *pseudocode* or in structured English. There also are generators that will use screen specifications and data structures and create the program code needed to generate the screens. As the following diagram of a COBOL code generator indicates, good inputs are needed for the generator to create good outputs. The phrase "garbage in, garbage out," certainly applies to a code generation system.

COBOL rules and constraints
↓
Data structures → Code generator ————→ COBOL code
↑
Procedures (pseudocode or structured English)
or
Screen specifications

One key factor in using regenerators is to know what *not* to regenerate. There often is a need for manual intervention to regenerate code, and some code is beyond the capabilities of regenerators.

The cost of regenerating code can be quite high. Performed as a service, it can cost $1 to $4 per line of COBOL code. If purchased, a complete regenerator package may cost $150,000 or more. The purchaser of such a package must be sure that the resulting code is really structured.

Although code generation will continue to be an endeavor attracting much attention, developers still must come up with a set of system specifications. Systems development workstations can assist in this task.

Systems Development Workbenches

There is much tedious and time-consuming work in systems development. This especially is true in developing and maintaining system documentation. For example, as any data flow diagrammer knows, it takes a great deal of time to draw and redraw the many levels of data flow diagrams. Making data dictionary entries and keeping the entries up-to-date is a task that many developers dislike. A means of easing this work load is an *automated systems development workbench,* often called a ***CASE (computer-aided software engineering) workstation***. The automated workbench is a combination of a microcomputer system and a software program designed especially to aid the work of the systems developer.

The automated workbench allows the systems developers to place and move diagramming symbols on the computer screen with a mouse pointing device, add labels to diagrams, explode items on the diagram to show greater detail, and place all items shown in a data dictionary for further description. The description can include data elements within data structures needed for certain routines which will allow the workbench to actually generate COBOL data divisions.

The greatest advantage to using such a workbench is that it makes a current working set of documentation on the system available to all team members. It makes implementation of the concepts discussed in Chapter 3 on a database for systems developers feasible and operational.

The automated systems development workbench can provide other aid such as error and consistency checking. For example, the automated system can check data flows at different levels to assure that data is "conserved" or shown at each level.

The workbench will allow various outputs of the data stored in the system. Hard copy reports of diagrams and other data can be easily printed. Every set of system documentation can follow a standard for content, order, and appearance. Using a microcomputer linked to a projector unit, the system documentation can be called up and displayed to a large audience. This is particularly helpful in doing team product reviews.

In the future, these workbenches will be integrated with other systems development aids. A likely future direction will be the linking to project management and estimating tools. An integrated workbench will indicate which deliverables are completed, whether they were completed on schedule, and then make any alterations for the future. The workbenches could serve as input devices to code generators and even have test data generated from data descriptions included in the development database. These are some of the most exciting possibilities for the future.

Artificial intelligence and expert systems can and will be a part of future systems development. Not only will systems developers be called on to incorporate expert systems concepts into systems they build, but there also will be activity focused on building expert systems for use by developers. Developers are not immune from use of methods they advocate for others. Expert systems have already been built for hardware configuration. A goal will be an expert system for all phases of systems development.

Techniques like requirements defining using interactive dialog, introduced in Chapter 6, may be a good place to start.

LEARNING HOW TO LEARN ABOUT SYSTEMS DEVELOPMENT

A major challenge in any field is to keep your knowledge and skills current. Knowledge is perishable in a rapidly changing environment. The systems field has some basic concepts that developers can learn from this book but there will be new releases of technology, software, and techniques that systems developers will want to discover. The following are sources of this knowledge:

> *Newpapers*—business sections of local daily papers will include information on major happenings in the technology industry. Many of the articles will focus on new releases of microbased hardware and software. A paper such as the *Wall Street Journal* will help an analyst keep up with happenings across the computer industry.
>
> *Computerworld*—This is a weekly newpaper tabloid that reports exclusively on happenings in the information industry. The paper's frequent "In-Depth" sections often explore systems development topics in detail.
>
> *MIS Week*—this is a weekly newspaper tabloid that focuses on the management issues and technology trends in the industry.

The readers of *BusinessWeek* and *Fortune* magazines will find features under the information and technology subheadings. Important product releases and industry trends are reported.

Trade journals, including *Datamation, Infosystems,* and *Computer Decisions* feature articles and news of the information management industry. These trade journals feature advertising on information management products, including items from computer room supplies to announcements of large mainframe vendor releases.

Vendors of certain software or hardware also publish periodicals informing the reader of new product releases and successful applications using their wares. It is best to check with sales representatives to discover such publications.

Specific sizes of computers are the focus of some weekly and monthly periodicals. *PC Week, Personal Computers,* and *MACUSER* are examples of such publications. The best method of finding out what is available in this area is to check with a large bookstore in their computer magazines area.

Periodicals oriented to systems practitioners which are not trade journals include the *Journal of Systems Management* and the *Journal of Information System Management.*

Systems developers should pay some attention to research in the systems development areas. Significant academic journals include *MIS Quarterly, Journal of Management Information Systems, Information and Management, IEEE Transactions on Software Engineering,* and various publications of the Association for Computing Machinery (ACM), including *Communications of the ACM*.

Other academic journals which are not focused on information systems, but have occasional articles pertinent to systems developers include *Harvard Business Review, Business Horizons, Administrative Science Quarterly, Decision Sciences,* and the *Academy of Management Journal.*

Systems developers also should be aware of associations and organizations where persons with an interest in systems will gather. Significant organizations include the Association for Computing Machinery, Association for Systems Management, Data Processing Management Association, and the Society for Information Management. All these organizations hold national, regional, and local meetings that include speakers and presentations of interest to members. Meeting persons with common interests at these meetings will help you establish your own network of persons that you can learn from. The trade journals mentioned above also contain listings of national meetings. Often, a local professor of information systems can inform you about the activities of such organizations.

The systems developer also should be aware of gatherings such as trade fairs. The largest of these is the National Computer Conference (NCC), but there often are such shows of new wares on regional and local levels.

All of the above material would be of interest to the general systems development audience. As well, there are groups and seminars which focus on specific topics such as computer security, specific programming languages, and specific applications such as expert systems. The informed analyst will keep his or her eyes and ears open and discover areas of special interest. The challenge will be to be selective as there are so many things to know.

YOUR CAREER IN SYSTEMS DEVELOPMENT

The reader of this chapter should form his or her own opinion about where the systems development field is going. An individual plan for your future should be established. Find out what you think you can do well and focus on it. Try to build on your strengths and support your weaknesses. If you have a technical bent, focus on some area of specialization such as the hardware and systems software side of systems development, but don't ignore your behavioral skills. If you have a behavioral bent, try to focus on a specific area, such as organizational design. Don't be afraid to take coursework in the behavioral sciences or in management topics such as organizational design. But don't ignore your technical skills.

Information centers or user-functional units will also give the developer an opportunity in the future to work with persons interested in using the benefits of modern technology. In some organizations, the information systems unit may be more of a data processing group working on transaction processing systems. This may not be detrimental, but will not be "where the action will be" in the future.

You should inventory your own skills as a systems developer. Important characteristics for a systems developer include:

Familiarity with modern development methodologies
An understanding of business in general
An understanding of accounting principles
An understanding of politics of business units and position holders
Knowledge of business practices and culture in your organization
Knowledge of hardware and software
Knowledge of database organization and usage
Technique skills, including how to run meetings and product reviews
Communication skills, including speaking and writing English and "computerese"
An ability to listen
An ability to work with persons at all levels of an organization
An ability to lead others
An ability to come up with creative solutions
An ability to see the big picture as well as detail
A positive attitude
Patience

Compare your own skills with the above list and decide which ones you should work on to grow as a systems developer.

As a new developer and organization member, you may be enthusiastic about using your new skills and aiding others to do the same. But remember that organizational change in the systems area may come slowly. This topic is examined in the next section.

INTRODUCING CHANGE TO SYSTEMS DEVELOPMENT GROUPS

One thing you will face in your future is introducing change to systems development groups. By progressing through this book, you have met up with many new techniques and approaches to systems development. You may think many of the approaches mentioned in this book are widely accepted but systems developers are as reluctant to change as anyone else. Many are not using the most up-to-date approaches to systems development. Since you will be working with these persons, it will be of value to speculate why change has not taken place.

One reason is that techniques were introduced over a number of years. Structured programming came first and made a big splash in the early 1970s. Since a program is needed to make the computer perform, many persons thought that structured programming would solve all systems development problems. Actually, this is as incorrect as believing that a good carpenter could build a good building if he or she had a bad blueprint or no plans at all. A design is still needed.

In the mid-1970s, an approach to solving the software design problem was introduced. This was the use of structure charts to represent the structure of a computer program. This graphic program blueprint could be evaluated for program module cohesion, or how well a computer program module "stuck together" and whether it performed only one function, and module coupling, or how modules could be linked together to avoid spaghetti-like connections. Again, many people got on the bandwagon. Many of the excellent system solutions represented by structure charts and structured programs solved a problem very elegantly, but sometimes it was one that the user did not really have. Systems developers had built the building very well, but the user may have wanted a barn and got an office complex.

In the late 1970s, another set of techniques appeared that approached the problem of developing a user needs specification without having a novel-sized book of "specs" users never understood. These were the techniques of structured analysis—data flow diagrams, data dictionaries, process logic tools, and team product reviews.

However, this piecemeal appearance, solving the least important problem first (at least in users' eyes) left many unsatisfied developers and project leaders. They had heard of too many "solutions" but still had problems. Many developers wondered what was next and when this trend would end. This hindered acceptance of the techniques. Life as a developer was in a constant state of change, with many of the advocated approaches falling by the wayside.

Another reason why structured techniques did not create a revolution is that there was a change in the time spent in different life cycle phases. More time was needed doing up-front analysis defining user needs. This meant that it would take longer to get to the steps of writing a computer program. However, many organizations measured systems department productivity by the number of lines of program code that were produced. This made many project managers nervous. They were not comfortable planning when they could be building. If there was pressure to produce the program code, it was easy to dismiss the planning activities and get on with writing programs. Bad code was better than no code at all. This has been referred to as the "code is where the tire meets the road" syndrome.

There also was resistance to change among the systems development community. Systems developers had to change the way they had done things for years. There was an increased demand for human interaction skills. The behavior of machines that programmers worked with were easier to understand than the behavior of the fickle human users. The machine always let you know if you were right or wrong when you submitted a program.

As a beginning analyst, you may be more willing to accept change. If an experienced analyst is comfortable representing systems as physical models in the form of systems flowcharts, developing logical models in the form of data flow diagrams will be more difficult. Unlearning something that has worked in the past is not easy. Experienced developers may have to give up something they currently have to assume ownership of something new.

When the going gets tough and deadlines loom and pressure mounts, people have a tendency to go back to the familiar and comfortable ways that have worked in the past. The belief is that you won't take the unfamiliar shortcut, even if the road is smooth, if the old way might work. Change takes time and effort.

Finally, some of these techniques have been misused. The best example is team product reviews, which also have been called *structured walkthroughs*. The idea of the review is to have an early review of a product, such as a data flow diagram, before the developer spent much time refining it and getting his or her ego into the product.

Managers were not encouraged to attend reviews because they would stifle interactions between peers, and evaluate people, not products. What happened was that managers *still* attended and stifled communications. Developers wanted to look good so they polished their deliverables and got their egos into the product. Suggested changes were seen as personal attacks and the whole process turned into what many referred to as "structured walkovers." The helping attitude was lost. The technique was blamed for all the misfortunes. Having learned these approaches correctly and formally will give you the advantage of having a deeper understanding of the concepts underlying the techniques. You can aid in the introduction of new approaches and serve as a changemaker, but this task will not be an easy one.

Yourdon (see References) makes some suggestions on how to implement new development techniques in an organization. He suggests:

Ensure that management understands the new approaches and is willing to provide complete commitment and follow-through.

Don't introduce too many new techniques at once.

Start with a technique such as team product reviews where the results of finding errors should be obvious to all participants.

Ensure that adequate training and tutoring is available (reading a book is not enough).

Introduce structured analysis and design before structured coding.

Choose one or more medium-sized, safe pilot projects.

Groom some "local experts" to help others.

Management must be supportive and willing to do what is needed to install a new approach. This means giving up some short-term results for long-term benefits while learning and adaption take place. (For further discussion of these topics, see two references to Yourdon at the end of the chapter.)

By introducing new approaches, using them successfully, and spreading them to others in your organization, you *will* influence the future. Good luck in this endeavor. You can meet the challenge.

SUMMARY

It is clear that the future systems development field will be one of excitement. The challenges faced by new systems developers are sure to make the field anything but boring. New technology and the realization that systems development can be done better will provide many opportunities for the future.

The new analysts who desire change will face many challenges. There are many people who would prefer to maintain the status quo. However, systems users and our organizations must look to improvements and progress in the future. The world is moving too fast for us to stand still.

REFERENCES AND FURTHER READINGS

Brownstein, Irv, and Nancy Lerner. "Nurturing Your Own Productivity," *Computerworld,* In Depth section, April 25, 1983, pp. 31–34.

Carlyle, R. Emmett. "Can AI Save COBOL?" *Datamation,* September 15, 1985, pp. 42–43.

Grant, F. J. "Twenty-First Century Software," *Datamation,* April 1, 1985, pp. 123–126+.

Jenkins, A. Milton. "Surveying the Software Generator Market," *Datamation,* September 1, 1985, pp. 105–107+.

Yourdon, Edward. *Managing the Structured Techniques,* New York: Yourdon Press, 1979.

———. "The Second Structured Revolution," Yourdon, Inc., internal paper, 1979, 10 pages.

REVIEW QUESTIONS

1. Why will system performance not be as critical of an objective in the future?
2. State some ways in which systems development will change in the future.
3. Why are the results of systems analysis so critical to the success of a development project?
4. Why will systems development projects become more risky in the future?
5. What are some specialized development jobs that may evolve in the future?
6. What systems development activities may users perform in the future?
7. Why would the use of a regenerator be economically feasible for an organization with unique applications written with outdated and unstructured code?

8. How might systems development workbenches be integrated with other systems development aids?

9. What are some guidelines for the introduction of new systems development methods?

DISCUSSION QUESTIONS

1. Do you believe that systems development is more of an art than a science? Relate the characteristics of an artist mentioned in the chapter to what you know about the work of a systems developer.

2. Do you feel maintenance will be a major objective of systems development in the future? Why or why not? Are there exceptions where performance will be more important in some applications?

3. The author believes a certain "development elite" commanding great respect from other organization members will evolve in the future. Either defend or refute this belief.

4. Take a side in the issue as to whether users or developers will be more alike in the future.

5. What tasks do you feel are tedious in systems development? Which of them could be automated?

EXERCISES

1. Add any characteristics that you feel are important to the list for a successful systems developer given in this chapter. Do a self inventory to determine your strengths and weaknesses. What can you do to strengthen your weaknesses?

2. Attempt to find some literature on a systems development workbench. Try to get access to a workbench and report your reactions

3. Visit your library to determine if the publications mentioned in this chapter are available. Make a list of the publications. What articles did you find that are relevant to systems development?

APPENDIX A

A Case Study to Be Used for Systems Analysis

THIS CASE STUDY, based on an actual business, provides a training ground for developing systems analysis skills.

The Good Fit Shoe Store is a company which needs a systems study. You are one of the project leaders for the project. Your task is to establish some preliminary documentation. At a minimum, you should include:

A logical model of your vision of the existing system. This likely will include a context diagram, a data flow diagram, and some data dictionary entries.

A requirements model for the proposed system, including some quantified business objectives, specific business tactics, and measurable system objectives. You may have to create some "fiction" when quantifying the business objectives.

A set of directions and cautions for the future in dealing with the project. For example, would you recommend hiring a computer programming student or quickly buying some computer hardware?

THE GOOD FIT SHOE STORE CASE

The Good Fit Shoe Store is a small retail business with two full-time and four part-time employees. One of the full-time employees is the owner, Greg Slater. Greg is proud of the number of satisfied customers the store has served. He feels this satisfaction is due to the personalized service his store offers. In his opinion, discount stores and chain shoe stores are more concerned with quantity sales, without providing assistance from persons who know shoes and feet. He tries to train his employees to ensure a "good fit" of size, style, and cost.

Greg is an energetic fellow in his late twenties. He got started in the shoe business by working for one of the chain shoe stores. The main function of a clerk in the chain store was to ring up sales and bag the shoes. Greg felt a lot of people were buying inappropriate sizes and styles of shoes that did not fit their needs. After the chain shoe store experience, Greg took a job in a small clothing shop where he started and built up an outstanding shoe department. He found that care and personal attention to the customer led to repeat sales.

Greg worked part-time at the clothing shop while he finished his geology degree at the state college. He and his family did not want to leave their home town to take a geology position, so he was in a state of confusion as to what to do to support his wife and two children. His wife wanted to spend more time at home and not have to work the night shift at the local hospital. The clothing shop job would not allow the Slaters to live in a manner they desired. His future was influenced when his father-in-law approached him with the idea of starting a new shoe store. His father-in-law had money he wanted to invest in a new business. The local banks were also supportive of two local residents who wanted to boost the economy.

Building store business was not difficult, since a locally owned business was patronized in the city of 18,000 where the store was located. Keeping up with demand and getting good help was another matter. The local cannery paid much better than Greg could pay, so he was often left hiring people who would not have been his first choice. The business continued to grow and thrive, but not without problems.

First, the "books" were taking more of Greg's time than actually meeting customers and promoting the business. Then Greg saw a TV ad showing a hat store faced with many of the same problems that he had. The hat company got a computer and their business became more organized. This led Greg to believe his business could be run more efficiently by having a computer to help, especially in the area of accounts payable and inventory management. Because of keeping the books and increasing competition from discounters, Greg felt the need to record some of his current activities to see if they could be computerized.

CURRENT ACTIVITIES AND DATA

Greg recently wrote down some things about his current practice of ordering, receiving, selling, and paying for merchandise at Good Fit. His intention was to hire a student from the local technical school to write a computer program to do many of the things that are currently done manually.

To order shoes from vendors, Greg telephones the order to the vendor, or verbally gives it directly to a sales representative. To keep track of the vendors, Greg maintains a file box with vendor business cards stapled to an index card. As sales reps change, he staples new cards to the index card.

Greg keeps a list of orders placed and expected delivery dates. He calls this the "open order list." This list contains the vendor information from the business cards, the order details including the date of the order, the styles, colors, sizes, and quantity of merchandise, the cost, and the anticipated date of delivery.

When the ordered merchandise is received, the packing slip from the vendor is compared against the open orders. Packing slips usually contain the vendor name, the date shipped, the date of the order, the order reference such as the phoner's name or the name on the written order, and a list of the merchandise, including the styles, colors, and sizes, and whether the ordered items were filled, back-ordered, or canceled. Items that match are crossed off the open order list which is then typed to create the closed order list. The closed order list contains the date the things are received, order number, date of order, vendor name, styles, colors, and sizes of merchandise, and quantity received.

The merchandise is priced and placed in storage or on the shelves for sale. The inventory of what is in stock is kept in Greg's memory. This bothers him since he would like to take a vacation and go rock-hunting in the Grand Canyon. He feels that things would be so far out of control when he returned that he would rather stay at the store and not worry from afar.

When a customer buys a pair of shoes, the seller records on a clipboard the date, vendor, style, color, size, and price to create a transaction record. The customer receives a sales receipt with the date and amount of the sale, including sales tax. The cash register also records a copy of the receipt. The clerk marks on the register receipt whether the sale was cash, check, or charge card. The transaction record is reviewed by Greg, who mentally notes any changes in the inventory. If the seller records the transactions and Greg takes the time to review the record, Greg feels he knows the sizes, styles, and colors, the cost, the selling price, the vendor, and quantities of items in the store.

Lately, Greg could not believe that some items were not in stock since they were neither on the transaction record nor could he find them in the store. There were so many items missing that he was confused, since sales receipts from the cash register, and the transaction record were fairly close.

When an invoice is received from the vendor, it is compared against the closed order list. A match results in the invoice being filed in the accounts payable file drawer according to the due date. Greg keeps a running total of the monthly accounts payable, including the discounts available if he pays by a certain date. When the due date comes up on an invoice, a check is written and sent to the vendor. The monthly balance due is updated. A copy of the check is made and the amount is posted to the checking account balance and to the appropriate account balance. This data, including check number, discounts taken, date of payment, vendor name, amount, invoice numbers, and account posting, is all kept in the check register.

PROBLEMS AND OPPORTUNITIES

Greg feels there are some real problems with the way the business currently operates. He really wants and feels he needs to take a vacation. Things are not going well at home. He constantly gets calls at home from his clerks because they are not sure of what to do. He has had more and more stockouts of some items and too much inventory of others. The transaction records just do not seem to be very accurate. Greg feels a computer could help.

Greg came in one morning last week after taking an afternoon off the day before to go on a picnic with the family. He found that an order from a vendor had arrived and had been opened. Items seemed to have been sold, or at least were not there according to the packing slip. The vendor has not been very accurate, but Greg does not know if it was the vendor, the failure to fill out a transaction record, or if things are "disappearing." There also were some shoes in a bag in the back room that he knows were sold last week. He does not know what is going on with these shoes and one of his part-time people who only comes in once a week was working that night. Greg doesn't like calling people at home.

One of the local running groups was in a few weeks ago asking for a discount for their members, which was granted. Now it seems that every other order for any type of shoe shows a discount. This group has bought very heavily, so Greg does not want to offend them. Maybe he should issue discount cards and numbers?

To complicate things further, one of the local physical education teachers has mentioned to students that she buys her shoes at Good Fit. This has influenced the students to patronize Good Fit. The store now is getting so much business that some of the old order policies from vendors are not keeping enough inventory in the store. Greg never thought that this kind of good news would cause him problems.

Computer sales people have approached him and said that a computer will solve many of his problems. These people cautioned Greg against using a computer student to write programs for Good Fit. Greg has talked this over with his father-in-law and come to the conclusion that he needs some business help before he needs computer help. Greg is willing to spend time with someone who can help him. He is so flustered that he feels his world is collapsing. Success sure does come at a cost.

The Small Business Administration and local Chamber of Commerce has retained you to head a consulting team to aid small businesses such as Good Fit with systems problems. Since Good Fit is in another city, you are to prepare for your first meeting with Greg by developing some summary models of the business for review by him at your meeting.

APPENDIX B

A Real World Systems Project

THIS SECTION PRESENTS a tested format for conducting a systems analysis on an actual existing system. This type of challenge allows students to gain experience that many employers desire.

Many students have discovered that the best method of anchoring any learning is through actual doing, not just reading and listening. This appendix will give you details on how to find and conduct a systems analysis project in a real world environment. The method presented here has been tested in several locations. The participating students have claimed that the project was the key means of building confidence and the belief that they understood and actually could do systems development work. The results of the team projects have been gratifying. Several students have taken their project results into job interviews to exhibit to employers they have more than "book" knowledge. Students should view this experience as a real opportunity to learn in a safe environment where you can seek guidance from both your classmates and instructor.

A TEAM PROJECT

Systems analysis work in the real world typically is done in teams. Teams also will be used in this real-world project. You will apply the knowledge and skills you will be learning within a small group.

You will be responsible for forming and organizing your team and finding a project. You *must* have three or four members on your team.

Each team will develop a number of products that would represent "deliverables" in a real project. Student teams will share these "deliverables" with both the company where the project takes place and the rest of the class. The instructor will make additional comments and attempt to enhance the learning experiences.

Your team must produce a final report that will be the basis for your team project grade. Your presentation to the class also will influence your grade. Near the end of the semester, each team member will be given a grade by the other team members. This feedback will be used to adjust your individual team project score.

AN OVERVIEW OF THE REAL-WORLD PROJECT

In general, the class project is the documentation of an existing system with techniques learned from the textbook and class. You will be required to produce a business model, a data flow model, any helpful data relationship models, descriptions of items on the data flow model, a requirements model linking the organization to the information subsystem, and any suggestions for improvements (which could include some suggestions for a new logical design). Your team might include some suggestions for continuation of the project if this is deemed a reasonable thing to do.

The subsystem you will document should be in place in an organization in the local area. The subsystem should be of importance to the organization. You should select one specific subsystem within the organization such as the billing, inventory, or order-taking system. Do not take a broad view of representing the entire organization as a system.

You should have an agreement with someone within the chosen organization to spend some time with you to aid you in understanding the system and providing you with any existing documentation. This contact person is essential to project success.

You will benefit from the project because you will have a chance to apply your learning from this class. You will have an opportunity to work as a member of a three- or four- member team and will be exposed to the pleasures and difficulties of team work. Remember that you are a representative of the school you are attending and should behave as a professional. All of our reputations are on the line in this kind of endeavor. If you perceive a problem arising, call or see your instructor.

The organization should benefit from this project since they will have three or four bright minds examining an existing system and leaving the organization with lasting documentation that many organization members will be able to understand. This is not to be a "make-work" activity. The deliverables should serve the organization as a record of what they are currently doing and could include some indications of areas where improvement can take place.

The first step in the project is to form your teams and to choose a project, not necessarily in that order. You are free to choose your own teams unless your instructor tells you otherwise. Look for diversity and try to making this a learning experience for all concerned. Since your team members will grade you on your contribution, working together is a necessary endeavor. Be sure you can turn out a good product. This project should be fun, not drudgery.

By the time you finish the material in Chapter 5 of this book, your instructor should receive from your team a document with the following information:

1. Names of the team members performing the analysis.
2. Name and location of the organization where study will take place.
3. Name, position, work address, and work phone number of the primary contact person within the organization.
4. The subsystem you will analyze within the organization. Include a brief description of the subsystem and why it is important to the organization.
5. Any bottlenecks or fears the team has about the chosen project.

Your team should begin thinking about the final written and oral report to be presented this term. There will be *no* incompletes given for the project. The project must be finished approximately 2 weeks before the end of the school term. Both written and oral reports must be of professional presentation quality.

Your team and its members should think of yourselves as unpaid consultants aiding an organization by analyzing and documenting one of their subsystems. You likely will find the project one of the most challenging and rewarding endeavors of this class.

A SCHEDULE OF EVENTS

Your project should progress through various stages.

Stage 1: Initiate Systems Learning, Find Project, and Form Team

A. Understand Systems and Development Process: This is done by reading and understanding the material at least through Chapter 5.
B. Search for Projects: Projects can be found in local businesses, the university or college environment, or in organizations such as fraternities, sororities, or student clubs.
C. Select Project and Form Team: The team may be formed and then a project sought, or a project may be found and then a team formed. It may be best not to form a team with just your friends—you may learn more from others you have recently met. Remember that class schedules are critical in considering team members. They must be able to attend team meetings.
D. Develop Project Statement: Guidelines for this statement are found in the previous section.

Stage 2: Continue Learning and Develop Intermediate Products

A. Organizational or Business Model: This may include an organization chart and some job descriptions.
B. Data Flow and Data Structure Models: Chapter 5 provides aid in defining and developing these models. You likely will have at least a context diagram and a top-level data flow diagram. You may want to do a second level of the data flow diagram for one or two processes to serve as an example for the organization.
C. Requirements Model: Chapter 6 provides help in developing this model.
D. Class Discussions on Progress to Date: Some questions to consider include:
   - What existing documentation did you find?
   - What has surprised you the most so far in your project?
   - What tasks have you done correctly so far in your project?
   - What things have you done that you would like to do better next time?
   - Any lessons learned to share with the rest of us?
   - What are your current fears and concerns?

   Be prepared to share some of this information with your classmates and instructor.

Stage 3: Review Intermediate Results

A. Team Product Reviews: These reviews will be conducted according to the procedures presented in Chapter 7. Some reviews will be conducted in the classroom to serve as examples and models of proper review execution. You may want to conduct some of these reviews outside class using both your team members and persons from other teams.
B. Directions and Summary for the Future: Chapter 8 and beyond may be useful to you in establishing a future plan for the project. Once you have had experience on a project, you may want to consult Chapter 14, which gives some guidelines for managing a systems development project.

Stage 4: Final Report and Presentations

A. Create Final Report: You should be ready to put your findings into a final report form. Be sure to use your report writing skills. You may find some hints for writing in Chapter 10 in the section on Manual Writing. Your final report may include:
   I. Executive summary
   II. Background on project (including Who?, When?, Where?)
   III. Models of System
      A. Business or organizational models

B. Logical models
C. Requirements models
IV. Future directions (including what to do and resources needed)
V. Summary and conclusions

Copies of the report will not only go to the instructor, but to your project sponsor. You may want to save a copy of your report for your own files.

B. Give Final Presentation: Aid in giving presentations can be found in Chapter 7. Try to make your presentation as professional as possible. You will be asked to give the presentation to the class. You may want to talk to your instructor about inviting your users to your presentation, including your project contact. Some students have found videotaping to be useful in preparing their presentation.

SOME HINTS AND CAUTIONS

1. In selecting a project, your project sponsor's commitment and enthusiasm is essential. The project sponsor must see the project as an opportunity, not a problem. Be sure time is available for you to make contact within the organization.
2. You may be faced with the dilemma of whether to choose a company where you may want to seek employment. This can be dangerous since the class project is a place to make mistakes and learn. You may be better off in an environment where you can learn by experience without having to be cautious about every move.
3. Be sure your team can meet outside of regular class hours. This may mean that the minimum allowable team size may be an advantage, rather than a disadvantage. Look for diversity in your team member skills so all strengths can be gathered and weaknesses can be supported.
4. Your first contacts with your sponsor are critical. Be sure to dress right so you will feel right. *If you do not know something, say so.* You are in a learning environment. A kickoff memo (see Chapter 4) may be appropriate.
5. You may discover that the users do not have business objectives and tactics at the tip of their tongue. Explain the concepts, share the requirements dialog, and attempt to understand the organizational mission together.
6. Do not make promises you cannot keep. Remember that you have limited time to conduct your project. Your primary mission is to document a system. You are not charged with building new systems or doing programming unless this is part of another agreement with the organization. Users can become excited with some of your preliminary results and may have great expectations. Your

task is to manage those expectations. Remember—communication is often the key to eliminating misunderstandings.

7. Do not become discouraged. Read and believe the following.

A STUDENT'S VIEW OF THE REAL-WORLD PROJECT

Once we become familiar with some activity, we can disassociate from it and really enjoy it. During running, disassociation takes place when everything is in perspective and balance. There are no distractions and worries. Pain is absent. There is a state of unconscious competence where perfect coordination of all body parts leads to a synergistic flow. But, I learned to enjoy running a long time ago and it wasn't easy at first.

The project was as painful as some early runs. Many things were getting in the way. We had too much data, bad data, incomplete data, uncooperative users, poor understanding of data, etc. We were overwhelmed.

But then the pieces started to fall into place. We moved from unconscious incompetence to conscious incompetence to conscious competence. We first didn't know what we didn't know, then knew what we didn't know, and now have newfound knowledge. Confidence and competence have been built and things have started to click. The unknown is becoming obvious. The fog is clearing. After several false starts, I now feel like I could run for miles.
—Court Allen, University of Colorado, Boulder.

APPENDIX C

An Example of a Student Team's Completed Real World Systems Project

THIS APPENDIX CONTAINS the results of a systems analysis project completed with the directions included in Appendix B. Except for improving the quality of the figures and exhibits and some minor editing, the student product has not been enhanced by the instructor/author or the editors. The material is what the student team accomplished and submitted during a one semester undergraduate Systems Analysis class at the University of Colorado in Boulder, Colorado. The project results are not intended to be an example of perfection, but are intended to exhibit a typical high-quality product by a student team. None of the students was a professional systems developer, yet the results clearly indicate the knowledge, skill, and motivation that would make a systems project manager (and a professor) proud. It is hoped that other students and instructors can learn from the exhibited results.

This appendix is shown with the permission of Lisa Van Vorous, E-LINE SYSTEMS, INC., and University of Colorado/Boulder students Eloy Caro, Hank Gonzales, Mike Robertson, and Kathy Stevens.

E-LINE SYSTEMS INC.: AN ANALYSIS OF THE ORDER PROCESSING SYSTEM

E-LINE SYSTEMS INC.
TABLE OF CONTENTS

SECTION ONE: EXECUTIVE SUMMARY

Started in September 1986, E-LINE SYSTEMS, INC., has developed as a growing member of the import-export sourcing market. E-LINE was started within a larger company called Vacuum, Inc. Vacuum was originally set up for exporting, marketing, and consulting. As Vacuum was involved with quite a bit of overseas work, colleagues would ask the representatives of Vacuum to pick up various items for them ("as long as you are going to Hong Kong, could you look into this for me?"). Realizing that Vacuum was actually doing quite a bit of this, the president of Vacuum decided to set up a spin-off company of Vacuum which would take over some of these added duties which the representatives of Vacuum were performing. Thus, E-LINE SYSTEMS, INC., was established as an import-export sourcing company.

As the term "import-export sourcing" may be unfamiliar to most, a brief description might be helpful. Essentially, the range of E-LINE's activities include being contacted by a company in the United States who needs some kind of product exported from overseas. E-LINE would take the company's product specifications and match them up with an exporter overseas who could best fulfill the needs of the importing company. E-LINE finds the export source of a company's import product needs and negotiates a contract which will meet the price and product specifications for all parties involved in the transaction. Currently, E-LINE works with approximately 15 countries around the world, and imports products ranging from paper products to computers and furniture (for more information see Section Seven—Products/Nations Reference).

Although E-LINE is a young company, the years, contacts, and experience that began under Vacuum have given E-LINE an edge that most beginning import-export companies do not have. Currently E-LINE is working toward expanding into more consulting work (particularly between two countries outside of the United States so as not to have to go through the trade restrictions of the U.S. government) and more sourcing for companies requesting orders of 1,000 items or more (see the requirements model in Section Three to examine the business and system objectives and the business tactics that will be applied toward this end). Eventually E-LINE would like to expand to have another home office based in England where sourcing for countries in Scandinavia, Africa, and the Middle East would be facilitated.

SECTION TWO: HIERARCHY DESCRIPTION AND ORGANIZATION CHART

E-LINE SYSTEMS, INC., as an organization, is comprised of four primary positions (see Figure C-1). The president makes all final decisions and functions as an overseer for all operations. The overseas export director aids in the decision making process and advises on overseas operations.

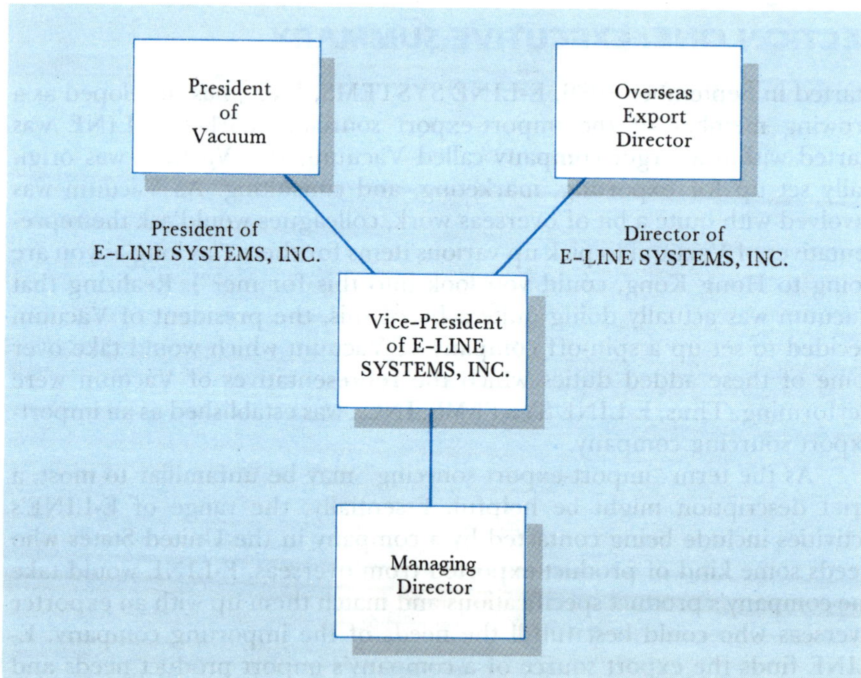

FIGURE C-1
E-LINE SYSTEMS INC. organization chart.

The vice-president keeps operations running, insuring all is in order and executed in a timely manner. The managing director aids the vice-president in operation and is responsible for market and product sourcing.

SECTION THREE: REQUIREMENTS MODEL

The requirements model is the deliverable in which each group quantifies what they would like to see happen in the business to increase revenues and decrease costs (their business objectives). Then the company specifies what they can and/or will do to aid in achieving these objectives. These are the business tactics. Finally, the company is given the opportunity to express what they would like to see an installed system be able to do to help perform their business tactics. These are the system objectives.

Writing out the requirements model with E-LINE's executives really helped pinpoint a focus for our project. Our group could better understand where E-LINE currently stood in their own minds, and where they would like to go. It was also a great help in having them understand just what we as a group would be doing on this project. That is, we wouldn't be installing a new system within E-LINE, but that we would analyze the workings of their current system and help them focus in on areas for potential improvement and growth. In coming up with system objectives, we were able to work on ideas for a potential new computerized system (what they would like it to do for the company).

Business Objectives

1. Increase the number of customers by 50% to increase revenues by the same amount by August 198x.
2. Expand E-LINE's market share of the import-export business by 25% to aid in increasing the number of customers (who might deal with the new markets) and thus, potentially increase revenues as E-LINE would have more to offer potential and present customers by January 198x.
3. Decrease the overall access time of locating the source of a product by 25% in order to decrease the costs of doing so by the same amount. Goal date is January 198x.

Business Tactics

1. E-LINE's salesperson will be in charge of doing some advertising and direct mailings to past and potential customers (importers) of products for which E-LINE typically sets up contracts. Also, information should be gathered on these potential and past customers as to their names, typical products, general product and quality specifications, general price range to work in, responses from direct mailings, who the company works through at present, what the price the company is working through (with the rival company), etc.

2. Examine other markets to determine their ability to satisfy the typical needs of E-LINE's present/potential customers. Increase the number of overseas contacts in order to more easily tap into these other markets (set up contacts within these new markets). Currently this is accomplished through information, samples, and company names brought back from overseas by friends in the import-export business.
3. Centrally organize information on past used sources of various products, as well as information from export books such as a particular country's export trade directory (i.e., the Korean Export Trade Directory). Information such as the export company name, product, particular company requirements (i.e., 2-month prepayment), product development availability (i.e., how much time is needed to make and send a certain standard size of an order), and any other information necessary for a particular company for exporting. Other information generally includes quality of product (if known), prices, shiptime, shipping costs to importer, etc.

Typically all of the above information will grow with each new order or contact that E-LINE is involved with.

System Objectives

1. Have the ability to store customer information (both present and potential customers) so that reports on the needs and product specifications of the customers can be generated when needed. Reports should have the ability to be generated so as to print out different reports per customer status (such as present customer, potential customer responding to mailing, potential customer not responding to mailing, etc.).
2. Have the ability to produce reports quickly on lists of potential markets in order to facilitate the weighing of options, advantages and disadvantages of expanding into the various markets looked at by E-LINE.
3. Be able to produce reports generated from some key value such as "Eelskin Handbags," which would give the above information for companies so as to facilitate the matching up of a customer's requests for their products (i.e., price, quality, time to receive the product, and any other special considerations the import company needs fulfilled) with what the various export companies have to offer.

Of course, achieving a decrease in time would depend on what the order is (i.e., an unusual product that E-LINE would have no starting information and contacts for). Basically, however, these will be of a particular aid when the order might be something which could be considered a fairly standard import (handbags, calculators, etc.) that E-LINE probably has had experience dealing with before.

SECTION FOUR: CONTEXT DIAGRAM

An Example of a Student Team's Completed Real World Systems Project

The context diagram is a top level representation of the E-LINE order processing system (see Figure C-2). It shows data with its sources and destinations. Inputs for the order processing system come from potential customers, customer sourcing, foreign contacts, product shows, and export directories. Future contacts and E-LINE accounting both receive outputs from the system.

Potential customer is defined as an individual or business that contacts E-LINE to find available products overseas. Customer sourcing provides customers who are interested in an item E-LINE has marketed to a target group. Foreign contacts are individuals living overseas that E-LINE depends on for to-the-minute information concerning foreign markets. A product show is a gathering of producers which gives E-LINE a chance to

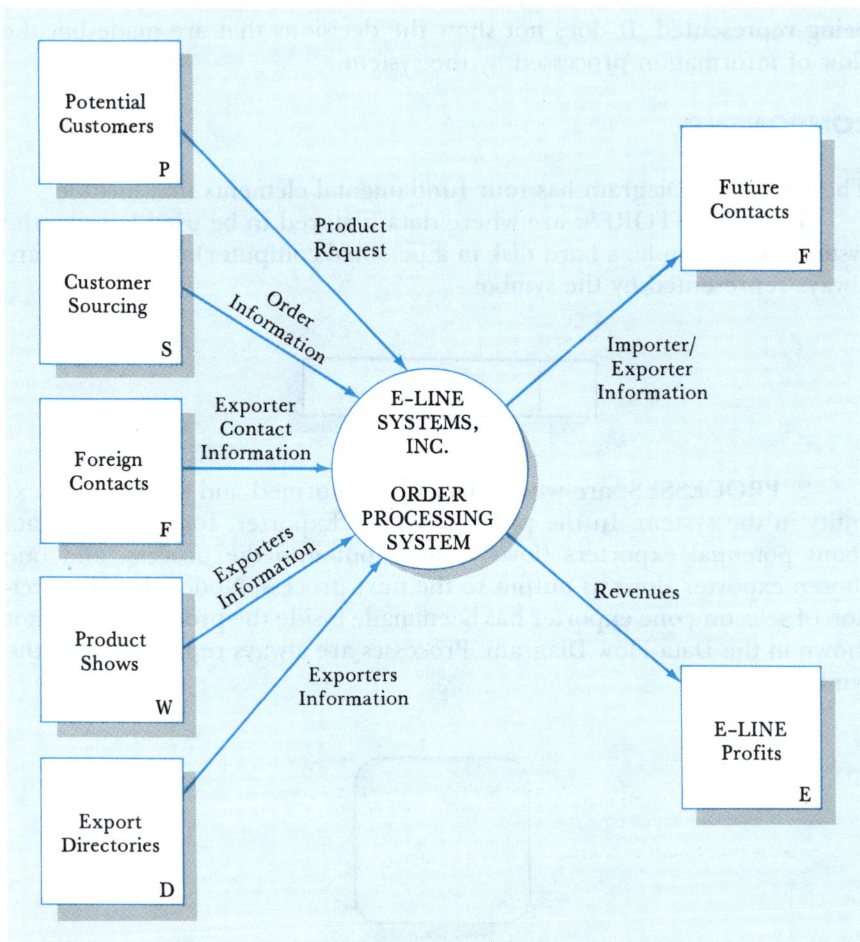

FIGURE C-2
E-LINE SYSTEMS INC. context diagram.

see what a country's industry is offering that year (i.e., annual Hong Kong trade show) and export directories are a listing of "who produces what" by country.

Outputs are the result of inputs and processes. The E-LINE order processing system produces importer/exporter information for future contacts, which provide a source of future reference in international trade, and revenues, which make E-LINE profitable.

SECTION FIVE: DATA FLOW DIAGRAM (LEVEL 01)

Explanation of Data Flow Diagrams

DEFINITION

A Data Flow Diagram is a graphical representation of how data flows in a system. In other words, it represents the data network of the system that is being represented. It does not show the decisions that are made but the flow of information processed by the system.

COMPONENTS

The Data Flow Diagram has four fundamental elements that include:

1. DATA STORES: are where data is stored to be used later by the system (for example, a hard disk in a personal computer). Data Stores are always represented by the symbol

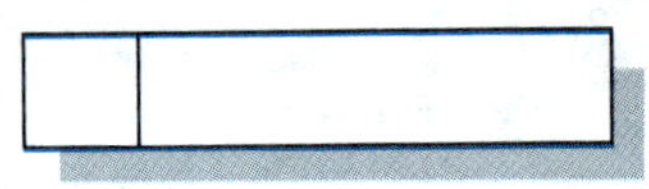

2. PROCESSES: are where data is transformed and sent to the next entity in the system. In the process Choose Exporter, for example, data about potential exporters flows as an input into the process, and one chosen exporter flows as output to the next process. Notice that the decision of selecting one exporter has been made inside the process but it is not shown in the Data Flow Diagram. Processes are always represented by the symbol

3. EXTERNAL ENTITIES: are sources of information into the system or destinations to which information flows outside the system. For

example, Potential Customers are an external entity because they do not belong to the system. Data about product characteristics flows into the system from the Potential Customer, and that data will be processed by the system. External entities are always represented by the symbol

4. DATA FLOWS: are movements of data inside the system, movements of data that flow from outside the system into the system, or movements of data that flow from the system to an external entity. For example, when a potential customer provides information to the system the data is transferred through the system by data flows. Data flows are always represented by the symbol

Figure C-3 shows the top level data flow diagram for E-LINE SYSTEMS, INC. order processing system.

DATA DICTIONARY

I. EXTERNAL ENTITIES

CUSTOMER SOURCING

Description: Customer sourcing provides the majority of E-LINE's importer contacts, and encompasses all active promotion of the company, including mass mailings, personal contacts, and salesman contacts. Market sourcing provides 80% of E-LINE's initial contacts. Sourcing may include:

1. *Mass Mailings:* Letters sent to a wide variety of potential importers, usually promoting a particular product or products and containing an order form for the named item(s). Mass mailings are sent to businesses in the customer file and also businesses sourced through the phone book, American Business Lists, Merchandise Mart, and library references including Contacts Influential.
2. *Personal Contacts:* Personal contacts are connections made through channels including friends, business associates, and informal communication with E-LINE's parent company, Vacuum Inc. Personal contacts provide E-LINE with its most valuable sourcing information. Additionally, every time a contract is negotiated, personal contacts and outlets for future contacts are established.

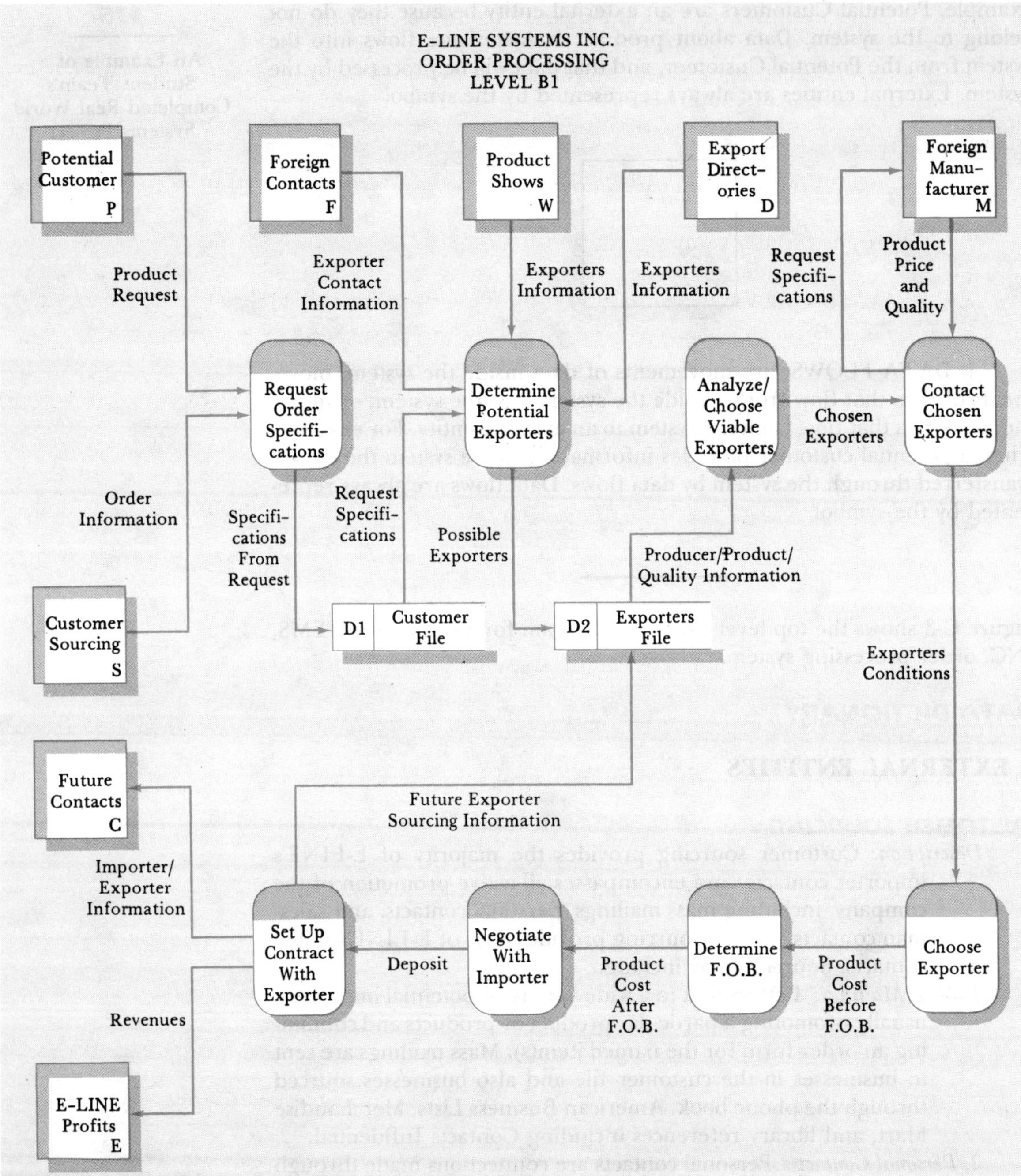

FIGURE C-3

E-LINE SYSTEMS INC. order processing system level one data flow diagram.

3. *Salesman Contacts:* E-LINE employs a full time salesperson who establishes contacts through visits to area businesses, phone contacts, and field sales. The salesperson is able to keep a close eye on local demand and trends.

E-LINE PROFITS

Description: E-LINE builds a profit buffer into the cost it charges an importer for setting up a deal, and the F.O.B. price of delivery from the foreign manufacturer to the product's destination.

EXPORTER DIRECTORIES

Description: Another means of finding potential exporters is through directories offered by countries listing the items the nation's private industry produces. In the Eastern Bloc, nations such as Poland must be accessed through the nation's Consulate before any business can be conducted.

FOREIGN CONTACTS

Description: Foreign contacts are overseas manufacturers that E-LINE has had prior contact with, or has reliable references which assure the company's accountability. Another form of foreign contact is individuals who live overseas and are in touch with markets and producers. E-LINE has established a base of foreign contacts through international trade shows and the transactions of Vacuum, Inc.

FOREIGN MANUFACTURER

Description: After viable foreign manufacturers are chosen, they are given the product specifications to develop a prototype and product price. The interaction between E-LINE and the manufacturer is high at this point and negotiations are critical at this stage. For any given order, E-LINE may negotiate with up to 20 different overseas manufacturers before one producer is chosen.

FUTURE CONTACTS

Description: After a contract has been completed, all of the individuals and businesses that have been researched are documented and placed in the customer or exporter file for future reference. By keeping track of all of its past business associates, E-LINE expands its base of contacts for future business.

POTENTIAL CUSTOMER

Description: A potential customer is a domestic person or business with an interest in importing goods through E-LINE. Potential customers contact E-LINE through the channels of mail or telephone, and inquire about a previously unsourced good which is produced or can be obtained overseas. The clarifying difference between a potential customer and a contact established through market sourcing is the method of original contact. Potential customers contact E-LINE on their own initiative, after having heard of the company through reputation, the phone book, or their own research.

PRODUCT SHOWS

Description: Product shows are conventions that allow manufacturers from a particular country to show products that will be offered that year. These shows offer an excellent opportunity for making contacts with producers.

II. DATA FLOWS

CHOSEN EXPORTERS

Description: Exporters which make the "second cut" from process 3 (analyze/choose viable exporters). Chosen exporters are those considered worth getting price quotes for the desired good.

Source: Analyze/choose Viable Exporters (Process 3).

Destination: Contact Chosen Exporters (Process 4).

Composition: List of one to four exporters who are good prospects for the customer's product.

DEPOSIT

Description: A price agreement deposit is an agreement that the importer will pay for all products ordered prior to any manufacturing. Usually a letter of credit from the importer's bank is required by the country of the supplier. The letter of credit certifies that the importer has sufficient financing to pay for the goods ordered, and guarantees that the money will be frozen until time of payment.

Source: Negotiate With Importer (Process 7).

Destination: Set Up Contract With Exporter (Process 8).

Composition: Letter of credit.

EXPORTER CONDITIONS

Description: After product price and quality are known, manufacturer conditions are considered. Conditions include the time it will take to deliver a product, how large a deposit will be required to start work, and what terms of payment are required.

Source: Contact Chosen Exporter (Process 4).

Destination: Choose Exporter (Process 5).

Composition: Time required for delivery, amount for deposit, terms of payment.

EXPORTER CONTACTS INFORMATION

Description: When looking for an item overseas, the first source of information is foreign contacts who are intimately familiar with the availability of new items. The information is eventually stored in the Exporters File and includes: who has a product, who can get or make it, which firm to avoid because of a poor past track record, who can offer the most favorable terms, and the quality of product a company produces.

Source: Foreign Contacts (Input).

Destination: Contact Potential Exporters (Process 2).

Average Time: 3 to 50 hours.

Composition: Supplier information, dependability, and optional sources.

EXPORTER INFORMATION

Description: Exporter information comes from market research through established channels including trade directories and consulates for Eastern Bloc countries. Exporter information is relied on when foreign contacts with prior knowledge of an overseas company are not available.

Source: Manuals and Catalogs (Input).

Destination: Contact Potential Exporters (Process 2).

Average Time: 3 to 50 hours.

Composition: Name, address, telex, and products offered.

FUTURE EXPORTER SOURCING INFORMATION

Description: Every time a contract is made with an exporter, a great deal of information is discovered which will be of value for future exporter sourcing. This information is compiled after the contract is completed, and put in the exporter file.

Source: Set up contract with exporter (Process 8).

Destination: Exporter File (Data Store 2).

Average Time: The task of updating the exporter file is done once and takes a full day to finish manually.

Composition: Insight on supplier quality, time required for an order, and any problems encountered with the exporter.

IMPORTER/EXPORTER INFORMATION

Description: The steps required for import sourcing and order processing provide a great deal of incidental data which can be used in the future. E-LINE is able to expand by using this data and as the company obtains a wider base of clientele.

Source: Set up contract with exporter (Process 8).

Destination: Contacts Reference (Output).

Composition: Data which could be of value for future reference.

ORDER INFORMATION

Description: Order information comes from an importer who was contacted through customer sourcing. The importer has already been contacted by mail, a personal contact, or by saleperson; therefore, the product to be imported has already been established. The information received is used to determine potential exporters which will be later contacted.

Source: Market Sourcing (Input).

Destination: Request Order Specifications (Process 1).

Average Time: Varies with order.

Composition: Price, quantity, ship time, availability, quality, style, color material, country.

POSSIBLE EXPORTERS

Description: Potential exporters are those overseas manufacturers or suppliers who have the ability to supply the desired good. They have been picked through information from foreign contacts or through research companies. All the information discovered about potential exporters is stored in the exporter file (Data Store 2) for future reference.

Source: Determine Potential Exporters (Process 2).

Destination: Exporters File (Data Store 2).

Composition: Suppliers who are still feasible after an initial study.

PRODUCER, PRODUCT, AND QUALITY INFORMATION

Description: A breakdown of the potential exporters from process two (determine potential exporters) which goes to process three (analyze/choose viable exporters) where the data is further scrutinized before the exporter is contacted.

Source: Exporter File (Data Store 2).

Destination: Analyze/choose Viable Exporters (Process 2).

Composition: Suppliers who are still feasible after an initial study and any product information available about them.

PRODUCT COST BEFORE F.O.B.

Description: Product cost before F.O.B. is the total cost of a product if it were bought in the nation it was produced in. Delivering the item F.O.B., however, will add to the per item cost.

PRODUCT COST AFTER F.O.B.

Description: Total order cost is the cost from the overseas supplier plus tariffs, duty, shipping, and clearance.

Sources: Determine F.O.B. (Process 5).

Destination: Negotiate with Importer (Process 6).

Composition: Item costs plus tariffs, duty, shipping, and clearance.

PRODUCT PRICE AND QUALITY

Description: The price quote which a chosen exporter gives E-LINE for the good designated by the product specifications.

Source: Foreign Manufacturer (Input).

Destination: Contact Chosen Exporters (Process 4).

Average Time: Varies with order.

Composition: Includes price quote, conditions of trade, how soon the product can be available, and supplemental or similar product descriptions.

PRODUCT REQUEST

Description: When an individual or business contacts E-LINE on its own accord, the potential customer will make a product request by providing E-LINE with information and descriptions of the desired good.

Source: Potential Customer (Input).

Destination: Request Order Specifications (Process 1).

Average Time: Varies with order.

Composition: Price, quantity, ship time, availability, quality, style, color, country, material.

REVENUES

Description: E-LINE marks up the total cost of importing a good to cover its costs and a profit. Usually a 30% markup is required to cover fixed costs (i.e., telex, telephone, rent, heat, and lights). Any additional markup is E-LINE's profit. Negotiations with the importer will determine how much profit E-LINE can make on a given deal.

Source: Set Up Contract with Exporter (Process 8).

Destination: E-LINE Profits (Output).

REQUEST SPECIFICATIONS

Description: Request specifications are composed of the information which is sent to foreign manufacturers to describe the product desired. Request specifications are first documented and stored in the customer file (Data Store 1), and then sent to potential exporters to determine if the good can be produced or obtained by that source.

Source: Customer File (Data Store 1).

Destination: Contact Potential Exporters (Process 2).

Composition: Quality, price, style, color, country, material, quantity, availability.

SPECIFICATIONS FROM REQUEST

Description: Request specifications are composed of the information which is sent to foreign manufacturers to describe the product desired. Specifications from requests are first documented and stored in the customer file (Data Store 1), and then used to find potential manufacturers (see request specifications) to determine if the good can be produced or obtained by that source.

Source: Request Order Specifications (Process 1).

Destination: Customer File (Data Store 1).

Composition: Quality, price, style, color, country, material, quantity, availability.

III. PROCESS DESCRIPTIONS

PROCESS ONE—REQUEST ORDER SPECIFICATIONS

Description: This process starts off the entire order processing data flow diagram. Once E-LINE is contacted by an importer, the first step is to telex the company to determine exactly what product specifications they are looking for. E-LINE's vice-president is generally responsible for the correspondence with the company.

Source: There are two main sources for this process. These are the contact from the potential customer, and contacts E-LINE has made through market sourcing (E-LINE contacting various companies, offering a product idea and waiting for a response).

Destination: Information from this process flows into D1, the customer file.

Average Time: Approximately one hour.

Composition: Information determined in this process includes product name, desired product quality and price range to work within, order quantity, and time frame reference for desired receipt of goods.

PROCESS TWO—DETERMINE POTENTIAL EXPORTERS

Description: In this process, E-LINE takes the information gathered in process one concerning the product specifications of the importer and matches these up with information from foreign contacts, and manuals and catalogs to come up with a list of the best potential exporters to contact. The number of potential exporters cannot be quantified in the general sense as the length of the list depends on such things as—is this the first time that E-LINE has worked with this particular product? How unique the product might be?, etc.

Source: The inputs into this process on the data flow diagram are the request specifications from the customer file, E-LINE's established foreign contacts (see previous data dictionary description), and looking up exporter information in the various manuals and catalogs (of particular noted use is the Contacts Influential for exporter sources).

Destination: The information stored in the Exporters File.

Average Time: Varies with order.

Composition: Information gathered will pertain to the subjects which are of concern to the particular importer (i.e., product, price, quality, etc.) in a general sense. In other words, this list will contain exporters who meet the basic requirements of the importer.

PROCESS THREE—ANALYZE/CHOOSE VIABLE IMPORTERS

Description: This process essentially extends process two in that it takes the list of possible exporters in the file and looks into them more in depth. This process narrows down the list of possible exporters to establish a list of the exporters that will best fulfill the needs of the importer.

Source: The information in the Exporter File (D2).

Destination: Process 4, where contact will actually be made with the exporters on the further broken down list created in this process.

Composition: The list will include specific information as to why the particular exporter best fits the needs of the importer (i.e., the price offered is lower than that specified by the importer).

PROCESS FOUR—CONTACT CHOSEN EXPORTERS

Description: In this process E-LINE actually makes contact with the exporters on the narrowed down list. At this point E-LINE will establish the willingness and ability of the exporters to meet the specific importer needs at that point in time.

Source: The list of the exporters from process three.

Destination: Process 5 where the final exporter to work with will be chosen.

Composition: Additional information is to be determined which covers the ability of the exporter to meet the importer's specifications at that time. Of particular interest is information on time for delivery and specific price.

PROCESS FIVE—CHOOSE EXPORTER

Description: In this process the final match up of the importer specifications with the total information on the exporter is made and a final exporter is chosen and contacted.

Source: Information on the final list of exporter's conditions comes into this process from Process 4.

Destination: The final product price from the chosen exporter is sent to the next process which will use this information to determine the F.O.B. price for the importer.

Composition: Complete information on the chosen exporter which is gathered in all of the previous processes is conglomerated here.

PROCESS SIX: DETERMINE F.O.B.

Description: In Process 6 all of the costs associated with bringing the product to the importer are calculated. Aside from the price quoted by the exporter, calculations such as tariff and duties charges, shipping costs, and clearance company costs must be calculated in order to send the final product cost to the importer.

Source: Process 5 where the exporter was chosen so the exporter's price quote could be sent into this process.

Destination: Process 7, where the total determined price is negotiated with the importer.

Composition: Price quote from Process 5, determined tariff and duty charges, shipping costs, and clearance company costs. See Process 6 explosion as well as explosion diagram for more detail.

PROCESS SEVEN: NEGOTIATE WITH IMPORTER

Description: This is the process in which E-LINE discusses a final price between the importer and exporter. There definitely is no set way of doing this particular process as much of what goes on depends quite a bit on the reasonableness and desires of the importer and exporter in each individual sourcing operation.

Source: Process 6, where product cost after F.O.B. was determined.

Destination: Process 8, where the price agreement from this process will be added into the final contract agreement between the exporter.

Composition: The main components in this process are the determined product cost from Process 6, paired with the results of contracting the importer and exporter for negotiations.

Average Time: Dependent on the importer and exporter involved.

PROCESS EIGHT: SET UP CONTRACT WITH EXPORTER

Description: This final process in the whole order processing schedule is where the final contract between the importer and exporter is drawn up and signed.

Source: Process 7 where a price agreement was determined.

Destination: What flows out of this process is essentially what flows out of the system as a whole. That is, the future exporter sourcing information is sent to be recorded in the exporter's file data store. Another output from the whole system is that E-LINE has perhaps established new contacts with an importer and with several exporters that might prove useful in future import-export sourcing operations. Finally, of course, E-LINE's pay comes out of the final price agreement in the contract (normally about a 30% mark-up).

Average Time: Dependent on the particular order and importer and exporter involved.

SECTION SIX: DATA FLOW DIAGRAM (LEVEL 02)

Explosion of Process 6: Determine F.O.B.

The explosion of Process 6 on the data flow diagram simply breaks down the process of determining the free on board price of the order into a deeper level of explanation. When a process is exploded from the 01 or main level of the data flow diagram, another (lower level) data flow diagram is created which breaks up the main level process into greater detail. Explosions provide a clearer understanding of what is going on in some of the processes in the main data flow diagram. Here in the explosion for Process 6, one can see that quite a bit more actually goes into determining the F.O.B. price than is shown on the main data flow diagram.

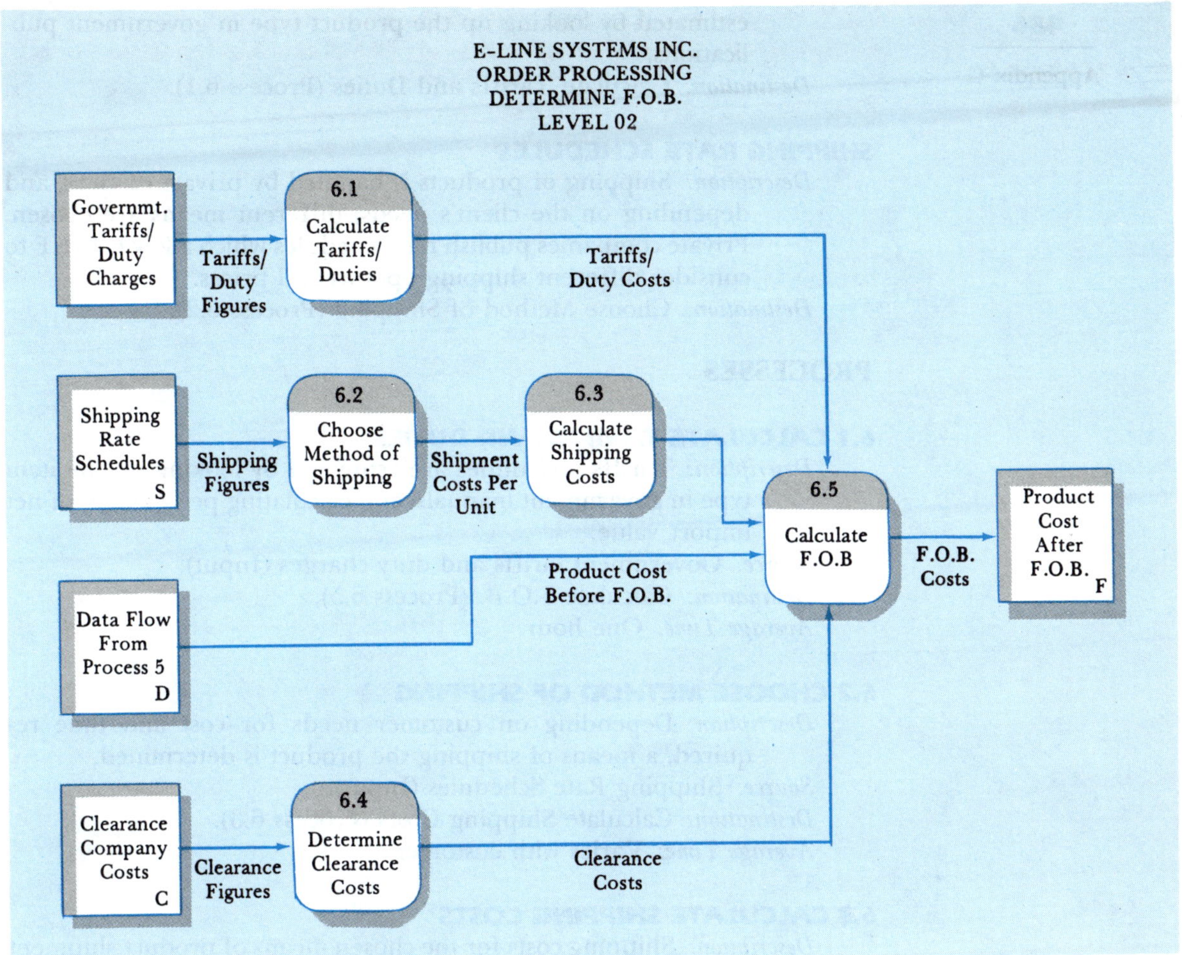

FIGURE C-4

E-LINE SYSTEMS INC. order processing system explosion of Process 6.

Data Dictionary: Process 6 Explosions

INPUTS/DATA FLOWS

COMPANY CLEARANCE COSTS

Description: A clearance company is used to handle customs procedures. A.J. Fritz Inc. is used by E-LINE for Denver area imports.
Destination: Determine Clearance Costs (Process 6.4).

GOVERNMENT TARIFFS AND DUTY CHARGES

Description: Products brought into the United States are taxed to make domestic products more price competitive. Tariffs are estimated by looking up the product type in government publications.

Destination: Calculate Tariffs and Duties (Process 6.1).

SHIPPING RATE SCHEDULES

Description: Shipping of products is handled by private carriers, and depending on the client's needs, different means are chosen. Private companies publish rate schedules which allow E-LINE to consider different shipping options and prices.

Destination: Choose Method of Shipping (Process 6.2).

PROCESSES

6.1 CALCULATE TARIFFS AND DUTIES

Description: Tariffs and duties are estimated by looking up the item type in government manuals, and calculating percentages of net import value.

Source: Government tariffs and duty charges (Input).

Destination: Calculate F.O.B. (Process 6.5).

Average Time: One hour.

6.2 CHOOSE METHOD OF SHIPPING

Description: Depending on customer needs for cost and time required, a means of shipping the product is determined.

Source: Shipping Rate Schedules (Input).

Destination: Calculate Shipping Costs (Process 6.3).

Average Time: Varies with customer.

6.3 CALCULATE SHIPPING COSTS

Description: Shipping costs for the chosen means of product shipment are determined using the product weight, quantity, volume, and packaging.

Source: Choose Method of Shipping (Process 6.2).

Destination: Calculate F.O.B. (Process 6.5).

Average Time: One hour.

6.4 DETERMINE CLEARANCE COSTS

Description: A clearance company such as A.J. Fritz is contacted and a quote of the charge for services is received.

Source: Clearance Company Costs (Input).

Destination: Calculate F.O.B. (Process 6.5).

6.5 CALCULATE F.O.B.

Description: The product price before F.O.B. is added to shipping tariff, duty, and clearance costs to project a total product cost.

Sources: 6.1 Calculate Tariffs and Duties.
6.3 Calculate Shipping Costs.

6.4 Determine Clearance.
Destination: Product Cost After F.O.B.

DATA FLOWS

CHOSEN SHIPMENT RATE

Description: The preferred means of shipping is determined and its rate is carried to Process 6.3 (calculate shipping costs).
Source: Choose Method of Shipping (Process 6.2).
Destination: Calculate Shipping Costs (Process 6.3).

CLEARANCE COSTS:

Description: The costs for the clearance company which E-LINE chooses.
Source: Determine Clearance Costs (Process 6.4).
Destination: Calculate F.O.B. (Process 6.5).

CLEARANCE FIGURES

Description: The quote given to E-LINE by a clearance company for the cost of their services.
Source: Clearance Company Costs (Input).
Destination: Determine Clearance Costs (Process 6.4).

F.O.B. COSTS

Description: The cost of shipping an order to Boulder (or the destination E-LINE specifies).
Source: Calculate Shipping Costs (Process 6.3).
Destination: Calculate F.O.B. (Process 6.5).

SHIPPING FIGURES

Description: Rate listings for different shipping companies and different forms of shipping.
Source: Shipping Rate Schedules (Input).
Destination: Choose Method of Shipping (Process 6.2).

TARIFF AND DUTY COSTS

Description: Tariff and duty charges are a form of tax added to the cost of an import. They are paid for by the importer in addition to the cost of the goods.
Source: Calculate Tariffs (Process 6.1).
Destination: Calculate F.O.B. (Process 6.5).

TARIFF AND DUTY FIGURES

Description: Tariff and duty figures are used to calculate tariffs and duties (Process 6.1).
Source: Government Tariffs and Duty Charges (Input).
Destination: Calculate Tariffs and Duties (Process 6.1).

Appendix C

Item	*Source*
Accessories	Hong Kong
Bicycles	England
Brass products	Thailand
Canvas/vinyl	Hong Kong
Clothing	Hong Kong
Computers	Hong Kong, Taiwan
Computer boards	Far East
Copiers	Far East
Cookware	Far East, Scandinavia
Decorator items	All countries
Eel skin	Korea
Electronics	Far East
Engraving (wood)	India/Central–South America
Furniture	All countries
Handbags	Far East
Hard drives	Far East
Jewelry	All countries
Leather	South America/India/England
Machines	Scandinavia
Metals	All countries
Modems	Far East
Monitors	Far East
Off shore manufacturing	All countries
Optical	Far East
Paper products	Far East
Plastics	Far East
Porcelain	Scandinavia/Far East
Printers	Far East
Scientific	Far East
Silks	Far East
Sporting goods	Far East
Tiles	Near East
Vacuum	Far East
Watches	Far East

Countries/Sources
Hong Kong
Korea
Thailand
England
Denmark
Greece
Spain
Sweden
Norway

Countries/Sources
Chile
Taiwan
India
Arabia
Egypt
Japan

SECTION EIGHT: E-LINE ORDER PROCESSING FORMS*

CUSTOMER CONTACT REPORT: The customer contact report is used to record the name and address of the customer and exactly who E-LINE will be dealing with. Any special type of equipment and/or instructions required of the customer are also listed.

CUSTOMER SOURCING MAIL FORM: The customer sourcing mail form is sent out when E-LINE conducts a mass mailing for potential customers. The form requests that the customer specify what type of business they are interested in, be it import sourcing or off-shore manufacturing, and what type of products and expected volume they would like to be dealing with.

COMPANY SERVICES and PRODUCT SALES: This information sheet is sent along with the customer sourcing mail form. It describes the services E-LINE has to offer such as import sourcing, off-shore manufacture, export market consulting, or technology exchange. The Product Sales portion lists a few of the companies and/or distributors that E-LINE deals with.

SECTION NINE: SUGGESTIONS TO E-LINE'S ORDER PROCESSING SYSTEM

Our analysis team considered several alternatives to improve the order processing and sourcing system. We will discuss changes we consider practical and economically feasible.

E-LINE SYSTEMS INC. is a service organization. The business does not carry inventory or manufacture products. Instead, E-LINE's lifeblood is applying its expertise in negotiating contracts between importers and exporters. To maximize profits, E-LINE employees must spend as much time as possible pursuing prospects, and, conversely, minimize time spent researching and finding overseas suppliers to meet their domestic client's needs.

Modifications to the current E-LINE order processing system could increase efficiency, and in the long run increase profits (by leaving employees free to pursue contracts) and decrease costs (in lost person-hours).

*(*Book Author's Note: Actual copies of the forms were included with the report*)

Potential modifications would include database maintenance on both customer files and exporter files. In doing so, the reports in the system objectives section of the requirements model could be easily provided.

The database on customer information would include information on the present customers, and any information gathered on potential customers by E-LINE's employees. Present customer information would outline more specifically the present customer's order and complete specifications and needs of the importing company. Database information on both present and potential customers would include such information as name, product(s), general order quantities, etc.

Determining potential exporters (Process 2) and analyzing/choosing viable exporters (Process 3) and their inputs/outputs are shown in Figure C-5.

The exporter file is used to store data on exporters that E-LINE has worked with in the past and those who E-LINE's research might indicate a potential to use in the future. Although only one exporter is eventually

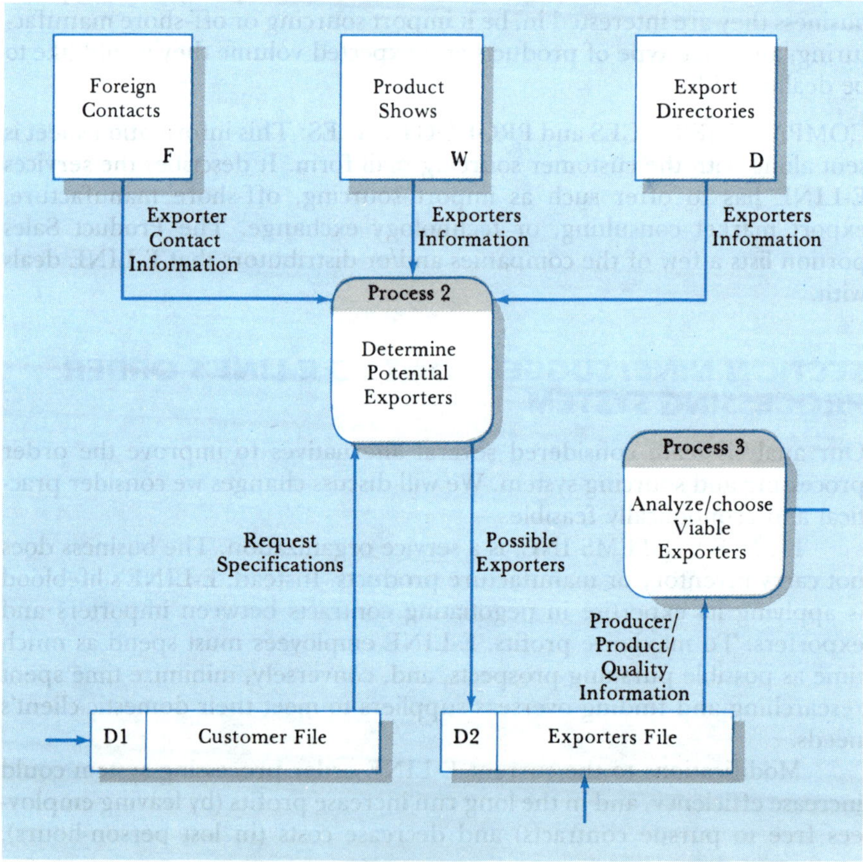

FIGURE C-5

E-LINE SYSTEMS INC. data flow diagram for a potential area for automation.

used per order, data on others researched is stored for future reference. The ability to reaccess this data quickly and efficiently would allow E-LINE employees to spend less time determining and analyzing exporters.

Implementing a computer database containing the exporter file would make storing and searching for past data easier and more efficient. E-LINE employees could search for information on products by key fields such as continent, country, product, and manufacturer. Automating the exporter file would be particularly valuable as both E-LINE and their base of contacts grow.

SECTION TEN: GROUP SUMMARY ON PROJECT DEVELOPMENT

In carrying out our semester-long systems analysis project, our group learned a great deal about systems analysis as well as team systems analysis dynamics. None of us had ever done a project where we analyzed a system within a company, nor had we done an analysis of any kind in such detail.

As we worked on our project we came to realize that there is a great deal of detail involved in even the seemingly smallest of tasks. Often the extent of detail put into an analysis can be of extreme importance in understanding a company. In determining the level of detail, we had to first establish the boundaries of the E-LINE system we would analyze. This was perhaps the most difficult part of the project; for in order to narrow down a project, one must first understand the company as a whole. After two meetings (one with the president of E-LINE, and one with the vice-president), our group felt that we had a fairly good grasp on exactly what E-LINE did and what subsystem we wished to analyze. We chose to analyze the order processing system as it seemed to be at the heart of E-LINE's activities.

In creating the deliverables on the project, we became familiarized not only with what should be included in each deliverable (and how to go about creating it), but also the importance of working with the company at each step of the analysis process. For example, in creating the Data Dictionary from the Data Flow Diagram, although it was established that the diagram was exactly what the company's order processing looked like, we were not 100% sure about what some of the data flows and processes were comprised of. Thus, we met with the vice-president to step through each level of the data flow diagram. This gave us a more than adequate understanding of E-LINE's activities. With each deliverable it seemed as if we received a more and more detailed understanding of E-LINE from several different aspects of the organization (i.e., how things are done now, who does what tasks, how they would like the system to work in the future, and what the long-range goals are which the company is striving to work toward).

This project also gave each of us a good understanding of the group dynamics involved in performing a systems analysis. This is not to say that none of us knew anything about working in groups before, but more that we now realize that there are certain subtleties involved particularly in analyzing a system within a group (just as a group construction project would have dynamics unique to a construction job). For example, in assigning tasks, some tasks can be divided up and researched by individuals (such as the requirements model), and others need to be more of a group effort (such as the data flow diagram which really involves knowledge of the flow of the entire system, thus needing input from the entire group).

Something else that our group learned to do extremely well was to schedule and plan the project. Assignments for the accomplishment of such activities as deliverables and documentation were divided up equitably, and in accordance with particular skills individuals possessed (i.e. one person might be skilled with words—thus he/she would write documentation, someone else might be more technically oriented, so he/she would do the data flow diagram on Excelerator, etc.).

Another important group dynamic which our group performed extremely well involved the importance of trust in working on the group project. Everyone had their tasks done at a scheduled time, and the tasks were accomplished to the best of the individual's ability. Things were obviously not done just for the sake of having a finished deliverable or documentation.

Meetings with E-LINE's representatives were also run very efficiently. E-LINE was contacted in advance as to when the meeting could be scheduled as well as informed as to what we as a group wished each meeting to accomplish. Therefore, research could be done prior to our meeting. This would allow concepts to sink in such as listing business objectives, or there would be a certain deliverable that would be discussed which we had to have ready. Thus, the particular information necessary to complete the objective of the meeting was ready by the time the actual meeting took place.

Overall, we were lucky to have approached E-LINE, as they were receptive to our ideas and efforts. E-LINE's executives were more than willing to give our group any of their time that we needed, which was a great help in scheduling meetings and finding information. Our group also worked together very well, particularly as far as the important issue of trust was concerned. Both of these factors were of extreme importance and influence towards our accomplishment of a successful project system analysis.

INDEX

A

B

C

D

E

F

G

H

I

J

K

L

M

N

O

Q

R

S

T

U

V

W

Y